*f*P

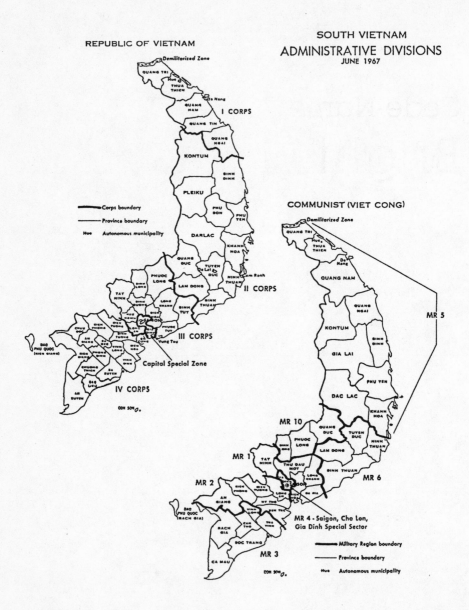

SOUTH VIETNAM
ADMINISTRATIVE DIVISIONS
JUNE 1967

Code-Name
Bright Light

The Untold Story of
U.S. POW Rescue Efforts
During the Vietnam War

GEORGE J. VEITH

THE FREE PRESS
New York London Toronto Sydney Singapore

Manufactured in the United States of America

ISBN 0–684–83514–2

To my loving wife Gina Kathryn,
whose husband was often a prisoner to the research and writing of this book,
and to my beautiful daughter Analiese Caroline,
whose father was frequently missing in action.

Contents

Preface: 30 Kilometers West of Soc Trang, Mekong Delta, South Vietnam

0900 hours, October 8, 1966

The light observation plane lumbered slowly over the Viet Cong prison camp that lay expertly camouflaged within the dense jungle growth and green bamboo thicket below. Hidden somewhere in the maze of grassy fields and thick strands of rain-soaked brush, an American soldier was being held prisoner. At the plane's controls sat Air Force Colonel Heinie Aderholt. In the seat behind him, a sergeant using a hand-held camera quickly snapped photo after photo of the surrounding area. Aderholt kept the plane on a steady course and a discreet distance away, trying not to raise the suspicions of the camp guards. Just another airplane flying through the humid, monsoon-laden air of South Vietnam's Mekong Delta.

In September, Aderholt had become the first commander of the newest section of one of the most top secret and elite American military units in Southeast Asia, the Studies and Observation Group (SOG). SOG was a highly classified intelligence and commando unit that specialized in quick-strike raids and clandestine reconnaissance against the enemy supply columns that snaked down the Ho Chi Minh Trail.

Aderholt's section was called the Joint Personnel Recovery Center (JPRC). The JPRC was a small staff office recently set up to analyze intelligence reports and then organize raids using troops from SOG to recover the growing number of American prisoners of war (POWs) being held in Southeast Asia. To Aderholt and the SOG commander, Army Colonel John K. Singlaub, SOG's unconventional nature made it perfectly suited for the same style of lightning attacks envisioned by the Military Assistance Command, Vietnam (MACV) to rescue American prisoners. The JPRC's charter was to develop intelligence on the status of American POWs, plan rescues for those in captivity, and coordinate the recovery of shot-down airmen after normal Air Force or Navy Search and Rescue (SAR) efforts had failed or were otherwise canceled. Despite struggling to establish and staff a new office, in its short existence the JPRC had already conducted several post-SAR attempts to recover airmen trying to avoid capture by hostile forces.

Now the JPRC was planning its first assault on an enemy POW prison. As the plane moved beyond the unseen camp, Aderholt reviewed the events of the last weeks. The rescue mission had been code-named *Crimson Tide* by Aderholt, after his beloved University of Alabama, but various problems had delayed the operation. Planning for the mission had begun shortly after August 30, 1966, when a seventeen-year-old Viet Cong (VC) guerrilla named Pham Teo had "rallied," or defected, to the South Vietnamese government.[1] The rallier claimed to have seen a black American prisoner only five days before. Although Aderholt wanted to immediately launch a rescue operation, the SOG staff believed more intelligence was needed before sending troops in to raid the camp. Based on Teo's description of the area where he saw the prisoner, an Air Force reconnaissance plane was ordered to fly over and take aerial photos. The pictures, however, had proved useless in pinpointing the exact spot. Having never seen high-altitude photos before, the former VC had been totally at a loss when shown the overhead shots. Moreover, the Air Force had taken pictures of the wrong area. After SOG intelligence had reinterrogated the rallier to again confirm the site, Aderholt decided to fly the reconnaissance mission himself and take lower-level, side-angle pictures called "obliques."

The cumbersome Army bureaucracy had also contributed to the month-long delay in launching the raid. Since the rallier's information had provided the first chance for the U.S. military to test the JPRC and the concept of a POW intelligence and rescue unit, the operation had attracted a great deal of high-level attention and everyone at MACV headquarters wanted to be involved. To get final approval for the rescue plan, Aderholt had to hand-carry a draft to all the different staff sections at U.S. military headquarters. Despite the high interest in the raid, his first visit did not go well. When he stopped to see Army Major General Joseph D. McChristian, who headed military intelligence in Vietnam, McChristian refused to see him; Aderholt was shocked. He was forced to simply drop the plan off. After an interminable wait of several weeks, McChristian and the MACV staff finally authorized the plan. As the plane continued toward the airfield at Soc Trang, Aderholt hoped the delays had not ruined the JPRC's first opportunity, and he wondered if the American prisoner was still in the camp where the seventeen-year-old VC said he was.[2]

1100 hours, October 11, 1966, Can Tho

JPRC intelligence analyst Sergeant Alden Egg stared intently at the VC rallier, watching for any signs that Teo was lying.[3] Egg's job was to identify the black American prisoner. Only three black Americans were currently being held prisoner in the Mekong Delta. Based on the VC's description, Egg believed that it was Edward R. Johnson, an American sergeant captured near Can Tho in South Vietnam on July 21, 1964, while serving as an advisor to the South Vietnamese Army. SOG intelligence, however, disagreed and thought it was James E. Jackson, a medic who was captured on July 5, 1966. Besides Jackson and Johnson, Sergeant Joe Parks was the only other black American known to be held in the Delta.

Egg quickly put together a thick file of reports on Johnson from several VC POW camp guards who had defected and from various South Vietnamese prisoners who had escaped after being held with him in the dreaded "Forest of Darkness," the impenetrable mangrove swamps of the Mekong Delta forest called the U-Minh. The U-Minh was a legendary hideout for thieves and assassins. Now it hid the elusive VC.

From reading the reports, Egg learned that Johnson had resolutely defied his captors, refusing to provide any information while also resisting their persistent attempts to politically indoctrinate him. To the VC, Johnson was a "stubborn" and "undesirable" prisoner who frequently voiced anti-communist opinions. To them, such resistance was unacceptable.[4]

Then his VC interrogators discovered his weakness. Johnson was deeply afraid of the water, and under the pretext of "teaching him to swim," the VC repeatedly threw him in the numerous canals and small bodies of water that flowed through the Delta. They used the threat of additional swimming lessons to torture Johnson until he became more receptive to their propaganda instruction. They also tried to use his race against him. Johnson's wife was German, and the communist manipulators taunted him about his marriage to a white woman. "Who is she sleeping with tonight?" they asked. "Do you think she's waiting for you?" The VC interrogators constantly goaded Johnson, painting the United States as a racist country that didn't value his life and didn't care that he had been taken prisoner. Only revolutionaries like us can be your friend, they whispered, only we can help you understand the truth about the war and your country.[5]

As he watched the rallier study the new photos, Egg realized that Teo was trying hard to help. Teo had worked for the VC since he was fourteen, but had grown tired of the difficult and dangerous life of a guerrilla. Hearing of the South Vietnamese amnesty program for Viet Cong soldiers, he had decided to desert. After the fiasco with the overhead aerial photos, however, SOG intelligence wanted to be completely certain that Teo was telling the truth, and they forced him to take a lie-detector test. He passed. When Teo was shown the low-level pictures, he was able to easily point out the camp location. Further, he agreed to lead the U.S. troops to the camp where he had last seen the American. As he studied Teo closely, a small hope began to grow within Egg that Sergeant First Class Edward R. Johnson, a man who had suffered immensely during his captivity, might soon be free.

1330 hours, October 18, 1966, Soc Trang Airfield

Army Captain Frank Jaks, Operations Officer of SOG's Forward Operational Base 2 (FOB2) at Kontum in the Central Highlands of Vietnam, hurried across the Soc Trang runway toward the UH-1 "Huey" helicopter.[6] The Huey was the workhorse of the Vietnam war and was designed to ferry troops into battle. Along with a hundred-man company of SOG mercenaries from Kontum, Jaks had been ordered only three days ago to prepare for a POW rescue mission. Although the morning had started out badly with an agonizing two-hour delay, the raiding party had finally left Kontum and traveled first to the city of Can Tho. There, Jaks had received a final intelligence briefing on *Crimson Tide* from a colonel whom he had never met before. From Can Tho they had proceeded on to Soc Trang. A heavy monsoon storm had prevented the helicopters from lifting off on schedule, but now the weather was finally clearing. A dozen of the Huey helicopters were loaded with his waiting men. Four gunships provided armed escort.

Jaks had mixed feelings about this mission. Most of the final coordination had not been done by him but had been made by the JPRC with the American Senior Advisor for IV Corps, the Vietnamese Military Region which covered the Mekong Delta. He could only hope everyone had done their job properly, as the sudden order had left him little time to prepare for the mission. To make matters worse, SOG intelligence could not precisely pin-point the camp location.

Jaks was even more anxious about the combat reactions of his troops. They were used to warfare in the mountains of Laos, but now they were being asked to fight in the swampy lowlands of the Delta. Plus, his commander, Major Francis Sova, had told him that the rallier had recently revealed that the American was a possible deserter who might be trying to lure U.S. aircraft into VC ambushes. Although Sova suspected a trap, he grudgingly ordered the operation to continue based upon the analysis of the new photos by SOG intelligence. "Expect almost no resistance," the unknown colonel at Can Tho had told him. "You should be done in thirty minutes."

Sova had created a raiding party with one platoon from A Company and two platoons from B Company to conduct the POW raid. Each platoon had thirty to forty men, but the men were armed only with light infantry weapons. The three platoons were composed of hired Chinese mercenaries called Nungs. The Nungs were from the Cholon district of Saigon and were considered by many to be the fiercest fighters in Southeast Asia. Their fighting ability, coupled with their willingness to undertake dangerous missions for pay, made them perfect soldiers for covert warfare. The SOG recruiters had been busy and many Nungs had joined the secret unit.

A native of Czechoslovakia who as a child had escaped from the communists, Jaks was an outstanding combat leader who thrived in the covert world of SOG. He was also instinctively cautious, and for this mission had decided to do without the normal food ration; he ordered his men to carry a double load of ammunition instead. The ground plan called for two platoons to act as blocking forces while the third platoon swept toward where the American was believed to be held. The excellent aerial photos Aderholt's sergeant had taken showed typical Delta terrain: flat, grassy fields, with a distinct tree line, and heavy jungle growth where the camp was suspected to be.

Jaks was not the only American going on the raid. Each Nung platoon had several U.S. leaders. Another American, Sergeant First Class Frederick Lewis, the SOG camp engineer at Kontum, had begged to go along to see some "real combat." Jaks agreed, believing that the operation would meet little resistance, but he put Lewis with the 1st Platoon, which was headed by one of his more experienced NCOs, Sergeant First Class Charles Vessels. Vessels' platoon was acting as one of the blocking forces. Jaks was surprised, though, by an unexpected passenger. As his "Huey" lifted off, he noticed that Teo was riding in the next helicopter. Although the VC rallier had accompanied them to Soc Trang, Jaks was unaware that Teo was going on the rescue mission. A good sign, thought Jaks. *Maybe we aren't riding into an ambush after all.*

1400 hours, October 18, 1966, Bien Hoa Airport, Saigon

Aderholt cursed the Air Force again. The Seventh Air Force (7th AF), the USAF headquarters in South Vietnam, had refused his request for prop-driven A-1s to support *Crimson Tide,* choosing instead to use F-100 jets. Aderholt had tried to plan the air-support portion of the raid, but that segment had been taken over by 7th AF. They told him to mind his own business; "our more than adequate staff would determine the type of aircraft needed for the mission." Typical service rivalries, Aderholt thought. With a high-profile mission like a POW rescue operation, the Air Force coveted part of the action. Aderholt had wanted the slower, more maneuverable A-1 aircraft because the low cloud ceiling from the monsoon rains at this time of year often made it too difficult for jets like the F-100s to operate effectively. Unfortunately, Lieutenant General William W. Momyer, the commander of the 7th AF, had a well-known preference for jets over propeller planes and he had spiked Aderholt's request.

To further complicate matters, the Air Force plane sent to carry the SOG commandos from Kontum to Can Tho had been delayed due to poor planning. Some "idiot"[7] at 7th AF had decided that since the plane was going to Kontum, it might as well carry some cargo. By the time the plane was finally off-loaded, the flight had been delayed several hours. Poor weather in Soc Trang also set the mission back by an hour. Aderholt had flown his O-1 light observation plane down to the area to observe the operation, but the delays had created a fuel shortage for his plane and he was forced to fly back to Bien Hoa. Sergeant Egg and another SOG captain who had done much of the planning for *Crimson Tide* had also tried to reach Soc Trang in a helicopter, but the weather was so bad that they were unable to land. As Aderholt's plane touched down at Bien Hoa airport, he cursed the meddling Air Force bureaucrats once more.

1425 hours, Command Helicopter, South of the Landing Zone

The flight from Soc Trang had been uneventful, the monsoon clouds creating a heavy overcast. Now, Jaks' formation was nearing the landing zone (LZ) and the VC prison camp. Without warning, a heavy rainstorm hit, making navigation extremely difficult. Jaks was in the lead helicopter and the rest labored to stay in formation around him. Approaching from the south, Jaks could see his LZ ahead. As he peered through the rain-splashed cockpit, off to his right he spotted the tree line. Nothing was moving.

As his helicopter came in to land, enemy machine-gun fire suddenly burst from the trees, the tracers from the bullets making a bright green glow through the tropical rain as they streaked toward one of the gunships. Shocked, Jaks watched as the rounds tore into the helicopter. Chunks of metal flew off as the bullets ripped open its side, sending the helicopter crashing to the ground. The machine-gun fire from the tree line increased and more small arms began shooting at the approaching helicopters. One of the gunships opened up with rockets, trying to suppress the barrage. Helicopters began maneuvering wildly to avoid the fire as others started landing and discharging troops. When his helicopter touched down, Jaks jumped out, stepping into about an inch of standing water left after days of torrential rainstorms.

As the rest of the helicopters carrying the 2nd Platoon landed, his men leaped off and scrambled for cover in the grassy field. While Jaks struggled to organize the chaos around him, Nung voices from the 1st Platoon started screaming for help on the radio. They were pinned down by concentrated fire from other VC. In the confusion at the primary LZ, the Huey pilots carrying the 1st Platoon had swung away to find another landing spot and had unwittingly put the Nungs down between two hidden VC units. A small canal covered by grass and not visible on the aerial photos divided his landing zone from the trapped Nungs. Jaks radioed the gunships to provide support to the 1st Platoon, but a fierce VC salvo drove them off. Lewis, the camp engineer who had always wanted to see some real combat, stepped from the door of his helicopter and was instantly cut in half by a burst of enemy machine-gun fire. Shortly after Lewis was shot, Vessels was also killed, leaving the 1st Platoon leaderless. Vessels' body was later found among a group of Nungs. It looked like he was trying to make a last stand.

Now Jaks could hear mortar rounds exploding in the distance. Instinctively he knew the shells were pounding the exposed soldiers of the 1st Platoon. His own situation wasn't much better. Although the 2nd Platoon had finished landing, they were still taking intense fire from the tree line and his men were trapped against the canal. Only thin scrub bushes and small thickets of bamboo along the canal provided any protection for Jaks' men. As he ran for cover, Jaks realized that any chance to rescue this lone American prisoner was quickly fading.

1600 hours, Tree Line

Despite the savage enemy volley, Jaks had gathered the 2nd Platoon and assaulted the VC position in the tree line under withering covering fire from the gunships. Fortunately, the VC had only one machine gun. Jaks' platoon captured two prisoners and questioned them for information on the American POW. In a search of the area, no prison camp or American was discovered. Teo pointed out an underground hospital complex and several booby traps near the hospital bunkers, but Jaks had a more immediate problem. The canal prevented him from linking up with his 1st Platoon, which was still pinned down and taking heavy casualties from the other VC. Jaks used his radio to contact a Forward Air Controller (FAC) overhead in an O-1. To help the Nung survivors of the 1st Platoon, Jaks wanted the circling F-100s to bomb the entrenched enemy. Responding to his request, the FAC ordered the F-100s to strike the VC positions. Within seconds two F-100s came in low and fast, their bombs tumbling quickly toward the ground. Loud explosions rocked the area. Jaks groaned: the jets had missed the VC and hit the Nung platoon instead. Just as Aderholt had feared, the broken cloud cover had prevented the pilots from getting a good fix on the location of the friendly forces and the pilots had dropped their bombs short of the intended target, landing them instead on Jaks' men. The O-1 pilot called off the jets.

Jaks sized up the situation. He was outside friendly artillery range, direct air support was no longer available, and his unit had no heavy weapons. His 1st Platoon was surrounded, and with his radios unable to reach SOG headquarters to request help, Jaks knew he would probably have to spend the night facing methodical elimination of his men by a superior VC force. *Crimson Tide* was a disaster. From the VC prisoners he learned that the JPRC's first POW rescue mission had landed his men in the middle of the rest area for two enemy battalions, including one of their most feared units in the Delta, the elite U-Minh 10 Battalion. Gathering the members of his 2nd Platoon into a defensive perimeter, Jaks wondered how, or if, they would survive the inevitable night attack.

Acknowledgments

While this work bears my name as the author, in reality it is the combined efforts of many people. For me, the most enjoyable part of writing this book is the opportunity to acknowledge my family and the individuals whose tremendous support led directly to the creation of this study.

First and foremost, my deepest thanks go to my parents, George C. and Joan A. Veith, who gave me so much and who taught me the lessons that prepared me for life. My aunt Caroline, my sister Christine, her husband Jim, and their daughter Lauren always provided kind words and encouragement.

Early in this project I was fortunate to meet three people who acted as more than mentors; they also became good friends. Dr. Timothy N. Castle, currently a Professor of National Security Studies at the Air University at Maxwell Air Force Base, provided motivation and the occasional swift kick to help me complete this book. Dr. Castle always insisted on precise scholarship and attention to detail, and his sage advice steered me past several low points as I labored with the challenges of writing and researching this work.

Garnett E. "Bill" Bell, a former long-time member of the U.S. government's efforts to solve the POW/MIA mystery, was instrumental in helping me grasp the nuances of the issue. His expertise on Vietnam was invaluable to my comprehension of that distant country, and when I struggled to grasp the complexities of the war and the motivations of the communists, he was unfailing in providing guidance, wisdom, and behind-the-scenes insight.

If there are any unrecognized heroes of the wartime efforts to assist American

POWs, Claude L. Watkins must surely sit in the front row. So often the works of good men go unnoticed in this issue, buried under the seal of classification. He generously shared his knowledge of the enormous national-level efforts to support our POWs, an enterprise never truly recognized before.

Many others deserve important recognition for their assistance. I am especially indebted to three archivists from the National Archives, Richard Boylen, Clifford Snyder, and Charles E. Schamel, and to Herb Rawlings-Milton in NARA's Declassification Section, who always responded to my frantic requests. Others who were instrumental include the author John Prados, who helped develop the overall theme of this book, and Randy Rakers at Carlisle Barracks, who provided insight into their vast holdings. Steve Sherman of Radix Press in Houston and Darrell Whitcomb helped enormously in locating many individuals, while the noted Vietnam historian Douglas Pike also served as a mentor and was always willing to share his vast knowledge of the war. Jerry Mooney's courageous revelations of the highly classified efforts of the National Security Agency helped immeasurably in gaining an in-depth understanding of the NSA's role. Gary Linderer from *Behind the Lines* magazine provided moral support as well as a veteran's perspective.

I would be remiss if I did not thank some of the many other people who have guided me along the way. Ann Mills-Griffiths, who has toiled so long and hard in the service of the POW/MIA families as Executive Director of the National League of Families, deserves special note for her sound counsel and humor. Dino Carluccio, Legislative Assistant to Senator Bob Smith of New Hampshire, and Al Santoli, veteran and author, are noteworthy for their unceasing efforts to ensure that the U.S. government remains committed to the "fullest possible accounting." Dolores Alfond, Chairperson of the National Alliance of Families, also provided welcome and direct support. I especially want to thank my editor at The Free Press, Mitch Horowitz, for believing in this project.

Lastly, I want to thank the men of the JPRC and those who led the raids to free their fellow soldiers for spending so much time with me reliving often painful memories. You are my heroes.

1. Introduction

The revolution pertains to the people. The people undertake the revolution only when they are assimilated with revolutionary thought. The propaganda and indoctrination task plays a very important role in this. It constitutes the most essential link and always leads the way in the revolutionary movement. The propaganda task also involves the political indoctrination and leadership of the people's ideology to crush the enemy propaganda which poisons the people's minds. . . . Ultimately, by understanding the ideology and characteristics of the enemy, we can crush his spirit and defeat him. Thus, use the enemy to defeat the enemy.
—*Captured enemy document, circa 1965*

More than two decades after the end of the Vietnam war, the POW/MIA issue continues to divide Americans in a manner reminiscent of the war itself. While the Vietnam war is more of a peripheral issue compared to such enduring American controversies as racism and abortion, the societal fallout from the war remains firmly embedded in our culture. Passions about Vietnam are still periodically rekindled, both deliberately and by happenstance, and never more intensely than over the unresolved issue of still-missing American servicemen. Like many of the legacies from that bitter conflict, it is an emotional and complex subject, awkwardly reminding us of debts still owed—at times seemingly inconvenient for those more interested in pressing their political and economic agenda to open diplomatic relations with Vietnam or planning ambitious business ventures in the region.

Skeptics and those with less charitable agendas point out that, despite the prayers and persistence of so many, in the years since the last American helicopter lifted off from the rooftop of the American embassy in Saigon, no ghost has materialized from a forgotten jungle outpost to rejoin his comrades and family, save one lone Marine in 1979, Robert Garwood. Why then, many cynics ask, is it so difficult for the remaining advocates of the missing to agree, at long last, to view Vietnam as a country and not a war?

The answer resides partially in the American military's commitment to never abandon a fallen comrade. That commitment continues today in the sense of responsibility for a full accounting for the missing felt by a regrettably small number of U.S. government officials. It is fueled by thousands of American citizens and veterans that, despite repeated claims to the contrary by the communists, the Vietnamese or Laotians do possess detailed knowledge on the fate of many American POW/MIAs. Ultimately, though, what sustains this issue is the love and devotion of families searching for answers, bolstered by the belief that the truths can still be discovered, and that eventually the full story of Vietnam's and Laos' duplicity regarding the fate of many Americans will be exposed.

Many Americans wonder why or how the issue has continued to this day. Although two full Congressional committees have investigated the issue, both struggled under accusations of malfeasance. Despite these investigations, from a historical perspective, the one area still most glaringly unexplored is the content and direction of American wartime POW intelligence and, concurrently, the U.S. military's covert wartime rescue efforts. These efforts have remained a mystery, hidden since the end of the war by the cloak of national security and buried under the duty to avoid disclosing important intelligence methods and sources.

This book, however, reveals that secret history—the story of the immense, often highly classified efforts to identify, locate, and rescue American POWs. This study probes the history of the U.S. government's intelligence programs, botched rescue efforts, failed ransoms, and futile attempts at diplomatic swaps. While this study endeavors to show that the Vietnam-era military did not break faith with their missing or captured comrades, it also does not gloss over their mistakes or conceal their failings. The total effort was simply too riddled with bureaucratic and service jealousies, too compartmentalized, and too exposed to local and national political considerations, both in the United States and in Southeast Asia.

In essence, the military did their best to recover American POWs—and yet they completely failed. The fact that the military failed shows how overwhelming the odds were, no matter how great the sacrifices to recover them or how much resourcefulness, dedication, and tenacity were displayed. Some of the barriers were self-imposed, for the military's POW endeavors often operated without a much-needed integration of resources, intelligence, and experience. However, despite every obstacle imaginable plus the frequently grudging cooperation of our Asian allies, the military tried desperately. But even failure can teach a great lesson, and because we failed does not mean we should not keep trying. The previously secret knowledge amassed from these activities has never before been thoroughly examined. If the hard-won lessons of the past can be applied to a future war, perhaps this country can avoid enduring another painful and lingering thirty-year controversy.

MACV-SOG, the Joint Personnel Recovery Center, and Search and Rescue

Understanding the many facets of the POW/MIA issue often seems to require a crash course in military jargon, plus a handbook to help the uninitiated comprehend the blizzard of acronyms, various layers of bureaucracies, and multitudes of organizations and units. The following sections are designed to provide the reader a basic grounding in the issue and the war.

MACV-SOG was established on January 24, 1964, when President Lyndon B. Johnson authorized covert operations against the North. The Military Assistance Command, Vietnam's (MACV) Studies and Observation Group (SOG) was designed to disrupt the enemy's sanctuaries clandestinely by conducting commando-style raids across the Laos–South Vietnam border to destroy or gather intelligence on supplies moving from North Vietnam through Laos along the Ho Chi Minh Trail.

To accomplish that difficult mission, SOG was granted authority to operate across the national borders of the other Southeast Asian countries, something normal U.S. ground units were forbidden to do. Because of the political sensitivities involved in attacking North Vietnamese Army (NVA) sanctuaries located across the borders in Laos and later in Cambodia, SOG was among the most secret, tightly held operations in the war.

Ostensibly, the Joint Personnel Recovery Center (JPRC) was a small staff office within the headquarters of the Military Assistance Command, Vietnam that handled POW intelligence. Only its relationship to SOG was classified. Within SOG, the JPRC was called the Recovery Studies Division, or OP-80.

While much of this book focuses on the efforts of the JPRC, other important search-and-rescue activity occurred in the years before the JPRC was set up. There were also critical activities that impacted the POW effort at the national level outside the purview of the unit, and covert actions in Vietnam that swirled beyond its reach during the unit's existence. The State Department, the CIA,[1] and the Defense Intelligence Agency (DIA) had a great deal of involvement in those actions, and while the JPRC was often center stage, ultimately it was only one player among many. However, because of its highly classified relationship to SOG, little has been officially released on the JPRC's activities or is known about the exploits of this critical section responsible for rescuing captive Americans. Its vast efforts over its six years of existence have, until now, been no more than a footnote in the larger volumes on Vietnam or a paragraph or two in the postwar books on POWs and MIAs.

Essentially, the JPRC was the military's response to an almost impossible situation. North and South Vietnam, Laos, and to a lesser extent Cambodia each presented the U.S. military with a set of unique political, cultural, and geographic obstacles to overcome in recovering captured personnel. The difficult terrain and dense foliage, the secret war in Laos, and the political ramifications of sending troops into North Vietnam were just a few of the major problems the U.S. military faced in trying to identify, locate, and rescue its prisoners. Throughout its existence, the JPRC launched a number of raids aimed at retrieving Americans in communist prison camps, maintained intelligence data on the locations where POWs were kept and their status, and developed various Escape and Evasion (E&E) programs. It also briefed air crews on survival techniques, recovered the remains of American servicemen, and helped free almost five hundred South Vietnamese soldiers and civilians. More important, the knowledge of its presence and E&E procedures significantly helped the morale of the aviators flying and fighting the air war.

The inability to develop accurate and timely intelligence on the precise locations of POW camps where Americans were being held, especially in South Vietnam, was the single most influential reason for the failure of the U.S. military to rescue even one single prisoner. While the same can be said about the entire U.S. war effort, the lack of precision intelligence often compelled the JPRC to send combat teams on raids into areas where a camp was only *thought* to be, essentially hoping to get lucky.

Bright Light was the unclassified code-name given to intelligence developed on prisoners or prison locations or, in the early days, to designate a rescue team. The term *Bright Light* had several meanings. Initially it referred to the SOG teams waiting on standby that were sent in to recover a downed pilot if the regular Search and Rescue (SAR) forces were unable to recover them. The term also signaled to analysts reading reports the presence of intelligence relating to American POWs so that this intelligence could be acted upon immediately. It was not restricted solely to American personnel: the term *Bright Light* was generic for any intelligence report on friendly military or civilian prisoners. However, it was generally used only within the Indochina theater. The major U.S. intelligence agencies in Washington rarely used the term. For instance, the National Security Agency (NSA), which was responsible for intercepting the enemy's electronic transmissions, used the code-name *Songbird* to identify intercepted enemy radio transmissions that discussed any U.S. prisoner or the shooting down of a U.S. airplane.

Historically, the United States Air Force (USAF) was responsible for most POW matters. Using the experience developed from past wars, the Air Force taught U.S. airmen critical lessons on how to avoid capture and stay alive after being shot down by hostile fire. These lessons came under the umbrella of a program known as Escape and Evasion. Air crews were taught how to signal Search and Rescue aircraft, how to evade enemy forces, how to overcome the difficult physical conditions of shock and injury, and how to locate food and water.

Search and Rescue was among the most important missions in Southeast Asia. After an aircraft was reported missing, helicopters were sent to search for the missing aircraft. If a pilot was shot down and managed to eject safely, an electronic beeper was activated that would send a signal to other orbiting aircraft. Once on the ground, the pilot used a hand-held radio to establish voice communication with the SAR helicopters. Because rescuers always suspected that the enemy had captured the pilot and were forcing him to use his radio to lure in the rescue helicopter, authentication procedures were established that enabled the SAR crews to confirm the identity of the pilot before pick-up. Other means of signaling and authentication were also devised, such as symbols on the ground, but these will be explained in later chapters.

The Navy also ran an efficient SAR organization, using specially modified helicopters launched from destroyers that sailed close to the North Vietnamese shore when carrier-based planes were making air strikes. The Navy designated three points in the Gulf of Tonkin as staging areas. These were known as South SAR, Mid SAR, and the famous North SAR. In early 1966, the Navy established Helicopter Support Squadron 17, or HC-17, to handle its SAR efforts.[2]

Terminology and Geography

Although PAVN, for People's Army of Vietnam, and PLAF, for People's Liberation Armed Forces, are the proper terms for the armed forces of North Vietnam and the guerrillas of South Vietnam, the commonly used American terms are NVA and Viet Cong, or VC, and I have used these more familiar terms in this book.

The VC and the NVA were not two separate communist military forces. The Viet Cong were Southerners, either local youths recruited to fight in the guerrilla war or "regroupees," individuals who were born in the South and who had moved north after the end of the French Indochina War only to return later to fight against the Western-allied government of Vietnam (GVN). While some southern elements of the revolution may have entertained thoughts of quasi-independence from the North, the communists in North Vietnam harbored no such illusions about their southern comrades. Despite the wartime rhetoric and the delusional thinking of some Americans in the peace movement, the revolution in the South was instigated and completely controlled by the Politburo in the North.

For the South, the primary target other than the communist military forces was a nebulous entity known as the "VC Infrastructure," or VCI. The VCI was the political and administrative organization through which the North sought control over the South. It embodied a typical parallel Communist Party control structure, which included a command and administrative apparatus, the Central Office for South Vietnam (COSVN), under the leadership of a front organization, the National Liberation Front (NLF).

The Lao Dong Party was the communist organization that held sway in the Democratic Republic of Vietnam (DRV)—North Vietnam to us. In the 1930s and '40s, the Indochina Communist Party attempted to unite all the communist parties of the peninsula under one umbrella organization to overthrow both the French colonial rulers and later the Japanese, who conquered Southeast Asia in the early days of World War II. After the return of the French, the communists launched an insurrection to gain Vietnam's independence. This eventually resulted in the Geneva Accords of 1954, which partitioned the country into North and South Vietnam at the 17th parallel.

The communist term for a person in a leadership role, either a military officer or a Party official, is *cadre.* Cadres are Party members who were the managers of the revolutionary forces and directed their political education. The communist viewpoint discussed in this book comes directly from their writings, which are revealed in thousands of documents captured by U.S. forces. I have tried to spare the reader what is often called "cadrespeak," the Vietnamese version of an Orwellian misuse of language and twisting of words. This is meant to clarify for the reader the tortured syntax and opaque verbiage of communist officialdom so prevalent in their documents, for understanding their views helps us to comprehend their motives and actions.

The political arm of the Laotian communist forces was called the Neo Lao

Hak Sat (NLHS), which in English means "Lao Patriotic Front." In Western circles they were referred to as the Pathet Lao (PL), which translates as "Lao Nation," but the actual Pathet Lao were simply the Laotian communist army. Militarily, the PL were trained, supplied, and advised by the North Vietnamese armed forces, and the handful of Lao who formed the inner core of the NLHS were completely beholden to the North Vietnamese Lao Dong Party. Overall, the Pathet Lao military forces were only slightly stronger than the Royal Lao Army (RLA), and without the stiffening of their North Vietnamese advisors they would have crumbled quickly.

The communists who rose to power in Cambodia were different from their Lao counterparts. While supported by the North Vietnamese, the Khmer Rouge nursed ancient grudges against them, which occasionally sparked armed clashes. But as long as fighting the American-supported Lon Nol government was the central aim of both parties, this animosity was muted.

During the war the hill tribe in Laos that fought so valiantly for the United States was known by the term "Meo," which translates to the lowland Lao as "barbarian." The correct name for the "Meo," however, is Hmong, and out of respect for their gallant wartime service to this country I have used that term throughout the book. To maintain accuracy and the flavor of the time I have kept the word "Meo" if it is used in a quoted cable or document.

The Army of the Republic of [South] Vietnam was generally called by its acronym, ARVN. As the United States pushed the South Vietnamese to extend their control into the countryside, the GVN built up irregular militia forces known as Regional Forces (RF) and Popular Forces (PF) to guard the villages against VC attack. South Vietnam itself was divided into four separate Military Regions, also called Corps. The northernmost section of South Vietnam, from the Demilitarized Zone (DMZ) down to Quang Ngai province, was called MR 1, or I Corps. Heading southward, there was II Corps and then III Corps. Finally, IV Corps covered the area known as the Mekong Delta.

The communists also divided South Vietnam into Military Regions, and added another designation called a "Front." The B-2 Front comprised the provinces from the southern rim of the Central Highlands down to the tip of South Vietnam. MRs 1 through 4 were in North Vietnam, while MR-5, which initially included all the northern portion of South Vietnam, was further divided up into three separate commands in early 1967. Later, MR-5 shrank to contain only the eastern provinces of the Central Highlands and the coastal provinces in central South Vietnam. The Western Central Highlands and the tri-border area was known as the B-3 Front.

Research

While the government's wartime security classifications of POW intelligence were understandable, one major factor that sparked the growth of the POW/MIA conspiracy theory was the continued postwar classification of POW material long after the end of the war. Initially, the government had a variety of reasons for maintaining the classification of POW intelligence. Many of the sources who had provided us with information were still alive, and one of the cardinal tenets of intelligence work is to not reveal sources and methods. But, after President Nixon had assured the nation that all our prisoners were safely home, for most Americans the POW issue and the painful war were now thankfully over. Plus, an unclassified successor organization to the JPRC was now operational, one whose stated purpose was to handle the humanitarian aspect of remains recovery and coordinate with the families of those still missing.[3] Thus, continuing to classify POW intelligence led many to believe that the government was hiding evidence.

Only very recently has that veil of POW/MIA classification begun to lift. Although the Department of Defense (DOD) in 1978 released fifteen large volumes of wartime intelligence reports under pressure from the POW/MIA families, the government's massive database of POW files has generally remained classified. However, one of the witnesses at the first hearing of the Senate Select Committee on POW/MIA Affairs in November 1991 was Garnett "Bill" Bell. At that time, Bell was widely considered to be the foremost expert in the government on the Vietnamese and the POW/MIA issue. Because of his expertise, he was chosen to head the first official United States office opened in Vietnam since the fall of Saigon, the U.S. POW/MIA office. During questioning at the first hearing, Bell recommended that all of the POW/MIA material accumulating in government files be declassified except for active live-sighting investigations.[4]

The Senate Select Committee agreed, and in 1992 they were able to achieve the declassification of much POW material though a presidential Executive Order. Although this Executive Order (EO) directed the release of all POW intelligence documents, much information was blacked out in a security process called redacting, which excerpted those portions that revealed intelligence sources and methods or unduly compromised a family's privacy.

Although the Vietnamese for years denied they possessed POW files, recently they have begun to release some POW-related material to the U.S. government. An undercover operation helped force the Vietnamese to reveal these files. In 1991–92, Ted Schweitzer, a DIA contractor posing as a private American researcher, discovered and copied thousands of wartime photographs and documents regarding American POWs.[5] Since then, more access to Vietnam's archives has been granted to official U.S. researchers. Unfortunately, few of the over 30,000 documents and photographs released by the Vietnamese actually pertain to missing Americans.

With such a glut of anonymous government bureaucracies and highly classified data, how could one hope to accurately re-create what has been hidden and forgotten for so long? Early in my research on the POW/MIA issue, I was fortunate enough to stumble upon a vault of information that had not been provided to the Senate Committee, despite its request to DOD. Contained in the Vietnam room of the Center for Military History at Carlisle Barracks at the Army War College in Pennsylvania were the majority of the JPRC weekly and monthly reports detailing their recovery efforts. These reports were scattered among thousands of other original documents that had been flown out of Saigon in the waning days of the war. By searching through every single document I was able to discover over 80 percent of the previously missing JPRC reports. Oddly enough, these documents had been declassified in 1985 by the CMH staff, who were simply following normal declassification procedures. All the while the families and activists were pushing for the release of classified documents, a literal treasure trove of material lay declassified but untouched.

Further, since these were the original documents, they contained the signature blocks of the officers who served in the JPRC. Through the use of national telephone directories, and the kind assistance of several current military officers, I was able to locate and interview almost all of the officers and NCOs who had served with the JPRC. Their insights were invaluable and their oral histories are an indispensable part of this effort. Almost to a man, they still expressed great frustration and bitterness at not having rescued any of their fellow Americans.

Other critical oral sources are the interviews with the individuals who managed the national POW programs, the men who synthesized the various forms of intelligence on U.S. POW/MIAs and provided it to the highest levels of the government. Finally, the stirring accounts by the men who actually participated on the raids, or who were taken prisoner, provide the gripping details that no documents could ever furnish.

The "McCain Bill," a law written by Senator John McCain, a former POW who served on the Senate Select Committee, was based on an earlier proposal by then Congressman Bob Smith. It stipulated that the vast amounts of POW/MIA data that were being declassified and released by various government agencies must be housed in a suitable library. The Library of Congress (LOC) was chosen, and through the diligent efforts of both the Photo Duplication Service (PDS) and the Federal Research Division (FRD), thousands of pages were copied onto over 900 reels of microfilm and indexed.[6]

The bulk of these documents consist of thousands of postwar sightings, called *source reports.*[7] These came mainly from Southeast Asian refugees who had either seen or heard about American POWs. The second major group consisted of the case file on each individual MIA. McCain's bill, however, cleverly authorized DPMO to only release the case files of men still missing as of the date of the legislation and only with the permission of the family. Therefore, no files on any of the returned men were released. The final tally amounted to less than half the total casualty files held by DIA on American POW/MIAs.

In an unusual and welcome move, the Senate Committee, at the urging of its vice-chairman Senator Bob Smith, voted to immediately open its files to the public after they ceased operations.[8] The Committee files and much declassified material was transferred to the National Archives Record Administration (NARA), where I found many critical documents in the voluminous files of Frank Sieverts, the former Special Assistant to the Secretary of State for POW Affairs.

Another find of great importance in understanding the government's efforts is the massive POW/MIA files of the Central Intelligence Agency. In response to a Freedom of Information Act (FOIA) request in 1984 by the Executive Director of the National League of POW/MIA Families, Ann Mills-Griffiths, the CIA searched through its enormous Vietnam and Laos Operational files and created over two hundred large bound volumes of POW/MIA-related documents, which are currently warehoused by the CIA's Office of Freedom of Information and Privacy Coordinator. I was able to search each volume individually, taking home almost a thousand pages of fascinating material.

Of special interest are the documents available at the Presidential Library of Lyndon B. Johnson in Austin, Texas. I was able to uncover previously unknown State Department documents at the LBJ Library, most notably message traffic from the U.S. Embassy in Vientiane pertaining to the loss of men in Laos. Open source material, such as books by former soldiers, papers from academic conferences, and dozens of articles on the POW issue contributed much corollary information.

Also extremely useful was Douglas Pike's Indochina Archive. The Archive consists of his enormous personal collection of material gathered while working from 1961–1975 as an employee of the U.S. Embassy in Saigon. Mr. Pike is considered by many to be one of the top Vietnam experts in the United States. His huge accumulation of official wartime government publications, newspaper articles, captured enemy documents, and communist media monitored by the CIA's Foreign Broadcast Information Service (FBIS) is sorted into various categories, including a major section on POW/MIAs. Mr. Pike recently donated a large portion of his collection to Texas Tech University's Center for the Study of the Vietnam Conflict, which is rapidly growing into America's premier research facility on the war.

Conclusion

It is impossible to adequately describe all the different raids and valiant efforts to recover American POWs. There are far too many documents scattered in too many archives, too many untold stories or memories fogged by the passage of the years or the unwillingness to dredge up old emotions, and probably still other documents too important or too forgotten to declassify.

Any historic account should recapture the great efforts as well as the honest mistakes and outright blunders of the people who both made the decisions and carried out the orders. Judgment should be tempered by the passage of time. Unfortunately, in the highly emotional atmosphere surrounding the issue of American POWs and MIAs, with its charges of governmental cover-up and countercharges of activist fraud, it seems that little room is left to uncover any semblance of the truth for the missing men, their families, or this nation.

2. 1961–64: Early Losses

They told me that since Voice of America had already announced my execution,
no one knew I was alive or where to look for me, so I might as well cooperate
with them.
—*Charles Klusmann, a Navy aviator who was shot down in Laos and who later*
  escaped, describing his interrogator's reasoning as to why he should make a po-
  litical statement in favor of the Pathet Lao

The experiences of the first American captives in South Vietnam and Laos provided an ominous warning for the future as their Vietnamese and Laotian captors
were intent on coercing American prisoners into making political statements for
the "revolutionary forces." The interrogators of the Viet Cong (VC) guerrillas
and the North Vietnamese–supported Pathet Lao (PL) who captured them attempted to manipulate the American POWs into signing propaganda statements
or into making radio broadcasts denouncing the United States. The main themes
for these political statements included praising the "revolutionary forces" for their
humane treatment, condemning U.S. involvement, or depicting how despised
the GVN or Royal Lao governments were among the populace. Most Americans
resisted making such statements, although a few felt compelled to sign them to
survive; upon release, they all immediately repudiated them.

Although the communists had accomplished much indoctrination success with
the French POWs from the first Indochina War, and despite receiving advice from

the communist Chinese (who shared their Korean War experiences with the Vietnamese), a similar indoctrination attempt failed with the early American POWs.[1] The NLF hoped this political instruction would lead the POWs to work for the antiwar movement in their home countries after their release. This miscalculation of the level of cooperation of American POWs forced the VC to carefully reevaluate their policy of early release. Although their program initially failed, the VC continued to study the psychology of the American soldiers they captured and they reoriented their POW education techniques, if not their entire fighting strategies, accordingly.[2] The communists would get plenty of future subjects for testing. As American advisors became more involved in helping the South Vietnamese military fight the VC, they became targets for attack and capture. Later, as the U.S. involvement grew heavier in Southeast Asia and more American troops became engaged in direct combat, U.S. servicemen and contract civilians started to be taken prisoners of war or were listed as Missing in Action in ever increasing numbers.

Unfortunately for the early American POWs, U.S. ability to provide effective rescue operations was almost nonexistent. In Laos, short of direct intervention by American combat forces, there was absolutely no hope of a combat raid to rescue any of the Americans held by the Pathet Lao. Moreover, the administration of President John F. Kennedy was extremely reluctant to undertake any such action, mainly to avoid a conflict with the Soviet Union or to compromise the neutrality of the fragile Lao government. The Royal Lao Army was far from an effective fighting force and incapable of such action, and the Hmong, a tough tribe who lived in the mountains of northern Laos and who eventually became the primary adversaries of the NVA/PL, were not well-equipped enough for such operations.

The situation in South Vietnam was somewhat better, but the American forces were so few and the South Vietnamese so weak that without proper intelligence, the chances of rescue were slim. Still, local American led forces launched immediate searches for U.S. soldiers and civilians when they were captured.

The Plain of Jars

Some of the first captures and combat deaths of Americans during the Indochina conflict occurred in Laos in the context of the fighting in 1961–62 between the Pathet Lao, the neutralist forces under rebel Captain Kong Le (then allied with the Pathet Lao) and the Royal Lao government. One of the major geographical features in central Laos is the Plain of Jars, an open grassy plain where thousands of large earthen jars dot the landscape, remnants from the ancient Kingdom of Laos. Like a chess master who understands that controlling the center of the board often leads to victory, the competing factions understood that tactically the Plain of Jars was essential in holding northern Laos. Despite increased clandestine American support for the Royal Lao government, which included the presence of roughly four hundred U.S. "advisors" under a program code-named *White Star,* in the latest dry-season offensive the combined North Vietnamese/Pathet Lao and neutralist Kong Le troops had quickly overrun the poorly led Royal Lao soldiers and occupied the strategic Plain.

Apparently the turmoil was not enough to deter the adventuresome spirit of Charles Duffy, a civilian who worked for the American Embassy. On January 13, 1961, Duffy left on a hunting trip from the Lao capital, Vientiane. He departed in a rented jeep and was accompanied by a Lao guide. Several days later, the guide returned with the jeep and informed the American Embassy that Pathet Lao forces had stopped them outside the capital and had taken Duffy away. Duffy became the first American missing in Laos and he remains missing to this day.[3]

Since the United States was backing the Royal Lao government, the Soviets weighed in on the rebels' side with heavy material support, thereby presenting JFK's new administration with its first Cold War crisis. To monitor the Soviet supply and communist military activity, the U.S. Embassy in Vientiane began a series of reconnaissance flights over the Plain using a specially equipped Douglas C-47 cargo aircraft named *Rose Bowl.* For the past several months the airplane had been conducting photographic and electronic surveillance missions over the Plain. Recently, the U.S. embassy had been attempting to locate a beacon the Soviets were using to guide their resupply aircraft into a small airstrip at Xieng Khouang, a town located near the Plain.[4] The Plain was known to be ringed with enemy AAA guns, but so far the communists had not fired on the unarmed aircraft with its clearly visible U.S. markings.

That was about to change. On March 23, 1961, the aircraft departed Vientiane and was traveling to Saigon with its normal crew of six, plus two passengers, Army Major Edgar Weitkamp, an administrative assistant in the attaché's office, and Army Major Lawrence Bailey, another assistant in the attaché's office. As the plane began its pass near the town of Xieng Khouang, antiaircraft guns fired on it, hitting a wing. Bailey, who was the only one wearing a parachute, jumped from the plane as it began to spiral toward the ground. His left arm was broken as he exited the plane, and his ankles and legs were badly bruised on landing. Unable to move, he was quickly captured by neutralist troops. Bailey was the flight's only known survivor, although much speculation has arisen in the last several years that Weitkamp may also have survived, at least initially.[5]

Bailey's first interrogation was by Pathet Lao and Neutralist officers who attempted to ascertain the size of the American contingent in Laos, U.S. policy toward Laos, and U.S. support of Vang Pao, the Hmong leader who had been recruited by the CIA to raise a guerrilla army. After several days, he was flown on a Soviet-built AN-2 "Colt" to the town of Sam Neua, the capital of Sam Neua province (now called Houa Phan) and a Pathet Lao stronghold. His broken arm in a cast, Bailey began a long ordeal in Pathet Lao captivity. As a prisoner, he endured disease, hunger, solitary confinement, and very difficult living conditions.[6]

Bailey was the first American captive of the Pathet Lao, but their numbers increased on April 22, 1961, when a team of American Special Forces under the command of Army Captain Walter H. Moon were riding in an armored car which was ambushed by communist forces in the battle of Vang Vieng. These Army advisors were in Laos assisting the RLA as part of the *White Star* program. Moon, who suffered a bad head wound, and Sergeant Orville R. Ballenger were captured. Two other sergeants, Gerald M. Biber and John Bischoff, are believed to have been killed although their ultimate fates remain unknown.

Several weeks later, an H-34 helicopter was also shot down; it was carrying two Air America employees and an NBC newsman named Grant Wolfkill. The three Americans, plus Moon and Ballenger, were held separate from Bailey at a prison camp called Lat Theung, located south of the Plain of Jars. Bailey continued to be held in Sam Neua, farther to the north and closer to the Vietnamese border. A total of six Americans were now held by the Pathet Lao. The CIA was unable to locate any of them, although they did receive sporadic reports indicating that Americans were being held in Nong Het, another town near the Vietnamese border.[7]

The Pathet Lao interrogated Walter Moon using a questionnaire probably developed with North Vietnamese help.[8] He never fully recovered from his head wound and the injury made his behavior increasingly erratic. When Ballenger later returned to U.S. control, he stated that the Pathet Lao guards had begun to fear Moon's odd behavior and killed him after an aborted "escape" attempt. Wolfkill also reported hearing several rifle shots and witnessing a bloodied Moon being carried from the prison building where they were being held.[9] The PL told the American government that Moon was buried outside the prison, but several attempts by the U.S. government in 1991–92 to locate and excavate his grave failed. The sites shown to the team were empty.

With the signing of the Geneva Accords on Laos in August 1962, the remaining prisoners were released and returned to Vientiane. During the Lao civil war, the United States had no functional Search and Rescue capabilities that could have assisted the captured Americans. When the CIA sent Air Force Major Heinie Aderholt undercover to Laos, Aderholt told Bob Weaver, another undercover officer, to instruct the Air America pilots in simple Escape and Evasion techniques, such as signaling their location to search aircraft with a mirror. Some instruction was better than none. Although a Peace Accord had been signed, the halt to the fighting was only temporary. While the *White Star* teams were withdrawn, American support for the Royal Lao government continued and military aid increased. Laos, however, had not seen the last of Americans fighting in their country, nor had America seen the last of its POWs in Pathet Lao hands.

Communist POW Policy

To grasp communist POW policy, it is important to understand their motivations and methods for handling POWs. The North Vietnamese organizations that controlled American POWs and, just as importantly, their remains and personal effects, were controlled either by the security forces, known then as the Ministry of Public Security (MPS) and renamed after the war the Ministry of the Interior (MOI), or by the military.

The full extent of the Vietnamese organizational structure set up to exploit American POWs has never been completely determined, but basically the MPS ran the prisons while the military was responsible for indoctrination and intelligence interrogations. A political organization within the army called the General Political Directorate (GPD) articulated the military's POW policy. The most important factor in understanding Vietnamese behavior toward American prisoners is that the Communist Party dominated all aspects of the war. The Party viewed the military as the "tool of the Party," and the security forces as the "absolutist tool of the Party," which meant that the military and security forces within the North Vietnamese state were completely subordinate to the goals of the Party. Moreover, within the ranks of the military the Party leadership installed Political Officers (PO) who acted as a separate and superior chain of command.

With almost religious fervor, the Party sought to undermine or convert the enemy forces through a process called "proselytizing." Proselytizing was a series of propaganda acts aimed at either motivating a targeted group, such as the civilian masses, to change sides, or modifying the belief system of the POW so that he became a supporter of the "revolution" and its goals. The section within the GPD that directed this propaganda warfare against U.S. soldiers and also handled POW affairs was called the Enemy Proselytizing Department. An Enemy Proselytizing officer was assigned to each NVA unit down to Battalion level. At lower levels, the political officers handled prisoner duties.

The basic communist intentions toward POWs were revealed to U.S. intelligence through the capture of dozens of POW policy documents in South Vietnam. For example, one document comments on the importance of carrying out the correct POW procedures. "The policy essentially aims at attacking the enemy's morale. To implement the policy well is to contribute actively to the destruction of the enemy's idea of resistance and to introduce the idea of surrendering into the enemy ranks."[10] Other policy documents state that "To faithfully carry out the Party's POW policy . . . means to . . . hit right at the enemy's vulnerabilities . . . to launch a vital blow that will divide their ranks both in ideology and organization and create favorable conditions for our political struggle." In essence, "The problem of POWs and defectors is important and complicated since it is the basic content of our political offense against the enemy."[11]

The communist POW policy was directed not just at enemy soldiers, but at all elements of the enemy's society. "The proper implementation of our policy toward prisoners can also exert a great political influence on enemy soldiers' dependents, the people in SVN controlled areas, the American people, the people of satellite countries, as well as the people of the world. Through our humane treatment of enemy PW's and explanation of our PW policy, we can enlist more support from foreign countries. This contributes to making the anti-U.S. war movements in the USA and in the world increasing strong and further isolating the enemy."[12]

It is beyond doubt that the communists sought to use the POW issue to foment and drive the antiwar sentiment in the United States. Their releases later in the war of POWs captured in North Vietnam directly to antiwar activist groups were designed to increase the stature of the protesters and to affect the American strategy, both in war and at the Paris Peace Talks. The Vietnamese are masters at examining their enemies for flaws, a process refined from, as the old Vietnamese saying goes, "always having lived in an armed camp."[13] The assumption that the POW/MIA issue is without complexity or depth is totally false. In fact, the exact opposite is true. The communist policies toward POWs display a carefully conceived plan to strike at the emotional core of the enemy, both the Americans and the South Vietnamese. Further, the conception that the communists were ragtag guerrillas running around unorganized in the jungle is also wrong. The communist logistics systems, training programs, and organizational abilities were far more complex and well thought out than we have ever given them credit for. In many ways, the communists were bigger bureaucrats than we were. The DRV intelligence services are among the best in world, and the United States has been ill-served by our constant underestimation of them.

Into Vietnam

George F. Fryett, Jr. became the first American prisoner of the communist insurgents in South Vietnam. Fryett was a young enlisted man with a high-level clearance who worked as the top-secret-document control clerk at the U.S. Military Assistance Group headquarters in Saigon. On December 24, 1961, he was riding his bicycle to go swimming at a pool in Thu Duc on the outskirts of Saigon when two members of the VC Saigon-Cholon-Gia Dinh Special Zone, also on bikes, surrounded him. One used a hand grenade to hit Fryett on the head, wounding him and knocking him unconscious. Intelligence reports of his being exhibited in villages north of Saigon by his captors triggered a sweep by large forces of Vietnamese troops.[14]

Fryett was transported to the main POW camp of the communist Central Office for South Vietnam (COSVN), which at that time was located near the Cambodian border. Due to the lack of trained personnel, in May 1962 Colonel Le Chan, Chief of the COSVN Political Bureau, assumed the additional duties of commandant of this POW camp.[15] Fryett spent six difficult months at the camp, where he became ill and lost much weight. The camp political cadre pressed Fryett to make various statements supporting the communists' cause while describing their lenient treatment of him and asking for his freedom. Several weeks before his release, Liberation Radio broadcast the contents of letters they claimed were written by Fryett, including an announcement to his wife that he was alive and being treated well. Although he was released on June 24, 1962, the NLF continued to broadcast his "statements," including a plea by Fryett for the United States to leave South Vietnam.

What the NLF didn't know was that Fryett was divorced. His parents immediately recognized the error and used this to deny that their son had been "brainwashed." Back in Saigon, Fryett publicly denied that he had signed anything while a captive. However, the U.S. military's Code of Conduct provided guidelines for prisoner behavior that specifically precluded making any such political statements. Because of the broadcasts, Counter-Intelligence (CI) in Saigon suspected that Fryett had violated the Code. Given his high clearance, they subjected him to a thorough debriefing. Due to his claims of illness and weight loss, CI ordered a complete physical examination. The exam noted that although he had lost weight, he was in very good condition.

This finding generated even more suspicion and the CI began to press him over the radio broadcasts. According to a CI document, during his debriefing Fryett reported that he was "subjected to three major interrogations. On one occasion he stated he was given a written examination, which he was required to complete. He gave only personal information in response and claimed he answered all questions concerning military information with a negative reply. . . ."[16] But, Fryett admitted, while he was ill, "Because of the prolonged interrogations and indoctrination to which I was subject, I must, in all honesty, recognize the fact that a possibility that I made or signed statements does exist." He denied that he was approached or recruited to act as an intelligent agent. With no further evidence of any misconduct by Fryett, CI allowed him to return to the States without pressing any charges.

Before Fryett was turned over in June, however, another loss and release incident occurred. After the decision by the communists to release him had already been made, a broadcast by the NLF radio station announced that it "was being held up because the truth had not been told about the release of the other two Americans."[17] That event involved an American Special Forces unit on patrol in the more northern South Vietnamese province of Quang Nam. Four American NCOs from the CIA-directed Combined Studies Division (CSD), which was the forerunner of SOG, were captured in an ambush. George Groom, Francis Quinn, James Marchand, and James Gabriel were on a training patrol with a platoon of Vietnamese militia called Popular Forces. The platoon included a Vietnamese translator and a radio operator. They were captured on April 8, 1962, because, as Groom said, "we broke all the rules."[18]

Together, Groom and Quinn had linked up with Gabriel and Marchand the day before. The Vietnamese radio operator had convinced the four to stay in the same location for two consecutive nights and to acquire some food supplies for a party the next day. As Groom recalls, "On the morning of the 8th, a couple of natives from the nearby village of An Chau came over to our camp. Marchand and the interpreter were talking to the villagers about buying some food, when suddenly the VC opened fire on us. We retreated with the platoon to a tiny wooded area that offered the only cover in the immediate area. Gabriel was on the radio, trying to call in that we had been attacked. Then he was shot on the right side by someone. Marchand picked up the radio next, and then he was hit in the leg. By this time we were surrounded by VC holding rifles pointed at us.

"The VC cleaned up the battlefield quickly, and when he left they made Quinn and I carry the two wounded Americans. We carried them for about one half mile before they ordered us to leave them by the side of the trail. I set Marchand's leg, which was broken. He told me that our radio operator was the one who had shot him in the leg. I had also seen some of our platoon helping the VC carry equipment away. Quinn tried to patch up Gabriel, who was in much worse condition. We didn't want to leave them, but they insisted and told us that other VC would come by later and pick them up. We had no choice, so we left them by the trail. A little while later, Quinn told me he heard shots."

The patrol's home base was outside of Danang. Alerted by the radio call, the camp informed Major Harry Munck, the Executive Officer of Combined Studies, that the patrol was under attack. Munck immediately ordered Major Jack Warren, the camp commander, to form a search team using Vietnamese helicopters and hired mercenaries. Tracking the Americans to the village, they followed the trail used by the VC unit and discovered the bodies of Gabriel and Marchand, each killed by a bullet to the head. After following the trail several miles deeper into the mountains, it disappeared in the thick jungle growth. Despite the lack of intelligence on their location, and having few resources, Munck kept sending patrols out to look for them until the day Groom and Quinn were released. As Munck recalls, "It was too early in the war for any large effort; we could only use what we had within our own small unit plus whatever the South Vietnamese had available."[19]

Groom and Quinn were marched for two days to a temporary camp in the mountains. None of the VC spoke English, so the VC used the South Vietnamese interpreter to translate for them. The VC repeatedly asked Groom "what type of plane they had flown in on, what were the markings on the plane and what were the nationalities of the pilots that flew us in. They wanted to know what camp we belonged to, what kind of training we had and what we specialized in. Later, the Camp Commander asked us if we would stay with them and train their people. We just laughed and told them no." Other than these few questions, the VC seemed indifferent to gathering military intelligence from the prisoners. Apparently, this could be explained by the ease with which the Viet Cong were able to obtain this type of intelligence from other sources.[20]

The VC continued attempting to indoctrinate the pair, using every opportunity to change their outlook. When a South Vietnamese Air Force plane dropped bombs very close to the camp about a week after they were captured, the VC insinuated that the South Vietnamese had deliberately tried to kill Groom and Quinn. "They told us that to our face," remarked Groom.

About four days after they arrived in the camp, a Vietnamese man appeared. Although he didn't speak English, he told them through the interpreter that he was a schoolteacher from Danang. He said he had just come to observe them and see if they were getting enough to eat, since the rations of the VC were barely enough to keep the VC alive, let alone a much larger American. Shortly thereafter, he disappeared. However, this was no ordinary "schoolteacher." He was either the Danang City Party Committee chairman, Nguyen Thanh Nam, or more likely a very high-ranking communist cadre named Professor Ho An, a teacher at Danang University. Professor An was an undercover member of the NLF Central Committee; later he traveled extensively to the Military Region 5 (MR-5) POW camp to conduct propaganda training and he would help to arrange the release of other American POWs later in 1967. Professor An, however, was fluent in English and was also the head of the Vietnamese-American Friendship Society in Danang.[21]

The decision to release Groom and Quinn came directly from the National Liberation Front (NLF) and MR-5 headquarters. During their time in captivity, the VC had expended most of their indoctrination effort on trying to explain to Groom and Quinn why they were fighting the South Vietnamese government and trying to convince them that their cause was just. When they asked them if they understood, Groom and Quinn just nodded their heads in agreement. The VC seemed to naively accept this. However, even though the communists consistently attempted to coerce Groom and Quinn into signing political statements, the VC weren't the only ones capable of cunning manipulation. Groom remembers that "through our interpreter, we kept telling the VC they could make a huge propaganda statement by releasing us on May Day, the day of the communist commemoration. We could see them thinking about it. Two days before our release on May 1st, they had us start doing exercises, gave us extra food and shaved us."

On the day before their release, Groom and Quinn were seated at a table outside and were told they had to sign statements before they could be set free. A cameraman started taking photos. "I looked over at Quinn. He was holding his pen in his left hand instead of his right, so I put my pen in my left hand also. After a while, the VC caught on. They were plenty mad." Despite catching their ruse, the VC still forced them to sign the documents.[22]

As a condition for leaving the camp, Groom and Quinn were required to carry pamphlets printed in English to hand out to other American troops. Groom noticed that the pamphlets were "nicely printed, like on a typewriter," and he felt they might provide intelligence on the thinking of the VC. Groom and Quinn tucked the pamphlets in their boots and covered them with their trousers to hide them from any ARVN soldiers. Despite their precautions, the ARVN troops who found the pair noticed the pamphlets in their pant legs and confiscated them.

When Groom and Quinn returned, the Army military-intelligence debriefing team wanted to know everything about the camp, what weapons they had and what kind of questions they were asked. Groom and Quinn informed the debriefers that the VC had mentioned that they were holding one other American

POW, undoubtedly George Fryett, and told them about the pamphlets. When a press conference was held several days later, however, their debriefers instructed them to deny any knowledge of the leaflets, fearing that the media would print the VC propaganda. Despite these efforts, shortly after the release of the pair a CBS reporter discovered the existence of the leaflets and broadcast the contents. The military was forced to admit that Groom and Quinn had been ordered to cover up the presence of the pamphlets.[23] When this decision to lie about the pamphlets was revealed, the VC announced a delay in setting Fryett free.

After the release of Groom and Quinn, on May 30, 1962, the VC attacked a leprosarium near Ban Me Thuot in the Central Highlands of South Vietnam, capturing three Christian missionaries, Dr. Eleanor Vietti and two male assistants. The VC also took large amounts of medical supplies and stole the sanitarium's truck. Alerted to their kidnapping, the Embassy ordered Major Harry Munck to begin a search. "The son of another missionary and I went to Ban Me Thuot to locate the three," said Munck. "We contacted the Rhade, a local Montagnard, (a group of non-Vietnamese peoples who live in the mountainous areas of Central Vietnam), and discovered the missing missionaries were still alive. The rumors we were getting from the Rhade were that the VC wanted to use them to treat their wounded and sick. In connection with other operations in the area, we attempted to rescue them." On June 12 and 13, the Embassy noted that the U.S. Special Forces "conducted an operation in the Ban Me Thuot area following up on reports of the sighting of three. Reports were evidently correct but the VC and their captives had left prior to the arrival of the forces."[24]

One reason they were not immediately released like the other POWs is that the VC didn't reap the expected propaganda bonus they had hoped for from the others. Reports from local informants concerning the three stated that "the VC intended on releasing Vietti and her companions, but had changed their minds after Sergeant George Fryett had 'broken his promise' to the VC and had said things that he had promised not to say."[25] Ominously, the NLF radio station hinted that American prisoners now held in South Vietnam or captured in the future would not be released so quickly.[26]

While the NLF did make future releases, the missionaries never returned home. The Christian Alliance continued for the next ten years to follow up on reports of their continued survival, but most reports were unclear. In later years the communists have offered differing versions of their fate. One source interviewed in early 1993 stated that they were killed by the VC raiding party about 500 meters from the compound. Another source, the former Province Communist Party Secretary, stated that the three were killed by bombs from a South Vietnamese aircraft and buried next to a river bank.[27] Harry Munck was convinced they were alive at least until mid-June 1962, and he questions the communist versions of their deaths. "They could well have been killed in a bombing or strafing raid, but I find it difficult to believe they were killed shortly after leaving the compound. Why didn't the VC just kill them when they overran the place? Our information was accurate, but our rescue attempt just missed them." For this most intriguing and difficult Missing in Action case, no clue has yet been uncovered that provides the definitive answer.

The last case in 1962 involved another U.S. Special Forces advisor captured by a VC patrol. On July 23, 1962, Sergeant Roque Matagulay was hunting near Pleiku when a VC unit spotted him walking alone. The *New York Times* noted that, like the others, Matagulay resisted signing statements but finally signed "only when I believed I was at the end of my physical endurance. Sgt. Roque Matagulay said . . . that when he signed four documents he had a severe case of malaria and other diseases and had dropped from 185 pounds to 145 pounds. He had been a prisoner four months. The sergeant said he believed that the communist guerrillas had tapes of his statements."[28] He was released on December 24, 1962.

Even though communist POW policy encouraged the capture of prisoners and expressly forbade the killing of prisoners, the VC had executed Gabriel and Marchand. Party political officers immediately set about correcting such breaches by increasing training in POW matters and emphasizing the Party policy that stated that "US POW's must be properly handled, well fed, and made to write letters praising the lenient policy of the Front towards US POW's, for international purposes, and to encourage their fellow countrymen to go back to the USA and stop committing crimes against the Vietnamese people."[29] VC political cadres were instructed to "popularize" the "effect of the recent release of captives . . . to local units."[30] If POWs were to be executed, it was to be with a specific purpose in mind, not wanton acts of murder by undisciplined troops. Though not always well adhered to, Communist Party POW policy toward Americans was nonetheless consistent and motivated by the Party's intense desire to use POWs to gain a political advantage in the war against the GVN and the U.S. imperialists. The coming years would give them their chance.

The First Civilians

Although the missionaries had disappeared, the early pattern of quick release continued with the first American and foreign civilians to be taken prisoner in South

Vietnam. An Australian, Wilfred Arthur, was captured and released in October 1961. A Philippine national, Alfred Mungada, who worked as a surveyor, and a German, Olaf Mueller, a tourist, were also taken prisoner and released. Mungada was captured on December 9, 1961, and released on February 20, 1962. He was held for a time with Fryett. Mueller was on a sightseeing tour to a Buddhist shrine just north of Saigon when the taxi he was riding in was stopped by VC guerrillas dressed in South Vietnamese uniforms. Marched for days through the jungle, he and the taxi driver contracted malaria and underwent political indoctrination. When they were released on June 9, 1962, they were marched to a road where the VC flagged down a car, which took them to a nearby village. "At the village, he said, 'I hired a car and returned to Saigon as I left—in a taxi.'"[31]

The seizure of Arthur A. Krause, the first American civilian captured by the VC, eventually led to a stunning VC proposal. Krause was working for Philco as a contract engineer for the U.S. Army building bridges and roads and expanding Special Forces camps. He was seized on June 8, 1963, about forty-five miles southwest of Danang while inspecting a bridge that had been blown up by the VC. He was also scouting for a gold mine that was rumored to be in the area. As he was leaving the destroyed bridge, his jeep was surrounded by six guerrillas. He was unable to flee or resist. The VC tied a rope around Krause's hands and neck and led him to a nearby village, where he spent the night.[32]

On the third day, the group linked up with a man who spoke broken English. Apparently the VC in Military Region 5 had not improved their English-language capability since the capture of Groom and Quinn, and it would not be until the second month of Krause's captivity that the VC found a competent English-speaking interrogator. They "conscripted a Mr. Phan Tu, who was doing newspaper work at the time, to serve as a translator for the captured American. The Front also chose him because he had worked with French POWs in the 1950s."[33]

Before the arrival of Tu, who called himself "Bon," the VC officer who spoke the broken English constantly accused Krause of being a spy.[34] Krause related that "since they accused everybody of being a spy, I just ignored them and kept denying it." What the VC didn't know was that in fact Krause was a spy. Krause had been working for three years as a clandestine asset of Army intelligence under an experimental program to recruit promising civilians who worked in areas of civil unrest.

The VC interrogation consisted of repeated questions about the fortifications of the various camps Krause had worked on. They were especially interested in any tunnels that had been dug. "I tried repeatedly to convince Bon that there were no tunnels. He just wouldn't believe me. He kept saying the French had dug tunnels, why didn't the Americans?" Krause reported that the VC had also attempted to indoctrinate him, but generally refrained from the harsher political reeducation attempted with the other Americans. Tu stated that the NLF eventually decided to release Krause because it was determined he was a civilian contract employee and not a military advisor. More important, Tu said, "during the detention period the captive had ample opportunity to see how well local people interacted with the NLF forces," and he "could return to U.S. control and inform the American people" about the war.[35] How did the VC know Krause was only a civilian, as he claimed? "When they interrogated me," states Kause, "they knew everything about my work for Philco. Obviously, they had access to my 201 Personnel file at the Philco offices in Saigon. Since we had over ten local Vietnamese working for us, it didn't surprise me."

Shortly before his release, Tu made a bold offer. The Saigon embassy reported that Krause was informed by Tu/Bon "that if Krause returned he could arrange the release of U.S. captives of the VC. Bon explained that VC had no desire continue hold prisoners who established the *[sic]* identity as military personnel or civilians with a legitimate reason for being in Vietnam. They would continue to hold those they considered to be spies. When Krause raised questions of missionaries Bon was less forthcoming and professed not to be fully informed. Bon told Krause the VC wanted a secure method to release prisoners which would not expose the VC nor endanger the lives of prisoners whom they said might be killed by ARVN. . . . Bon told Krause he was speaking with the authority of Nguyen Huu Tho, the Chairman of the Central Committee of the NLF."[36]

When Krause was released near Danang on November 22 he was immediately flown to Saigon, where he underwent a lengthy debriefing by his friends at Army intelligence. Mentioning the VC offer, he was taken to see the American ambassador, Henry Cabot Lodge, and the CIA station chief. "When I told Lodge about the plan, Lodge was very surprised and wanted to pursue it. Even Lodge's British advisor, Sir Robert Thompson, was generally for it, although he warned me it could be dangerous. The CIA chief, however, seemed almost indifferent." Krause volunteered to stay in Vietnam to assist other POWs in gaining their freedom, but in February 1964 his offer was politely declined. "Lodge never told me the reason why, he just said we can't do it. I always believed that the GVN squelched the offer because they didn't want to present any opportunity to grant the slightest recognition to the NLF."

The NLF, who had devised the plan, had stipulated one condition that made the Americans suspect their motivations and that led to the U.S. disapproval. The

NLF wanted no ARVN involvement, fearing that the ARVN would kill the prisoners and blame it on them. To the heightened political senses of the communists, who were constantly attempting to shape the perceptions of the peasants, such an event would provide propaganda fodder for the South Vietnamese. The Embassy thought it was a smoke screen to gain direct negotiations with the United States, but Krause believed them. "They told me that such an incident had happened before when they had tried to release a GVN District Chief. Bon seemed quite fearful of ARVN treachery, to the point that the release point had to be in an open field where they could watch the POW physically get into the helicopter and depart. Therefore, they only wanted to release POWs to the Americans. While I'm sure there was a hoped-for element of political recognition in their plan, Bon seemed quite sincere to me in his desire to avoid the ARVNs for the reasons he stated."

Krause eventually left Vietnam and returned to the United States. In September 1964 he decided to visit Washington on some business matters. Surprisingly, while he was in the city he was contacted by three men—two military-intelligence officers and a State Department representative. The three quizzed him about the original VC proposal and he reiterated to them the VC offer to set up a secure channel for releasing American POWs. Secretary of State Dean Rusk queried the U.S. Embassy in Saigon about the possibility of exchanging prisoners. In October, Rusk noted to the Embassy that "Govt. and public interest in U.S. prisoners in Vietnam has increased over past several weeks. . . . Is there any possibility that exchange of significant hard-core Viet Cong who have proven intractable could be privately arranged by GVN for . . . Americans?"[37] But Krause had told the State representative that Bon had not asked for exchanges. "He simply wanted to get rid of POWs that were a drain on their meager resources. He also was afraid that if some POWs died, they would be blamed for it and lose political face." After a negative response to any exchanges by the Saigon Embassy, the decision was made by State not to further pursue the NLF offer.

Whether the NLF was truly interested in finding a mechanism to release POWs or whether this offer was simply the first in a long line of dangled bait is unknown. In reviewing the subsequent diplomatic record, one is led to believe that the Front was more interested at this time in achieving propaganda gains than in holding captives long-term. A captured document dated December 1963 clearly outlined their goals. "The recent release of prisoners received a favorable reaction . . . and the common policy was clemency. Take advantage of prisoners for international propaganda purposes. You must understand the experiences and procedures for the release of prisoners in order to provide the necessary documents in the propaganda program."[38] Remarkably, even at this early stage of the war the experiences of the Viet Minh forces with the French POWs during the early 1950s and the lessons learned by the Chinese with foreign POWs in Korea were being applied to American POWs. The guerrillas of the NLF and their masters in Hanoi were seeking public recognition, and by loudly proclaiming a policy of mercy toward POWs they hoped to foster sympathy for their cause in the court of world opinion.

Eugene Debruin

In Laos, the cease-fire brought about by the Geneva Accords was rapidly falling apart. In the northern part of the country, Vang Pao's Hmong were gaining strength under the CIA's clandestine build-up and were continuing to make attacks against the North Vietnamese–backed Pathet Lao forces.[39] In the south, the beleaguered Royal Lao Army (RLA) could only hold certain key outposts and mainly survived through continual resupply from aircraft of Air America, the CIA's contract airline. Although the CIA and the U.S. Embassy maintained tight security about American involvement, some incident was bound to occur that would reveal the covert U.S. presence.

On September 5, 1963, an Air America C-46 carrying rice and buffalo meat to resupply RLA troops in Savannakhet province in southern Laos was shot down by a PL unit. The crew included three Americans, one Chinese, and three Thais. Initial reports from villagers in the area indicated some crewmen survived, but their number and their identities were unknown.[40]

When informed about the loss, the CIA immediately attempted to locate the crewmen. The next morning, two Air America helicopters placed a search team close to the downed plane. Shortly after reaching the site, the team was forced to withdraw due to heavy enemy fire. It was discovered that the American pilot and copilot had been killed in the crash, but the other American, Eugene Debruin, and four other crew members survived and were captured by Pathet Lao forces. After the extraction of the team, the dangerous local situation forced the U.S. ambassador to Laos, Leonard Unger, to order that no more searches be conducted.

The Pathet Lao took the POWs to a prison camp near the PL-controlled town of Tchepone adjacent to the famed Ho Chi Minh Trail, where CIA informants watched them being escorted into the camp. Because the PL had complete control of the area, the "informant doubts that it would be possible to raid the camp and rescue the prisoners. The most serious obstacle to a successful raid is the difficulty that would be encountered in an attempt to get a raiding party into the area."[41]

The Pathet Lao moved quickly to reap propaganda benefits from the unexpected presence of the Americans, and Pathet Lao leader Prince Souphanouvong, a member of the Lao royal family who led the communist Lao faction, began broadcasting accusations of renewed U.S. military interference based on documents found in the plane crash. Since it appeared that any rescue operation was impossible, the only reasonable alternative was to find a diplomatic solution. Ambassador Unger's first move was to attempt to establish contact with the prisoners. He sent a telegram to them via the Pathet Lao offices in Khang Khay and he requested that the Debruin family also send mail.[42]

The CIA, meanwhile, continued to track the location of the prisoners and discovered that the PL were telling the local people that the POWs would be released soon, assuming a "proper" request was made.[43] Unfortunately, no response by Eugene Debruin was received to either Unger's telegram or any letters from his family, although a PL propaganda photo was later found showing him and the captured crew. After repeated U.S. Embassy attempts to gain their release, by December the Embassy had "reached unhappy conclusion that survivors will not be released until PL believes there is something they can buy therewith . . . speculated that this might be withdrawal Air America."[44]

The Embassy's conclusion was prophetic. Debruin, who was known to be alive and a prisoner until August 1966 (when he was last seen by an American prisoner who was escaping from the camp where they were held together), would never come home, nor have his remains been returned. The Eugene Debruin case haunts U.S.-Lao relations. Despite repeated American requests for information, the Lao government has steadfastly maintained that Debruin perished in the 1966 escape attempt and denies any knowledge of the location of his grave. His brother, Dr. Jerry Debruin, continues to press both the American and Lao governments for help in finding the ultimate truth about Eugene's fate. To this day, he is still trying to find out what happened to his brother.[45]

Overrun

In the waning months of 1963, two separate groups of U.S. Special Forces advisors were captured when the Vietnamese units they were part of were overrun by larger VC units. On October 29, 1963, Captain Humberto "Rocky" Versace, Lieutenant James "Nick" Rowe, and a medic, Sergeant Daniel Pitzer, were captured when their Civilian Irregular Defense Group (CIDG) unit in the Mekong Delta was decimated in combat. The CIDGs were a collection of Vietnamese and Cambodians recruited to fight the VC for control of the local villages. Rowe, Versace, and Pitzer were accompanying the CIDG unit on a mission to destroy a reported VC outpost in another village several kilometers away. Although the initial assault went well, the VC quickly regrouped and surrounded the CIDG unit, trapping them against a canal. While trying to escape, Versace was wounded in the leg. He and Rowe were captured together. Pitzer was also seized.[46]

One month later, another group of four Americans were captured at the village of Hiep Hoa, 46 kilometers northwest of Saigon. In a surprise assault on November 24, 1963, the VC used mortars and more than four hundred men to attack and for the first time overrun a Special Forces camp. The first mortar rounds struck directly on target, and the presence of firing inside the camp aimed at the defenders strongly suggested that enemy agents were assisting the VC attack.[47]

The plight of Sergeants Issaac Camacho, Claude McClure, Kenneth Roraback, and George Smith, plus the saga of Versace, Rowe, and Pitzer were the beginning of a true odyssey for American POWs in the South. The days of early release were over. The tempo of the war was increasing and despite the escalating American involvement, the GVN was starting to crumble under the rising communist military/political pressure. Although McClure, Smith, and Pitzer would eventually be released, the communists were by now far more adroit at stage-managing the POW releases to squeeze every ounce of political drama out of them. As U.S. involvement in the war continued, the early pattern of quick VC release of American POWs slowed almost to a complete stop. Given the horrible conditions that most of the POWs endured, combined with the death in captivity of so many prisoners, the initial failure to follow up on the Krause initiative coupled with the additional refusal in 1964 was, in hindsight, probably a serious mistake. Although it undoubtedly would have entailed providing the NLF with some propaganda success, only the inflamed sensitivities of the GVN would have suffered any damage, either real or imagined. While the U.S. embassy in Saigon was interested in gaining the release of the American POWs, they were, ultimately, unprepared to risk or trade the political legitimacy of the Saigon regime to achieve the POWs' freedom.

The MIA List Starts to Grow

The USAF suffered its first MIAs in Southeast Asia on September 2, 1963, when a B-26 carrying three Americans, including Lieutenant Howard "Phil" Purcell, and one Vietnamese disappeared en route to the Danang air base. Although their unit, the famed 1st Air Commandos, dropped almost 500,000 leaflets offering a reward for information on the missing fliers, no word was received on their fate nor was the plane found.

As an example of how the Vietnamese could easily have resolved the suffering of many families years ago, Garnett "Bill" Bell, then the head of the U.S. POW/MIA

Office in Hanoi (then part of the Joint Casualty Resolution Center, or JCRC), recounts how in March 1992 his Vietnamese POW/MIA office counterparts informed him that remains probably belonging to this missing aircrew had been recovered. He traveled to meet a village committee in Kontum Province to receive the personal effects and discovered that "the weapons could still be fired, the leather boots were not rotted, and the pages of the flight manuals were in pristine condition. The Vietnamese actually claimed to have recovered the remains five months before in an area of Vietnam that has one of the heaviest rainfalls in the world. They expected us to believe that they had just recovered these items from the jungle. Plus, they had washed the bones in soap, obviously hoping to remove any traces of the preservative we have found on many skeletal remains turned over to us by the communists."

To ensure the remains were in fact from the crew, DNA testing was conducted on the bones, which confirmed it. After the funeral, Purcell's mother told a reporter, "It's been a long thirty-three years. Until you really know, you never quite give up. My head told me it was over with, but my heart didn't. I only had the one boy, and I thought the world of him. Now I can go up to the grave and know he's there beside his Dad. I'm really relieved that he's here. I wanted him with his Dad."[48]

Much like Laos, for the U.S. military in Vietnam in the early years Search and Rescue (SAR) units, with one small exception in Saigon, were almost nonexistent. Detachment 3, Pacific Air Rescue Center, was not established until April 1, 1962, when South Vietnam and the United States signed the Joint Vietnamese/U.S. Search and Rescue Agreement.[49] However, when another B-26 crashed in January 1964, the SAR forces had improved to the point that the USAF was able to immediately launch a dedicated SAR helicopter to find them. Unfortunately, when they located the downed plane, they were unable to find the occupants. The pilot, Captain Carl Berg Mitchell, would be the subject of several future live-sightings, but he never came home and is still listed as MIA.[50]

Another American pilot, who became the longest-held American prisoner of the war, was Army Captain Floyd Thompson. A Special Forces officer who was flying an L-19 light observation plane with his copilot, Captain Richard Whitesides, he was shot down on March 26, 1964, in Quang Ngai Province. Thompson was told by his captors that his copilot was dead. For years Thompson was also listed as MIA, although he was held in South Vietnam until March 1970 and then moved to North Vietnam, where he was released during Operation *Homecoming*.

One of the great fears of the U.S. military was the possibility that some American POWs or soldiers would succumb to the skilled enemy proselytizers and collaborate. Personnel who merely deserted and went to live in run-down suburbs of

Saigon, while an annoying indicator of low morale, didn't pose any direct threat. But Americans who willingly fought or aided the enemy against their own countrymen were a far different matter. Rumors continually abounded concerning white or black Americans seen with communist troops or carrying weapons. For years, many had considered two Marines, Robert Greer and Fred Schreckengost, to be potential collaborators. Both men disappeared on June 6, 1964, while riding their motor scooter to take a sightseeing tour of some ruins outside of Danang. Their bike was found the next day, but the men had disappeared.

In 1990, Bell was Chief of the JCRC investigation team searching for the pair. He reports that the Vietnamese told the JCRC that the two Marines had been killed during an escape attempt. The Vietnamese took Bell's team to a grave in an open field that was near a Vietnamese cemetery. The JCRC excavated the grave site and found only some cloth scraps. The next day, the Vietnamese told Bell that "grave robbers" had moved the remains to another location. Bell was shown a nearby sweet-potato patch. When Bell walked over to view the location, he noticed the ground was soft and recently cultivated. Although the JCRC team did uncover the remains, Bell believes the Vietnamese "salted" the bones into this new location where the JCRC could find them to prevent the Americans from knowing what had really happened to the two Marines.

Yankee Team Recon

Any pretense to peace in Laos was shattered on March 16, 1964, when a combined North Vietnamese/Pathet Lao force attacked across the Plain of Jars, driving their former allies, the Neutralists, out of the area. At the battle of Tha Thom, the Royal Lao Army also melted away, despite increasing support from Hmong guerrilla ambushes of the communist soldiers. In response to the loss of the town, the U.S. Embassy—which controlled all U.S. military activity in Laos—stepped up the secret bombing of the NVA/PL using Royal Lao aircraft piloted by contract Americans based in Thailand.

The U.S. government had been contemplating further covert action in Laos since November. They had a pressing need for accurate intelligence on the communist movement of supplies and men into South Vietnam, on enemy military capabilities, and on the increase in Chinese road-building in northern Laos. National Security Action Memorandum No. 273, upon which much of the early course of the war was based, called for MACV and the CIA stations in Laos and South Vietnam to develop a program to send small American-led teams of raiders across the border from South Vietnam into Laos to conduct intelligence gathering operations against the Ho Chi Minh Trail.[51] The first six-man group was launched on June 15, 1964, around the Laotian town of Tchepone to gather intelligence on the movement of NVA supplies and men into the South.[52]

Intelligence-gathering missions by ground teams are limited to the small area they can cover and pose the danger of discovery and capture. Aerial reconnaissance, however, can cover a wider spectrum. On May 19, the U.S. government ordered reconnaissance flights using Air Force RF-101 and carrier-based Navy RF-8A aircraft over the Plain of Jars to locate enemy troop positions.[53] The operation was given the code-name *Yankee Team.* Although airplanes carried the risk of being shot down, U.S. ambassador to Laos Leonard Unger attempted to overcome that peril by restricting the airplanes to certain heights which were out of the range of the bigger-caliber AA guns. Still, with the U.S. role in helping the Royal Lao government fight the combined NVA/PL army mushrooming, and the military capabilities of the communists also rapidly growing, an incident was inevitable.

On June 6, 1964, a Navy RF-8A from the carrier USS *Kitty Hawk,* which was stationed in the Gulf of Tonkin, was ordered to conduct a photo recon of the area around Khang Khay, an important Pathet Lao–controlled town deep in rebel territory. Lieutenant Charles Klusmann was flying near the city around noon when his aircraft was hit several times by ground fire. Forced to bail out, Klusmann landed in a tree, bruising his legs and ankles. When his wingman reported him down, a nearby Air America C-123 cargo plane immediately responded and went searching for him.[54] The plane found his location when Klusmann used a mirror to signal his position.

Alerted by the Mayday, two Air America helicopters from Thailand flew to the scene. Because of the political importance of maintaining the facade of Lao neutrality, however, the U.S. Embassy had recently imposed a "no fly" restriction over Pathet Lao territory for the Thai-based American piloted Royal Lao aircraft. Since Klusmann had landed in an enemy region, the Air America helicopters were forced to land and wait for clearance from the U.S. Embassy.

By the time the rescue was approved, Klusmann was already captured. He was taken to a temporary prison camp, where he was first "interviewed by a civilian official who advised him that further disposition and treatment of him would depend on US withdrawal from all efforts in Laos."[55] The Pathet Lao were obviously very interested in Klusmann, since he was the first American military man they had captured since the signing of the 1962 Geneva Accords. Although his guards did not treat him very well, Klusmann's true importance to the Pathet Lao was confirmed when later in the summer he was visited by a high ranking PL military officer whom he later identified as General Singkapo Sikhotchounamaly, the chief of the Pathet Lao military in the northern part of Laos. Klusmann recalls that "Singkapo actually visited twice. He was fairly pleasant and asked if I was being treated okay."[56] Singkapo's first visit resulted in an inspection of the camp and a dressing down for the PL unit guarding him. The same PL unit that had captured Klusmann had remained as his guard unit, following him to each camp during his internment. A tongue-lashing from Singkapo made the guards quickly improve his living conditions.

The day following the meeting with the civilian, Klusmann met his interrogator, an English-speaking man who said his name and rank were "Captain Boun Kaham." Klusmann was kept in solitary confinement and interrogated steadily until early August. However, "right after Ed Alvarez was shot down and captured in North Vietnam in the beginning of August, Kaham disappeared and I never saw him again. I always wondered if he went to work on Alvarez."[57]

Following the interrogation pattern of the VC, the Lao asked Klusmann only a few questions about military intelligence matters. Instead, "They wanted to know information on my friends and family and what it was like in America. The guy already had plenty of military information. He showed me a fairly recent CINCPAC organizational manual, which was still classified Confidential. Then he really shocked me. He knew what carrier I was on, the *Kitty Hawk,* and he told me the exact night my ship had passed through the Bashi Channel in the Philippines when we were sailing for Vietnam. I mean, how does this guy in a mud hut in the middle of nowhere in Laos get that kind of information?"

While concerned about the fate of the pilot, the U.S. Embassy in Vientiane was even more determined not to provide the Pathet Lao with any propaganda bonus from the shoot-down. Unger moved quickly to exert damage control on press reports of the crash by issuing a statement that the aircraft was an unarmed recon plane. He was furious, however, when State and DOD gave the press a background identification of the downed aircraft as a fighter. On June 8, Unger wrote that "I am at a loss to understand why this was done. As long as our previous line was maintained we could pass off bombing and strafings in PL area as work of T-28s [training planes modified for use as bombers] however much PL presented eyewitness accounts of U.S. jet involvement. Now, however, we have virtually acknowledged that U.S. aircraft have been bombing and strafing in Laos."[58]

Despite Unger's manipulation of the press, Captain Kaham, was still pressing hard for a political statement, and the Pathet Lao were turning the psychological screws on Klusmann. On June 26, the Voice of America broadcast that the Pathet Lao had executed an American pilot.[59] Kaham used that announcement to apply pressure on Klusmann to make a broadcast, telling him that since no one knew he was alive, he should cooperate and make a statement so that his family would know he was okay. As a defense against Kaham, Klusmann had resisted by feigning sickness, but suddenly he did become very ill. He had contracted malaria. "One day when I wasn't feeling very well, they took me over to the building where they conducted the sessions. They started pressing me pretty hard to make a broadcast. For some reason, I just stood up and said to Kaham, 'I'll make a broadcast when hell freezes over,' and I walked out the door. Surprisingly, he never bothered me again." Still, Klusmann was forced to sign a letter describing his good treatment.

After recovering from his bout with malaria, Klusmann and two jailed former PL soldiers held with him in the camp and whom he had befriended escaped by digging through the walls of the mud hut and loosening the barbed-wire perimeter fence. They escaped on the night of August 30. Two days later, they stumbled into a friendly guerrilla unit. Klusmann was immediately evacuated to Thailand, given a medical check-up, and sent home. His ordeal, however, was not over. Concerned that he might have violated the Code of Conduct, military intelligence personnel in the States questioned him harshly about his possible cooperation. Klusmann was astonished at his treatment. "The interrogation I went through when I came home was tougher than anything the Lao ever did to me."[60]

Klusmann's was not the last American-piloted plane shot down, or the last *Yankee Team* recon loss. In August, a T-28 flown by an American was hit and downed in eastern Laos. Since only Washington could grant permission for Americans to pilot rescue helicopters in Laos, Ambassador Unger was forced to request State Department approval for the use of an American-flown helicopter to rescue the downed American. Because of the intense enemy fire, the presence of communist ground troops near the downed pilot, and the time difference, Washington's decision was delayed. Due to the extreme urgency of the situation and unable to wait for their response, Ambassador Unger risked his career and the secret American involvement by unilaterally making the decision to send in the Air America helicopter. It was shot down almost immediately with two American pilots on board. Then the situation grew even worse. Two other T-28s, also piloted by American airmen who were providing close air support, crashed due to mechanical problems. In desperation, Unger ordered napalm to be used if necessary to suppress the enemy fire.[61] Eventually, all the pilots were rescued, but the confusion resulted in a reconsideration of the tight leash Unger was on in using American-piloted aircraft. After considerable discussion in Washington, in late August Unger noted that he had been granted "discretionary authority . . . use Air America pilots in T-28s when I consider this indispensable to success SAR operations."[62]

In October the Joint Chiefs of Staff authorized the expanded use of Air America SAR aircraft "to include . . . cross border operations . . . to protect our interest."[63] Unger, however, was deeply suspicious that the military's cross-border operations might transgress on his control of the war in Laos, or worse, interfere with the plausible deniability of the secret war so carefully built up by him. He took the authority granted him in August to conclude that he alone would make the decision on using Air America SAR helicopters to rescue personnel on cross-border operations in Laos. He would make that decision based on the loss circumstances.[64] This was a decision that would have far-reaching effects.

Although Unger was concerned about the loss of American lives and took precautions to avoid putting Americans in danger, both he and Washington were more worried about exposing the U.S. role and safeguarding the secret U.S. presence in Laos. Losses were to be expected, Unger felt, given the risks inherent in clandestine conflicts. For instance, Klusmann notes that "when I got back, the Air America pilots told me they had sat on a ridgeline for an hour waiting for authorization to cross the 'no fly' line. Finally, they said screw it and came after me, but by then it was too late."[65]

In November, another *Yankee Team* plane was shot down. This crisis forced the American military to completely revamp their Search and Rescue priorities and dramatically increase the SAR forces. The continual need for intelligence on the communists and the deepening American military involvement in Laos and South Vietnam were making direct U.S. combat intervention inevitable. Yet, despite the growing awareness and interest in American POW in Washington, the military's growing need for a unit dedicated strictly to rescue operations was still not being addressed.

3. The First Angry Family

Mrs. Hertz said she hoped that a meeting with the President would not occur after her husband's execution, with the President attempting to present her with a posthumous medal.

—*National Security Council (NSC) Memorandum recounting a conversation between Mrs. Gustav Hertz, the wife of a captured civilian in South Vietnam, and NSC official Chester L. Cooper, after she was refused a meeting with the President to discuss her husband's case*

In 1965, the status and location of American prisoners of war remained only one priority among many to the U.S. military in Vietnam. The United States was facing a guerrilla war that it was completely unprepared for in a country that it was totally unfamiliar with. With the logistical infrastructure of South Vietnam overwhelmed by the massive infusion of American men and materiel and with the GVN's political institutions teetering, the American military was trying to fight the war while simultaneously creating the foundation for a South Vietnamese nation. Committed to and tied down in the rapid build-up of forces, DOD deferred to the State Department concerning POW affairs. Internally, however, DOD had growing misgivings about State's envisioned diplomatic solutions, especially in compelling the North as signatories to the Geneva Accords to provide the privileges granted POWs under the accords. As the State Department's overtures fizzled against communist intransigence, DOD began prodding State to consider more aggressive actions, including direct military responses for communist transgressions, to gain the release of the POWs or at least improve their conditions.

Even though it was military men who were becoming prisoner or missing in action in increasing numbers, DOD deferred to the State Department because State, as the diplomatic arm of the U.S. government, possessed unquestioned control over the efforts to obtain the return of POWs. Although State was stymied by the DRVs refusal to engage in face-to-face negotiations over POW matters with the U.S. government in a standard diplomatic forum, it still exercised its authority by working through the offices of such international bodies as the International Control Commission (ICC), a committee designed to oversee the implementation of the 1954 Geneva Peace Accords, which ended the war in Indochina between the communists and the French. State also continually urged other international institutions, such as the International Committee of the Red Cross (ICRC), to press the DRV/NLF to abide by the rules of the Geneva POW Convention. Like the military, however, in the early stages of the conflict the State Department also viewed the POW/MIA issue as only one among many clamoring problems.

With no formal declaration of war in Southeast Asia, the North had proclaimed that the American POWs were "war criminals" and insisted that the Geneva requirements did not pertain to the prisoners. Suddenly confronted with the executions of several American POWs in South Vietnam in mid-1965 by the VC, and faced by the DRV threat of war-crimes trials for American pilots shot down in the North, the State Department finally began focusing its attention on the POW issue. Eventually, in mid-July 1966, State acknowledged this new mind-set by also adjusting its public rhetoric (after Congress modified the Missing Persons Act to make the language used to describe the prisoners more accurately reflect their true status), and began referring to the American airmen as POWs instead of "detainees." The LBJ administration hoped this would put the communists on notice that they would be held legally accountable for any actions that violated the provisions of the Accords.

Despite the refusal of the DRV/NLF to comply with the Geneva Accords, the NLF's relatively quick liberation of American prisoners in 1962–63 had altered the American government's expectations concerning prisoner releases. U.S. diplomacy regarding American POWs in Vietnam changed so that now its primary objective became the release of POWs before the cessation of hostilities rather than exchanging them at the end. Of course, it hoped to accomplish this feat without engaging in any direct dialogue with the NLF, mainly so as to avoid offending the South Vietnamese government. Faced with a guerrilla-style conflict, and with only limited American military forces available for rescue attempts, and unable to rely on the weak ARVN or Royal Lao forces, the State Department viewed the issue of POW recovery as a matter for negotiations that only periph-erally involved military action. Therefore, State's reaction to the POW issue was legalistic and followed the normal diplomatic channels.

The entry of major American combat units into South Vietnam in February 1965, however, ended the days of quick release. Now the VC were looking for more concrete results from the release of their American POWs. This new pol-icy quickly bore fruit after the GVN announced the impending execution of several imprisoned communist terrorists; the NLF immediately threatened to execute three American POWs. The new South Vietnamese military govern-ment, determined to halt a wave of VC terrorist attacks in Saigon, ignored American pleas to halt the executions and put to death several captured VC ter-rorists. The VC then carried out their threats by killing three American POWs, Rocky Versace, Kenneth Roraback, and Harold Bennett. Under more strenu-ous American diplomatic pressure, the GVN ceased the executions of the com-munist cadres and eventually agreed to consider the VC offers for POW exchanges.

The NLF undoubtedly hoped that such exchanges would provide them with de facto political recognition. While State wished to discuss the POW/MIA issue directly with the DRV, State refused to meet with the NLF, afraid that a meeting would be construed as recognition. The U.S. government feared that such recog-nition could ultimately lead to worldwide appeals to cease the fighting, accept the NLF as a legitimate political party, and hold elections within South Vietnam that included the NLF. None of those prospects interested the United States or the GVN, but the executions of the three Americans in the summer and fall of 1965 forced a temporary reevaluation of the policy of no direct talks with the NLF. While both sides were interested in exploring the possibilities of an exchange, se-rious channels would not develop until January 1966.

Despite internal DOD complaints about State, the military also acted slowly to address the POW/MIA problem. Early in 1964, for instance, the Air Force Ad-visory Council on Prisoners of War recommended the establishment of organiza-tional focal points in the Office of the Secretary of Defense (OSD) and the offices of the Service Secretaries to monitor POW actions, E&E training, and intelli-gence liaison, but no action was taken within DOD.[1] A year later, DOD recog-nized the growing problem and "some departmental working groups were established and internal changes were made which significantly improved some functions in the Department."[2] The Army, however, didn't start holding monthly POW conferences until September 1965. Yet, the history of the Korean War and the obvious use by the communists in Southeast Asia of the POWs as propaganda pawns should have alerted State and DOD much earlier to the urgency of the situation. Even though the numbers of POW/MIAs were small and the problem overshadowed by the expansion of the war, the political importance of the POW issue should have provided a glimpse into the future and launched the U.S. government into stronger action sooner than it did.

The Kidnapping of Gustav Hertz

The time from the summer of 1964 to the spring of 1965 was a relatively quiet one for the POW/MIA issue. The NLF had floated the idea for POW exchanges via the Bon proposal, but the State Department decided against following through even after revisiting with Krause in September. When State did turn its attention away from the escalating war toward POW affairs, their priorities were geared toward forcing the NLF to allow mail to flow to the prisoners in the South and receiving a complete list of POWs held by the communists. In the DRV, the first American prisoner, Navy Lieutenant Commander Everett Alvarez, seemed to be receiving mail without too many problems; little had been heard though, from a second American, Navy Lt. Cdr. Robert Shumaker, who had recently been shot down and captured.

This almost laissez-faire attitude abruptly changed when a senior civilian member of the U.S. Embassy in Vietnam was kidnapped on February 2, 1965. A Foreign Service officer named Gustav Hertz, assigned to the United States Agency for International Development (USAID), was riding his bicycle on the outskirts of Saigon when he was seized by the VC. The Embassy alerted the Vietnamese police and signaled the intelligence networks to uncover his whereabouts. Reports soon began to filter in that Hertz had been seen moving with VC units toward COSVN headquarters in Tay Ninh Province on the Cambodian–South Vietnamese border. The Embassy and CAS Saigon decided against a rescue attempt, fearing the VC would kill him before any such operation could be mounted and because there were some early indications that the VC might decide to release him.[3]

These indications were coming from a CIA informant, who on March 2 relayed information that he could contact Hertz and bring back a note bearing his signature as proof of his contact. The informant said he would do this within fifteen days, but expected to be paid VN $20,000 (about $200 U.S. at that time) to cover his initial efforts to locate Hertz. If this effort resulted in the release of Hertz, he wanted an additional VN $250,000 reward, to be paid afterwards.[4]

On a parallel track, the U.S. military was pushing the State Department to consider the possibility of exchanging POWs. In a joint State/Defense message from Secretary Rusk to the Embassy in Saigon developed shortly after the Hertz kidnapping, Rusk wrote, "It has been suggested that if key members of the Viet Cong or elements allied to them could be secured they could eventually be exchanged for American prisoners. . . ." Rusk, though, was wary of the impact on U.S.-GVN relations and was still lukewarm to the idea. Indirectly, he provided the Embassy a convenient out. "It seems likely . . . that an extraordinary effort over and beyond normal military operations in the South would be necessary to acquire 'negotiable' prisoners. It would also have to be understood that we be prepared to negotiate some of these against GVN prisoners in the hands of the Viet Cong."[5]

Shortly after Hertz was kidnapped, and in reaction to the landing of U.S. Marines near Danang, the VC began a wave of terrorist bombings and drive-by shootings in an attempt to topple the weak Saigon government and deter the United States from committing further troops to the war. On February 11 the VC blew up the American officers' billets in Saigon. The death toll was high, and a subsequent manhunt caught the VC bomber, a man named Tran Van Dong. On March 30 a bomb exploded in a stationary car in front of the U.S. Embassy, destroying large sections of the building. A high-ranking VC terrorist named Nguyen Van Hai was captured as he tried to pick up the vehicle's driver. The GVN military immediately demanded that actions be taken to suppress the VC terrorism. The shaky civilian government quickly acquiesced and put Hai on trial. At his hearing, his lawyer, a former South Vietnamese diplomat, asked for clemency because Hai was only the pick-up man. The court refused. Hai was found guilty and sentenced to death.

Little else was heard about Hertz until April 7, when the NLF radio announced that Hertz would be executed if Hai was killed. The NLF broadcast said that "The fate of G. Hertz is decided by the United States itself."[6] Just as the U.S. government was seeking to tie the POW actions of the VC guerrillas to their commanders in Hanoi, the North was actively painting the GVN as the "puppets" of the U.S. government. The announcement sparked an immediate demand from the Hertz family to see President Johnson to ask what measures the United States was taking to free him. Johnson refused to respond, believing that if any White House involvement became known it would only complicate matters. Instead, he sent Chester L. Cooper from the National Security Council to meet with the family.[7] At the meeting, Mrs. Hertz "explained that her lack of confidence in present efforts in her husband's behalf was prompted by her inability to get any significant military action at the time of his disappearance. . . . Mrs. Hertz noted that she had been unable to get any information of any consequence . . . from the CIA. In fact, at a later date she had to recall to CIA officials details of her husband's disappearance which she had a right to expect they would have clearly remembered."[8]

Despite the efforts of Communist Party cadres to train their forces in proper POW handling procedures, since the Gabriel and Marchand murders other local guerrillas had also bound and shot captured American prisoners. The embassy, therefore, took the execution threat seriously and pressured the GVN not to execute Hai, asking them to regard Hertz as a "special case," i.e., a civilian prisoner under threat of execution. Although the GVN relented and delayed carrying out the death sentence, U.S. concern for Hertz increased when it was learned that another American USAID worker, Joseph Grainger, who had also been taken prisoner, had recently been killed by the VC. Grainger was captured on August 8, 1964, when the jeep he and two companions were riding in was ambushed by the VC. After an unsuccessful ground search by ARVN forces, the American Embassy printed a reward leaflet with photos of Grainger and the other captives. After the leaflets were dropped by airplane the other two, a Filipino and a Vietnamese, were released on December 28. Grainger however, remained captive. According to intelligence reports, in response Grainger began a hunger strike on January 1 to protest his continued imprisonment. On January 5, he managed to escape. Although he successfully hid out for a week, a VC patrol eventually caught up with him as he was washing himself by a stream. When he refused to return to captivity, he was shot twice and killed. "His body was buried at night," a VC rallier reported, "and the grave was flattened to conceal it."9 His wife traveled to Vietnam in 1966 and paid the VC to have his body disinterred and returned to her.10

By June, it became clear that the CIA's attempt to ransom Hertz had failed. The CIA informant, a woodcutter with ties to the Viet Cong, had arranged for the VC to bring Hertz to the Ban Me Thuot area on June 8, but the VC never showed. Apparently, the VC Public Security agency (An Ninh) had discovered the attempt to buy out Hertz and stopped it. In a document signed in September and captured by the U.S. 9th Infantry Division (ID) in October, a message was sent to all district-level security sections warning them to be vigilant against such bribery. "It has been reported that recently the US imperialists . . . have been actively engaging in buying off dependents of cadres and soldiers in charge of guarding American surrenderers in an attempt to release these captured Americans. With a view towards preventing this from happening, it is requested that agencies concerned maintain closer contact with the detention camps. . . ."11

The Hertz family believed that time was running out given the increasing NLF threats. In early June, the family asked Senator Edward Kennedy to approach Algerian Foreign Minister Bouteflika to intercede with the NLF representative in Algiers on behalf of Hertz. The NLF had diplomatic stations in several Iron Curtain countries, but as a fellow "revolutionary" Algeria hosted one of only two stations the NLF had outside the communist bloc. The NLF replied that they would release Hertz and at first asked for nothing specific in return, but it was obvious they were seeking some sort of propaganda benefit from the circumstances of Hertz's release. Desperate to gain the freedom of a fellow Foreign Service officer, both State and the Embassy agreed to pay a propaganda price for Hertz if that was what the Viet Cong wanted.[12] The NLF then informed Bouteflika that they would release Hertz only if they were assured the Americans were directly involved and if the GVN agreed to send him out of Vietnam. However, the new American ambassador, Maxwell Taylor, unaware that the same NLF concerns had earlier been voiced to Krause, was confused by such a request. He cabled, "We anticipate no difficulty in getting GVN agreement when required. Request for assurances . . . makes no sense to us. In fact this alleged requirement on part Viet Cong casts doubts on whether Bouteflika knew what he was talking about."[13]

While the Embassy had hopes that the CIA ransom effort would still bear fruit, they wanted to gain Hertz's release without having to exchange him for Hai. Taylor wrote, "Since Bouteflika did not link Hai with Hertz we should *not* do so in response to Bouteflika's initiative."[14] State was concerned not only with appeasing the GVN but more importantly with not setting a precedent for more VC hostage taking. If the United States were seen to have caved in quickly to VC threats, every American civilian in Vietnam could be in danger of kidnapping. While the NLF initially appeared interested in releasing Hertz, the fall of the Algerian government on June 19 put a temporary halt to this promising channel.

"I'm just trying to find my brother"

Hertz's relatives weren't the only family concerned about the disappearance of their loved one. An Air Force pilot named Daniel Dawson had disappeared on November 6, 1964, while flying an O-1F on a routine road reconnaissance mission in South Vietnam. Dawson and a Vietnamese observer had departed Bien Hoa airport in the morning. When their aircraft was overdue, an extensive SAR effort was launched. Since the probable crash location was deep in VC-controlled territory, no ground search was conducted and eventually the official search ceased after failing to locate the plane or Dawson and his observer. After several months of waiting, his brother Donald Dawson became actively engaged in attempts to locate him. Although Donald was married and the father of four small children, he quit his job, cashed in the family savings, and traveled to Vietnam to hunt for his brother. His dedication in pursuit of his brother's whereabouts earned him the admiration of many of the local American pilots. He was continually persuading them to take him aloft in their spare time to search for the crash site. Frustrated by what he perceived as a lack of formal effort by the U.S. military, he printed leaflets offering a reward for his brother, the remains, or information on either. He was convinced the VC knew what had happened to his brother, but despite his appeals and requests, the VC denied any knowledge of the incident.

Dawson's repeated efforts to contact the NLF made them begin to suspect, in their typical paranoid way, that he was a spy. The NLF decided to lay a trap for him. In late March word was sent that the communists had found his brother's remains. In desperation, Dawson sought help from a Roman Catholic priest, Father Nguyen Thinh Doan, who arranged a meeting with the communists. The local VC agreed, and asked that he come with the priest and a translator. Dawson enlisted the services of a college student, a young French-Vietnamese woman named Collette Emberger who had mysterious links to the revolutionary forces.

On April 26, 1965, with Emberger acting as his interpreter, Dawson and the priest entered VC territory. Before he left, Dawson told some friends that if he wasn't back shortly he was probably a captive. His suspicions proved true, and in early May word reached Saigon that Dawson and Emberger had been arrested by the VC. They were marched to the main American POW camp in Tay Ninh Province, where he and Emberger were held until the NLF was convinced he really was just a civilian looking for his brother. In August the NLF released them both.[15] Later, in 1973, after a VC rallier provided information that he had witnessed the crash and that both pilots had died and were buried next to the plane, Donald Dawson returned to Vietnam to persuade the American and Vietnamese authorities to again search for his brother's crash site. It was still not located. Other witnesses in 1992 stated that Dawson had survived the crash but had succumbed to his injuries several kilometers from the plane wreck.[16] He is still among the missing today.

"No one even cried": The First Raids

With few ground forces in country capable of performing rescue operations, the U.S. military was forced to rely almost exclusively on ARVN combat forces for such missions. Although general sweep operations had been conducted previously for captured men, the first formal raids of the war occurred on December 23 and 25, 1964, when raids were conducted by ARVN infantry in the Camau Peninsula in the Mekong Delta and in Tay Ninh province respectively. The ARVN raiders were supported by American helicopters and the ARVN's American advisors.

Although little is known of the attempt on December 23, the assault was designed to rescue the men in the Rowe camp. Rowe's book provides the best description of the attack, and apparently it came close to recovering the men.[17] Significantly, both missions used tear gas to immobilize the guards, although the results, as National Security Advisor McGeorge Bundy wrote to the President, "are reported to have been very slight."[18]

The raid in Tay Ninh province was assisted by American advisors in a "combined operation . . . on 25 December 1964 with the hope of freeing U.S. personnel in a suspected VC detainment camp."[19] In an operation code-named *Hung Vuong I* (after a Vietnamese king), sixty-six helicopters, including thirty armed gunships, staged from Tay Ninh on Christmas morning to airlift elements of the 33rd ARVN Ranger Battalion into landing zones south of Tay Ninh city in an area known as the Bo Lu woods. During this operation, Vietnamese troops employed three hundred pounds of bulk tear-gas powder and several hundred gas grenades.[20]

The tear-gas powder dispensed from the helicopters set off a political firestorm in March 1965, when the VC charged the United States with engaging in chemical warfare, an accusation resurrected from the Korean war. Dismissing the VC claims, Bundy further wrote to the President, "In neither case was there any effective contact with the enemy or success in the rescue of the prisoners. It sounds to me as if no one even cried." Despite the poor results obtained on the two raids and the political backlash caused by the communist propaganda, President Johnson and the military continued to authorize the use of tear gas during SAR operations and POW raids.

On March 14 the 3rd Airborne Battalion of the ARVN 22nd Division made a helicopter assault on the village of An Nhin (for which the operation was named) in Binh Dinh province. Intelligence indicated that two American POWs were being held in a camp just north of the village. At 0930, gunships from the U.S. 52nd Army Aviation Battalion made strikes into locations adjacent to the landing zone. The 3rd Airborne made a heliborne assault, sending two companies into the area seeking to attack one VC company that was reported to be providing security for the area. Upon landing, the ARVN unit was informed by the local villagers that the VC and the two American POWs had been moved twelve hours prior to the operation.[21]

Although the ARVNs just missed the two American POWs, they did rescue 38 South Vietnamese civilians held in the camp. The After Action report, however, noted some problems with the ARVN commanders in conducting the mission. "The condition of the village and POW camp showed that it had been evacuated quickly, therefore some degree of surprise was achieved. Unfortunately all planning on division level was done by American advisors, and most of the execution on Division level was accomplished by Americans. Because Americans seemed to be running the operation Major Dieu, the battalion commander, became very disgusted and seemed to be against the operation at the beginning."[22]

Even when allied forces received accurate intelligence on the location of American POWs, the mobile VC simply faded into the jungle to avoid the assaults directed against them. That the VC had moved just prior to the operation would be a result that repeated itself throughout the war.

A Hot Summer

Despite instituting stricter security measures, the civilian government was unable to halt the VC terror bombings and was forced to resign by the South Vietnamese military. On June 16, 1965, the new military government responded to the continued VC terror campaign by announcing a decree stating that any communists captured while committing acts of terror would be executed. To demonstrate their resolve, on June 22 the new government, in one of its first acts, publicly executed in Saigon's central marketplace Tran Van Dong, the bomber of the American officers' billet. In retaliation, on June 24 NLF radio announced the execution of Sergeant Harold Bennett, an American captured on December 29, 1964. Later, the NLF announced that Bennett had been shot specifically for the execution of Dong.[23]

The execution shocked the U.S. government, and the combination of the kidnapping of a senior civilian like Hertz and the revenge killing of Bennett may have been the turning point for American POW policy in the war, or at least marked the end of giving POW affairs a low priority. The U.S. government described Bennett's death as "a wanton act of murder." It immediately ordered the CIA to produce a study detailing the current intelligence on the whereabouts and status of the Americans held in South Vietnam.[24] But the U.S. government could not yet bring itself to publicly admit it was ready to begin exchanging prisoners. In reaction to Bennett's shooting, the State Department spokesman, Robert J. McCloskey, remarked at a press conference that "he knew of no efforts so far to arrange an exchange of prisoners in Vietnam. Efforts to release American POWs have been made periodically through the Red Cross, but without success."[25]

Combined with a terrorist bombing at the My Canh restaurant, which also resulted in massive casualties, Bennett's death placed the U.S. Embassy in Saigon in a difficult situation. A long cable from Ambassador Maxwell Taylor outlined the quandary faced by the United States. "Viet Cong execution of Sergeant Bennett closely followed by My Canh restaurant atrocity brings into sharp focus blackmail potential VC and Hanoi possess in numbers of US hostages in their hands and the usefulness of this blackmail to a stepped-up terrorist campaign, since they well aware we place higher value on human life than they do, Hanoi/VC prepared use this weapon to own advantage. They have evidently decided that execution of US prisoners will be very sensitive issue for USG, and their experience with Hertz case in which they undoubtedly aware that we have caused GVN to delay execution of Hai, may have led them to believe that we will pay very high price to prevent execution of our personnel. They thus hope to cause political problems between US and GVN, to stir up US public opinion against Vietnam policy, to damage US troop morale, and also raise morale their terrorists cadre by showing their ability to retaliate for GVN executions. . . . We cannot permit ourselves to be placed in position of paying blackmail for lives of US prisoners in form of preventing GVN from executing terrorists. . . . We would soon find the price raised to some other even less acceptable level."[26]

Escapes

Not all the POW news was bad, however. On July 12, one of the four sergeants captured at Hiep Hoa in Hau Nghia province in October 1963 escaped. Sergeant Issac Camacho slipped away at night and managed to avoid the VC patrols and return to U.S. control. Camacho had loosened his restraints and slipped out during a rainstorm. The other American POWs in the camp blew out their lamps and stayed behind to cover for him. Stumbling around in the jungle, Camacho finally came across a road. Luckily, a car passed by driven by a French national. Signaling the car to stop, Camacho asked the driver to take him to the nearest Americans. The Frenchman willingly obliged and drove Camacho to a nearby Special Forces camp. Camacho became the first American serviceman to escape from the VC.

Several other American civilians also successfully escaped or were rescued. On October 8, 1965, Joe L. Dodd, an employee of the RMK Construction company, was returning by motorcycle from Cam Ranh Bay to Saigon when he was stopped at a VC roadblock. He was held for several days with another South Vietnamese Army sergeant, but managed to escape on October 25 when his guards fell asleep. Dodd was the first civilian to escape his VC captors. On his return he was held incommunicado for several weeks so that American intelligence could debrief him. Two other Americans, Marine privates Joseph North, Jr., and Walter D. Hamilton, were captured in the Danang area on October 18. They managed to escape on October 29.

Another American soldier who was fortunate enough to have guards with poor sleeping habits was Sergeant Pedro Crisostomo of the 1st Infantry Division. While his platoon was assaulting a bunker complex, he was wounded when a mine went off behind him, peppering his back with shrapnel. The mine killed the man he was with, and as he looked around to see if any of his fellow soldiers were still alive, he was hit again, this time by a rifle bullet in his shoulder. Pinned down and unable to move because of the enemy fire, he lay there wounded until darkness fell. As he carefully began to move back toward his own lines, several VC found him and dragged him into a nearby bunker. About an hour later, one of the guards fell asleep. When the other guard momentarily put down his rifle, Sergeant Crisostomo picked up a nearby entrenching tool and banged the guard on the head. Running out of the bunker, he spent "most of the rest of the night—almost 'passing out a number of times'—to make his way about 150 yards to his battalion position."[27]

Later in the year, fortune also smiled on several other American construction workers. On December 21, four other men who also worked for RMK had gone out to inspect a quarry about twelve miles from Saigon when three men dressed in short-sleeved shirts and denim shorts stepped from the jungle and pointed pistols at them. Unable to turn the car around, the Vietnamese driver was forced by the VC to the side of the road. Recounting his predicament at a news conference, Henry Hudson described how his VC captor ordered them to walk into the jungle. "We told them we wouldn't go a step further. One of the VC said, 'I'll count to three and you can make up your minds.' We started moving before he started counting."[28]

The VC took their boots so that the Americans wouldn't leave shoe prints on the jungle trails. Later that night while they were walking along a road, heavy-weapons fire opened up on the VC column. They had stumbled into an American ambush. Hudson, another American named Edwin Jones, and the Vietnamese driver dove into a ditch. The other RMK employee, a Canadian named Otto Shulten, was shot in the back by one of the VC guards. After a brisk firefight, the VC melted away and the American unit recovered the captured construction workers.

"Right through the front and grab the American"

While these men had managed to escape their captors, one American medic was not so fortunate. An enlisted man named James McLean was a medic stationed at the Duc Phong outpost in Phuoc Long province. At midnight on February 10,

1965, his outpost came under heavy mortar attack and was overrun by the VC. The next morning, an ARVN unit was airlifted into the town and it was soon learned that McLean was definitely a POW. On numerous occasions over the next few months, he was reported to be alive and in VC custody by both VC deserters or by released ARVNs who had been held with him.

On September 27, 1965, two ARVN soldiers were released by the Viet Cong from a POW camp near Song Be in Phuoc Long province. The two reported that the camp contained ten prisoners, including one American. The local U.S. Special Forces detachment was informed, and they immediately arranged to take the two ARVNs up in an airplane to attempt to identify the area. The ARVNs quickly pointed out the specific camp area. The Song Be Special Forces contacted the intelligence section for III Corps, which discovered additional intelligence reports indicating that other released POWs had mentioned a camp in the same area. Based on these reports and the overflight, a plan to raid the camp was developed and sent to the III Corps senior staff for approval. Once they agreed, permission for the plan was also required from the U.S. Senior Corps Advisor.[29]

Finally, on October 10, an experienced Special Forces sergeant named Paul Rusidorf, who commanded one of the Song Be "A" teams, was asked to lead the raid. As Rusidorf remembers, "A major who I had known previously came to my camp. He took me off to the side and asked me if I would go get this American POW. He briefed me on the intelligence on the camp location and what the ARVNs had said. There was supposed to be one American POW. He was tied to a bamboo bed by bamboo around his ankles. I told the major it sounded like a temporary camp to me and that we needed to move quick. I asked him if they had any heavy weapons or if any airplanes flew over the camp regularly. He said no. I said okay, let's act like we're a lost airplane. We'll fly straight over the camp once the night before to do a recon. My entire "A" team volunteered to go on the mission, and we also had some Montagnards with us. There were very high trees near the area and the drop zone (DZ) was pretty small, so I requested smoke jumpers' outfits in case we missed the DZ and had to parachute through the trees. My plan was nothing fancy, just blow through the front, grab the American and go right out the back and across a rope bridge that crossed a river. On the other side was a clearing in the jungle for the helicopters to land and pick us up, even though I doubted they would show up on time. But I wanted to do this because he was an American."[30]

After training for the mission, Rusidorf and the officer went up in the airplane. "I only wanted to fly over once because I was afraid we would arouse the suspicions of the camp guards. We flew past the camp and all of sudden I feel the plane turning around. I started yelling at the major that you can't do this. He said yes I can. As we were coming around again a .50-caliber machine gun opened up on us. I could see the tracers coming up from the ground. When we got back to Bien Hoa, I discovered we had been hit twice, once in the prop and once in the wing. I starting yelling pretty good at the major, and I told him, that's it, mission canceled. I said to him, 'I thought you told me they didn't have any heavy weapons.' I'm lucky he didn't court-martial me for what I said, but we never did the mission."

Whether McLean was still in the camp is unknown. The headband from his helmet was found much later by an American recon team in Cambodia. The possibility exists that the VC deliberately released the two ARVNs, in order to trap some unit attempting to make a rescue. If it was a trap, the slow response by the Army bureaucracy must have totally confused them. The McLean case provides another example of Vietnamese excuses regarding known POWs. McLean was never released, nor have his remains ever been returned. One Vietnamese cadre interviewed in 1993 stated, "He was killed by a wild tiger after he was moved during a bombing attack by US/GVN forces on the camp in mid-1966."[31] Another interview with a high-ranking communist cadre indicated that McLean was killed in the same bombing raid on the camp. One laughed when told about the "wild tiger" story. According to the cadre, McLean's buried remains would be almost impossible to locate now.[32] Significantly, both individuals admitted that McLean was held in a camp controlled by the communist Public Security forces. In the South, American POWs were normally held in military-run camps. A captured document from 1966 confirmed that McLean was undergoing an investigation by communist security personnel.[33] Whatever his ultimate fate, he never came home. Despite being a high-priority case of the U.S. government for over seven years, no American search team has been able to locate his grave or find out what happened to James McLean.

"Running through the jungle blindly"

Four USAF sergeants returning from R&R at the Vietnamese coastal resort town of Vung Tau were also among those who were in the proverbial wrong place at the wrong time. On October 31, 1965, the four were riding back to Saigon in a truck driven by a Vietnamese friend. They were about 30 miles outside of Saigon when they were stopped by a roadblock of the VC Ba Ria Province Main Force Battalion. USAF Sergeant Jasper Page and his three friends "were sitting in the back when I heard the truck stop. I looked out the window and I saw this guy yank the driver out. I saw two VC on the other side of the truck who looked like Mexican bandits because they had crossed bandoliers on their chests. I was carrying a pistol, and I pulled it out to shoot one of the guys holding the driver. Just as I drew a bead on him, the VC on the other side of the truck saw me and yelled to their friends. The back door flew open, so I stopped. They pulled us out, slapped us around a bit and tied us up."[34]

They were split up into pairs, bound together and blindfolded and then put back into the truck and driven down a dirt road. After a while, the truck became stuck and they were led into the jungle on foot. Page remembers that "they had an interrogator who spoke English. He wanted to know what unit we belonged to, what our jobs were and what we thought about the war. He gave us some pamphlets written by these two Americans, Smith and McClure, which basically said we shouldn't be in Vietnam. They asked us to tell them how good the pamphlets were."

Several nights later, two of the sergeants who were tied together, Page and Samuel Adams, made an escape attempt. A tropical rainstorm had hit and only three guards were watching them. Unnoticed, they had managed to loosen their ropes. When their guards momentarily put down their weapons, Page and Adams jumped them. Page grabbed one guard's weapon, but was unable to fire it because the safety was on. When he saw that another guard had recovered his weapon, and that Adams was running into the jungle, Page also started running into the thick growth. Blindly racing through the jungle, he heard shots fired in his direction. He listened to Adams shout "No," and then he heard several shots. Believing Adams had been killed, Page kept going.[35]

"I kept the weapon the entire time," Page remembers, "even though I only had a few rounds. You can't imagine how your sense of security increases when you are carrying a weapon." Page managed to avoid the VC patrols, although he was spotted once by some kids. "I was at a rubber plantation when we saw each other. I tried to communicate with them but they took off. Since the area was filled with VC, I ran into the jungle and camouflaged myself to blend in. A few minutes later two guys on bicycles came riding along. Luckily, they didn't see me."

On November 4, "his clothes crusted with mud and in a state of shock and dehydrated after being without water for more than a day in the tropical heat," Page crossed an oxcart trail. Following the trail, he came to a U.S. outpost.[36] "I was afraid to drink the water because of the possibility of dysentery. The only thing I drank was a little rainwater that I caught with my hands." He was examined by a medic and then flown by a VNAF helicopter to Tan Son Nhut air-base. Page was immediately debriefed by U.S. intelligence where he pinpointed on a map the location where he was captured, plus the last location of Adams and the others. His return sparked an extensive air and ground search for the other three. Helicopters flew over the area and began broadcasting a message that the Americans wanted to trade for the POWs. The offer was food or medical supplies in exchange for the American prisoners. Later that month, however, an NVA rallier disclosed that the guards had panicked after Page's escape and had shot the remaining American POWs. The communist Vietnamese government claims not to know the location of their graves. Despite several U.S. search attempts, their remains have never been returned.[37]

Roraback and Versace

If the execution of Bennett and the kidnapping of Hertz were not the turning point for U.S. POW policy, the executions of Sergeant Kenneth Roraback and Captain Rocky Versace undoubtedly were.[38] Continuing political unrest in South Vietnam sparked further reprisals against captured "terrorists," and the GVN executed three fishermen from outside Danang who claimed to be protesting American destruction of their property. Although the U.S Embassy had managed to convince the GVN to postpone the execution of Nguyen Van Hai because of the threats to Hertz, further U.S. appeals to stop the execution of Tran Van Dong had failed. Consequently, the VC executed Harold Bennett. Now, continued American protests to the GVN that further executions might have dire repercussions for the other American captives continued to fall on deaf ears, and the Embassy was powerless to prevent the execution of the three involved in the Danang protest.

Again the VC demonstrated their determination to carry out their threats; they murdered Roraback and Versace. The announcement of their deaths came on September 26 over NLF radio. "Our people have wholeheartedly applauded this stern measure of the Liberation Armed Forces and have been extremely enthusiastic over this appropriate punishment for the U.S. aggressors' crimes. However, until now, the NLFSV has always implemented its policy of leniency toward the aggressors. This time, to punish the U.S. aggressors and their lackeys for having massacred our compatriots indiscriminately, the Liberation Armed Forces command ordered the punishment of the two . . . aggressors. This action was entirely correct."[39]

The executions shocked the world, which saw them as cold-blooded murder.

In reality, it was not only cold-blooded murder, but also cold-hearted political calculation. Instead of informing the International Red Cross when an American POW died, they deliberately hid his death for some possible future need. A captured document dated December 21, 1965, clearly spells out their plan. "The killing of U.S. POWs . . . created a great shock in the capital of Saigon. From now on, all units are instructed to strip all the necessary papers from U.S. soldiers killed in action, carefully bury them. This should be kept secret in order to make believe they are still alive and held in captivity. We will 'kill' these dead again should the need arise. Unit commanders must secretly recover the corpses of U.S. soldiers killed in action and bury them. Their graves should be correctly marked for future recognition. Only in this way can we make the enemy believe that the dead are still alive and held in captivity."[40]

In response to this second execution, and combined with the rumors floating out of Hanoi of impending trials of captured American pilots as war criminals, Washington finally awakened to the realization that the situation had become quite grave. One of the first steps taken by the U.S. government in response was to prod the GVN to rapidly improve treatment of NVA/VC prisoners. In late July 1965, after numerous press reports of GVN torture of VC captives, Secretary of State Dean Rusk met with Samuel A. Gonard, the head of the ICRC, to discuss "moves to improve the treatment of prisoners by both South Vietnamese authorities and the Viet Cong."[41] Shortly thereafter, on September 27, the MACV commander, General William Westmoreland, and GVN Chief of the Joint General Staff Nguyen Huu Co signed a Joint Interrogation Agreement specifying that all captured enemy POWs would be turned over to the custody of the South Vietnamese. Additionally, Westmoreland reminded all American military forces in Vietnam to treat enemy POWs in accordance with the dictates of the Geneva Convention. Prompting the U.S. actions were "reliable indications that DRV may proceed soon to try US airmen now held prisoner in Hanoi. This lends urgency to need for GVN and US record to be as favorable as possible on POW issue."[42]

The Joint Chiefs of Staff (JCS), also reacting to the executions of Roraback and Versace, ordered a fresh look at the twin issues of accurate accounting for the growing numbers of missing Americans and the feasibility of an American prisoner-rescue outfit. Although the services were now holding a monthly meeting to discuss the POW/MIA issue, on October 5 the JCS instructed the office in charge of personnel, called the J-1, to begin establishing a project that listed all Americans by country of loss who were not known to have been killed, plus the amount of contact between them and the Red Cross or their families. While not wishing to absolve the Services from their normal accounting responsibilities, "it is entirely possible that the Chiefs will become involved should further prisoners be executed or our prisoners tried as war criminals."[43]

The First Attempt: The Joint Recovery Center

Some mechanisms to gather intelligence and increase coordination were already under way. Each Embassy has a political officer called the POL/MIL (political/military) whose job is dedicated to handling military affairs. In September 1964 a Foreign Service officer named H. Fremen Matthews arrived in Saigon to assume the post of POL/MIL. Matthews was thrust into the middle of the Hertz dilemma, "since it was no longer a purely military problem."[44] Matthews recalled that "Gus Hertz was a well-known guy in the Embassy, a good man and fairly senior. He wasn't undercover CIA, and we had believed that the VC didn't want U.S. civilians."[45]

In response to the threatened execution of Gustav Hertz, the U.S. Mission Council, a body comprising the highest-ranking members of the American hierarchy in Vietnam, ordered the Embassy in May to establish a committee to make recommendations and begin coordinating U.S. POW actions. Matthews helped organize the Committee of Prisoners and Detainees, which was later renamed the Study Group on Prisoners and Detainees.[46] The committee was the U.S. authorities' initial effort in Vietnam to deal with the growing problem of American prisoners. By early June, after reviewing the failures of *An Nhin* and the raids in late December 1964, the Embassy committee recommended to Ambassador Taylor that a prisoner-rescue unit be created to include representatives from the CIA, MACV, the Embassy, and other prominent American agencies. The unit was to be named the Personnel Recovery Center. MACV quickly recommended that the unit should be manned strictly by military people. Taylor agreed; however, he wanted the unit to report directly to him.

On June 14, 1965, the formation of a nascent "Joint Recovery Center" was announced. Maxwell Taylor then sent a message to William H. Sullivan, the new American ambassador to Laos, discussing the proposed effort and its need to take unhindered action across borders, especially into Laos. "Mission committee," he wrote, ". . . has responsibilities for whatever action mission may be required to take concerning U.S. prisoners or detainees in Third countries, specifically Laos. . . . Such action would of course be coordinated with AmEmbassy Vientiane and other US commands concerned. . . . Resources and assets of Joint Recovery Center would be available for use on behalf such prisoners and detainees. JRC would in effect take over when SAR efforts presently stop. Since one of JRC's most important assets will be collection and analysis in one place of all available information from agencies concerning prisoners and detainees, mission would appreciate Vientiane's furnishing whatever information it has concerning such prisoners and detainees in Laos."[47]

Despite Taylor's plea for overall command, Ambassador Sullivan was not about to relinquish any authority or allow a recovery force to cross into Laos without his permission. The political realities of the war were such that any rescue force would only have authority to initiate rescue operations in South Vietnam. He replied, "We appreciate Saigon's solicitude for U.S. prisoners and detainees in Laos but feel that on balance, we are better equipped to look after these people than Saigon would be."[48]

While the unit could operate independently within South Vietnam, the more politically sensitive missions into Laos or North Vietnam would still require specific approval either from the ambassador in Laos or from Washington. Normal SAR responses would also remain divided, as Sullivan considered the recovery of downed air crews in Laos a function of his office. Finally, in the scorched-earth writing he became famous for (some officers jokingly referred to his cables as "Sullies"), he finished with this observation: "We note that 'JRC would in effect take over when SAR efforts presently stop.' As far as Vientiane concerned, SAR efforts for prisoners and detainees in Laos never repeat never stop. Suggest you revise JRC terms of reference accordingly."

Taylor's earlier cable also noted that "JRC cannot function with maximum effectiveness until DOD has acted on request for assignment of Director of JRC." By September, however, given the resistance by Sullivan and the apparent reluctance of the military to have the JRC reporting to the Embassy, "the embryonic effort was discontinued because of a lack of trained personnel."[49] In reality, the military had simply dragged their feet until the JRC command arrangement was more to their liking. On September 17, General Westmoreland re-proposed that "MACV undertake planning for and execution of detainee recovery operations in RVN in lieu of establishing separate organization responsible directly to Ambassador."

At first the Saigon Embassy did not reply, but Westmoreland persisted and repeated the same message on November 15.[50] The Embassy finally relented and remarked on November 30 that "any measures which COMUSMACV proposes to institute to discharge the functions originally described in terms of reference . . . will be satisfactory." Westmoreland was now free to begin creating a recovery force dedicated to recovering American POWs, although it would take another year to complete.

Organizationally, MACV had also started taking steps to assign the POW/MIA issue a higher priority. The military staff section for intelligence, the J-2, ordered the 704th Intelligence Detachment to begin creating folders on each individual POW or MIA.[51] The J-2 had already allocated one staff officer to be the "Detainee Recovery Officer," and in mid-1965, Major Arthur J. Kyle assumed those duties, replacing Captain Marvin Gibbs.[52]

Even as the U.S. military was taking the first steps in implementing active measures to recover American POWs, they were still having a hard time positively identifying where the POWs were being held. While Alvarez and the growing number of prisoners in North Vietnam were suspected to be held in Hanoi, their exact locations were still unknown. The USAF 1127th Field Activity Group (FAG), which was the main service intelligence unit in Washington actively concerned with the locations, treatment, and conditions of the POWs, queried the Air Force in the Pacific in September 1965 for any information in their files concerning the locations of American POWs in North Vietnam and Laos. In reply, the Pacific Air Force (PACAF) responded, "Very little info is available here concerning POW camps. We have probable locations for POW camps in Laos but none for North Vietnam."[53]

Smith and McClure Are Released

Of the four men captured at Hiep Hoa, only Smith and McClure remained in captivity, heavily guarded by the VC after Camacho's escape. They were being held near the Cambodian border in Tay Ninh province in the main American POW camp of the NLF along with several other American POWs.

On November 28, Smith and McClure were released in a propaganda attempt to regain some favorable exposure after the negative reaction by the world press to the earlier executions. The NLF used the release to reinforce communist POW policy on their own troops. "Our recent release of POWs and surrenderers has a very large impact. According to higher headquarters, we will badly need US POWs for use. In the battles, our armed and paramilitary forces must try to capture POWs from the US satellite forces, keep them carefully, observe, implement properly our POW policy, and evacuate them immediately to Military Proselytizing agencies to use them in necessary missions."[54]

After the capture of the four, the National Liberation Front used the incident to increase morale among their own troops and cadres.[55] Many captured enemy documents make mention of the successful indoctrination of Smith and Mc-Clure. After their release, Smith and McClure held a press conference and made statements praising their treatment by the VC. Additionally, they spoke against continuing U.S. involvement in South Vietnam. Their remarks caused considerable furor in the American military and there was widespread talk of a court-martial for both of them. However, after several months of being held virtually incommunicado on Okinawa, Smith and McClure were given general discharges and abruptly released.

4. The Men in the Caves of Laos

The NLHS Representative denied any knowledge of the broadcast but at the same time asserted that this meant the USAF pilot was alive. He also referred vaguely to large numbers of other U.S. prisoners whose aircraft had been shot down by Pathet Lao anti-aircraft defenses. Ninety-five percent of the pilots whose planes had been hit did not survive according to Sot. I purposely did not press him about the five percent of pilots who have been captured because I believe this is part and parcel of the exaggerated Pathet Lao claims of U.S. planes shot down.
—*U.S. Embassy officer in Vientiane, recounting a conversation with Pathet Lao representative Sot Phetrasi after a radio broadcast by captured U.S. pilot David Hrdlicka*

The issue of the ultimate fate Americans lost in Laos has been the subject of intense speculation ever since 1965. It remains the most contentious and emotional POW/MIA dispute from the Vietnam war outside of the argument over whether men were left behind in captivity. While the problem echoes back to January, 1961, its true genesis is the events that followed the loss of two Air Force pilots, Charles Shelton and David Hrdlicka, in April-May 1965. Known POWs who were held in the caves of northern Laos in the Pathet Lao stronghold of Sam Neua province, Shelton and Hrdlicka never came home. Eventually, they became the postwar poster children of the POW/MIA issue.

The mystery surrounding their fate, coupled with the return in 1973 of only ten men from a group of just over six hundred MIAs in Laos, is a paradox that has never been adequately explained by either the North Vietnamese, who controlled roughly 80 percent of the territory where the MIAs went missing, or the Laotians. The vast majority of these losses were pilots from shot-down aircraft or helicopters. The remainder were ground losses of Special Forces personnel engaged in reconnaissance of the Ho Chi Minh Trail. While roughly 40 percent of the six hundred were determined at the time to have died in their loss incident, the fate of the rest was simply unknown, with many, perhaps close to one hundred, for which there was evidence that they may have survived, at least initially.

Additionally, the few prisoners who did return in 1973 were dispatched to Hanoi, incarcerated there, and released from North Vietnam. No one came home from a Lao prison, and since the completion of *Homecoming* the Laotians have repeatedly denied holding any other Americans besides Debruin, Shelton, and Hrdlicka during the war. They further claim that Shelton and Hrdlicka died in the 1960s, their grave sites destroyed by U.S. bombing, which obviously prevents them from returning their remains.[1]

What is known about Laotian communist wartime POW policies is that in many respects it mirrored that of the North Vietnamese. In their public announcements the same theme was repeated: halt the bombing and we can talk about POWs. If the U.S. stopped the bombing and agreed to talks, the theme became: end the war and we will release the POWs. Despite these Lao positions, most U.S. intelligence officers believed that the Laotians turned over their U.S. prisoners to the North Vietnamese on a fairly regular basis, especially during the last half of the war.

The U.S. government's response to the POW problem in Laos has been sharply debated for many years. It refuses to acknowledge that rescue operations were ever attempted for the POWs in the caves of northern Laos despite numerous statements to the contrary in diplomatic and CIA cables. Indeed, the record shows that plans for rescue and intelligence-gathering attempts were ongoing from 1965 through at least 1971, and probably longer. Despite these unusual government denials, the loss of Shelton and Hrdlicka marked the beginning of a lengthy effort to identify and locate the men held in the caves that dot the craggy limestone cliffs of Sam Neua province.

Just as significant, the available documentary evidence indicates that although the United States did possess important intelligence on captured airmen in northern Laos, they were unable to precisely identify who was being held in the caves save those two pilots and possibly one other. One of the main reasons was the Pathet Lao's refusal to allow any correspondence from the prisoners. Unlike the North Vietnamese, both the communist Laotian media and the official organs of their government rarely publicized the names of captured Americans, believing this was the one card they could use to halt the U.S. bombing. Despite repeated attempts to gather intelligence on the men in the caves, this intelligence failure to identify, coupled with the impact of the "secret war" policy and the perceived roadblocks thrown up by the turf-defending CIA and U.S. Embassy, hamstrung the American efforts to recover or assist these men. Therefore, the inability to obtain confirming evidence of a prisoner's identity means that the collected wartime POW information remains in the realm of probable, not conclusive, intelligence. This represents the true heart of the MIA dilemma in Laos for the U.S. government and the families: while the mass of data acquired provides strong circumstantial evidence that would lead almost all reasonable people to accept that more POWs than Sheldon and Hrdlicka were held, that evidence does not meet the more rigorous standard required for proof.

Some of the difficulties the U.S. government faced in acquiring confirming intelligence were the inhospitable and often remote terrain where many pilots went down, the low population density, the lack of Pathet Lao or Royal Lao control over large swaths of the country, the hardships encountered by enemy forces in moving American POWs to central control, and the lack of discipline of many PL troops, which may have led to a swift execution for some captured Americans. All of these contributed to the paucity of answers. Many Americans, for instance, may have successfully escaped their burning aircraft only to perish while attempting to evade enemy forces, or succumbed later to injuries, their locations perhaps forever unknown. While all of these factors must be entered into the equation, both the communist Lao and Vietnamese should still be able to provide answers as to the ultimate fate of many Americans, answers which have so far not been forthcoming.

The CIA was initially given responsibility for developing intelligence in Laos on the status and whereabouts of any American POWs missing in that country. Between 1965 and 1967, the CIA procured critical intelligence on Americans being held in caves in northern Laos. CIA case officers created, and worked closely with, Hmong units in northern Laos. These Hmong teams had access to the POWs in Sam Neua province through bribery of the Pathet Lao soldiers guarding the Americans. Additional intelligence began flowing in late 1965 when Pathet Lao defectors reported that more Americans than just Shelton and Hrdlicka were being held in this area. The CIA recorded this information in a series of cables that were dispatched to the military and other U.S. agencies as part of the intelligence sharing process.

The POW information contained in these CIA intelligence cables originates not only from interrogation reports of these defectors and captured enemy soldiers, but from local village informants used by the Hmong as spies against the communists. The villages that were overrun in the annual North Vietnamese "Dry Season offensive" contained an intelligence network that provided information on North Vietnamese troop concentrations and locations.[2] With the 1968 "Dry Season offensive," however, the NVA began a scorched-earth campaign in Sam Neua, driving out the local Hmong villagers aligned with Vang Pao. Only Pathet Lao sympathizers remained, and the CIA's intelligence on POWs in northern Laos slowly dried up. In the south along the Trail, no locals were allowed near the Trail except those pressed into force labor. Ultimately, the Hmong were unable to mount a successful rescue, either because of the inability to pinpoint which cave complex in the Sam Neua/Ban NaKay area the American POWs were being held, or because of the high concentration of enemy forces.

Sullivan Takes Over

In November 1964 William H. Sullivan replaced Leonard Unger as the American ambassador in Laos. The change in ambassadors, however, did not change the Embassy's attitude toward the military. Like Unger before him, Sullivan was committed to maintaining the image of Lao neutrality and the policy of no overt American military involvement in Laos. At the same time, his mission was to interdict the flow of supplies into South Vietnam and also to fight the combined Pathet Lao/ North Vietnamese. To accomplish that task he used the CIA and their clandestine assets backed by U.S. air-power to fight a "secret war."[3] Acknowledging an American military presence would shatter the Lao pretense of neutrality.

It was Sullivan's implementation of that policy, however, that quickly led him into severe disagreements with the military, especially over POWs. It can be argued that Sullivan possessed a cold, albeit accurate assessment of the harsh realities in Laos, namely that in fighting a war continually disavowed by the U.S. government, casualties among and sacrifices by the men doing the fighting were inevitable if the secret war was to preserve its deniability. Some military officers who worked with him, notably General Westmoreland, were much less generous in their estimation of the man. Many officers felt that Sullivan badly impeded the battle in Laos and severely damaged the overall war effort. "Whose side is he on?" was a refrain often heard.

Much of the acrimony stemmed from Sullivan's arrogant personality, which, combined with a witty and sometimes scathing writing style, created an intense dislike of him among many of the senior military officers at MACV. They sneeringly called him "Field Marshal" behind his back. In retrospect, the military's disgruntlement with Sullivan was based primarily on the galling thought of someone from the "striped-pants crowd" being given the authority to dictate the use of power, especially when they disagreed with how he used and applied that force. While he was probably more concerned about the welfare of the POWs and aircrews than the military gave him credit for, he managed to make even that care sound parochial.

Although Sullivan's attitude toward the military, and SOG in particular, was often one of disdain, he was also operating under tight instructions from the Royal Lao government headed by Laotian Prime Minister Souvanna Phouma and from Washington. His disposition and predicament comes across best in his own words. Writing in March 1965, just before the start of the bombing campaign in the *Barrel Roll* area of northern Laos, Sullivan stated, "It should be recognized that our air operations in Laos are entirely dependent upon the political authority granted us by Prime Minister Souvanna. The fact that this card-carrying neutralist permits US aircraft to conduct combat missions against enemy targets on Laotian soil is the result of very carefully nourished relations which my predecessor skillfully began and which I have attempted to perpetuate. It bespeaks Souvanna's . . . remarkable confidence in the United States." Sullivan went on to point out that "This means, in my opinion, that we must bend over backwards in executing our military missions so that we maintain this unique and essential political foundation for our operations. It means that we must sometimes sacrifice maximum military opportunities, in order to temper them to the political climate."[4]

While Unger faced the occasional crisis caused by an aircraft loss, Sullivan bore the brunt of the war. But he was no trailblazer, and his responses mimicked Unger's. For instance, as the bombing tempo increased in North Vietnam under the February 1965 *Rolling Thunder* campaign, the aerial assault in Laos concurrently grew and so did the losses. In northern Laos, a Navy A-1 was shot down on April 2 and a B-57 was lost on April 7. SAR helicopters were unable to locate the pilots for either aircraft. Without any contact from the crews, Sullivan realized that official announcements concerning their loss could potentially be destabilizing to Prime Minister Souvanna Phouma's government. Like Unger before him, Sullivan pressed for continuing the ruse either that they were unarmed reconnaissance planes, or "that they were lost while performing combat missions over hostile territory." Admitting the loss of a B-57 in Laos especially "would scuttle our reconnaissance cover story on which Souvanna insists."[5]

Sullivan believed the Americans were able to "get away with all this by elaborate dissimulation, tight discipline over loose talk, and a sprightly collusion with our Lao hosts." If exposed, "it would be inevitable that many of our activities would have to be suspended. Those of us who conduct these operations harbor the illusion that they are of some value to the United States and cause some annoyance to our enemies. On the basis of this assumption, we require scores of Americans to risk their lives every day and a few every month give their lives in an effort to carry out this program."[6]

His main anxiety was about sending American soldiers on the SOG *Shining Brass* cross-border raids. He limited their movement to an operating zone restricted to within 20 kilometers of the border, not only to reduce the risk of exposure but also so as not to interfere with the CAS [Controlled American Source, code-word for the CIA personnel overseas] units known as *Road Watch* teams, also operating along the Trail. Sullivan expressed his concern when he wrote, "As for region in vicinity Route 9, I am convinced it is so sensitive and so well guarded . . . to send Americans would, in my view, be suicide and would also be politically counterproductive."[7] Ambassador Sullivan's overriding desire was to conceal the American presence in the secret war, and he was fearful that "U.S. personnel captured during these operations would be flagrant violations of 1962 Geneva Accords. An exposure in this form would not only prove highly embarrassing to U.S., but also to the Lao government."[8]

At the same time, MACV was painfully aware that cutting the flow of supplies down the Ho Chi Minh Trail was an important key to ending the war. They pushed Sullivan for an expanded use of SOG recon teams along the Trail, hoping to develop additional intelligence and to strike at the enemy supply movements and the NVA sanctuaries in Laos. MACV continually prodded him to increase the depth of the operating zone for the *Shining Brass* cross-border operations.

Sullivan believed that the potential for losing Americans in SAR attempts to rescue SOG teams in trouble was very great and thus risked exposing America's secret war and consequently destroying the delicate facade of Lao neutrality. He noted that SOG now had more targets than it could reasonably attack, so it made little sense to him to let SOG roam deeper into Laos. Eventually, however, he relented and allowed MACV to expand the zone from 20 to 50 kilometers in from the border. On several occasions in the future, though, his unwillingness to commit American or Vietnamese-led recovery teams for downed fliers in trouble [he preferred to use the indigenous CAS teams first], or his decision to let them enter Laos only after he had carefully weighed the political ramifications, which thus badly delayed their entry, eventually became a source of deep friction between Sullivan and the military.

Charles Shelton and David Hrdlicka

USAF Captain Charles Shelton was flying a reconnaissance mission over Laos near Sam Neua, the provincial town that served as both capital for the province and surrogate headquarters for the Pathet Lao, when, on April 29, 1965, his RF-101 reconnaissance airplane was badly hit by AAA fire and he was forced to bail out. Poor weather in the local area made it difficult for the SAR helicopters to find him, although his beeper, a device carried by aircrews to electronically signal their location to the SAR forces, was being intermittently picked up but was too weak to permit triangulation.[9]

For the next several days, the helicopters kept searching for Shelton but they were hindered by the continuing poor weather. Because of their numerous contacts with the villagers in the area, a Hmong guerrilla team operating nearby was moved into position to conduct a possible rescue attempt. By May 5, the Hmong team determined that Shelton had been captured. One of the Hmong guerrilla team members was brought out on a SAR helicopter to provide a report. He informed the Embassy that his unit had learned that Shelton was being held in one of the numerous caves in the vicinity of Sam Neua.[10] Interestingly, the Hmong reported that much like Klusmann earlier, the "pilot was to be interviewed by highly-placed PL leaders in the near future."[11]

Sullivan seemed as worried about the strain on his meager SAR resources as he was about Shelton's loss. One of the propeller-driven A-1 escorts suffered a hit while guarding the SAR helicopter picking up the Hmong guerrilla. It was forced to crash-land at one of the nearby friendly airstrips called *Lima Sites.*[12] Sullivan complained to Washington in a cable about the drain on his air assets in conducting those rescue attempts, never failing to remind State of the dire consequences of the discovery of U.S. involvement in Laos. "During past few weeks," Sullivan wrote, "I have been required ever more frequently [to] authorize use of Air America pilots flying RLAF (Royal Lao Air Force) T-28s to provide low cover for helicopters engaged in rescue attempts. . . . Every time I authorize Air America pilots in RLAF planes, I am consciously jeopardizing entire Air America operation in this country and am risking severe embarrassment to both U.S. and Lao governments." After mentioning the T-28 plane damaged in picking up the Hmong, Sullivan went on to note that "There are four of them in the air right now on a rescue mission near Sam Neua and we risk always the possibility that next shoot-down will be in enemy rather than friendly territory."[13]

The rescue operation was for David Hrdlicka. On May 18, 1965, Hrdlicka was the pilot of the lead aircraft in a flight of four on a bombing mission when his plane was also hit by AAA fire. Like Shelton, he also bailed out successfully. Fifteen minutes after watching him land, Hrdlicka's wingman noticed him surrounded by people from a nearby village. Two helicopters and four T-28s shortly arrived on the scene to conduct the SAR pickup, but could not locate him. When one helicopter landed at a nearby friendly village, they learned that Hrdlicka had been captured by the Pathet Lao. Fortunately for Hrdlicka, his wingman was able to watch him land safely, which helped establish that he was captured since no beeper or voice communication was heard from Hrdlicka after he bailed out.

Carol Hrdlicka was a young wife with three small children living near McConnell Air Force Base in Wichita, Kansas, when David was captured. Carol remembers vividly the day an Air Force officer came and told her that her husband had been shot down in Laos. "At first, they didn't know if he was being held by friendlies or unfriendlies. They told me he had been seen hitting the ground and walking away. I looked at the officer and I told him, you tell me the truth, no matter how bad it is, I will deal with it. Well, they started to patronize me anyway. Don't worry, they said, he'll probably be released in a year."[14]

Carol tells of a slow change in describing the POWs that went from "detained to interned to captured." The Air Force also maintained the fiction that David was on a reconnaissance mission. "It wasn't till years later that I learned that he actually was on a bombing mission."

Later they informed Carol that attempts were being made to get David released. "When an old friend of ours came back from Thailand, I asked him directly what was being done. He told me privately that teams on the ground had access to the prisoners. He called them 'ghost teams.' I was also in touch with other pilots coming back from Vietnam who were providing me information on David outside the normal casualty channels. They also told me that rescue attempts were being made on David. However, when I asked the government in 1991 whether there ever was a rescue attempt for David, they denied that any attempts were ever made."[15]

Why would the government deny that an operation to rescue Shelton and Hrdlicka had been conducted? Perhaps the seeds of that denial can be seen from the following. As the American bombings began to take a toll on the communist supply systems, in late April photo interpreters noticed that the NVA were using transport planes to send supplies into the city of Sam Neua. The available documents seem to indicate that the operation, code-named *Duck Soup,* was designed to coordinate an attack by U.S. fighters to shoot down the DRV supply plane at the Sam Neua airport. Shelton in fact may have been on a photo mission for *Duck Soup,* since the first mention by Sullivan of the operation is an April 23 cable where he references a prior discussion on enemy supply planes at the recent Southeast Asia Coordination meeting.[16]

Although the official documents do not mention either Hrdlicka or Shelton or any rescue attempt, for years the *Duck Soup* operation has been rumored to have been a cover name for a rescue operation for Shelton. Most recently, a reporter from the Riverside, California *Press-Enterprise* newspaper described how USAF Lieutenant General Clifford Rees, who retired as Vice Commander of the USAF in Europe in 1992, admitted that he was part of *Duck Soup* and that the mission was a rescue attempt.[17] Although DPMO [the government agency handling POW/MIA matters] denied that *Duck Soup* had any relation to Shelton, it is clear from the cable traffic that other messages exist, especially the appraisals from CINCPAC and the USAF base at Udorn, Thailand, on the feasibility of the strike against the North Vietnamese supply plane. Certainly the testimony of a former high-ranking USAF officer should have instigated a more thorough study. However, after the DPMO denial, the matter was quietly dropped.

Despite the DPMO denial, rescue operations by the Hmong teams were ongoing and the American prisoners were accessible. A cable from Sullivan states, "Our mighty Meo report from one of their outposts in Sam Neua that they have succeeded in recapturing one of the U.S. pilots captured during past few weeks by Pathet Lao. . . . I would like to stress overwhelming importance that this rescue not repeat not be given publicity. . . . This officer is only one of three for which we currently have Meo rescue operations in progress."[18]

Given the growing war and the possible POW problem in Laos, an ICRC representative visited Vientiane early in the summer of 1965 hoping to discuss the POW situation with the Pathet Lao. Unaware of the other Americans, his main goal was to visit Debruin. The U.S. embassy in Vientiane at first did nothing to provide him with more current information. With Washington apprehensive over revealing the American bombing in Laos, State had cabled the Embassy questioning "whether it desirable at this time to have ICRC raise with PL names of those presumed dead. Also since there is still some chance Shelton might be rescued it does not appear wise present his name at this time."[19] Sullivan stated he was "inclined agree preferable at this time not to ask ICRC raise with PL names of those presumed dead and will not do so unless instructed otherwise."[20] Moreover, Sullivan was so convinced that one of the men in northern Laos had been recaptured that he also reported to State that "[Embassy officer] did not mention names of Hrdlicka or Shelton since as Dept. now aware from messages other channels we are not yet positive which one of these two men is believed to be accessible to friendly forces. We hope to have definite information on this individual in near future. . . ."[21]

However, by August Sullivan wrote that, "We have reluctantly concluded that original report received here about June 21 concerning recovery of missing USAF pilot by friendly team was based on faulty information and must now be considered untrue. Several attempts to confirm or follow up this report have proved fruitless and passage of time makes it most unlikely that friendly forces had in fact recaptured an American pilot. Therefore believe we can turn over names of two pilots missing over Laos (Hrdlicka and Shelton) to ICRC rep for investigation with PL authorities."[22]

Whatever immediate attempts were made to rescue Shelton and Hrdlicka, either *Duck Soup* or something as yet unrevealed, they ultimately failed. The pair remained in captivity at the Pathet Lao headquarters, which was eventually moved from Sam Neua to Viengxai, about thirty kilometers away. Sullivan tried to quietly intercede with Sot Phetrasi, the local NLHS representative in Vientiane, to bring mail to the men in the caves. Phetrasi, who later in the war became a central figure concerning American POW/MIAs, refused, and with no American pressure possible, the men imprisoned in the limestone caves continued to wait.

The Men in the Caves

At the end of December 1965 the first reports were received that provided details of the capture and confinement of Shelton and Hrdlicka. A defector, a Pathet Lao captain who was stationed in Sam Neua province until June 1965, stated that he had witnessed the arrest of two American pilots on separate instances in late April–early May near Sam Neua. The officer gave precise details about Shelton and Hrdlicka, showing American interrogators the entry in his diary listing Hrdlicka's name. The PL defector mentioned that the Americans "were interned separately in caves 400 meters northeast of Ban Nakay Tay, about 28 kilometers northeast of Sam Neua. . . . A Vietnamese officer . . . and a Lao officer from the intelligence section of Pathet Lao Headquarters . . . interrogated the two Americans."[23] In a haunting similarity to Klusmann, and reportedly Shelton, Hrdlicka was interrogated "in English. Most of the questions were of a political/propaganda nature and Hrdlicka answered only that he knew nothing of politics."[24]

Further reports from additional PL defectors from the area indicated that the group of Americans had now grown. In January 1966, a Pathet Lao corporal who was a truck driver in Sam Neua/Houa Phan province saw "four Americans pilots taking a bath in a stream near a cave called Sadet fifteen kilometers southeast of Sam Neua." Due to the American bombing the PL "had moved their command post to the cave . . . called Tham Sadet."[25]

Later, in March 1966, a North Vietnamese soldier captured in a battle near Sam Neua reported that he was part of a search for an American pilot who was captured on January 16. The pilot's plane "bore the marking 'F-105.'"[26] A close examination of the record of losses shows that USAF Captain Don Wood was shot down while flying an F-105 fighter on this date in nearby Xieng Kouang province. Additionally, Pathet Lao radio broadcast that an American pilot had been shot down on January 16 and captured, a claim quickly parroted on January 18 by Peking radio. A postwar refugee report indicates an American pilot was captured alive during this time.[27] The source was part of an undercover Royal Lao Army reconnaissance team when he spotted the Caucasian pilot being held by a combined NVA/PL guard force. Although no beeper or voice contact was established with Wood, the JPRC searched his crash site in 1971 and found no remains. Later, his ID card was displayed in a Pathet Lao film and found in a Hanoi museum.

Aerial photography was used to verify the stories being told by the PL defectors, especially accounts of the enlargement of caves for Pathet Lao offices. It appeared that a radio station, a bank, and a large tunnel were being constructed to house the few high-ranking PL officials. They were reportedly guarded by three to four battalions of North Vietnamese troops plus PL security forces. A March CIA cable notes that the tunnel headquarters "is considerably larger than the former one at Tham Sadet."[28]

Although the January report stated that four Americans were being held, most reports from PL defectors noted that there were only three Americans in 1966 in the cave area.[29] A former teacher for the Pathet Lao defected in early August to a friendly guerrilla unit and noted the presence near Vienqxai of the Americans, plus one Thai and other foreign nationals.[30] The Agency considered that the "best report available on location pilots was from [redacted, i.e., blacked out by censors] PL schoolteacher who defected to Meo troops. . . . He actually saw pilots this location in Jan 66. . . ."[31] The Thai captive was confirmed in November 1966, when another prisoner of the PL later escaped and reported that he was told by a PL soldier that "three American prisoners were being held in a cave near Ban Na Kay as was a handsome Thai whom everyone came to look at."[32]

Ominously, the source reported that one of the Americans "had dies [*sic*] because he could not eat." In December 1966, other sources began reporting to the CIA that one of the American pilots had "died of stomach trouble. He was described as tall, heavily built, and balding."[33] Although the identity of this dead American has never been discovered, the reported death would spark CIA action to again attempt to rescue the men in the caves.

Hrdlicka Makes an Appeal

Notwithstanding Sullivan's apprehension that the Pathet Lao would parade captured Americans to expose the secret war, in reality the PL would not for some time acknowledge holding any American POWs. Further, for the previous two years the Pathet Lao had refused the request of the Far East representative of the ICRC to visit the PL-controlled city of Khang Khay to discuss Debruin's imprisonment. State also noted that "Propaganda exploitation of Debruin for example has certainly not materialized to degree expected during imprisonment," and that "PL detention of foreign prisoners is important humanitarian issue to us but would appear to have little intrinsic value to PL except as bargaining lever."[34]

Sullivan's dread of the PL using captured American POWs to expose the secret American war finally became real on May 22 when the Foreign Broadcast Information Service (FBIS), a CIA-financed agency that recorded and translated foreign media sources, monitored a broadcast from the PL radio station. The U.S. Embassy in Vientiene reported that the broadcast "provides passages from letter allegedly written by downed U.S. pilot to NLHS Chief Souphanouvong. . . . the serial numbers used correspond very closely to Capt. David Hrdlicka."[35] Sullivan anticipated inquiries from the press and devised the usual cover story for Hrdlicka's loss that referred to a reconnaissance mission over Laos instead of his true bombing assignment. He further used the incident to hammer the military over a recent slip in the story of U.S. noninvolvement after the casualty affairs branch accidentally notified a family member that their son had been lost in Laos. Sullivan wrote, "Release of letter and use of Hrdlicka's name by PL undoubtedly intended to be pegged on recent publication of Laos military air casualties. This unfortunate example of complications we can get into by one simple slip in public handling of air operations and casualties in Laos; in this case, dispatch of routine unclassified next-of-kin notice. This should remind us of need to tighten up all our procedures to keep quiet war really quiet."[36]

The same went for the families. Carol Hrdlicka was informed that "because of the secret war, they told me I couldn't talk to the press because we weren't supposed to be in Laos."[37] The Air Force had "provided next-of-kin with text of intercepted broadcast and requested that they do not discuss its contents since we do not know what the communists are planning and any statements affecting their plans might prejudice Capt. Hrdlicka's possible release."[38]

Sullivan sent an Embassy officer to discuss the Hrdlicka broadcast with Sot Phetrasi. Phetrasi denied hearing the broadcast, but mentioned that "he had heard from unspecified sources about the capture of 'four or five American pilots' in the environs of Sam Neua city. Phetrasi also stated that Debruin was alive and being treated fairly. Phetrasi agreed to take mail and packages to the POWs the next time he went to the PL Headquarters."[39]

Hrdlicka's broadcast was a taped radio address in which he read a letter he had allegedly written asking the communist Lao leader Souphanouvong to release him so that he could return to his family. Based on prior experience with the VC, the radio appeal made the military suspect that his release would be part of a propaganda ploy by the Pathet Lao. Surprisingly, the press took only slight notice. However, Hrdlicka was not released and the broadcast was repeated on July 26. On the second occasion, the *New York Times* reported the broadcast. They quoted an official who said, "If the Viet Cong had made that broadcast, I'd be willing to bet on a prisoner release. But with the Laotians you never can be sure."[40] The *Times* also reported that the pilot had stated he had taken off from a base in Thailand, but that "Military spokesmen in Saigon refused to comment on the broadcast or the possibility that an American pilot was missing in action over Laos. U.S. officials have never publicly acknowledged the air activity over Laos, although American planes have been known to be attacking in Laos for several months. Only recently it was learned that more than 100 strikes a day were being carried out there."

Were the Pathet Lao sending a signal that they wanted to release Hrdlicka? If so, why was he not released? Given the amount of intelligence on pilots being held in the caves, was the Embassy's response similar to the efforts made to recover the men in South Vietnam? Did they acknowledge them and make similar attempts to ransom or swap them out? No, because Sullivan believed, or at least reported, that the PL were ill-disposed toward making any deals, and more importantly, because overtly acknowledging the POWs might have jeopardized the U.S. policy in Laos, which was to interdict the flow of supplies along the Ho Chi Minh Trail and covertly support the Royal Lao government against the communist Pathet Lao.

Consequently, in that first year of captivity for the men in the caves of Sam Neua, no public forum was used to apply pressure on the PL to grant the POWs the privileges of the Geneva Convention, for doing so would have risked exposure of the secret American bombing in the country. In an October 1966 cable, Sullivan summarized the options: "Doubt feasibility of ransom of prisoners. PL taking increasingly hard line. Do not rule out some prospects of rescue. One case in particular under current study. We are planning raise prisoners soon with local PL representative, but have no high hopes."[41]

From the intelligence reports, the CIA was well aware of the pilots in the caves and apparently was trying to find a way to rescue them in the fall of 1966, but for a variety of reasons was unable to. The Agency reported, "Since 5 Aug. we have been endeavoring develop additional details [redacted]. Problem is not lack of info but rather overabundance of reports of PL/NVN Hqs, caves, and captured pilot locations. . . ."[42] One CIA document summarizes the POW intelligence for

1966. "During calendar year 1966, CAS has received numerous reports of American pilots being held prisoner in Sam Neua. Reports have placed pilots in at least four different locations and descriptions these locations have generally checked out on photography. These reports indicate these pilots are moved from time to time. Several reports indicate originally there 3 pilots but in recent months 1 died because he either would not or could not eat. All reporting locations have been within area containing greatest enemy concentration in North Laos with exception Khang Khay area."[43]

Going After the Men in the Caves

In September 1966, Richard Secord was a young Air Force captain assigned to the CIA operations at Udorn, Thailand. Secord, who eventually was promoted to major general, was the Chief of Air Operations for the CIA-run war until the summer of 1968. In 1992, Secord testified before the Senate Select Committee on POW/MIA Affairs that "we got the Meo to mount a . . . operation whereby we went to some sympathetic Pathet Lao guards that were there, and found one or two that were willing to talk, and they described these three airmen."[44]

Secord further recalled in a later interview, that "we had positive information on three men in the caves, to include names, shoot-down dates and a physical description given us by a guard. We had little trouble penetrating the PL areas; a bribe of food or gold coin was all you needed to get good information. The responsibility for POWs was given to me because they were airmen and I was the Air guy. Vang Pao had several very good teams in Sam Neua in those days. One in particular was run by a guy we called "Tall Man" because he was taller than the average Hmong. There was no doubt that there were three men, as we had done a fairly close recon of the area, plus all the personal details we had received from the guards.[45]

"The CIA guys at Udorn favored a quick raid into the area. We requested an American to lead the team and asked for an exception to the no-Americans policy. We asked this for several reasons. First, we needed a "stiffener" in case something went wrong. Second, we felt we needed someone to reassure the Americans in the caves that these little guys dressed worse than the PL were really there to rescue them. We also asked for family pictures to show to the POWs and we also had a picture of a bunch of Air Force fighter jocks at Tahkli [an air base in Thailand] standing in front of an F-4 [fighter plane] with a big sign on it with the POWs' names and a message saying 'Waiting for you to come home.'

"Our request was denied. Then a Special Team arrived from Headquarters at

Langley that we had never requested. This had now become a 'Foreign Intelligence Operation.' Their plan was to bribe the guards with gold coins to bring them out. The raid was 'too risky,' they said, 'it might get the POWs killed.' I thought their idea was terrible. They tried, but for some reason the effort failed and afterwards the PL moved the Americans."

One reason the plan may have failed could also be why the CIA has been so reluctant to release information about any rescue or ransom attempts. Almost half a dozen different reports gathered over the years indicate that during this time frame a PL guard either accidentally or deliberately shot and killed one of the Americans he was guarding. Could the CIA bribery attempt have been badly botched and resulted in the death of one of the POWs? The accounts differ enough so that any hypothesis is mere speculation, but enough reports have filtered out to lend some credence to the possibility.

Documents provided by Carol Hrdlicka support some of Secord's account of a rescue plan. One document from the Casualty Affairs office notes that "these photographs of the family of Captain David L. Hrdlicka are forwarded as requested. The request . . . has caused much concern on the part of the wife. Many questions have been raised that the Casualty Division is not able to answer. Please advise by return message reasons for and urgency indicated in your [message]."[46] The Seventh Air Force replied, "Picture to be used to establish bona fide relationship by a friendly who will attempt to contact our officer."[47] Letters in the case file of Don Wood record that his family was also asked in late 1966 to provide pictures, particularly right-angle [right-profile] photos.

Aderholt, who would take over the JPRC in September 1966, was also planning a raid to free the men. He reveals the reason for the pictures and the motive for having an American on the team. "In the spring or summer of 1966, Vang Pao had reported that he had gotten a message in to Hrdlicka and the messenger had even tried to convince Hrdlicka to escape with him, but Hrdlicka didn't believe the guy and refused, thinking it was a plot to kill him. Since I had worked in the CIA for so long, I had good access to their data. This is why we needed the pictures of the families. I told Singlaub to get permission for the raid while I drew up the plans. I had looked at the aerial photos of the area and the ground around the caves was wide open, so I recommended that we use tear gas to immobilize the guards. I presented a plan to Singlaub that was still pending when I left the JPRC."

Colonel John Singlaub, commander of SOG, delayed implementing Aderholt's plan, because since he was receiving "daily reports from Ted Shackley, the CIA Station Chief in Vientiane. Ted was working on getting the men out, and he believed they had a good chance at rescuing them. However, I was never that thrilled with the communications with the Hmong teams since it always had to go through Vang Pao's staff, which tended to exaggerate their intelligence and capabilities."[48]

It is logical to assume that the reports of an American dying probably spurred the CIA into taking action. Similar reports of dying Americans in 1970 helped create the urgency for the raid at Son Tay. However, the intelligence that one of the men had died was not totally accepted by Secord. "We continued to get reports of three men in the area through the end of the year."

Although the story surrounding *Duck Soup* remains a mystery, it appears that at least two full-scale rescue operations were planned to recover Shelton and Hrdlicka, one initially in 1965 and one later in 1966 for the three men in the caves. A handwritten note in the case file of Charles Shelton provides insight: "[redacted] 6136 (Sep 66) Collecting info to launch rescue of US pers in prison camps [word illegible] sent back into area." The second, a memorandum written on March 7, 1973, states, "At the request of Mrs. McAfee, DIA, a research [*sic*] was conducted to ascertain whether or not any rescue attempts was made on the prison camp located at Ban Nakay Neua, Laos to free Charles E. Shelton. . . . An intelligence-collection effort was conducted in September 1966 into this particular area but no actual attempts were conducted to rescue detainees in this camp."[49]

Given the testimony of Secord and the available documentation, the government denials of what formally constituted a rescue attempt may be simply a matter of semantics, but to continually refuse to even acknowledge the elements of rescue planning to a family member like Carol Hrdlicka is extremely odd.

Dieter Dengler Escapes from Laos

The most spectacular escape of 1966, and the only other American besides Klusmann to successfully escape from a Pathet Lao prison, was a Navy aviator named Dieter Dengler. Dengler was a naturalized West German who had only recently arrived in South Vietnamese waters aboard the aircraft carrier USS *Ranger*. On his first mission on February 1, 1966, he was shot down over the Trail area in southern Laos, very close to the North Vietnamese border. Dengler claims to have evaded enemy contact for several days, but was eventually captured. After his capture, Dengler was marched to a camp that held Debruin and the rest of the crew from the plane shot down in September 1963. Another American who was also being held at the Pathet Lao camp was a SAR helicopter copilot named Duane Martin. Martin was captured on September 20, 1965, after his H-34 helicopter was hit and crashed while trying to rescue several shot-down airmen. Martin's other crewmen were captured by the NVA and returned in 1973.

The jungle camp where the men were held was, in its conditions, more like those in South Vietnam than like those in the North, although the men received much more abuse from their Pathet Lao guards than what was dished out in the VC prison camps. The PL guards would beat Martin and would often fire bullets at the others in an attempt to frighten them. But the political desires of the PL were similar to the VC. Dengler later reported that "The apparent aim of the captors . . . was to persuade the prisoners to sign statements condemning United States actions in Vietnam."[50]

After Dengler's arrival, the POWs were been moved to a new camp called Houei Het. On June 29, although weakened by months of abuse and poor food, Dengler and the rest of the POWs broke out of the prison, in the process killing several of the PL guards. The group split up; Dengler and Martin went one direction while Debruin elected to stay with his Chinese crewman, who at the time was very sick. The three Thais split into two separate groups; two of these men were never seen again.

According to Dengler's account, he and Martin stayed together and worked their way eastward, hoping to reach safety. However, it was difficult for them in the dense jungle to determine their direction of travel. After several days they discovered they had been walking in circles. Near starvation, Dengler and Martin came across a village. They attempted to establish contact, but unknown to them the villagers were Pathet Lao sympathizers. When Martin attempted to speak with a young boy, a farmer attacked him with a machete, striking a blow to Martin's head and neck and killing him. Dengler escaped back into the bush and continued to evade the enemy patrols sent to recapture him.

After aimlessly wandering through the Lao jungle, and finally at the end of his endurance, Dengler crawled up on a large rock in a small streambed, close to death. Miraculously, a U.S. airplane flew over head and at precisely the right moment the pilot looked down and saw Dengler lying on the rock. The pilot quickly called for a SAR helicopter, which lowered a cable to Dengler and hoisted him aboard.[51]

Of the original seven who fled the camp, only Dengler and one of the Thais reached freedom. Martin was dead and Debruin and his sickly Chinese crewman and two of three Thais were never seen again. However, it must be noted that Dengler is not without his critics. Aderholt in particular disbelieved large parts of Dengler's story, especially regarding his first days. Aderholt had CAS send a friendly guerrilla unit into the area where Dengler crashed to check his story with the local villagers. The unit's report confirmed Aderholt's suspicions, as they informed CAS that the American pilot had walked into the nearest village and surrendered. Further, when the third Thai, Prisit, was rescued, his description of Dengler was not flattering.

Recently, an American investigator interviewed a Lao connected with the Martin-Dengler incident. The Lao stated that he had exchanged gunfire with some men, eventually chasing one to the river and capturing him. The other ran off. He put his rifle to the back of the captured man's head and fired, blowing his face off. Because of the severity of the wound, the Lao was unable to identify whether his victim was a Caucasian or one of the Thais. He buried the man next to a tree. After an extensive excavation, the U.S. team eventually recovered a set of remains from this grave location, which is near the prison at Houei Het. The government's forensic laboratory has been unable to conclusively identify the remains as Martin or either of the two Thais. However, one intriguing piece of evidence provides strong circumstantial information that the remains are Martin. The skull shows that the individual had a cleft palate. Unfortunately, Martin's dental records have been lost, but a note in his other records indicates that he did have a cleft palate. Additional and extensive background searches by U.S. investigators, however, have not turned up any conclusive proof that Martin had a cleft palate. If the remains are eventually proved to be Martin, Dengler's account will need a serious revision.

Mahaxay

The only successful U.S. prison raid in Laos, which coincidentally also released the largest number of POWs ever freed during the war, was conducted by the CIA. For once, friendly forces arrived in time and unlike the Vietnamese, the PL had not moved their semipermanent camp location. Unfortunately, no Americans were recovered, but one rescued POW was one of the Thai crewmen from the Debruin aircraft. In early January, "a Lao farmer arrived in Savannakhet and said that he had just escaped from a POW camp near Mahaxay. Furthermore, he believed that the other prisoners could be rescued with a small force, which he offered to guide."[52] The CIA officer in charge of the Savannakhet field office was named Tom Fosmire. According to Secord, the CIA men at Udorn were embittered over the earlier failure to rescue the men in the caves and jumped at the next opportunity for a rescue mission. "We decided to not even alert the Station in Vientiane for fear of having the operation turned down."

Fosmire quickly trained a ten-man team and helicoptered them to an area near the camp. No Americans were with the rescue unit. Using the cover of night, the group moved slowly toward the camp location. The CIA report states, "A Lao guerrilla team using carbines and hand grenades attacked a Pathet Lao prison at 2030 hours on 7 January 1967 and freed all 57 prisoners held there in three buildings. One PL guard was killed, and the rest, estimated to be eight, fled. The team and the freed prisoners left the prison area immediately, striking out for friendly held territory. . . . The team with 28 of the freed prisoners arrived at a friendly outpost at 1700 hours on 8 January. During the night, 29 of the prisoners had left according to the team. Many were criminals who had escaped from Lao government prisons and were afraid to return. Among the 28 freed prisoners reaching the outpost . . . a Thai national, who had been a kicker for Air America and had been on the C-46 [cargo plane] that was shot down in September, 1963."[53]

The return of this Thai national, a man named Pisidhi [also spelled Prisit] Indrahat, enabled the Agency to track the early movements of the C-46 crew. He also provided a differing account of the escape of Dengler and the rest the men held in the camp at Houei Het. Although Pisidhi had managed to evade the PL for over a month, he was eventually recaptured and placed in the camp at Mahaxay. Additionally, his description of Martin's death, which he learned from his PL guards, clashed with Dengler's. He accused Dengler of hiding in the bushes while Martin attempted to communicate with the Lao villagers, and claimed that Dengler had run away when Martin was hit by the machete.[54] Dengler denies Pisidhi's version.

POWs and Lao Politics

In reviewing the efforts between May 1965 and May 1966 there are significant differences between the attempts to recover Gustav Hertz and the other American POWs in South Vietnam, and those to regain Shelton and Hrdlicka and possibly Don Wood in Laos. Ambassador Sullivan, while interested in the POWs, was anxious to maintain the policy fiction that any lost American airmen were engaged in reconnaissance missions that were monitoring North Vietnamese violations of the 1962 Geneva Accords that ended the Lao civil war. Secord knew Sullivan well and believes that the ambassador also had "a personal stake in proving that neutrality worked, since Sullivan had assisted Harriman in drafting those Lao Accords and it was well known that Sullivan was a protégé of Harriman."[55] This desire to see the Accords work, Secord believes, led to many of Sullivan's decisions concerning military actions in Laos.

Singlaub was also a harsh critic of Sullivan's, believing that the "core of the problem was civilian-military turf jealousy. . . . every time one of my teams took out a lucrative target a few kilometers from the approved area of operations, we'd get a rocket of a telegram from the embassy in Vientiane. . . . He'd wallpaper the entire U.S. government with information copies as an ass-saving precaution. . . . When I'd see Sullivan at regional meeting, however, he would apologize for his excesses when we were washing our hands in the officers' club men's room and no one could hear him."[56]

Since the Pathet Lao were not exploiting the American POWs for propaganda purposes, Sullivan was probably happy not to have the issue become public. But it also appears that he was not willing to raise it privately, and he did not begin addressing the issue consistently with the PL until months after Hrdlicka's broadcast. Moreover, all efforts to discuss the fates of these men were directed at the Pathet Lao, yet it was well known even then that the North Vietnamese controlled the PL and most of the territory where the Americans went missing.

However, like Klusmann before them, Hrdlicka, Shelton, and any other American POWs must have been under continual pressure to give statements. The PL attempted to manipulate Klusmann into making broadcasts and signing statements by using the announcement of his death to coerce him. The Americans in the caves must have undergone comparable treatment, and the PL captain mentioned earlier, who defected in December 1965, indicated that Hrdlicka's interrogation had followed a similar pattern, at least initially. However, it was almost precisely a full year after he was captured before Hrdlicka made a statement over Pathet Lao radio. None was ever forthcoming from any other American POW in Laos. Why?

Klusmann offers some suggestions. "There are many reasons why the broadcast could have been made. They had tried to use the announcement of my death to manipulate me and they could have used the same trick by convincing him that no one knew he was alive. They kept telling me from the first day that I was going to be released and I kept saying okay, release me, but they didn't. You don't realize how persuasive they can be, especially when you're sick. After I got back, the head of the survival school said that my interrogation was right out of a Soviet interrogation manual, that this was a classic, textbook example of the Soviet method and they believed that Kaham might have had Soviet training."

Perhaps the Pathet Lao never held any other Americans long enough to make such broadcasts, since it has been reported through intelligence debriefing of PL defectors that PL POW policy was to turn them over to the North Vietnamese. But if there were at least two, possibly three Americans in the caves, why only Hrdlicka? Why not Debruin, who had been held much longer and was a civilian and not bound by the Code of Conduct? Maybe it was simply not in either North Vietnam's or the Pathet Lao's interest to expose how many POWs they had captured in Laos. If that is true, does that indicate a different plan by the communists for these men or was it a result of differing circumstances? After all, the DRV was also loath to reveal both the names and numbers of American POWs in North

Vietnam and its own presence in Laos. But the DRV also had a conflicting desire: to use POW statements to generate political sympathy among the countries of the outside world and to sow dissension in the United States. Part of that propaganda was for internal consumption, to bolster the fighting spirit of their own troops against the massive firepower of the American aggressors. Was Hrdlicka's broadcast a message meant as a morale booster for the PL troops undergoing relentless American bombing?

As for Sullivan's efforts, the loss of Shelton and Hrdlicka would be far more understandable if the Pathet Lao and the United States had been engaged in a truly secret war. But in fact the secret war was an open secret, a secret known and kept by everyone from the Chinese and the Soviets to the North Vietnamese and the Americans, because it was in all of their national interests to keep the fighting quiet. The Chinese were engaged in a massive road-building project in northern Laos and had thousands of construction troops and antiaircraft guns deployed in the country. The NVA needed the Ho Chi Minh Trail, and the Soviets feared replicating their own 1961–62 involvement in Laos, with its overtones of possible military confrontation with the United States. The *New York Times* for 1966 is replete with accounts of American planes bombing in Laos, and the only ones who appeared not to know the full extent of the fighting in Laos were the American people, the Congress, and the families of the men who were lost in that country. What Sullivan, and Unger before him, really feared was not that the secrecy would be uncovered, but that it would be publicized, a notoriety they dreaded the fragile Royal Lao government could not survive. Similar concerns over GVN sensitivities had derailed several efforts to help American POWs in South Vietnam, but the war in Laos was "secret" and "quiet." So were the efforts for any captured Americans.

For example, President Johnson had earlier appointed former Governor of New York and World War II Ambassador to Moscow W. Averell Harriman as the Administration's point-man on POW matters. Harriman considered asking Laotian Prime Minister Souvanna Phouma, during a visit by him to Washington, to begin speaking publicly about the condition of American POWs in Pathet Lao hands. When Harriman cabled Sullivan to solicit his views, Sullivan wrote back, "As you can readily appreciate, Souvanna can offer little more than sympathy re US nationals held by Pathet Lao. I am sure, however, that he would be willing cooperate in any way you consider helpful to their release. There are two features of problem on which I would comment. First is fact that publicity re US prisoners is obviously embarrassing to Souvanna. Dept.'s awkward handling of this subject last summer when spokesman revealed '30 US missing in Laos' was not rpt not helpful to our larger purposes in this country. Second point is that it would not rpt not enhance Souvanna's stature as independent statesman to have him come back from Washington acting overtly as attorney for US nationals."[57]

Once again, Sullivan had placed the fiction of Lao neutrality above the welfare of the Americans missing in Laos. Sullivan's words concerning a "larger purpose" are indicative of a mind-set that, if necessary, Americans in Laos would be sacrificed for long-term policy goals or the greater national interest.

5. State Begins to Act

Vietnamese circles here today rejected as ingenious but impractical the idea of placing American prisoners at points likely to be bombed in U.S. air raids. The humanitarian feelings of the Americans, they stated, are not just as highly developed as ours. They are likely to carry out their bombing raids just the same. And it is our duty not to jeopardize human lives in this way.
—French press report from July 22, 1966, quoting communist sources after stories began circulating in Hanoi that an American pilot might be placed at each fuel dump and each power plant and that three pilots might be placed on the Doumer Bridge in the center of town

The beginning of 1966 saw the emergence of the first serious efforts to arrange the exchange not only of Gustav Hertz, but also of many of the other American prisoners suffering in captivity in North and South Vietnam. The possibility of swapping American POWs for either NLF cadres or NVA prisoners held by the GVN became a theme that would continue to the end of the war. Despite the wartime attempts by the communists to create a fictional rebel organization in South Vietnam, all the major decisions on swapping for American POWs were made in Hanoi. Several postwar interviews with knowledgeable Vietnamese cadres confirm that the DRV's Politburo controlled all POW exchanges. Although little is known about the precise reasons behind each attempted channel or why it failed, the record indicates that in the early years of the war the communists were only interested in battlefield exchanges and rebuffed any attempt to engage them in a diplomatic forum. Initially the communists were mainly focusing their propaganda efforts on the citizens of South Vietnam, but as the war grew in intensity we can surmise that the communists wanted to legitimize the existence of the NLF by showing the world that it was a military and political force to be reckoned with. It also sought worldwide sympathy for the revolution by displaying its "humane" policies toward POWs, despite the "crimes against the Vietnamese people" those POWs had committed. By spreading the rumor that the VC treated captured soldiers with kindness, they also hoped to sap the fighting spirit of the opposing military.

However, exchanges were a complex matter. Determining the reasons behind the failure of most of these attempts has been difficult, but several possibilities can be discussed. For instance, some of the American POWs that the DRV hoped to swap may have died unexpectedly in the horrible, disease-ridden conditions of the communist jungle prison camps. More likely, though, the DRV was trying to elicit from the Americans a list of those who the United States government believed were dead. The communists would then have an easier time exploiting them if they were in fact alive. Klusmann's handling was an excellent example of this type of intelligence program. However, any conjecture concerning communist motivations at this point, in the absence of a review of contemporaneous Vietnamese records, remains pure speculation.

The State Department also made repeated attempts through the International Committee of the Red Cross (ICRC) to ameliorate the conditions of the airmen captured in the air war against the DRV. Despite several tantalizing initial ventures, however, all of these attempts fell apart due to the DRV/NLF refusal to engage the United States in negotiations or to acknowledge the applicability of the Geneva PW Accords to the American prisoners.

Efforts Through the Red Cross

Shortly after the release of Smith and McClure, DOD began pressing State to make a reciprocal gesture to the communists. Since an ICRC team was currently visiting South Vietnam to inspect the GVN's POW facilities, State decided to use the opportunity to prompt the GVN to release two NVA prisoners to ICRC custody for reparation. Release of these NVA POWs would be accompanied by press statements "expressing hope that this action would lead to further de facto exchange of prisoners." Moreover, "our objective in seeking these actions is . . . hopefully lay groundwork for further releases of US prisoners held by DRV/VC."[1]

Having previously been stonewalled by communist refusals of direct United States requests to grant mail privileges or access to the growing number of American POWs, following the execution of Bennett, Roraback, and Versace, the State Department turned to the ICRC as its only viable alternative for gaining proper treatment for the American POWs. The International Committee of the Red Cross had a historical mandate regarding POW care, and its actions and neutrality were part of the matrix of the provisions of the 1949 Geneva PW Accords. Although its principal role of succor to POWs during wartime has historically been respected by all combatants, its make-up and impartiality are the products of a European background and as such were either poorly understood or viewed with deep suspicion by Asian Marxists. Therefore, the DRV dealt with the ICRC only when it could foresee a possible advantage to itself. Otherwise it refused to accede to ICRC requests for prison inspection or to answer ICRC inquiries about the status or health of American POWs.

Although the ICRC had been able to do little for the American POWs in Indochina, by fortunate coincidence, the XXth International Conference of the Red Cross opened in Vienna shortly after the execution of Roraback and Versace. The United States introduced a resolution condemning the VC action, which was accepted almost unanimously by the member nations. Also during the conference, the American Red Cross asked the Red Cross Society of Cambodia to assist in getting packages and medical supplies through to the Americans held by the VC. The Cambodians had promised to see what could be done to deliver the packages to the National Liberation Front Red Cross for transmittal to the prisoners. But, like previous U.S. attempts, the Cambodians' efforts failed.[2]

The NLF voiced the usual litany of fears and excuses to the Cambodians in refusing their offer. The inherent difficulties of fighting a guerrilla war could expose the ICRC inspectors to wartime dangers, they said; moreover, the GVN would undoubtedly construct a devious plot to disrupt such a visit. In truth, while the main American POW camp was mobile, the NLF, like the DRV, wanted no interference in its attempts to indoctrinate the POWs and no outside "bourgeois" judgments on its treatment of POWs. Further, even though it had received condemnation from the ICRC for the executions, the NLF must have felt some satisfaction in halting the killing of its cadres by the GVN, a concession they achieved themselves after the ICRC's intercession failed to halt the executions by the South Vietnamese government.

Despite the inability of the ICRC to persuade the DRV to abide by the Geneva Conventions, Washington's concerns for its POWs led it to begin pressing the GVN to comply with the Accords. Matthews, the POL/MIL officer at the Saigon

Embassy, states that "suddenly, when civilians started becoming POWs, the concern was raised in Washington over GVN treatment of NVA/VC prisoners. We felt that maybe we could achieve a quid pro quo by improving GVN treatment."[3] As such, this stimulated the American government to pay closer attention to the GVN's treatment of its communist prisoners, hoping that if the South Vietnamese approached the ICRC's standards, this would shame the DRV/NLF into a parallel compliance with the provisions of the Geneva Accords.

Determined to show the ICRC that its POW house was in order, MACV began sending monthly reports to Washington for retransmittal by State to Geneva detailing the numbers, locations, and status of captured enemy prisoners. The U.S. Embassy in Saigon also assigned Matthews to monitor the efforts and to coordinate the attempts to persuade the ICRC that the GVN was following the Geneva Conventions. Although the State Department felt that MACV should handle enemy prisoners instead of turning them over to the GVN as the Westmoreland/Co agreement called for, the Embassy strongly disagreed. Henry Cabot Lodge had returned as U.S. ambassador to South Vietnam, and he wrote to Secretary of State Rusk that "We do not believe we should consider at this time stopping transfer of prisoners to GVN for following reasons: It would probably affront Vietnamese nationalist sensitivities and arouse a major controversy (at a time when we can least afford it), and it would probably reduce rather than increase pressures upon them to improve treatment of prisoners."[4]

With the threat of war crimes trials looming, discovering the whereabouts and conditions of the American POWs now became a critical task for U.S. intelligence. However, while U.S. intelligence was beginning to focus on the locations where Americans were being held, a series of events occurred that momentarily allowed the United States to believe that the DRV might be willing to exchange some of the American POWs. That belief would be fleeting.

Algiers

The combination of the executions and the threats emanating from Hanoi impressed upon the State Department the urgency in finding a solution to the POW issue. State's main problem, however, was in locating a suitable representative of the DRV/NLF to discuss POWs. Most of the diplomatic missions the NLF maintained were in communist countries, and when approached they refused to meet with U.S. representatives or intermediaries. Although the Algerian connection had lain fallow for a time after the fall of the Ben Bella government, when the Algerian government finally stabilized the United States attempted to resurrect Senator Edward Kennedy's previous discussions held in June 1965 on exchanging prisoners. During the ICRC conference in Vienna in October, State asked the ICRC to query the NLF whether it was still interested in swapping Hai for Hertz.

The ICRC agreed, and Washington asked Prime Minister Nguyen Cao Ky to release Hai in the event that the NLF decided to free Hertz. On December 12, 1965, Ky gave his approval for the exchange, and on January 4, 1966, ICRC representative Jacques de Heller spent two hours discussing the proposed swap with the NLF envoy in Algiers, Huynh Van Tam. Although Tam had expressed interest in the summer in exchanging Hai for Hertz, he now rejected a direct exchange, citing the poisoned atmosphere resulting from the earlier GVN executions of the terrorists. However, he broached the possibility of a larger exchange that included all prisoners and suggested that a conference involving the ICRC, the United States, and the NLF meet to discuss the POW situation.

The Embassy in Saigon was still worried that a direct meeting between the National Liberation Front and the United States would create problems with the government of South Vietnam. Lodge was concerned over how an American-POWs-only exchange would affect GVN attitudes, and he believed that "both Hanoi and Viet Cong are probably using prisoners in the sense of hostages and trying to drive a wedge between the U.S. and the GVN by pressuring us to place a higher value on U.S. than [on] GVN prisoners and to establish a higher priority for the exchange of U.S. prisoners."[5] While Lodge was not against following up on the Tam openings, he asked for time to gain GVN concurrence for a direct meeting. Moreover, he insisted that to maintain GVN goodwill, the Americans had to broach the subject of exchanging GVN prisoners.

The one question seemingly not considered by Lodge and the Embassy was if the ARVNs were themselves secretly exchanging prisoners with the VC. Who knows how many POWs were swapped between the two without American knowledge or approval? Since the numbers of South Vietnamese prisoners were substantially higher than the Americans, and given a historical and cultural acceptance for swapping prisoners, one can reasonably conclude that when it suited the interests of the South Vietnamese (while the United States was agonizing over possibly harming relations with the GVN if we didn't include their POWs in any swap), the GVN probably exchanged POWs with the NLF without informing the United States or considering the repercussions on American prisoners.

The Saigon Embassy, though, was still busily attempting to sensitize the U.S. government to the GVN's fears. But President Johnson's advisors believed the opportunity to open a channel for exchanging American POWs could not be overlooked, and the U.S. government made the decision to meet with the NLF together with the ICRC despite its long-standing policy against direct negotiations with them. National Security Advisor McGeorge Bundy recommended to President Johnson that "We felt that such a tripartite discussion, with the possibility of an early release of U.S. prisoners, was of such importance as to override our concern about confrontation with the NLF. We, therefore, determined that a prompt affirmative response was appropriate."[6]

In mid-January, Secretary of State Dean Rusk flew to Saigon to meet with Prime Minister Ky to discuss a wide range of bilateral matters. On the subject of the possible POW exchange meeting, Rusk reassured Ky that the United States would keep the GVN completely informed of the results of the talks and would keep strictly to the topic of POWs. Under those conditions, Ky agreed to a U.S.-NLF rendezvous under the auspices of the ICRC.

As NLF envoy, Tam had insisted to the ICRC representative that the proposed talks with the United States be held in the utmost secrecy. At the next opportunity, however, he revealed the essence of the negotiations to a private American citizen named Sanford Gottlieb, an official of the National Committee for a Sane Nuclear Policy (SANE). Gottlieb was in Algiers to see the DRV trade delegation that was currently visiting Algeria; during his stay he also stopped to visit the NLF representative. In the course of their conversation, Tam told Gottlieb, "The Front is prepared to discuss the exchange of all prisoners, including Mr. Hertz."[7] Gottlieb immediately held a news conference in which he described his talks with Tam and made direct mention of the proposed meeting between the National Liberation Front and the United States to discuss prisoner exchanges.

Although the Americans were shaken by the breach of secrecy, the confirmation by Gottlieb of the NLF's interest after the ICRC's meeting between de Heller and Tam raised the hopes of the U.S. government. After securing Ky's approval, Secretary Rusk immediately cabled the ICRC asking them to meet with Tam a second time to express Washington's willingness to convene with the NLF. On January 19, de Heller met with Tam to pass on the U.S. statement, and came away from the meeting "very favorably impressed with his conversation with Tam."[8] Tam stated he "had to transmit the information to the Front and receive definitive instruction," and that "he would have a definite answer within fifteen days."[9]

As the State Department began to prepare for the meeting with Tam, the NLF abruptly slammed the door on any conference. The ICRC received a letter on January 25 dated January 21 that completely contradicted Tam's earlier position. In the letter, Tam stated that he had told the ICRC representative that the NLF was not authorized to have any relations with the ICRC, nor would it consider any meeting with representatives of the American government. Stunned by the reply, the ICRC informed Washington that in its opinion, in "the very short time which elapsed between de Heller's Jan. 19 visit to Tam and the sending of this letter . . . Tam must have been in touch with his Headquarters, which must have refused to acknowledge the position he took. . . . De Heller has said that it is as if another man wrote the Jan. 21 letter. . . ."[10]

The Vogel Proposal

Although the Tam channel was closing, another door was opening in Berlin. While the ICRC was meeting with Tam, Wolfgang Vogel, an East German lawyer who had earlier been involved in arranging the exchange of spies between the communist bloc and the Western allies, approached the U.S. Mission in Berlin with a proposal to exchange American prisoners for North Vietnamese prisoners held in the South. Vogel claimed he had support from high levels in the East German government to mediate an exchange of ten American POWs for a like number of NVA prisoners. An integral part of the deal, however, included the exchange of two convicted East German spies held by the United Kingdom, a husband-and-wife team named Kroeger, for two British citizens convicted on espionage charges by the Soviets. As a preliminary good-faith step, Vogel asked for a list of POWs that each side desired released.

The State Department was unable to determine whether the exchange proposal was a genuine feeler or simply an attempt to get the Kroegers back, with the Vietnam POWs thrown in. Regardless, State moved forward to take advantage of the offer. Ever mindful of the insecurities of the South Vietnamese government, the U.S. Embassy recommended that a list of GVN prisoners also be included. The State Department also upped the ante by asking the Joint Chiefs of Staff to provide expanded lists of American POWs, including both known captives and those men who were simply listed as missing. Given the extreme reluctance of the British to release the Kroegers, State told Berlin to meet with Vogel and submit all the lists including the one containing the GVN prisoners, but to refrain from offering the Kroegers.

Upon receiving its instructions, the U.S. mission met with Vogel. They promptly presented the expanded group of lists, asked for a complete list of American POWs in North Vietnam, and inquired about including the GVN POWs. Vogel was dismayed by these two additional points and believed their introduction "stood a good chance of bringing the U.S. prisoners exchange scheme to naught.

. . . the exchange was now in a delicate stage. . . . the introduction of the additional elements such as the GVN prisoners would be highly unfortunate."[11] Vogel also mentioned that he believed that the Soviets were actively involved.

Vogel's anxiety caused the United States to immediately back-pedal. Rusk cabled Lodge that "our inclination would be not to press Vogel again to accept GVN list at this time. We have now made very clear our strong desire that GVN should be included if exchange materializes, and our overall reading is that Vogel may be engaged in serious effort that may have some bearing on Soviet/DRV relationships."[12] Rusk added that if the U.S. deal went through, they could always raise the matter of the GVN POWs later.

Suddenly faced with the prospect that the Saigon Embassy's previous insistence on including the GVN POWs might scuttle the Vogel channel, Lodge quickly agreed to Rusk's decision. Changing tack, Lodge wrote back, "In view Vogel's firm and explicit statement that insistence on inclusion GVN prisoners might queer any prisoner exchange, we concur that Berlin should not press Vogel further on this issue now. . . . We believe GVN reaction will be one of disappointment, but we have always felt GVN much less interested in prisoners than we are."[13]

After the first meeting, the United States impatiently waited, but nothing further was heard from Vogel. On January 30, the Berlin mission again initiated contact with Vogel to discuss the proposed exchange. Vogel stated that he was waiting for a DRV response and that the list was under consideration, but that "not all of those mentioned on the list are in DRV hands."[14] Further, Vogel said, the DRV wanted the exchange held in Vietnam; any NVA prisoners would be disguised as Viet Cong, and the NLF would be in charge of the swap, with no direct DRV participation.

Unfortunately, the DRV never responded to Vogel, although Vogel tried to resurrect the talks in mid-June 1966. No adequate explanation has ever been provided by the communists for their blunt dismissal of the Tam and Vogel channels. Either Tam had acted without prior knowledge of the Central Committee, or some other unknown element was involved. Whether the communists were ever truly serious is another factor, since every time the United States began to discuss the specifics of POW exchanges, the DRV/NLF backed away.

Whether the Vogel exchange fell victim to the same problem as the Tam channel is also unknown. If these were genuine feelers, the efforts may have represented authentic divisions among the DRV leadership over American POWs. That such divisions were real and still evident until late in the war was revealed in a high-level DRV document found in the Russian archives in April 1993 by Harvard researcher Dr. Steven Morris. It became known as the "1205 document" because the numbers of American POWs given by the author as being currently held by the DRV were far higher than the number of those who came home. The author, a high-ranking NVA general, mentioned that differences of opinion existed between various factions in the DRV leadership over the policy toward POWs, with some advocating a more lenient response to the U.S. proposals at the Paris Peace Talks.

In 1992 Vogel told author Craig R. Whitney that the Americans had only handed him a list of eleven pilots, five Navy and six Air Force. According to Whitney, "Vogel's recollection years later was that the American authorities may have been testing intelligence reports that the men were being held or treated in hospitals in East Germany . . . but by the middle of 1966 it was clear that those of the pilots who were alive must be in Indochina, not in East Germany, and that the Vietnamese were not interested in letting the Soviets have any of them."[15] The more likely probability is that the Vogel offer was the opposite, a carefully crafted intelligence ploy designed by the Soviets to draw out from the U.S. side who it believed were held prisoner in the DRV.

While disappointed by the failures of the two conduits, State continued to explore every option to establish contact with the DRV and the NLF in order to discuss the POW problem. The problem was still in getting the communists to talk.

Opening Other Channels

One of the Geneva Accords provisions allows for a neutral country, called a "Protecting Power," to represent the interests of enemy POWs held by a hostile country. The United States had canvassed several neutral countries to act in such a capacity, but they all declined the U.S. request. Finally, the United Arab Republic of Egypt accepted. In mid-January, the leaders of the DRV flatly refused the request from the Egyptians to act as a "Protecting Power" for the POWs in North Vietnam. Unable to find another suitable country, the United States pressed the ICRC to assume that function. In May 1966 the ICRC agreed, but its offer to the DRV to act as the "Protecting Power" for the POWs was also refused by the communists.

Stymied by the lack of progress, and in response to growing pressure from the DOD and congressional leaders like Senator Kennedy, President Johnson in mid-May appointed former ambassador to the Soviet Union W. Averell Harriman to become the U.S. government's policy coordinator and spokesman for POW affairs. After reviewing all the different American approaches currently being considered, Harriman decided to proceed immediately with two options. The first involved using the U.S. Embassy in Laos to contact the DRV office in Vientiane. The second was to make contact with the NLF through a private citizen.

The State Department also explored the idea of using public pressure to embarrass the DRV/NLF into discussing the POW problem. Elements in the State Department believed that one side effect in using a publicity campaign against the communist behavior or announcing the failure of the exchange attempts would be to quiet the growing criticism within the American government over State's handling of the issue. However, the Saigon Embassy was emphatically against any such publicity. Lodge wrote, "We also believe that publication of exchange would add fuel to question of VC representation at eventual peace conference. . . . Our agreement to meet with VC without any Vietnamese representation present could be construed by some as important weakening of our present publicly stated position on VC representation. We would also be concerned about GVN and Vietnamese public reaction to the release of this exchange. When we made proposal to . . . Ky we assured them that everything would be done with minimum publicity. On that basis Ky gave his approval of our proceeding on proposal to Secretary Rusk."[16] The Embassy's strong stance against publicity effectively killed that option, although word was quietly leaked in Washington concerning the efforts to trade for American POWs.[17]

Hamstrung by the Embassy's opposition to a public campaign, Harriman's first attempt was to ask Sullivan to make an inquiry with the North Vietnamese in Vientiane concerning POWs. Sullivan replied that he felt it best to make this communication "direct and official." Sullivan also recommended that any meeting at first be handled by his chargé, since the DRV ambassador was currently absent and he himself was going home soon on leave. Finally, he asked for a piece of paper to hand to the North Vietnamese so that the U.S. message was precise, plus he requested time to allow him to brief Souvanna and the other friendly embassies. He didn't expect much from the attempt, he wrote, believing that the "North Vietnamese themselves would probably be totally negative. Only question is whether they would also be abusive, either privately or publicly, for the sake of their Peking audience."[18]

Sullivan's second-in-command delivered the note on June 13, 1966. Surprisingly, when the Embassy chargé handed the note to the DRV representative, no mention was made of the Americans in Sam Neua, nor apparently were they part of the equation for the various exchange channels. The note generally expressed "our concern about the fate and welfare of U.S. pilots captured in North Vietnam, asking for improved treatment in matters such as mail, gift packages, visits by the ICRC, and lists of prisoners. The note also said we would like to obtain the release of the prisoners and that we were prepared to enter into discussion on this subject at a place and level agreeable to the other side."[19] The note was accepted by the DRV chargé, who carried it with him on the International Control Commission (ICC) flight back to Hanoi. Apparently the effort was again rejected, for when the DRV chargé returned in mid-July he made no effort to contact the American Embassy. After waiting several days, Sullivan's people tried to contact the DRV embassy, but their note asking for a meeting was returned unopened. Hanoi had once again declined an invitation to talk.

Harriman's second approach was to the NLF. He picked a foreign citizen: Wilfred Burchett, an Australian communist newsman who, along with two Cuban journalists, had already interviewed Smith and McClure in the American POW camp in Tay Ninh province in early 1965. The first contact with Burchett was made in Phnom Penh, the capital of Cambodia, in early July by Robert Shaplen, the respected Far East reporter for the *New Yorker* magazine. When approached by the State Department, Shaplen agreed to act as a go-between. Following his instructions, Shaplen asked Burchett to contact the NLF regarding a possible exchange of prisoners for materials, including "the supply of drugs."[20]

The State Department did not want to simply offer money for the men, and Harriman asked the Joint Chiefs of Staff for their views on the desirability of ransoming American prisoners for commodities. In 1963, the U.S. government had ransomed the Cuban prisoners from the Bay of Pigs incident for material goods; now they wanted DOD's opinion on proposing a similar exchange. In State's view, any exchange would only be in nonmilitary materials such as medical supplies, foodstuffs, or pesticides.

The State Department was fully aware that such a barter might be construed as giving "aid and comfort to the enemy," and State was not proceeding without DOD's concurrence. DOD was ambivalent about ransoming, noting that MACV had already attempted such an endeavor without success. Further, they were concerned that troop morale might be effected, since the men in the North were officers and the men in the South were generally enlisted soldiers. Although DOD was lukewarm to the proposal, State went forward anyway and informed Shaplen to proceed. Surprisingly, Burchett agreed to the proposal and carried the request to the NLF representative in Cambodia, Tran Buu Kiem. True to form, Kiem responded negatively to Shaplen in a letter on July 15. Like the DRV, the NLF wasn't interested in talking.

The Threat of Trials

While Harriman was seeking to establish a means of communicating with the DRV/NLF, the U.S. government was confronted with a far more serious problem, the threat of DRV criminal proceedings against the airmen captured in North Vietnam. As the bombing grew in ferocity, the North Vietnamese began to make increasingly strident threats about the Americans it held captive. War-crimes trials became a real possibility. The DRV refused to accept the Geneva Convention provisions concerning the legitimate rights of servicemen engaged in military actions against the territory of North Vietnam, referring to them instead as "war criminals." Lists of names, most mail privileges, and ICRC inspections were all denied by the North Vietnamese under the blanket statement that since no formal notification of war had been declared, the men were not POWs and were therefore liable for punishment under the DRV penal code. Matters became worse in June, when DRV interrogators began extracting and publishing "confessions" from captured Americans stating that they had bombed civilians and asking for forgiveness from the North Vietnamese people.

The harshness of the DRV propaganda machine reached new heights on June 16 when the military paper *Nhan Dan* reported a campaign to sign petitions urging the DRV government to bring the POWs to trial. When several days later the USAF bombed the DRV's oil reserves near Hanoi and Haiphong, huge crowds were reported marching in the cities shouting "Death to the imperialists!" The culmination of the public campaign was reached on July 6, when the communists paraded dozens of American POWs through the streets of Hanoi before angry mobs who cursed and shouted threats at them. Several POWs were also beaten by the crowd.

The next day, the Czech news agency claimed that the DRV intended to hold trials for the captured Americans. In response, Secretary of State Rusk launched an all-out diplomatic effort to convince the North of the magnitude of its mistake. U.S. embassies around the world began informing every single government that had relations with the DRV that the United States would retaliate for this gross violation of the Geneva Convention. Previously, without independent, neutral confirmation of the health and status of the POWs, the State Department found it difficult to sustain any world outrage against the behavior of the DRV, but this time the stakes had been raised and the world community was now paying close attention. Through this diplomatic offensive, the United States sought to apply the full force of its diplomatic weight to dissuade the communists from holding trials.

The military, naturally, were appalled at the prospect of trials and further potential executions of American prisoners. In response to a query from State, CINCPAC cabled the Joint Chiefs that "should such trials take place, with possible subsequent executions, it is encumbent upon the U.S. to take necessary actions against NVN. To do anything less could have adverse effects on the morale of our fighting men as well as on families back home."[21] As to direct military actions, the commander of CINCPAC recommended that the U.S. military bomb buildings in Hanoi and mine the harbors of Haiphong, actions currently forbidden to him.

But the U.S. civilian government wanted to avoid making open threats of military retaliation until the lives of the POWs were directly threatened. To ensure that no spokesmen accidentally sent the wrong signal, both State and DOD issued orders to all their personnel to refrain from making any statements concerning possible U.S. reactions to the trials. Deputy Secretary of Defense Cyrus Vance further reinforced this with a "single spokesman" decree on July 26, naming Averell Harriman as the only individual authorized to speak publicly on U.S. POW policy.

Eventually, the U.S. diplomatic "Mad Minute" paid off and the DRV backed away from its threat to stage war-crimes trials. On July 24, 1966, Ho Chi Minh cabled CBS news that "no trial in view." Lodge quickly presented Rusk with his assessment of the DRV change of heart. "Hanoi has always counted on and still doubtless hopes that U.S. public will tire and bring pressure to bear . . . to terminate U.S. commitment in South Vietnam. In minds of leaders in Hanoi experience with French domestic opinion in 1954 still serves as model. . . . However, we believe that primary reason for Hanoi's backing off on this matter was regime's concern over adverse U.S. public reaction which would have been followed by increased U.S. military pressure. . . . In sum, this most clear-cut change in Hanoi internal policy in reaction to external pressure that we have seen in some time. It reflects, we believe, Hanoi's awareness that it had misread domestic U.S. attitudes, and that it decided not to alienate further any goodwill NVN cause had accumulated in past. It also shows Hanoi retains flexibility for quick reassessment and change of major policy, even a disregard of own domestic propaganda campaign."[22]

Since the beginning of the year the DRV/NLF had rejected at least four different approaches concerning the release or exchange of POWs, had rebuffed any attempt by the ICRC to admonish them for violating the Geneva Convention, and had slammed the door on repeated American offers to negotiate on POWs. The U.S. government had exhausted every avenue to convince the DRV/NLF to abide by the Geneva rules and had spared no effort to achieve some knowledge of the whereabouts and status of the American prisoners. While historians can argue whether another approach, nuanced slightly different, could have produced better results, the simple fact remains that the communists were given ample opportunity to engage the United States in a dialogue about the POW situation. Whether the result of a deliberate calculation or gripped by wartime hysteria, the reasons for the communists' refusals remain unknown.

Questions About American POWs: Finding Out Who Was Alive

Although hinting at possible "brainwashing" at the hands of the communists, in their public statements in the first half of 1966 U.S. officials appeared uncertain how the DRV was extracting confessions from the American prisoners, let alone what condition they were in or how many were currently in DRV hands. Then, when the various "confessions" from POWs starting appearing in both the communist and free world media, the U.S. military became determined to discover how the POWs were being treated, especially whether they were undergoing "brainwashing" or torture. Besides discovering how the men were being treated, the other major problem was finding out who was alive and where they were held. Acting in conjunction with the CIA, the military embarked on an intelligence-collection program that used over a dozen methods, including many open source materials such as films and pictures of POWs, to determine the status and whereabouts of the prisoners and especially to determine if they were captured or dead. Even though the DIA was responsible by regulation for tracking POWs, the USAF's 1127th Field Activity Group (FAG) at Fort Belvoir, Virginia, eventually become the clearinghouse in Washington for POW intelligence. The 1127th was a collection unit composed of intelligence analysts and former POWs from earlier wars.

Many have assumed for years that it was the debriefings of the returned prisoners which provided the conclusive intelligence that enabled the U.S. government to state that all its prisoners were home. Only partially true. Through a highly classified and still tightly held prisoner communications program called the Combined Services Support Program (CSSP), the U.S. military knew, before the main POW release in 1973, the identity of every prisoner who returned home from Indochina save one man. From a historical perspective, this prior knowledge is the great unknown factor behind the government's stated assurances that no prisoner remained in captivity after April 1973. To the pilots who were instructed in this method, it was jokingly known as the *Can't Say Shit Pal* program, although its name may have been changed in recent years to the Special Access Program.

Letters provided the most expeditious way to confirm whether a POW was alive or dead. But they also furnished a means of covert communication and for passing intelligence. Using a method known as "double-talk," a meaning hidden within a phrase or group of words that someone not native to the language would probably not comprehend, the POWs were able to provide prisoners' names, locations, and the type of treatment they were receiving. This program was originally developed by the British. It was through this method that the U.S. government first discovered that the POWs were being tortured. Although the first instance of torture occurred in late October 1965, the U.S. government did not confirm that its men were being brutalized until December 1966. Later, it was published that the government first discovered that the POWs were being tortured when Navy aviator Jeremiah Denton was seen blinking out the word "torture" in Morse code during a televised event. They have since used this incident as a red herring to publicize their discovery of the harsh treatment without jeopardizing the real source of the intelligence.

This program, of course, rested entirely on the mail being forwarded. One communist POW-policy document, dated January 1966 and captured in I Corps, reveals that the Vietnamese held back letters from those considered "obstinate," and to prevent the United States from discovering who was a prisoner. "In general," the document states, "the prisoners may send and receive letters. But it is necessary to maintain secrecy, names, and numbers of prisoners in order to prevent them from establishing contact with the enemy. The letters written by the prisoners not known by the U.S. to be in our hands, or by the 'obstinate' ones, will not be forwarded and [will be] kept for study. As regards to the 'progressive' or overt prisoners, we may hand them the letters sent to them or forward their own letters on the occasion of the holidays. We do not stop reactionary prisoners writing letters but we do not distribute letters to them or send their letters. We distribute letters only when they are advantageous to us."[23]

Another unexpected intelligence bonus came in July 1966, when Hanoi paraded the American POWs through the streets of Hanoi. Many prisoners were identified via the films of the parade made by the communist-bloc media, although at this time the U.S. could only identify with certainty thirty-five POWs. However, American intelligence on camp locations and prison conditions was so minimal that the U.S. government temporarily believed several sources who reported that the prisoners were being treated humanely. In mid-May 1966, a Polish diplomat reported to the ICRC a conversation with a North Vietnamese diplomat who informed him that the DRV had already captured more than two hundred American pilots, although the diplomat also claimed that many of the American pilots had expressed willingness to remain in North Vietnam to train North Vietnamese pilots.[24]

The more important sources were Western journalists who were allowed to travel to Hanoi. These were generally pro-communist writers from European newspapers. In August, a French correspondent reported to U.S. officials that he also believed there were between two hundred and two hundred sixty POWs in North Vietnam. This report led DOD officials to inform the press "that they aren't being treated too badly . . . no brainwashing—apparently no torture."[25]

Another French journalist, Madeleine Riffaud, who had spent the summer in Hanoi and had visited about twenty of the POWs, also provided information. Riffaud was a hard-line communist and her writings were definitely slanted in favor of the DRV position. After she printed an article in the French Communist Party newspaper *L'Humanité* describing her interviews with various American POWs, the U.S. Embassy in Paris asked her for an interview. She agreed, and in response to questions from the Embassy officer, Riffaud stated that she believed that more than one hundred fifty American POWs were then being held in the DRV, a number consistent with earlier reports by the Polish diplomat and the other French journalist but well above the number of men held at the time and who eventually returned home. However, she reported that they were being held in small groups, and although they suffered from the heat they were being treated well and adequately fed, even better than the average North Vietnamese.[26]

She also reported that she felt that most men were in fairly good health, except James Kasler, a pilot who she believed was arrogant and cold. Kasler had been severely injured on ejection and the communists had declined to provide medical treatment for his wounds except for the most rudimentary care. When Kasler refused to meet with the French correspondent, his North Vietnamese captors would not tolerate it, and the communists took advantage of his wounds to torture him into agreeing to meet with her. Whether Riffaud knew this about Kasler is unknown; she certainly never published or gave any indication of Kasler's predicament.

Besides attempting to gain their early release, the U.S. government spent much diplomatic energy trying to force the DRV/NLF to allow the prisoners to send and receive mail. In the years before 1967, mail was sporadic in both frequency and numbers; following communist policy some POWs were able to send and receive mail on a regular basis while others were completely refused the privilege. But in May 1965 the DRV for a time completely cut off the mail channel. Previously, letters and parcels had been shipped through the offices of the ICRC, but now the DRV did not want the ICRC involved in transmitting mail; they wanted all mail to come directly to North Vietnam. Although the U.S. government feared that the communist jailers were using the letter-writing privilege as an inducement to cooperate, thereby hoping to gain propaganda statements from the captives before allowing them to send or receive letters from their families, the potential for intelligence-gathering overrode this apprehension. The U.S. Post Office was asked to quietly set up a means to convey letters to North Vietnam, and an appropriate channel was found through Hong Kong. The families were informed they could use this route or any other they could find.

By using the route through Hong Kong to the address in the DRV, some mail was now starting to get through, and one of the Navy's intelligence officers decided to take a high-risk gamble to get a message in to the POWs. Commander Robert Boroughs was the Navy's intelligence officer assigned to the Interagency POW Intelligence Working Group, which later became a more full-fledged POW intelligence committee. The intelligence community noted that mail to and from the prisoners seemed to pick up around the Thanksgiving and Christmas holidays. Working closely with the wife of Navy POW James Stockdale, in late 1966 Boroughs clandestinely placed a message on the back of a photograph.[27] As Boroughs recalls, "I knew we were pushing our luck and risking Stockdale's life, but we were willing to try anything to achieve some success."[28]

In Stockdale's return letter home, he secretly passed the names of several other Navy officers held captive in Hoa Lo, the infamous main prison called the "Hanoi Hilton." As a result of Stockdale's clandestine communication, in February 1967 Navy Casualty abruptly changed the status of three men from believed dead to captive. The *New York Times* noted that this was the first time since World War II that a serviceman's status had been reversed. "The Defense Department gave no explanation of how it had learned that the men, who went down in North Vietnam in Navy planes, were alive. A terse notation in the regular casualty listing said that their status had been changed 'as a result of information recently received.'"[29]

While Boroughs was sneaking a message in to Stockdale, the USAF 1127th Field Activity Group was also gearing up to gather intelligence on American POWs through this clandestine channel. The 1127th's main job for years was to support the Defense Attachés in each overseas embassy. One of its smallest but most important sections was the Escape and Evasion (E&E) branch, part of the plans section of the 1127th. Plans was headed by a World War II veteran, USAF

Colonel Bob Work. Work had been one of the chief interrogators of high-ranking German POWs at the end of that war and he saw a growing need to update the resistance training of American pilots headed for Vietnam.

"Except for small pockets of the service like SAC," Work notes, "there was little recognition of E&E in the services. When I arrived at the 1127th in 1965, there were no written requirements and the 1127th only had one guy working E&E matters, and he had many other duties. I finally had to assign unwritten E&E responsibilities to my other staff. When I saw the growing POW/MIA dilemma, I began to build up the section to start solving the problem."[30]

One of Work's best moves was to rehire a savvy ex-POW named Claude Watkins. Watkins had retired from Air Force active duty in the summer of 1965 as a master sergeant, but Work sought him out in July 1966 to help upgrade the E&E program. Watkins had spent almost a year and a half in a German POW camp during World War II after being shot down while flying in a B-17 bomber. Shortly after his capture, while he was being held in solitary confinement at a Luftwaffe interrogation center, Watkins kept hearing tapping on the walls and pipes. Later, when he was transferred to a Luftwaffe hospital, he met a British pilot who taught Watkins that the tapping was a clandestine communication method the British pilots were using to pass critical information back and forth to each other. Intrigued, Watkins learned the British "tap code" and brought it back to the United States.

Based on his POW experience, Watkins for many years taught a course on E&E procedures to Air Force pilots. By chance, one of his students was a USAF officer named Carlyle Smith Harris. Harris was eventually shot down over North Vietnam on April 4, 1965, while piloting an F-105D, becoming the sixth American POW held in the DRV. During the time Harris attended the E&E course, the Air Force would not allow Watkins to teach the "tap code" because it was not part of the official syllabus. Despite the order, Watkins would always mention his World War II experience with the British pilot to his students. During a lunch break, Harris stopped Watkins and asked him how it worked. Watkins took Harris into his office and taught Harris the "tap code." Apparently Harris paid attention, and while a prisoner in Hanoi he began to teach it to the other Americans. Stockdale mentions in his book *In Love and War* that he began using the "Smitty Harris tap code" in August 1965.[31] Watkins recalls, "When the POWs came home, they told me that the tap code was the lifeblood of the prisoners in the North."[32]

Like the Navy, the Air Force also instituted a secret communication program with the POWs. "Our first indications of the POWs trying to tell us something," Watkins remembers, "was from the wives coming to the Casualty Affairs officers with letters from the prisoners that had sentences that didn't make any sense to them. We discovered that the POWs were using 'double-talk' in their letters to pass information to us. Our first indication that the Vietnamese were torturing our men came from some 'double-talk' in a letter from Edward Alan Brudno, an Air Force pilot lost over North Vietnam in October 1965."

As Watkins explains, "All letters went to Casualty Affairs first, then to DIA and then to us. When I got the call from DIA about Brudno, probably in the fall of 1966, I traveled to New York to see Mrs. Brudno. She cooperated with us and eventually we got another letter from Brudno that provided the first good intelligence that the North Vietnamese were torturing our men. The communists allowed the men to write during Christmas, and in Brudno's Christmas letter he worked in a sentence about 'that live stereo performance by the Orcheringtay Igspay Latin [torturing Pig Latin] dance ensemble . . . last year in Scarsdale, NY. . . . '33 In the same letter, he mentioned his 'old problem of fags [meaning cigarettes] has finally disappeared from my skin.' [The cigarette burns had healed.] The information we got from Brudno and the chances he took were unbelievable. Once, FBIS picked up a radio broadcast in which he said that the North Vietnamese 'Thanksgiving dinner was great, just like the barf my mother-in-law used to make.' He also put in phrases like 'I just enjoy watching the animals wandering about. They are very gross animals, like most everything here by the way.'34 But the wildest one we ever got was when he stated, 'The next time you see Mrs. Johnson, who lives on Lyndon street, tell her son to keep it up with vim, vigor, and fukkho [fuck Ho].'"

As more mail from the POWs arrived, the intelligence community expanded the clandestine-communications program. The program was critical for U.S. intelligence in its attempts to overcome the North Vietnamese political use of POWs and was instrumental in discovering the use of torture on Americans. But the most important intelligence aspect was determining who was a prisoner. Based on letters from POWs like Stockdale, men who were listed initially as dead had their status changed to captured based on the clandestine writings. Despite the North Vietnamese policy to not furnish the names of captured pilots to the ICRC or to U.S. officials, the covert communications of the POWs enabled the government to learn the identities of many of the men. Eventually, the type of sources available to DIA and the 1127th to identify POWs and their locations grew to over a dozen. According to Watkins, one example "was a guy who wrote a letter to his wife telling her to make sure when she sold the VW Bug to use the license plate. Then he wrote the number. Turned out to be the authenticator code for one of the guys who was listed as MIA."

Raid in Phu Yen: Looking for Evidence Against the VC

The expanding military tempo found American troops plus ARVN units pushing deeper into previously uncontested VC territory. Not surprisingly, both allied military forces began to stumble upon enemy POW camps with increasingly frequency and many of the POW raids that occurred in 1966 uncovered horrible scenes of deprivation. The Embassy in Saigon immediately began to use pictures and testimonials from the freed captives describing the terrible camp conditions to embarrass the Viet Cong. More important, the Embassy wanted to prod the ICRC into taking a harder line against the communists over their treatment of POWs.

In February 1966, in the northern part of South Vietnam, a Marine reconnaissance patrol stumbled into a village used by the VC as a prison camp. They freed thirty South Vietnamese and uncovered an "elaborate tunnel system and a set of prisoner stocks such as were used by early American settlers to detain prisoners by the wrists and ankles."[35] On October 10, American soldiers from the 1st Cavalry Division, engaged in a combined operation with South Korean Marines near the city of Qui Nhon in central South Vietnam, overran another enemy camp. They found an even greater scene of horror, similar to the brutality uncovered in February. The fleeing North Vietnamese guards had murdered twelve of the prisoners, who were found chained together. Only seven survived the massacre.[36]

One of the worst prisons uncovered was a camp in Phu Yen province in the Central Highlands of South Vietnam. At the end of September, two NVA had deserted to the 3rd Brigade Headquarters of the 101st Airborne Division and told their interrogators that they had been guards at a prison camp in the mountains a short distance away. More importantly, the guards had said the camp held two Americans and one South Korean Marine, and one of the NVA had offered to act as an escort. Sergeant Charles McDonald of 2nd Platoon, Charlie Company, 1/327 Infantry, 101st Airborne Division, had been ordered to take the rallier and join up with the Brigade's reconnaissance element, Tiger Force, to raid the camp.

McDonald had been ordered to conduct the raid on the afternoon of October 1. He now was hurrying his battle-weary platoon across the broad Tuy Hoa valley in Phu Yen province to link up with Tiger Force. Night was falling rapidly, and unable to raise Tiger Force on the radio, McDonald lagered his platoon near the entrance to a small canyon. The next morning, his men linked up with Tiger Force, which had spent the night encamped only a short distance away.[37] The combined forces worked their way through an abandoned minefield, avoided five VC carrying bamboo, and came upon a well-worn trail leading into the mountains and toward the camp. As time was of the essence, the team decided to use the trail. Moving forward, Tiger Force encountered several NVA soldiers in a guard post located inside a cave. Mistakenly, a young Tiger fired a round and shot one of the guards. Realizing that the prison camp had probably been alerted by the sound, the Americans decided to risk an ambush by moving as rapidly as possible up the trail toward the camp.

By mid-afternoon the American soldiers reached the camp.[38] Most of the prisoners had already been moved. Only the weakest remained behind, unable to make the journey. "The sight of those people was unbelievable," MacDonald remembers. "Several dead bodies lay wrapped up and tied to poles. They had starved to death. The ones still alive were emaciated and near death. Off to one side we could see a significant number of graves. We didn't want to dig into the graves and we didn't have time to burn the prison. We could hear the voices of the NVA guards in the distance. We tried to follow the escaping guard force for awhile, but after we found and stopped to help several more POWs who had dropped out of the column, it was getting too late to catch up with them. We gave the freed POWs what little food we had, put them on our backs and carried them back down the trail. We never spotted the two Americans or the Korean."[39]

On October 4, the *New York Times* published an interview with one of the inmates, who reported that seventy-five prisoners had died in the camp over an eleven-month period. They noted that the American soldiers had swept into a VC prison containing starving Vietnamese civilians and that almost two hundred prisoners had once been held there, the rest having been "converted" to the VC cause and released.

Later in October, forces from the ARVN 9th Division attacked another VC prison in Vinh Binh province. The camp contained a 64-year-old South Vietnamese nun named Sister Rosa who taught first-graders in a local school. The communists had arrested her a year earlier as a "spy," a typical terror tactic used by their security forces to harass and intimidate the local population. In North Vietnam, the Ministry of Public Security (MPS) viewed the North Vietnamese Catholics as one of the greatest threats to their internal security, since the Catholics were the most anti-communist bloc of the population. Consequently, the communist security forces in South Vietnam targeted Sister Rosa as a potential roadblock to their proselytizing campaigns to influence the South Vietnamese peasants and decided to remove her. She endured a horrible ordeal and she believed she would die in the camp. Only her faith, she said, had kept her alive.

While courting the world press, the U.S. Embassy in Saigon was pushing the South Vietnamese government to upgrade their prison facilities. The U.S. military had also been instructed to gather as much evidence as possible detailing communist prison atrocities, and the rapid discovery of Viet Cong prisons filled with mistreated and massacred prisoners offered Harriman in Washington and the American Embassy in Saigon the opportunity to contrast the GVN treatment of Viet Cong POWs with the recently discovered VC prisons. In late fall, Harriman began a new effort with the ICRC to compare the GVN's lackluster treatment of their POWs with the torture and cruelty of the DRV/NLF's camps. The Embassy lost no time in alerting the ICRC about the conditions of the VC camps, sending pictures and testimonials from the recovered POWs both to the ICRC and to the world press.

Although the GVN were still dragging their collective feet, the South Vietnamese had made great strides in improving the conditions in many of their POW camps. But fearful of losing its image of neutrality, the ICRC was slow to give any public praise to the GVN. The American Embassy's public-affairs office, however, lost little time in trumpeting the contrast with the North to anyone who would listen. The strategy behind the Americans' public-relations blitz was to convince the ICRC to bring more pressure on the insurgents to comply with the Geneva standards, and also hopefully to shame the DRV into upgrading the conditions of the American POWs in North Vietnam. Unfortunately, neither ploy was successful, nor did they serve to mute the press criticisms of the South's POW treatment.

From 1962 through the summer of 1966, all U.S. diplomatic undertakings had crashed against the wall of a calculated DRV/NLF intransigent stance on POWs. The DRV propaganda machine had promised to tie American POWs to bridges and place them in the Hanoi power plant to prevent American bombing attacks, and threatened to convict them as war criminals, even as the DRV security apparatus was currently engaged in a systematic campaign of torture and deprivation to produce politically charged statements. The time had come for new approaches.

6. The Joint Personnel Recovery Center

The purpose of the Joint Personnel Recovery Center is establish a capability with MACV for personnel recovery operations after termination of search and rescue (SAR) efforts.
—JPRC Terms of Reference, message from CINCPAC to JCS, August 16, 1966

The failures of the State Department negotiations convinced the Department of Defense that more aggressive measures were necessary. The DOD's litany of the DRV's transgressions included the executions of the three American servicemen and threats of war-crime trials of POWs, plus the recent "confessions" forced from American airmen held captive in the North. The DRV/NLF continued to refuse any ICRC visits or to afford the POWs any of the Geneva Convention protections. Increasingly, the U.S. military believed that State's diplomacy was not alleviating the plight of the captives and they felt compelled to act.

The military's response was to create a unit in September 1966 called the Joint Personnel Recovery Center. But the JPRC was not an operational unit and commanded no combat forces. It was a small staff section in an office in Saigon manned by officers and enlisted personnel from all branches of the U.S. armed forces. No Vietnamese served in the JPRC. Its main function was to act as a clearinghouse for the flow of intelligence on American POWs, determine the validity of the information, and then organize rescue attempts employing either SOG forces or local troops.

Within South Vietnam, each military service already had the initial responsibility to search for and recover its own personnel. In developing the JPRC, the decision was made to allow any Search and Rescue (SAR) forces a maximum of 72 hours to complete recovery attempts after an aircrew was shot down or a serviceman was lost in a ground action. After those 72 hours had passed and the normal Search and Rescue forces had failed to find the individual, the JPRC would then become responsible for organizing rescue teams to conduct operations in a post-SAR environment. The JPRC became involved only after SAR forces had completed their efforts, when a possible prison facility was detected, or when the movement of prisoners was suspected. When intelligence was developed on a prison location, the JPRC provided the intelligence to a nearby unit and effected coordination across the various staffs and political bureaucracies.

The JPRC depended on other intelligence units and agencies to perform basic POW intelligence collection, as the JPRC had no internal collection assets of its own. The problem was how to get the other intelligence agencies to provide the POW intelligence to a unit more highly classified than they were. Unfortunately, most of the POW intelligence received by the JPRC was of such poor quality and so outdated that the forces sent into areas to look for POW camps were often simply sweeping general areas instead of making pinpoint raids. Nevertheless, the military was determined to begin attacking the VC camps.

Bringing in the Cavalry: Activating the JPRC

In April 1966 the Joint Chiefs of Staff formalized organizational responsibilities relating to American prisoners of war.[1] All the staff elements were assigned functions and the DIA was directed to coordinate POW intelligence and to ensure that a high priority was given to POW intelligence collection. DIA was ordered to direct the "Combined Services Support Program . . . and other clandestine communications with U.S. prisoners of war."[2]

The CIA had also begun to formalize the POW information it held. In the beginning of September, the CIA reported that in the past "3 ½ months approximately 3000 pieces of information have been screened for pertinence to this program. The materials exploited include intelligence reports, cables, ground photography, aerial photography, maps and charts, domestic and foreign newspapers, books, pamphlets, magazines, etc. The [redacted] collection was organized to tie in all information possible to an individual prisoner, hence the creation of the U.S. POW Profile Card."[3] The CIA queried other intelligence organizations; all were found to have similar collections.

The Hrdlicka broadcast forced the Air Force to take another look at how it was internally handling POW affairs. Shortly after Hrdlicka was heard on the radio, Phillip Hilbert, the Under-Secretary of the Air Force, wrote to the Chief of Staff of the Air Force. "The circumstances of the capture of our people and the activities in which they were engaged, as well as the very peculiar and undefined nature of this undeclared war, require special handling which I do not believe is well arranged at present. The direct activity of the State Department and the Embassies in the POW handling is obvious . . . based on high-level interest, again I urge that one office be directed to assume responsibility (for POWs). . . . the responsible office should maintain a file on each case."[4]

In December 1965 the military command in the Pacific region [CINCPAC] held an Escape, Evasion, and Personnel Recovery conference to discuss methods to solve the problem. At the meeting, it was pointed out that a need still existed for an element devoted to identifying and locating the camps where the men were being held. In response to the conference recommendation, the staff of the Special Assistant for Counterinsurgency and Special Activities (SACSA), a unique and highly classified office that dealt with all aspects of Unconventional Warfare (UW) and reported directly to the Chairman of the Joint Chiefs of Staff, ordered CINCPAC to begin creating a suitable POW intelligence/rescue unit.

The conference focused the military's attention on the need to identify and locate its suffering prisoners and rescue them if possible. The attendees endorsed the concept of an organization to plan and develop rescue operations in Southeast Asia. The earlier planning for a Joint Recovery Center was updated and the proposed organization was given the new name of Joint Personnel Recovery Center. The slight change was designed to include the South Vietnamese, recognizing that they were also interested in recovering their people and were extremely sensitive to the smallest indication that the United States was not viewing them as an equal partner.

However, when CINCPAC asked for recommendations on who should command the JPRC, in typical bureaucratic tradition arguments broke out over which service should be the controlling agency. Both MACV and the Pacific Air Force (PACAF) at CINCPAC believed that they should be the one to direct this unit. Finally SACSA weighed in, stating that MACV should be in charge, but that since the majority of prisoners were Air Force, and since the Air Force traditionally was in charge of POW matters, an Air Force officer should head the organization.

When the decision was finally approved, the Air Force was charged with providing the officer to lead the unit. USAF Lieutenant Colonel Barney Cochran immediately nominated Heinie Aderholt. Cochran was currently working at SACSA and had served with Aderholt in the 1st Air Commando Group at Eglin Air Force base in Florida in the early 1960s. Cochran recalls, "We had no concentrated effort to try and get back our POWs and we needed something. The State Department was engaged in these half-assed attempts to get guys out and had failed. Heinie was then Director of Operations for 13th Air Force at Clark Air Base in the Philippines. Aderholt was the best man for the job, plus I knew he wasn't very happy at Clark, so I called him one night about three o'clock in the morning his time and got him out of bed. I asked him if he wanted the job. He said 'Hell yes, be glad to.'"[5]

Based on Cochran's recommendation, General Hunter Harris at PACAF HQ in Hawaii formally asked Aderholt to take over the reins of the new unit. Aderholt agreed, but only under certain conditions: he wanted his next assignment to be the command of a Fighter Wing. Harris okayed the request, although the future wouldn't quite work out the way Aderholt hoped.

MACV also accepted Aderholt as Chief, JPRC. While the JPRC was still being formulated, however, the Embassy Study Group was determined to continue rescue efforts using 5th Special Forces personnel. The Study Group ordered the Combined Intelligence Center, Vietnam (CICV), a joint U.S.-GVN-run intelligence center through which flowed most of the intelligence on the location, size, and strength of the enemy forces, to "complete a study on VC POW camps at the end of March. The 5th Special Forces want to, and are confident that they can raid these camps and liberate the Americans being held . . . Colonel Aderholt should arrive in the very near future to assume command of the Joint Recovery Center."[6]

Little is known if any attempts were made in the first half of 1966 by the Special Forces. Aderholt went to work in early April 1966 at the MACV staff office and quickly formulated a concept involving a combination of Army Rangers backed by air assets. He traveled to Hawaii and presented this idea to General Harris, but Harris' Director of Intelligence, USAF Brigadier General Ernest Johns, didn't want the Army involved. Aderholt remembers, "When I proposed the organization, I wanted to be in business the next day. But Johns wanted the Air Force to control the operation. I replied that the Air Force didn't have those kind of forces. He said 'We'll train them.' That's not necessary, I said, those kind of forces are already in theater." Aderholt says he "wanted a dedicated force assigned to the JPRC. I didn't want to have to always request forces to launch a raid. So I asked for the Rangers, but the Army replied, 'Don't tell us who to put on a recovery mission,' so I didn't get them and we never got dedicated forces. In hindsight, it was a big mistake."[7]

After talking to Harris, Aderholt flew back to Vietnam and spoke to Air Force Major General George Simler, who agreed with Aderholt's vision. His next stop was to see Army Colonel Donald Blackburn, the SOG commander. Blackburn also gave his approval for Aderholt's concept, but by now the Army had refused the request for the Rangers. Blackburn, however, was scheduled to leave SOG shortly and Army Colonel John Singlaub had been nominated to be SOG's new commander. While Singlaub was at MACV attending various briefings he met Aderholt for the first time. According to Singlaub, "Aderholt informed me that the current situation was unsatisfactory and that we needed to do something for our POWs. The Air Force was arguing that they should run the show, but this went against Unconventional Warfare doctrine. E&E was our function, because we could place covert assets in areas to help downed airmen. This ultimately wasn't successful in North Vietnam because in 1954 we loaded all the anticommunists on ships at Haiphong and moved them to the South. Our compassion really helped their security services weed out the bad elements for them, but stripped us of the ability to create agents that could have helped our downed airmen."[8]

As the new head of SOG, Colonel Singlaub was one of General Westmoreland's favorite officers. Westmoreland, though, needed no doctrinal prodding from Singlaub as he was pushing to control the JPRC. But the fierce interservice jockeying for control was badly delaying implementation of the unit. Finally, on April 27, CINCPAC reached a compromise. MACV would run the organization, but the Terms of Reference would also recognize Air Force functions and responsibilities for SAR matters.[9]

However, once MACV was assigned the responsibility for the JPRC another internal struggle developed, this time between SOG and the MACV J-3, the operations section. Although Westmoreland initially picked SOG to handle the unit, according to the 1966 MACV *Command History*, that summer "there was a difference of opinion between SOG and MACJ3 as to the establishment of the JPRC. MACJ3 recommended that the JPRC be a separate organization with assets earmarked for recovery operations; these forces would continue with their normal training activities, but would be on call in response to plans prepared by the JPRC."[10] The Air Force also attempted to regain control of the JPRC and recommended that the 7th AF be in charge. However, by August, General Westmoreland "reaffirmed his prior support of the JPRC as an element of SOG, noting that SOG was the logical agency to assume responsibility for JPRC functions."[11]

MACV and the Army had won the battle for control of the JPRC, but it had taken almost eight months of bureaucratic wrangling to achieve victory. While the generals were turf fighting, Aderholt had an embryonic plan and was waiting impatiently to begin operations. Essentially, a trade-off had allowed an Air Force officer to command the unit, thus providing the Air Force an important voice within SOG. Also, the JPRC would be a multiservice organization, ensuring that credit for any successes would be spread around.

Based on Westmoreland's guidance, Singlaub turned to one of his Air Force staff officers, Major Lester Hansen, to write the Terms of Reference, which was in essence the organization's job description. "In July," remarks Hansen, "Singlaub asked me to take over writing the JPRC Terms that some Air Force major had been sitting on for months. I worked with SOG Plans to develop the different types of scenarios we would probably face and how we could overcome them. Based on looking at those scenarios, we proposed a set of definitions in August to CINCPAC, which they accepted."[12]

The JPRC was tasked to develop requirements for the collection of intelligence and other data necessary for operations to rescue POWs. It was to perform collation, analysis, and evaluation of intelligence concerning detained and missing personnel and prepare basic operational procedures and plans for the assistance of detained personnel. The office was also to coordinate and establish liaison with U.S. and allied agencies to insure maximum utilization of available resources and, most important, to minimize reaction time for launching recovery operations.

Its command structure, however, mirrored the political realities of the war. Ambassador Sullivan had again voiced his concerns over the intrusion of military forces in Laos without his approval. Therefore, his cables discussing the JPRC authorization include phrases like "The diplomatic aspects of recovery operations are within the purview of the State Department," and "The JPRC concept as now outlined precludes military incursion into matters of primary State Department interest and insures coordination and approval prior to initiation of operations."

Ultimately, the decision was that within South Vietnam, recovery operations needed to be coordinated only with the Ambassador prior to launch, but in Laos the JPRC had to coordinate with both Saigon and Vientiane *plus* get CINCPAC approval before a *Bright Light* post-SAR team or a POW raid could be launched. In North Vietnam and Cambodia, both Saigon and CINCPAC needed to approve the operation and Vientiane had to be consulted if the operation overflew Lao territory.[13] The JCS basically agreed to the Terms, but in early September, DIA inserted a paragraph that asked the JPRC to "Provide DIA with the requirements for the collection of intelligence in excess of local capabilities and other data."[14]

On September 16, 1966, CINCPAC ordered MACV to implement the

JPRC. Several days later, MACV responded that "the JPRC was established interim basis on 29 Aug 66, and officially activated on 17 Sept upon receipt of the . . . message. Liaison is being effected with all MACV components. . . . Initial conceptual planning will be the responsibility of the JPRC. When SOG resources are utilized in recovery operations, the operational planning and execution will be the responsibility of the SOG staff. . . . In summary the JPRC is active on a limited basis at present. . . ."[15]

The JPRC Swings into Action

Les Hansen, who helped draw up the Terms of Reference for the JPRC, was asked by Colonel Singlaub to transfer from SOG Plans to the new unit. He remembers that "the first couple of months of the JPRC was pure chaos. We certainly didn't get much sleep. Aderholt was the first man in the JPRC and I was the second. Our first 'office' was a couple of desks and chairs with two partitions to form a space in the hallway on the top floor of SOG Headquarters. Besides letting the intelligence units and major MACV and subordinate commands know we existed, we were scurrying around gathering supplies and filing cabinets. We also had a clerk/typist named Robert L. Williams. Fortunately, the third officer in the JPRC was an Army major named Charles Boatwright. When he joined us he greatly assisted with the coordination and liaison work."

Boatwright was working in the Counter-Intelligence Branch of MACV J-2 when he accidentally bumped into Singlaub at the PX. He had known Singlaub previously, and after talking to him for a while asked for a job. Singlaub agreed, and several weeks later orders came down to report at once to SOG. Immediately Boatwright, who had been in Army Military Intelligence for some time, used his network of friends and contacts to rapidly "put the JPRC on the map. I went around to the 149th and 135th MI Groups, the interrogation and document centers, MACV J-2, the SIGINT units and many other places to alert them to our existence and to get them to send us POW intelligence. Everyone was very enthusiastic and offered to help."[16]

The JPRC became semioperational on August 29, 1966.[17] Most of the first few weeks were spent on training exercises and in gathering casualty and intelligence reports. By the middle of September, the JPRC was ready to handle some of its responsibilities, and interest at the upper echelons of the military was extremely high. CINCPAC requested a weekly update that covered three areas; Recovery Operations, Other Activities, and Problem Areas.[18] In addition, they sent another message announcing that all cable traffic discussing POWs carry the identifying code-word *Bright Light.* The code-word was unclassified and was to be used by all the major commands to alert the reader that POW information was contained in the message.

Appropriately, the first three JPRC missions were post-SAR *Bright Light* missions. Dubbed Operation *No. 1,* Operation *No. 2,* and *Canasta 572,* the JPRC and the SOG *Bright Light* teams responded well, but the out-of-country command arrangements rapidly proved cumbersome. Operation *No. 1* commenced on September 23, when a weak beeper signal was heard by an aircraft near the general location of the loss on September 12 near the Lao/North Vietnamese border of a USAF F-105D piloted by Captain Robert Waggoner.[19] A request was made the next day to CINCPAC for a recovery operation, which authorized it, "contingent upon approval from American Embassies in Bangkok and Vientiane." Approval was finally granted and on September 26, three days after the beeper was heard, the team went in. They searched the general area and interviewed "village informants," but the search was negative.

According to Hansen, the search was negative "because Sullivan played around for three days. Laos was like a fiefdom to him. We sent a flash message to Vientiane and they didn't answer. We tried calling them on the scramble phone but the connection was very bad. We had little leverage as we barely had our feet on the ground as an organization. Sullivan finally decided they had a team nearby, so he sent them to look for the pilot. By then it was too late."

Operation *No. 2* which occurred on September 29 sought to recover two pilots who had parachuted out of an F-4C into Laos. A *Bright Light* team was sent in the next day and recovered one pilot and the body of the other. Boatwright recalls that "these missions were basically training missions for us. I was a little leery about *No. 1,* I never really thought we had anything. But recovering the pilot and the body of the other guy really gave our morale a boost. We had trained several teams in post-SAR efforts, but we had no formal unit assigned to us. Whoever was available went. We picked the code-names for the first month or so, then CINCPAC decided they would choose the names." These operations provided a chance for the new unit to fine-tune the system and discover any flaws. The obvious one was the long response time from the embassy in Laos. But the JPRC could not change the command structure of the war, and Sullivan's extended decision-making process during which he weighed the various political/military ramifications would continue to jeopardize the success of recovery missions. But the war would not wait for either Sullivan or the JPRC, and the initial two operations were just a warm-up for the JPRC's first major post-SAR efforts, Operations *Canasta 572* and *Commando 01.*

Crossing Borders—*Canasta 572* and *Commando 01*

On October 12, a Navy A-1H pilot named Robert Woods was shot down in North Vietnam, at a point roughly halfway between the cities of Vinh and Thanh Hoa and about fifteen kilometers inland from the coast. Lieutenant Woods was flying "a morning road recon mission when I was hit from behind by antiaircraft fire. I bailed out pretty low, and my chute had just opened when I landed in a tree in a fairly dense, large forest. I wasn't hurt too bad, so I swung over until I could reach the tree trunk. I released the parachute harness and shinnied down the tree. When I got to the bottom, I threw my helmet and gear one direction and I went the other. I kept going for about fifteen minutes and then I just collapsed from the shock and fatigue."[20]

Lost in the jungle, Woods had been unable to contact his wingman, who had returned to the carrier and reported that he believed Woods had gone down with the plane. By late afternoon, however, Woods had luckily managed to contact another Navy A-1. The airplane quickly radioed for the Navy rescue helicopter at North SAR to attempt a recovery of Woods. "By the time they got there, it was starting to get dark. They were already low on gas, and I was having to maneuver them to me by their sound, since I couldn't see them through the thick growth. There was so much radio chatter I was having a hard time breaking in to guide the helicopter. By the time I got them maneuvered over top of me, the local militia was closing in and they started firing at the SAR helicopter." To help pinpoint his location, Woods fired his pen flare. "That did two things. First, it told the Vietnamese exactly were I was, and second, it caught the jungle on fire. I think the Vietnamese spent half the night trying to put it out."

Unable to rescue Woods because of the enemy fire, the SAR helicopter departed. In Saigon, Les Hansen started getting "messages about every ten minutes detailing what was happening. After the Navy helicopter failed, Heinie was out of town so I went straight to Singlaub and said this was an operation that was right up our alley. He agreed and told me to go down to the Navy's 'Detachment Charlie' at Tan Son Nhut airport and tell them we can put a team on their carrier that they can ferry in at first light. I had never heard of Det C, which turned out to be the Navy's liaison office with MACV."

Major Les Hansen drove out to Tan Son Nhut and found the Navy office. He met the commander of the unit, Captain Buddy Yates, and tried to explain the concept to him. "Yates had never heard of us either. He looked like he simply didn't believe what the hell I was trying to tell him. I told him we were this new unit and we had forces that could help him. Finally, Yates got in touch with the

Admiral who was commanding the carrier task force at *Yankee Station*. The Admiral agreed to the idea. Singlaub already had Team *Ohio* from Kontum on standby. Team *Ohio* was commanded by one of the true legends of the war, Dick Meadows.[21] We arranged for the Navy to have the Carrier on Demand (COD) airplane ferry them to the ship. The pilot's call sign was 'Canasta 572,' so that's what I named the operation. By the time the Team got to the carrier, it was midnight, so I went to bed."

Two hours later, Hansen was awakened and told to report to the Green Room, the secure communications facility at SOG headquarters. "It was CINCPAC, they wanted to know where was the team. I told those idiots, 'On the carrier!' Well, because these teams consisted of two American NCOs and twelve Nungs, and because they were going into North Vietnam, somebody well above CINCPAC said that we couldn't send in the Americans. When the Nungs found out, they said they weren't going if the Americans weren't. So the team sat there all day, waiting for authorization. Eventually, Washington gave in and allowed the Americans to go in, but they were under a strict time and distance leash."[22]

Woods, meanwhile, had waited patiently all day, not moving far from his spot. "I was hiding in some pretty dense growth and I could hear them looking for me. Once, this kid carrying a pitchfork stepped right over my leg. I could see his face, he was scared out of his mind and looking straight ahead and not down, so he didn't see me. I figured I needed to move, so the next morning I had gone about 150 yards when I came to a jungle trail. Just as I stepped out onto the path these three North Vietnamese regulars stepped onto the path at the same time. As soon as I saw them, I broke the antenna off my survival radio."

Singlaub recounts that Meadows knew that the pilot had been captured but that Meadows had entered North Vietnamese territory hoping to ambush the enemy column containing Woods.[23] The scenario, according to the *Command History*, was that the "recovery team was helilifted to the area of the downed pilot and landed at a point approximately 800 meters from his last known position. Approximately 100 meters from the target, the team encountered a large trail under the jungle canopy. After fifteen minutes, a North Vietnamese uniformed patrol, obviously engaged in a search, approached within 10 meters of the team and the team leader thought they had been detected. The patrol was engaged and all four members killed. The team leader requested exfiltration, feeling that the team was compromised. During the exfiltration, one helicopter was hit by ground fire at the exfiltration point. On the flight out, the helicopter was hit again and three team members received minor wounds. The helicopter was eventually lost. It was learned later that the pilot who was the object of this operation had been captured."[24]

Woods believes that the NVA probably tried to use his damaged beeper to lure the rescue force into a trap. "When the three saw me, as I raised my hands over my head I broke the antenna off, but it will still continue emitting a weak signal. It was still pretty dark out and the three NVA really couldn't see me that well, but I know they were as scared as I was since their AKs were shaking. I'm just lucky they didn't cut loose on me."

The killing of the four-man patrol by the team, one of whom according to Hansen was an NVA captain, may have helped spark the later North Vietnamese reactions toward Woods. He was paraded in front of villagers on his way north, with the cadre using loudspeakers to whip up the frenzy of the peasants at each stop. "The day after I was captured was particularly bad. They held a mock execution in front of a ditch and they were throwing all kinds of crap at me." Woods was imprisoned in Hanoi until the end of the war.

Damaged by enemy fire, the rescue helicopter carrying Team *Ohio* was forced to ditch next to the carrier. Later, Hansen debriefed the team and wrote a fifteen-page report on their actions. "The Admiral was very impressed with what had happened and requested that the JPRC permanently assign a team to stay on the carrier. Although we had to refuse, he understood and we continued to make flights out to the carriers to conduct E&E briefings."[25]

The political ramifications of placing Americans on the ground in North Vietnam had delayed the operation by at least one day and probably led to Woods' capture. Aderholt, discussing another mission, recalls that "Americans in North Vietnam were only allowed to go so many meters away from the rescue helicopter lest it be considered an 'invasion.' This is the kind of bullshit we had to work under."

The political restrictions in Laos were not much different. Although the JPRC was attempting to work with the Embassy in Vientiane, Ambassador Sullivan preferred to use the indigenous CAS guerrillas or local RLA soldiers, since much of the border area of southern Laos was completely controlled by the enemy. Both CAS and the Embassy were generally willing to attempt rescue operations if they were positive that someone was evading, but the delay between an aircraft going down and the subsequent deployment of Lao military forces was often too long for the fleeing American, especially if the rescue forces did not have a good fix on his location.

A typical incident occurred on November 16, 1966, when an A-1E carrying three crewmen was shot down in southern Laos. The entire crew escaped the damaged plane and the pilot and copilot were picked up by a SAR helicopter fairly quickly. The pilot told the rescuers that the crew chief, a man named Alan

Pittman, had left the plane first and was seen with a good chute.[26] The search was called off when the SAR helicopter was hit by ground fire.

The JPRC was notified and sent a Flash message to Vientiane, which in turn alerted the RLA forces nearby. According to Chuck Boatwright, "Vientiane was very hot to get this guy, as they believed he was alive." The operation was called *Commando 01,* after the call sign of the plane. That night, an Air America plane flew over the area and broadcast a message through a loudspeaker for the airman to build a fire, since low-level reconnaissance would be flown over the area that night and friendly guerrillas would be inserted the next morning.

What happened next is unclear, as the CIA version and the MACV *Command History* differ. Apparently, over two hundred fifty RLA troops were brought in to search the area, but were eventually withdrawn. On November 18, sixty Lao irregular guerrillas also entered the search area, but Pittman was not found; nor did he signal on the night of November 16. The CAS guerrillas stayed several days and eventually discovered information on the fate of Pittman. According to the CIA South Lao Operational Report, "on the morning of 22 November, [redacted] reported in to Thateng with a plausible story of Pittman's death. [Redacted] related the story; Pittman was captured on the morning of the 17th, stripped down to his shorts, and was shot by one of the VC assigned to that area."[27] The JPRC and CAS accepted the story, but despite the presence of Vietnamese troops, neither Mr. Pittman nor his remains have ever been recovered.

Changes to the Escape and Evasion Program: Code Letters

While Major Chuck Boatwright was integrating the intelligence network on the Army side, Les Hansen was developing contacts with the Air Force and the Navy. Hansen held many meetings with Navy intelligence and the 7th AF. He recalls, "One of Heinie's first orders was to revamp the entire Escape and Evasion program. The Joint Search and Rescue Center (JSARC) were among the most admired people in the theater because they saved hundreds of downed airmen, and one of the first things we did was reassure them that we wouldn't interfere until they asked us to. But we had no rally areas, no markers, no reward program, only the old bloodchits [a piece of silk carried by pilots that guaranteed a reward for anyone who helped a downed aircrew member escape] the Air Force had been using for ages. JSARC had told us one of their big problems was locating guys beneath the triple-canopy jungle. Aderholt tried to get SOG to develop something you could use as a marker, but nothing worked. We were looking for something that was small enough to carry but could still penetrate through the brush and then explode, leaving a residue to mark your spot. They tried paints and all kinds of powders, but they all failed."

Aderholt wanted even bigger changes in the E&E program for downed pilots. On September 12 and 13, 1996, the JPRC participated in a conference with officers from the Navy, the 7th AF, and the JSARC. The agenda included discussions of JPRC intelligence requirements and SAR termination procedures and operations.[28] What eventually came from this conference was the realization that a system was needed for pilots to signal their locations to passing aircraft if they were unable to transmit using their hand-held radios, and especially if they had managed to evade to one of the new Selected Area For Evasion (SAFE) areas. In the typical dry language used by the military to describe a procedure, SAFE areas were designed "to provide aircrews encountering an extended evasion situation with a means to return to friendly control."[29] Basically, they were remote locations that contained few people and were positioned near significant geographical features to assist the pilots in navigating cross-country to find them.

Hansen attended the meeting, and it was "damn productive. We were breaking new ground, and everybody, I mean everybody wanted this to work. It was sort of like being for motherhood. On the second day, a Navy intelligence officer from one of the carriers came up with the idea for laying symbols on the ground. We thought that was a great idea and after playing with it for a while, we tried testing aluminum foil. We had planes fly over Tan Son Nhut at varying heights taking pictures and we had pilots try a visual to see how well it could be seen. The foil didn't work worth a damn. Finally, the SOG photo interpreters came up with a list of natural materials a pilot could use to signal from the ground, basically what stuff worked best in different situations. The main point was to use contrasting colors, a dark letter on a light background, for instance.

"Each month had a primary and a back-up letter. The system went into effect in the beginning of October 1966. At first, we picked the letters, but then CINCPAC took it over. PACAF supplied the SAFE area locations. SOG insisted that no letters with curves be used and that they all had to be straight lines, except we couldn't use the letter *I*. After the system went into effect, I started briefing all the incoming pilots about the new system. I flew to Thailand and out to the Navy carriers at Yankee Station to talk about how to use the program and what materials they could use. It was one of the most successful things we did." By year's end, as part of their additional duties, six SOG Teams, called Safe Area Activation Teams (SAAT), were developed and trained to enter the SAFE areas and recover airmen.

Hansen was constantly flying around Southeast Asia briefing Aderholt's new E&E program to the incoming aircrews and to the ones who were in-country.

The PACAF and SOG photo interpreters were now carefully watching both the designated SAFE areas and the aerial photography for signals. Additionally, the JPRC was also in the process of packaging thirty air-deployable kits which were "designed to drop to downed airmen when a code letter has been sighted. They will be prepositioned at several different sites to provide a capability for immediate reaction. . . . PACAF has furnished several sample materials which may be suitable to use in constructing the monthly emergency code letter."[30]

By the end of January, five separate instances of code letters matching the correct month had been discovered via photography by Air Force reconnaissance aircraft. These sightings were immediately passed to the JPRC, but three of the symbols proved to be false alarms. The first incident happened in mid-December, when two USAF planes returning to NKP spotted the letter *V*, which was the back-up signal for the month. It was quickly determined that a CAS Road Watch team had inadvertently constructed the symbol.

However, two other sightings seemed somewhat more promising. On December 31, the JPRC received a message from the 67th Recon Technical Squadron (RTS) based in Japan stating that a readout of photography from Christmas Day "revealed possible E&E code letter for December (*K*) very near designated pick-up point for NVN Safe Area #6. Recce pilots reported that code letter appeared to be natural phenomenon consisting of a ditch and stones."[31] Unable to determine if the symbol was deliberate or naturally occurring, the JPRC requested additional photo missions over the area. Unfortunately, poor weather delayed the new mission until January 15, 1967, when another readout failed to locate the original symbol.

The more interesting mission was an operation called *Teamster*. On January 27, a back-up code letter *V* was spotted in Laos and a fire was sighted near the code letter. CAS at Udorn was alerted and they indicated they had assets in the area if "photo/visual recce positive."[32] Photos from the next day were negative, and a Forward Air Controller (FAC) flew a visual over the area and reported that he had received ground fire and that any symbol was gone. The JPRC "speculated that evadee captured." Hansen believed someone was there, but the closest air loss to the location was an Air Force pilot who was downed in an O-1 on January 17. If it was a legitimate symbol, who this individual was remains unknown.

The rapid discovery of five symbols—two of which were natural, two formed accidentally by CAS forces, plus the mystery of *Teamster*—indicate that the new E&E program was a double-edged sword. While it provided an easy means of signaling by downed pilots, it was very difficult to distinguish between natural growth and an actual symbol, not to mention the accidental misuse of the system by other forces. Unfortunately, the sudden flurry of false alarms had a severe dampening effect on the enthusiasm of the photo interpreters and the recce squadrons and they quickly lost interest. The next symbol would not be listed in the JPRC reports until October 1968.

Battlefield Exchanges

One of the main reasons Heinie Aderholt wanted to be part of SOG was that he believed its high level of classification would protect knowledge of the unit from the communists. Today we know that the DRV/NLF security forces were well aware of the presence of SOG, so the question arises, when did they become cognizant of the new rescue unit? Also, what was their reaction to the JPRC? Despite repeated attempts by State to create a forum for direct exchange of POWs, the leadership in Hanoi had refused every overture. Now, with the NLF feeling the punch of the American military machine, they were suffering growing losses of senior cadres. Suddenly, offers of a trade of American POWs and VC leaders proliferated between U.S. military intelligence units and enemy forces. Was this sudden emergence of clandestine offers coincidental with the development of the JPRC or was it something more?

The available declassified record shows that from October 1966 and continuing almost to the end of the war, various ransom and swap attempts would be raised only to eventually fall apart. Only a few of the swap attempts can at best be construed as moderately successful. However, several of the senior Vietnamese cadres interviewed under the Oral History Program (OHP) initiated in 1993 by Bill Bell hint at still hidden, more direct swaps of prisoners.[33] Whether a given swap offer was a clever intelligence ploy on the part of the communist security services, a genuine attempt to trade Americans that simply fell apart, or an elaborate fabrication designed solely for monetary gain, the men in the JPRC still gamely followed up on every development, in some cases risking their lives pursuing flimsy leads.

The first mention of a battlefield exchange occurred in the JPRC weekly Bright Light report for mid-October. On October 13, the Headquarters of the Marine Forces in Vietnam, which were fighting in the I Corps section of South Vietnam, advised the JPRC that a Catholic priest near Hue named Father Dong had been contacted by the VC regarding the possibility of exchanging two American prisoners held by them for a VC captain and lieutenant. The JPRC contacted the Embassy in Saigon for instructions. Aware that enemy POWs captured by U.S. forces were turned over to the South Vietnamese under the Westmoreland-Co agreement, the Embassy "decided it would be desirable to secure VC officers for possible exchange from prisoners recently captured by U.S. forces and not yet turned over to ARVN control."[34] The MACV J-2 informed the 135th MI Group that although political cadres were excluded from the exchange, as were using the offices of the ICRC, it hoped to keep the possibility of negotiating through Dong open until J-2 could provide suitable enemy prisoners. Obviously, the U.S. Embassy wanted to conduct this operation without first obtaining GVN acceptance, which is a curious position given their earlier insistence both on receiving the South Vietnamese government's blessings and on their stance on the need to include GVN prisoners in any contemplated POW exchanges.

It was some time before two POWs were found who matched the VC requirements, and even they were found only after the JPRC was forced to request appropriate VC POWs directly from the ARVN 1st Division, which also operated in the area. The mission was given the code-name of *Swap,* and on November 10, the Hue field office of the 135th MI Group was told to provide the priest the names and backgrounds of the two VC POWs. Unfortunately, the two VC escaped and little further cooperation on furnishing VC POWs was forthcoming from the South Vietnamese. The ARVN continued to stall, and by the end of January 1967 the operation was at "a standstill due to lack of suitable VC prisoners for possible exchange." Further, "the Senior Advisor to the 1st ARVN Division is of the opinion that this unit is perhaps not cooperating fully in the attempt. . . . This attitude may stem from the fact that certain . . . ARVN officers may be resentful of the fact that their counsel and aid were not solicited at the outset . . . and all planning was taking place without their knowledge. He is of the further opinion, however, that disclosure of sufficient information to secure ARVN support would very probably result in a compromise of the Catholic priest acting as the go-between in these negotiations and place his life in jeopardy. In light of this, the Senior Advisor recommends that disclosure of information be withheld until such time as suitable VC prisoners become available."[35]

In frustration, the JPRC ordered the 135th MI Group to ask the priest to find our whether VC POWs from some other Military Region would suffice. Although Father Dong initially replied that the VC would accept officers from other regions, in mid-May the VC informed the priest that the deal was off because the two Americans had escaped.[36] However, no successful escapes by Americans occurred during this time. The use of a Catholic priest as an intermediary is not surprising. While the communist security services had targeted the Catholic Church for repression, it had also sought to coopt them. Dawson in 1964 had been lured into VC captivity partially through the efforts of a Catholic priest. Was this conduit a genuine offer or an intelligence feeler? Neither Boatwright nor

Hansen believed the priest was neutral although, according to Boatwright, the "135th thought highly of him. I wanted to polygraph him, but the priest got offended. He didn't think it was appropriate and his refusal made me suspicious." Regardless, the JPRC had felt obligated to make the attempt.

Money for a Map

In the meantime, Chuck Boatwright was working on another ransom attempt involving Americans held in the Delta. He recalls, "The 135th had developed a source in Can Tho who had contacts with the VC. He wanted one million piasters [the South Vietnamese currency] for information that would lead us to the location of two Special Forces NCOs in the Delta. He gave them directions to meet and insisted that whoever came carry no weapons. The 135th wanted me to go to the meeting. I told Heinie I wasn't going without a weapon, so he okayed a .45 in a shoulder holster under my jacket. Our new NCO rode down in the jeep with me. He was armed with a Swedish K [a light automatic weapon], and I told him if I wasn't out in thirty minutes, come in shooting. I was really leery of an ambush or kidnapping.

"We drove to a small village and found the building, a two-story hotel, a type which was very unusual. I walked in carrying the piasters in a briefcase. Behind the counter was this very tough-looking guy. He never said a word, he just raised his hand and pointed up the stairs. I climbed the stairs and saw this hallway that had four doors, only one of which was open. I walked into the open door and inside the room was this old woman sitting on a chair next to another chair and a table. I sat down and nobody said anything for a few minutes. Finally, in good English she asked me if I had the money. I said yes and she pulled out a hand-drawn map on onionskin paper showing locations, where the guards were, the usual stuff. I looked at it and I couldn't figure out where she was talking about, but after she drew in some more items I started to believe her.

"Suddenly, I heard this noise underneath the table, which really was a kind of low-setting chest. I jumped up and pulled out the revolver, scared half out of my mind. As it turns out, the old lady had been to the market before she had come here and she had two chickens tied up and inside the chest. After things calmed down, I arranged for a second meeting with her. I wanted to compare the map against our aerial photography to pin down the area. I only gave her a little bit of the money and she got upset because she wanted it all, but she eventually agreed to meet again. When I got back, we couldn't match the hand-drawn map to any map we had. I went back to see her at the appointed time, but she never showed up. I was carrying the military maps and the rest of the money, but there was no-body around. I never figured out whether the meeting was just for show or what. Worse, after it got out that we were offering money for Americans, that's when all the crap starting coming in."37

Cobra Tail and *Hot Snap*

Many of the American POWs in the South were being held near the South Viet-namese/Cambodian border in Tay Ninh province; they were often reported being moved or seen in the area. One of the closest calls the JPRC would ever have in attempting to rescue American POWs was their first cross-border raid, dubbed *Cobra Tail.*

Hansen had just arrived back in Saigon from Udorn, where he was briefing the Thai-based aircrews. Boatwright informed him that "two men from the 135th MI Group were waiting to take him to a safe house in the Saigon suburbs to meet a Vietnamese man who swore that he had seen two Caucasians being held pris-oner in a camp near the Cambodian border. The Vietnamese was a walk-in, a source who shows up at your door with information. He was a tinker, a traveling repair shop who went into the remote border areas sharpening knives and selling needles, pins, and small household items. It was during his travels that he had seen the prisoners.

"He had seen them more than once, the last time about five days before. Trying to pinpoint the location was a bitch, as the guy had never seen a map before. Fortunately, the 135th had a set of large-scale pictomaps of the area. We spent most of the day trying to locate the encampment, but I finally got a pretty good fix on it. It was three kilometers inside the Cambodian bor-der."38

The location was an isolated hamlet called Ba Thu near the Parrot's Beak area. Earlier, on December 18, the source had been polygraphed and no deception was found. Hansen had SOG fly an aerial mission and take oblique photos of the camp. The source was debriefed again using the photos and the camp location was established at a point only 30 meters inside the Cambodian border. The source drew a very precise sketch of the camp layout, including the guard loca-tions and the approaches to the prison. On Christmas Day, the Saigon Embassy granted permission for a recovery operation.

Hansen went to see Colonel Singlaub and briefed him on the operation. Singlaub was enthusiastic, and together they went out to see the commanding general of the 25th Infantry Division, who agreed to launch the raid using his forces. Hansen spent the next three days with the 25th Infantry planning the operation. The raid was scheduled for December 30. On the eve of the raid, Hansen was joined at division headquarters by one of Singlaub's most trusted officers, First Lieutenant Fred Caristo.

Caristo had been working in SOG sending OP-34 commando teams into North Vietnam. Someone was needed on this raid who was a combat veteran and who could speak both Vietnamese and Cambodian. Caristo fit the bill.[39] He had been detailed to assist the 25th Infantry in their planning, especially since they had done few helicopter-insertion-type raids. Caristo had recommended that the 25th change their original plan to go in at first light and instead attack at noon, hoping to catch the enemy resting in their hammocks after lunch.

When the flight took off, Caristo was in the lead helicopter. As the helicopter came in flying low and fast, Caristo had climbed out onto the skid. Just as the helicopter was about to touch down, the pilot realized he was on the wrong side of the LZ, a clearing next to the hut containing the Americans. As the helicopter flared to make its landing, Caristo jumped, not knowing that the pilot had at the last second decided to turn around and set down on the other side. Landing in the rice paddy, Caristo turned to see the helicopter lift away. Instead of the helicopters landing the troops and attacking the hut, the element of surprise was now gone. Even worse, instead of a small camp guard unit and a nearby reaction force, dozens of NVA troops poured out from bunkers and started firing at the retreating helicopters.

Caristo was out in the open, alone. A horseshoe-shaped minefield was between him and the hut. Caristo remembers thinking, "They're going to kill the prisoners." In an unbelievable feat of courage, he jumped up and ran across the minefield directly for the hut that he believed held the two Americans. Miraculously, he was unharmed by the enemy fire and his churning feet never touched one of the deadly mines. Reaching the hut, Caristo never bothered to stop and ran right through the back wall of the bamboo shack and leveled a rifle at two people, an elderly man and a young boy. Caristo recalls, "I kept shouting 'Where are the Americans, where are the Americans?' but I didn't realize that I was shouting in Vietnamese and they were answering in Cambodian. When I finally understood the problem, I asked the old man in Cambodian 'Where are the Americans?' The old man looked at me, pointed at two pieces of rope laying on the ground and said 'Gone.' My heart sank. I asked him when did they go, and he said 'late last night.'"[40]

Les Hansen had been invited to listen in on the raid at Division Headquarters. After about 45 minutes of intense radio chatter, the troops of the 25th Infantry had managed to assault the camp and captured a number of enemy soldiers. As he listened, Hansen heard the "last words I wanted to hear. Someone said, 'What we came for is not here.' I felt like hell. I really believed that we were going to get a couple of our people back with this effort, but it was not to be. A few weeks later, we received a message from State and another from Sullivan asserting that they had been informed that an armed incursion had taken place into Cambodia. I was tasked to draft the reply and I responded that the border in that area was ill-defined and that as far as MACV was concerned, no border violation had knowingly occurred. A small lie, but Sullivan was such a pain in the ass that it didn't matter to me. We never got any other intelligence that we could even remotely link to the two Americans. To this day, I wonder what happened to them."

Caristo was also convinced that they had just missed the pair. The two-week delay in getting approval, planning, and then launching the raid had probably cost them the chance to recover the two Americans. For his extraordinary courage, Cristo was awarded the Distinguished Service Cross. It reads in part, "Through his heroic and unselfish efforts, Major [then 1st Lieutenant] Caristo saved numerous United States military and noncombatant lives. Although the prisoners were not recovered, Major Caristo's valorous actions were the single outstanding factor of the operation and reflect great credit upon him and the U.S. Army."[41]

Shortly after *Cobra Tail* ended, Chuck Boatwright was involved in an operation to rescue POWs lost from the First Cavalry Division. At the very end of December, "reports were received from three separate sources concerning 6 US POWs being held by an NVA Bn [Battalion] in the 1st Cav area. These prisoners believed to have been taken when 1st Cav Artillery emplacement overrun on 27 Dec. On 31 Dec 1st Cav requested JPRC permission to conduct personnel recovery operation based on above information."[42]

The 1st Cav sources were two defecting NVA soldiers and an ARVN who had escaped from an enemy prison camp. One of the sources referred to the prisoner as a Negro. The Cav later discovered they were only missing one man from the unit that was overrun, an enlisted man named Luis Ortiz-Rivera. Ortiz-Rivera was Puerto Rican and was later released in January 1968.[43]

Boatwright was sent to monitor the operation. After attending some meetings, he thought the planning "looked fairly decent and in-depth, so I returned to SOG. By the time they had finished the planning and launched the raid, it was too late and they didn't find anyone. The intelligence was good, they just waited too long to make the attempt."

Crimson Tide

The JPRC's first major POW raid (see the beginning of this book) had turned into a bloodbath. As Frank Jaks watched the dawn slowly chase the night from the Mekong Delta, he knew his company had lost many men. By the time they had swept through the tree line and the hospital complex, he had lost contact with his 1st Platoon. All attempts to raise them had proved futile. While his 3rd Platoon had taken only a few casualties, they had remained in their positions and refused to move, even after Jaks had ordered them to link up with him. Deciding that strength lay in numbers, Jaks instead shifted his platoon to link up with the other platoon before nightfall. They had been forced to wade through a swampy, water-filled area to reach the 3rd Platoon, but they did manage to link up. Expecting an attack, Jaks had formed a defensive perimeter.

The night had been one of the worst of Jaks' career. Too keyed up to sleep, he had maintained radio contact with some orbiting flare ships. The airplanes kept up a continual stream of parachute flares, illuminating the darkness and helping to keep the VC units from attacking. The pilots on the flare ships had made it a point to continually reassure him that they wouldn't desert him and his men and that help would arrive at daylight. Jaks was grateful for both the flares and the pilots' attitude. Since Jaks had ordered a double load of ammunition, no one had brought any food and his men were very hungry after the heavy fighting. To make matters worse, around midnight their mosquito repellent ran out and thick swarms of the hungry insects had descended to further torture the wet and exhausted men.

Finally at daybreak the gunships reappeared. As Jaks' soldiers began to inspect themselves, they found that they were covered with leeches. Jaks discovered over a dozen leeches on himself. At midmorning the Hueys arrived. He learned that only six men out of forty had survived from the 1st Platoon. They were all taken straight to Vi Thanh, the capital of Chuong Thien province, loaded on a SOG C-130, and flown directly back to Kontum. The body bags containing the dead were loaded together with the SOG troops on the plane. It was a long, very quiet ride back.

As Jaks recalls, "When we got back to Kontum, the Nungs performed the Chinese death rituals. Sova was there, and the only thing he said, the only thing he could say, was 'I'm glad to see you're back.' We were absolute wrecks from the operation. We were only three platoons against two VC battalions, and one of them had heavy weapons. The gunships saved my ass on that landing zone, as they got the VC in the tree line on the run and enabled us to charge it and drive them out.

Otherwise, the same thing would have happened to us as [to] the 1st Platoon. At the formal debriefing in Saigon, Aderholt told me that I had 'done the best you could have under the circumstances,' but his praise didn't matter to me. I was devastated by the losses, especially Lewis, who just wanted to come along to see a little action. The American people should know that those Nungs fought and died trying to rescue an American POW. You don't understand how dedicated they were, how faithful they were to us. Just like the Montagnards and the Hmong, and we abandoned them after they fought so hard so that American soldiers didn't have to die."

Aderholt recalls that late in the afternoon, he and Colonel Singlaub went to see General Westmoreland to tell him about the problems on *Crimson Tide*, but Westmoreland took it in stride. "Westmoreland said, 'These things happen in war.' He was upset about the losses, but understood that in a combat situation there are always risks. However, the next day, I got a call from General Momyer's office. I was to report immediately and explain the failure of the operation.

"Momyer was upset and very vocal about the close air support, especially the F-100 dropping the bombs on the Nungs. When I told Momyer his staff had refused our request for A-1's, he tried to defend them and place the blame on us instead. But between the photos to loading cargo on the ferry aircraft to the close air support, the Air Force had botched their part of the job. If they had listened to us in the first place, this would not have happened."

Singlaub also recalls that "the operation became a source of embarrassment because of too much Air Force involvement. The ARVN 21st Division lost quite a few helicopters that day, and they weren't too happy about it and made their views known, and to top it off, Momyer was angry because we had used the ARVN's instead of U.S. helicopters. Regardless, I believe flying the O-1 probably violated the operational security of the mission and the prisoner was moved prior to the assault."

Finally, Success

Despite the JPRC insistence on deferring to the Search and Rescue control center, post-SAR was still a difficult concept for some of the Air Force people. Given all the near misses and the disaster of *Crimson Tide*, Aderholt and Hansen, though not wishing to step on the toes of the JSARC people, nonetheless were chafing to accomplish something positive. Aderholt states that "we would watch the reports come in on the various SAR missions. I could see instances where we could have helped and I was always trying to get JSARC to stand down earlier than the required 72 hours so we could go after somebody. We finally got one right in late October 1966, when a SOG O-1 flying near Attapeu in Laos saw an F-105 pilot eject in the Bolovens Plateau area. As it was late in the day and the Air Force did not operate rescue helicopters at night, I asked the 7th Air Force to terminate SAR so we could have a crack at rescuing him."

The backseater in the SOG O-1 was the commander of FOB2, Francis Sova. After witnessing the ejection of the pilot and his good parachute, Sova called Frank Jaks at the Operations bunker at their launch site at Dak To. Jaks had returned to duty after spending several days recuperating from the raid in the Delta. He remembers, "Sova called me and gave me the coordinates. I looked at the map and I was stunned. They were about 10 kilometers SW of the town of Attapeu, which was well beyond our helicopter range. Even our gunships couldn't go that far. I radioed him back and I said, 'Do you know where this is at? We can't get there and back.' He says, 'Figure something out,' so I sent two helicopters from the VNAF 219th Squadron carrying fuel drums and hand pumps to land on a LZ about fifteen kilometers from the pilot. I covered the LZ with gunships and A-1 Skyraiders. I then had two Hueys fly out to get the pilot. I was in the lead helicopter.

"It was getting dark when we finally got to the pilot, a Major Robert Kline, flying on one of his first missions out of Korat, Thailand. He was hidden in the wood line and when we picked him up he was amazed. He said to me 'I didn't realize American helicopters were in this area.' I said we aren't, just be happy we're here and forget the whole thing. We flew to the LZ pretty low on gas, hand-pumped the fuel as fast as we could into the Hueys, and then took off for Dak To. We took the hand pumps, but we left the fuel drums behind with a nice surprise underneath. We were extremely lucky the enemy didn't spot us. When we got back, I had to radio Saigon and tell them what had happened. After I gave them the coordinates, they called me back. They didn't believe me. I spent almost an hour on the radio convincing them what I said was true. This was the craziest thing I did in the war, but the key is you have to make fast decisions in situations like that. Saigon wasn't too happy, but you can't beat success. I'm sure if I had failed, though, I would have been swinging from a pole."[44]

Jaks' daring rescue of Major Kline was the sort of high-risk operation the JPRC had been designed to handle. However, according to Aderholt, "the 7th Air Force people gave me hell because we used an Army helicopter to recover the pilot. Interservice rivalries are the worst."

By the end of November 1966, the JPRC was now organized and running fairly smoothly, but with several serious problems. With the inception of the JPRC, MACV had informed all the major commands that the order to launch a POW raid could only be given by the JPRC. The rationale was that the JPRC could provide the necessary intelligence and coordination, but in reality the dictum took the initiative away from the units and slowed the reaction time of the combat elements. The battlefield intelligence that several units received was extremely time sensitive and often came directly from prisoners who had just escaped or guards who were defecting. Since the enemy moved their camps almost immediately, rapid response was critical. The raid in Phu Yen province was an example. If McDonald's platoon had been notified the same day the ralliers came into the camp, they would probably have recovered all of the prisoners. The delays in granting approval for cross-border raids were even longer.

The ever-present threat of ambush, however, was a major reason why some maneuver commanders did not immediately react to POW information. Many requested more intelligence, such as aerial photography or helicopter support. The cumbersome Army command structure, plus the added burden of gaining Embassy or national command approval for most operations, put a severe brake on the speed of operations. The failure of *Crimson Tide* was a classic example, as the foot-dragging of the MACV bureaucracy ensured its failure.

Aderholt had had enough; he wanted to return to flying airplanes. Disgusted by the slow-moving Army command, stymied by the lack of dedicated forces, and having made a mortal enemy in General Momyer, commander of the 7th AF, he called in his promise from General Hunter Harris at PACAF to command a Wing. He requested his release from Singlaub, who was extremely disappointed to lose him. Aderholt left SOG in early December 1966 and Hunter Harris sent him to Udorn, Thailand, to take over the *Lucky Tiger* operation, a special-project counterinsurgency unit which later became the 56th Special Operations Wing.[45]

Colonel Heinie Aderholt's impact on the organization of the JPRC and the military's new aggressive policy on rescuing its POWs was immeasurable. He had created a small but vitally important POW intelligence/coordination section from scratch, designed its structure and midwifed it through birth. During his short tenure, Aderholt's aggressive nature had led to the implementation of a new Escape and Evasion program in Southeast Asia that eventually grew into one of the most successful SAR/E&E operations in the history of air warfare. Although his no-nonsense leadership style made him a legend among the Air Commandos, it probably also prevented him from reaching higher rank. He was a propeller pilot in an increasingly jet-oriented Air Force, an Air Force managed by bureaucrats extremely uncomfortable with his fiery style. Aderholt was a throwback to the aces of World War I, and his departure would set the JPRC back for months. More important, the high losses of *Crimson Tide* would cause the military to exercise even more caution in launching raids, and without Aderholt's strong leadership to counterbalance that attitude, the failures would continue to mount.

7. Reciprocal Release

We cannot, of course, know that release to the VC forces of two POWs who remain loyal to the VC cause would induce them to release further U.S. soldiers. We can be sure, however, that to do what the Embassy and the GVN propose is to give the VC nothing of value. How we can defend that as a serious effort to bring about the release of U.S. personnel is a mystery to me.
—George Aldrich, Legal Advisor to the Secretary of State, responding to the U.S. Embassy's refusal to pressure the GVN into giving up VC prisoners

Despite the strenuous efforts of the U.S. military, no American POWs were rescued in 1966, although the JPRC had come close on several occasions. In many ways the first half of 1967 would not see an improvement in the unit, nor would the military or the political mandarins who ran the war build on the lessons of the earlier mistakes. The losses of *Crimson Tide* and the resultant in-fighting and finger-pointing between Momyer and Aderholt had caused many commanders to think twice about undertaking risky POW rescue missions. Always aware of their "Efficiency Reports," the senior commanders unfortunately drew the wrong conclusion from *Crimson Tide;* instead of launching during the critical first few hours before the VC could move the POWs, military commanders began demanding more photo missions, more detailed intelligence on locations, more Order of Battle (OB) studies. Subconsciously, the generals in charge of the maneuver units began to weigh the risks involved in rescuing prisoners, the enormously difficult decision whether to gamble the lives of an entire unit in attempting to free just one or two men from the clutches of the enemy. For some the choice was easy; for others, much more difficult.

Improving the E&E program

After Operation *Hot Snap,* no other JPRC-directed raids were launched until April. The frenetic days of organizing the unit while concurrently launching missions slowed considerably as a new JPRC commander took over. In mid-December, Aderholt's vacated position as Chief, JPRC was filled by another Air Force colonel, Allan Sampson. Sampson was then the SOG second in command. He was a fine officer, but the difference in his leadership style was soon felt, and, by January, Sampson was slowing the previously fast-paced JPRC operations. Boatwright remarks, "The two were 180 degrees apart. Aderholt was a hell-bent-for-leather guy, while Sampson was a full-file, take-an-in-depth-look-at-a-situation type. Many times we never had the full picture or a complete intelligence profile. When you start second-guessing every operation, the tempo naturally decreased."

As a fellow "blue-suiter," Les Hansen felt he was closer to Colonel Sampson than the other officers. He believes that "Sampson simply didn't have Aderholt's clout. Aderholt was a legend and Sampson didn't have that kind of pull." But even Hansen was puzzled by some of Sampson's decisions. In a typical but unfortunate bureaucratic style, Sampson decided to shake up the personnel in the JPRC by swinging an ax, firing one of the Army officers and an Army NCO. Plus, the personnel turnover that so plagued the whole military effort during the Vietnam war also began to damage the JPRC. Sergeant Alden Egg, the Army intel analyst who had worked so hard on *Crimson Tide,* departed in December shortly after Aderholt. Several of the other enlisted soldiers left in February 1967. Although their positions were filled, it took time for the new men to get acclimated.

By the end of January the strength of the JPRC was only eight men—five officers and three NCOs. MACV recognized the enormous demands being placed on these few individuals and expanded the unit by three men. By late 1967, the unit was divided into three basic sections: Intel, Operations and Plans, and Admin. The Chief, one Army NCO, and a clerk/typist from the Navy comprised the Admin section, while the Intel section had two officers, one Army and one Navy, plus two Army NCOs. The Operations and Plans section had one Army and one Air Force officer and another two Army NCOs.

Initially, the JPRC design called for a Navy officer. When MACV recruited the first group of JPRC personnel it was discovered that, based on the requisite qualifications, the Navy officer chosen did not have the correct credentials. However, after *Canasta 572* it was recognized that Navy input was needed and a new slot was added for one Navy officer. Lieutenant Commander Charles "Rod" Foster joined the JPRC in early January. Foster was an experienced aviator who had flown missions from carriers; his knowledge of Navy procedures proved valuable in the months ahead.[1]

Foster immediately went to work to further refine the E&E program. At the end of January 1967, thirty survival kits were deployed to airbases in South Vietnam and Thailand for use by the SAR forces. Half the kits were designed for a high-speed drop from jet aircraft while the other half were deployed from slower planes. Further testing by Foster revealed that the kit had a better survivability rate if dropped in a modified fuel pod. By March, the new kits were ready for use.

Also in early January the first Reward Program was implemented to help recover American air crews. Ambassador Lodge signed a leaflet that was dropped by the millions over North Vietnam offering $5,000 in gold to anyone assisting in the recovery of a downed pilot.[2] In April, the JPRC asked for an expansion of the leaflet program to South Vietnam which provided for immediate monetary rewards to any persons who helped American airmen or any missing personnel to return to U.S. control, or provided information or returned equipment or other evidence which revealed their status or disposition.[3] The reward program included Laos, but there the monetary reimbursements were significantly downgraded: only $2,000 in gold would be given to a Lao who helped an American. Sullivan's reason was that he wanted to avoid "psychological shock" among the Lao population and military forces over the large amount that would be paid for an American as opposed to nothing for a Royal Lao soldier.

In May 1967 the program was approved for South Vietnam. However, the reward program became another double-edged sword. On the one hand, it was hoped that it would spur the local population into helping American POWs escape or airmen evade; on the other hand it swamped the JPRC with false claims. Word of the reward was spread primarily through the leaflet drops. Thirty-six million leaflets were dropped over Vietnam in July and August, another three and a half million over Laos. The program quickly ran into snags in Laos when Prime Minister Souvanna asked the U.S. government to stop dropping the leaflets. He was afraid that the communists would use the leaflets as propaganda fodder, alerting the world to the presence of American military personnel in "neutral" Laos.

Sampson assisted Foster in upgrading the E&E program further by having the Pacific Jungle School begin instructing newly arrived pilots on the Fulton Extraction System. The Fulton was a James Bondish contraption: a downed pilot inflated a balloon and released it on the end of a long rope; the pilot then strapped himself into a chair attached to the rope and waited while a specially equipped HC-130 cargo plane flew by and snagged the rope; the crew of the plane then winched the pilot on board. However, the Fulton had two major flaws. First, a large balloon tethered to a rope was like a gigantic neon sign signaling to the enemy "Here I am!" Second, if the enemy fire was so intense that a rescue helicopter couldn't make it in, how was a slower-moving, bigger-target HC-130 cargo plane going to survive? Regardless, the Air Force forged ahead with training in the Fulton System.

In March the JPRC, in conjunction with the Pacific Air Force command, produced a film called *There Be Tigers Here* to depict the latest E&E programs and the JPRC's role. Several former VC participated in the movie, playing Viet Cong chasing the downed pilot. Meanwhile, Foster was assigned to ensure that the SAFE areas stayed current and that photo recce flights were flown over them on a regular basis.

Going into North Vietnam

The parajumpers and pilots who flew the SAR missions called recovering a downed airman a "save." Search and Rescue operations are always among the most dangerous of missions, and the closer to Hanoi the tougher the save. The JPRC was alerted several times in 1967 by USAF SAR forces to have *Bright Light* teams on standby, but in each instance the SAR forces were able to return the next day and pick up the downed pilot.

It was for the more difficult missions into the heavily defended air space of the Hanoi/Haiphong area of the DRV that the SAR units requested JPRC assistance in rescuing downed airmen. Two operations in the space of three months would test the courage of the SAR forces to the very extreme and prove the worthlessness of the Fulton Extraction System.

All of the downed flights involved Navy aircraft. As a result of the positive experience of *Canasta 572*, the Navy was much more willing than the Air Force to terminate SAR actions and turn to the JPRC. On April 24, an A-6A bomber carrying two pilots, Michael Christian and Charles Stackhouse, went down about forty miles northwest of Hanoi. The crew ejected safely and were in voice contact with their wingman. The Navy commander of Task Force 77.0, the carrier group located on *Yankee Station* in the Gulf of Tonkin, immediately requested the JPRC to alert a *Bright Light* team for insertion. Given their location near the capital and the concentrated AAA and SAM defenses, Hansen felt there was little hope of rescuing the downed airmen. Sampson, however, recommended that an attempt be made using the Fulton System—but the pilots were captured before the effort was made. They later returned at *Homecoming*.

The most difficult post-SAR rescue mission, and another case that illustrates the MIA dilemma, is that of James "Kelly" Patterson and Eugene "Red" McDaniel from the carrier USS *Enterprise*. On May 19, 1967, they were hit by a SAM missile in their A-6A attack plane while attempting to bomb a vehicle-supply depot. Their plane damaged by fragments from the missile, Patterson was heard to say on the radio, "Okay, Red, let's get out of here, huh?"[4] Both crewmen ejected safely and landed near the center of Safe Area #9. It was an excellent area for evasion, but Patterson unfortunately broke his leg upon landing. Further, he and McDaniel were separated by a ridge line and were unable to establish communications with each other.

Kelly's older brother George "Luck" Patterson was a Marine infantry lieutenant who was serving in South Vietnam at the time when Kelly went down. He had last seen Kelly several weeks before when Kelly had come to visit him at his base. Kelly even accompanied Luck out on a patrol. "I last saw Kelly as he was riding on top of an Amtrac [a Marine armored vehicle] heading back to the base," Luck remembers. "We talked before about the possibility of him being captured and Kelly said he feared it more than anything else."[5]

No Navy SAR helicopter was sent in, mainly for two reasons: the toll of pilots lost that day was extremely high, plus the growing SAM deployment in the DRV had made the area Patterson and McDaniel went down in a high-threat area. Despite the danger, the next morning a fellow squadron member named Nick Carpenter, who had watched the two land, launched from the *Enterprise* escorted by USAF F-4s from Danang. He located Patterson's downed chute and reestablished voice contact with Patterson. Kelly stated he had not seen McDaniel.[6]

After contacting Patterson, the Navy petitioned the JPRC for assistance. Hansen was aware of the growing problem from following the message traffic. Upon the Navy's request, Hansen went to the Joint Search and Rescue Center (JSARC) to plan a rescue operation. "At first we wanted to try and get him at night. JSARC turned that idea down since they had no night capability. Then we thought we could create diversionary air strikes to draw away the majority of AAA and SAMs while the rescue helicopter came in from the west under the cover of additional air strikes. This plan was approved when suddenly the JSARC people informed me that Momyer had called the mission off because he didn't want to risk the SAR helicopters. I was furious. Since he was then in the JSARC, I stormed in to see him. After a heated exchange, he said we could use the Fulton. I told him this was the first day I had ever been ashamed to wear the Air Force uniform. How I wasn't court-martialed I don't know, I guess he figured I was too small fry to worry over."

A full day was lost trying to arrange the Fulton effort. By the morning of May 21, Patterson had already spent two days without food and water while nursing a broken leg. Foster arranged for the Navy to have Carpenter fly in the backseat of an F-4 fighter carrying one of the new air-droppable survival kits and a Fulton pod. Carpenter later wrote a detailed statement of his actions, stating, "We located him by mirror flashes and dropped the kits to him. They landed in a clearing about 100 yards down the side of the hill from him."[7] Later that night, Carpenter flew as a passenger in the specially equipped HC-130 cargo plane to pick Patterson up in the Fulton. The F-4 fighters that had escorted him the previous day went on ahead to relay to Patterson the time for the HC-130 pick-up. Upon arriving at his spot, they learned from Patterson that the Vietnamese had captured the kits before he could get to them. In response, Patterson retreated up the hill for safety.

The message was relayed to the HC-130, which aborted the Fulton attempt. The consensus was that nothing further could now be done for Patterson. The morning of May 22 another *Enterprise* airplane flew into the area and received no transmissions from Patterson. In the afternoon another visual and electronic search was conducted with negative results. James Kelly Patterson was gone. Alive and on the ground, he never returned and he has never been accounted for.[8]

Another similar post-SAR attempt reveals the JPRC's growing powerlessness to rescue men shot down near Hanoi and the port city of Haiphong. On July 18, an A-4E from the carrier USS *Oriskany* was pulling out from a bombing run when it was hit by flak and shot down near Hanoi. The pilot, Lieutenant Commander Richard Hartmann, call-sign "Magic Stone 404," was seen to parachute out. Voice contact was established and the Navy's North SAR helicopter attempted to retrieve him, but it "was suspended until first light on the morning of 19 July due to heavy automatic weapons fire in the vicinity of the downed pilot. JPRC was queried as to the availability of a Bright Light team or other possible JPRC assets. It was determined that the use of a Bright Light team was not feasible due to the hostile anti-aircraft environment."[9]

Against the JPRC recommendation, the strong concentration of enemy forces, and because the Air Force had once again turned down the SAR request, the Navy decided to send in its own helicopter to recover Hartmann. As the rescue ship was maneuvering over a ridge to locate him, it was hit repeatedly by heavy volleys of AAA fire, crashing to the ground and bursting into flames, presumably killing all four men aboard. The NVA had set up a "flak trap" for the rescue helicopter and destroyed it. The JPRC explored the possibility of employing the Fulton, but realized that it was useless. Contact was maintained with the pilot on July 19 and through the morning of July 20. He radioed that he was "all right and in good spirits." Unable to do anything for the pilot, in deep frustration Hartmann's fellow Navy aviator Rod Foster wrote, "There has been no further word from Magic Stone 404."

Several days later, Hanoi Radio announced the capture of Hartmann by name. In 1994 a former NVA soldier, Nguyen Xuan Tuyen, reported that he had personally observed a pilot as he lay in the back of a Chinese-manufactured truck. The pilot was wrapped in white bandages from his shins to his mid-chest. Unfortunately, the man who had radioed that he was "all right and in good spirits" after watching his rescue helicopter crash did not survive his treatment. Hanoi Radio noted that he had "died in captivity on 22 July." When his remains were returned in 1974, the DRV included a death certificate and a file record summary of his treatment which indicated that Hartmann died from "acute inflammation of the lungs" suffered from an infected leg wound.[10]

Afraid to Pull the Trigger

The few JPRC efforts in the first half of 1967 were generally fruitless, mainly because the long planning time was badly delaying the launch of a raid after intelligence was gleaned about a camp location. The only successful raids were those initiated by heliborne infantry units in immediate reaction to intelligence. Twice during the year using this formula, the 101st Airborne raided camps and recovered POWs. On February 10, 1967, they attacked a camp near Saigon and rescued 51 POWs. They found an unusual scene of brutality. "One prisoner, his body covered with sores, said the camp had been the scene of at least thirty executions in the last year."[11] On July 29, the 101st assaulted another camp-and-hospital complex and recovered 22 POWs.

Although the number of American POWs in the Delta was relatively low, the Navy SEALs surprisingly were not used until mid-June 1967. Code-named *Grenade,* the first SEAL efforts to rescue American POWs occurred when the 135th MI Group element in Can Tho received a report on June 8 of two U.S. POWs being held near the town of Sa Dec. The information was furnished by a Vietnamese who had escaped from the camp. An aerial photo mission was immediately flown and the escapee's information proved accurate. The JPRC wanted to infiltrate a SEAL team into the area and attack at first light on June 13. During the afternoon of June 12, however, a visual recon by the SEALs together with the rallier noted that, despite the earlier assurance by the photo people, the area described by the rallier and the area photographed were not the same.

A 24-hour delay was needed to permit additional photography and planning. On the 14th, the SEALs attacked a VC camp site and destroyed several huts. The source, who had "accompanied the raiding force . . . after entering the alleged camp site, determined it was not the location at which he had been held prisoner."[12]

Angler was another operation that highlights the growing frustration of Hansen and the JPRC with the slow pace of raid planning. In early February, the 149th MI Group informed Hansen that they had a Montagnard under their control who claimed to have seen two Caucasians being held prisoner by the Viet Cong. Hansen was sent to the same safe house where he had interrogated the tinker for Operation *Cobra Tail.* The Montagnard did not speak Vietnamese, so two translators were necessary; the first from English to Vietnamese, and then from Vietnamese into the source's language.

The source was a charcoal peddler who plied his trade in the mountains between Danang and Quang Ngai province. "Quite by chance he came upon a small group of VC who apparently permitted him into an area where he saw two Caucasians caged in bamboo enclosures," according to Hansen. "He assumed these were U.S. prisoners. The Montagnard said the camp was located atop a knoll near the junction of two large streams. Unlike the Cambodian operation, this was a very small camp.

"The terrain was so difficult that a large-scale operation was out of the question. After various trips to the J-staff to show the aerial photos, I was sent to brief Marine General Lewis W. Walt, the commander of I Corps. We talked for about half an hour and at the end he said that our information was good, but that the sighting was pretty stale and given the nature of the terrain, he was not certain about launching a rescue operation. I agreed with his evaluation, but we wanted to at least try.

"We decided to send the source back in carrying a homing device in a walking stick. The plan was that if he found that the POWs were still there, he was to activate the transmitter and leave it concealed as near to the camp as he could without undue risk. If the POWs were not there, or if the camp had been abandoned, he was simply to carry his walking stick with the device back out. By the time this planning was accomplished in early June, I was departing Vietnam."[13]

Although the peddler had seen the Americans in early February, it was not until late June that the man was sent back in carrying the homing device. He returned on July 14 and told the debriefers that he "arrived in the camp on 2 July, found the prisoners were gone and did not activate the UHF homer. The source stated that the US prisoners departed the camp on 30 June accompanied by 500 VC headed towards Laos."[14]

Like *Angler,* other operations were developed over a five-month period that were not conducted, ostensibly for lack of intelligence. Operations *Sycamore* and *Wigwam* were planned but not run. Because the JPRC was unable to pinpoint the precise locations, no forces were inserted into the area. Many of the American POWs, the JPRC believed, had been moved into Cambodia. "Intelligence reports increasingly indicate that sizable numbers of U.S. POWs are being held near the Cambodian border or within Cambodia proper. Although it is difficult to con-clusively confirm the validity of these reports, the fact that they are being received in quantity tends to establish a presumption of some validity. It is felt that pres-sure should be brought to bear on this problem at the highest level."[15] It was. The exchange game was back in business.

Reciprocal Release: Scales and Monahan, Crafts and Womack

Although the DRV refused to acknowledge the presence of its military personnel in South Vietnam, after the release of Smith and McClure the new U.S. policy was to request the GVN to release VC prisoners in response to similar actions by the NLF. The GVN, however, was extremely reluctant to give up anyone who might be of value to the shadowy Viet Cong. This attitude was supported by the U.S. Embassy, which resisted State's request to press the GVN for prisoner re-leases. The Embassy believed that its working relationship with the GVN would be severely damaged if the United States pressured the South Vietnamese govern-ment on this issue.

Earlier, in May 1966, two American construction workers named Thomas Scales and Robert Monahan were driving in a jeep from Saigon to the port city of Vung Tau when their battery overheated. Getting out, they went to get some water from a nearby pond and found themselves surrounded by ten guerrillas. The pair were held until January 5, 1967, when they were unexpectedly released. To further display the NLF's humane POW policy, a Filipina woman was also let go, although her husband, an employee of Air America, had died in captivity.

Sensing an opportunity, State asked the Embassy to persuade the South Viet-namese to publicly announce the release of a like number of Viet Cong, hoping a goodwill gesture would encourage the NLF to release more American POWs. The South Vietnamese government agreed, but the resultant release of three for-mer VC guerrillas directly back to their families was a showcase of GVN disregard for American concerns. The South Vietnamese military freed several NLF POWs, but tied the release to the Tet holiday and not specifically to the release of Scales and Monahan, thereby negating any practical benefit. Additionally, the prisoners whom the GVN had released declared that they had no intention of returning to the ranks of the rebels.

Secretary of State Rusk was furious. He immediately cabled Ambassador Lodge, stating, "I am disturbed by way in which recent release of three VC PW's was handled by GVN. . . . the actual operation was still far from reciprocal gesture we had in mind following release Scales and Monahan. Statements by released VC PWs that they had no intention of rejoining VC . . . destroyed in advance any hope that operation could encourage release by VC of other U.S. prisoners. That such a hope was admittedly a thin one seems to me beside the point. There is so little we have been able to do for our men held by the VC . . . that we must explore every avenue that might benefit them including anything that might lead to exchange or mutual release of prisoners. I would not of course recommend releasing hard-core terrorists or cadres, but some of the smaller fish who would have returned to VC control might have served as bait for further releases without creating serious military risks. I know that you feel deeply the need to do something for our men held by the VC and the DRV. . . . I would appreciate your taking a personal look at the situation to see whether the GVN can be brought around to our point of view. If not, they should put no obstacles in our path when we wish to take unilateral actions that could benefit Americans captured by VC."[16]

Lodge responded, "I believe we would have had real difficulty in dissuading GVN from its insistence that PWs be given into the custody of relatives. . . . I would be on difficult ground in demanding release of VC to our custody for our exclusive release. . . . Basically, I am inclined to doubt whether these details of release are very persuasive one way or another with the VC. I should think the significant thing for them would be the nature of the bait rather than how it was made available. I agree with you wholeheartedly that we must neglect no opportunity to do what we can for our people in the hands of the VC, but I wonder whether this sort of gesture, though worth trying, is not of limited value. I believe it is of far greater importance that we push ahead with our approach to . . . develop diplomatic campaigns to establish status and treatment of Americans as PWs . . . and ultimately secure repatriation of all American PWs. To this end we must . . . start giving GVN and ourselves some measure of public support."[17]

Despite the GVN's actions, Averell Harriman tried to put the best spin on the release of the VC POWs. He contacted Burchett again and asked him to take a letter to the NLF thanking them for the release of the three and pointing to the reciprocal release by the GVN. Although the U.S. government received no reply from the communists, Harriman believed that the message had gotten through. Several weeks later, on February 23, two more American POWs were released, this time military prisoners.

The State Department now felt even more strongly that a crack had opened in the previously closed door of the NLF. The next day, the U.S. government announced its intention to release two POWs in return. But despite Rusk's plea to Lodge, the ambassador refused to push the GVN into freeing prisoners that might immediately rejoin their comrades. He instead backed the South Vietnamese plan to liberate another two repentant prisoners to their families.

By March 2, the exchanges between State and the Embassy had become increasingly sharp and the two sides had reached an impasse. Harriman's staff pressed him to lean harder on the Embassy. In a memo from George Aldrich, State's legal advisor, he wrote, "In the most recent message in the long series dealing with our efforts to respond to VC releases of U.S. prisoners by reciprocal releases of VC prisoners, the Embassy in Saigon has told us in no uncertain terms that its view, not ours, will prevail. The essence of this disagreement is that we propose to give the VC something they want in return for their giving us something (two U.S. soldiers) that we want, but the Embassy refuses to ask the GVN to give *anything* to the VC. We want to bring about *de facto* exchanges. The Embassy remains adamant that we not ask the GVN to change its plans, which are to release to their families two VC who do not wish to return to the VC ranks. We cannot, of course, know that release to the VC forces of two POWs who remain loyal to the VC cause would induce them to release further U.S. soldiers. We can be sure, however, that to do what the Embassy and the GVN propose is to give the VC *nothing* of value. How we can defend that as a serious effort to bring about the release of U.S. personnel is a mystery to me."[18]

Harriman sent a further cable to the Embassy on March 8, asking them to explain to the South Vietnamese government that the American government felt compelled to insist that two prisoners be released. The GVN rejected Harriman's request with the same line that only "repentant" VC POWs would be released. Seeking a compromise, Harriman's assistant for POW Affairs, Frank Sieverts, asked DOD to consider releasing two captives still being processed by U.S. military forces. He wrote, "It has not been easy to get the GVN to make the reciprocal release in good faith. They are unwilling to release prisoners to return to VC custody, and they strongly prefer to release only reformed VC who can be expected not to want to return to VC ranks. In our view this GVN attitude sharply undercuts the effect of this policy. Unless the releasees want to return to the VC, and are able to do so, the gesture is meaningless, except for superficial propaganda. Consequently, we are proposing that MACV itself make the releases. . . . The Defense Department has just given its agreement to this policy, and we hope it will be put into effect soon."[19]

However, the South Vietnamese government still refused to be swayed, and now the Embassy was almost in open revolt. After another State telegram requesting the Embassy to intercede with the GVN, they cabled back, "We have not yet complied with the Department's instruction . . . because we are concerned that the requested approach to the GVN at this time might jeopardize excellent progress we have been making with GVN on other aspects of PW question. We don't question that release of hard-core VC might provide greater inducement for VC release of more significant prisoners than they have released so far, but we feel that it may well antagonize the GVN and cause a reaction that could be detrimental to our efforts to ensure their cooperation in other aspects of the PW question."[20]

Further, the Embassy recommended that MACV not unilaterally release any captured VC prisoners; the Embassy was also against the policy of reciprocal release. "We see at least two major dangers inherent in policy of passing message to VC that we are prepared to reciprocate release of US prisoners. It could easily lead us down a dangerous road where VC would be encouraged into thinking it useful for them to have significant US prisoners to hold as hostage for release of any prominent VC who might fall into our hands, and GVN on its part likely be concerned about how far we might be prepared to go if we started bargaining with VC for release of prisoners. They might question whether we would content ourselves with simply asking for 'hard-core' VC or would begin to go farther, asking for release of high-ranking VC officers, convicted assassins, etc. This sort of cooperation from GVN has not been achieved easily and it works toward increasing pressure on NVN and on VC for better treatment of PWs they hold and for release of sick and wounded."[21]

Despite Aldrich's pressure to take a strong stand against the Embassy, in May 1967 Harriman backed down from the new American ambassador, Ellsworth Bunker, who had assumed the post earlier in the month. Sensing the futility of further argument, State believed that it was now too late to change the mind of the GVN and the Embassy. Thinking that the VC would continue to release American POWs, State believed the most logical time to send a new message to Saigon was when the VC made further releases of American prisoners. It would be November, however, before the VC would try again.

The Hunt for Douglas Ramsey and Donald Cook

The capture of Gustav Hertz had created fears at the U.S. Embassy that American civilians would suddenly become targets of a wave of VC kidnappings. Although these fears never came true, the VC did capture another senior American advisor, a Foreign Service officer named Douglas Ramsey. In a strange way, Ramsey became almost like Hertz's twin and the pair were the constant focus of attention among the civilians in the Embassy and at State.

Speaking fluent Vietnamese, Douglas Ramsey had been working in the country for several years as the senior economic advisor for USAID in Hau Nghia province. He was captured on January 17, 1966, north of Cu Chi, when his jeep was ambushed by a VC guerrilla unit while delivering a load of rice, sauce, and cooking oil to some local peasants. The jeep was set afire and left to burn. His Vietnamese driver was wounded in the leg, but was left by the side of the road. About an hour later, the driver managed to report the attack and kidnapping.

Nothing was heard of Ramsey until February 1967, when Privates First Class Charles Crafts and Sammy Womack were released by the VC from a POW camp believed to be in Bien Hoa province. Crafts and Womack were immediately taken to Okinawa for debriefing. They stated that they had been held together with both Ramsey and a Marine, Captain Donald Cook. Ramsey, they reported, was in bad shape mentally and physically, having just recovered from a severe malaria attack. According to Crafts and Womack, the VC did not like Ramsey because of his knowledge of their language and history.[22]

Unknown to the communists, Crafts smuggled out three letters, two from Captain Cook and one from Ramsey. Ramsey's letter was to his father, relinquishing power of attorney to him for his financial affairs. Cook wrote one letter recommending medals for various POWs and another to his wife. Crafts also brought out proof of the death of another American, Captain John Schumann. Crafts recalls that "I was next to Schumann when he died. He told me before that if anything happens to him, you take my ring and make sure my wife gets it. Apparently this was an old German tradition. He had married a German girl and he wanted her to know what had happened to him.[23]

"Captain Cook actually was the first to tell me that he thought Sammy [Womack] and I were leaving. Shortly after that the interpreter and the Camp commander told me, 'You're going home.' Captain Cook was a very smart man, but secretive. The Vietnamese never knew he was a Marine, they thought he was Army. I found out after we got back that he was fluent in Chinese and had attended Intelligence training. When the Vietnamese told us we were leaving, I offered myself instead of Captain Cook because I wasn't married while he had a family and four children. They turned me down. I guess Womack and I were picked because we were lower-ranking enlisted men."

The JPRC was alerted on March 10, 1967, that "the debrief of Crafts and Womack had narrowed the location of the prison camp from which they were released to five possible locations. All locations lie within a square-kilometer area. . . . a detailed overlay and summary would be forwarded as soon as possible. JPRC has ordered aerial photography of the suspected campsite area and hopes to have this on hand for immediate collation when the overlay and summary arrives."[24] The operation was initially given the code-name *Chinook,* and then later, when the operation was actually launched, *Gray Bull.*

By the following week, the aerial photography had been received. The preliminary readout was inconclusive, but eventually some of the details furnished by the pair were confirmed. JPRC then tasked the CICV to create an Order of Battle (OB) study of the area.

Finally, on March 29, the 5th Special Forces Group was ordered to raid the area to rescue Ramsey and Cook. First, they sent an agent into the area to attempt to further pin down the camp location. He returned several days later "with the information that there were hostile forces in the area, but was unable to confirm the presence of U.S. POWs." State was more cautious, counseling the mission against taking actions which would focus too much attention on Ramsey. Their theory was that his best chance lay in convincing his captors that he was not worth hanging on to, and that instead they should release him for what ever propaganda value they could get.[25]

Despite this recommendation, it was decided to launch a rescue operation.[26] The camp location had been narrowed down to an area in Binh Long province. The plan called for using a rescue team comprised of experienced American Special Forces personnel plus Montagnards. They would walk to a point near the camp and then attack at first light. Tear gas was to be used to "incapacitate the majority of the Viet Cong propaganda team and Security Force thus minimizing resistance."[27] On April 5, the team was moving toward its night objective when it was attacked by a small VC unit. One of the Americans was slightly wounded, but the group continued toward their night objective, a position a few hundred meters away from the suspected POW camp. Very carefully, the team occupied their predawn attack position, but did not sleep that night as they could hear many bird whistles, which were often used by the guerrillas as signals.

At first light on April 6, the rescue team "penetrated the objective area and traversed it to the stream but found no indications of a PW camp." Although the "most experienced SF personnel were used for this operation and they were 'keyed' to successfully accomplish this mission, they were disappointed, to the man, because the two US POW's were not in the objective area." Further, the team "recommend that on future missions of this type, a small recon force be employed to determine if, in fact, the target does exist before the operation is executed."[28]

On April 7, the day after the attempt, Ambassador Lodge informed State of the raid's failure. "The raid had been planned very carefully. I had reviewed it personally in detail, and had been pleased by the extreme care being taken to try to ensure the safety of the prisoners. I suggest that this information be passed to the Ramsey family. Even though this raid was unsuccessful, it may reassure them to know that everything possible is being done for him, and that we never forgot." Lodge then added a small footnote, a detail which is surprising in its naïveté. "The family should be urged to hold this information in strict confidence, because enemy knowledge that raids are being launched to recover prisoners would greatly prejudice their prospects for success. . . . FYI. The outcome of raids staged thus far has been such that we have reason to believe the enemy does not know the objective of the raids."[29]

Secretary of State Dean Rusk did not respond until the end of April. "Mission should know that after careful consideration Washington agencies decided not to follow recommendation of informing Ramsey family of unsuccessful rescue attempt. Decision based on chance that family would be unable to keep attempted rescue secret, thus unacceptably prejudicing success of future attempts to rescue Ramsey and others; dubious nature of reassurance, since raid was unsuccessful, which would raise questions on details of operation in family's mind which we would not wish for security reasons to answer. We have other means of assuring family we have not forgotten and we are in frequent touch with them."[30]

What "security reasons" could Rusk have been referring to? A cryptic note in the SF operation plan makes mention that the "prisoner security force . . . may attempt to kill the Americans in the event surprise is not achieved regardless of the involvement of the Camp Commander in the plan for their liberation." Did Crafts and Womack bring out a message from the camp commander indicating he wanted to defect with the POWs? Ramsey recalls that the camp commander at this time was Le Huy, and does not believe that he would have been involved in such a scheme.

Both Crafts and Womack deny carrying any such message, but was there a code in Cook's letters? This is not without precedent, as several similar incidents would occur later in the war. If so, nothing has ever surfaced regarding a defection or trade this early for Ramsey, but since his name would appear later in the year in reference to another swap attempt, the possibility exists.

The Stratton Incident: Brainwashing or Torture?

Despite the setbacks in 1966, President Johnson's POW policy coordinator, Averell Harriman, continued to push for better treatment of American POWs. Since the POW parade in Hanoi the previous summer, the only public indications that the North Vietnamese were brutalizing the men were drawn from the growing number of "confessions" and criticisms of U.S. war policies made by captured pilots. One brave Navy officer, Commander Charles Tanner, managed to emphasize the fraudulent nature of his statement by addressing his "confession" to his colleagues "Ben Casey" and "Clark Kent." The CIA was assigned the task of comparing the POW statements to determine if a trend could be established. When all the statements were analyzed closely, it was unclear if the "confessions" were products of the old-style communist "brainwashing" treatments or were something more sinister, since "it appears to be communist practice to rework any given statements for release at frequent but unpredictable intervals." However, "current intelligence and overt evidence both suggest that Hanoi is engaged in a propaganda offensive which involves the systematic exploitation of the POWs through an organized, controlled effort to 'elicit' their cooperation."[31]

Although Brudno and Stockdale had previously indicated that torture was ongoing, few letters were being received. By June 1967, out of a known population of 180 prisoners, only 42 POWs had been allowed to write letters, whereas 68 had made statements or broadcast over the radio. Further, the communists were manipulating the tapes by splicing in phrases or shifting words in published statements to create "new" ones, all in the hopes of generating propaganda.

Then on March 6, 1967, the DRV made their first major mistake in their handling of the POW issue. At a conference for foreign newspapermen, the communists paraded a number of American POWs including Navy Lieutenant Commander Richard Stratton, who had been shot down on January 5, 1967. For his part, Stratton put on an acting display worthy of an Oscar. Faking robotic movements, his eyes glazed, bowing from the waist repeatedly toward the audience, his puppet-like actions seemingly directed by a DRV officer while his "confession" played over a loudspeaker, Stratton gave every appearance of one who was mentally controlled by his captors.

The conference was attended by a journalist from *Life* magazine, Lee Lockwood, who passed information privately back to the U.S. government on the conditions of the POWs. Watching Stratton's performance, the French cultural attaché turned to Lockwood and exclaimed, "Frightful!" Many photographers took pictures and film of the news conference, and when they were shown on American television the public's outcry was swift. State's response was more muted, however, restrained by Harriman's reluctance to take any steps that might worsen DRV treatment of the POWs. Moving cautiously, State turned to its old ICRC channel: Harriman sent a letter of protest through the ICRC to the DRV on March 24th, stating that "the NVN authorities have made statements both public and private to the effect that their policy regarding treatment of US PWs is a humane one . . ." but because of their "refusal to permit representatives of a neutral country . . . to visit the US PWs . . . it has not been possible to verify the NVN claims of humane treatment."[32]

Further, Harriman indirectly referred to the intelligence the United States was starting to gather concerning torture of the POWs. "In recent weeks information has come to our attention which casts the most serious doubts upon the NVN statements that US PWs are being treated humanely. We have reluctantly come to conclusion that some of the US airmen are being subjected to emotional or physical duress. . . ." Harriman also noted to the Saigon Embassy that "We all remember the ugly record of 'brainwashing' during the Korean War. It would be a matter of gravest concern if North Viet-Nam were using similar means against the prisoners."[33]

Harriman's letter, a summary of which was printed in the April 7 issue of *Life*, was a pale response to stronger internal warning of evidence that the DRV "may soon mount a major psychological offensive. Overall, a parallel with communist behavior in Korea is emerging. . . . We know now that physical and mental torture was used to elicit the confessions; these same pressures are being used against U.S. prisoners today. North Vietnam's violations of the terms of the Geneva Convention regarding prisoners duplicate those committed in North Korea. Indeed, Hanoi apparently has learned little new and is aping the psychological tactics and procedures used so successfully by Pyongyang."[34]

The DRV moved to counterattack the bad publicity it received over the press conference by having selected POWs meet with left-wing journalists. On April 17, 1967, a Cuban journalist published an interview with Stratton, who denied he was "brainwashed" and supposedly ridiculed the notion that he was acting under duress.[35] The communists believed they had successfully overcome the previous mistake, and again paraded a group of badly wounded American POWs in front of reporters in May. The outcry was again severe, and for a time the DRV stopped publishing the confessions and retreated into sullen silence.

Forming the First POW Committees

Recognizing that closer internal planning on POW policy was needed, both State and DOD implemented committees designed to internally coordinate their actions. On April 29, 1966, the State Department created a group called the Interdepartmental Committee on Prisoners of War. The group's purpose was to discuss finding some method of communicating with the communists. Meetings were held twice a mouth and the committee included representatives from the military. Since it was chaired by State, the focus still revolved around finding diplomatic solutions. In June 1966 the committee attempted to enlist the cooperation of a close friend of Charles de Gaulle, a French former high official in Vietnam from the old colonial days, Jean Saintény. Saintény was scheduled to fly to Peking and possibly on to Hanoi for a visit. State had the U.S. Embassy in Paris query the French government whether it would be willing to have Saintény ask the DRV for a list of American prisoners. The French proved reluctant; they believed that they had repaired relations with the communists and were unwilling to possibly jeopardize their image of neutrality with the Hanoi regime.

Although the individual services began holding monthly meetings in the last part of 1965, during 1966 the military began joint DOD-level meetings to formalize their POW policies. The OSD (Office of the Secretary of Defense) initiated monthly Conferences on Detainees and Prisoners in Vietnam. Basically, the conferences sought ways to support State's diplomatic efforts and help the families of the POWs deal with their loss.

Realizing that POW intelligence was also desperately needed, an Interagency POW Intelligence Working Group was formed in late 1966 that sought to provide information to the national intelligence agencies to help determine the locations of prison camps and whether specific men were POW or MIA. This group was chaired by a CIA officer, Edwin Buchanan, and included representatives from the services and from DIA. It was hoped that "this Committee (would get) many small but, in the aggregate, important things done which would otherwise almost certainly fall by the wayside. . . ."[36]

Bureaucratic foot-dragging, however, quickly made itself felt. For instance, the Working Group wanted to create a database that included family information. They discovered that most of this type of information was lacking, and although the Navy had furnished most of its next-of-kin addresses, the "Air Force has not been able to muster the manpower to dig it out of personnel files. . . ."37 Despite repeated requests by the Working Group to the services to create this database, it was not accomplished. Finally, after failing to force the services to take more interest in the Working Group, the CIA sought to embarrass the services by circulating a memorandum entitled, "Deficiencies in POW Intelligence Collection Program." The memo "was distributed and quickly brought results. The Air Force sent an additional and more senior representative to the next Working Group meeting to note for the record that two extra men had been assigned."38

Despite the immediate response to the memo, the CIA was rapidly growing weary of heading and hosting a committee that dealt essentially with a military problem. By April, Buchanan noted in the Monthly Report that "If any committee is symbolized by the camel, then the Interagency committee, which joins the labors of four military services and two intelligence agencies, deserves to be represented by a cross between the griffin and the distelfink, or so we have tentatively concluded after several weeks of hassling over the status of the Interagency POW Intelligence Working Group. Not that there has been anything finkish in the behavior of the various members of the Working Group themselves, the problem rather has been a failure of support at the supervisory level in the military services."39

The CIA began pushing for an authorization for the group, hoping to place the burden squarely on the military. "Another concern of the Working Group is the need for a charter which will establish the authority needed to levy requirements upon which DIA and the Services can act. DIA can issue such a charter, but only as the result of high-powered requests from the Services. An Air Force (OSI) representative stated that the entire OSI command complement of general officers favors giving the Working Group a charter and would make an appropriate request of DIA in the future."40

The Air Force kept its promise and Brigadier General Stewart L. McKenney, Assistant Director of DIA for Collections, wrote a memo to the Director of DIA stating, "Despite its achievements, however, the effectiveness and possibly the existence of the Working Group are in immediate danger because of manpower problems in the Military Services. For example, a request by the participating ONI component of the Navy for a needed person to work was turned down on the grounds that there was no record of a requirement to do such work. Representatives of the Air Force have indicated that they too may soon find it impossible to sustain their present level of participation unless the Working Group receives official recognition. . . . Under the circumstances, it is requested as a matter of some urgency that DIA ask the services to regard the Interagency POW Intelligence Working Group as fully authorized body which acts in support of a top-priority national intelligence requirement."[41]

The Power Behind the Throne

By the end of the summer, after the usual interservice sniping and Washington game-playing between agencies, the CIA-managed Interagency POW Intelligence Working Group gave way to an intelligence committee that both had the power to levy requirements and was the final authority on POW intelligence in Washington. Terms of Reference were agreed upon to form a new committee called the Interagency Prisoner of War Intelligence Ad-hoc Committee (IPWIC).

The group was established on August 23, 1967, by order of the Director, Defense Intelligence Agency (DIA). The committee was composed of members from each of the service intelligence agencies plus a representative from the CIA. Its purpose was to be a focal point within the government for all intelligence concerning American personnel, missing in action or prisoner, including civilians. A DIA officer, Navy Captain John S. Harris, was the chairman.

IPWIC's primary function was "an intelligence support and coordinating group whose principal task is to augment and facilitate the flow of appropriate PW/MIA intelligence . . . and provide a central point of reference for intelligence concerning U.S. PWs to include intelligence on their status, location, and treatment. In addition, the CIA is requested to provide technical and specialized support [for] authentication, psychological assessment, and other aspects. . . ."[42]

Air Force Colonel Rudolph Koller was reassigned in the summer of 1967 from his position as Deputy Director of Collections at USAF Intelligence to be the new commander of the 1127th. One of Koller's first assignments was to appoint the Air Force members to IPWIC. He nominated Major James Westbrook and Claude Watkins, the E&E expert from the 1127th. In recounting the early days of IPWIC, Koller remembers that "at first, IPWIC was very partisan, everyone was turf conscious. For instance, before they would totally believe us about torture we needed several more POWs to pass this information to us. Robbie Risner [an Air Force POW] got one 'double-talk' message out that said, 'Our treatment is great, just like the Apaches used to give us on the farm.' Another guy clinched it when in referring to painting a car, he said, ' *T*ell *O*ld *R*ichard *T*o *U*se *R*eal *E*namel.' "[43]

IPWIC remained in the shadows for the entire war, its members monitoring the flow of POW intelligence. Much of its activities remain classified, including operations directed against some of the American antiwar activists who were entering North Vietnam and leaving with POW information. One major covert operation involved delaying a well-known antiwar protester's traveling party at the Customs gate at a U.S. airport when they returned from a trip to Hanoi. While the group was arguing with Customs, DIA operators sneaked into their luggage, took all the film the group had made of POWs, copied it, and then surreptitiously replaced it. The group was then allowed to leave, never knowing that DIA had rummaged through its baggage.[44]

Still Searching in Laos

Despite having several American POWs in their hands, the Lao communists had refrained from the political theater of staged news-conference "confessions." They had limited themselves to propaganda broadsides aired over Pathet Lao radio detailing highly inflated numbers of American planes shot down, plus the occasional printed pamphlet. In late April, PL radio announced the downing of the 500th American plane, stating that they had "shattered the nibbling attacks by the U.S. and its puppet and smashed the U.S. Air Force's prestige. . . ."[45]

As for the American POWs in Laos, despite a continual flow of CAS intelligence, little was being done for them. Prime Minister Souvanna continued to pressure Ambassador Sullivan to avoid exposing the American presence in Laos, which placed the U.S. government in the difficult position of not being able to raise a public outcry against the POWs' treatment. Denied the stick of public embarrassment and hampered by the secret war policy, Sullivan's options were limited. To prevent possible disclosure of the war, he was continually maintaining the line against further American military encroachments onto his turf in Laos to interdict NVA supplies on the Ho Chi Minh Trail, and was adamant in his refusal to permit further expansion of the SOG cross-border raids or other military proposals that "take no account of political considerations."[46]

The first positive information concerning American POWs came when the ICRC representative for Laos informed his headquarters in Geneva on May 5, 1967, that the PL had finally acknowledged holding two American prisoners, Ernie Brace and David Hrdlicka. Hoping to learn more, State pressed the ICRC to badger the PL into confirming the status and locations of the other Americans, especially those missing. The ICRC reluctantly agreed, but no word was received from the PL over the early summer months. Finally, in August the State Department addressed a list of 33 Americans missing in Laos to the U.S. Embassy in Geneva and asked them to pass the list to the ICRC representative for Laos "expressing appreciation for initiative to gain information about missing personnel."[47]

Although CAS was still receiving reports on the POWs, the PL had moved the American prisoners to a new area. After searching for them, new intelligence was received that pinpointed the men. In a lengthy cable on August 13 to the Director of the CIA, CAS reported "our efforts locate pilots, authenticate informants and obtain new intel. On 15 June two [redacted] were sent . . . with mission locating U.S. pilot prisoners previously reported to be imprisoned in cave on banks Houei [stream] Vong north of Ban Kang Muong. These [redacted] reported that local villagers had told them pilots had returned to cave . . . after spending few days somewhere in Ban Nakay area. One [redacted] said that two pilots were still in good health. He said that former chief guard had been discharged and no longer in this area."[48] The cable went on to list the numerous reports that had been received on the presence of American pilots. In summary, CAS now "believes that all reporting indicates two separate groups of pilots. Request JPRC comments on Sam Neua group." Further, CAS believed, their informants "were reporting truthfully."

What intelligence was CAS receiving? What sparked these CAS attempts to locate American POWs? In April, a PL defector who is described as a policeman/chauffeur from the Ban NaKay police station told of attending "a ceremony held to welcome Prince Souphanouvong, who had come to visit the three American prisoners held in a cave near Kang Lit . . . [redacted] said the Americans seemed to be happy and cheerful and in good health. They joked and smiled when they talked with Souphanouvong. One of them had tapped [redacted] on the back and shook his hand."[49] Another source indicated that the Kang Lit cave complex was on the Houei Vong near Ban Kang Muong, and that "although he had seen only two pilots in November it was his understanding that there had been four rather than three pilots at Ban Nakay and that there were three pilots still alive and being held in a cave near the Houei Vong segment of river Sim . . ." and that "one of pilots had died en route. . . ."[50]

Immediately CAS ordered aerial photography flown over Laos based on the above source reports of the area. The source's description proved very accurate. He also relayed that the Pathet Lao sergeant in charge of the prisoners "sometimes entertained the pilots at his home in Ban Kang Muong."[51] Another cable indicates that in May CAS sent someone in to confirm these reports. They reported that "a rice farmer [redacted] who had been a PL officer until about 1966, told him that on 20 April 1967 one of three Americans being held captive in a cave at Kang Lit . . . had died. On 22 April Master Sergeant Chingan, the chief of the Pathet Lao guards detailed to the American prisoners, was transferred to Ban NaKay Teu because he apparently failed to notify the proper authorities immediately upon discovering that one of the pilots was ill. Khambai, a PL officer, arrived the same day to replace Chingan."[52]

Information was also received confirming earlier reports that PL General Singkapo was involved with Hrdlicka and Shelton. "In May 1965 [redacted] the home of General Singkapo. Two Americans in flight suits . . . were being held under armed guard in the General's house. . . . The pilots were quiet and looked worried."[53]

By the fall of 1967, many other reports had been received by CAS concerning the death of an American pilot and the presence of three or four other American pilots in that part of Laos. Apparently, the PL had a series of cave complexes and they shuttled the prisoners among them, but despite repeated photo missions, "the cave cannot be positively identified in available aerial photography."[54] In reaction to Washington interest, the CIA station in Vientiane produced a summary listing of all enemy prisons reported in Laos. "The list is provided only as a guide. Prison locations are unverified and there are instances where two or more entries probably refer to the same installation."[55] In November, the CIA began to database all prison locations, assigning the letters "L" for Laos, "S" for South Vietnam, "N" for North Vietnam, and "C" for Cambodia. The camps were each given a number and were listed in the order in which they were reported. In November, over thirty reports had been received on prison camps in Laos, many of which contained references to Americans, generally either the Sam Neua group or the Dengler-Debruin camp further south.

What transpired on the CAS May-June missions remains unknown. That teams were sent to look for American pilots based on numerous reports of their presence in a specific area is indisputable. The CAS Hmong teams had so thoroughly penetrated the Sam Neua cave area that, by combining their intelligence with aerial photography, the CIA at Langley was able to construct "a very realistic model of the Sam Neua caves in northeastern Laos, which are known to house a major Pathet Lao headquarters as well as American PWs."[56] Again, the new reports of Americans dying probably prompted the dispatch of the teams.

Meanwhile, Ambassador Sullivan continued to maintain a close watch over any possible unfavorable publicity. When the Royal Lao Army wanted to display captured NVA soldiers, Sullivan stepped in "to express misgivings over planned display . . . and could have adverse effects on RLG and US POWs. We believe that the physical presence of these prisoners is important to us and the RLG as living evidence of North Vietnamese aggression. . . . They should receive decent treatment because of the possible impact on US prisoners in Laos and North

Vietnam. Finally, we believe they should be kept alive for possible negotiating purposes in the future vis-à-vis Americans who are carried as 'missing in Laos.'"[57]

End-game for Hertz

Despite the rhetoric of war and the continual failures in exchanging prisoners, the U.S. government remained very interested in finding a negotiated settlement to the POW problem. To their fellow Foreign Service officers, the cases of Hertz and Ramsey were especially sensitive as they could readily identify with their plight.

At the end of May 1967, the NLF immediately reacted when the GVN again sentenced three captured terrorists to death. On June 15 the Front's radio station broadcast a message threatening to retaliate and implied that Hertz might already have been killed. "The Front allowed McClure and Smith to return to the United States. However, the examples of Kenneth Roraback and Gustav Hertz are still fresh in our memories. Let the US aggressors and butchers, Thieu and Ky, ponder this. If the Americans, Thieu, and Ky stubbornly continue to remain idiotic and frenzied, to kill people and plunge themselves into blood, Ramsey and other US criminals will be unable to avoid the shameful death as did [*sic*] Roraback and Hertz to pay the blood debts they incurred with the Vietnamese people."[58]

Washington was surprised by the radio broadcast and also confused, since the broadcast implied that Hertz was dead. The *New York Times* reported that the US government believed "a tacit agreement [existed] between the United States and the Viet Cong that Mr. Hertz would be kept alive as long as the South Vietnamese did not execute a Vietcong terrorist, Nguyen Van Hai. . . . "[59] Anxious to determine whether or not Hertz was still alive, State cabled Saigon about the possibility of sending a message through Cambodia urging the NLF to consider the idea of exchanging Hertz, Ramsey, and Marine Captain Donald Cook for GVN-held terrorists.[60] Saigon proposed instead that State send its message through the "ICRC channels and that US delay efforts re an exchange because of SVN political implications. State accepted Saigon's advice and acted accordingly."[61] Apparently, the US Embassy still was not prepared to pressure the GVN over the welfare of the American POWs.

By July, an interview of Stockdale in the *New York Times* by a Polish journalist, plus another DRV press conference using visibly wounded American POWs, was causing increased concern. Also, new intelligence indicated that American POWs were once again being placed by the DRV near the Hanoi power station to prevent U.S. bombings. The White House publicly issued a plea for the DRV "to permit the impartial inspection of American prisoners" and also "reiterated its desire to negotiate a prisoner exchange 'using intermediaries or directly, by public means or private.'"62

This was a significant move, and represented the first time since the July 1966 Manila Conference that the President had called for negotiations over the POW issue; more importantly, it was the first call by the Johnson Administration for direct talks with the NLF. But to the Hertz family, the declarations were not enough. The family wrote letters to the NLF embassy in Moscow on July 23 and to Prince Sihanouk in Cambodia on August 1, asking both to press the NLF on the status of Gustav Hertz. A reply was received back from Sihanouk, who stated that in mid-July the NLF had indicated that Hertz and Ramsey were alive and in good health.

Despite the Saigon Embassy's continued reluctance to intercede forcefully with the GVN, State continued to look for opportunities to create a dialogue on exchanges. Toward that end, in the beginning of July, when forty VC District and Regional level cadres were captured in sweep operations in the Saigon area, State queried the Saigon Embassy about the "desirability and prospects to exchange certain of these senior cadres on a one-for-one basis for (1) Ramsey, Hertz, if he is still alive, and other civilians held by VC; and (2) for American military personnel held by VC. Advantage of this idea is that these are senior VC officials whom VC probably really want back and not just terrorists whose return would be useful primarily for morale effects on terrorist units. They are also in our terms civilian rather than military personnel, though we realize VC do not make clear-cut distinction between categories. Thus an exchange for civilians held by VC would have some inherent equity. Exchange for military personnel, on the other hand, would have as rationale lack of distinction made by VC. . . .

"We are also aware of disadvantages. GVN would be reluctant to give up cadre and when exchange became known would have difficult public relations problem as to why GVN officials kidnapped by VC were not exchanged. Equating American civilian officials to VC cadre is distasteful to say the least. Such equation could also lead VC to step up attempts to kidnap Americans. Nonetheless, plight of our prisoners held by VC, as evidenced by reports and by VC executions and threats, is such as to require us to explore this idea further. Great care would have to be taken to obtain GVN clearance discreetly at highest level, and to select VC cadre for exchange who would be of maximum interest to VC and of minimum potential danger to ourselves and who had been well treated by GVN."63

The State cable prompted action. This time, Saigon was willing to act.

State Continues to Deal: The *Buttercup* Exchange

Based on State's continual urging, CAS Saigon arranged for the release from jail of the wife of a senior member of the NLF's Central Committee, Tran Bach Dang. According to a former high-ranking NLF cadre, Dang was "the permanent Party secretary for the Saigon/Cholon/Gia Dinh region."[64] The operation was code-named *Buttercup* and was designed to create an exchange channel directly with the leaders of the NLF at COSVN Headquarters. The United States was accepting the communist condition of no intermediaries and had decided to deal directly with the NLF. Dang's released wife was told to take a message to the NLF indicating American interest in opening a secret channel to discuss finding a diplomatic solution to the POW issue.

At first, the NLF did not reply, but shortly thereafter, Dang dispatched an emissary to convey to the American Embassy a proposal to negotiate for an exchange of POWs only. Dang's network of senior cadres in the Saigon area had been badly hurt by the recent GVN police raids, and now he saw an opportunity to recover some of his losses. Additionally, these valuable cadres would be needed for the upcoming Tet offensive in 1968.

Unfortunately the messenger, a communist named Sau Ha, was caught during a GVN police sweep. But Ha was no ordinary low-level courier. To demonstrate his interest, Dang had sent one of his senior deputies. In Ha's possession was a letter he was preparing to send to Ambassador Bunker. Since the letter requested secret and exclusive talks between the NLF and the United States, the usual South Vietnamese insecurities arose. Although the GVN police chief passed a copy of Ha's letter to CAS Saigon on August 19, the South Vietnamese closely monitored the development of the *Buttercup* channel.

Ha's letter asked Ambassador Bunker to release eight communist cadres, whom he identified by name. In exchange, the NLF would release an unspecified number of their American prisoners. The letter stated that any one of three men taken from the eight named NLF prisoners of the GVN could act as an intermediary for Tran Bach Dang. CAS Saigon immediately informed Bunker of the letter's contents. Needing the approval of the South Vietnamese, Bunker sought an audience with the GVN leadership, which agreed to release one of the three, a man named Truong Binh Tong. Tong was freed on September 9, and was sent on his journey bearing a letter from Bunker offering three options for conducting further negotiations. Due to heavy fighting, Tong was unable to reach COSVN and he returned to Saigon. CAS Saigon then arranged for MACV to declare a two-day cease-fire under the cover of allowing any potential *Chieu Hoi*'s [VC defectors] to rally.

Tong departed again and this time completed his trip on October 11. Two weeks later, he returned to Saigon and delivered the NLF's reply. Dang claimed he had complete authority to negotiate. He asked for the release of Sau Ha and good treatment for the remaining communist cadres, and if these conditions were met, Tong would return to COSVN to arrange for the release of some American POWs.

Unfortunately, one of the main American POWs needed for the exchange, Gustav Hertz, apparently had died. Prince Sihanouk mailed a letter to Mrs. Hertz stating that Nguyen Huu Tho had sent word that Hertz had passed away on September 24 after a short but fatal attack of malaria.[65] More roadblocks surfaced near the end of November, when press reports in the Saigon newspapers stated that the Americans were engaged in secret talks with the VC. According to one CIA official, "Despite the significance of the overture, not everyone in Saigon and Washington was receptive. . . . Thieu was reluctant to release the . . . prisoners on Dang's list because all were dedicated communists and foes of his regime. CIA officials sympathized with his view. Only after considerable debate was a deal arranged."[66] Further difficulties were encountered when the GVN police chief resigned to express his "unhappiness with the prospective release of Sau Ha and continuing American pressure to release additional prisoners. . . . Thieu considers [this] to be a political challenge to himself [by] the police and military, and we are now confronted with the task of salvaging the operation with the minimum risk to President Thieu's political position."[67] The GVN fears of direct U.S./NLF talks were playing their usual damaging role.

By early December, the press reports were being openly discussed in the GVN legislature, and the American Embassy was forced to "deny that any meetings had taken place."[68] Although the *Buttercup* channel was now partially blown, the messenger kept shuttling back and forth between Saigon and COSVN. In particular, the Embassy wanted Tran Bach Dang to provide the American authorities with a list of American prisoners.

On January 3, 1968, five letters were drafted in Washington and sent to Saigon along with $1000 for delivery to five American POWs. Tong was sent back to COSVN. On January 20, Tong returned to Saigon and related that he had been "chastised for accepting the letters and money."[69] However, despite Tong's report of his poor reception and the NLF's outrage in January when three cadres, two of whom were named in the *Buttercup* messages, were murdered by the GVN in a van on its way to a police station, Dang released two Americans on January 23, 1968, several days before the Tet Offensive.

In February, the Embassy wanted to continue the process and sent Dang a list of ten American prisoners. Secretary Rusk cabled Ambassador Bunker that "List of names to send . . . should be drawn from list of US prisoners we have identified as held by VC. Since Dang has been specific with his lists we believe we should also be precise. We recognize problem of choosing among prisoners, and accordingly propose that we select those who have been held two years or longer."[70]

Under American pressure, the GVN secretly released three of the POWs on Dang's list in response to his release of two U.S. enlisted men.[71] Tong was dispatched again on February 22 with the list of the ten American POWs the Embassy wanted back, but he never returned. Undoubtedly, the continual fighting in the first half of 1968 stymied any more exchanges, but *Buttercup* would continue to percolate throughout the war. In the meantime, it wasn't the only exchange game in town.

8. "Colonel, how many men do you think one American is worth?"

When I finished my briefing Westmoreland asked, "Colonel, how many men do you think one American's life is worth?" I said if I have to put a number on it, probably 6 or 7, but that's not the point. A captured man, he has to know that somebody is always out there coming after him, he has to have that hope. He has to know that we are his last hope.
—Lieutenant Colonel Horace J. Reisner, the new JPRC commander, briefing General Westmoreland on whether to continue the JPRC operation

Changes continued to roil the JPRC in 1967. The last of the old guard, Major Les Hansen and Major Charles Boatwright, departed within days of each other in June, leaving Lieutenant Commander "Rod" Foster as the only officer with any institutional memory. The Air Force sent Lieutenant Colonel Horace J. "Jack" Reisner to replace Allan Sampson as Chief, JPRC. Like Heinie Aderholt, Reisner was an E&E expert. A lanky six-footer, he was a combat veteran of the skies over Europe during World War II, having flown B-24 bombers over the Romanian oil fields at Ploesti on some of the most dangerous bombing raids of the war. Korea had been more of the same, and the combat missions over the first Cold War battlefield had put silver in his dark hair. From 1956 to 1960 he worked for the National Security Agency, and he was now considered one of the best-versed officers in the Air Force on intelligence matters. Reisner's tenure would be one of the most intense periods in JPRC history, a time of tremendous stress with rescue operations conducted at a furious pace.

Saving the JPRC: Reisner Briefs Westmoreland

After the go-slow early months of 1967, a new group of officers arrived in the summer to revitalize the unit. Les Hansen was replaced in June by another Air Force officer, Captain Dave McNabb, who had been working at the Public Affairs office trying to improve the leaflets urging the VC to surrender. Captain Fred Seamon, an Army military-intelligence officer, was assigned to replace another JPRC Army captain, who had been sent home after hitting a Vietnamese with a jeep. When Army Lieutenant Colonel Charles Ogle arrived to replace Chuck Boatwright in August, the JPRC was again at full strength.

Jack Reisner came on board in midsummer and his first priority was to get a handle on the unit. "Sampson gave me a complete briefing but there was still so much to learn. I decided to look at the POW problem from an overall perspective, but there were several big contingencies. First, were all the POWs being taken to Hanoi? In my opinion the answer was no, as guys were being held in the U-Minh Forest and in Laos. Why? Well, the men held by the VC were being used as negotiation bait while the Laotians had five guys in the Sam Neua caves. As I looked at the Vietnam situation, I swore that what had happened to the French would not happen to us."[1]

The JPRC's failures, however, had not gone unnoticed. In the beginning of September, a team from SACSA composed of Aderholt's old friend Barney Cochran, Edwin Buchanan (the CIA officer who had chaired the original POW Intelligence Committee), and several others traveled to Saigon on a fact-finding mission. Cochran recalls, "We came out to brief the JPRC on the latest intelligence. Buchanan carried a scale model of Ap Lo, which was a POW camp near Hanoi, plus a composite of what we knew of the other POW camps in North Vietnam. We also wanted them to know about the torture going on that was passed to us in the prisoners' letters. We understood that the JPRC had an almost impossible task, but we were trying to find out what was happening to see if we could help."

Buchanan's report noted that the JPRC was not receiving all the necessary intelligence reports, and even when it did get them, it was too limited in space and personnel to adequately address them. Overall, he felt that "although many leads for the rescue of U.S. PWs have been followed and some attempts have been made, no actual rescues so far have yet been achieved. No simple or single reason for this can be given at this time. It is suggested, however, that the JPRC could benefit by the assignment of a full-time [DIA] officer acquainted with the files and material available in Headquarters and competent to collate and analyze all the pertinent intelligence material. It is felt, also, that steps could be taken locally in Saigon, by JPRC, by the Embassy, or by the military commands, to increase the flow of information. . . ."[2]

No DIA officer was ever assigned. Buchanan also brought with him the CIA's realistic model of the Sam Neua caves plus a DIA questionnaire. The tone of the questions indicated that DIA was concerned about the effectiveness of its assistance, and the JPRC's curt responses suggested that the input from the military's intelligence arm was not solving its biggest problem, the lack of reliable intelligence. DIA's main question was "Is there any additional PW intelligence which . . . would assist that organization in its mission?" The JPRC responded, "More intelligence information—particularly details—is always needed. . . . There is so much false info that it could occupy the entire time of all JPRC personnel to check out rumors and vague reports. *Detailed,* reliable info is sorely needed."[3]

After the team's departure, Reisner was ordered by the MACV staff to provide a briefing to General Westmoreland on the JPRC's effectiveness. The string of failures combined with the major slowdown in operations brought out the critics, and the bureaucrats at CINCPAC and MACV wanted to disband the operation entirely. According to Charlie Ogle, Reisner "was being forced to justify the existence of the JPRC. MACV policy required that all personnel-recovery operations in the theater of operations be conducted under the auspices of the JPRC. The JCS guys thought this orientation was wrong, since nobody could do anything without JPRC approval. This was badly delaying operations and stymieing the field units. Further, in the mid-sixties DOD was governed by a 'systems management' approach, and we, as part of the system were not producing any 'recoveries.'"[4]

Crimson Tide was also still haunting both the military and the JPRC. Dave McNabb remembers how heavily the early disaster weighed on Sampson. "This was always given as an example of why we should be so cautious about launching raids."[5]

Colonel Reisner was granted fifteen minutes to brief General Westmoreland. He decided that his approach would be to simply provide the general with the "absolute facts. I mainly wanted to present the history of the unit and remind Westmoreland that this was his idea, and that in one of his messages he noted not to have very high expectations, that historically this type of operation was not very successful.

"When I walked into the room, there was about thirty people. Basically, I was having to justify Aderholt's prior decisions even though I had never met the man. While I didn't agree that the JPRC should be in SOG, which had been the Air Force's position from the beginning, I felt it was worthwhile to continue the JPRC. After I finished, Westmoreland asked a few questions, specifically about the operation last year [*Crimson Tide*] that had lost so many men."

The commander of MACV asked Reisner if he believed the losses from that operation were justifiable. Reisner answered that it appeared that U.S. intelligence was unaware that the two VC units had moved into the area and he felt it was unfair to comment on his predecessor's decisions. But the general continued to press Reisner. Looking right at the new JPRC leader, Reisner recalls, "Westmoreland asked, 'Colonel, how many men do you think one American's life is worth?'" The briefing had reached its climax and the future of the POW rescue unit hung on Reisner's answer. "I said, 'Well, if I have to give a number, six or seven, but that's not the point. From a morale standpoint a captured man has to know that somebody is always out there coming after him, he has to have that hope. He has to know that we are his last hope.' After a second Westmoreland, ever the Virginia gentleman, said, 'You're doing a fine job and we'll continue to back you 100 percent.' I sat down and the meeting broke up a short while later."

"You're a crazy son of a bitch": Planning to Raid Ap Lo

The scale model of Ap Lo brought by Buchanan was not just for show and tell. According to Watkins, a letter written in July 1966 from Alan Brudno, the same POW who first alerted them about torture, contained hidden references to the camp's existence. Watkins recalls that Brudno also used the "double-talk" ruse. "We went back and examined his old letters. At first, we couldn't figure out his letter. Sometimes deciphering was difficult. On the second page of the letter to his wife it read, 'Remember when the policeman stopped us? *Sue* told him, in her ridiculous Jewish accent, *oi*. And you were so calm and friendly and said *hi*. But I had to ruin everything and embarrass you with a loud *damn*.' He later talked about 'hills' and the 'number nine' and 'filling up our tic-tac-toe board.'[6] We were discussing this one day with the head of FBIS when he mentioned that a district of Hanoi in North Vietnam was called Suoi Hai. We immediately started looking at aerial photography of the area, and sure enough we discovered a prison that was laid out like a tic-tac-toe board. Nearby was a dam. The prison was Ap Lo."

Three years before the most famous POW raid of the Vietnam war—on the prison in Son Tay in 1970—the JPRC was ordered to plan an assault on Ap Lo prison in the DRV. Although he was just getting settled in as chief, Reisner recalls that Colonel John Singlaub called him into his office and told him to begin the planning for a raid in the North. The assignment was passed to Ogle.

Lieutenant Colonel Charlie Ogle already had a long career in the military. At the age of sixteen he joined the Merchant Marine and spent a year in the Pacific during World War II. After leaving the sea, he enlisted in the Army right before Korea and later, during the war, received his commission as an infantry officer. His previous combat experience helped him understand the problems inherent in prisoner-rescue operations. He spent over two months working on the Ap Lo mission, planning the routes in, locating the AAA gun positions, and working on a myriad of other details, including bombing the dam to cut off NVA reinforcements. As always, service rivalries played a role.

"My planning consisted of using Army forces to go in to get the POWs," Ogle recalls, "but I realized that I needed Air Force expertise and so I worked closely with four Air Force officers. Weather was one big problem. I felt we only had a narrow window of opportunity to get in and out. But my larger concern was about their radar. When I expressed my anxiety to the Air Force guys, one officer said to me, 'Look, we can shut down their radar screens, don't you say anything about it, but for this we'll do it.'

"Because we were so highly classified only a few people could attend our briefings. One day I went to the MACV J-3 to give an update on my plan. When I finished, this Army colonel turned to me and said, 'You're a crazy son of a bitch to try this.' I said 'Colonel, if you're refusing, the Air Force would be happy to take over this mission.' He immediately changed his attitude."

Reisner, however, was firmly against attacking Ap Lo as he considered it too heavily defended. Eventually, his opposition killed the plan. How much of the JPRC's original planning was incorporated into the later Son Tay mission remains unknown.

"In the Central Highlands forever": The 4th ID Wants Its Men Back

While the debate raged on between the State Department and the Embassy in Saigon over the policy of reciprocal release, the recommendation for attempting battlefield exchanges was being revived. The first possibility arose on July 12, 1967, when a platoon from the U.S. 4th Infantry Division (ID) was ambushed and overrun by a large NVA force. By late July, the Embassy reported to State that intelligence was received "indicating that two personnel, David W. Sooter . . . and Joe L. Delong, are being held by NVA troops in Cambodia along with as many as seven others. . . . Commanding General 4th ID asked that the information be conveyed to Governor Harriman . . . with a view to contacting the North Vietnamese. We have asked the 4th ID to look into communicating locally with the enemy commander regarding a battlefield exchange."[7]

Although State was dubious about the reliability of the information, the Embassy was convinced. "We believe our information on the PWs is sufficiently reliable," they wrote, "identification of Sooter and Delong by NVA PW was quite definite. . . . We are still exploring the possibility of exchange, including delivery of leaflets or go-betweens."[8] Harriman agreed, recommending "that main emphasis be placed on careful exploration of possibility of battlefield exchange. We have suggested this before and believe this may be suitable occasion to try. . . . Message would be brought to VC/NVA commander by one or more VC/NVA PWs in our hands. Believe this might be preferable to leaflet drop, since latter might be taken as propaganda initiative."[9]

The Embassy ordered the 525th Military Intelligence Group and the CIA to locate and recruit a Montagnard or Cambodian to take a message to the local NVA commander. Between mid-August and mid-October these agencies unsuccessfully sought a candidate. In frustration, the 4th ID commander asked permission to capture and release their own POW. In mid-December, a North Vietnamese POW who had been captured one month earlier at the battle of Dak To agreed to take a message in both English and Vietnamese requesting a one-for-one exchange of POWs.

In January, 1968, the operation first discussed over the summer was now ready to begin. On January 30, a private named Nguyen Van Be was released with the message, which stated that the 4th ID was prepared to execute a direct exchange of one NVA officer and eight NVA enlisted for one U.S. warrant officer and eight enlisted men held captive by them. The NVA commander could communicate his reply by either messenger or radio. Radio frequencies, dates and time for communications were included in the note.[10] The next day the enemy's Tet Offensive smashed across South Vietnam. Despite constant monitoring of the radio frequency, no reply to this message was ever received from the North Vietnamese.

Although Sooter eventually returned at *Homecoming*, it was already too late for Delong. On November 9, 1967, Sooter, Delong, and another American, named Richard R. Perricone, tried to escape from the camp. Sooter and Perricone were immediately recaptured, but Delong managed to evade the guards hunting for him. According to Martin Frank, another of the POWs being held at the prison camp, the VC returned several days later. They showed the other American POWs a burlap bag containing the black trousers Delong had been wearing when he escaped. The trousers were bloody and full of bullet holes. "Delong," the NVA camp commander told the remaining POWs, "would be in the Central Highlands forever."[11] He remains Missing in Action to this day.

Dealing with Thieves

Although the area along the border between Cambodia and South Vietnam was hotly contested, a part of it was relatively free of communist guerrillas. The Delta provinces of Chau Doc and An Giang were populated by a religious minority called the Hoa Hao, a militant Buddhist sect founded in 1939 by a young mystic named Huynh Phu So. Initially, the Hoa Hao supported the communists in the war against the French and later against the regime of Ngo Dinh Diem, but the fiercely independent group also resisted the VC's attempts to convert them to the Party. Trusted by no one, the Hoa Hao turned to banditry to survive and began attacking both sides. In response, the VC ambushed their leadership, killing Huynh Phu So. Immediately, the South moved to repair relations with the Hoa Hao and by early 1967, the Saigon government had organized the Hoa Hao into nine battalions of local militia. Rearmed, the Hoa Hao sought revenge and drove the VC almost completely out of the two provinces.

On June 27, the JPRC received a report that a Hoa Hao platoon working with a group of Khmer Serai, another religious minority group given to lawlessness who inhabited the ill-defined border area, had fought a VC unit about twenty kilometers inside Cambodia and had recovered nine American POWs. The JPRC immediately dispatched an agent to try and identify the Americans. The source relayed that the Khmer Serai wanted to exchange the American POWs for permission to enter South Vietnam and work with the Hoa Hao. Although Reisner wasn't involved in the early negotiations, he recalls that "they also wanted a huge supply of guns and ammo."

Given the shady history of the two groups, the State Department was cautious. Although "we are greatly interested in recovery of any POWs," State did not want any border incidents with Cambodia. Secretary Rusk sought to limit direct U.S. government involvement with the two groups but authorized the JPRC to investigate.

On July 11, in an operation code-named *Bandito,* JPRC and Vietnamese representatives met in Can Tho with a Hoa Hao leader named Tam. Tam was told that negotiations for the Khmer Serai to enter South Vietnam could begin once proof of the nine American POWs was received. The next day, Tam departed Can Tho. He returned on July 25, stating "He had run into 'difficulties' and was unable to obtain the identifying data on the US PWs."[12] He was sent out again and told to return by August 3 with photos of the Americans.

U.S. Ambassador Ellsworth Bunker wrote to Rusk, "We are not in a position to assess the good faith of the Hoa Hao and Khmer Serai personnel involved. We would have to rely on the safeguards proposed—avoiding any direct U.S. relationship with them, and having the GVN warn them against any across-the-border operation. While we cannot foresee precisely the details of the release of U.S. PWs or the entry of the Khmer Serai units into SVN, we do not believe there will be any difficulty with the press about U.S. involvement. We can simply make it clear that the only U.S. role was to receive the PWs."[13]

Tam met with the commander of the Khmer Serai, a man named Ruen. Ruen refused to furnish proof of the Americans because he "did not believe that the Khmer Serai would be permitted to enter South Vietnam with the Hoa Hao." Plus, since the GVN didn't believe him about the Americans, he would not release any of the U.S. PWs and he was terminating negotiations.[14]

The negotiations ended, but in the byzantine atmosphere of Indochina the trading was not over. On October 23, a Vietnamese male named Le Van Phuoc was brought to the JPRC. Phuoc claimed that the Hoa Hao had eight American POWs under their control. Additionally, Phuoc was carrying a letter verifying his credentials from a relative of the wife of Prime Minister Nguyen Cao Ky. Because of the similarity to *Bandito,* Reisner was intrigued.

He sent Ogle to investigate. Ogle was taken by a CIA officer to a safe house in Saigon to meet with Phuoc. He quickly became convinced that Phuoc was lying. "He wanted a enormous amount of weapons, plus $30,000. I was very skeptical from the start, having read beforehand in the old files about a similar operation." After several meetings "investigations of the new source revealed him to be a prevaricator who had fabricated his bona fides."[15] According to Reisner, "Although frauds, we had pretty good intelligence that the Hoa Hao did actually have at least two Americans, a black officer and we thought one of the civilians, maybe Hertz. You have to understand that these people had no compunction about trading POWs like goods at the market. Unfortunately, we never could get to the right people or get any proof."

The Return of Jackson, Johnson, and Pitzer; Finding Nick Rowe

In November, one of the most significant releases of the war occurred when the NLF freed three of the men held in the Delta: James Jackson, Edward Johnson, and Daniel Pitzer. Although the secret Embassy and CIA *Buttercup* negotiations were still ongoing, these men were released outside that exchange channel. Why they were not included as part of those negotiations remains a mystery, but one strong possibility is that the worsening illness of Johnson convinced the NLF to release them, hoping to achieve a propaganda coup before more of their "assets" perished. Several POWs in the Delta camps, including Orien Walker, Leonard Tadios, and Joe Parks, had already died of malaria and malnutrition.

The first hint that the communists intended to release the men came over Hanoi Radio. Shortly thereafter, the CIA reported a conversation between the NLF representative in Phnom Penh and a high-ranking Cambodian official. The NLF "intended to liberate more American prisoners for humanitarian reasons but with the ultimate aim of encouraging Negro movements in America, which in fighting against racial discrimination have expressed themselves as being against the US war of aggression in Vietnam.

"Formerly, liberated American prisoners were immediately handed over to the American officials, who kept them out of reach of the public and took measures to prevent them from freely expressing their ideas. The US was trying to minimize the effects of the release by the NLF, who intended it to show international public opinion . . . that the NLF had always treated its prisoners well. Therefore, to succeed in its aim of publicity, the NLF has in mind a new procedure consisting in freeing the prisoners directly to their families or to pacifist Negro organizations in the US. . . ."[16]

But the target was not just American blacks. Jacqueline Kennedy, the widow of President John F. Kennedy, was visiting Phnom Penh at the time and the NLF undoubtedly hoped to make a favorable impression on her. Sihanouk took the occasion of Mrs. Kennedy's visit to express annoyance at U.S. violations of Cambodian borders and refused any future assistance to American POWs. His bombast was refuted a few days later when the three Americans were released in Phnom Penh.

While traveling to Phnom Penh, Pitzer and Jackson, both medics, were told by the VC to keep Johnson alive "or else." Upon arrival in the city, the three were released to one of the fiercest American opponents of the war, Tom Hayden. In an interview with the *New York Times,* Hayden said the "the idea of releasing the men as a gesture toward the peace movement and the Negro struggle in the United States was first broached by . . . a member of the Central Committee of the NLF,"[17] thereby confirming the CIA intelligence report.

Immediately stories appeared in the press that American officials in Saigon were accusing the VC of "brainwashing" the men. The genesis of the "brainwashing" story was a press interview with a rallier named Phung Van Tuong who had been an interrogator in their camp. Tuong recounted how the indoctrination sessions were held even before interrogation and that the political instruction consisted of five distinct lessons, the last of which was on "the duties and responsibilities of American prisoners who have been graciously released by the NLF to return to their families. . . . When they are released they are not to rejoin any fighting arm of the US, they are to convince many others of the wrongness of the American cause. . . . [T]hey are to stress that the war must stop to save the lives of thousands of American children. If they do these things then they can help to awaken the heroic American spirit to get Americans to fight for the right cause."[18]

When the press stories broke in November, Reisner was furious. "Nick Rowe, the remaining American prisoner in the Delta, was an object of great interest to us and the CIA had been sitting on this guy [Phung Van Tuong] since he rallied in February. Further, when we asked to interview him, the guy disappeared and the CIA would not let us near him. At the next SOG staff meeting, which always included the CAS Special Assistant to Singlaub, I blew up and accused them of not being truthful, timely, or complete in their reporting to us. Singlaub threw me out of the meeting, but my point was made."

The debriefing of the three POWs was initially delayed because Johnson and the other two were in the hospital recuperating from numerous diseases, including severe dysentery and malaria. After regaining some strength, the three pinpointed the area where they believed that Rowe was still being held. The Army reported to the CIA that "The three PW's were moved around often. Pitzer was held in eight different camps, Jackson in three. The treatment of the PWs was fair, considering that both captors and captives were living in such poor conditions—Johnson was initially subjected to torture."[19]

By early December, the JPRC review of the debriefs concluded that Rowe was being held in the U-Minh Forest and "periodically moved from one camp location to another. . . . the Sgt.'s believe that all the camps . . . are located within a fifty-square-kilometer area. Recovery of Cpt. Rowe presents a three-part problem: precisely fix the location of the camp in which Rowe is located; seize the camp and its guards before they have an opportunity to murder Rowe to prevent his escape; and then extricate Cpt. Rowe and the members of the recovery party before the VC have an opportunity to react decisively to the situation. Locating the campsite is the key and the most difficult."[20]

The JPRC called the operation to recover Rowe *Black Knight*. Although the debriefs had given them a good fix on the camp, Nick Rowe would have to wait in a POW camp for another long year.

Post-SAR Success and Failure

Just as the record for raids in 1967 was poor, so was the number of escapes. However, another of the many strange occurrences that seemed to be a matter of routine in Indochina occurred in October 1967. On October 18, a villager reported that two Americans were trying to get into South Vietnam from Cambodia. The report was passed through Special Forces channels to the JPRC, which promptly alerted all the military units along the border. Two days later, the JPRC was notified that a white man had appeared at a border post.

According to Reisner, "When the man appeared at the border everyone assumed he was an escaped GI. I was sitting in my office wondering who it was when I heard Foster answer the phone. Suddenly Foster shouts, 'Great fuck, a Hungarian.' Everyone in the whole building must have heard him, as we had most of SOG in our office within a matter of minutes."

The Hungarian, a man named Istvan Pivik, had cleverly eluded the Cambodian border authorities and turned himself in to a Vietnamese outpost in Chau Doc province. Pivik had a wild tale to tell. He had joined the French Foreign Legion after escaping from a prison in his native Hungary shortly after World War II. He claimed to have fought with the French in Vietnam and to have been captured by the Vietnamese, who promptly shipped him back to Hungary. Sneaking out of Hungary, he stowed away on a ship that he thought was heading for America but that was in fact steaming back to Cambodia. After the authorities there arrested him, he was awaiting deportation when he again escaped, along with another individual. Pivik decided to head for Saigon in the hope of finding his old girlfriend. Although he had no knowledge of any American POWs, after his debriefing he was transferred to CAS control and disappeared.

The quick JPRC response with the Hungarian was followed by a major post-SAR success, the recovery of Private Roger Anderson, a soldier from the Army's 9th ID. Anderson was rescued from VC control in a way that would have done Hollywood justice. He was on guard duty about sixty-five miles south of Saigon when he disappeared from his post on January 3, 1968. Since he was due to depart Vietnam within a week, his unit believed that he had been kidnapped. A search the next day failed to locate him, and Anderson's fate as a POW appeared to be sealed.

Five days later, the 9th ID received an agent report that Anderson had been sighted with a VC column. "An American POW, name Anderson, was sighted while walking in a northerly direction. . . . Individual was wearing white shorts and no footgear."[21] His unit asked for JPRC help and Seamon was sent. "We discovered that Anderson had been kidnapped by the VC using the old 'honey trap,'" Seamon recalls. "A girl came out to the edge of the woods and signaled to Anderson, who then left his post. Upon reaching the girl, he was jumped by a bunch of VC.[22]

"I figured that Anderson was probably being taken toward Cambodia, so I contacted all the helicopter units in IV Corps to search along the border for him. A couple of days later one of the pilots, who was known as a real hotshot, was flying along a canal when he buzzed a dugout canoe being paddled by two men. After he buzzed them, they started hauling ass for the shore. He circled around and strafed the sampan. The two VC dove into the water. The door gunner kept firing and killed one of the VC. The other VC escaped. All of a sudden they see this head pop up out of the bottom of the sampan. Anderson jumped up and ripped off his shirt to display that he was an American. Anderson was uninjured and one lucky s.o.b."[23]

The reward program that had been instituted earlier in the year came tantalizingly close to achieving success in late December. On December 20, an F-100F with two Americans aboard was shot down by ground fire in North Vietnam. After intermittent beeper contact, an electronic search was conducted the next day and voice contact was suddenly established with one of the two pilots. Surprisingly, the downed pilot indicated that he was captured but that his captors were amiable and had allowed him to keep his radio. Then one of the National Security Agency listening posts eavesdropping on the conversation reported that one of the Vietnamese guards stated on the radio, "that if anyone could hear him, he would be listening on the morning of 22 December and was willing to discuss the situation and compromise. . . . Collateral reports indicated that the North Vietnamese captors and one captured U.S. pilot talked with other U.S. pilots airborne over NVN that day."[24]

After making positive identification of the American, the pilot in the orbiting U.S. aircraft attempted to make a deal with the guards for the captured pilot's release by offering the gold reward. One guard sarcastically answered that the pilot could be picked up in Hanoi, but the pilot continued to claim that his two captors seemed to be in a bargaining mood. Although one of the U.S. aircraft dropped below the cloud cover and was immediately met with AAA fire, the decision was made to continue the negotiations.

Alerted to the crisis, Reisner moved swiftly. He contacted the SAR forces to have a helicopter standing by while he drove to the Embassy to get the gold. Reisner remembers "when I got to the Embassy, everyone was out at some Vietnamese celebration. Finally I found a clerk and when I tried to explain the situation to him, he wouldn't let me have the gold! I had to write a personal check for $5,000 before he would give it to me. I put the bars in my car and drove out to the helicopter. They took off and headed for the coast of North Vietnam. Standing off the shoreline, they hovered until they raised the Vietnamese guards. They asked to speak to the pilot, but they wouldn't let him. When the SAR pilot asked for the proper authentication, the Vietnamese were unable to give it. Fearing a trap, we had to reluctantly call off the mission."

Shortly thereafter, another post-SAR operation led to a major blowup with Ambassador Sullivan, one that would have dire future consequences. Late on January 14, 1968, an electronic-surveillance plane was shot down over North Vietnam near the Laotian border. Four crew members ejected from the bomb bay, followed by three crew members from the pilot's compartment. The weather was dismal in the area and the SAR helicopters were unable to get in. The next day the weather cleared somewhat but the rescue helicopter crashed en route.

The SAR forces requested JPRC okay to cross into North Vietnam. To reach the crash site, the helicopters had to use the dirt airstrips in Laos called Lima Sites, which required prior approval from Ambassador Sullivan. Reisner tried like hell to get permission from Vientiane. "I was the only guy who had the authority to send rescue forces into North Vietnam, but I still had to get the okay from Sullivan to use the Lima Sites. The damn secure phone wouldn't work, so I ordered them in under my authority. I told Singlaub if anything goes wrong, I'll take the blame, but if we have to wait for Sullivan we will never rescue the men."

Over the next two days, the large rescue helicopters flown by the SAR pilots called "Jolly Greens" managed to recover all of the SAR people plus three of the original seven-member crew. But four crewmen were still missing and by January 19, Singlaub realized that any hope of finding them lay with sending in a *Bright Light* team. General Momyer was briefed and approved any necessary air assets. The next day, two teams departed Nakhon Phanom (NKP), a major American airbase in Thailand. But when they reached the insertion area they were unable to find a suitable landing spot. Running low on fuel and fighting the growing darkness, the helicopters were forced to return to base.

Unable to do anything else for the four remaining survivors, the SAR commander at NKP called off any further missions. On January 22, however, a strong beeper signal was received from the area. Captain John Alison was chosen to pilot a SAR helicopter back into the area. "We flew up there not knowing what to expect," Alison recalls, "The Sandys [A-1s used to provide covering air power] went into the area to check it out first. They reported no movement so I came in. I flew across this open area to where we thought they were. Just as I came to a hover, all of these small arms opened up on us. I took off immediately. We got hit about a dozen times, including twice in a droppable fuel tank, which started to leak. It was the classic trap. The bad guys had the beeper and used it to lure us in."[25] Fortunately, the four survivors returned at *Homecoming*.

Reisner remembers that Sullivan was furious at his decision to send in SAR forces without his approval. "I received several nasty messages from Sullivan over treading on his turf. Even today I can recall almost the exact wording of one message. 'I don't work for MACV, CINCPAC, or the JCS, I work for the President and I want all of you to remember that.'"

The incident sparked the creation of a Memorandum of Agreement (MOA) between the JPRC and the U.S. Embassy in Vientiane, which provided streamlined procedures between SOG and Vientiane for the insertion of *Bright Light* teams. Unfortunately, the Agreement broke down immediately under its first test, one that may have cost a man his life.

On February 27, a Navy OP-2 "Neptune" plane was shot down on a sensor-laying mission over the Ho Chi Minh Trail in southern Laos. Of the nine crewmen on board, seven managed to bail out and were rescued by SAR helicopters. One man, John Hartzheim, was badly wounded and went down with the plane. The pilot was a different story. The SAR forces picked up a strong beeper from a survivor, thought to be the pilot, Paul Milius. Contact was lost before they could rescue him. The next day, the SAR forces requested that the JPRC provide a *Bright Light* team to recover the survivor. Code-named *Texas Crest,* the plan was to insert the team at the man's location to conduct a limited-area ground search. Ogle was ordered to escort the team to NKP. Unable to get Sullivan's approval to proceed into Laos, the team waited all day in Thailand. Permission was finally granted on February 29 and the team was briefly inserted that morning but was extracted because of heavy enemy fire.[26]

Westmoreland was outraged at Sullivan's dithering. He sent a cable to Vientiane expressing dismay at the length of time needed to authorize the JPRC *Bright Light* team. Sullivan, trying to justify his actions, smoothly wrote back that "I am puzzled by your statement that there was 'misunderstanding' concerning proposed Bright Light rescue effort. . . . All information which we have received here concerning Navy crash indicated that seven crew members bailed out and that two remaining (both wounded) were trapped in forward compartment. . . . I have received distinct impression that chances of their having successfully bailed out were very slim. While it is true that SAR personnel reported seeing somebody on the ground near the crash site, there was never any confirmation that this person was a crew member. . . . Nevertheless, because of that sighting and the slim chance that it could have been a crew member, I authorized the Bright Light mission.

"The authorization was delayed because of confusion resulting from MAC-SOG failure to follow procedures prescribed in JPRC Memorandum of Agreement. . . . In my view, mission might have been able to move into crashsite on same day if proper coordination procedure had been followed. . . . From a political point of view . . . SAR rescue forces are USAF personnel . . . to which RLG has given its consent. JPRC forces are Vietnamese Special Forces teams whose introduction into Laos is always a matter of utmost political sensitivity . . . because of fact that there exists no rpt no understanding with RLG that they can be used in Laos. Hence: it is categorically not possible to permit them carte blanche to operate in Laos where a crash occurs."

Westmoreland fired back. "I regret to say that we may have missed the opportunity to pick up a survivor through procedure problems, in spite of our exchange of messages . . . voice, radio, and visual contact established with an eighth man. Eighth man was able to fire flare on command and vector overhead by radio, when contact was lost because of hoist problems, impending darkness, and possibly a broken radio. JSARC and 7th AF authorities believed excellent chance of recovery with a ground search team working closely with SAR forces."[27]

Westmoreland went on to mention that the Navy plane was only a "secondary objective." Wasn't Milius the object of the search, wasn't his the strong beeper signal picked up? The answer is no. In December 1994, a JTF-FA team researching the loss interviewed villagers who had witnessed the crash of the Navy plane. The villagers related that the eighth man got out of the plane but his parachute did not fully deploy. The locals buried the body nearby. Whose, then, was the strong beeper? Who was in voice contact and firing a pen flare? After discussion of the case with a DPMO researcher and her resultant check of the SAR logs, she discovered that "the contact with the unrescued American was a significant distance (38 kilometers) from this loss incident. The contact appears to be solid, but does not appear to be Milius. This . . . may correlate to Refno 1063 (Gilbert S. Palmer or Thomas T. Wright), an unresolved RF-4C loss."[28]

The unresolved RF-4C case was an Air Force plane carrying two men, Palmer and Wright, on a photo mission when it disappeared the same day as the Navy aircraft. One officer was black, the other white. A wartime interrogation report of a captured NVA soldier reveals he saw several American POWs, including one black man, in a temporary NVA prison camp near the loss incident. This report was correlated to Wright, the black officer. Did Wright survive the loss incident of his plane only to disappear forever into the jungle of Laos? In SAR operations, time is of the absolute essence. Obviously someone was alive, on the ground and signaling, but Sullivan's refusal to immediately allow the *Bright Light* team into Laos because of "political sensitivities" and "procedural problems" may have cost a man his life. Plus, Sullivan was confused over the JPRC objective, which wasn't the Navy plane but the man who fired his flare on command. Neither pilot from the RF-4C, Wright or Palmer, returned at *Homecoming* or has ever been accounted for.

"We just can't do it": Disaster in Hue

While Colonel Jack Reisner was attempting to get the CIA to share intelligence with the JPRC to recover Nick Rowe, the massive enemy attack that became known as the Tet Offensive disrupted the JPRC's normal intelligence channels, especially in the city of Hue in the north of South Vietnam. Inside the city, the Army's 525th Military Intelligence Group detachment was captured by enemy soldiers, a potentially disastrous compromise of intelligence operations. Reisner realized that the fluid combat situation created by the enemy assault offered a rare opportunity to recover some of these men and other Americans recently captured in the heavy fighting. To escape the fighting, the enemy soldiers had to march their new prisoners on foot toward their camp areas, thus exposing themselves to aggressive attacks.

Reisner carefully watched the intelligence reports flowing in. Spotting several lucrative targets, he dispatched Captain Fred Seamon first to the Song Be area and then later to Ban Me Thuot. He sent Charlie Ogle to the Danang-Hue area to help track down leads on Americans missing in that location. If any POWs were spotted, Reisner wanted the two officers to be in position to immediately coordinate recovery operations using any available local forces. In doing so, they would be involved in some of the most desperate rescue attempts of the war.

Seamon went to Song Be to meet elements of the 1st Brigade of the 101st Airborne. On February 11, the unit received a report that a POW camp with thirty Americans was located along the Song Be River. Upon arriving, Seamon learned that "the source had told a Vietnamese Catholic priest one of the VC interrogators was going to defect and confirm the existence of the camp. The source could actually read a map, which was very rare. He drew a sketch of the camp, gave us the defensive positions and descriptions of the POWs. He also agreed to lead a recovery force to the area. I wanted to debrief the source further, but the Brigade chaplain, a Father Murphy, had established a rapport with the guy and he wouldn't let me. Murphy was an odd character. He carried a weapon and didn't mind a fight. Since I was raised a good Catholic and having graduated from Notre Dame, I wasn't prepared to disagree with him.

"When the interrogator didn't show, I organized a rather large force to raid the camp. Just as the unit was getting ready to depart, the American leading the group turns to his interpreter and says, 'Tell this guy [the source] that I will be right behind him, and if he leads us into an ambush my first bullet is going right into the back of his head.' Murphy went absolutely ballistic, threatening this SF officer with all kinds of terrible consequences if anything happened to the source. They launched the raid anyway but came up with a dry hole."

Meanwhile, Ogle was also deeply involved in rescue efforts. On February 6, two French Catholic priests were released who had been held captive by an NVA unit. They reported that seven American personnel were being held in a house south of the Redemptionist Seminary in Hue. The prisoners were tentatively identified as seven of the military-intelligence personnel missing from the 525th MI unit in Hue.[29]

Ogle received this information on February 8. Word was also quickly passed by MACV to the 1st Marine Division to make every effort to recover these personnel as rapidly as possible. Ogle immediately contacted the commander of the 1st Brigade, 1st Marine Division. "I asked him for a Marine rifle company to go in and get these guys. He looked at me and said, 'We're fighting for our god-damned lives here, I just can't do it.' I understood completely. In my entire year in the JPRC, this was the only time I was ever turned down for an operation. Hue was a disaster, bodies were still lying in the streets, some parts were secure and others weren't. The Seminary was in the unsecured part. When I went up with several other Americans to do a recon of the area, the guy standing right next to me was shot by a sniper. Afterwards, we started looking for some of the missing people. One was wounded and in U.S. custody. We found one dead in the streets. The body had already turned green. Later, I helped dig up the grave of another one. His hands were tied behind his back with commo wire and he had been assassinated."

Ogle hung around the area hoping for another chance. He got it on February 23, when two of the 525th MI soldiers escaped from their guards. Robert Hayhurst and Edward Dierling knocked out their lone guard after they were sent to wash their rice bowls in a nearby stream. Both were able to account for the whereabouts and conditions of the other American POWs recently captured in Hue along with the number of guards and the column's probable route.[30]

It was the precisely the situation Reisner had been looking for, but now it was a race against time. Nineteen Americans were being guarded by only four enemy. The escapees had pinpointed the area where only two days before they had last seen the prisoners. Despite the heavy fighting and the enormous drain on the American combat forces, Reisner badgered his superior, Colonel Singlaub, into diverting two teams of Nungs from another vital mission to intercept the POW column. Ogle also convinced the 1st Cav to supply a reaction force if heavy contact was made.

By February 25, everything was set in motion. In an operation code-named *Duval Sands,* two SOG *Bright Light* teams were to insert by helicopter and assault the column at first light the next day. This was a golden chance to recover a significant number of Americans, but Reisner was deeply worried about the weather. "I had seen the fog in that area and I knew it was a problem, especially since the day before had been clear. I was begging the communication officers to keep a circuit open. I tried to maintain constant contact with the operations officer at Phu Bai, the base where the helicopters were staged at. When the comm guys shut me down I turned to the NSA guys, who had their own commo, and begged them. They were also concerned about some of their people in the Danang area, but the station commander had managed to get them out."

Reisner sat up all night watching in growing frustration as the hourly weather reports came in. The haze was mounting. By first light the conditions had been reduced to "zero zero," no visibility and no ceiling. Impossible flying weather. According to Reisner, the Ops officer called him and said, "'We just can't do it.' This was a major blow and I felt like a deflated balloon. I had been awake for two days and nights living on coffee, Cokes, and cigarettes. I believed it was a sure thing, one of our best opportunities. We were getting lots of support because one of the POWs was CIA, and the CAS folks wanted him back because he was a guy who they felt was very important."

Despite the tremendous efforts of Ogle and Reisner, the enemy had slipped away under the cover of the morning fog, taking the nineteen POWs to their separate fates. The JPRC, however, still had one last chance.

Searching for Civilians: Blood, Benge, and Olsen

As heavy fighting continued to rage around Hue, the North Vietnamese offensive was creating havoc in other areas as well. The city of Ban Me Thuot in the Central Highlands, the scene of the 1962 leprosarium attack, was partially overrun. Mike Benge was the head of USAID in the city and was one of the senior ranking Americans there. He had served in Vietnam previously, and remembers that "every Tet, a good friend of mine and I would celebrate the holiday together at my house. We always used to remark how Tet would be a perfect opportunity for the communists to attack, as there was so much gunfire from the carousing ARVN troops that you could never tell if any real fighting broke out."

"Although I warned the intelligence people over a build-up of NVA troops that the Montagnards had informed me about, they ignored me. So this Tet was no different. We were sitting on my balcony having a drink, listening to all the Chinese firecrackers, when I remarked how the VC had missed another great opportunity to overrun the city. We raised a toast to each other, and just as we clinked glasses an eight-one-millimeter mortar round exploded in my front yard. I said 'Shit, maybe this is the year!'

"After a firefight that night, the next morning I called the MACV compound to find out what was happening and what to do about the civilians. They didn't know, so I got in my jeep and started rounding up people. I had no clue that most of the city had been overrun."[31]

Benge drove out to various parts of the city to help move the American civilians toward the more secure MACV compound and also to find volunteers to assist at the local hospital, since he thought the fighting had probably caused heavy casualties. On his last stop to visit some American civilian volunteers, he was attempting to turn his jeep around "when a thirteen-man NVA psy-op team jumped up from a ditch and pointed their weapons at me. One had a B-40 [an antitank rocket] aimed directly at me. I had a small pistol with five rounds in it. My math skills instantly divided five into thirteen and came up with 'I'm in trouble.' The scene was almost surrealistic. The leader of the team had a haircut like Hitler complete with a little Hitler-style mustache. He points his AK-47 at me and says in this heavy Oriental accent, 'Surrender, humane and lenient treatment.'"

Benge was moved to an NVA HQ. From there he was marched to the leprosarium, where he watched nightmarish scenes: The NVA executed several Montagnards, including one of the guards at his own house. He was threatened with a loaded pistol against his head while being interrogated by an English-speaking NVA cadre. Finally he was moved to a temporary camp, where he witnessed the execution of another Montagnard. Several days later, two American missionaries, Henry Blood and Betty Olsen, were brought into the camp.

After the raid at Song Be, on March 20 Reisner sent Fred Seamon to help recover the three civilians lost at Ban Me Thuot. An escapee from a VC prison reported that a large number of American, Vietnamese, and Montagnard POWs were being held in an area to the east. A recon team from the nearby Special Forces camp was moved into the area. A thousand meters from the camp they ran into a VC patrol, but they managed to escape under the cover of an air strike. The attack, however, enabled an ARVN NCO to escape from the VC camp and he also reported the presence of the three Americans. The 173rd Airborne Brigade immediately landed two companies to conduct a sweep of the area, but found that the camp had already been moved.

On April 3, one of the Montagnards who worked for Benge as a translator escaped from the new camp location. He reentered friendly lines on April 6. Seamon quickly returned to Ban Me Thuot and he and the Province Senior Advisor coordinated a raid for the night of April 7. The Montagnard guided the helicopter assault and there was a brief contact with a VC element when the force landed. The camp was entered but was found to be recently abandoned. Pigs and chickens were found caged and a large rice stock was located. POW buildings were open, and the layout was as described by the source. He was rewarded with $18,000 SVN ($153 US).[32]

The JPRC continued to watch for any additional information. On the first attempt, they had gotten near. On the second, they had just missed them by a day. Benge recalls that "After the Montagnard escaped, the VC moved us deeper into the mountains. We were taken to a cave and camp complex where I contracted cerebral malaria. I was delirious for five weeks, but the VC allowed Henry Blood to go to one of the other camps." From this camp, two more Montagnards escaped on May 3 and brought word of the Americans.

Seamon hurried back to Ban Me Thuot for the third time. The plan, dubbed *Rayburn Cane,* was delayed for five days after one of the Montagnards got sick. Using the time to further interview them, Seamon discovered that the men had not actually seen the cave, they had only heard about it. On May 25, two Special Forces CIDG teams led by American personnel were inserted. One team was immediately engaged by an enemy unit and a reaction platoon was sent in to assist them. After driving away the enemy forces, the team remained in the area for several days searching for the cave. Finally on May 30 they stumbled into two Vietnamese men being used as slave labor for the camp complex. Using these men as guides, they carefully reconnoitered the area and picked up additional Vietnamese prisoners. One of these men was recognized by one of the Montagnard sources. The team was then led to the cave, only to find it recently abandoned. In the weekly report Reisner stated, "This area remains of intense interest to the

JPRC. It is a known VC PW detention area and the VC are unlikely to leave the area. . . ."[33]

Seamon and the JPRC had just missed the three again. "I remember spending so much time in the Ban Me Thuot area looking for them. My only satisfaction was in recovering the Vietnamese. The VC were using them as slave labor to farm the local area. When I came back I was exhausted from the continual attempts to rescue them. It was heartbreaking to me that we didn't recover the three civilians."[34]

9. The Year of Releases

I consider reference telegram, which declines to pay First Class travel for released pilots in event they travel commercial, to be just about the most penny-pinching piece of bureaucratese I have ever encountered. . . . If Defense declines to pay more than Tourist Class fare, my entire country team has volunteered that we will take up a collection to pay the difference from our own pockets. I suspect I could get a great many other volunteers throughout CINCPAC command who would be happy to chip in to buy one-way tickets (First Class) from Washington to Hanoi for the green-eye-shaded penny pinchers who drafted reference telegram.
—Ambassador William H. Sullivan, reacting in a cable to the initial refusal by
a DOD official to pay first-class airfare for three American POWs just released
from Hanoi

The State Department continued to face a door locked against any access to the DRV's American prisoners. The U.S. government demanded the North Vietnamese allow the International Red Cross entry into the prison camps, and had repeatedly called Hanoi's attention to its obligations under the Geneva Convention. The requests for increased mail privileges, prison inspections, and a list of POWs and dead were immediately rejected. At the end of December 1967, President Johnson suggested that the Vatican send a mission to both North and South Vietnam to inspect the prisoner-of-war camps. Despite the Pope's personal plea, the North refused to allow a Vatican representative into their country and refused any Red Cross inspections. Nothing moved the DRV.

While the North Vietnamese were trumpeting to the world their "humane and lenient treatment" for the American war criminals who had bombed their country, in reality the men in the filthy cells of the DRV prison system were systematically undergoing brutal torture and degradation. America was seemingly helpless to prevent such treatment. The State Department's only success was in generating a storm of protest over the DRV's proposed war-crimes trials and forced public confessions. Additionally, the U.S. military and the Embassy personnel in Saigon put a great deal of energy into improving the South's POW facilities, hoping to focus world attention on the contrast between the GVN and the DRV.

Despite the tumultuous events it held in store, 1968 would be a year of releases and escapes, allowing the U.S. government to believe again for a brief moment that its efforts to bring about the early liberation of American POWs were finally paying off.

Releasing Prisoners: Two Pairs from the South

The *Buttercup* channel bore more fruit on January 23, 1968, when two Americans held prisoner in the MR-5 camp were released. Marine Lance Corporal José Agosto-Santos and Army Private First Class Luis Ortiz-Rivera returned to U.S. control after being released by their captors about fifteen kilometers west of Tam Ky in Quang Ngai province. Both were immediately given a military intelligence escort and taken to a hospital for medical checkups.

Unknown initially to their debriefers, these were the first released Americans who had been heavily indoctrinated. Both men lied concerning the location of their POW camp and whether they had seen any other American POWs. They claimed to have walked for eight days and knew nothing of the location of their camp or other Americans. However, two days later under increasingly "detailed examination, Agosto-Santos changed his story and admitted walking only four days from the camp, and stated ten other U.S. PWs were in the camp. He could identify three, and confirm the death of one other. . . . When confronted with this evidence, Ortiz-Rivera also changed his story. He produced a written list naming ten U.S. PWs alive in the camp, confirmed the death of another (same man as Agosto-Santos named), and gave information which may lead to the identification of a Caucasian living with the VC guards at the camp."[1]

The debriefings of the two produced some startling insights. Agosto-Santos claimed he was released because he obeyed all camp rules and helped prepare NLF propaganda material. "At a release ceremony, he agreed to return to Puerto Rico and instigate rebellion against the existing government. He said he would have done anything they wanted him to in order to be released. . . . Among those PW's they identified were two Marines, Corporal Earl Weatherman and Private Robert Garwood, who they claim are not being treated as PW's and have free run of the camp. They report that Garwood occasionally accompanied VC units on operations and that Weatherman. . . lives with the guards rather than the other US PW's. Santos also stated that he and Rivera agreed between themselves not to provide info to US authorities concerning identities of US PW's and locations of PW camps. Santos' reasons were his disenchantment with the US military . . . and the initial obligation he felt towards the VC for saving his life. . . . A psychological study could be written on Santos. . . ."[2]

The Army reported that Ortiz-Rivera "had no idea of PW camp locations. He cannot read maps, and has no concept of distance or directions. Subject did identify all PWs in the camp and provided descriptions of camp personnel. Subject also provided sketches of all five camps of his internment. The subject reported that he believes the VC maintain records on the PWs and send monthly reports to NLF Hqs."[3]

After the two enlisted men were freed, another major release in the South occurred when the Hanoi news agency responded that the NLF had decided to release two American civilian females captured in Hue, a Quaker schoolteacher named Sandra Johnson and Doctor Marjorie Nelson. This release was another pure propaganda ploy. The women had been carefully treated and deliberately picked for release because of their known sympathy to the VC cause. A German nurse named Renate Kuhnen, who was abducted when the Pat Smith hospital in Kontum was overrun, was not released despite appeals by the Bishop of Kontum that she was not an American and did not work for the GVN. Eventually, she was let go a year later, after she made propaganda statements for the NLF.

On the morning of April 1, the VC placed Johnson and Nelson on a bus heading for Hue. They were in good health but initially refused to participate in any intelligence briefings. Jack Reisner remembers that it was obvious the women had been well treated and were a propaganda tool. They made taped propaganda broadcasts for the NLF which were prominently played on Hanoi Radio. "When we wanted to debrief them, one said to me 'I promised I wouldn't say anything.' We could have picked up some good intelligence from them, but they refused to talk to us." Eventually, the women did agree to speak with Army intelligence, but little was gained. "They were able to give the

names of several POWs who were with them but would not give camp locations or the names of their captors."[4] It was obvious that the communists were
carefully choosing who would be released. Both sets of POWs were, in the
minds of the communists, sympathetic to their cause. The Party policy of "humane and lenient treatment," which was being repeatedly instilled in the releasees, was starting to pay off.

. . . and Three from the North

To draw American attention away from the impending Tet Offensive, the DRV
decided to release the first set of POWs from the prisons in the North. Hanoi
Radio announced that Air Force officers Captain John Black and Major Norris
Overly plus Navy Ensign David Matheny would be released in keeping with its
"humanitarian and lenient policy" and because they "had shown a repentant attitude during the period of detention."[5]

In keeping with their new policy of trying to release POWs directly to antiwar
groups, Hanoi contacted David Dellinger and asked him to arrange for the transfer of the POWs in Hanoi to an antiwar group. Dellinger designated the "Committee for Support of Released Prisoners," who chose Professor Howard Zinn of
Boston University and Father Daniel Berrigan of Cornell to travel to Hanoi and
receive the three American POWs. The two departed New York on January 31
and arrived in Vientiane on February 2.

The only available air transportation from Vientiane into Hanoi was an International Control Commission (ICC) flight. The Tet Offensive had forced the
cancellation of the flight on February 2 and 6, and to prevent the movement of
capital out of the country from the many wealthy Saigon merchants the GVN
had banned all commercial flights out of the city until the fighting died down.
Without air transport, the release of the pilots appeared to be in jeopardy.

Reisner was ordered to get the ICC plane out at all costs. "I called in every chit
I had in-country to get that plane out of Saigon. I went to see the ICC people to
send their crew out for the next flight on the ninth. They said it was too risky, so
I offered to send a guard force. They accepted. I called an old friend in the Australian Embassy to convince the Australian ICC officer to leave on the plane.
Talking directly to another Embassy without going through our Embassy was a
major no-no, and I was really risking my neck. I had to coordinate across the different command elements to line up support. Finally, I had to get the South Vietnamese government to allow the plane to leave [for Vientiane]. General Ky lived
on Tan Son Nhut, and I literally begged the Commander of the 7th AF to go see

him to get the plane released. He agreed, and eventually President Thieu allowed the plane to depart on the ninth.

"The normal flight schedule allowed the plane a thirty-minute window to leave Saigon. They were guaranteed protection from all sides if they left during this time frame. I was in the control tower when we got final authorization. Just as the plane began moving, this guy comes running out trying to catch the plane. He was smuggling gold in his suitcase and overcoat. The police snatched him up and arrested him. The window was closing, less than a few minutes remained. The ICC people wanted to stop. I started yelling 'No, don't stop, keep going!' Finally the plane began taxiing and took off. It was nip and tuck getting that plane off to pick up the three Americans."

The POWs and the two antiwar activists arrived back in Vientiane on February 16 and were met at the airport by Sullivan. Reisner had earlier arranged for the POWs to be returned to the states via U.S. military aeromedical aircraft, but Zinn and Berrigan preferred to go commercial. Sullivan reported, "It took forty minutes after arrival ICC plane before I could obtain clear decision from pilots that they preferred travel by U.S. military aircraft. I wish to stress, however, that delay was entirely due to dialectic diddling by Zinn and Berrigan, which placed serious burden on pilots' conscience. . . . Nexus of discussion was fact that North Vietnamese authorities had told pilots that they preferred pilots accompany Zinn and Berrigan on commercial aircraft and 'indicated' their action would have bearing upon their decision with respect release other prisoners.

"It was clear that Zinn and Berrigan had played very heavily upon this feature in their conversations with pilots during flight from Hanoi. . . . After pilots chose air-attaché plane, both Zinn and Berrigan advised me that they felt compelled to tell press I had used pressure, and had 'destroyed basis of past two weeks work.' It is unfortunate but perhaps inevitable that squabble took place in this way. Zinn had been prepared to accept pilots' decision . . . but Berrigan emotionally balked, and because of his vociferous protest, matter ended on a sour note. I would recommend the Vatican put him on Chaplain's duty in Khe Sanh."[6]

The initial debriefs of the three produced a surprising amount of intelligence. They enabled the military to change the status of 39 pilots previously listed as MIA to captured and confirmed that 63 other pilots currently listed as captured were indeed alive.[7] Further debriefings produced 172 names of men they had either seen or heard about. Also, the three officers were also able to confirm the Hanoi prison camp located in the Citadel, called the "Country Club." This confirmation was aided by the camp mock-up provided by the CIA. To aid in the debriefing, the Agency also provided photographs of Hanoi and photos of suspected and confirmed prison camps.[8]

More than just camp layouts was gained from the debriefings. According to Claude Watkins, one piece of very important information was revealed. "This was the first direct confirmation that the POWs were using the tap code. However, we couldn't understand their version. Then Bob Boroughs, the Navy officer who earlier had smuggled in the note to Stockdale, determined that the POWs had reversed the letter sequence. After that, we knew they were successfully communicating and our hopes for them rose."

Sullivan attempted to analyze the communist strategy in releasing the three men. It appears, he said, that "Hanoi is sensitive to needling. Free world rejection of earlier photo's (e.g., Harriman's statement that they were 'travesty') struck home and caused them decide release some prisoners who would bear out their statements about good treatment. . . . Other consideration, perhaps for frank appraisal with Zinn, is probability that Vientiane release point served Hanoi quite well. First, they got considerable publicity. Second, as bonus, they got contradictions between peace group and US government due to dust-up over travel plans. It is interesting to note that Hanoi broadcast on subject of release made no mention of travel on military plane, which was central point on Berrigan rhubarb. I wonder how much of this Zinn-Berrigan created by their own initiative, getting Hanoi officials to endorse their own patent desires to carry these three boys home as trophies. This question arises particularly because DRV embassy reps watched and noted in detail all preparations made in dry run last Friday when attaché plane was conspicuously standing by. . . ."[9]

As much as Hanoi wanted the antiwar effort to swing American public opinion, the peace crowd wanted it even more. According to one captured document, "The anti-war movement of the American people is growing. The various U.S. organizations have often requested us to provide them with souvenirs and papers with personal handwriting or other items found on dead or wounded U.S. soldiers such as: ID cards, letters, photos, personal papers, handkerchiefs with embroidered initials, military badges, notebooks, diaries, etc. They will be used as evidence for motivating the American people to oppose the U.S. aggressive war in Vietnam. The troops should be encouraged to collect more of these items and send them for study and subsequent help to the U.S. anti-war organizations."[10]

For Hanoi, the true strategy behind these releases was simple. Another captured document declared, "It is imperative that we try to gain the sympathy of the . . . American people and the people of the satellite countries and make them oppose the United States policy in Vietnam. This sympathy holds some prospect of gaining ground. As a consequence, we should have an appropriate policy designed to win over and weaken them. . . ."[11]

The Next Release

Following up on their attempt to gain a battlefield edge on the U.S. government with a prisoner release during Tet, the North Vietnamese tried to influence the just-started Paris Peace Talks with the release in July of an additional three Americans from the cells of Hanoi. Again, the DRV requested that the pilots be turned over to American pacifists.

USAF officers Major James F. Low, Major Fred N. Thompson, and Captain Joe V. Carpenter were to be escorted home by Anne Scheer, the wife of Robert Scheer, editor of *Ramparts* magazine, Vernon Grizzard, an antidraft organizer, and Stewart Meachum of Philadelphia, a Quaker who was Secretary of the American Friends Service Committee and who had close ties to Averell Harriman.

The vast majority of POWs in Hanoi, almost all of them officers with college educations, had strenuously tried to abide by the Code of Conduct, with varying degrees of success. Article Three of the Code stated that a prisoner could not accept parole. Some from the first group, particularly Jim Black, claim they had no idea they were being released. The second group, however, was very different. Lieutenant Colonel Ted Guy, one of the few to be captured in Laos, ordered Major Low not to go. Guy recalls, "I was the ranking officer in the prison section where we were being held at. When I ordered Low not to leave, he told me, 'Fuck you, Colonel, I'm going!'"[12]

As chief POW policymaker and negotiator, Harriman was deeply concerned about the travel of the pilots from Vientiane back to the United States, in view of the major flap that had so angered the antiwar groups after the last release. Zinn and Berrigan told the press that the decision by the pilots to return via military transport was an example of the U.S. military's "cold-hearted brutality," forced upon the pilots by Sullivan. Harriman sought out Colonel Ha Van Lau of the DRV's Paris delegation to clarify matters. In discussions, Lau expressed no preference as to how the pilots traveled. Harriman was "informed that the civilians could return with the pilots on a military plane if they wished to do so and that they had been so informed."[13]

The peace delegation specifically flew to Paris, however, to meet with Harriman and clear up the travel issue. Anne Scheer agreed that while the DRV "had put no conditions on the method of return . . . their people had made it clear to us that [they] were unhappy over the way the last prisoners were handled in February." Furthermore, "It would be a proper gesture to Hanoi to permit the pilots to fly commercial."[14]

Again, it seems that the return arrangements were more important to the antiwar protesters than to Hanoi. The reason they wanted to fly commercial was simple: publicity for them and their movement. "Hanoi and the peace movement are agreed that the men must be allowed to come to this country on a commercial flight so that they can hold an immediate press conference," Robert Scheer said. "The last group of pilots freed by the North were picked up by the military and never heard from publicly. If this were to occur again it would be very difficult to arrange future releases, since it would be interpreted as a victory for the Government rather than a sign from Hanoi to the American peace movement."[15]

As soon as the Americans arrived in Hanoi on July 18, a ceremony was held formally releasing the men from their DRV prison. The men thanked the Vietnamese people and the camp commander for their good treatment. Captain Carpenter promised to "explain the attitude of the Vietnamese people and their great determination in the fight for the independence and unification of Vietnam against the U.S. aggressors."[16] According to the French reporter on the scene, the men were turned over initially to a "Vietnamese Committee for Solidarity with the United States People" who then released them to the Americans.

The North was taking no chances that the American peace delegates would fail to understand the importance of the POW release. The DRV had activated this front organization in October 1967 "to meet the pressing requirement of a friendly relationship between the two peoples, and the intimate interest of the drive of the American people against the war of aggression waged by the US government in South Vietnam." Its main purpose was to "maintain relations with, and assist, all social organizations and progressive workers, intellectuals, servicemen who wish, together with the entire people of South Vietnam, to coordinate the struggle with the American people in order to end the war . . ."[17] After the war, this committee was absorbed by the Vietnam-American Association.

The State Department immediately determined that the appearance of this committee "was obviously timed for the anti-war demonstrations scheduled this week in the United States . . . The establishment of the Front Committee, coming on the heels of a meeting between Hanoi-Front representatives and American citizens at Bratislava [a Czech town where Tom Hayden and others had gathered to plot antiwar strategy], further indicates that Hanoi and the Front have decided to intensify their effort to make and maintain direct contacts with anti-war groups in the U.S. and elsewhere."[18]

The ICC flight had no trouble this time in lifting off from Saigon, but the released pilots and the antiwar group did not arrive back in Laos until August 2 due to delays by the North Vietnamese. Against the advice of Sullivan, the pilots decided to fly home in a commercial plane. Upon learning that some DOD accountant had denied first class travel fare back to the States, Sullivan flew into a rage and offered to pay for the difference in cost by collecting money among his embassy staff. DOD quickly corrected the error, but was more concerned, given the POW's earlier statements, that the choice the pilots had made indicated that they might have been heavily indoctrinated, despite the DRV assurances that no pressure had been brought to bear on them.

After arriving in Laos, the group chose to remain overnight in Vientiane. The pilots stayed in the home of the Embassy air attaché, Colonel Robert Tyrell. Tyrell reported back through Air Force channels the results of an informal briefing with the three ex-prisoners. He wrote that "All three appeared in excellent spirits, good health both mentally and physically. . . . One of the most predominant facts presented concerned good treatment they received throughout captivity. They gave impression that good treatment for most prisoners is rule rather than exception for those slated for release.

"Thompson's pick-up as follows: He was taken to a village where he was overnight guest. . . . He was then moved to an intermediate location and interrogated for five-day period. Because of poor English on part of interrogators, questions were written and Thompson required to provide written answers. At completion he was forced, under duress of a guard bayonet pointed at his temple, to sign questionnaire. Throughout this period, interrogation seemed to emphasize personal rather than technical or military matters.

"Thompson and Carpenter believed they were earmarked for possible release very early in their captivity. They feel that how one reacts during capture and screening process sets stage for treatment thereafter. . . . During the frequent interrogations or conversations, no Russians or Chinese were observed in or around the compound. . . . Low estimates the total prisoner population to be around 700. . . . He [Low] is firmly convinced the US needs the complete list and must take a hard stand in getting prisoners released. He reported there is talk that some pilots will be tried and unless we know who is there and insist on release, they may spend a long time in captivity."[19]

Besides the intelligence gained from the three pilots, the Quaker Stewart Meachum was also secretly providing information to the United States. Through his ties to Harriman, he agreed to be debriefed by State. "Mr. Meachum stated that during his second interview with the releasees a Caucasian [male] tape-recorded the interview. One of the North Vietnamese told Mr. Meachum that the man was a 'cooperating' prisoner. Mr. Meachum did not offer any further information on this prisoner. Meachum did state that the North Vietnamese made no conditions whatever regarding the release of the PWs."[20]

With the release of the two groups of POWs, the State Department once again attempted to prod the North into more releases by raising the possibility of reciprocal releases. This time, however, the United States would use the few NVA captives it held in custody, a group of 14 NVA seamen captured on the high seas after their PT boats had been sunk by the United States Navy. Since these men had not been captured in South Vietnam but instead on the open ocean, MACV decided that the agreement that the U.S. armed forces would turn over all prisoners to the GVN did not apply.

When informed of the U.S. decision to release the NVA sailors, the GVN quietly acquiesced. Initially, Secretary Rusk had hoped to quickly return the men via the same ICC flight channel, but the DRV chargé in Vientiane expressed Hanoi's refusal to receive the men, especially if any publicity was involved. Finally, after much discussion of a safe means to return them plus a lengthy delay that eventually involved the ICRC interviewing the seamen to see whether or not they desired to return, they were sent home on October 21 in a small boat that was launched from a Navy ship 15 miles off the coast of the North Vietnamese city of Vinh.

Once again, the United States had tried to coax the DRV into creating some mechanism for exchange, only to be soundly rebuffed. The North was only interested in releasing prisoners to peace groups for the purpose of achieving favorable publicity to counteract charges of POW mistreatment or failure to implement the Geneva Accords. At the same time they were hoping to buttress the antiwar movement and thereby bring pressure on the U.S. government at the Paris peace talks. While each individual effort probably accomplished little, in the aggregate the North's actions supplied the doves with all the ammunition they needed to continue their vociferous protests against the war. Right or wrong, they were playing into Hanoi's expressed desires to use the POW issue to foment domestic turbulence in the United States.

But Hanoi had another agenda. They hoped the POWs would act as agents of influence in their native country. While their efforts were generally unsuccessful with the American POWs, one captured document outlined their intentions succinctly: "We release POWs like raising pigeons to be released; later they will bring back the flock to our house."[21]

Escapes

More Americans escaped in 1968 than all the other years combined. All escaped from communist captivity in South Vietnam, mainly due to a lack of vigilance by the guards. It appeared that, finally, the United States was catching up with the odds.

At the same time as Santos and Ortiz-Rivera were released, two other Americans escaped from their captors on January 22 in western Quang Tin province in I Corps. The two men, Marine Corporal Steven Nelson and Private First Class Michael Roha, had been held for two weeks by the VC. They told a story of such a remarkably easy escape that, at first, the military-intelligence personnel were suspicious. According to the two Marines, their two guards became very lax, one leaving them for thirty minutes to return the lunch bowls while the other slept. After the noon meal, they were not checked again until late in the afternoon.

Determining their guards' pattern, the Marines one day slipped past the sleeping guard and headed in the direction of the sun. Successfully evading the VC, they finally stumbled into a Marine outpost. At their debriefing, the men said "they were treated like guests by the VC—given clothes, three meals a day, vitamin pills, and sandals for their bleeding feet. They were not pressed for information and efforts at indoctrinating them were mild. . . . The unanswered question is whether they were allowed to escape with their tale of good treatment for propaganda purposes, or was their guard really sleeping?"[22] According to the JPRC report, Nelson had been reported killed when he was lost. Like Mark Twain's, the report of his death was premature.

Another Marine, William Taliaferro, escaped or was released by the VC on February 13. He was carrying two handwritten documents in Vietnamese, one a release order and the other a description of medical treatment provided to him.

A more intriguing story of capture and escape occurred when on the afternoon of April 15, Specialist/5 Donald E. Martin managed to elude his guards and return to American control. Martin had been captured on March 2 in Lam Dong province. After he had spent several days in captivity, an English-speaking cadre named Yem was assigned to him. Yem showed Martin the ID card and other personnel property of a man from Martin's unit named Robert Cline. Martin believed he recognized Cline and knew that he had been killed in action earlier. Ominously, Yem showed Martin a small black-and-white photograph of two Americans standing with a group of VC. He was told that one of them, a Negro, had been a sergeant in Special Forces, but had joined the VC to fight with them. The other, who looked "Spanish, Negro, or Puerto Rican," deserted from the U.S. Army. One of them was dressed in black pajamas, the other in NVA khaki-type uniform. They were carrying AK-47s with magazines and were wearing enemy-style field gear. He was not told the names of the individuals or when the picture was taken.[23]

His guards also told him he was being moved toward the Liberation Army Headquarters. In making his escape, Martin claimed to have killed two of his guards while the other three were asleep. A Vietnamese civilian aided him in reaching an outpost of U.S. Advisory Team 38. A reward was paid to the man who helped Martin make his way to freedom. Martin claimed not to have seen any other POWs; however, on the afternoon of March 27 or 28 he was told that he was one thousand meters from a hospital where two wounded American POWs, a lieutenant and a PFC, were being held. The JPRC believed they were probably Lieutenant John C. Dunn and Private First Class James M. Ray, captured nearby on March 19, 1968.[24]

The JPRC attempted to locate the hospital using infrared and camouflage-detection photography but were unable to find it in the dense jungle growth. Shortly after Martin escaped, another enterprising specialist/5 named William B. Taylor made his break for freedom when U.S. gunships strafed a VC base camp in Kien Giang province in the Delta. Taylor had been MIA since March 20, when his airplane was lost on a recon flight. The pilot was killed in the crash.

Later in the month, another two Marines used their wits to escape from communist control. Sergeant Albert J. Potter and Corporal Frank C. Iodice were captured on May 30. The pair told their debriefers that the cadre in charge of the escort party asked the two what they thought of the war. The Marines replied that "two countries simply disagreed so they fought. The cadre said 'this is not correct.' The cadre said they were fighting injustice. He then asked subjects to lay down your arms and fight for the Liberation Army or prepare to go to Hanoi.

"Potter and Iodice reported that during the day the high cadre commander conducted brief (approx. 15 min.) interrogation. Subjects were interrogated separately. During the course of interrogation subjects disclosed no information. The cadre knew personal data which could only have been obtained from a source with access to subjects and their assignments."[25]

During an ARVN attack, the VC attempted to hide the Americans by shoving both into a nearby hole. A cover was placed on top and they were told they would be shot if they tried to leave. Despite the guards' admonition, the two attempted to move the cover but were unable to dislodge it. Fortunately, a nearby air strike badly weakened the structure and the two managed to remove it. The two low-crawled about a hundred meters, then bumped into an ARVN patrol. At their debriefing, the two related how the guards had told them that "five

U.S. POWs had been captured and were hiding nearby. However, the location of the captured U.S. could not be fixed with enough accuracy to warrant making a recovery attempt."[26]

Finally, Sergeant Buddy Wright, engaged on a long-range reconnaissance patrol, was captured on September 22 in Cambodia when he became separated from his fellow patrol members. Several days later, he untied his ropes and successfully evaded the enemy for ten days, returning to American lines on October 6.

The quick thinking and resourcefulness of these men saved them from the horrors of captivity. The remark by the enemy cadre in charge of Potter and Iodice about fighting for the revolution remains a fascinating detail, as does the picture shown to Martin. Unfortunately, this important information concerning possible American collaborators remains almost totally unexplored by the author and other researchers because the vast majority of POW debriefs remain highly classified. The two Puerto Ricans, Agosto-Santos and Ortiz-Rivera, also described the collaboration of two Americans held at their camp, Earl Weatherman and Bobby Garwood. Apparently, the communists were succeeding in convincing more Americans than just those two to work for the VC cause. How many more is still one of the great secrets of the war.

Improving the JPRC: Keeping the Pressure On

Reisner decided to conduct a review of the past efforts of the JPRC to determine if any improvements could be made. Ogle refloated Buchanan's idea of changing the MACV policy to permit local commanders more flexibility in conducting raids. MACV agreed, and in April a message was sent to all field commanders encouraging them to act quickly to recover POWs when perishable information was acquired. The previous requirement of JPRC authorization for POW recovery operations was removed, and close coordination was increased in order to lower reaction time and multiply the probability of recovering American POWs.[27] The JPRC developed maps for each Corps area showing the probable locations for POW camps while the CIA put together a "Summary and Location" document listing intelligence reports in chronological order and detailing eleven primary target areas, including Sam Neua.[28]

As a former employee of the National Security Agency (NSA), Reisner also hoped to prod that Agency into supplying more POW information. The NSA is one of the most secretive of U.S. intelligence agencies. It was established by presidential directive in 1952 as a separately organized agency within the DOD under the direction, authority, and control of the Secretary of Defense.[29] The

NSA is responsible for the collection of foreign Signals Intelligence (SIGINT), which results in the production of Communications Intelligence (COMINT) for the government. NSA produces SIGINT in accordance with the objectives, requirements, and priorities of the Director of Central Intelligence (DCI), as the CIA sets the agenda for the intelligence-collection priorities of the United States. Each military service also has signal intercept units, but these units report directly to the NSA.

Reisner first came to Vietnam in 1964 as the Air Force liaison to the NSA and he helped set up some of the early monitoring stations, especially around the Danang area. Every day, he recalls, he went down to the communications center to "bug them for information. I knew some of these guys personally. I had worked for NSA in Europe and when I left JPRC and went to PACAF I was the top SIGINT officer in the Pacific Air Force. Even though the NSA had a hell of a lot of equipment in Vietnam, we never got much from them. There were always huge internal battles over using SIGINT real-time. The services complained bitterly about NSA siphoning off money and people and then wouldn't give them any intelligence back. I think the first time we got anything was some shoot-downs near Hanoi, but there was never any specific instance of POW movement."

The SIGINT capabilities of NSA during the war were enormous, ranging from specially designed aircraft-collection systems to the more standard unit, the field intercept station. Although field stations had been the backbone of NSA since its inception, NSA also sent aircraft on SIGINT reconnaissance missions along the periphery of Vietnam and over other parts of Southeast Asia on a daily basis. These aircraft included the manned hi-tech EC-135 *Combat Apple,* the U-2 *Olympic Torch,* and the EC-130 *Comfy Gator.* The collection capabilities were so unique that the airplanes were virtually flying antennas. This massive electronic intercept capability not only represented the largest SIGINT collection effort ever mounted against a target nation in wartime, but also was the most productive and successful effort ever mounted in the area of intelligence analysis in support of the national interests of the United States.

However, its efforts were directed more at logistics flow and the movements and locations of enemy units than at tracking POWs. Eventually, Reisner's efforts paid off in July 1968 when NSA published a list of SIGINT POW intelligence requirements. The NSA directed its field stations and airborne collectors to "provide any pertinent communications concerning U.S. PW's. . . . The above information is required by the Joint Personnel Recovery Center to assist in the recovery of U.S. missing/captured personnel. Intelligence concerning U.S. PW's and camp locations has been very sparse and sporadic. Particular emphasis should be placed on [redacted] the Delta area of South Vietnam, along the South Vietnam/Cambodia border areas, and the Sam Neua area in Laos where there are collateral reports of U.S. PW sightings."[30]

Despite the constant activity in South Vietnam, Reisner had not forgotten Laos. He was especially anxious about the Sam Neua area. "We had continual reports of between 3 to 5 guys in that area. I wanted to keep the pressure on CAS to keep looking for them." Reisner sent JPRC Captain Dave McNabb to one of the CAS-SOG coordination meetings at Udorn to begin planning to free the POWs in the cave area, to begin confirming the presence of U.S. POWs in various locations in Laos, and also to begin cleaning up the list of camps. A meeting was held with CAS and Embassy Vientiane representatives in Udorn on June 8 to discuss the location and identification of POWs in Laos.[31]

The first priority was gathering a complete list of names of POWs and MIAs. By late July, the JPRC sent their list for comparison to the CIA Chief of Station (COS) in Vientiane, Ted Shackley.[32] Shackley cabled CIA HQ at Langley, Virginia, that "JPRC has compiled an updated list . . . on PW/MIA in Laos as a result of our request for comments on accuracy and completeness of the list provided. . . . Additional comments from JPRC indicate [name redacted] and Milius, Paul L. [the Navy OP-2 pilot lost in February] are listed by the JPRC as KIA because their aircraft exploded on impact. . . . The JPRC list is unofficial and not releasable to the public; but it does represent their best estimate of the current status of US MIA and PW detained in Laos and is continually revised."[33]

Another matter of concern was the list of enemy POW camps in Laos. The JPRC had already compiled a list of POW camps in Indochina based on defector interrogations and escapee reports. Under Ambassador Sullivan's direction, CAS and 7/13th AF, the Air Force headquarters in Thailand, had placed the Lao POW camps as off-limit targets in the Bombing Encyclopedia (BE), which was a list of targets developed for each country. Regardless of the veracity of the sighting, however, POW-camp sightings automatically generated a no-bomb area, and eventually the communists figured this policy out and began moving their logistics facilities close to these areas.

In response, the Air Force began requesting reevaluations of some specific sites. But the problem of no-bomb areas kept growing and by September Sullivan was soliciting comments on this policy. Admiral Thomas H. Moorer, the Chief of Naval Operations, responded that "I concur with this policy. . . . I do not believe at this stage of the war that we should jeopardize the lives of either US or friendly POWs. . . . In considering the criteria used to establish the status of POW sites, I

am convinced from reading statements of US escapees that US personnel captured in southern Laos are being moved frequently and that established prison
compounds probably do not exist. However, in the absence of positive information to confirm the disestablishment of known POW sites, we should assume that
it continues to exist regardless of the passage of time. Until some reliable means
have been devised to establish prisoner activity in a known site, we should exercise prudence. It appears to me that additional effort is needed to verify the existence of POW sites in southern Laos. I would propose, therefore, that specific
reconnaissance efforts be mounted, with the resources now available to Ambassador Sullivan, to provide information on the existence of active POW sites."[34]

The decision was made to allow 36 months to elapse before bombing could
be resumed in an area reported to contain a POW camp. The military was at first
more concerned with southern Laos, and in December 1968 CAS forces reported that only four prisons existed in that area. These contained roughly three
hundred Lao military prisoners, none of whom were Americans. This was veri-
fied by a PL captain assigned to the PL South Laos Regional Headquarters who
rallied in September 1968, and who showed the CAS guerrillas the "supply requests submitted to South Laos Regional HQ during March 1968." The captain
also confirmed the presence of Americans in the Sam Neua area during late
1965.[35]

The problem of verifying POW camps and forbidding bombing attacks would
crop up again, and when Admiral Moorer became Chief of the JCS he did not
forget the men in the caves of Laos.

Debacle in Laos: The Loss of Site 85

As the bombing of North Vietnam intensified and the DRV's air defenses continued to grow stronger, American air losses began dramatically increasing. The Air
Force decided to engage in more night strikes and attacks in poor weather, both
of which required precision guidance. To provide the extremely accurate directions needed for these missions, the Air Force convinced Sullivan to allow them
to install a portable version of a highly sophisticated radar/navigational device on
a mountaintop deep in enemy territory. The peak, called Phou Pha Thi, was considered sacred in the Hmong religion. It was also about twenty-five miles east of
Sam Neua city, close to the North Vietnamese border.

It was an audacious gesture to put a small military outpost in the heart of
enemy territory. It was also a clear violation of the 1962 Geneva Accords on Lao
neutrality. The mountain was chosen because it was considered virtually impreg-

nable by both the CIA and the military; it had a sheer escarpment on one side and steep cliffs on two others. The fourth approach was heavily guarded by approximately seven hundred of Vang Pao's Hmong soldiers, which were later reinforced by a Thai infantry unit. Since it was also the base for a Hmong guerrilla outfit, CAS gave it the name Lima Site 85. It was one of the most top-secret installations in all of Southeast Asia and vitally important to the air war.

The Air Force was granted permission to install the advanced radar equipment on Phou Pha Thi along with a navigational system known as the Tactical Air Navigational system, or TACAN. The Air Force sent about sixteen "civilians" to run the installation. Eventually, the Air Force also assigned a Forward Air Guide, an Air Force officer located on the ground who called in air strikes in defense of the site when enemy forces began closing in. Two other Americans, CAS advisors who worked with the indigenous forces, completed the complement of U.S. personnel.

The TACAN site on the mountain was built in August 1966, although the radar did not became operational until November 1, 1967.[36] It was the only functional radar site of its type in Laos, although three other TACAN sites existed, including one at the town of Muong Phalane in southern Laos. Obviously aware of the importance of the TACAN sites, the communists decided to knock out the Muong Phalane site first. They feared that it might be involved in supporting an aerial counterattack against communist troops in the central and southern part of South Vietnam during the upcoming Tet Offensive. They attacked on Christmas Day, 1967, with a precision barrage of mortars followed immediately by an infantry assault. Most of the structures were damaged or destroyed, but not the TACAN equipment, which surprisingly emerged unscathed. However, two of the American technicians were killed in the attack.

The U.S. government's attempts to hide American military involvement in Laos included a practice known as "sheep-dipping," whereby military men were temporarily transferred out of the service and into a civilian position for a specific tour of duty. The men who occupied TACAN sites around Laos were provided with Lockheed Corporation identity cards and wore civilian clothes. The dead men now presented a political problem: how to properly account for them after the press reported the Pathet Lao attack.

At first, the State Department wanted to avoid referring to the two dead as Lockheed employees. Vientiane cabled back that they were "puzzled" by such a request, since "rather elaborate arrangements have been made to 'cover' certain personnel as Lockheed employees and they carry Lockheed identity cards. If they have been captured, they will probably say and their identity cards will substantiate that they are Lockheed employees. Believe we should stick with to this arrangement. With regard TACAN believe it would be preferable to refer to it as an Air America communication facility."[37]

When the RLA forces recaptured the village housing the TACAN site, they found the two dead Americans. But the Embassy and State had already determined the pattern regarding American losses in Laos; the sheep-dipped personnel would stay sheep-dipped.

The NVA, however, knew about Site 85 and intended to destroy it. On January 12, the North Vietnamese used two Soviet-built AN-2 "Colt" aircraft to bomb the installations on Phou Pha Thi. The Colt was a single-engine biplane that was modified by the NVA to carry 120mm mortar rounds releasable through a tube in the floor. The rounds would arm in the slipstream and detonate on impact. It was shades of World War I, with roughly the same results. Only slight damage was done to the TACAN site, but several Hmong were killed by the exploding ordnance. The two planes were shot down.

Despite the poor accuracy of their aerial bombardment, the North Vietnamese were not easily discouraged. Their excellent intelligence services were aware of the more important facility on Site 85, the radar/navigational system. A general offensive was currently under way, and as part of their strategy their ground forces began encircling the mountain. Planning to destroy the site undoubtedly began prior to Tet because the North Vietnamese strategists knew that Tet would result in the resumption of heavy bombing raids in the DRV in retaliation; without the site's radar guidance, however, the majority of American bombers would again have to attack in daylight, thus exposing themselves to the potent NVA air defenses.

Steadily pushing back the friendly forces, the combined NVA/PL offensive had almost completely surrounded the mountain by the end of February 1968. It was obvious to everyone involved that an attack against the site was imminent. An internal State Department document noted: "The enemy has been completing elaborate preparations, including the building of roads, to make a ground assault against the site. . . . Sullivan believes this will take place within two weeks."[38]

Richard Secord was watching the enemy maneuvers with growing apprehension. According to his memoirs, he and the CAS staff at Udorn had insisted to everybody and anybody who would listen that Site 85 was in grave danger. However, the use of the top-secret equipment on the site was so important that the risk to the station was justifiable. In spite of the warnings, the Air Force refused to withdraw the men and equipment from the mountain.

The direct enemy attack never materialized, although the communist forces engaged a Hmong unit at the base of the mountain the night of March 11, 1968. Instead, in the early morning hours of March 12, a twenty-six man raiding party led by NVA Lieutenant Truong Muc climbed the sheer cliff previously thought unscaleable and attacked the radar site. Heavy fighting ensued, but Muc's well-trained sappers overwhelmed the Air Force technicians.[39] Muc's original plan called for him to be gone by sunrise, but the difficulty of climbing the cliff and the stiff fight put up by the Americans badly delayed his timetable. Apparently he was still on the mountain when dawn broke. At first light, the Air Force lifted off the few American survivors by helicopter and then began pounding the hill with a withering barrage of U.S. air strikes, trying to destroy the valuable equipment and all evidence of the American presence.

With the Air Force smashing the physical evidence, Ambassador Sullivan went to work assessing the potential political harm. Earlier in January, Vientiane and the U.S. Air Force had worked out a press statement to be employed if Site 85 were overrun, and now Secretary Rusk wanted to use it. Sullivan, however, felt that "In current circumstances, I feel no statement should be made by U.S. spokesmen anywhere. . . ."[40] He was waiting to see what move the North Vietnamese and Pathet Lao would make. He briefed Souvanna, who had not been previously informed as to Site 85's true capabilities or the number of Americans at the secret base. Souvanna noted that the enemy now "could make some pretty damaging statements."

Yet once again the Pathet Lao refrained from making a major propaganda coup out of the discovery of the American presence. They did announce over PL radio the capture of Phou Pha Thi and claimed that twenty American advisors had been killed. Rusk stated, "If PL claims get no more specific than this, believe we . . . could in most cases deny charges, standard reply to press queries referring to such allegations is that we do not comment on communist propaganda."[41]

Sullivan agreed with Rusk and noted the "singular lack of interest in these broadcasts" by the press. Although he was waiting for the communists to make a big press splash, he still advised patience. Perhaps based on his prior experience, it was almost as if he knew the communists would not create a major propaganda display of American artifacts from the site. "Therefore, my strong recommendation is to have all the nervous Nellies sit tight and wait till we see what develops. As for the loose ends mentioned, if this were the only loose end in Laos, you might arouse my interest. As it is, if all the loose ends in this country were laid end to end, we could knit gags for every public-information officer in the government."[42]

Eventually, neither the DRV nor the PL used the evidence from the radar site to create any political furor. The 11 missing men were quietly declared dead and death benefits paid to their families. But for years rumors have circulated that several Americans survived the assault. In 1972, a PL platoon leader who defected claimed to have "encountered a small Pathet Lao element taking a male Caucasian to the headquarters area at Ban NaKay. The individual was bound, did not seem to be injured, and was wearing light-colored frame glasses. . . . The Pathet Lao escorting the individual stated that he was an American whom they had captured near Phou Pha Thi. . . . JPRC records do not indicate any prior report concerning US personnel captured, missing, or killed at Phou Pha Thi."[43]

The CIA agreed that the JPRC was kept in the dark, stating, "An NVA prisoner captured in November 1972 provided the first nonsensitive information on possible capture of an Air Force employee at Phou Pha Thi (LS-85) in 1968; previously all personnel not recovered were presumed dead. The case was so sensitive that JPRC did not have any record of the incident. [Sentence redacted]. Five USAF personnel were successfully evacuated from the TACAN site, and 14 or 15 others were MIA. . . . Some of the USAF defenders were holed up in a bunker part way down the cliff. They were spotted by the NVA and blown off the cliff by fire. One might have survived. [Redacted] said the report from the captured NVA matched all the facts he knew."[44]

Since then, more intelligence has come to light concerning whether men were taken from the hill alive. In August 1990, an Air Force captain named Timothy N. Castle was finishing his doctoral thesis on U.S. military aid to Laos during the war. Castle speaks fluent Lao, and while traveling in the country he was granted an interview with Pathet Lao General Singkapo. Singkapo was the PL commander of the military region in which Site 85 lies, and he was previously involved with American POWs, including Debruin, Klusmann, and probably Hrdlicka and Shelton. Finding Singkapo "consistently clear and precise in his recollection of wartime events," Captain Castle questioned the general regarding the events at Phou Pha Thi. Singkapo recalled that "some injured Americans were captured at the site and sent to North Vietnam." In summing up his interview, Castle wrote, "Despite General Singkapo's declaration . . . of willingness to discuss his knowledge of the captured Americans with U.S. MIA/POW experts, the Lao government consistently blocked access to the general. Senior officials in the Lao government told U.S. representatives that Singkapo was senile. Finally, a year later, General Singkapo was interviewed . . . and claimed that he had been 'misunderstood.' I believe General Singkapo . . . was quite open and did not consider the ramifications of his remarks." Castle, like many others, went on to ask whether "there will ever be a complete account of the attack on Phou Pha Thi."[45]

The Lao government allowed Muc to accompany a JTF-FA team to Phou Pha Thi in December 1994; however, no remains were found at the spots where Muc claimed his team had buried the dead Americans.[46] While many reasons can be postulated why no human skeletons could be found in the thin mountain soil, the most probable is that the Lao in 1977 recovered any remains left on the mountain. NSA-monitored Lao transmissions, available to DIA shortly after they were intercepted but only recently declassified, indicate that in the spring and summer of 1977, the "Lao People's Liberation Army (LPLA) Company 18 has probably been assigned the task of recovering the remains of American personnel killed in the Phou Pha Thi area. . . ."[47] In July, NSA further reported that "the remains of some American war dead had been taken to 'Office 208' [redacted] somewhere in Houa Phan (formerly Sam Neua) province."[48]

Muc's account has also been severely questioned by independent scholars and several of the family members of the missing men, especially Ann Holland, wife of Melvin Holland, one of the missing. The loss of the men was considered so sensitive that the deaths of the men were kept off the casualty rolls, and in 1968 Mrs. Holland was told point-blank to remain quiet about Mel's job and his loss. Only in 1982, under the threat of her lawsuit, did the U.S. government publicly concede that men had been lost when Site 85 fell. The names of the eleven were finally added to the roster of men Missing In Action.

Mrs. Holland provides a glimpse of the effect the government's cover-up of Mel's loss has had on her. "Twenty-seven years ago today, Mel and I left to go to Washington, DC for the briefing for this last assignment. I guess it's a good thing a person cannot look into a crystal ball and see what life has in store. I was twenty-seven years old with five small children. I have now spent half my life trying to uncover the truth about what happened to my husband."[49]

Brigham, Smith, and Jones

The last prisoner release of the year occurred in December 1968, when the NLF announced over Liberation Radio that it desired to release three American POWs held in the South. The NLF initiative was unexpected, but in retrospect can be seen as part of their overall strategy to wrest political recognition from the United States for the communist-supported movement in the South. With the Paris Peace Talks frozen for two months over the issue of NLF representation, the communists hoped to break the deadlock by pursuing de facto recognition.

On December 18, the NLF made two broadcasts, the first announcing the release, the second detailing the procedure for the U.S. command to receive the POWs. Basically, the NLF wanted to meet near a VC stronghold in Tay Ninh province, and if the United States was interested it should send a delegation on Christmas Day.

This was the first open offer of direct battlefield negotiations, and the implications for GVN-U.S. relations were enormous. The GVN had earlier balked at any form of direct NLF-U.S. overtures, and the recent *Buttercup* exchanges were still fresh in everyone's mind. Rusk cabled both Harriman in Paris and Ambassador Ellsworth Bunker in Saigon for their opinions. Bunker as usual was flatly against the idea of direct talks. "Obviously we must do everything reasonably possible to facilitate earliest return of US prisoners," he wrote in a cable, "but we should also be aware that the enemy's purpose may be to embarrass our relations with the GVN and to use the prisoner release as a means to force us to recognize status of NLF as separate from and equal to Hanoi. . . . It seems to us therefore that the unusual procedure by the enemy may be intended to lead us into some kind of ceremony . . . or other arrangements designed to enhance their status at a time when the Paris talks are deadlocked because of U.S. and GVN refusal to acknowledge that we are fighting two separate enemies. Accordingly, our preferred procedure would be to . . . handle the entire matter in Paris."[50]

In essence, Bunker was prepared to reject the prospect of reclaiming three American POWs from the jungle camps of the VC only because such an event might embarrass the GVN or lead to a propaganda victory for the NLF. Granted, the Paris talks had reached a stalemate, but shortly power was to pass to a new Administration, which undoubtedly would chart its own destiny and policies. Given the history of the exchange attempts, Bunker's continuing opposition is at best puzzling, especially since the U.S. government internally agreed in mid-September "that U.S. public opinion would not permit U.S. authorities to refuse to accept released PWs."[51]

Harriman, on the other hand, was not inclined to let this opportunity slip by. He replied to Bunker, "I thoroughly disagree with the proposal contained in reference telegram. To make an issue of the NLF status in connection with their proposal for release of prisoners would be to play directly into the hands of the NLF. . . . Certainly, the NLF will attempt to portray prisoner exchanges as enhancing their status, but the more we make of it, the greater the enhancement. . . . We should not quibble with the NLF over the terms and conditions of prisoner release unless they propose some clearly outrageous or humiliating conditions. The American public would never understand the delay or refusal to accept the release of U.S. prisoners because of our unwillingness to meet in the field. I would think that from the GVN's standpoint that direct negotiations between the US and the NLF in Paris would be much more sensitive than . . . meeting on the field of battle."[52]

Bunker visited President Thieu, who agreed to cooperate but warned Bunker that "the NLF will try to obtain mileage out of it, and we have to move carefully." Rusk then directed Bunker to proceed with the arrangements. The text of an answering radio message was completed and subsequently broadcast over Armed Forces Radio agreeing to the meeting place.

General Walter T. Kerwin, the American commander of III Corps, was ordered to pick a five-man team to rendezvous with the NLF representatives. The head of the U.S. delegation to the operation now known as *Chicago Fire* was Lieutenant Colonel John V. Gibney. The Embassy told Gibney to avoid all courtesies such as handshakes, offers to partake of food or drink, or even sitting down with the enemy so as not to give the appearance of negotiating, since that could be construed as political recognition. The Embassy emphatically did not want the press involved, and if the enemy brought their press or were flying the NLF flag Gibney was to protest that these items were "superfluous to purpose of meeting." A local cease-fire was in effect, but only for a short time.

On December 25, when other Americans all over the world were celebrating Christmas, Gibney boarded a helicopter in Saigon for the ride out to the meeting. As they approached the landing site, they spotted a large NLF banner flying in a field. Gibney ordered the helicopter to land on the opposite side of the open area. Getting out of the helicopter, Gibney and his team observed two men come out of the woods and begin walking toward them. Gibney and the American officers moved to meet them halfway. Upon meeting, the VC interpreter indicated that his leader would like to sit down with them at a table they had set up a short distance away, in the woods. Gibney refused, provided his name and rank, and asked for the prisoners.

After a short wait, a man described as the NLF leader came out of the woods and offered his hand to Gibney. Following his instructions, Gibney declined, stating, "I have no time for amenities." When the NLF cadre offered to sit down at their table and have a drink, Gibney curtly replied, "I have no time for protocols."[53]

The Vietnamese instantly became angry, stating that it appeared that Gibney "had a bad attitude . . . [and] that I thought I was superior to them." The meeting continued to deteriorate, but Gibney, although desperate to recover the men, held fast to his instructions and refused to sit down or discuss any protocols with the communists. After several hours of fruitless arguing, with Gibney refusing to engage in any dialogue or formalities with the NLF representatives, the Vietnamese broke off the meeting. They stated that they would inform the Americans by radio broadcast if they intended to meet again.

With no POWs, Gibney returned in the helicopter to Saigon, hoping he had done the right thing. The American side had secretly tape-recorded the event. Undoubtedly so had the communists. After listening to the tape, Gibney was convinced that the communists had not intended to release the Americans that day and were engaged in some sort of "game." On December 28, NLF radio broadcast a message blaming the Americans' "bad attitude" for the Christmas Day failure. Still, the NLF was willing to meet again with the U.S. team on January 1, 1969, another American holiday.

Under pressure from Harriman because of their strict instructions to Gibney, the Embassy reacted to the radio message by stating that "The behavior of the US military representatives at all times was dignified, correct and businesslike. Lt. Col. Gibney said that the turnover of the three was a simple matter and repeatedly asked that a date, time, and place be set for their release. In accordance with his instructions, he did not allow himself to be drawn into discussions or situations that were irrelevant to the purpose of the meeting and were obviously intended to be exploited for political and propaganda purposes."[54]

The communist leader had mentioned that if the U.S. "had the correct attitude, that we could build bridges here, and this could lead to other negotiations in other tactical areas. If the initial meeting went well, meaning if we had the right attitude, then this would be building bridges in other areas for extensive releases in the future."[55]

Ambassador Bunker was not buying it. "Our two main concerns in instructing our team were to get prisoners released and to avoid a succession of meetings with the VC. . . . What we expected was that the VC would try to engage our team in discussions designed to enhance or establish the NLF as an independent entity which the U.S. is dealing with bi-laterally. . . . The NLF could exploit and would elevate a simple exchange into a major political problem for us in South Vietnam and further complicate our problems with the GVN in relation to the Paris talks. We could see precedent, once established, being repeated in one area after another as they dribbled out three or four prisoners at a time seeking to establish their presence and control of territory in different parts of the country. . . . I believe we have complications enough in our relations with the GVN, without adding to them at this point. Had the Paris talks been engaged in substantive discussions we would have been somewhat more flexible in our instructions. There is nothing that the other side could not have said to us standing up that they could have said sitting down."[56]

Harriman was furious, but the Embassy held to its position. While they allowed Gibney more flexibility in his next meeting, the ground rules were the same; no gestures or concessions to the NLF. The team flew back to meet with the communist cadre on the morning of January 1. This time a press contingent went out with them in a separate helicopter. When the team landed, the cadre marched into the field to meet Gibney. After a short discussion and a one-hour recess, the Americans were brought out: three enlisted men, James Brigham, Donald Smith, and Thomas Jones were returned to U.S. control. Gibney signed the receipt for the prisoners, placed them on the helicopter, and the group returned to Saigon.

The three were not in great shape from their jungle sojourn. Brigham had a severe head wound, which a communist surgeon had operated on but which had become infected. As soon as he returned to the States American surgeons attempted to repair the damage, but he lapsed into a coma and died a week later. The communists instantly accused the Americans of "murdering" Brigham because he had agreed to work for the "cause of peace" in the United States.

The three had in fact been heavily indoctrinated. Because Brigham was black, the communist interrogators leaned on him especially hard, but the other two also divulged information and made statements. On December 25, the same day as the first meeting, the Americans captured a document that recorded an interrogation of Brigham.[57] In it, he was asked many questions concerning his views on the war, the Saigon government, and the effects of the antiwar movement at home. Apparently the communists were questioning the prisoners to improve their knowledge of the mentality of American soldiers and to gauge the effects of the growing antiwar movement on soldier morale.

Back in Saigon, the press film of the second meeting was shown to a high-ranking communist defector, the former Deputy Political Officer (PO) for one of the communist political zones around the capital. Lieutenant Colonel Tran Van Dac was a veteran of the war against the French, a native South Vietnamese who had marched north across the DMZ with his unit in 1954 and then returned to the South in January 1962. He served in a variety of PO positions until April 1968, when he grew sick of the communists and defected. Watching the film, Dac felt that "In releasing three American captives, the VC intended to force the U.S. to recognize the NLF as a political entity possessing real assets. By doing this the Front hoped to create a more favorable climate for the NLF delegation in Paris. In short, the prisoner release was a politically motivated move to force the Allies to recognize the existence of the Front and to improve the status of the Front at the Paris Peace Talks. . . . Source was positive that the release took place for political and propaganda objectives on the part of the VC and not out of a humanitarian spirit."[58]

Unknown to Gibney and the American command, the communist interpreter during *Chicago Fire* was Lieutenant Nguyen Hung Tri, an Enemy Proselytizing cadre who was previously the deputy commander of the American POW camp in Tay Ninh province. His current assignment was to write articles for the Front's news and print media. The NLF leader was Major Nguyen Van Tuoi, a cadre from COSVN's Enemy Proselytizing Office whose sister was married to an American major assigned to MACV HQ in Saigon. The actual release had been coordinated by the Chief of the Enemy Proselytizing Office, Senior Colonel Tran Van Luc, who was later killed in an air attack. His deputy chief was one of the enemy soldiers taking photos.[59]

The gathering of senior cadres from the COSVN office responsible for handling American POWs indicates that perhaps the communists had been prepared for more extensive negotiations. The actions of the U.S. team, however, dissuaded the communists from ever again attempting a face-to-face meeting. While the propaganda aspects of the meeting were obvious, in their haste to prevent the NLF from gaining any political capital, did the American negotiators inadvertently shut off a channel that would have led to the release of more prisoners? In hindsight, was it worth closing a conduit that might have freed American prisoners in return for some nebulous political gain by the NLF? Unlike the exchange negotiations conducted elsewhere, where the DRV/NLF had refused to talk, since 1963 the United States had been offered repeated opportunities in South Vietnam to regain POWs in exchange for captured communist cadres, yet the GVN's fears and the advice of the Embassy forced the U.S. government to walk away every time.

10. Camp of the Week

He [Rowe] immediately volunteered to lead troops back into area of his impris-
onment. He is confident there are two U.S. PW there but cannot pinpoint their
location since he has been in isolation for the past year. He is eager to return to
duty and help JPRC recover more prisoners. JPRC would be proud to have him.
—JPRC message to CINCPAC the day after Nick Rowe escapes after five years of
* captivity in the Mekong Delta*

As 1968 gave way to 1969, immense changes occurred in the war and in the efforts being made for American POWs. At the national level, talks began on ending the fighting and a new Administration was elected. The JPRC again
underwent profound changes, including constant command shuffling, changes
which ultimately shaped the efforts to hunt for POWs.

The primary concern in the JPRC became recovering Nick Rowe. The Americans learned from the debriefs of Jackson, Johnson, and Pitzer that the terrible
conditions in the Delta camps had already caused the deaths of several American
POWs. The Vietnamese prisoners held in the U-Minh "Forest of Darkness" fared
even worse.[1] Consequently, the JPRC directed nine raids in the course of eight
months trying to rescue Nick Rowe. Eventually the constant JPRC pressure
helped bring about the most spectacular escape of the war and the end of the five-
year ordeal of Nick Rowe.

The Peace Talks Open

After years of fruitless attempts to coax the North Vietnamese into discussing a set-tlement to the war, the Paris Peace Talks finally began in May 1968. Johnson ap-pointed Averell Harriman as the main negotiator for the United States. At the same time, Harriman still carried his original portfolio as coordinator of POW af-fairs. While he was determined to bring the prisoner issue to the forefront of the talks, he wanted to put it on the table in the same manner as he had represented it before: with a low public profile so as not to injure any constructive dialogue with the communists. He believed the few indirect contacts the U.S. government previ-ously had with the North Vietnamese confirmed that they also favored minimiz-ing publicity. Doing so, as the Americans later discovered, played straight into their calculations; the DRV/NLF's vulnerability to world opinion became appar-ent from watching their overwrought reaction to several calculated American ef-forts to publicly condemn them for their mistreatment of the American POWs.

Harriman went to Paris with no illusions about the communists and the pris-oner issue. But in his years as principal POW negotiator, he also had grown weary of the constant suspicions of the South Vietnamese that prisoner-exchange talks might lead inexorably to a negotiated settlement. Harriman was no longer con-cerned that direct U.S. negotiation about Americans in captivity with the NLF would somehow lend support to the communist fiction that the Viet Cong in-surgents were strictly a South Vietnamese–inspired revolutionary group directed against the GVN. The DRV's vehement claims that North Vietnamese military forces were not engaged in combat in South Vietnam had long ago been exposed as lies, and it was now well understood that Hanoi directed the war and the poli-cies of the guerrillas in the South. Whether Harriman also understood that all POW policies were also directed by Hanoi is another matter.

Harriman summed up his feelings as the last days of the Johnson Administra-tion drew to a close. Responding to a joint State-DOD message on POW issues at the Paris talks, he wrote of the U.S. negotiation strategy, "We should press hard for agreement on POWs prior to agreement on other matters, [and] we certainly agree that release of POWs is a matter of high priority that should be taken up early . . . and at the highest level. However, agreed plan is to make restoration of the DMZ and mutual withdrawal of forces as first priority items. We doubt if there is much chance on POW release until there is progress on an understanding re mutual withdrawals.

"We are quite clear that we should deal with Hanoi bilaterally to obtain release of US pilots held in North Vietnam. We do not know what position the DRV will take or what quid pro quo it will demand for release of our pilots. We frankly do not know at this time how best to deal with the question of release of US/FW [US/Free World] prisoners held by the NLF. We believe it is best to remain flexible, to try . . . to get a feeling for the situation. How the NLF intends to deal with the POWs is unclear. They evidently had something in mind regarding prisoner releases in calling for the Christmas meeting in South Vietnam, but we missed the opportunity to explore in that meeting and the New Year meeting what their intentions were.

"We recognize that GVN felt the NLF would attempt to obtain propaganda out of the prisoner-release process, but we have never been very impressed with the value or importance of that factor. After all, VC is a fighting force which together with NVA has captured our men. Dealing with them on POW issue cannot have significant propaganda advantage unless we make it so. The important thing is to get our men out. Our negotiators here should not be hampered in trying to achieve this objective by GVN supersensitivity about NLF."[2]

Several days later Harriman got his chance to ascertain the DRV's position on POWs. At a meeting with the DRV negotiators, he "opened by saying we would like to raise the question of US pilots who are in DRV custody. . . . The second question was how and when the DRV visualized an appropriate time for discussion of the release of all the pilots they hold. . . . Thuy [the second-ranking Vietnamese negotiator] replied that the DRV considers pilots captured over the DRV as . . . war criminals and, therefore, has not treated them according to the Geneva Conventions. . . . This question, Thuy said, actually depends on the attitude of the United States and on the question of a peaceful settlement of the Vietnam problem. . . ."[3]

Like the North Korean negotiators before them, the DRV authorities were far from willing to treat their primary bargaining asset as a separate issue. Nor were they ready to make any concessions on such matters as visits by the International Red Cross. Harriman would spend the remainder of his time as Paris negotiator locked in the same endless quarrels over protocol as over POWs, all brought on by a Vietnamese negotiation tactic called "talk and fight." This tactic, poorly understood by Americans, called for continued battlefield engagements and combat pressure combined with repeated public announcements of their willingness to discuss a cease-fire—only, of course, if certain preconditions were met by the United States.

In essence, Harriman's arrival in Paris marked the beginning of the end of the State Department's dominance in the POW arena. Harriman would also soon begin leaving more of the work on the issue to his assistant, Frank Sieverts. Eventually, Dr. Henry Kissinger at the White House and the new secretary of defense, Melvin Laird, would wrest the initiative away from the bureaucrats at State. In retrospect, while State can be seen as having explored every avenue to gain early release for the POWs or to ameliorate their conditions, little could be accomplished against the determined intransigence of the communists. Additionally, the secret war policy in Laos precluded most public efforts for Americans held in captivity there.

Worse, the persistent obstruction of the attempts at early release by the Embassy in Saigon was perhaps just as damaging. When the U.S. ambassadors to South Vietnam and Laos were obliged to make a choice between helping the POWs or supporting the deeply flawed policy goals of the Johnson Administration in Southeast Asia, the two men, while obviously interested in the welfare of the men and willing to work for their release, made their views clear. From the available documentary evidence it appears that they were willing to sacrifice the POWs, rightly or wrongly, to their perception of the national interest and current policies of the United States. Hindsight always seems perfect, but how many more men would have come home if Bunker, and the other ambassadors before him, had been more willing to stand up to the GVN? How many more Americans may have been identified in Pathet Lao hands if Sullivan had been less committed to doggedly pursuing a hypocritical policy that had all the earmarks of the old tale about the Emperor's new clothes? It is a question which lingers to this day: What is the government's responsibility when its moral imperative appears to be in conflict with the national and policy goals?

Turmoil in the JPRC

After a year of frenetic activity, Colonel Jack Reisner's one-year tour was over. In early July he rotated back to Hawaii, where he became the head of the E&E branch of the Pacific Air Force.[4] The commander of SOG, Colonel John Singlaub, also left in the late summer of 1968. He was replaced by Army Colonel Steven Cavanaugh. Reisner's departure, unfortunately, would set off a chain of events that severely weakened the JPRC. Over the next year, the JPRC would have a series of five different commanders, a situation that—starting in early 1969—began to slowly degrade the effectiveness of the unit.

Reisner's replacement was on board for only six weeks before a serious eye ailment cut short his tenure. By mid-August, the position of Chief, JPRC was filled by its Navy officer, Dickinson Prentiss. Prentiss rotated out in December 1968 and was replaced for one month by a SOG officer, Irving MacDonald. In January 1969, the SOG Deputy, Colonel Robert Gleason, switched MacDonald to SOG Intelligence and brought in Lieutenant Colonel Robert Bradshaw. According to Bradshaw, he and Gleason did not mesh well together, and Bradshaw requested a transfer. He was moved to a different position at MACV headquarters in late February.[5]

With Bradshaw's departure, the senior ranking man was now Lieutenant Colonel John Firth, who had replaced Charlie Ogle and who by default now became head of the JPRC. The JPRC had undergone a slight change of authorization in late 1968, and the position of Chief was now called Director. Firth held command of the Center until his departure in July 1969.

Although the JPRC's officers were moving around, its NCO corps stayed relatively stable. One of the new NCOs was USAF Tech Sergeant John Mitchell, who served in JPRC from June 1968 until April 1969. Under the direction of a hard-charging Special Forces sergeant named Gordon Rozell, Mitchell began the first coordinated attempt to create a systematic filing system at the JPRC. Mitchell recounts taking the many POW-sighting reports and attempting to correlate them to individuals, often writing POW biographical information directly on the reports. He and another JPRC NCO decided to divide the responsibilities for Indochina in half. Mitchell took North Vietnam and Laos. He recalls, "I thought our intelligence on U.S. POWs in Sam Neua was excellent. It also appeared the communists had a POW holding area near Tchepone on the Trail."[6]

Mitchell's belief is supported by source reports from Laos. One example is a CIA report from COS Vientiane which states "source knew of a temporary internment center for American POWs located on the bank of the Se Bang Hieng (river) in Tchepone District in 1966. Source said it was controlled by North Vietnamese who used it as a temporary holding area and preliminary interrogation center. Source said he believed this location was used exclusively for foreign prisoners." The report ends cryptically. "Station [redacted] directing Op exclusively to [redacted] U.S. prisoners. Will keep headquarters informed."[7]

Changes were also under way at the Saigon Embassy. The Embassy political/military (POL/MIL) officer was now Robert Shackleton, a career Foreign Service officer. Shackleton states that "in a larger Embassy, the POL/MIL job could mean just about anything, depending on the country in question. In Saigon, the majority of my time was spent on POW matters. However, coordination was often on a need-to-know basis. Bunker was a flinty, secretive man who ran a very tight, compartmentalized ship.

"The JPRC was another matter entirely. I took the JPRC very seriously and fully supported their efforts. I worked closely with Dickinson Prentiss, but quite simply, the JPRC task was impossible. The intelligence was just too dated and imprecise."[8]

Shackleton was also placed in charge of the Detainee Committee in Saigon, but with the JPRC handling prisoner rescue operations, the Committee's focus turned to improving the GVN's POW camps. "My priority was the POW issue, but from a political viewpoint it appeared hopeless. The VC allowed no Red Cross visits, let alone had made any sort of attempt to adhere to the Geneva Convention, so we concentrated on improving GVN treatment and prisoner releases in the hopes of modifying VC POW behavior. We coordinated all POW activity to bring the GVN camps up to ICRC standard, hoping it would put pressure on the communists to do likewise. One major vehicle which we used to accomplish this was the U.S. Military Police, with whom we worked very closely. We succeeded in this project admirably but it did little good for our missing men. The communists weren't interested in improving treatment, they were interested in propaganda."

Camp of the Week

Fortunately for the JPRC, Captain Dave McNabb applied for a one-year additional tour and in the process became the longest-serving JPRC officer. Eventually, he and newly arrived Captain Robert Lunday would become the dynamic duo of the unit. As the others departed Vietnam, McNabb, as the officer with the most experience, naturally became the driving force in launching rescue operations.

McNabb had volunteered to go to Vietnam as part "of the effort to put down communism." Before he came to Vietnam he had been a backseater on an F-101 fighter plane. To fill the empty slot created by the loss of another officer, SOG detached a Special Forces–trained captain named Robert Lunday. According to McNabb, "Lunday was very optimistic about our chances. He believed you could do anything once." As McNabb and Lunday worked together and grew closer, they were encouraged by John Firth to develop plausible raid scenarios and then look for a force to launch missions into enemy territory.[9]

McNabb notes, "As Lunday and I began to talk, we felt the key to this was to operate in the enemy's territory, that if you could keep the pressure on them something would give. So we dreamed up 'Camp of the Week,' a concept where we tried to overcome the normal inertia of not committing forces by keeping U.S. or U.S.-led forces in constant activity. But the reluctance of some commanders often prevented us from carrying out our plan.

"Lunday and I concluded that after we proposed an operation, if they started asking questions the mission would be killed. As an example, Lunday and I had intelligence on a POW who was supposedly tubercular and being moved from Tay Ninh towards the Parrot's Beak area. We meet with General Kerwin, commander of III Corps, who authorized us to use his forces if we could get good intelligence. Lunday was anxious to recover the guy and he went to Tay Ninh to work the problem. Several days later the phone rings and I pick it up. It's General Kerwin on the line. He says to me rather bluntly, 'Are you and Lunday trying to run my Corps?' That ended that operation."

McNabb received other excellent advice from Bill Buckley, the CIA officer in the *Phoenix* pacification program, who was later killed while a hostage in Lebanon. He recommended that McNabb use the old French maps of the country, since they often indicated where the VC had their base areas. One of Buckley's innumerable contacts, a geographer from Kansas, looked at the maps and told them to find the areas where government control was weak, especially along political or military boundaries. It was there, he said, that you would find the enemy's base camps.

From McNabb's perspective "these maps provided us with very good information. The location of the camp Rowe was held in was on the map with a notation citing 'Camp for political detainees.' But enemy POW facilities were not normal prisons. We weren't looking for the county jail, we were looking for caves, slit trenches, and huts."

Captain Charles Roberts was the Army Military Intelligence officer who replaced Seamon. Previously, he had been the Laos country officer for the 319th MI Group in Hawaii working Order of Battle (OB) and the movement of supplies down the Trail. He quickly bought into McNabb's concept and concentrated his efforts on "looking for camp movement patterns, not individuals as much. I tried to gain access to all the intelligence I needed to help them plan raids, especially CIA information. When I was in Hawaii, I had the definite feeling that the CIA was holding back information on Laos from the military."[10]

Roberts also agrees with McNabb about the reluctance they often faced in running raids. "The feelings from U.S. commanders was, 'Won't they kill the guys?' This was the first line of resistance. The second was, 'This is in the heart of bad-guy country.' The third always was, 'How good is your intelligence?' Many commanders were gung-ho, but many also weren't. We ran ops into II and III Corps, but not much in I Corps as the Marines didn't agree with us very often. But the bulk of our time was spent in the Delta."

Besides the reluctance of the Marines, one other reason the JPRC turned its attention away from I Corps was a CIA report delivered in the annual fall visit by SACSA and the CIA. The report, entitled "Movement of American Prisoners into North Vietnam," was developed using interrogation reports of enemy POWs. The first draft was completed in July 1968, and was discussed with JPRC and CIA Vietnam Station officers in September.[11] The report's conclusions were that "the North Vietnamese were moving prisoners into North Vietnam . . . for two reasons; (1) Growing number of prisoners, and (2) Greater security and better prisoner exploitation opportunities in rear areas." The report went on to point out that the number of American MIAs in Laos and South Vietnam had doubled within the last year. Therefore, it was logical to the CIA that the North Vietnamese had partially solved this problem by transporting at least the I Corps–area prisoners to secure areas within North Vietnam.[12]

But the main explanation for why the JPRC spent so much time concentrating on the Delta was acting JPRC head John Firth. Firth "was obsessed with getting Nick Rowe back," Mitchell recounts. "He had been Rowe's Executive Officer when Rowe was captured, and now that the others had been released from captivity he was determined to get him back. He spent all of his time looking for Rowe."

Roberts also recalls that "Lunday and Firth were chasing off to the Delta every week looking for Rowe." Firth's fixation would drive the JPRC for the next six months, leading to several successful POW raids in the Delta that recovered almost a hundred Vietnamese. The continual JPRC pressure plus an ARVN offensive into the U-Minh Forest forced the Rowe camp to begin moving. Although it was the pressure of the raids that allowed Rowe to make his dash for freedom, he escaped by using his own remarkable poise and courage to seize the opportunity presented to him.

Beating the Bush for Rowe

Recovery operations had been targeted at the Rowe camp, however, even before the release of Jackson, Johnson, and Pitzer. Fred Caristo, the SOG officer who had just missed recovering two Americans in Operation *Cobra Tail,* led one non-JPRC POW operation into the Delta in the fall of 1967 that turned up nothing. Many years later Caristo was interviewing Daniel Pitzer, the Special Forces medic released in November 1967, when he learned a remarkable fact. Caristo had just asked Pitzer if anyone had ever come close to rescuing him. Pitzer recalled that he had heard firefights on occasion, but only one time did he remember U.S. forces coming near.

"Pitzer told me," Caristo said, "how several months before his release a raid had come very close to him. When the troops landed, he was in a concealed underground bunker with a cocked pistol held to his head. He could hear people walking around searching the area. A short time later he heard an American voice nearby talking into a radio requesting helicopters to leave the area. Later he heard the choppers come in, pick up the troops, and depart. Afterwards, Pitzer said, he cried.

"That American was me," said Caristo. "I can't believe how close I came to rescuing him and never knew it."

The JPRC's first attempt to rescue Rowe was Operation *Lucky Leaf.* In late August 1967, the 135th MI in Can Tho contacted the JPRC with another report of a Vietnamese escapee from a prison camp. A Popular Force soldier who claimed to have been held since 1962 said he had been able to escape while fishing. The source reported that two U.S. POWs, a black master sergeant and a Caucasian captain, had been brought to the camp in April 1965.[13] The JPRC had an aerial photography mission flown plus the usual visual reconnaissance. The pictures were shown to the source and this time a polygraph was also used. He passed.

The 5th Special Force (SF) was tasked to run the raid. Because of the difficult terrain, the 5th requested and was granted two weeks to plan and rehearse. A battalion from the 9th Infantry Division (ID) was to act as a reaction force.

On October 2, the SF team was launched into the area and searched for 36 hours. No camp was found. The source was flown over the area in an attempt to locate the camp site. Four different locations were pointed out by the source, all of which had been previously searched by the SF. It became obvious that the source could not locate the camp.

The JPRC suspected a trap, and the source was turned over to the ARVN IV Corps G-2 for further interrogation. The ARVNs discovered that the source, "in all probability, was not an escapee, but had been released, for one reason or another, by the VC. . . . It is possible that Source was, and is, being used by the VC."[14]

The JPRC was beginning to suspect that the VC were playing a cat-and-mouse game with them. Then in November the NLF released the three Americans, Reisner launched Operation *Black Knight,* and the hunt for Nick Rowe began anew.

Tightening the Noose

Dave McNabb's first major operation was also one of the most successful raids launched by the JPRC. On August 28, 1968, he received a report from Can Tho that two Vietnamese had escaped from a POW camp in Chuong Thien province in the Delta. They reported that the camp contained 8 Americans and 35 Vietnamese.

The escaped prisoners had first stumbled into an ARVN outpost, where they were transported to the headquarters of the ARVN 21st Division. The 21st declined to launch the raid, because the camp was across a river and in enemy territory. Apparently the ARVN had good reason. "Chuong Thien," according to Richard Childress, who became a District Senior Advisor in Chuong Thien province in November and later served as the Director of Asian Affairs at the National Security Council in the Reagan Administration, "was rated by CORDS as the second-least pacified province in the country."[15]

McNabb flew down to Can Tho. Balked by the ARVN, he arranged for the transfer of the escapees to the local CIA-sponsored Provisional Reconnaissance Unit (PRU). The CIA maintained an extensive infrastructure of officers in South Vietnam and to a lesser extent in Laos. In South Vietnam, CIA officers were found in every province and they developed the indigenous-manned PRUs, which were paramilitary units recruited to fight the VC. These units were used as part of the highly classified and ultimately infamous *Phoenix* program, which was designed to pacify the South Vietnamese countryside.

After the debriefing, McNabb and the PRU unit planned a raid, code-named *Cranberry Bog*, for the night of August 30–31. The raiding party consisted of the American PRU advisor, the two escapees, and nine PRU. McNabb arranged for special equipment recently added to the JPRC stocks to be available, including portable radios, a small life-raft, explosive bolt cutters, and starlight scopes. The team went back to the ARVN outpost, which was only 3,000 meters from the POW camp. At midnight the team began their infiltration to the camp under the cover of a U.S. Forward Air Controller (FAC) employing the starlight scopes, who provided night surveillance and also acted as a radio relay. The raft was used to transport the radios and weapons across the river to the POW camp.[16]

McNabb flew with the FAC. He recalls, "The PRU advisor was a Navy SEAL. He had to swim across the river towing this bright orange raft we stole from an RF-101 survival kit. Afterwards we got some black-colored ones, but on this occasion we had no other choice but to use the orange raft. The SEAL had to swim across the river at night towing this orange-colored raft into VC territory with the PRU clinging to the sides because they couldn't swim."

At dawn, the raiding party attacked the guards and killed two VC. The other guards ran. A reaction force of 60 PRU supported by four gunships landed near the campsite and cordoned off the area. There were no friendly casualties. A total of 49 Vietnamese POWs, mostly ARVNs, were found shackled and standing in trenches filled with chest-deep water. They were interrogated immediately regarding the U.S. POWs, but it was determined that they had been removed on

August 28 by enemy forces in estimated battalion strength and taken in an unknown direction.[17]

McNabb regrets that he didn't just take the PRU unit right then and head toward Rowe's camp. "I had the PRU for another two hours, but by the time the raid was over at 1000 hours I had been up for thirty-six hours. We had a pretty good idea where Rowe's camp was, but certain higher-command elements were afraid to let us attack it for fear that the guards would kill him. We were going to have to prove we could get him out without him being killed before we would be authorized to hit it."

Over the next two weeks the JPRC showered the *Cranberry Bog* area with reward leaflets. CAS Saigon promptly reported to Langley that the liberated Vietnamese had tentatively identified two Americans from photos shown to them. In turn, the CIA noted, "This action considered success even though U.S. prisoners moved prior to raid and proved raids of this type can be launched effectively with combined efforts Station intel input, JPRC advice and actions of PRUs."[18]

Unfortunately, the presence of the Americans was a complete fabrication. After the war, one of the Vietnamese who had been liberated from the camp was interviewed to determine who the eight U.S. personnel might have been. He related that the two original sources "had made false statements concerning the presence of U.S. PWs at their camp in order to exert pressure on U.S. officials to have a rescue operation mounted against their former detention facility. . . . In summary, there never were any U.S. PWs at the camp raided on 30–31 August. . . ."[19]

After the success of *Cranberry Bog*, the JPRC continued pressing hard in the Delta. The new reward program was bringing in its fair of share of fraudulent claims but it was also producing important new information. On September 17, a Vietnamese female prisoner escaped from a VC camp in An Xuyen province at the southern tip of Vietnam. She said the prison held almost a hundred Vietnamese prisoners and two Americans and she was willing to lead a team back in.

Code-named *Azalea Creek*, the mission was launched at first light on September 21. A Regional Forces company with their American advisors were landed in helicopters. Tactical air and naval gunfire were on standby. When the forces landed, they discovered that the camp had been recently abandoned. When the troops searched the nearby elephant grass, twenty-five Vietnamese prisoners were found being guarded by one female VC. Ominously, the prisoners revealed that someone had informed the VC of the impending raid. The VC had removed one group of POWs at midnight and were last seen heading in the direction of the U-Minh Forest. The prisoners had heard of Americans in the area but had never seen any. The female escapee was rewarded with VN $20,000 piasters.

In early October, another PRU unit acted on a recently acquired piece of intelligence and unilaterally conducted a prisoner-recovery operation against a VC camp on Dung Island, located at the mouth of the Bassac River. The whereabouts of the camp were provided by a woman who had received a clandestine message from her husband, who was held there. She reported the information to the PRU, who then passed it on to their U.S. advisors. The PRU under the command of Navy SEAL Scott Lyons struck the camp at first light and freed 27 Vietnamese POWs.[20]

The JPRC group was ecstatic. Three successful recoveries had been made in little over a month. Although no Americans had been liberated, the concentration on the Delta was paying off. New information was pouring in, gathered by the increasingly effective 525th MI agents and other sources. Every week brought a fresh piece of intelligence. The circle was closing around Nick Rowe.

On October 15, the JPRC received an intelligence report that a woman claiming to be the wife of a VC camp guard alleged that there were five Americans and 80 Vietnamese in a heavily guarded prison in the Delta. In return for a reward and his freedom, the VC guard had agreed to protect the prisoners during a rescue attempt. The women also said that one of the Americans was a captain in poor health. She had to return to the camp the next day, as she was only out of the camp on a 48-hour medical pass.[21]

Three days later Operation *Sage Brush* was launched. A 120-man PRU force under U.S. leadership searched the area for four hours without locating any POW camp or enemy activity. Extensive debriefing of sources, guides, and village residents was conducted in order to determine the causes and motives for the apparent deception and compromise. A preliminary investigation indicated that a camp was widely rumored to be in the area, and the "VC guard" and his female relative thought that a large operation might locate the POWs and they would get a reward.[22]

On the heels of *Sage Brush*, another raid called *Juniper Berry* was launched in late October. A woman escapee from this camp, who also was the wife of the ARVN chief of staff for Ba Xuyen province, reported that the camp contained one American and almost eighty Vietnamese. A PRU company was landed on the target but it did not appear to be a POW camp.

Two dry holes in a row suddenly lowered everyone's expectations—except Firth's. On December 1, he got another chance to recover Rowe. An ARVN private managed to escape from the camp *Sage Brush* was originally aiming for. The source was extensively interrogated and polygraphed. He had been in the camp at the time of the October raid and heard the loudspeaker aircraft which had been employed over the area. He estimated that the actual camp position was about fifteen hundred meters from the site raided and confirmed that there were three American prisoners in the camp.[23]

Sage Brush II commenced at noon on December 8, 1968, with one PRU company and two mobile-strike-force companies. The camp was located within three minutes but had been abandoned at least twenty-four hours earlier. It was exactly as the escapee had described it. Twenty pounds of documents and samples of leg stocks, leg irons, and medicines were captured. The camp was set on fire and destroyed. Two hours later a helicopter sighted another previously unknown camp and personnel close by. The guards and approximately sixty Vietnamese prisoners fled. Seven Vietnamese civilians were recovered. Battlefield interrogation of the seven prisoners recovered revealed no knowledge of American prisoners.[24]

After the raid, information continued to filter out of the area. The JPRC reported that "Local inhabitants have stated that seven VC cadres were killed by the gunships. . . . They further stated that the prisoners were moved because of a planned naval operation in the area. They had no forewarning of the recovery operation. . . . Initial readout of the documents reveal there is a complex of six separate camps in the area containing 444 prisoners."[25]

The JPRC was 900 meters away from Nick Rowe. Why Firth didn't move toward Rowe's camp at that time is a mystery to McNabb. "We had a pictomap on the wall with the eight-digit grid coordinates that Pitzer had given us, which later proved extremely accurate." But a recent ARVN offensive into the U-Minh Forest, which included devastating B-52 strikes, had caused the camp with Rowe to change position. They wandered around the area for several weeks. On December 30, however, Rowe and his guards moved into a camp close to the *Sage Brush* location. His long wait for freedom was almost over.

"Wouldn't you want to rescue a lieutenant just like you?": Rowe Tastes Freedom

In reality, the Delta had two main U.S. POW camps, one in the Ca Mau peninsula in An Xuyen province and one in Kien Giang province in the dreaded U-Minh Forest. At first, Rowe had been held in the Ca Mau prison, but in 1965 he had been moved north to the U-Minh Forest camp. After the release of the three other Americans, he had been alone for almost a year, suffering from skin diseases and malnutrition. Even though Rowe had resisted the VC indoctrination, the NLF informed him in early November 1968 that they were considering releasing him. Before doing so, the communists decided first to check his background by using their contacts in the United States. Then someone in the States apparently betrayed him. The VC informed Rowe that they had learned, through the help of American antiwar protesters, that he was not a simple engineer as he had continually told them but was instead a Special Forces officer.[26] Rowe feared he had been targeted for execution when he discovered, after rummaging through the camp documents during the guards' lunch break, that he was to be transferred to the Civilian and Enemy Proselytizing section at Region Headquarters.

While Rowe was contemplating his impending transfer and possible execution, Firth had traveled to the Delta town of Muc Hoa. Firth was looking for a young Special Forces lieutenant named John Regan. Regan had been fighting with the 47th Mobile Strike Force, a unit made up primarily of ethnic Cambodians. He did his job well and had made serious inroads into VC control of the area.

"One day this guy Firth came to Muc Hoa looking for me," Regan remembers. "I didn't even know who he was or why he picked me, but he wanted me to run the raid to rescue this POW. At first I wasn't sure, but he looks at me and said, 'Wouldn't you want to rescue a lieutenant just like you?' How could I say no to that?"[27]

Oddly, for two weeks Firth had Regan's soldiers make amphibious landings on twelve different beachheads along the coast. Finally, on December 31, he was told to bring his unit to a staging area. "I picked my best Cambodians to go with me. These men were great fighters and extremely loyal. They would fight to the death for you, and I wanted to have those kind of men around me when we landed." Regan kept his notebook from that day and his writings reveal the details of the operation. "50 VC—20 armed. Camp at VC 949788. Three LZs, Alpha, Bravo, and Charlie. Sweep LZ Charlie and secure it. Extract from LZ Alpha. Be prepared to assist A or B." His troop briefing was equally succinct. "No shooting. Normal LZ procedures. Watch friendly positions. Move fast, sweep clean." Regan's code-name on the radio was "Irish."

An unnamed colonel in a sanitized uniform provided a last briefing to Regan and his men on the morning of December 31, 1968. The plan called for one of the CIA's PRU companies to land on LZ Alpha and directly assault the camp. Another platoon from Regan's Mike force, led by Lieutenant Buck Littell, would land on LZ Bravo and block any escape from the west. Regan's Cambodians would secure the eastern perimeter of the camp on LZ Charlie. Additionally, a line of tear gas was to be laid south of the camp to prevent escape in that direction.

Now it was time to load up. The ride to LZ Charlie was uneventful, the faint sun hidden behind some clouds. When the assault group reached the camp area, the initial attack worked perfectly and all three units hit their LZ at the same time. As Regan's helicopter came in to land, however, he noticed they were right in the middle of a bunker complex. As his troops began to disembark from the helicopters, VC civilians began pouring from the bunkers, trying to surrender. Some began throwing their weapons into a nearby canal. Within minutes Regan had captured over 30 VC prisoners. Unseen from the air, the bunkers Regan's men had stumbled into belonged to a VC hospital complex.

As Regan struggled to gain control of the area, Buck Littell on LZ Bravo had met no resistance and had quickly reached the edge of the POW camp. He radioed Regan that they had found 20 Vietnamese prisoners chained together in the prison, but they had not found Rowe. He informed Regan that the newly freed South Vietnamese had said that the VC had just moved the "white man out." The VC guards had taken Rowe and fled. Then Regan overheard one of the command helicopters radio that "the PRU had got off the helicopters and went the wrong direction. Instead of directly attacking the camp, they had gotten lost. The plan was completely blown. When I heard how screwed up everything was, I decided to advance towards the camp and seal off the back side. I thought that if Rowe was still alive, his only hope of rescue was for us move forward and intercept the fleeing column. But to get to him, we had to attack across an open field and through some elephant grass. I couldn't leave the prisoners, so I had to drag them behind me. We formed a skirmish line and moved out. I had 30 VC POWs to my rear, plus who knew how many more were still hiding in some spider hole. We were completely exposed, and as we began moving through the elephant grass my heart was pounding in my chest. I was scared to death. We were totally out in the open. I thought the VC would start firing at us at any second."

Moving through the open field, Regan thankfully reached the edge of the camp without incident. He was ordered to hold his position. The PRU had finally reoriented themselves and were directed to attack the camp, even though Littell and Regan had essentially captured it. With the camp secure, Regan watched the Chinooks come in and pick up the captured VC and the freed South Vietnamese. Because he had not found Rowe, he desperately wanted to turn around and go back to the bunker complex to look for him. But the Americans commanding the PRU element ordered Regan and Littell not to engage in any hot pursuit. The PRU would do that. According to Regan, "The CIA definitely wanted the credit for rescuing Rowe."

Unknown to Regan, Rowe and the camp guards were only a short distance away. Regan later heard that Rowe and his guards were actually in the bunker complex that Regan landed on. Rowe was hidden inside one with a shotgun pressed against his head. When Regan moved off the LZ, Rowe and his guards fled in the opposite direction.

Upon hearing the helicopters and watching the insertion of the troops, Rowe convinced one of his guards to leave the main group and travel alone before they were all killed by the gunships searching the area. After artfully leading his lone guard away from the main group and waiting until the guard had his back turned to him, Rowe picked up a fallen branch and smashed it into the base of the guard's skull. Running about fifty meters to a clearing, he stopped and began waving his mosquito netting in the air. After a short while, a gunship spotted him. Mistaking him for a VC, they were moving in for the kill when the helicopter troop commander decided he wanted a prisoner. As the helicopter landed, the crew realized he was an American. He jumped in and the helicopter took off. After five years as a prisoner, Nick Rowe was a free man.

When word reached JPRC headquarters that Rowe had been recovered, Mitchell remembers that he and Firth jumped into a jeep to meet him at the airport. "Firth had vowed not to leave Vietnam until Rowe was rescued, he had spent months launching raids to get him out, and now it had finally happened." The JPRC immediately fired off a message to CINCPAC and SACSA. The short JPRC message read, "Fittingly, the first U.S. PW recovered by an aggressive operation is Major James N. Rowe, USA. . . . At 311340H Dec 68, JPRC was notified by IV Corps that Rowe had been recovered. . . . Area still being swept for possible additional PW."[28] The JCS alerted presidential advisor Walt W. Rostow, who in turn called President Johnson. Johnson wanted to know what medal Rowe was going to get. At first, "MACV has no plans at this time," but later Rostow noted that "We are attempting to assemble data necessary for a recommendation for the award of the Medal of Honor."[29]

The helicopter that picked up Rowe came from Troop B, 7th Squadron, 1st Air Cavalry, which was supporting the 32nd ARVN Regiment of the 21st ARVN Division. John Regan felt the CIA had too much influence on the operation. "They definitely wanted the PRU to get the credit for a successful recovery. My men could have immediately pursued Rowe but we were told to hold. Even before I got back to Muc Hoa, Rowe had called the base and told my XO [Executive officer] he had seen my name tag, that's how close we were to him."

There was one last piece of unfinished business. According to a message sent immediately after he was debriefed, Rowe "has contributed information on basis of which ARVN 21st Division is conducting operations in U Minh Forest area. . . . He immediately volunteered to lead troops back into area of his imprisonment. He is confident there are two U.S. PW there but cannot pinpoint their location since he has been in isolation for the past year. He is eager to return to duty and help JPRC recover more prisoners. JPRC would be proud to have him."[30]

The escaped ARVN private who had led *Sage Brush II* had said there were three American prisoners in the area. One, of course, was Rowe. The camp documents recovered indicated an extensive prison system, one under the control of the province security forces. Also, the source's description of the camp was "exact." Rowe believed there were two more American POWs in the area, and in later years was adamant, based on his experience, that men had been left behind. Rowe mentions in his book *Five Years to Freedom* that he saw several other American POWs while attending an outdoor movie, although he was unable to see them clearly nor was he allowed to speak with them. In the euphoria of Rowe's recovery, were two more American POWs, men who never came home, left behind somewhere in the Delta?

Searching for Bodies

The JPRC reward program did produce some results, mostly in the recovery of American dead. The program basically awarded $5000 for a live American, $500 for a body. One of the areas that seemed to respond well to the program was near Can Tho. On September 1, the JPRC was told that a defector at Can Tho had led a team which recovered the remains of an American. The defector had also stated that the individual was killed in a helicopter crash on February 2, 1968. The deceased was identified and $500 was given to the 525th MI Group for them to reward the defector for his efforts.[31]

Several fishermen helped to find bodies that had washed ashore from crashed aircraft or men who had been hit and fallen overboard in engagements on the many streams and rivers in the Delta. While successful on some occasions, the reward program could also create dangerous situations and lead to unscrupulous attempts by Vietnamese criminal gangs. Fred Caristo, the hero of *Cobra Tail*, who was by now working for the 525th MI Group, recalls that "the Vietnamese were going out to old French cemeteries digging up bodies to turn in. We had to be constantly on the lookout for scam artists. I was almost kidnapped once by four guys who claimed they had information on some POWs. We had gone to meet them at a hotel and I wound up having to shoot my way out."

In fact, Caristo was involved in an even more dramatic remains-recovery mission, the recovery of Private First Class Timothy Kapun. Kapun was killed in February 1968 during a VC ambush while assigned to a boat conducting river patrol. While Kapun's body was being returned to his home base, it was accidentally washed overboard. His lieutenant signed a statement regarding the circumstances, but the company commander, first sergeant, and battalion commander asserted that the body had been placed on a helicopter and sent to the mortuary located on Tan Son Nhut air base. The family continued to press the Army for the remains, and under this pressure the Army launched an investigation.

In mid-December, a 525th MI agent reported that a farmer in a village near Can Tho had found a body in his rice paddy and buried it. The agent brought out a name tag and one dog tag. Caristo, his sergeant, Terry O'Keefe, and the agent were dispatched to recover the body.

"We flew down to Can Tho and then caught a pedicab to a spot near the village," Caristo recalls. "We walked about two miles to the village, where we met the village chief and the farmer who had buried the body. We all went into a hut to negotiate the return. About four of the local Self-Defense people joined us, armed I might add. We were in civilian clothes and I had five hundred dollars and my nine-millimeter pistol in an attaché case I was carrying. After we enter the hut and sat down, the village chief informs me he is going to negotiate for the farmer. He asks for five thousand dollars. I told him we didn't have that much, plus the standard reward was only five hundred. We continue to carry on this conversation in Vietnamese, and as we're talking more and more of the Self-Defense people start crowding into this hut, all of them armed. Eventually there are close to twenty-five of these characters in the room.

"Well, the chief kept insisting on five thousand dollars even after I had showed him how much I was carrying. As we're talking, I heard this one guy say out loud, 'Let's just kill them and take the money.' I slowly opened the case and pulled out my nine-millimeter. I chambered a round and put it up against the chief's head and said, 'I'm leaving here in five minutes either with your body or the American's.' He said, 'Reach under the bed you're sitting on.' I slowly put my hand under the bed and touched something wrapped up in a plastic tablecloth. I pulled it out and handed it to O'Keefe, who opened it and confirmed it was a Caucasian by looking at the shape of the skull. Then they handed us the other dog tag. I gave the guy two hundred and fifty dollars and told him the farmer would get the rest when we confirmed the identity. We got up and left. The Self-Defense guys just moved out of our way. We caught a cab back to Can Tho and several weeks later the mortuary called and said it was Kapun."

The reward program actually first paid for a body recovery in December 1967, when two Montagnards were paid $500 U.S. when they returned the body of Private Jonathan Blue of the 4th ID. But the return of dead Americans was not tracked until May 1967 when the JPRC reward program was approved. The first official payment in Laos was made in early August 1968 to a CAS guerrilla team who recovered the body of a Navy commander missing in Laos since January 1967. In accordance with Sullivan's rules, they were paid only $200 U.S.

Sullivan Remains Untouched; Arthur Hesford Visits Laos

Even the loss of the men and valuable equipment on Site 85 did not diminish Sullivan's prestige or power. President Johnson, preoccupied with his decision not to run again, plus the imminent start of the Paris Peace Talks, probably had no stomach for the fight that would inevitably have occurred if he had sought to limit Sullivan's or any other ambassador's powers. Worse, Sullivan's disdain for the military, and SOG in particular, was becoming increasingly evident. He wasn't even bothering to hide it anymore.

The Air Force had recently introduced into the air war a new type of aircraft, the swept-wing, all-weather F-111 bomber. One was quickly lost, apparently over the Trail in Laos. The military was desperate to keep this important piece of hardware out of North Vietnamese hands, especially since they hoped the new "terrain-hugging" flight technology would enable U.S. Air Force planes to easily penetrate Soviet air defenses if a war with the USSR broke out. Since the NVA's air defenses were an exact duplicate of the Soviets', the Air Force was using the Vietnam war as a test track for their penetration strategy against So-viet air defenses.[32]

When SOG requested permission to enter Laos to search for the wreckage, Sullivan wrote back, "When first F-111 aircraft was reported missing, I received a message from my favorite instant correspondents, MACSOG, indicating they would like to send one of their Batman teams into South Laos to look for the wreckage. After Hanoi announced shooting down plane over NVN, matter apparently became academic and correspondence did not flourish. . . . In order clarify situation with respect to Laos and avoid future rhubarbs or recriminations, I would like to set out my position on contingencies in this message. That position, in essence, is that I would not rpt not be prepared to accept the risk of inserting Americans on the ground in enemy-held areas for the sake of searching for or sanitizing wreckage of an F-111. I would, naturally, accept such risk for the sake of rescuing crew members."[33]

The next day, Sullivan recounted, at a cocktail party at the Polish embassy he and the DRV chargé were engaged in a conversation when they were joined by several others, including the Soviet military attaché. The DRV chargé "shifted to a bantering line, thanking us for delivering an F-111 to them so that they could study its electronic system. He asked the Soviet attaché whether Soviets had yet received a full briefing on the system." Foreseeing nothing but more North Vietnamese insults, Sullivan reports that he then broke away "in search of vodka."[34]

While Sullivan and the military continued to butt heads over rescue operations, the status of POWs in Laos still worried the JPRC. Based on the JPRC's June 1968 request to check out Sam Neua, the CIA was still attempting to locate American prisoners in Laos. In November at the CAS-SOG coordination meeting held at Udorn, CAS presented a status report on their attempts to locate American prisoners alleged to be held in the vicinity of Sam Neua. They had two teams near Sam Neua who had the task of locating and identifying American personnel detained there, as well as Road Watch and other duties. In addition, the CIA reported, penetration agents were being recruited and trained for the specific task of locating the POWs.[35]

Despite the continual JPRC efforts to press CAS to locate American POWs in Laos, effective U.S. assistance for the POWs was still hampered by the political aspects of the war. In April 1968 a policy paper was developed for DOD by its general legal counsel which addressed itself to the peculiar position of American POWs in Laos who had been lost and/or captured while overflying a neutral third country. The paper concluded that the U.S. government could insist that these persons be afforded full coverage of the Geneva Convention but that unfavorable political consequences would result. DOD realized that, because of the political nature of the war, the problem was ultimately a political one and final resolution rested with the State Department. The only actions open to them were to urge State to take whatever steps it deemed necessary to obtain diplomatic recognition of the POW status of American personnel lost in Laos.[36]

But convincing Ambassador Sullivan to raise the issue of American POWs in Laos without jeopardizing the secrecy of the war was another matter. While Harriman was arguing with the Vietnamese in Paris, he cabled Sullivan asking about the growing numbers of Americans missing in Laos. Sullivan replied to his old mentor, "I appreciate your expression of concern re U.S. pilots held prisoner in Laos. It is one of the most vexing and least tractable problems with which we are faced. In assessing how we might stimulate release by Pathet Lao, I have naturally been drawn to compare situation with that which prompted releases by North Vietnamese. Unfortunately, there is practically no parallel in Pathet Lao situation. . . . Moreover, situation is complicated by evidence that a number of pilots missing in Laos are captives of North Vietnamese. . . . Other possible angles such as using NVA prisoners held here in Laos have been fruitlessly examined. Only leverage which has some similarity with North Vietnamese situation is possible Pathet Lao sensitivity to Red Cross appeals. ICRC representatives . . . have always been received courteously, but without any evidence that Pathet Lao are embarrassed by their refusal to permit Red Cross visits. . . ."

Sullivan went on to ask for an envoy, either a genuine pacifist like Stewart Meachum or perhaps a family member. Sullivan insisted it should "be done quietly, and on behalf of some pilot families, rather than at behest of USG. . . . We have just learned that Arthur Hesford, brother of Peter Hesford (one of our downed pilots), is coming to Laos in the near future. We will try out various approaches with him, including our continuing efforts to send packages and letters to our pilots. . . ."[37]

Arthur Hesford was the first of many family members to make the trip to Vientiane seeking information from the NLHS concerning their loved ones. His brother, Peter Hesford, and his copilot were Missing in Action after being shot down in Laos while on a night strike on March 21, 1968. Although the FAC stayed in the area for two hours listening for beepers, none was heard.

Arthur Hesford and his father, however, believed that Peter had a good chance of survival. "Within a couple of weeks I got a visa and flew to Vietnam to talk to Peter's squadron mates, including his wingman, who told me what had happened that night and that they had not heard a beeper," Arthur remembers, "but I researched the F-4 ejection sequence and was told that if the plane hadn't hit the ground yet, he stood a good chance of getting out. I decided I wanted to find out more about his loss and asked the Embassy for help."[38]

The Embassy sent a letter to the Indian ICC commissioner, who agreed to ask Sot Phetrasi, the head of the NLHS delegation in Vientiane, for information. Sot told the Indian that the PL knew the plane had been shot down but he didn't know whether Peter Hesford was alive. Unaware of this information, Arthur Hesford decided to fly to Vientiane in July. He arrived on July 3 and was granted an audience with Sot on July 5.

He recalls, "The Embassy people were very nice, especially Jim Murphy. He arranged for an interview with Sot Phetrasi and for a translator, a Reverend Roffe, who had spent a great deal of time in Laos and who was well known. When I met Phetrasi, he agreed to find out about Peter if I wrote a letter addressed to Prince Souphanouvong. He promised he would do his best to find out any information and if I came back, he would let me know. The fact that he knew my brother's name so quickly led me to believe Sot knew what he was talking about and gave me some hope." While the Embassy representative was present, Phetrasi repeated the NLHS POW line, which mirrored the DRV's POW policy. The "first step," according to Phetrasi, "in solving POW question was 'lessening' of U.S. hostilities in Laos. Only after these actions could the subsidiary question of pilots be taken up."

In September, Sot Phetrasi began telling journalists that Hesford was alive. In an interview with a French journalist named Max Coiffait and a later one with a Reuters stringer named Ky, Phetrasi stated that Hesford was alive. When pressed on how he knew, Phetrasi said he had information from "Headquarters."

The Embassy informed Arthur Hesford of Sot's declarations. Encouraged, Arthur returned to Laos in November and stayed for a month. He had three meetings with Sot Phetrasi. At his first meeting with Sot on November 23, 1968, Hesford recalls that Sot said "'Yes, I have information on your brother. To the best of my knowledge, your brother is alive.' After we left, the Reverend Roffe told me to be careful about what Sot said, that he was isolated. But I knew he had a radio and a mail pouch. I also asked about Peter's backseater and Sot said he thought he was also okay, but he seemed much less sure."

Arthur Hesford proposed to Sot that he trade places with his brother. Sot was surprised by Hesford's request but turned him down on the basis of Buddhist principles, which state that a man cannot pay for the crimes of his brother. Feeling he could do no more in Vientiane, on his return flight from Laos he wanted to meet Averell Harriman and stopped to see the Governor in Paris. Vientiane reported to State that he intended to ask "Harriman to make a direct appeal to Souphanouvong for information regarding the status of US pilots missing in Laos. His rationale was that despite Hanoi's influence a message directly to Souphanouvong from a responsible US official would avoid dealing with question of NVN/PL relations. Comment: We told Arthur that given relationships of PL to NVN, Souphanouvong could not be expected reply to any contemplated official US communication without consulting Hanoi. We were noncommittal as to desirability of such a step."[39]

Although willing to attempt this direct communication, Sullivan was afraid that such a letter might be used in the current NLHS media campaign against the increased U.S. bombing in Laos. Having ceased bombing in the DRV, the Air Force and Navy were free to devote their full attention to attacking the Trail and other targets in Laos. Of course, "If we are interested in sending letter, Ambassador Sullivan will . . . have to discuss matter with Souvanna in advance."[40]

In April 1969 UPI reported that Sot Phetrasi [now being spelled Soth Petrasy by the press] was continuing to demand the unconditional cessation of U.S. bombing before "discussions on the release of American prisoners of war held in Laos could begin. . . . Colonel Petrasy said that the prisoners were detained in caves in northern Laos. Observers here believe that Colonel Petrasy has a limited knowledge of the number and whereabouts of United States POWs in Laos."[41]

Hesford returned to Vientiane in September 1969 to deliver another letter he had written to Souphanouvong. On September 6, Soth met with Hesford for a little over an hour. Soth said he did not have any more information on Peter. However, Soth "admitted that the Lao People's Liberation Army had a list of prisoners missing in Laos which was available to Prince Souphanouvong. As a policy matter, Soth explained that the LPLA would not make this list available while the bombing was going on."[42] The Embassy further noted that "Soth's admission that withholding names was a policy decision confirms past conversations of Embassy and more recent information."

An Embassy officer visited Soth Petrasy to discuss the letter and discovered that "Soth's tone about his failure to provide info regarding status personnel on POW lists seemed more defensive than in past conversations. . . . Although suggesting POWs are kept near point of capture, Soth referred to moves for security. Perhaps Soth was alluding to transfer of U.S. POWs from Laos to NVN."[43]

The reference to the possible transfer of American POWs to North Vietnam was not an idle comment. In fact, the CIA had recently received reports that a number of American POWs in Laos were being moved to the DRV. But the NLHS was also simply following a combination of communist NLF and DRV POW policies: use the POW issue to stop the U.S. bombing (the DRV position), and to then gain political recognition (the NLF program).

Arthur Hesford's repeated visits had an extremely important effect on the POW/MIA issue in Laos, as his efforts forced both the Pathet Lao and the U.S. government to publicly acknowledge the continued loss of American pilots over that country. At a November 1969 press conference, Soth Petrasy made a statement that "more than 158 American airmen are held prisoner in Laos. . . . For the first time, Soth said he would make efforts to forward letters and telegrams sent him by the relatives of U.S. airmen believed shot down in Laos. In the past, he has always rejected such requests. . . . U.S. officials have never admitted to any American air activity over Laos other than reconnaissance flights. But allied sources have disclosed that U.S. air strikes, including support missions for ground forces, involve as many as 500 planes a day over Laos."[44]

Never Give Up Hope: Code Letters and Post-SAR Attempts

While the JPRC was papering South Vietnam with leaflets concerning the reward program, the bombing halt over the DRV ordered by President Johnson on

October 31 brought a stop to the program over the North. The JPRC also began developing a psy-ops program to advertise the reward program for Laos. The leaflet included a basic message urging communist soldiers to defect with American POWs. One unique feature was a map showing how to escape to friendly territory.

Despite the JPRC's intention that the reward leaflet program include Laos, on November 28 the U.S. Embassy in Vientiane turned down a MACV/JPRC request to employ reward leaflets in Laos. Vientiane responded by saying that "for a variety of internal political reasons and the probability of increasing the jeopardy of the downed U.S. pilots in Laos we do not want any reward leaflets addressed to the problem of U.S. captured personnel in Laos produced or dropped at this time."[45]

The no-publicity policy was severely tested when in December 1968 the *New York Times* noted the increasing air war in Laos and printed an article describing SAR forces rescuing Americans who were flying bombing raids from bases in Thailand. "Most of the air rescue work now is over eastern Laos, in the vicinity of the enemy supply network. . . ."[46] In response, a joint State-DOD cable asserted that "There will be no change in current policy regarding release of information on Americans shot down in Laos. . . . It will continue to be policy not to announce publicly any losses in Laos as they occur."[47]

In response to the joint cable, the Embassy requested new SAR procedures for Americans, especially use of the Forward Air Controllers (FAC) working exclusively in Laos, who were known as the Ravens. A joint Air Force/Embassy meeting was held at Udorn on January 15 to discuss "prerequisites for initiating USAF SAR. . . . recovery of Raven FACs who fly unmarked O-1s armed with rockets and accompanied by Lao observers was vital. Proof of US military flying armed aircraft from Laos must be withheld from the enemy. Therefore every reasonable effort should be made to initiate SAR despite lack of beeper or radio contact or proof that survivors exist. Recovery of bodies is desirable however undue risk of SAR resources is not anticipated. Request SAR procedures be amended to include authority to initiate USAF SAR to recover Raven bodies."[48]

The Embassy's insistence on the necessity to hide the presence from the enemy of Americans flying armed aircraft from Laos was simply a matter of continuing to comply with U.S. government policy. Americans shot down flying from bases in Thailand could be explained away, but Americans flying aircraft off of Lao bases was a clear violation of the by-now frayed Geneva Accords. Of course, the enemy had plenty of downed aircraft and equipment to exhibit to the world press any time they wanted to no matter how the Americans modified their SAR procedures. The communist media continually trumpeted reports such as "On 22 January 1969, the Lao army and people blasted down the 1,000th U.S. aircraft over Savannakhet."[49] Even their families now knew where the airmen had been lost.

Although the requirement to maintain the SAFE areas in North Vietnam was dropped with the bombing halt, the image interpreters were now free to spend more time looking for symbols. Incidents of code letter sightings suddenly picked up in the period between October 1968 and April 1969. One curious event occurred in late October 1968. While reviewing film of Haiphong on October 31 that was taken on October 1, "a possible code letter" was noticed. "The photo revealed the letters *A* and *K,* code letter and back-up for June, laid out on the rafters of a bombed-out building on the outskirts of Haiphong. Request research photography taken this area to determine initial time of placement of code letters."[50] The JPRC passed the information to CAS, but no mention is made of the outcome.

In the first half of 1969, several code letters were spotted on the ground in Laos. On March 13 the code letter *T* was spotted. CAS was alerted and discovered it was a group of RLA troops and their dependents who had gathered to be evacuated from enemy attacks.

On March 19 the code letter *N* was reported at grid XC 9314. The letter was confirmed by visual reconnaissance. JPRC alerted the 7th AF, which immediately dispatched two F-4s to deliver survival kits. The kits were placed on the target three hours later. They remained unopened but the next day an orbiting F-100 FAC "reported seeing a parachute shelter and receiving mirror flashes from grid XC 1286 in Laos. JPRC asked 4802 JLD to investigate the sighting and requested 7th AF continue fly VRs [visual recon] in the area. JLD is preparing a team for infiltration and is scheduled to launch the team on 27 Mar 69." However, for unknown reasons the team was delayed until March 31. The kits remained unopened and were destroyed by napalm on April 8.

On March 31, the Air Force reported that film recently taken just north of the DMZ showed a possible evader symbol. Since the location was in North Vietnam, the 7th AF wished to obtain more photo coverage before committing additional assets. On April 7, fresh coverage confirmed the symbol and the commander of the 7th AF directed an E&E kit be dropped. On April 8 the weather was terrible, however, and the kit wasn't dropped until the next day. The Air Force flew repeated missions over the area but no visual or electronic contact was established with the evader. The search was suspended on April 11.[51]

Why was it taking so long to respond to possible E&E signals? Why did it take CAS ten days to launch a search team to investigate someone signaling with a mirror, especially since that was a common procedure? The answers are difficult to ascertain, but several possible reasons are the dangers involved, the presence of a possible enemy trap, the previous lack of results, and the continued political ramifications of putting Americans on the ground in Laos. But if DOD and State were so adamant about not revealing the presence of Americans to the enemy, and the military had modified the normal SAR procedures to attempt to recover "Raven" FACs even if no beeper was heard, why the slow response to these signals?

Unfortunately, the post-SAR picture would be no different. Three major post-SAR rescue attempts were conducted in 1968, all of them in December and all in Laos. The first was a USAF RF-4C reconnaissance plane shot down on December 11. The front-seat pilot ejected and was rescued by SAR forces on the morning of December 12. There was no sign of his crewman, Russell D. Galbraith, but the pilot said he had definitely ejected but that he had not seen him after he landed. The Joint SAR Center (JSARC) immediately requested JPRC assistance.

Within four hours JPRC had notified the embassies in Vientiane, Bangkok, and Saigon plus queried CINCPAC to obtain the necessary clearances. A Vietnamese-manned *Bright Light* team was pre-positioned at the U.S. air base at Nakhom Phanom (NKP), Thailand. Vientiane, however, already had a CAS Road Watch team in the area and that team was ordered to search the area. They located the pilot's radio and parachute but were unable to find any trace of Galbraith. Sullivan then refused permission for the *Bright Light* team to deploy to assist in the search. The team returned to Danang.

Another post-SAR mystery occurred the following week when a Navy A-6A was shot down. The pilot ejected and although he twice scanned in a 360-degree circle, he was unable to locate his backseater, Michael L. Bouchard. The pilot was picked up by SAR forces, but the "second crew member could not be positively located even though a beeper was heard and the signaler responded to commands. The JPRC notified Udorn and requested they launch a search team into the area."[52] Three teams were sent in for several days to look for him, and a loudspeaker on an airplane was also used, but no sign of Bouchard was found.

Writing to Bouchard's son, the pilot tried to explain the circumstances of his father's loss. His poignant letter was quoted in the Senate Select Committee report. "What happened to your Dad and I was the real definition of rotten coincidence. . . . As we rolled in and released the bombs, two antiaircraft rounds struck the airplane on the right side. . . . The explosion caused the engine to explode and the right wing blew off at the fold. At this point, we looked at each other and ejected from the aircraft. I went out a second or so before Mike and wound up on the west side of a small river. He was on the east. . . . the material and the people we were after were there. . . . There was enough evidence that Mike might be held in the general area where we were hit that a 'bright light' team was inserted in an attempt to find and rescue him. . . . They found nothing indicating his having been there. . . . It was hard to accept, but I feel he was killed that first night . . ."[53]

Finally, on December 24, Charles Brownlee, flying an F105D, was also hit and bailed out over Laos. SAR forces discovered the pilot hanging in a tree. He was described as "inert." A parajumper, Charles King, was lowered down the helicopter's hoist to bring him on board. King then radioed he was wounded by ground fire. The helicopter attempted to winch him and the pilot on board but the cable broke and both fell ten feet to the ground. Under an extremely heavy enemy barrage, the SAR helicopter was forced to pull away. A short beeper was heard ten minutes later. The JPRC staged a *Bright Light* team to NKP, but due to the enemy presence Sullivan refused to allow them to go in.

Currently, Galbraith, Brownlee, and King are considered "Priority Discrepancy Cases" by the U.S. government. These are cases in which the United States believes the Vietnamese and Lao governments should be able to provide quick and easy answers to the fate of MIAs since they were lost in close proximity to enemy forces. Strangely, the Bouchard case is not on this list, although the SAR forces reported a beeper and the signaler responded to commands. Regardless, the communists have denied any knowledge of what happened to these men.

Van Putten Escapes

In March 1969 the German nurse Renate Kuhnen, captured a year earlier during the Tet Offensive, was released in Kontum, the city where she was captured. Kuhnen stated that "she saw no US PWs but heard that a US Negro had been held at one of her camp sites. She stated she had been indoctrinated and had made releases for radio and TV broadcasts. An Embassy rep indicates her comments to the press will not favor the US position. He also stated that a Military Intelligence session might prove counterproductive so a request for a formal debriefing was not pursued."[54]

On April 17, a young Army enlisted man named Thomas H. Van Putten, assigned to the 79th Engineer Group, escaped from a VC prison camp on his third attempt. Van Putten had been captured on February 10, 1968, when his convoy was ambushed and overrun by a company-sized element. According to Van Putten, "The day I escaped I had left the chain around my ankle unlocked and the guard didn't check it. Later in the afternoon when he left, I took off. I eventually came to a creek and followed that to a river. I just floated down the river until one day I heard helicopters. It was a hunter/killer team. I took off my shirt and started waving it at them. At first they thought I was a VC and they were lining for a firing run when the pilot saw that I was an American."[55]

He had been evading for 21 days and was suffering from malnutrition and dehydration. He was immediately debriefed by Military Intelligence specialists and revealed that he had been interrogated for military information only in the beginning; the remainder of his interrogations had been the usual attempts to gain propaganda statements. Fortunately, none of the interrogators spoke English very well. Only the camp commander spoke "passable English."

Back in the States, Van Putten worked closely with a CIA Identikit specialist attempting to create composites of the camp commander and his interrogators. This was a technique that had been used in the past by the Agency. The CIA was trying to build a database of enemy POW officials to use during debriefing sessions with released POWs, especially prisoners from the North.

His debriefing revealed that there were seven other American POWs held in the camp. He was moved between four or five prisons during his captivity. At his last camp he was held in an underground bunker covered with logs, with a trap door to get in and out through. Van Putten knew the names of four POWs and provided enough information to tentatively identify a fifth. The four included Norman Brookens and another civilian, Michael H. Kjome, plus the two Army POWs Dunn and Ray, whom the JPRC had gone after when Donald Martin escaped in April 1968. The VC would not permit Van Putten to speak with the "Army major," but the JPRC determined that it was probably Raymond Schrump.

Based on Van Putten's information, a recovery operation using the 1st Cav was planned, but the NVA First Division moved into the area and the operation was indefinitely postponed. Charles Roberts remembers that he was the one who "called off the operation when the NVA moved in. We were after at least three U.S. POWs. The escapee had given us a good location on the camp and I believed this was one of our best chances. I felt terrible for a long time afterwards."

Interestingly, Van Putten's camp was very close to the Ba Thu area. American prisoners had possibly been held there at least since late 1966, when *Cobra Tail* was launched. In fact, an intelligence survey done of the Ba Thu area notes that in December 1966, "Ba Thu was subsequently identified as one of several transshipment points for ordnance entering into SVN. . . . For this reason Ba Thu is classified as a major base area which provides strategic support for enemy units operating in III and IV Corps. . . . In addition, Ba Thu has been alleged periodically to contain POW camps housing both US and ARVN personnel."

The additional sightings of POWs, most of whom returned at *Homecoming*, by American observers confirms that the NVA were using the Ba Thu area as a base area and had a series of POW camps in the area. In September 1968 an escaped ARVN reported two Americans, Brookens and Richard W. Utecht, also in this area.[56]

Who were the two men sought during *Cobra Tail?* Fred Caristo has steadfastly maintained, based on the description of the POWs' uniforms by the source, that the two men were Army aviators. "The source reported the POWs were wearing one-piece flight uniforms," Caristo recalls. "When I was debriefing him, we had some pilots nearby, so I showed the guy the cloth and he said that's it, that's the uniform. One of the reasons I was so eager for this mission was that I thought I was going to rescue some Army guys."

Case files and wartime sighting reports indicate that the two men could possibly have been Charles Dale and David Demmon, two Army aviators lost on June 9, 1965. An aerial search failed to locate their crash site. Both Dale and Demmon were tentatively identified by U.S. intelligence as prisoners in the Delta when a camp guard defected in February 1966. Demmon in particular was reliably reported alive and being held in Cambodia in 1971 and was the object of a major POW raid. The two are considered a Priority Discrepancy Case by the U.S. government.

On the other hand, according to the Vietnamese 1995 unilateral investigation into the loss of Dale and Demmon, they state their plane crashed two to three kilometers off the coast of Vinh Binh province and witnesses claimed both pilots were killed. The local villagers were interviewed and said that one body washed ashore and the other was found entangled in parachute webbing out at sea. Both were buried on the beach, but two large-scale excavations found nothing. The communists have turned over one document that pertains to Dale, but its contents are unknown. The Vietnamese have recommended that the case be closed as the "remains are unrecoverable."

In 1971, an American military officer discovered a wrecked aircraft on the beach in Vinh Binh province that he believes was the Dale-Demmon crash site. (This is discussed in a later chapter.) He spoke to a local fisherman who told him that the VC forced him and others to drag the wreckage off the beach and hide it in the nearby swamp. While the fishermen agreed both men had been killed, his description of the events once again calls into question the accuracy of Vietnamese cooperation, especially on a high-profile case like that of Dale and Demmon.[57]

11. MACV for JPRC

Dellinger said that the NVN delegation gave him no encouragement on the question of lists of American prisoners. He said that he emphasized the painful uncertainty the absence of such a list brought to many Americans, but that this merely produced an emotional response from the NVN delegation to the effect that those Americans should think of how many Vietnamese know that members of their families are dead. Speaking from notes, Dellinger quoted an unnamed NVN officer as saying, "Tell those relatives that, if their men are held in the DRV they receive the most humane treatment possible."
—State cable recounting conversation in Paris between Ambassador Lodge and
    peace activist David Dellinger shortly before the release of an additional three
    U.S. POWs from Hanoi

After the success of Nick Rowe's escape and recovery, the number of rescue attempts dramatically slowed in the first half of 1969. As the United States began to withdraw its ground combat forces under President Nixon's plan for turning the war over to the South Vietnamese, the combination of reduced numbers of American troops and the decline in the morale and cohesiveness of the remaining U.S. maneuver units had a debilitating impact on the capability of the JPRC to recover POWs.

In April 1969 CINCPAC noted the slowdown and wanted some answers. The JPRC responded that "the reduced Bright Light activity is the product of many factors of which three are cited. First, decrease in post-SAR activities is due to enhanced capabilities and techniques applied by SAR forces. Second, reduction of deep penetration missions in NVN decreases exposure to heavy opposition and missions in Laos are closer to neutral or friendly territory resulting in a reduced number of unrecovered aircrew. Third, the decline in information on PW's in SVN is due to the temporary tactical situation. A review of past indicators and history of increased enemy activity shows a direct relation between increased enemy activity and reduction in number of reports concerning enemy PW activities. As the enemy withdraws, PW info will increase, providing better definition of targets, which in turn will increase Bright Light activities."[1]

Despite that prediction, the number of raids continued to slacken. The attitude of unspoken reluctance that McNabb and Roberts had earlier encountered further hardened after a raid launched in July 1969 recovered a lone American POW suffering from a severe head wound inflicted by a VC guard's machete a few moments before rescue troops reached the prisoner. By the end of 1969 the JPRC found it increasingly more difficult to convince American commanders to launch raids into enemy territory. To reflect the reduced activity, a major change was recommended in JPRC reporting procedures. Since its inception, the JPRC had been reporting to CINCPAC on a weekly basis. In the fall of 1969, the JPRC advocated that it submit monthly reports instead. The suggestion was accepted by SACSA, and starting in December the JPRC reports were rendered monthly.

Fortunately, the Air Force was sending a new commander for the JPRC to once again revitalize the unit. Lieutenant Colonel George R. Reinker had previously served a tour in intelligence working with the Air Force Security Service, the SIGINT arm of the men in blue. Currently, he was on flying status but was looking for a new job. One day he called an old friend in Personnel and volunteered to go to Vietnam if they had a good staff intelligence job.

Several days later, his friend called him back. "How about rescuing POWs?" he asked. Reinker immediately accepted. Before he left for Vietnam, he was sent to SACSA for an orientation tour. After he was given an overview of the unit, Colonel Don C. Hatch, who replaced Cochran at SACSA, told him to "keep us advised and let us know if you need anything." It was all the encouragement he would get for a long time.[2]

Getting the CIA More Involved

The military's joint intelligence service, known as the Defense Intelligence Agency (DIA), was the focal point for all military-gathered intelligence. Theoretically it operated closely with the CIA, but in the reality of the ever-present Washington power struggles the two intelligence agencies were major competitors. Often, the flow of information between the two was restricted by security measures and the effects of the unspoken rivalry. Even though a CIA officer was a member of DIA's POW intelligence committee, IPWIC, one of DIA's great concerns was ensuring that the CIA was forwarding all POW information directly to them, particularly intelligence on Laos. In late February 1969, DIA compared its own Lao intelligence holdings against the latest published CIA semiannual intelligence round-up on enemy prison facilities in Laos. DIA's survey indicated that they lacked information reports on almost half of the CIA-listed camp locations.[3] A letter was sent to the CIA member of IPWIC, Richard Elliot, requesting these reports and any additional information that would augment the intelligence database that DIA held on Laos.[4]

Internally, DIA was furious at Langley and made its views known. The CIA did not want to be accused of withholding information on a high-visibility subject like POWs, and quickly moved to patch relations. A courtesy visit was paid to DIA on April 2 by a senior CIA official and the discussions clarified the necessity for providing DIA with all possible information from CIA files on this subject. The CIA immediately provided DIA with a computerized listing of reports on POWs and prison camps in Laos. In addition, they made a great show of asking the CIA station in Vientiane for any additional information held at that station on POW locations.[5]

DIA wasn't the only customer looking for help from the CIA. Frank Sieverts at State was pushing the intelligence community to start including civilians in their POW accounting procedures. In January, Sieverts began a major campaign to include civilian MIAs in DIA's database. He especially wanted photos of civilians published in DIA's booklet of unidentified POWs.

Meeting with some inertia, he began pressing harder in March 1969 to get DIA and CIA to establish the responsibilities of the three agencies with regard to civilians. It was agreed that DIA would distribute photos of civilians with the regular military debriefing kits prepared for returnees and escapees while DIA would maintain skeleton files reflecting physical descriptions and basic information jackets on each civilian. The State Department was responsible for action on civilians, but the CIA would maintain the main intelligence files on them.[6]

Pleased that he had raised the issue of civilian POWs to a higher profile, Sieverts immediately began collecting photos of missing employees from American businesses that had lost personnel. Many civilian employees of U.S. companies had disappeared, especially during the fighting during Tet in 1968.[7] "It was only reasonable for civilians to be included in the DIA photo book," Sieverts believed.

"I turned to CIA to handle the civilians because DIA had difficulty with nonmilitary personnel as their computers wouldn't accept the coding for them."[8]

But the CIA was balking at Sieverts' informal request. An internal CIA report mentioned that "State has not yet communicated a formal request to CIA for handling of intelligence files on civilian PWs. At a meeting on 9 June 1969, Mr. Sieverts reiterated his position that State was not equipped to handle intelligence files on PWs, that he hoped CIA would fill this function, and that he was formulating a letter . . . on this subject. Mr. Sieverts was told some time ago that we could take this additional responsibility only if formally tasked to do so. Meanwhile, DIA has become much more active with regard to civilians."[9]

In Vietnam, the 525th MI Group was also expending additional efforts to identify missing civilians. Rumors began circulating, however, that the JPRC and the 525th were not concentrating on civilians, especially in the I Corps area; many civilians were lost in Hue during the Tet Offensive. Sieverts fired off a letter to the Embassy demanding an explanation. The Embassy responded that "Shackleton looked into the matter and confirmed our understanding that JPRC indeed continues to have responsibility for gathering and collating information on civilian PWs. . . . I think there is no real need to ask MACV to cover civilians since Shackleton tells me that he has always relied on JPRC for information and has never found their files wanting. . . . JPRC has no explanation for the impression that your informant received. . . . The unfortunate fact is that we receive practically no information about U.S. civilians in VC hands, but if any problem arises, we will let you know."[10]

Sieverts' lobbying of the two intelligence agencies to include civilians in the POW equation had paid off. The intelligence community was now aware of the problem and would, in the future, pay greater attention to their plight. Eventually, Sieverts would expand that concern to include foreign civilians lost in the maelstrom of the war. By 1972, the issue of missing civilians, especially journalists lost in Cambodia, was every bit as important to the U.S. government as its missing military men.

Death of a POW

Despite the recovery of Rowe, the JPRC persisted in emphasizing the Delta, recovering 10 ARVNs in a raid by the US 9th Infantry Division on March 23, and another 48 in separate raids by the 21st ARVN Division in early April. However, only occasional efforts were made for American POWs held in the areas north of Saigon.

One of the few non-Delta raids that reacted swiftly to current intelligence was

Monroe Bay, an operation to recover two aviators whose O-1 was lost on April 3, 1969. The two men, Arthur G. Ecklund and Perry H. Jefferson, made radio contact at 0730 hours and then disappeared. An extensive three-day aerial search failed to find their plane.

On April 15, a Vietnamese source reported a conversation he had with a Montagnard fighting for the communists who claimed to have shot down an aircraft on April 3. He related that two Americans had been wounded but were captured alive. Reacting to this information, JPRC requested that a SOG *Bright Light* team be inserted to search for the downed airmen. At midnight on April 17, a 25-man team moved into the area.[11] The team conducted a thorough sweep and encountered no enemy. After checking the reported enemy campsite and failing to find the crash site the team was extracted and the operation terminated.[12] Despite the excellent intelligence on the capture of the two men, they never returned home and are oddly not on the U.S. government's Priority Discrepancy Case list.

The most notable quick-reaction raid was attempted in July 1969. On July 1, a Vietnamese named Vo Ngoc Chau rallied to an ARVN outpost in Vietnam's northernmost province, Quang Tin. He had seen an American POW in a hospital only a few days before. Without waiting for authorization, elements of the Recon Company from the 5th Regiment of the Second ARVN Division, some PRU, and helicopters from the U.S. 101st Airborne immediately assaulted the camp area. Chau led the forces into the hospital complex. During the operation, six NVA were killed and several others plus their weapons were captured. Because of the difficult terrain, an ARVN soldier was lowered by a rope into the jungle from a hovering helicopter to reach the POW, Larry D. Aiken. An American trooper rappelled down another rope to assist. Aiken was found lying face down outside the hut where Chau had reported seeing him. He was unconscious and suffering from a fresh head wound. The two soldiers then carried him 300 yards down a stream bed to a waiting helicopter. Aiken was admitted to a military hospital, where he remained in a coma until his death on July 25. Hospital officials concluded that he died of an open skull fracture and brain damage inflicted by his captors prior to his rescue.[13]

Although the raid was launched without JPRC assistance, the death of Aiken caused great concern at MACV and SOG. Reinker remembers, "The first day I walked into the JPRC was the day they made the recovery attempt on Aiken. Everyone was very down about the results of the operation and it definitely colored the attitude towards successive missions."[14]

It was decided a reward of $5,000 in gold was to be presented to the source by a JPRC officer. Dave McNabb's replacement, Air Force Major Daniel Scott, was sent. McNabb departed in June 1969 after two years in the JPRC. Scott had been the flight navigator for General Harold Estes, then Commander of Military Airlift Command. Although he had no experience in covert warfare, he nevertheless thrust himself into the JPRC operations with enthusiasm.

Scott flew to Tam Ky with the money in gold "chiclets," small pellets of easily transportable gold. "We held a ceremony in a schoolyard. When I wanted to give the gold to the source, I was told to present it to the ARVN sector commander, which I did," Scott recalls. "God only knows if the source ever got any of the money."

About three months later, JPRC received a memo from the American Embassy in Saigon regarding the operation. Scott remembers, "The embassy asked for our reasoning in the matter. We were informed that they had received an inquiry from the soldier's congressman, Gerald Ford. Mr. Ford questioned the rescue effort because the man had been killed as a result of the raid. He thought it would have been better if we had waited until the end of the war and the soldier could have been returned through the normal prisoner-exchange process. Obviously, he had no clue as to the conditions in the VC camps. Also, one of the most important axioms of the Vietnam war was that if you were ever captured, the allied forces would never cease looking for you. It was imperative that those in combat knew that they weren't alone. But this was typical of the thinking of some civilians. I had to write back essentially denying that we were involved, which was the truth, but it still really upset me."

Monteray Angler: Trying to Solve the Problems

Although Aiken was killed as a result of the raid, the excellent response displayed by the ARVN unit highlights the main obstacles to successful POW recoveries: the twin problems of rapid enough reaction to POW intelligence reports and accurate enough determination of the source's validity.

Both SOG commander Steven Cavanaugh and his deputy, Air Force Colonel Robert Gleason, believe that at this point in the war the JPRC should have been transferred to the SAR units. Gleason states, "JPRC was not a priority, it was the stepchild of SOG. The enemy POW camps moved too quick and traveled too lightly. Our biggest problem was in getting real-time intelligence. The language, cultural, and educational problems presented by the average source combined with the mobility of the camps presented tremendous odds to overcome, plus the constant danger of flying into a trap. Despite the poor results, the JPRC people tried their damnedest."[15]

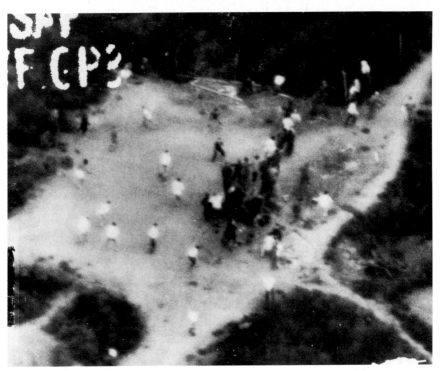

The so-called "volleyball" picture showing "20 non-Asians and their guards." This photo was taken on October 11, 1969, by a RF-4C reconnaissance plane over northern Laos, very close to the reported detention site of American POWs. Two months later a CIA report described 20 American POWs being held in this same area. If these were POWs, none ever came home. *(confidential source)*

The photo shown to George Reinker in the summer of 1969 that the 7th AF photo interpreters believed were "probable Caucasians" and "probable POWs." Note the white shirts similar to the ones in the "volleyball" photo. *(confidential source)*

Frank Jaks and VC rallier at Kontum the morning of Operation *Crimson Tide.* *(courtesy Frank Jaks)*

These leg stocks were found abandoned in the POW camp raided on December 8, 1968, during Operation *Sage Brush II.* *(courtesy Fred Hopewell)*

Prisoner hut and sleeping mat made of bamboo from the same camp. *(courtesy Fred Hopewell)*

Nick Rowe's prison camp the morning he escaped. *(courtesy John Regan)*

Left to right: Major Chuck Boatwright and Major Les Hansen, standing in front of the JPRC office, Spring 1967. *(courtesy Tom Pushak)*

JPRC group, mid-January, 1968. *Standing, left to right:* Capt. Dave McNabb, Cdr. Dickinson Prentiss, Lt. Cdr. Rod Foster, SSGT William Maddox, Capt. Fred Seamon. *Kneeling, left to right:* Sp/7 Willie Ourada, Sp/5 Roger Testerman, LTC Charles Ogle, 1SGT Gary Donelson. This photo was taken by LTC Jack Reisner for LTC Ogle. The plaque Foster is holding was given to each individual in the JPRC when he left. Prentiss is Foster's replacement. *(courtesy Dr. Charles Ogle)*

JPRC group, January 1970. *Standing, left to right:* Sp/4 Helring, the 519th MI database coder who later drowned, Maj. James Rabdau, SFC John Schermerhorn, LTC George Reinker, Maj. Dan Scott, MSGT Thomas Henry, Capt. Gary Mears, LCDR Charles Young. *Kneeling, left to right:* ISGT Sebastian Deluca, Sp/5 Anderson, 519th MI database coder, SP/5 Darrell Vasey, Yeoman Donald Richardson. *(courtesy Thomas Henry)*

JPRC group, March 1971. *Standing, left to right:* Capt. Carl Kraft, LTC James Black, LTC Gerald McImoyle, Maj. Fred Hopewell, LCDR John McFadyen, Maj. Robert Mann. *Kneeling, left to right:* T/SGT Curtis Woodall, Jr., SSGT Howard Rounds, 1SGT Sebastian Deluca, Yeoman Clifford Buccione, SSGT Billy Rowland. *(courtesy Fred Hopewell)*

JPRC group, October 1971. *Standing, left to right:* LTC Andy Anderson, Lt. Cdr. John McFadyen, T/SGT Francis Glaude, SSGT Howard Rounds, Maj. Gerry Bauknight. *Kneeling, left to right:* MSGT Salvatore Rende, Capt. Kevin Kelly, SSGT Billy Rowland, Yeoman Clifford Buccione. *(courtesy Gerry Bauknight)*

Funeral ceremony for Sebastian Deluca, July 17, 1971, Saigon. *(courtesy Gerry Bauknight)*

Cavanaugh agrees. "The recovery efforts were virtually impossible due to either poor or late intelligence or compromise. I was unable to devote as much time to the JPRC as I wish I could have. At any time I had twelve teams on the ground, of which 25 percent were in trouble. I would spend four or five nights out of each week trying to get them out. Consequently, the JPRC probably suffered."[16]

Should the JPRC been moved under the command of the SAR unit in 1969? Certainly the question should at least have been discussed by MACV. Given the record of three years of continuing failure, why the military didn't seriously reconsider the organizational viability of what it supposedly deemed a very important mission is odd.

Another major issue was the continuing problem of the high security classification of the JPRC because of its relationship to SOG. To combat that, Reinker dramatically escalated the number of briefings given by the JPRC in an attempt to increase its visibility. According to Reinker, "When I arrived, MACV thought we weren't being aggressive enough. I felt that the bigger problem was that we needed to move out of the shadows and decentralize to reduce the secrecy. Unfortunately, we also had to live under the realities of the war, which was to keep casualties down. There was an unspoken rule that even if you had a fixed location, if you ran the risk of taking fifty percent casualties the operation was not done." Scott also recalls that active U.S. combat operations became rare from around Christmas 1969 onward.

Reinker quickly moved to solve this problem. In August, every major command in the Vietnam theater down to division level was ordered to appoint a JPRC liaison officer. A message was sent under the signature of General Creighton Abrams, the new commander of MACV, reiterating the importance of the JPRC and the need to keep the recovery unit abreast of all POW information. "The JPRC element of MACV remains the focal point for PW recovery operations. Prior approval of JPRC for a recovery operation is not required and commanders are strongly encouraged to initiate unilateral actions. Messages and reports concerning prisoner intelligence or prisoner recovery operations (successful or unsuccessful) will include an information copy flagged BRIGHT LIGHT, COMUSMACV for JPRC."

In March 1970, to reemphasize to the remaining ground units the importance of taking quick action on perishable battlefield intelligence, Reinker resent the same message, again noting that the "factors of continuing high-level interest, and growing international interest, in all aspects of PW matters dictate a high priority for the conduct of recovery operations. . . ."[17]

In October 1969, Reinker began discussions with the SOG S-3 [Operations] to furnish concrete solutions for the ground commanders. Their answer was to create blank Operations Plans (OPLANs) that provided preapproved authorization for launching raids with any available forces.

The blank plan was code-named *Monteray Angler.* Major James Rabdau had been the Executive Officer of Command and Control North (CCN), the SOG base in Danang, and he knew that SOG still had many fine soldiers. He wanted the SOG forces to have first crack at using this concept. "Aiken's death greatly influenced the development of *Monteray Angler,*" Rabdau states. "We knew we could get into a camp, but since there was no guarantee of safety for the POW, ground commanders were wary of launching an operation. I believed the solution to reducing POW raid reaction time was to institute a program whereby Colonel Cavanaugh could react to new intelligence by immediately dispatching SOG forces." When presented to Cavanaugh, Reinker states he had no problem "clearing it with Chief, SOG. The idea was to tie in SOG assets with any available ground forces. We had blank OPLANs flown to the three SOG bases. Abrams gave blanket authorization to use up to battalion-sized elements as backup if necessary."

Despite their best intentions, however, the OPLAN was barely used. The problem of reaction was becoming overshadowed by the bigger problem of fraud. Numerous sources were offering information on U.S. POWs, but very little of it proved worthwhile. Much of the information flowing into the JPRC was a complete fabrication by sources hoping only to obtain a monetary reward. Telling the good intelligence from the bad was sometimes impossible. Worse, the good intelligence was often dated, sometimes by as much as three months. Another significant portion of the sightings reported were so fleeting they were useless. It was almost as if the JPRC were cursed.

Escapes and Recoveries

Despite all the problems, the one area of continuing good news was that there were actually a few escapes and releases in South Vietnam. Some of the escapees or evaders were assisted by South Vietnamese civilians, who were promptly rewarded by the JPRC for their assistance. For example, around midnight on May 6, a sailor named Adrian G. Eisenland fell overboard from his River Assault Craft, which was anchored in My Tho harbor. He managed to reach the shore and wandered along the bank for five hours. At five o'clock in the morning he encountered two men out fishing in a sampan. Neither could speak English, so they escorted Eisenland back to their village to meet a woman who did. She provided

Eisenland with dry clothes and arranged for him to be returned to his base at My Tho. She was given 18,000 Vietnamese piasters for her aid.

Bodies continued to be recovered and the reward program was instrumental in helping retrieve remains from several crash sites in Laos. In June 1969 the JPRC reported that "the psy-ops directorate has begun a long-range review of the psy-ops and reward programs with the end in mind of making the entire program more effective. Major areas for review are: media, themes, target audience and locale. This review is expected to take several months and is expected to produce a more comprehensive psy-ops and reward program."[18]

Code letters continued to appear sporadically, mostly in Laos. On November 13, 1969, the JPRC ordered two E&E kits dropped in the vicinity of a code letter laid out in a creek bed. Photo coverage of the area revealed that the kits had disappeared but nothing further was seen or heard from possible evaders. Several days later, an E&E kit was dropped on a possible symbol near the crash site of "Misty 31," a plane downed in Laos. That kit too remained unopened and disappeared one week later.

The best news concerned the few men who escaped. Shortly after the escape of Van Putten, the engineer who was picked up by a helicopter after his guard left his ankle chain unlocked, the *New York Times* reported that Sergeant Kenneth R. Gregory "was crying for joy when he was rescued on a jungle trail by a U.S. helicopter . . . four days after escaping from Vietcong captivity. . . . Sergeant Gregory was rescued 12 miles northwest of Tay Ninh City when an Army helicopter crew spotted him on a bamboo jungle trail. . . ."[19] According to Gregory, he was scheduled for release the next day if he signed a propaganda statement, but he slipped off his chains that night and escaped.

Several groups of prisoners were freed, but not by the direct exchange route used for Brigham, Jones, and Smith. The communists apparently decided against further direct meetings based on the American reaction at the last release. The untimely death of Brigham also played a factor. The NLF would now limit themselves to holding the release ceremony in private and then broadcasting it over the radio. Under this new policy, Jessie B. Harris was the first American POW released after the New Year's Day ceremony. He had been captured on June 8, 1969, when he became lost from his unit of the 101st Airborne as they were conducting a sweep near Danang. In late October 1969, Harris suddenly appeared at an LZ of the 101st. Somewhat confused after wandering around the jungle, Harris stated that he had not been held with any other American prisoners. Suffering from malnutrition and malaria, he had "no knowledge of camp locations. He was moved several times and spent approximately two months at the last camp. . . .

He mentions a relatively elaborate release ceremony at which he was presented a handkerchief and some propaganda leaflets. The leaflets are particularly interesting due to mention of the recent antiwar demonstrations in the U.S."[20]

Although no radio broadcasts were made that directly mentioned Harris, on October 27, 1969, NLF radio explained their new release policy by referring to Brigham. Stating that he had been in good health when released, the communist news statement accused the United States of using the pretext of further medical treatment to kill him because he had vowed to work against the war. The communist broadcast further warned American commanders to ensure the safety of released POWs and help them to return home.

The NLF played up the propaganda aspects of the next two groups' release. This was the "dribbling out" of POWs that Bunker had feared. The second of the two groups, helicopter crewmen Warrant Officer Michael T. Peterson and Sergeant Vernon C. Shephard, were released in mid-December 1969 near the Cambodian border. The pair had been shot down on November 2. After being held for only 38 days, the two said "they would not go to war again against their captors because of the good care they had received."[21] In a press conference at Tan Son Nhut airbase, the two expressed deep appreciation for their care and excellent treatment.

The first liberation under the new NLF policy, however, occurred earlier, in November 1969. This release of three Americans resulted in another major JPRC effort that ended in spectacular failure. On November 5 three enlisted soldiers named Willy Watkins, James A. Strickland, and Coy R. Tinsley walked into a South Vietnamese militia post near Tam Ky after being released from a communist prison camp. Watkins and Strickland had been held since January 1968, while Tinsley had been captured in March 1969. A medevac helicopter was immediately requested.

Captain Gerald A. Hamm was the Sector Intelligence officer who came out to meet the men. He reports, "I would like to point out here that to me the Americans did not look in any type of ill health and the gigantic rush to get a dust-off for these men was not needed as much as certain people anticipated. I was especially surprised at the condition of the two Americans that had been captive for 22 months. All three of the men appeared quite healthy. The only visible signs of ill health were that two of the men had swollen feet. The three stated that they had been to a detention camp, location unknown. They were treated well, were not tortured, heavily questioned, or made to do hard labor. They ate well (which was evident by their appearance). They were liberated on 24 October 1969 and had been walking since."[22]

The men had been held with twelve other Americans and they reported these names to their debriefers. Based on their information, the JPRC began to look more closely at I Corps, which had been virtually ignored since the fall of 1968. Major James Rabdau would eventually spend most of his six months in the JPRC attempting to raid those three men's camp in an operation code-named *Oak Circle*.

Growing Frustration: *Oak Circle*

Rabdau was an interim replacement for a JPRC Army officer who had been medically transferred when he developed a severe blood-sugar disorder. He arrived in December 1969, and was on the final leg of an eighteen-month tour of Vietnam when he was assigned to the JPRC. He had been a battalion executive officer in the 23rd "American" Division and had seen the destructive racial conflicts and escalating morale problems in the ground units. These problems, he felt, were exacerbated by the short six-month tours of the commanders. The short tours destroyed continuity, resulting in bad leadership which ultimately harmed the efficiency of the units. Acutely aware of the situation in the combat units, Rabdau spent much of his JPRC tour in the field with the ground commanders, working with them to increase their efforts to recover Americans. Despite his best efforts, however, he was running into a wall.

He describes the situation as "one in which most commanders weren't interested unless you had 'hard' intelligence, something which we almost never had. The Army was in bad shape; we had progressed from the best Army in the world when I was in Vietnam in 1966–67 to one, in some cases, teetering on the edge of collapse. The commanders were more interested in body counts and getting their Silver Stars and then moving on. Whatever portion of their unit was still willing to go out and beat the bush was not generally sympathetic to attacking a base camp deep in enemy territory unless you could precisely pinpoint it. Many officers were trying to get their ticket punched; being diverted from their primary mission to go on a wild-goose chase, especially after Aiken was killed, would not look good on their Officer Efficiency Report."[23]

After the debriefing of the three, Reinker sent Rabdau to I Corps to coordinate with his old unit, the Americal, to launch a raid on the camp they had been released from. The first attack against this prison began after an NVA rallier claimed to have recently been in the POW camp. He offered to lead the raiding party back to the camp. The Americal launched a raid on February 22 and found a number of buildings but no evidence of POWs.

Realizing the futility of running around the jungle, the JPRC "began an intensive study of that region in general, primarily to northwest of 22 Feb raid. Evidence that recent releasees (Tinsley, Willy Watkins, and Strickland) were held in general area, plus other low-grade reports, has prompted detailed study to attempt pinpointing camp locations."[24]

Rabdau began working with the Americal planning the follow-up operation, code-named *Oak Circle.* The prison holding the Americans belonged to one of the seven primary POW camps used in communist MR-5. Pinning down which one was currently holding the U.S. prisoners was the difficult part. The Americal's idea was to specially train several four-man recon teams to infiltrate the area to locate the camp. The JPRC believed that "Any raid will necessarily be a one-shot affair since any successful results demand an insertion on target. Any warning to the NVA-controlled camp will undoubtedly result in movement of PWs into even more inaccessible areas."[25]

By the end of April, the JPRC reported that the Americal had added a "Montagnard guide to four man recce team. The group has completed training and insertion is awaiting improvement in tactical situation in the area. Americal Division will support team insertion and appropriate diversionary action. JPRC project officer completed study of all available intelligence on the camp and gave update briefings to I Corps supporting agencies on 9–10 April. With exception of recce teams, this will be an all U.S. operation."[26]

Delays in the team insertions were encountered as the plan was being continually modified. Rabdau decided to equip the recce teams with mini-ponders emplaced in bamboo walking sticks. The beacons would be activated if the camp was found.

Finally, almost six months after Willy Watkins, Strickland, and Tinsley were released, the "ground reconnaissance phase of Operation *Oak Circle,* designed to locate an enemy PW camp in Southern I Corps, was initiated on 29 May 70 and terminated 11 Jun 70 with negative results. The operation was fully coordinated with, and supported by, the Americal Division. . . . Ground reconnaissance teams were provided. . . . Had the camp been located, it was planned to conduct a swift raid utilizing an Exploitation Company raiding force. . . ."[27]

Rabdau remembers *Oak Circle* as a perfect portrayal of a too-lengthy, brief-everyone-in-sight, drag-them-by-their-heels kind of operation. "This was a classic example of units over-planning an operation, fearful of the consequences of a potential screw-up."

In May 1970, another slow reaction to POW intelligence probably just missed the COSVN U.S. POW camp. A retired American intelligence officer named Zalin Grant was hired by the President of *Time* magazine to search for Sean

Flynn, the journalist who had disappeared in Cambodia. Grant had served previously in Vietnam and spoke Vietnamese. In the process of looking for Flynn, Grant interviewed a rallier in Tay Ninh city who described how he had helped build bunkers for a new POW camp at a location in Cambodia. He had also observed 11 U.S. and 80 ARVN POWs on May 4 en route to the new camp. Grant was shocked to discover that the 25th Division had interrogated the rallier earlier but had failed to quiz him on POW information.

The JPRC reacted quickly, sending a SOG recon team into the area. Their report notes, "The bunker complex was located; however it had been vacated and there were no signs of PWs in the area. CG, II Corps, noted that failure to include questions probably resulted in losing an opportunity to liberate 11 US PWs and about 80 ARVN PWs."[28]

The Families Demand Action: Laird Goes Public

Because the State Department's approach to the POW/MIA issue was one of "quiet diplomacy," the missing men's families were advised by government officials to maintain a low profile and refrain from publicly voicing their concerns or making critical statements. The POWs' families, however, had no formal outlet to vent their growing frustrations, especially as evidence continued to mount that the POWs were being tortured. With little government contact outside of visits by the casualty officers and occasional letters from military officials, the families began raising an increasing chorus of doubts over the benefits of State's policy. Slowly, under the guidance of Sybil Stockdale and others, the families began to organize. Mrs. Stockdale began initially by writing letters to Averell Harriman discussing her efforts. At first, Harriman attempted to ignore her correspondence, but eventually he grew to respect the tenacity and organizational skills of the families.

By early 1969, the wives had created an informal organization in Southern California known as the League of Wives of American Prisoners in Southeast Asia, which, in May 1970, became The National League of Families of American Prisoners and Missing in Southeast Asia.[29] In March 1969, two League-driven events would help put the Nixon administration on a new course, that of wide publicity about the treatment of American POWs. First, a letter was sent to the DOD POW Policy Committee inviting one of their representatives to meet with the League in San Diego. Second, a campaign was mounted by a group of families to inundate the North Vietnamese delegation in Paris with cablegrams expressing concern over the fate of their loved ones.[30]

The new secretary of defense, Melvin Laird, strongly disagreed with Harriman's policy of quiet diplomacy. Laird felt a "strong conviction that our responsibility to the servicemen who are prisoners of war morally obligates us to pursue and initiate all programs that might improve the welfare of our men in captivity and secure their release. The DOD's overriding obligations to its men who have risked their lives for their country require that we devote a high priority to prisoner-of-war matters."[31]

The meeting with the families in San Diego and their demands to increase pressure on the North Vietnamese, combined with the lack of any real progress in Paris, was all the justification Laird needed to begin publicly denouncing the DRV's use of torture and noncompliance with the Geneva Conventions. By early May, DOD and State officials were preparing a briefing that Laird would give to the press condemning North Vietnamese POW actions. "The main theme of the briefing . . . through pictures and other material lays greater stress on the question of prisoner mistreatment," Frank Sieverts wrote. "This is a tricky subject because it raises the question of *how do we know.* Our intelligence services have been long concerned to avoid any reference to the means by which we get information on our prisoners, on the ground that to do so could dry [the sources] up. The main sources have been (1) letters from prisoners; (2) debriefs of returned prisoners; (3) analysis of films, pictures, and other media material. This briefing makes use of the third type and avoids reference to the first two, which are obviously more sensitive.

"The briefing is strongly oriented towards our pilots in North Vietnam. I support this as a useful present windward tack. . . . At the same time, we should not lose sight of the hundred or so prisoners in South Vietnam and the unknown number in Laos, whose plight, man for man, may be worse, and whose prospects for release are dimmer than those of our men in the North."[32]

Suitably armed, Laird held the famous May 19 press conference, deliberately timed to coincide with Ho Chi Minh's birthday, in which he dramatically pointed out enemy mistreatment of POWs and demanded that they adhere to the provisions of the Geneva Convention. Laird also asked for the prompt release of the sick and wounded and demanded an accounting of the men listed as MIA. After the press gave wide circulation to Laird's charges, DOD and State officials fanned out to 21 different U.S. cities during the summer of 1969 to present briefings to the families.

Laird's broadside accomplished its goal. The United States was now firmly committed to the path of public attacks on Hanoi's treatment of American

POWs. Several months later, the pattern of widespread torture in the northern camps came to a halt.

Three More from Hanoi

The DRV's response to Laird was notably aggressive. They broadcast a series of prisoner statements describing "humane" treatment. Xuan Thuy, the North Vietnamese negotiator, immediately denounced the accusations and proclaimed that the DRV would never release the list of prisoners. Despite their thunder, the communists quickly moved to counter Laird's charges. Hanoi proposed to release a third group of three POWs, undoubtedly hoping to regain some favorable publicity to offset Laird's press conference.

The senior ranking POWs also ordered this group not to leave, with one exception, Seaman Douglas B. Hegdahl. Hegdahl was a Navy sailor who had been lost in the Gulf of Tonkin from the cruiser USS *Canberra*. He had been walking on the deck when the ship fired a gun during a naval engagement, blowing him overboard. Hegdahl portrayed himself as a simple sailor and the North Vietnamese believed he was worthless to them. What the communists didn't know was that Hegdahl had secretly memorized the names of over two hundred American prisoners being held in North Vietnam.

Following their earlier pattern, the communists contacted peace activist David Dellinger, asking him to send a group of antiwar protesters to Hanoi to receive the men. On July 3, Hanoi Radio announced the release of three men, ostensibly as a humanitarian gesture in observance of America's Independence Day. At this time the prisoners were not identified.

Traveling to Paris, Dellinger met with Ambassador Lodge to discuss the situation and clarify the travel arrangements. "Dellinger thought there would be no problem about the release since Harriman and Thuy had agreed last July that released prisoners would not be subject to pressure to return on military aircraft. . . . He said that the prisoners would come out through Vientiane, as before. . . . Dellinger said that the NVN delegation gave him no encouragement on the question of lists of American prisoners. He said that he emphasized the painful uncertainty the absence of such a list brought to many Americans. . . . Dellinger also raised the question of the ability of the released prisoners to talk freely to the press upon their arrival in the U.S. He said that last July prisoners had been surrounded on landing by U.S. officials and were placed under 'psychological pressures' not to talk. He said this question had not been raised by the NVN delegation, but rather by certain U.S. peace groups. . . ."[33]

The peace group, headed by Rennie Davis, left for Hanoi. The release did not occur on July 4 as planned, and Davis held a press conference to explain the delay. At the conference he was asked if he felt that he was being used for propaganda purposes. Davis replied that the release was "an expression of North Vietnam's attitude of sympathy and humanity toward prisoners . . . [and they] have demonstrated in the past a humanitarian policy towards prisoners."[34]

Three weeks later, on August 5, the peace group and three American prisoners, Navy Lieutenant (JG) Robert F. Frishman, USAF Captain Wesley L. Rumble, and Hegdahl returned to Vientiane on the ICC flight. Like the other American POWs who had been released through Laos, the ex-prisoners were faced with the choice of flying home commercial or military. The trio decided to fly back to the States by commercial aircraft, again fearing that they might compromise the possibility of more releases. Despite Dellinger's statement to Lodge that the North Vietnamese had not raised the question of which means of transportation to take home, Davis told the gathered newsmen that the communists had insisted the freed Americans travel commercial "in order that publicity surrounding its gesture not be choked off."[35]

The men also chose to remain overnight in Vientiane, where the air attaché interviewed them. He sent a message back to the Air Force describing Rumble as a "quiet man very much under control of himself. . . . He has a remarkable memory, had made a concentrated effort to memorize names of prisoners so he could pass on to U.S. authorities. . . . Frishman is in good spirits and very talkative. Would be excellent source for interrogation due to his willingness to relate his experiences. He is obviously very proud of himself as a military man and his ability to have survived his capture. He was most anxious to cooperate with U.S. officials, make any statement they wanted. . . . He related mental and physical abuse and was proud of his resistance to both. Hegdahl was interviewed only briefly. He may have considerable knowledge of other prisoners and conditions of imprisonment in that he was held in three different camps."[36]

In fact, while Hegdahl brought out over two hundred names of prisoners, it was Rumble who knew the longer list of POWs. But Hegdahl received more recognition, according to Claude Watkins, because he was an outgoing, personable individual while Rumble was withdrawn and only volunteered information when a question was directed at him. The amount of intelligence gained from these two was enormous from the standpoint of determining who was a prisoner in the DRV. Their release and debrief was probably the single greatest American POW intelligence coup of the war.

Additionally, the third group brought out a message from the prisoners. When the two previous groups of Americans had been released from Hanoi, the prisoners still in the Hanoi jail cells were aghast at their accepting release—a breach of the Code of Conduct. "What is the government's policy on early release?" the remaining prisoners wanted to know.

The DOD POW Policy Committee debated this question at great length, taking almost a year to decide on the answer. "The communication system arranged by the releasees was imprecise and reasonable doubt exists as to the exact language. . . . Due to this imprecision and due to the fact that another sensitive and reliable channel exists . . . no further action will be taken."[37] Eventually, the 1127th's Claude Watkins became deeply involved in determining the U.S. response. "I really agonized over this. Finally, I decided the Code of Conduct had to apply." The DOD committee sent a message to the POWs that the U.S. government "approves the return of sick and wounded and then others in order of longest time in captivity."

Godley Replaces Sullivan

In June 1969, G. McMurtrie Godley replaced William Sullivan as Ambassador to Laos. Sullivan had served almost five years in the post and now he was going back to Washington. Godley had experience in paramilitary activities, having served for two years as Ambassador to the (formerly French) Republic of Congo during some of that country's upheavals. Unfortunately, he maintained Sullivan's tradition of keeping the U.S. military at arm's length; worse, he continued Sullivan's reliance on the CIA for military assessments of the war. Little also changed for American policy toward its POWs held in Laos. In retrospect, only a shift in the "secret war" policy and opening direct talks with the Pathet Lao about ending the war in Laos might have affected American POWs there, and even that is debatable. Sullivan, of course, felt that he was carrying out his mission by representing his vision of U.S. interests, backed by the clandestine intrigues of the CIA. Unfortunately, while the North Vietnamese were thinking of Indochina strategically on a theater-wide level, Sullivan and the other ambassadors guarded their respective countries like feudal monarchs. Their impact on the war effort, let alone on POW recovery, can be seen in their legacy: a fragmented and overtly political approach to the war that helped hasten the defeat of the United States.

The JPRC, while reduced to the role of cheerleaders when it came to Laos, still maintained a keen interest in the country. Dave McNabb remembers plans being developed to raid Sam Neua, as "We believed that the PL moved the POWs into the town hotel on occasion. We had developed plans to go after them, but one day several Air Force planes were shot at from the area. They retaliated, violating the no-bomb line in Sam Neua, and accidentally destroyed the hotel."

One CIA report supports some of McNabb's story. The CAS source was a local informant of a Hmong Road Watch team operating west of Sam Neua. The team had reported reliably in the past. They stated that "A Meo villager from the vicinity . . . said that on 20 July 1967 six American pilots were being held prisoners . . . within the town of Sam Neua. The pilots were on the second floor of a two-story red building and many guards lived there. The pilots appeared to be in poor physical condition. . . . An enemy soldier told the villager that previously there had been eight pilots but two had died."

CAS commented on the report. "The same team had received and reported information from a different villager on 25 April 1967, to the effect that six American pilots and two Thais were being held in a cave. . . . Both reports probably refer to the same group of pilots."[38]

While noting the JPRC's continuing interest in Laos, the CIA made little effort to hide the fact that it considered that nation its private preserve. But the CIA-backed Hmong guerrilla units had been slowly pushed back by the North Vietnamese, and the local Hmong villagers in northern Laos, on whom the CAS teams depended so heavily for intelligence and supplies, were being systematically destroyed by a communist scorched-earth campaign.

Consequently, starting in mid-1968 the number and quality of the CIA's intelligence reports on POWs in Laos began to severely diminish. What CIA reports were coming through indicated that the PL were beginning to transfer American POWs to the DRV. Ernie Brace, who was being held by the North Vietnamese near Dien Bien Phu, had already been moved toward Hanoi. In early January 1969 the CIA noted that in mid-1968, "two of four American pilots held prisoner in Tham Sua cave, south of Ban NaKay Neua, Laos, were sent to Hanoi. Prior to being sent to Hanoi, one of the American pilots, described as an older man, killed three North Vietnamese Army soldiers when they attempted to interrogate him. . . . The killing occurred when the North Vietnamese attempted to chain the pilot to a desk—he overturned the desk on his captors and beat three of them to death with the chain before guards overpowered him. Following this incident, the elder pilot and one younger pilot were sent to Hanoi. The reason given . . . was that the two pilots were considered as incorrigible cases . . ."[39]

By the summer of 1969, another CIA report detailed more movement. "In late December, 1968, 27 Americans held prisoner by the Pathet Lao . . . were assembled in Ban Hang Long in Houa Phan province before being sent to North Vietnam. The 27 Americans represent all Americans the PL held captive in Laos. . . .

Before the American prisoners were released to North Vietnamese Army personnel, an agreement was reached between the North Vietnamese government and the Neo Lao Hat Sat Central Committee whereby all Americans captured in Laos would be sent to North Vietnam, where they would be used in prisoner exchanges. . . ."[40]

Prisoner exchanges notwithstanding, the Pathet Lao were following the negotiation lead of the DRV by demanding a total halt to U.S. bombing. In a rare interview in February 1970, Lao communist leader Prince Souphanouvong stated that "the problem of captured officers and pilots will be settled along with the settlement of the Lao problem, when the Americans stop bombing and shelling the Lao liberated zone, and end their intervention and aggression in Laos."

Like his predecessors, Reinker was determined to push CAS to locate and identify any Americans in Laos. The Air Force was also resolute. In October 1969, they would unite their efforts to try and determine what CAS knew or didn't know about Americans in Laos.

Updating the Lao Database

Despite the effort in 1968 to carefully monitor the growing list of POW camps, the Air Force remained worried about the continued expansion of no-bomb areas, which were areas around POW camps. The list had grown from an original group of only 18 in February 1967 to a total of 316 in September 1969. The inhibiting impact on combat air operations of a sizable number of off-limits targets was devastating.[41]

In October 1969, the 7th AF asked for a meeting with CAS, the JPRC, and the U.S. Embassy in Laos to discuss the problem. On October 1 the 7th AF published a lengthy computerized list of camp locations in Laos based upon reports from a variety of sources ranging from third-hand low-level informants to photographic imagery.[42] The Air Force call for action resulted in a conference at Udorn with representatives from each component. The Air Force complained of "the absence of a single executive agency within SEA [Southeast Asia] for PW camp deletion in coordination with AmEmb authorities, as well as a need for review of procedures for PW reports analysis, categorization of camps, follow-up reconnaissance, imposition of NBLS (no-bomb lines), and method of deletion."[43]

The conference attendees reached an agreement that "categorization, reports of PW sightings or detention facilities in Laos will henceforth be classified as follows . . . : Confirmed Alpha sites: Locations in Laos at which detained POWs have been reported by reliable sources on more than one occasion within a twelve-calendar-month period. Reliable sources would include first-hand information from escapees or other former inmates of the detention facility, tested reliable observer assets such as reconnaissance teams or Road Watch teams of CAS or DOD element concerned, proven clandestine assets, or photo imagery."[44]

The group also created confirmed Bravo camp sites, which needed only one reliable source, suspect Alpha and suspect Bravo sites, and a dumping ground called "historical." Time limits were placed on how long a camp could remain in each category. The JPRC was chosen as the "Executive Agent . . . as focal authority in SEA for additions/deletions to listings of PW camps in Laos. Airborne photo reconnaissance will be utilized to the maximum extent feasible to confirm/deny PW sightings reports." Surprisingly, the powers of the Vientiane Embassy were quite limited in their authority to formally initiate action to delete camps from the listing or to alter categories. Also, a new Special Joint Memorandum of Agreement was worked out in November 1969 between the JPRC and the Vientiane Embassy. Under the plan, JPRC would use SOG assets to ground check reported POW camps in the SOG area of operation in Laos and Cambodia, while CAS would use their assets to confirm or deny camps elsewhere in Laos.

The CIA had just produced their semiannual listing of POW camps in Laos and had 32 confirmed camps as of October 1969. This included all POW camps in Laos; only a handful were believed to hold Americans. The Air Force checked the CAS locations against their target list and under the new guidelines immediately asked for a reevaluation of five camp locations clustered together in an area near the Sam Neua caves. A FAC had spotted a lucrative storage facility and the Air Force was itching to bomb it. Looking at the sighting reports, however, it was determined that "site 210 at VH1262 was listed as a confirmed detention facility for four US pilots in a cave as of 15 Oct 68 and reaffirmed as a confirmed facility on 11 Apr 69. Under new criteria, conclude this location should be regarded as a confirmed Alpha site. . . . Our fundamental concern centers around probability of four US pilots held in a cave. . . ."[45]

The confirmed Alpha site appears to be in the Ban Hang Long area. The CIA report referenced earlier, concerning moving 27 American POWs to North Vietnam, gives the same location. Since the JPRC agreed that this area was holding American POWs, a no-bomb line was established centered on VH 125620, and it was agreed that the "site is to be classified as a confirmed Alpha facility probably housing U.S. pilots, last date of info is Aug 69. . . ."[46] By the end of November, a special 7th AF group using the new criteria had significantly reduced the number of listed POW camp sites. The new totals showed "forty-four confirmed Alpha sites in Laos. The Embassy in Vientiane agreed with the new figures and expressed appreciation for a very well done job. . . . The forty-four confirmed Alpha sites . . . is felt to be a much more meaningful list. . . ."[47]

Reinker attended the meetings and was privy to all the intelligence in Laos. He recalls that "when I first came aboard in July, I was shown an oblique photo recently taken in the Sam Neua area. I was only shown one, but I believe 7th AF had others. The photo showed several people standing next to a garden in the shadow of a karst [a limestone cliff, a geological formation common in Laos]. There was a three-foot-high fence surrounding the garden. The men were larger than the others standing around and the photo interpreters said they were 'probably' Caucasians and 'probably' POWs. The rating was 'probable' because of the quality of the photo, and although we requested follow-ups, we could never correlate the men to specific individuals."

Another picture was known as the "cabbage patch" photo. A team was dispatched to an area in northeastern Laos which appeared in late September 1969 to pilots and photo interpreters to show a number of mounds of earth, some bearing in mirror writing the letters "USS," plus another one that resembled a fighter plane. The team took over two months to reach the area only to find that the mounds were part of a cabbage farm. One local informant said there were no Americans in the area.[48]

However, there is an additional and more compelling photograph known as the "volleyball" photo, dated October 11, 1969, which the CIA reported shows "20 non-Asians accompanied by Pathet Lao guards near Ban NaKay Teu," the area near Sam Neua that was reported to be another detention site.[49] Two months later, the CIA received what appears to be remarkable confirmation of the presence of 20 American POWs in the same general area. A source report reveals, "About 20 United States Air Force pilots were imprisoned in a concealed section of the Ban NaKay area of Sam Neua province, according to two villagers who visited the region to buy a radio on an unstated date but possibly in late 1969 or early 1970. When the NVA guards noticed that the two villagers saw the pilots, the guards seized them and said they too would be imprisoned.

"The PL functionary, who was selling the villagers the radio, interceded. . . . the NVA guards released the villagers, but demanded they not tell anyone else about the location of the pilots prison camp. . . . [redacted] reported all the American prisoners held in Laos were taken to North Vietnam in late December, 1968. The 27 American prisoners that had been in Laos at that time were assembled in the Ban Hang Long area about mid-way between Ban NaKay and Sam Neua."[50]

The combination of reconnaissance imagery and source reporting is a strong indication that more men were captured and imprisoned in Laos than the communists have ever admitted. If these photos are displaying Caucasian prisoners, none of these men have ever returned home or been accounted for. However, there were enormous obstacles to proving conclusively that those men were American POWs. NVA security had grown so tight around the region that the Hmong team sent to investigate this report was unable to penetrate it and bring out corroborating evidence, such as a confirmed name or a second independent eyewitness.

One example of this difficulty is the discovery of a strange symbol—the stone outline of an airplane—that appeared on photos from the Sam Neua area in the spring of 1970. Jack Reisner spoke of a similar photo taken earlier that had been a total mystery to him: in the fall of 1967 a recce photo taken near Sam Neua showed a very clear, perfect outline of an F-105 made by large stones. According to Reisner, "We looked very carefully at this since we knew there were guys in the Sam Neua area. We inserted a CAS team into the area to check it out, but they didn't find anything. This was a mystery we never solved."

Scott recalls the 1970 incident. "As I was leaving JPRC in May 1970, I was called out to 7th AF intelligence at Tan Son Nhut to look at some photos in their possession. Photo recon missions of the Sam Neua region were taken on a regular basis as it was one of the most heavily fortified areas in enemy territory. The first photo I saw was an area of dense jungle in a mountainous area divided by a valley. A few glistening objects were seen. This was the sun shining through the tree canopy on a body of water. The second photo was taken some time later. This photo indicated that someone was clearing jungle out of a bend in the river. The third photo showed that the area had been tilled into a field. The fourth photo revealed that a crop of distinct figures had been grown which consisted of an outline of an airplane and the letter "F," plus some number I can't remember. Several cave openings were seen nearby. SOG Operations told me the area was too far north to even consider a recovery operation."

Just after Scott left, Reinker claims to have solved the mystery. "Although we couldn't figure this out, somehow the photos were accidentally shown to a Vietnamese Air Force intelligence officer, who said he knew exactly what they were. He claimed they were made by the Hmong for a religious ceremony. This was in almost the identical location of the symbols that turned up during the Senate Select Committee hearings. When I tried to alert them to this fact, no one would return my calls."

Given the evidence of the volleyball photo, many in U.S. intelligence in the last half of 1969 believed American POWs were still "probably" being held in northern Laos. An internal memo was sent at the end of 1969 to Richard Helms, the Director of Central Intelligence, indicating that "Except for prison facilities in North Vietnam, there is only one detention facility—a cave in Laos—located with enough certainty to warrant giving it a Bombing Encyclopedia (BE) number. The assignment of a BE number prevents targeting for American and Allied bombing and artillery attack."[51] Locating Americans in northern Laos was difficult; identifying them was even harder.

Out of the Stone Age: Creating the First POW Database

JPRC intelligence analyst John Mitchell was replaced in March by Master Sergeant Thomas "Jack" Henry, a career NCO with over twelve years' SIGINT experience working as a Soviet-bloc analyst in the Air Force Security Service. He also had served several years at the Air Force Mountain Survival School.

Henry witnessed the rapid deterioration of the JPRC after the rescue of Nick Rowe as acting CO John Firth lost interest in the unit. Henry quickly realized that the one-year tour was killing the institutional memory of the JPRC and that the earlier efforts of Roberts and Mitchell to create a filing system had been only moderately successful. The massive amounts of data that poured into the JPRC—including State cables, press releases, and FBIS media intercepts—was just too much for the JPRC analysts to keep up with.

Major James Rabdau agrees that there was "too much info for the very small JPRC staff to distill. We spent enormous amounts of time trying to determine what was bogus versus what was the truth. The rotation policy also killed continuity, leaving us no font of knowledge to turn to for answers. It often seemed like we were on our own."

Henry was determined to improve the situation. He felt that the intelligence the JPRC possessed "was being collected but was not in a usable form. The data pertaining to an individual was kept on three-by-five cards while the intelligence reports were kept in folders in file cabinets. The entire operation was a manual process that was being overwhelmed by the data backlog. The growing numbers of POWs and MIAs, combined with the constant rotation of personnel, made human recall and the use of three-by-five cards less than adequate for proper intelligence analysis. In my mind we needed the ability to generate an immediate response, in a fluid tactical situation, of either recovery forces or exploitation of previous intelligence. Operations before seemed to be just hit or miss."

Henry wanted to solve this problem by taking the large amounts of information that had been accumulating for several years and creating a computer database. "I had worked in Air Force Security Service for over ten years so I was familiar with what computers could do. The JPRC was still in the Stone Age. Optimally, I wanted the end result to be that everyone who was missing got categorized into either prisoner or killed in action, body not recovered (KIA/BNR). The worse thing was to be MIA. We needed to find out who was alive and where they being held. We needed to isolate the camps and determine who was in a given area. Basically, there were only two types of operations: the first against a known or suspected camp; the second type the post-SAR operation. If they were dead, then there was no immediate tactical need or basis in looking for them. Luckily, I found a great database person in Howard Daniel."[52]

Howard A. Daniel III was an Army master sergeant working in MACV's Intelligence Data Handling Systems (IDHS). IDHS sections provide the people, hardware, and software to enable consumers to query intelligence files for information. Daniel arrived in Vietnam in January 1966 and helped the Combined Intelligence Center, Vietnam (CICV) create the first Automated Database Program (ADP) for Enemy Ground Order of Battle. In the summer of 1968 he was transferred to MACV J-2 to work with their Top Secret Special Intelligence files. Daniel was perfect for the JPRC. He was interested in the POW/MIA problem and had the necessary clearances, a thorough knowledge of MACV operations, and a tremendous grasp of computer technology.

Working together, Henry and Daniel decided to code all the reports into three separate files, one for personnel, one for camps, and a general file they called "junk," i.e., intelligence reports that couldn't fit easily into either category. Henry designed "the personnel file as a working file at the field level. It was not concerned with the politics of the war other than observing the applicable security restrictions. Our use of KIA/BNR was analytical only and did not confer legal status. It simply had name and circumstances of loss along with other pertinent information."

Daniel recalls that it was often difficult to find personnel information. "We wanted to include dental records and other information to help identify a person. As I was looking at the very first printout, I noticed that many medical fields for MIAs were blank. The next day I was taking a break and was looking at the newspaper *Stars and Stripes* when for some reason I turned to the back page and looked at the section listing all the hold baggage in-country that had not been picked up. The list was by name and rank. As I'm looking through this list, I spotted about half a dozen names of guys who were MIA. I always shipped my medical records in my hold baggage and I wondered if some of these guys did also. I had JPRC send someone down to look through the baggage, and sure enough we found medical records and photos of guys that were missing. We used this information to update the database. Afterwards it became a regular tasking in JPRC to com-pare the POW/MIA list against the hold baggage list."[53]

The camp file was used to pinpoint the likely location of prisons. The junk file was for intelligence reports that didn't fit neatly into either category or were awaiting more analysis. Two men from the 519th MI Battalion were assigned temporary duty to assist Daniel in coding the files.[54] By January 1970 the system was semioperational and was able to provide "quarterly reports of PW camp sightings, publications of current PW/MIA listings, and special one-time data re-trievals based on requests from the field."[55]

Daniel enabled the system to transfer the grid coordinates from the camp files to a graphics plotter. Daniel recalls, "The graphics printer in the IDHS shop was running every hour every day, but I managed to squeeze in some time for the new JPRC system. At first we were looking for possible remains locations. The first map we used was too large, a 1:250,000 scale. The plotter made the map look black. So we started using 1:50,000 maps and the locations improved to the point where we began recovering remains."

Leaflets were targeted on select areas hoping that local villagers would come forward with information on grave sites. Using this system, Rabdau was able to recover the remains of two Americans POWs, Captain David Devers and Sergeant John O'Neill, who had been captured in 1966 near Hue. They had been paraded in front of several villages and then shot. In late December 1969 Rabdau was sent to I Corps "when a village chief asked for a reward to recover two U.S. bodies. The guy knew where they were all along but he was waiting until he felt it was safe. I had known Devers before. He was my driver when I was in Germany."

The JPRC also started plotting camp locations. Reinker remembers that the plots "showed dramatic potentials in I and II Corps area. Rabdau and Henry had maps all over the wall trying to pinpoint a location." This startling revelation came on the heels of the release of Willy Watkins, Strickland, and Tinsley. Reinker remembers that "the stuff from the U-Minh, MR IV, and Cambodia was constant. The JPRC hadn't looked at the north in some time."

Much of the information flow, unfortunately, was used only by the DIA and the delegation at the Paris Peace Talks. Daniel felt that despite thousands of man-hours logged in creating this database, only SOG Intelligence and DIA appeared interested in using it. Shortly before Daniel left Vietnam in August 1970, three full colonels from DIA flew out to JPRC to receive a briefing on the new pro-gram. As Daniel recalls, "The briefing was held at SOG, not MACV. At the end of my briefing, I informed them that the system still had many holes in the data, mainly from sources outside of Vietnam. We had all the information within

Southeast Asia, but we needed the intelligence on POW/MIAs gathered from Europe and elsewhere to make the picture complete. The colonels looked at me and said 'No, we're not giving it to you, you're on your own.' I was headed over the podium for them when Deluca grabbed me and said 'It's not worth it.' I never understood why they would not support us.

"Eventually one of these colonels was assigned to Paris and shortly thereafter a message came in to start sending printouts to the delegation. But nothing ever came back from them. It was a one-way street and I let everyone in hearing distance in MACV J-2 know about it, but no one ever did anything."

"We face a protracted struggle on the PW front"

In September 1969 Hegdahl and Frishman held a press conference to refute DRV claims of humane treatment of the POWs. Frishman in particular spoke eloquently of his harsh treatment, graphically describing several instances in which he had been tortured. Frishman also blasted the communists for their treatment of Lieutenant Commander Richard Stratton. According to Frishman, "The North Vietnamese tried to get Stratton to appear before a press conference and say that he had received humane treatment. He refused . . . [and was] tied up with ropes to such a degree that he still has large scars on his arms from rope burns that became infected. . . . Facing future torture, Stratton . . . got up before the press and intentionally walked around glassy-eyed, bowing as we are forced to do. . . . He told the North Vietnamese not to believe for one minute that he's cooperating with them. . . . [he says] the first chance I get I'm going to blow the whistle and tell the truth."

The antiwar crowd responded by attacking Frishman, calling him a liar and a stooge of DOD, but Frishman and Hegdahl had dealt a heavy blow to Hanoi's declared policy of humane and lenient treatment. In response to the DOD campaign, a new antiwar committee was formed in January 1970, called the Committee of Liaison with Families of Servicemen Detained in North Vietnam, more informally called the Committee of Liaison. The committee was headed by a woman named Cora Weiss. Its function was to act as a conduit between the prisoners, their families, and the DRV, especially in regard to mail and notification of a man's status.

The role of the antiwar activist groups was both secretly welcomed and publicly irritating. While any information from the DRV or an increased volume of mail was coveted, the method of receiving that information was just as important. DOD was well aware that the North Vietnamese wished to manipulate the next of kin to influence the U.S. government's Vietnam policies. Therefore, the DOD decreed that "no official change in status will be made as a result of information provide by these groups until such information is confirmed on an official government-to-government basis."[56]

To Frank Sieverts at the State Department, this new antiwar group indicated that "In spite of the relative success of US government public-opinion campaigns with regard to the plight of American prisoners in North Vietnam, we have no positive indication that these campaigns have resulted in better treatment for the PWs. We are no closer now than we were a year ago to the release of the PWs. There is no sign of change in DRV policy toward American PWs. The passing of time is a form of punishment for the PWs. . . . Technically our propaganda problem . . . is to indicate that the American PWs are of little value to the US and are a propaganda liability to the North Vietnamese. It is impossible, however, to do this when more than 1,000 wives want to be told that the most important item of business for the US government is release of the PWs in NVN." In essence, Sieverts said, "We face a protracted struggle on the PW front."[57]

Although the U.S. government's 1969 publicity campaign had generated some success in combination with the growing pressure by family members on the North Vietnamese delegation in Paris, the DRV had not succumbed to this pressure. Despite five years of effort, the government was still following the same three lines of activity. The State Department was engaged in a worldwide campaign to line up communist and noncommunist governments to support the U.S. demand that the DRV comply with the Geneva Convention. The intelligence community was still trying to locate and identify missing POWs, especially those who were being held but had not been acknowledged by the DRV. DIA had some success in this. Even in late 1968, DIA had "identified 316 US PWs in NVN and associated 152 of them with specific detention facilities. . . ."[58] Lastly, State and the U.S. Embassy were both pressing the GVN to treat their communist prisoners in accordance with the Geneva Convention.

Even after all the years of U.S. tact and diplomacy in dealing with the GVN, the South Vietnamese still remained quietly pessimistic over the policy of releasing NVA/VC prisoners in response to communist releases of Americans. An Embassy officer, meeting several senior GVN military officials, wrote afterwards that the GVN was especially adamant about the "release of able-bodied PW's, whom the communists would send back into the fight in SVN. . . ." Such a release "poses a real problem for the GVN because of the opposition of the Ministry of Defense. To illustrate the skepticism of the GVN regarding the argument that release of NVA PWs puts 'pressure' on the DRV to release American PWs . . .

quoted the Defense Minister as saying 'Rubbish. The Americans bombed them for years without putting effective pressure on them to change their minds. What makes the Americans think giving up our PWs will have any effect?'"[59]

In case the DRV did change their minds, contingency planning for any large-scale release of American POWs was under way. The military realized that the channels previously used for handling POWs were insufficient to deal with any sudden release of the POWs. In June 1968 and again in January 1969 the Deputy Secretary of Defense issued policy statements detailing the new procedure for processing returned POWs. Initially, MACV was tasked with the primary responsibility for establishing and operating a central processing center. In September 1969 a meeting was held at the hospital in Cam Ranh Bay to develop plans, procedures, and logistical requirements for processing large numbers of American returnees if the Paris Peace Talks suddenly bore fruit. The 12th USAF Hospital was designated as the collection point for the medical and administrative processing as well as initial debriefings prior to moving them home to the United States. The JPRC was to "monitor debriefings to insure the dissemination of information pertaining to the status of PWs who remain in enemy custody. . . ."[60]

By the beginning of 1970, DOD had issued new orders to update the procedures for early releasees. Previously called *Sentinel Echo,* the new plan was now called *Egress Recap.* JPRC developed and issued OPLAN J190, which outlined the program for reception, processing, and evacuation of recovered POWs. It provided guidance to U.S. forces in Vietnam concerning their responsibilities during the repatriation of any allied prisoner. However, it would still be three long years before the military could implement its plan. Meanwhile, the problems of American POWs and MIAs in Laos would continue to draw serious attention.

12. Every Message in Every File

Sometimes you can get unexpected results, like we did at Son Tay. The prisoners were grouped together and their morale and communications improved. Just because the raid failed doesn't mean we shouldn't try.
—Lieutenant General Leroy Manor, discussing the failed Son Tay raid

Reinker's departure in the summer of 1970 led to another command problem in the JPRC. Colonel John Sadler had by then replaced Cavanaugh as Chief, SOG. Sadler wanted a Special Forces–type officer to lead the unit. Although the Air Force had sent a replacement for Reinker, Sadler inserted his own candidate, an Army officer named Robert L. Morrissey, as Director, JPRC, leaving Reinker's replacement, Lieutenant Colonel Gerald E. McIlmoyle, to act as Operations officer.

Sadler believed that a Special Forces–trained officer would be more effective as JPRC Director, but he made a poor choice to fill that role. Morrissey had a serious drinking problem and often did not make it into the office. By October 1970, under Air Force pressure and now aware of Morrissey's health problems, Sadler relieved the Army officer and placed McImoyle in charge.

McImoyle was a heralded U-2 pilot who was on the Air Force fast track to general officer. The Joint Chiefs had pulled him off a very important position at the Air Staff to take over the JPRC. He had served in Vietnam earlier, in 1964 at Bien Hoa, as part of the first all-American unit to serve in the South. McImoyle states, "When I left the Air Staff, I told the Chief of Staff of the Air Force that I would do everything in my power to free someone. I was really driven to get someone out and we all worked twelve hours a day, seven days a week on this." His initial task was to familiarize himself with the files. As he remembers, "I wanted to know who was alive and who was dead so we could concentrate our efforts our recovering live POWs. Consequently, I read every single message in every file."

His staff included Major Fred N. Hopewell, who was Scott's replacement as the new Air Force officer. Charles Young was the Navy officer, but he left in November and was replaced by John B. "Smoky" McFadyen.

The first sergeant was now Sebastian E. Deluca, called "Top" for his rank, a longtime SOG NCO. Deluca, who had served in SOG at Ban Me Thuot, had become a fixture at JPRC. He was legendary for his ability to procure supplies and was worshipped by the soldiers who served under him and by many of the officers who worked with him. In due time he would be involved in one of the strangest incidents of the war—his own personal, one-man foray to rescue POWs in Laos.

Several major changes in JPRC procedures occurred under McImoyle's command. Hopewell was instrumental in changing the E&E program, as the original code letters had "caused a great deal of ambiguity, since other organizations also used letters to mark different ground areas. In early August, an aviator was shot down who had the code letter for the month written on a piece of paper that he had placed in his flight jacket. During his rescue he lost his jacket, so we had to assume that it was compromised. I developed new letters with curly ends so that they would be more distinct."[1]

Hopewell was also involved in developing the "Expedite Kit." This was a smaller kit which contained only essential items of equipment. The new E&E kits were carried by Forward Air Controllers, who could drop one immediately if—and where—a code letter was observed.

The main JPRC intelligence debriefing procedure was modified and updated. Also, the blank operations order called *Monteray Angler* was formalized into MACV OPLAN J201, *Bright Light,* and passed to all the field units. Lastly, beginning in November 1970, JPRC was responsible for collecting and publishing statistics concerning number of bodies recovered, U.S. military and civilians rescued, Vietnamese rescued, and the dollar amount of reward money paid. This information was for use by the Paris negotiators and was summarized each month in the Bright Light report.

The SEALs Get Involved

Two separate loss incidents in 1969 set off a continual series of raids and operations in the Delta that lasted into early 1972. The first incident involved a pair of advisors to the Vietnamese, Lieutenant Richard Bowers and Staff Sergeant Gerasimo Arroyo-Baez. Their unit was overrun on March 24, 1969, and the two were captured. The second concerned Captain Robert White, an Army aviator, and Lieutenant John Graf, a Navy intelligence officer, shot down on November 15, 1969, in an OV-1 in Vinh Binh province, the same region where Dale and Demmon were lost. The quest for these four men became the lengthiest manhunt since the search for Nick Rowe.[2]

The Navy officers who had previously worked in the JPRC were aviators, but unlike them Charles Young was a Surface Warfare officer. Young was given responsibility for operations in III and IV Corps. Although Navy SEALs had been used earlier in the war, notably during the fall and winter of 1968 when the JPRC was concentrating heavily on the Delta, they had been used only sporadically since. That was about to change.

Young believed that the SEALs offered the perfect rescue-force combination: a highly trained quick-reaction unit who were intimately familiar with the waterways of the Delta. Armed with the continuing flow of POW intelligence coming out of the Delta region, Young traveled to see the SEALs to rekindle their interest in launching POW raids. As always, they were enthusiastic to conduct JPRC operations. The first attempt was conducted in July 1970 by the SEALs Juliet Platoon. A *Hoi Chanh* [a rallier who was now actively working for the allied forces], acting as guide, raided a camp thought to contain two U.S. prisoners. The rallier precisely guided the SEALs to the prison camp, but it had been evacuated immediately prior to the arrival of the assault force. No prisoners were rescued.[3]

One SEAL who participated on this raid wrote that "A small campfire was still burning with fish and rice ready to eat in large bowls. The spot where the two Americans had been restrained was quickly located: bamboo racks off the ground that had larger ropes for the Americans' hands and feet."[4]

At the end of July 1970, the SEALs attacked another camp about thirty kilometers away. A SEAL team and one platoon from the 1st Cav were inserted. Another SEAL team was already in the area, having arrived by boat the night before. A search of the area found nothing, and interrogation of several captured VC suspects indicated that the POWs had been moved through the area within the past two days.[5] Like everyone else's, the SEALs' efforts were coming very close but were still agonizingly unsuccessful.

Two major POW raids, conducted by the SEALs in August and November 1970, displayed their abilities in conducting well-organized, lightning-fast raids. On August 21, a Vietnamese escaped from a POW camp near Vi Thanh, the capital of Chuong Thien province. A SEAL team under the command of Lieutenant Louis H. Boink III received the information at approximately 1800 hours. Operation *Story Book,* one of the finest POW raids conducted during the war, was under way.

Boink recalls, "When the source walked into our camp, I knew I had to move quickly. Everyone understood how high a priority POW raids were."[6] Boink spent much of the night coordinating with various units in the province who could provide support.

At 0918 hours the next morning, Boink landed his SEAL team and a Vietnamese Regional Forces (RF) platoon along a beach line six kilometers east of the reported POW camp.[7] Boink's plan was to hem in the VC guards on three sides with gunfire from Navy ships, Australian bombers, and Army helicopters while he assaulted the fourth side, hoping to apply sufficient pressure so that the VC guards would abandon the personnel. Naval batteries from the USS *Sutherland* fired to the south of the camp while B-57s from the Australian Air Force pounded a nearby canal. U.S. Army helicopter gunships strafed with rockets and miniguns to the north and east. The escapee led them directly into the camp, where they discovered that the VC camp personnel and POWs were fleeing southward. The guards had chosen to brave the offshore fire from the Navy.

According to one SEAL historian, "For two hours, the SEALs remained in hot pursuit through the swamp, following a trail of clothing and abandoned equipment. At 1245, they discovered twenty-eight Vietnamese prisoners whose guards had fled for their lives. . . . No Americans were discovered in the camp."[8]

Boink's team rotated back to the States in October. He recalls that the operation enabled "the team to end the tour on a real success. We were pumped up about this, and we wanted to form special teams to devote complete attention to POW raids. For some reason, our idea was shot down."

When the Navy rejected his idea, Boink turned to the CIA. According to a CIA memo, the SEAL platoon leader had "voiced a proposal that had been considered at various times. The platoon leader proposed the establishment of three four-man SEAL Bright Light teams, each to cover one of the southernmost provinces of South Vietnam. . . . The men would serve a six-month tour and devote their energies to nothing but prisoner recoveries."[9] Another report states that

"From contacts with Vietnamese while serving there, Lt. Boink developed information on a group of . . . American prisoners in VC POW camps located in the 3 or 4 most southern provinces in Vietnam. Lt. Boink and some USN SEAL colleagues approached higher Naval authorities with plans for a mission to liberate some of these prisoners, but their plans were rejected. Lt. Boink has since suggested that his information may be of interest to the CIA."[10]

Boink's request to the CIA was rerouted to SACSA, which also turned it down. Part of the information was incorrect, as Boink never claimed he had information on American POWs. But his design was reasonable and, given the SEALs' reputation and efficiency, should have been given far more serious consideration than it was. Vietnamization and the continuing troop drawdown probably doomed any employment of the plan.

Several other raids were run by the SEALs, but with no tangible results. Barry Enoch, one of the most highly decorated SEALs, recalls being sent on a mission that "was a complete fraud. We were shown aerial photos that included sampans and guard locations. There was supposed to be three U.S. POWs in the camp. We sent an ARVN company to sweep north of the area. We stayed behind to go in the next morning. When we got to the location, we swept back and forth four times and found nothing. We even matched the terrain to the photos to make sure, but I think it was a complete hoax."[11]

The last major SEAL raid of 1970 happened the day after the famous raid on Son Tay in North Vietnam, discussed later. Lieutenant Dick Couch had just arrived in-country with a new SEAL platoon. Earlier, two captured VC had provided information on the location of a camp in An Xuyen, a province on the southern tip of South Vietnam. The area was called the Ca Mau Peninsula and had thick jungle and treacherous swamps. While hunting for the suspected camp, Couch's unit captured a sentry, who revealed its location. Couch's platoon broke into the camp just before dawn and exchanged fire with 18 guards. The guards fled and the SEALs recovered 19 Vietnamese prisoners.

The SEALs had attacked one of the main prisons run by the communists in the Delta. The camp was subordinate to the Ca Mau Communist Party chapter and was run by the local area Security forces. One of the POWs was a former VC who had refused to accept any more military assignments after the heavy losses during Tet 1968. He was subsequently arrested by VC Public Security in late 1968. He reported that at the camp almost twenty men had died of malnutrition in the last year, while another sixty had been executed for various "crimes."[12]

The SEALs and the JPRC continued to work together in the Delta during the last few months the SEALs had remaining in Vietnam. On February 22, 1971, two ralliers claimed to know the location of a POW camp. Several days later, they led a SEAL team into the area but found nothing. Twice more SEAL teams were led into areas by ralliers. Each time, camps were discovered but the POWs had moved on.

The last effort of the SEALs came at the end of June 1971. On June 23, the Senior Advisor for "An Xuyen province reported that an agent knew the location of a PW camp . . . that contained 270 prisoners of which five were US. The agent was interrogated by Navy SEALs on 26 Jun and it was learned at this time that there were actually three camps in the area. One camp held the five US PWs as well as 75 Vietnamese PWs. The camp was located on the north side of a canal that emptied into the sea. The only possible way to get to the camp was by sampan due to the swampy mangrove terrain. A PW recovery operation involving US SEALs was planned for the morning of 29 Jun. The operation was canceled because, just prior to its commencing, the informant related information about guard posts and mines in the canal. These details had not been previously mentioned."[13]

The concept of the plan called for the SEALs to proceed to the canal entrance via sampans that were launched from an offshore Navy vessel. The SEALs would then swim to the camp along the canal edge and attack at first light. The signal to strike would be a diversionary air strike on a reported VC ammo storage area three kilometers away.

But even the SEALs weren't immune to the bad luck that had plagued the JPRC operations from the beginning. The Bright Light report noted that "en route from the Naval surface vessel the sampans experienced buoyancy problems and sank. It was decided that the noise created rescuing survivors compromised the operation so it was terminated. It is felt this compromise resulted in the PWs being removed. . . . if credible intelligence is received a future operation will be mounted."

The SEALs had successfully recovered 48 POWs in the last six months of 1970. When combined with the prisoners they freed during the months leading up to Rowe's escape, the SEALs accounted for a significant percentage of the total number of Vietnamese prisoners liberated during the war. While the two groups worked together on a piecemeal basis, the JPRC's failure to allow the SEALs free rein in the Delta and to coordinate their recovery efforts in advance is the most serious policy mistake the JPRC made. Plus, the Navy's refusal to authorize Lieutenant Boink's recovery-force concept is not understandable. Manning pressure should not have dictated rescue efforts. Of the four men lost in the Delta in 1969, only White returned at *Homecoming*. Although Graf probably died in February 1970 during an escape attempt, and Bowers was shot on the night of his capture by an angry VC guard, Arroyo-Baez lived on until August 1972, when he succumbed to disease. While it is easy to engage in second-guessing, most JPRC officers from this period believe that if the four-man SEAL rescue teams had been authorized, Arroyo-Baez would have come home alive.

Son Tay: The Daring Raid in the North

Much has been written about the massive effort to recover American POWs in the prison raid on Son Tay, many seeing it as the ultimate exercise in futility and another example of an endless parade of U.S. intelligence failures. Much has also been said about its unintended consequences: the consolidation of the prisoners into four separate camps, which enabled them to improve their internal communications and better their morale and treatment. Although the prisoners in Hanoi were aware of the battle, having noted the aerial assault conducted against the NVA air defenses, they did not know that a raid had taken place until December 1970, when they heard rumors from captured ARVNs, who had recently arrived in Hanoi. This information was finally confirmed in February 1971, when the government managed to get word into the camp using a particular intelligence method. This method was later discovered by the Vietnamese and resulted in a massive search of all packages addressed to prisoners, some of which later proved to contain radios and other communication devices hidden within various gift items.

How did the U.S. government first gain information on Son Tay? The prison did not actually become active until 1968. Research and personal interviews with former POWs and senior intelligence officers indicate that rescue information was relayed via a more elaborate and perhaps preplanned method of transmission than has ever been publicly acknowledged. For many years, people have believed that photo interpreters viewing imagery discerned that POWs were in the camp. In Benjamin Schemmer's comprehensive work on the Son Tay assault, *The Raid,* the author relates how several of the individuals working in the 1127th's E&E branch noticed on aerial photography that POWs were in the camp.[14] Most accounts indicate that it wasn't until mid-May 1970 that the Air Force confirmed the camp held POWs.

In reality, DIA informed CINCPAC on April 1, 1970, that Son Tay "has been confirmed as a currently operational PW camp for U.S. POWs. . . . Information from a sensitive source identified the camp as holding 55 U.S. PWs in late 1969."[15] The source was a letter writer who had managed to insert this message:

R E Q M A N O R S A R E P K M T B A V I. DIA was confused until a senior officer at the 1127th, Colonel George Iles, an ex-POW himself, and USAF T Sgt. Norv Clinebell, put it together. At first DIA thought the POWs were referring to a manor, i.e., a house, until Iles noticed the combination SAR and saw that it was "Man or SAR." Once that was understood, the rest fell into place: "*Req*uest *man or SAR east peak Mt. Ba Vi.*"

Ba Vi was a significant mountain near Son Tay. There was a prison on Mount Ba Vi that held Moroccan soldiers who had stayed behind after the French-Vietnamese war in 1954. On April 21, 1970, an NVA rallier gave a detailed report that a major prison for U.S. POWs existed on Mount Ba Vi. The 12th Recon Squadron flew a recce mission over the area but it was unable to locate the camp described by the source on their photography.[16] It was this mission that helped confirm the existence of POWs at Son Tay and that was later used as a cover for the real method of identification.

The decision was made to study the possibility of rescuing the men at Son Tay. After the Son Tay feasibility group was formed at SACSA, Claude Watkins says, the 1127th was cut off from any further input. Because the 1127th was kept out of the planning, that unit placed no great emphasis on continuing to monitor POW intelligence from Son Tay. The JPRC was also kept completely out of the planning for the Son Tay operation, although one JPRC officer recalls being asked to send all of their intelligence on the camp to DIA. The POWs had asked for sonic booms to be generated over the camp to alert them that the rescue operation was ready to commence.

Much is known about the planning and the operation of the mission. The great debate has always been over whether the Americans knew the POWs had been moved before the raid took place. Jim Westbrook, working with Claude Watkins in the 1127th's E&E shop, relates that they found out on the day of the raid that the POWs had been moved. "We had a backlog of letters from POWs in the office that we had not finished reviewing. One letter that had just come into the office was from a prisoner in Son Tay. In it was the message, 'We move early July.' I remember trying to inform DIA later that morning, only to discover the raid had just taken place."

The POWs who returned at *Homecoming* in the spring of 1973 were in fact moved in early July 1970. But aerial photos indicated that someone had moved back into the camp some time before the raid. Brigadier General Leroy Manor, overall commander of the Son Tay operation, noted to the *New York Times* that "It is very difficult to say exactly how long the camp had been vacated, but it was from several weeks to three months."[17] General Manor recently confirmed that statement, noting that "the vegetation had grown quickly in the courtyard, leading us to believe that no one was there. However, later photos showed that it was trampled down again and we thought someone had moved back in."[18]

Secretary of Defense Melvin Laird, defending himself against accusations that the Administration knew the prisoners had departed prior to the raid, said the "department had not known with precise information whether there were prisoners in the camp but was convinced the mission had a 50/50 chance of returning prisoners of war."[19]

If it was true that the latest aerial photos had given the DOD reason to hope that a group of POWs had moved back into Son Tay, who were these men—or were they the figment of a photo interpreter's imagination? Strangely, several wartime interrogation reports indicate that POWs had been returned to Son Tay for a specific purpose: to provide the setting for a mock press conference for peace activists.

In September 1971, an NVA corporal was captured in Tay Ninh province. He claimed that, subsequent to a Canadian delegation's visit to the Son Tay facility in October 1970, the American POWs were moved to another location and the facility was used for convalescing NVA personnel. Further, in March 1972, a rallied cadre stated that he had attended a lecture given by an NVA major at the Military Proselytizing School in North Vietnam shortly after the raid. The rallier stated that "some time previous to the assault on Son Tay there had been a press conference held at the camp for a number of foreign correspondents. In preparation for the press conference, which concerned U.S. prisoners of war, the North Vietnamese built a mock POW camp at Son Tay. . . . The purpose of the mock camp was to make the foreign correspondents believe it was a real POW camp. . . ."[20]

Lastly, another NVA rallier in January 1973 reported that he was attending sapper training on Mt. Ba Vi on the night of the raid. The source visited the camp after the raid. Shortly thereafter, a North Vietnamese group from Hanoi arrived in the Son Tay area and explained that an "American delegation had visited Son Tay approximately one month prior to the raid. . . . The North Vietnamese government suspected a CIA agent in the delegation and decided to move the camp. Source was told that the American PWs were taken by bus . . . and flown to an unknown location in Red China. . . . two weeks later, wounded NVA soldiers were moved into the Son Tay camp. . . ."[21]

Wild tales from ralliers trying to please their new masters? Possibly, but following a visit to Hanoi in July 1993, Senator Bob Smith asked his Vietnamese hosts how long before the raid they had moved the POWs. "A few days before, because of Cora Weiss and an intercept of your communications in Danang which mentioned the imminent raid," the Vietnamese replied. Senator Smith later noted that a Russian official and even Secretary Laird himself had testified that POWs were moved shortly before the raid.

As far as can be determined, Cora Weiss was not at the prison, but her husband Peter was in Hanoi on the night of the raid. Much discussion has revolved around the possibility of a second-tier prison system used to house American POWs that never came home. What with the aerial photos of renewed activity at the camp, and the rallier accounts and the postwar North Vietnamese admission to Senator Smith, the possibility of an unknown group of U.S. POWs, who may have been rotated into Son Tay and then taken to China, offers fascinating food for speculation.

The Vietnamese responded to the raid by implanting telephone poles in the open areas around POW camps. They also tipped off where they were holding U.S. POWs by improving their defenses around camps holding Americans. "According to a DIA post–Son Tay briefing for IPWIC members on 22 January, suspected prison sites at Dan Hoi and Ap Lo have been ringed with AAA guns. . . . There have been no similar changes detected around the known prison sites in Hanoi city. This photographic evidence suggests that both sites are currently holding American PWs."[22]

Even more interesting are the results of a postwar CIA study that was prompted by reports of American POWs still in North Vietnam after 1973. The study examined defensive measures erected around POW camps immediately after the raid. The report states, "An analysis of 19 camps not known to have contained Americans revealed inconsistencies in the various camps' reactions to the Son Tay raid. . . . Some camps reacted defensively to the raid, others did not. . . . only selected camps reacted initially to the raid. . . . the reason for this inconsistency in the various camps' reactions to the raid is not known. Because of this inconsistency . . . the possibility of a second prison system for the detention of American POWs cannot be disregarded."[23]

Claude Watkins remains angry about the failure of Son Tay and blames the stifling bureaucracy. "It was not an intelligence failure; we knew the men were there. But once it started being briefed all the way up the chain to Nixon, everybody had to put their mark on it under the guise of offering 'suggestions.' This dragged it out forever."

General Manor provides this final summation of the raid on Son Tay, and in some respects on all the failed raids during the war: "Sometimes you can get unexpected results, like we did at Son Tay. The prisoners were grouped together and their morale and communications improved. Just because the raid failed doesn't mean we shouldn't try."[24]

Other Raids

The first major raid initiated by the JPRC during 1971 was in January when a CAS source in Cambodia reported he had just seen four American POWs. JPRC intelligence officer Army Captain Carl Kraft met with the Vietnamese man and believed he was the most significant source they had received in a long time. The Bright Light report states, "The new source furnished the name of David Demmon, SP/4, USA, as that of a PW he had talked with two weeks earlier. Source picked out and positively identified Demmon's picture out of a group of dummy pictures displayed to him."[25] Moreover, "The source provided the phonetic name 'phan de Manh,' which translates to 'family name de Manh,' as one of the prisoners. Source stated he got name from the prisoner while talking to him on the first of December 1970. . . ."[26]

The next day the source was taken on a helicopter overflight, and he identified the village and the particular house where he had seen Demmon and the other three. Because the camp was located across the border in Cambodia, McImoyle needed permission from General Creighton Abrams to launch the raid. With Secretary of Defense Laird currently in-country, McImoyle briefed both Abrams and Laird. The SecDef gave his permission but limited the time on the ground to six hours.

Code-named Operation *Dai Phong* [literally "Big Wind," i.e., typhoon], the raid was launched using ARVN forces led by Lieutenant General Do Cao Tri, one of the most competent South Vietnamese officers and the commander of ARVN III Corps. The raid was carried out on January 17, 1971, by three hundred South Vietnamese paratroopers airlifted by U.S. helicopters. The raid, using American helicopter gunships flying as escorts, resulted in the capture of thirty enemy soldiers but did not find any POWs.[27]

The limits on the ground time prevented the ARVN troops from searching all the tunnels in the village. The JPRC noted that "later indications are that the PWs possibly were in the village in an underground bunker during the raid, and subsequently have been moved to an unknown location."[28] Additionally, the original "source's uncle was in village to learn the whereabouts of the PWs during the raid. Uncle went to village approximately 17 Jan 1971 but has not returned since."[29] When the source's uncle returned to South Vietnam, he had no new information. Together, "Source and uncle departed SVN for Cambodia to determine the location and status of the four U.S. PWs."[30] When they returned on March 12, the JPRC polygraphed the source and no deception was found. The combination of the correct name, recognition of Demmon's picture, plus the source's successful polygraph results, led the JPRC to recommend a change in status for Demmon from MIA to POW. Although Casualty Affairs wanted more information before agreeing to make the change, when the JPRC was queried again they continued to recommend the change to POW status for Demmon.

At the same time the raid for Demmon was being planned, in mid-December 1970 an NVA master sergeant had rallied. This source had been the medic at the main POW camp in communist MR-5 and he provided a detailed description of the layout and occupants of the camp, which he called the T-15 camp. He confirmed that eight American POWs were held there.

JPRC First Sergeant Sebastian Deluca had an enormous interest in raiding the MR-5 camp and he kept telling everyone in the JPRC he wanted to get that camp. For some reason the JPRC wasn't notified about the rallier until late January—which, according to one JPRC officer, Army Captain Kevin Kelly, infuriated Deluca. "Top believed people were sitting on their asses when it came to POW rescue operations," Kelly remembers. "It was bad enough all the lousy intelligence we got, but when we finally got something hot and it wasn't passed to us, you can imagine our frustration." Kelly further points out that when he and another SOG officer flew up to I Corps to coordinate the recovery mission and he asked the Marines to conduct the raid, "they essentially refused. The Marine general stated that there was no way he was sending his men out, they were in the middle of drawdown."

Kelly was forced to ask the Americal Division to conduct the raid. On February 2, the JPRC reported that the "source . . . flew a visual reconnaissance mission over the suspected PW camp. . . . On two separate VR passes both the *Hoi Chanh* and the pilot observed approximately 13 armed VC/NVA and a blond Caucasian about 6 feet 2 inches in height. A high-resolution photo mission was also flown but results were poor."[31] A building complex matching the POW compound was located. The camp was in steep, mountainous terrain with thick jungle. Based on the sighting "by the aero scout, a plan was prepared by the 198th Brigade to go after the camp on 3 Feb. However, the CG deferred the operation until . . . aerial photos could be taken. Soon after this, air assets were diverted north and then unfavorable flying weather" prevented the attack.[32]

Given the sighting of the "blond Caucasian," why the Commanding General deferred the operation is unknown, but his decision cost the JPRC the chance to recover the men being held in the POW camp of communist Military Region 5. The Caucasian spotted by the VR flight moving with a column of VC was definitely an American POW. He was Warrant Officer Frank Anton, a gunship pilot shot down on January 5, 1968. When Anton's helicopter crashed, his copilot went one direction and Anton and his two other crewmen went the other. His copilot was recovered by American forces later that night. At dawn on January 6, however, Anton and his two crewmates were captured by enemy troops.

During the three years since 1968 that Anton was held by the communists, he had watched eight other American POWs die from disease, starvation, and the loss of the will to survive. The MR-5 camp system had a mortality rate of almost 50 percent. Like everyone else in the camp, Anton had become riddled with various tropical diseases and he was extremely weak. He weighed barely one hundred pounds.

Anton clearly remembers the events of February 2. As he recalls, "I saw the Hueys circling up high above us. When the guards heard them, they panicked and everyone, including the POWs, ran into a nearby bunker. After the Hueys flew past, the guards started forcing us out. Since I was the first one in, I was pressed against the back wall. As everyone was leaving, I tried to hide but the last guard saw me and ordered me out. At first I refused, but he started poking me with a bayonet. As I walked out of the bunker, I looked up and I was staring right into the eyes of a black American infantry captain in the back of an OH-6 [a small observation helicopter]. I looked at him and just shrugged my shoulders. He shrugged also and then the helicopter took off. The rest of the American POWs were already about 150 meters ahead of me up the trail. We spent that night in a temporary camp about three miles away. The next morning, February 3, we moved back into the camp we had just left. The enemy told us then that we were going to Hanoi. We left several days later."[33]

If the Americal had attacked the next day, Anton believes, they would have landed right on top of them. But it wasn't until a month later that the American military finally moved to attack the camp. On March 9, 1971, the Americal air-assaulted an ARVN Ranger company into the area, finding a hastily abandoned camp site and documents indicating an NVA transportation unit was in the area, but none of the American POWs who had suffered so much in the terrible conditions of the camp. The long delay had destroyed any chance of freeing these men. Interestingly, in early 1972 a South Vietnamese unit captured a notebook of one of the MR-5 camp cadres. Even though no fighting had occurred during the 1971 raid, the cadre wrote in his diary that "I joined the security guards to bravely fight the enemy and secure the camp. The US soldiers were bad fighters. After suffering two KIA's, they withdrew." The cadre noted the U.S. POWs suffered from many diseases and that three had died.[34]

Sergeant First Class John Schermerhorn, who served for over a year in the JPRC with Deluca and knew him well, also recalls that the first sergeant was obsessed by the MR-5 camp, which he says Deluca called the Tam Ky camp because several Americans had been released in that area. Schermerhorn remembers that once, "Deluca got the idea to send me and Kuai, our German-speaking Nung, dressed as a Polish ICC team into the Tam Ky camp. I was to have a cast on my leg and carry a walking stick that had a beeper inside it. Once in the camp I was to turn on the beeper, allowing a *Bright Light* team to do its thing.

"The ICC had an office near the Golden Hotel in Saigon. From time to time Polish, Indian, and Canadian troops would stop by for a beer. Top was planning on having a Polish uniform made in a local tailor shop. I had no wish to end up as a PW myself. Half the VC cadres had been trained in Eastern Europe and would have known we were not real ICC. But Deluca was ready to try almost anything to locate that or any other camp."[35]

Chasing Deserters

Rumors of Americans fighting or working for the enemy had been floating around South Vietnam for years. Other rumors told of "bounties" and "kill-on-sight" orders for these deserters. Many sightings of collaborators had occurred, and on several occasions Marine patrols had run into and fired upon Caucasians moving with VC columns. Apparently someone was working for the VC, as captured documents even elaborated on the amounts of food and money to be spent per collaborator. One report stated that each U.S. deserter would receive a monthly allowance for pocket money, preventive medicine, and office supplies "for use in political indoctrination courses. They are also to be issued a suit and a set of pajamas per year."[36]

While it was proving difficult to pin down precisely who was actively aiding the enemy, one man in particular was sought by the JPRC. Marine Private Robert Garwood was repeatedly singled out as a collaborator by escaped Vietnamese and American early releases. Reportedly he had assumed the Vietnamese name of Nguyen Chien Dau (Nguyen the fighter). U.S. intelligence had accumulated dozens of reports of his working for the communist combined Enemy/Military Proselytizing section of MR-5 and later the Military Proselytizing section of Quang Nam province. In November 1970 the Marines captured a large supply of enemy propaganda documents in the province. They immediately requested a review to determine if any pertained to Garwood. One document indicated that Americans were aiding the enemy, but it was unclear if any of them was Garwood. A security directive from the Communist Party echelon in charge of the province stated, "The enemy was aware of the use of two Americans (possibly U.S. prisoners of war) by friendly [VC/NVA] forces to decoy the enemy. These two Americans were occasionally sent . . . [by the VC] to send deceptive messages by radios to US helicopters. The messages would request that the helicopters land in areas where friendly [VC] elements were ready to destroy them."[37] The security forces were ordered to find the leak.

Like most of the military, the JPRC badly wanted to recover one of these men, not only for the knowledge of the enemy they possessed but for what they could tell U.S. intelligence about other POWs. At the same time the MR-5 camp was being targeted, Air Force intelligence was receiving a growing volume of reports of Americans and one Korean having been seen moving freely with communist forces in November 1970 near the Phu Cat air base in II Corps. The 173rd Airborne Brigade was ordered to recapture these individuals.

For two months the 173rd combed the area but was unable to locate anyone. Then in late January the reports suddenly began pouring in, sometimes three or four a week. A total of fifteen sightings were received within a month. Most of the information was coming from one registered source, who was getting it from a VC commo-liaison cadre. The information varied, but generally talked about four "Americans" being seen northwest of the base accompanied by a large unit of North Vietnamese.

Patrols were again increased hoping to catch sight of the Americans. On February 20, the "101st Popular Force platoon sighted 2 U.S. and 7 VC soldiers in jungle fatigues. The PF PLT did not initiate contact with the element sighted because they thought they were part of a friendly reconnaissance team. When it found out later that the sighted element was not friendly, the PF PLT initiated pursuit. On 22 Feb the 101st PF again sighted the 2 U.S. with approximately 60 VC/NVA and initiated contact. The contact lasted for over 15 hours and 2 friendlies were KIA and 6 enemy."[38]

At the same time, the Americans were also spotted by two children. An intelligence officer reported their sightings. "One 'American' was identified as a Negro . . . wearing jungle fatigues, jungle boots, and a helmet with a camouflage cover. He was armed with an M-16 and was escorted by one VC/NVA type. . . . The other 'American' was identified as Caucasian, very thin, dressed the same as the Negro. . . . During contact between PF and RF units . . . two 'Americans' were again sighted that fit the description of the Americans sighted on 20 Feb 71. The 'Americans' were not armed; however, they were carrying heavy rucksacks, possibly containing radios. The Caucasian was observed 'popping yellow smoke' [detonating a grenade that releases a bright plume of colored smoke, used for signaling] during helicopter gunfire. The 'Americans' were believed by the Vietnamese to be POWs; however the American advisors believe they were cooperating with the VC."[39]

The sightings of the Korean also sparked a great deal of interest from the Korean military forces in the area. Kelly notes that he visited "the Koreans to get them to run an operation against the suspected base camp where we thought the Korean might be."

On March 7, the Koreans went looking for their countryman. A combat assault was conducted by a total of six companies from the 1st ROK regiment assisted by six officers from the 173rd. The assault was conducted simultaneously into three areas. Three ROK companies searched the areas but after an extensive examination of the objectives with no contact or indications that POWs were in the area, the operation was terminated.[40]

The number of reports on possible collaborators from 525th MI coded sources, CAS informants, and Air Force intel agents was mushrooming. Many concern Garwood, but most do not. It is extremely difficult to determine how many were fantasy, false information from agents trying to stay employed, or propaganda by the communist security forces. Some of the reports certainly have a ring of truth to them. How many Americans deserted or were originally prisoners and then converted to the communist cause remains one of the biggest mysteries of the POW/MIA story.

More Ransom Attempts

The efforts to exchange U.S. POWs for reward money continued to occupy the JPRC. One of the most dangerous efforts, undertaken by two JPRC members, first began on July 30, 1970, when a Vietnamese female contacted the JPRC and made an offer to repatriate some U.S. prisoners of war for the reward offered. "Since that time there have been extensive negotiations with this Vietnamese and other members of her group by the JPRC. . . . To date no tangible evidence exists that this Vietnamese has access to any US PWs, but negotiations are continuing in the hopes that some PWs can be recovered."[41]

At first, JPRC intelligence officer Captain Carl Kraft and First Sergeant Sebastian Deluca engaged in the negotiations with the woman. Kraft recalls meetings in Tay Ninh on several occasions to discuss the ransom. The negotiators finally agreed on $100,000 for a large number of Americans, several Thai, and forty Vietnamese. In late September, Kraft signed for the money, and then he and Deluca flew by helicopter to the prearranged site. The helicopter dropped them off with instructions to return in a half hour.

No one showed. Kraft states that "afterwards we felt betrayed. We took a foolish risk because we were so eager to try and get these guys back, Deluca especially. We were not as cautious as we should have been, and going out there by ourselves was not very smart."[42]

However, the game was not over. The Bright Light report states that the "JPRC representatives returned to Tay Ninh on 11 Oct to continue negotiations for repatriation of PWs. Letters signed by General Abrams were presented to the VC representatives to allay any doubts of the VC with respect to the validity of the reward offer or the sincerity of the U.S. representatives. The letters also expressed General Abrams' personal interest in the negotiations and his hopes for their successful conclusion. Direct JPRC questioning of the VC representative concerning U.S. PWs brought evasive answers and repeated reminders from the VC that negotiations would take time and must not be hurried. U.S. representatives were requested not to visit Tay Ninh again until they had been contacted. Arrangements were made for the VC to contact the JPRC through MACV Advisory Team 90. On 24 Oct 70 CAS officers near Tay Ninh were contacted by intermediaries for two VC requesting to know if CAS was interested in information on 21 U.S. PWs. It is not known what the VC intend by opening this second channel. JPRC and CAS are working closely on this matter and intend to make it clear to the VC that all U.S. agencies have a common purpose and negotiations for PWs will be made by one group."[43]

On November 7, the JPRC/CAS team met with the new CAS source. Nothing developed out of that meeting, although the JPRC continued to maintain contact with the first source. The JPRC had asked for a list of names of the U.S. POWs held in the camp, but the sources vanished, and there is no further mention in the Bright Light reports of this effort.

However, Deluca was intent on finding out if the VC were serious. He convinced the new Navy officer, John "Smoky" McFadyen, to join him in an attempt to pin down the VC offer. By January, their efforts were rewarded when a female VC who had recently rallied provided information about American POWs she had seen. She had been with the guerrillas since she was fourteen, working as a nurse on Nui Ba Den mountain in Tay Ninh province. As McFadyen remembers, "She was very young and had lived most of her life out in the boonies. She didn't own anything other than her black pajamas, so Deluca and I took her to the market. I bought her a dress and Deluca bought her dinner. She opened up to us and started telling us the locations of caves on the mountain. We showed her the POW/MIA photo book, and she picked out several

Americans she had seen in the caves. We believed her. The JPRC had good intelligence for a long time that U.S. POWs were held on the mountain. Of course, Nui Ba Den had been a VC stronghold for years, so we knew we were going to have to ransom them out.

"Deluca and I started hanging around Tay Ninh. We would drive out in this old yellow Datsun with Embassy plates. Deluca had the idea of meeting with the Cao Dai monks to see if they could help us. The Cao Dai are a major religious group in the area and they had great influence in Tay Ninh province. We met one monk who had been educated at Yale. He spoke fluent English and he introduced to us to some of the local villagers at the base of the mountain. We would sit around talking to these people and drinking tea together. Deluca spoke Vietnamese, so he carried on the conversations. Eventually we became so well known that when we would drive around people would start waving at us. They told us that three U.S. POWs were being held in caves on the mountain. After a while we showed the photo book to some of the villagers. One of the MIAs they picked out was one of the same people the nurse chose.

"Deluca sent word to the VC through the villagers that we wanted to trade for the POWs. To help build up their confidence in us, Deluca sent a peace offering of rice to the VC and the villagers. Somehow Deluca arranged for an unmarked SOG plane with Chinese pilots to meet us at Bien Hoa. He had 'procured' these fifty-pound bags of rice, which we then stuffed into the airplane. The plane was so overloaded I never thought we would get off the ground. Deluca flew out to this SF camp and delivered the rice, which somehow got to these villagers. A short time later, the villagers invited us back to meet a 'friend' of theirs. He was, or claimed to be anyway, a VC cadre in charge of the POWs. We had several long meetings with the guy, and eventually we agreed to swap three U.S. POWs for $100,000. The cadre also wanted to defect and go live in Paris.

"We decided to meet in two weeks to make the swap. The VC only wanted one of us at the meeting and we were to come unarmed. I checked the money out and put it in a briefcase. When we arrived at the last checkpoint before the village, I stayed there with the money and Deluca went forward. He came back a couple hours later and said the VC cadre never showed. Later we visited the Cao Dai priest and asked him to find out what happened. The priest made some inquiries and told us that an NVA cadre who would periodically inspect the POW camp had done so recently. During his visit he discovered the plot to ransom the POWs and promptly executed our contact. We tried to resurrect the exchange but we never could get anyone interested again."[44]

Buttercup Springs to Life

The *Buttercup* channel, which had lain fallow for almost a year, suddenly re-opened in late January 1969, when a French-speaking female who claimed to represent Tran Bach Dang, the high-ranking Vietnamese communist involved in the earlier *Buttercup* negotiations, telephoned the Embassy and proposed renewed discussions. The caller offered the exchange of four cadres in exchange for a number of U.S. POWs. Embassy officials told the caller they wished to identify the prisoners available for exchange. The CIA provided a list of twenty U.S. names with the demand that the NLF release ten of them in exchange for the four they wanted. The request evidently did not impress Dang and the emissary did not call back. With the talks broken off, the list was never passed to the other side.[45]

In July 1971 the communists "sent a letter to the Embassy requesting a special telephone number that could be used for continuing discussions of the prisoner issue. The Embassy duly supplied one, publishing in a bogus newspaper ad in one of the Saigon dailies. . . . For the next three months CIA operatives sat by an Embassy phone . . . but no one ever called. At last, in early October 1971, there was a surprise breakthrough."[46]

The breakthrough was the unexpected release of Army Staff Sergeant John Sexton. Sexton had been captured on August 12, 1969, when his tracked vehicle was hit twice by antitank rounds. Wounded, he remained near his vehicle but was taken prisoner that night when an enemy soldier found him sleeping and awakened him. On October 8, 1971, he walked into an ARVN outpost carrying three documents with him: two safe-conduct passes and a "rough sketch map of Route 7 between Mimot and Snoul [two towns in eastern Cambodia] showing a bridge crossing a river. . . . Sexton first explained map as being intended to describe place where persons named were to be delivered by helicopter at hour specified. At a later stage of debriefing he said . . . that he believed his release was intended as an exchange for the two persons named. He then added that he was told the US authorities were already informed of the planned exchange and he was to deliver the map. . . ."[47]

The Embassy was flabbergasted at Sexton's information and knew nothing about any exchange. Apparently, the NLF had managed to screw up the initial attempt. Sexton informed his JPRC debriefers that on "30 Aug 71 the camp political officer informed him that he was going to be released. . . . He was told that arrangements had been made with US authorities. . . ."[48] Sexton and his escorts then wandered around the jungle for over a month visiting several release points. No Americans ever showed because no one in the Embassy had any clue about the communists' intentions. Finally, in frustration, the communists took him to a point near an ARVN outpost and told him to start walking toward it.

The Embassy determined that one of the men the North Vietnamese wanted was a high-ranking cadre of the Saigon Communist Party chapter, Le Van Hoai. The communists, however, wanted the other man back even more. Nguyen Van Tai was a senior colonel in the North Vietnamese Ministry of Public Security who was currently assigned to COSVN. The GVN police had arrested him in Saigon on December 23, 1970 for carrying false papers. These two were among the highest-ranking cadres ever captured.

Once again, Ambassador Ellsworth Bunker was faced with having to request enemy POWs from the GVN to exchange for U.S. prisoners. When he went to see President Thieu to discuss the matter, Bunker learned that Thieu had no intention of giving these two up. Instead, he proposed releasing an NVA lieutenant named Ngo Vung.

Vung was one of the few NVA who were willing to return to the communist forces. He was taken by helicopter at the appointed hour to the specified area that Sexton's map indicated. He was carrying a note addressed to Tran Bach Dang suggesting one of his deputies call "Mr. Williams" at the Embassy for further dialogue on exchanges.

Dang's representative called on October 27. Helms informed Kissinger that the CIA "believes the call was genuine in the sense that the caller was acting on Communist Party instructions. As you will note, the caller proposed an exchange of an unspecified number of prisoners (presumably American) including '[redacted] of the CIA' for two Vietnamese. The caller proposed the exchange take place any day of our selection between 2 and 6 November in Tay Ninh."[49]

The Vietnamese wanted to trade Foreign Service officer Douglas Ramsey for their two cadres. Helms' recommendation, although censored by the CIA, is revealing. "While the opportunity to get Ramsey back should clearly not be lost, we believe there is a very serious risk indeed that if the communists are given both men they ask for in return, the channel will close and the dialogue cease. We are convinced that the man the communists most want back is [Colonel Nguyen Van] Tai. They will almost certainly sustain an interest in prisoner exchange discussions so long as he is held by the GVN. Furthermore, we believe there is an excellent chance that if the communists are apprised of the fact that we know who [redacted] they will accept an exchange of [redacted] for [redacted] to keep the dialogue going."[50]

Frank Snepp was a CIA officer who wrote an account of the fall of South Vietnam, including a discussion of the *Buttercup* exchanges, in his book *Decent Inter-*

val. He indicates that the CIA wanted to offer only Le Van Hoai for Ramsey, which seems to be borne out by Helms' statement above. Snepp writes, "As a senior agency official later explained to me, Tai was a top communist intelligence operative; Ramsey was 'no more than a Foreign Service officer.' Thus, to have exchanged one for the other . . . the communists would have gotten the better of the deal. Besides, the agency was hoping to trade Tai for a CIA officer [probably Eugene Weaver] captured during the 1968 offensive."[51]

But the CIA wasn't alone in wanting to play hardball with the communists. The military wanted an even better deal from the enemy. Admiral Elmo Zumwalt, then Acting Chairman of the Joint Chiefs of Staff, wrote, "Strongly recommend that every effort be made to persuade the White House to direct CAS Saigon to take a very firm stand in their negotiations with the NLF for the release of at least three US military PWs in addition to Douglas Ramsey and to obtain a list of all prisoners currently in their custody in exchange for Hoai. We should seek this as a desirable minimum. . . . My interest in this approach is based not only on our concern for our POWs held by the NLF but also out of consideration for their families and the political implications if it became known that we did not take a strong stand to try to obtain the release of some of our servicemen. . . ."[52]

Snepp's description of the agency's proposal to the NLF of trading Hoai alone for Ramsey is the only available account of the failure of the exchange. When Dang's emissary called again in late November, the CIA held firm to their offer of Hoai for Ramsey plus a list of U.S. POWs. Dang rejected the offer and the deal fell through. Douglas Ramsey would have to wait another fifteen months before he was freed.[53] No other CIA documents on *Buttercup* have been released.

13. Finding the Americans in Laos

When I finished briefing General Abrams he looked up at me and said, "This guy's got balls, we have to save him."
—JPRC officer Captain Kevin M. Kelly, relating the reaction of General Creighton Abrams to the report of the escape in Laos of USAF First Lieutenant Jack Butcher and his efforts to avoid recapture by North Vietnamese troops

Since 1967, the Joint Personnel Recovery Center had stressed increasing the efforts to discover the whereabouts and identities of American POWs in Laos. The Seventh Air Force conference provided the first opening for the military to improve its influence behind the previously closed doors of Laos. By October 1969, DIA also approved the Pacific Command's request for a directive to conduct agent operations in Laos and in North Vietnam. The Pacific Command pointed out the need for clandestine agent operations because the North Vietnamese had not divulged the identity and locations of U.S. prisoners. In Laos, two primary targets were established, Khang Khay and Sam Neua. This effort was the start of a high-level clandestine-agent operation to locate POWs, aspects of which remain classified.[1]

One area thought promising for determining a man's status was crash-site inspection. The Joint Chiefs asked CINCPAC to provide an outline of its capabilities to inspect confirmed or suspected aircraft crash sites for evidence that would support a determination of status. CINCPAC agreed: "As MACV crash site assets are degraded through programmed drawdowns, a viable PACOM crash site capability must be maintained. . . ."[2] This program required a large investment of time and valuable resources, and despite repeated CAS promises, only 11 out of almost two hundred crash sites had been inspected by the summer of 1971.

With Defense Secretary Laird's approval, in November 1971 CINCPAC held a conference to discuss plans for the follow-on crash-site inspection team. From that conference the plan for the Joint Casualty Resolution Center (JCRC) was born. CINCPAC OPLAN 5100 would eventually outline the structure of the JCRC, a unit that would have an almost twenty-year history of postwar attempts to solve the POW/MIA mystery.

Mysteries Without End

So many Americans disappeared into the thick jungle and craggy limestone cliffs of Laos that some activists in later years gave it the nickname "the Black Hole." As the U.S. government points out, the percentage of SAR saves was far higher in Laos than in North Vietnam, indicating that many of the six hundred MIAs listed at the end of the war probably did not survive their loss incident. Yet some from that group must have survived and been captured in the desolate and remote country of Laos. Much like rumors of lost cities, tales emerged of white men seen in cages or used as slave labor. Are these stories real or figments of a jungle-inspired imagination? Here are several of the more intriguing stories to come forth.

In 1970, a man named Kuno Knoebl published a book in which he recounted the story of a European military officer who actually visited the Ho Chi Minh Trail. A man in Knoebl's book named Lieutenant Blanchard outlined to Knoebl how he was shown a portion of the Trail. The officer accurately described the extensive camouflage, the massive road building, and the repair projects.

According to Knoebl, Blanchard described how he saw "a column of tall men coming down a narrow jungle path. At first I thought they were Chinese because they towered over the small Vietnamese. But then I saw they were whites, Americans, captured soldiers who were wheeling heavy loads of earth on bicycles. They were emaciated and exhausted and scarcely looked at me. They were bound by iron chains around their wrists to the bicycle frames. My Vietnamese escort told me they were prisoners paying for their crimes against the Vietnamese people."[3]

A CIA memo discussing this book states, "This is the only report we have come across of use of American PWs for forced labor. The only hard information we have that fits into this allegation is the repeated indication by Hanoi officials that recalcitrant PWs are punished in camps separate from camps for the average or cooperative PWs. If you have heard rumors of forced labor for American PWs in Laos, or seen reports to this effect, please call. We are quite interested in collecting whatever information may be available on this subject." A handwritten note at the bottom mentions that "We have fairly extensive coverage in this area by CAS Road Watch teams. No reports received which substantiate the text of this article."

Not only was Knoebl's account not believed by the CIA, another report, in March 1971, was also ignored, this time by the U.S. Embassy in Vientiane. A Thai prisoner of the North Vietnamese in Laos named Khamfone Sricharoen escaped from the communists after having spent five years in captivity performing slave labor on the Trail. An article in the *Bangkok Post* magazine section detailed his amazing story of capture, imprisonment, and escape. Mr. Sricharoen's tale included accurate descriptions of the area where he was held and the rigors of life working to build and maintain the communist supply line. More importantly, he told of two "white" prisoners whom he believed to be Americans also working on the Trail. He said, "The North Vietnamese tortured the white prisoners. The white prisoners were most of the time confined in underground cells. . . . When I last saw them, they were emaciated. Their faces were haggard and their skins stretched so tight over their bones. They were so skinny . . . I fear they may have died already."[4]

The State Department immediately asked for clarification from the U.S. Embassy in Laos. It wasn't until September, however, that the Air Force intelligence detachment in Thailand finally interviewed him. According to Sricharoen's recollection, he saw the Americans some time in December 1967. The Thai described the PL camp and the condition of the Americans and provided many other details. He overheard one of the guards call one American "Es Mo Set," but he had no idea if this was his name. The interviewer noted that while Sricharoen's description of time, distance, and location was at times weak, the area picked out by the Thai was near one of the confirmed Alpha POW sites in Laos, and that other reports had mentioned the movement of Americans through this area.[5] What happened to Sricharoen, or why his information was not believed, is unknown. Why it took U.S. intelligence so long to interview him is another matter.

Finally, one of the more exotic and possibly obscure stories involves a former communist author who defected to the GVN. The man, Xuan Vu, was a well-known writer in North Vietnam who once received a literary honor in Hanoi. As preparation for the Tet Offensive in 1968, he was sent to the South along with a group of writers, painters, and musicians to take over the Party's leadership in the arts once the offensive succeeded. After traversing the Trail and entering the South, he defected instead of entertaining the masses in communist artistry. He wrote and published in 1972 a memoir describing his long and difficult journey, a book called *Duong Di Khong Den* (*The Road that Leads Nowhere*). For his compelling account, he won another award, the GVN National Prize in Letters and Arts, 1972–73.

Somewhere in Laos along the Trail, he wrote, he came upon a strange scene. While halted at one of the numerous rest stops along the Trail called commo-liaison stations, he heard moaning, the sound of a human voice in agony. Following the sound, Vu and a companion found a Caucasian male trapped in a cage, hidden along a small side trail. His friend begged him to leave, afraid that they would be discovered by the local cadre. Shortly, one of the commo-liaison guards came looking for them and discovered them next to the cage. "Are you trying to liberate the American?" the guard asked. "No," Vu replied. "I just wanted to have a look at him." "Good," said the guard. "This pig is paying for his crimes against our people."[6]

Are these stories real or elaborate fakes? The answer is difficult to discover, but imagine the average intelligence analyst trying to prove or disprove these nightmarish accounts.

Finding a Solution

Despite the attempts of 7th AF to accurately determine if the burgeoning number of POW camps was accurate, the corollary issue of how to identify American POW/MIAs in Laos continued to present a serious problem. The military believed, with some justification, that it was having to continually push CAS for information and results on locating American POWs.

After several CINCPAC/MACV complaints the CIA furnished two explanations of its contributions to the POW problem. In February 1970, the CIA recounted its efforts to "collect intelligence information concerning American prisoners of war aimed at mounting rescue operations. No rescue operations are in progress at this moment because there is insufficient current, hard information to permit planning operations which would have a reasonable chance of success and would still not endanger the safety of the prisoners."

The Agency went on to mention that "Out of 34 prisons reported to be in Laos, only one can be considered as a confirmed prison site; this facility is a series of caves in a karst formation at Ban Nakay Neua. . . . The presence of American prisoners in or near this location has been reported since August 1966. The Station now has one intelligence team in the Sam Neua area of Northeast Laos sent there specifically to acquire information following a report that some 20 USAF pilots were prisoners in the Ban Nakay area as of late 1969 and early 1970."[7]

In April 1970, the CIA reported that "Chief of Station (COS) Vietnam maintains one officer [redacted] who is in charge of insuring that all pertinent Station assets are put at service of JPRC for the purpose of collecting PW intelligence and rescuing PWs. . . . Chief of Station Vientiane also cooperates closely with JPRC [redacted], as in the cases of the 'cabbage patch' and the caves at Sam Neua. COS Vientiane presses constantly for PW intelligence with all resources which can be spared from other operations. There have been escapes in Laos, but no successful operations to liberate American PWs. There has been at least one successful operation to liberate Laotian PWs. . . . All information obtained is either passed laterally to JPRC and other branches of MACV or dissemed as intelligence."[8]

To discuss the overall E&E problem, the JPRC held a four-day conference in Saigon in June with representatives from CINCPAC, Pacific Air Force (PACAF), and three personnel from Air Force headquarters. DIA's POW intelligence committee reported that the main purpose of the conference was to provide an opportunity to review current plans and policies and to discuss common problems and solutions.[9] The agenda included an update on the status of intelligence holdings on U.S. personnel, the problems of obtaining timely and valid intelligence, and a discussion of possible solutions. On the third day, the group flew to Udorn to meet CAS representatives from Vientiane and the 4802nd JLD to discuss the search of crash sites in Laos, use of reward leaflets in Laos, and rating and checkout of POW sightings or information obtained during debriefings of enemy personnel.[10]

MACV closely monitored the CAS follow-up efforts and continued to be dissatisfied. By August, CINCPAC concurred and made a strong recommendation that action be undertaken at the Washington level to reorder priorities in the training of CAS indigenous assets so as to more effectively accomplish the successful identification, assistance, and recovery of American POWs in Laos. The reason was that "the meager and in many cases outdated PW camp information has been 'spin-off' from road and trailwatch missions. Once entered in the Laos PW detention facilities list, the location of a reported sighting may provide the enemy sanctuaries that will remain free from air attack for up to thirty-six months. A timely and aggressive program to follow up PW sightings reports would enhance PW recovery chances. . . . All attendees at the Saigon/Udorn meetings were in agreement that field efforts should be intensified to improve the productivity of E&E/JPRC operations."[11]

In other words, despite CAS's continued assurances that POW collection effort was the highest priority in Laos, CINCPAC was claiming otherwise. The Joint Chiefs immediately ordered SACSA to reply. They recommended that native Lao agents be trained and infiltrated into areas along the Ho Chi Minh Trail where camps were suspected. However, they noted that after "extensive discussions CAS Washington regarding subject of US prisoners of war in Laos, CAS has expressed concern over the problems related to infiltrating assets into trail areas where suspected detention facilities may exist. They point out that present NVN tactics regarding transporting POWs is to restrict all Lao from vicinity of trails to be used for any NVN movement. This, plus the fact that most Lao civilians no longer habitate the logical areas for NVN POW detention, makes infiltrating Laotians into NVN ranks highly unlikely.

"From sensitive source activities in Southeast Asia, it is apparent that POW movements are known to only a few personnel in Hanoi and even they do not reveal exact positions during movement of POWs. Further, all efforts to infiltrate CAS assets into NVN/Hanoi have thus far proved unsuccessful. Coincident to the meeting with CAS Washington the new Vientiane Station Chief was undergoing preassignment briefings and has been apprised of the situation.

"Concur with your assessment that an aggressive effort should be pursued by forces in the field to follow up on any PW sighting reports. In addition, it is necessary to reemphasize and reindoctrinate *Prairie Fire* and CAS teams on the absolute necessity of aggressive and timely reporting of PW intelligence and quick reaction by JPRC. In connection with foregoing, you may expect an increase in effort and teams in the immediate future. CAS Washington has reasserted their complete understanding of the problem and has assured full cooperation of their field personnel. . . . This message coordinated with CAS and DIA."[12]

In the fall of 1970, SACSA sent Colonel Don Hatch to Laos to observe the situation. "Col. Hatch stated that the Joint Staff had noted an improvement in reporting from Laos on PW intelligence since his visit to CAS on 1 September 1970. At that time, Col. Hatch discussed with [redacted] the reply which SACSA was sending to a CINCPAC complaint of insufficient action by CIA in Laos; the complaint was based on talks at Udorn at the monthly meeting. Specifically, Col. Hatch stated that Joint Staff was pleased to note that [redacted] had been committed by Vientiane to the collection of PW intelligence. . . . there had been no basic change in the operational problems outlined except more NVA troops are now being captured and debriefed. We believe that the debriefing of these captives could be improved and would provide additional insight into the location and treatment of PWs."[13]

The continued lack of CIA POW intelligence in Laos and the ability to improve the prisoner intelligence collection effort would prove to be the key the military needed. The Embassy, however, was not allowing anyone onto their turf without a fight.

Pushing the Embassy

Despite the CIA's continual assurances that they would increase efforts to identify American POWs, both the State Department and the military remained skeptical. In February 1971 a draft cable was circulated among the JCS, State, and the CIA concerning the lack of intelligence on POWs in Laos. In early March, State sent the joint cable to the Embassy in Laos, noting that "Information about the release of all U.S. prisoners . . . is a matter of high national concern. In this regard, the situation in Laos is particularly difficult. Of the over 260 men lost in Laos, only three are listed as POWs in Laos. Three others were reported held in North Vietnam. There are indications that others have been moved to North Vietnam, but our information on this is limited. . . . We assume that other men have been captured and are held in Laos. Yet we have practically no information on the places in Laos in which these men are confined. . . . Request all elements of mission give this subject the highest priority possible under the current circumstances, with aim of identifying locations in Laos where US personnel are held, and establishing how many, and if possible, which ones are held at each location."[14]

The cable went on to offer some suggestions for improving the intelligence flow, including leaflets, interviewing of refugees, and insertion of more teams into areas suspected of holding POWs. Ambassador Godley immediately responded that "We share Washington's concern about American prisoners missing over Laos and are reviewing on priority basis procedures to gather intelligence. In this connection we assume Executive agencies are aware that information of this type already has highest priority in our intelligence effort and that all information is immediately passed to MACV, DIA and other addressees. . . . When information is hard enough to provide basis for considering recovery efforts, Washington will be alerted. Last year, for example, air photography of Sam Neua area revealed possible POW installation. [Next sentence redacted.] While this effort was unsuccessful we are continuing to look for other opportunities. In general, however, we believe that attention being given to PW question by all elements of mission reflects the importance and urgency we know the Administration attaches to this problem."[15]

CINCPAC was carefully following this message traffic and after State's March cable instantly offered to increase the intelligence and interrogation capabilities of the Royal Lao Army and their irregular forces by augmenting them with American resources. CINCPAC believed that a lack of intelligence on American POWs was the most significant factor hampering rescue operations and that the Embassy's refusal to allow more military help was contributing to that lack of intelligence. Admiral John McCain, the commander in the Pacific whose son was at that time a prisoner in Hanoi, wrote, "CINCPAC fully shares the concern expressed and concurs in the action proposed. . . . CINCPAC has the resource potential to provide a capability of collection on military targets in Laos. . . . On several occasions in the past when the need was not as urgent, CINCPAC offered to use these resources to assist in the collection mission in Laos but such assistance was not needed at the time. In view of current high national concern as evinced, CINCPAC is eager to provide trained and experienced military interrogators. . . ."[16]

By the end of March, the Joint Chiefs were requesting that CINCPAC specify which assets would be used to increase the Embassy's intelligence-gathering abilities in Laos. In mid-April, CINCPAC responded by outlining the different clandestine agents and collection nets it had available that could be applied to Laos, plus several internal interrogation teams that it could relatively quickly dispatch to Laos. The JCS coordinated this information with CIA and State, and another joint message was sent to the Vientiane Embassy offering the CINCPAC teams.

This was the military's strongest move yet to break through the sacrosanct barrier that the CIA and U.S. Embassy had erected around Laos. Under heavy JCS pressure, State cabled the Embassy suggesting it accept the interrogation teams. "The intense high-level interest in measures to recover US PWs and determine the status of those missing requires the use of all available intelligence-gathering assets. An expanded and coordinated program to inspect crash sites and to interrogate sources in Laos could lead to the recovery or determine the status of personnel missing. . . . It is also possible that such a program might yield additional information . . . of other personnel who may have transited Laos en route to PW camps in NVN. As the US withdrawal proceeds in Southeast Asia, some areas . . . may, in time, fall beyond the reach of direct US influence. While other areas may remain accessible, the diminished . . . strength of US forces may forestall inspection operations. Consequently, it is imperative to make the best possible use of available time."[17]

With State's backing of CINCPAC's offer to provide language-qualified interrogation teams and clandestine agents, the Vientiane Embassy was finding it difficult to refuse. But the Embassy intended to control this element as much as possible and was still reluctant to accept overt military resources in Laos on the grounds of the potential political hazards created by face-to-face U.S. interrogation of enemy soldiers.

Under considerable pressure, the Vientiane Embassy finally accepted a small Army team of interrogators that would work behind the scenes to improve the

RLA's interrogation techniques. By mid-May 1971 the "US mission, Vientiane, has established a working agreement . . . to more responsibly react to intelligence requirements concerning PWs and ralliers. There have been, as you are all aware, several proposals by intelligence-collection elements within the theater for the introduction of their personnel into Laos to conduct their own interrogations pursuant to the satisfaction of national intelligence requirements on the subject of American PWs. Vientiane mission response and the Ambassador's position have been that these collection agencies should levy their requirements on the Vientiane mission for satisfaction. The policy established with regard to US personnel conducting face-to-face interrogations of prisoners or ralliers has been that it is politically undesirable. . . . if US-conducted interrogation were exposed, [it] would have adverse repercussions."[18]

Although the U.S. Embassy had acquiesced to a military presence in Laos to assist in the collection of intelligence on American POWs, the operation wasn't fully staffed until late in the summer of 1971. The military interrogators, under the code-name *Project 5310-03-E,* eventually produced hundreds of reports dealing with POW information and other areas, such as Order of Battle and supply locations. Their success in gaining information from the few captured or rallied North Vietnamese was impressive, and even more so from the PL. For instance, in 1971 the death of the commander of the Pathet Lao South Lao Region caused most of the PL South Lao infrastructure to defect to the Royal Laotian Army. Much important intelligence on the Ho Chi Minh Trail was derived from their interrogations. It is not known whether the CINCPAC agent nets were ever used.

Looking at the Problem of Recovery Efforts

Intertwined with the discussion concerning the augmentation of the Vientiane Embassy's capabilities was the larger problem of actually recovering American prisoners. The drawdown clock was rapidly reducing the American forces and, just as importantly, weakening the political authority necessary to rescue any POWs in Laos. For instance, in February the Joint Chiefs of Staff (JCS) had rescinded permission for U.S. participation in the *Prairie Fire* area of operation, the fifty-kilometer strip lying along the South Vietnam–Laos border. Later, this ban was widened to include Cambodia. MACV interpreted this to mean that even the *Bright Light* teams led by U.S. personnel were not authorized to enter the country. Any American POWs held captive in this area would now have to be rescued by ARVN-led and -manned Special Forces teams.

The quandary was not just in Laos. In South Vietnam, the JPRC was experiencing the same dilemma: no U.S. forces available to conduct raids. On April 21 Defense Secretary Laird wrote a memo to Admiral Moorer in which he stressed the need for very rapid reaction capability and a force specially trained and selected for prisoner rescues. Moorer in turn queried CINCPAC and MACV for their thoughts on how best to approach this subject.

CINCPAC's opinion was that MACV should dedicate a force solely to prisoner rescue. They also wanted to upgrade all aspects of POW intelligence by using the CINCPAC agent nets. Since 1962, CINCPAC had attempted to insert agent operations into Laos and North Vietnam to collect military information, and had offered on previous occasions to provide trained interrogators to assist in the exploitation of sources. The recent approval of two interrogators in Laos was considered by CINCPAC to be only an initial step toward improving the POW intelligence collection effort.

Admiral McCain wrote a cable to Admiral Moorer explaining his views. "A sustained and integrated effort by the entire intelligence community is required to enhance the quality and timeliness of the PW intelligence product. Granting of recovery authorities and dedication of forces constitute . . . solutions to the problem."[19]

Moorer was sympathetic to McCain's idea and asked CINCPAC to provide a general concept for a new recovery force. MACV, however, felt differently about a dedicated reaction unit since any proposal was only a temporary solution, given that programmed reductions would render SOG virtually inactive by July 1972. General Abrams realized that "limited assets caused by redeployments preclude a totally dedicated task force for the sole purpose of PW recovery. Therefore, in view of the importance of this mission, a variation of the dedicated force concept is proposed."[20] Abrams recommended a version of the old JPRC theme—standby SOG units at each SOG base complemented by any available air assets. The on-call units would have a Command and Control element and would be able to gather, "on receipt of hard intelligence, within 24 hours to commence training and planning."

McCain wrote back to Moorer and included Abrams' comments. "The MACV concept is a pragmatic approach to the immediate PW recovery problem. . . . These forces can be assembled within 24 hours . . . [but] reductions in personnel strength anticipated by July 72 would eliminate MACV's capability to conduct PW recovery activities subsequent to the date. . . . The dedication of MACV assets can only be considered an interim solution. . . ."[21] To satisfy this critical requirement beyond July 1972, CINCPAC proposed to form a Joint Personnel Recovery Task Force dedicated to the location and recovery of

POW/MIAs in Southeast Asia. The Task Force would be directly responsible to CINCPAC.

At the end of May, Moorer took the short-term MACV solution and the longer-range CINCPAC proposal to Laird for approval. While the JCS approved MACV's plan to utilize SOG forces until July 1972, they were less convinced by McCain's idea for a CINCPAC-led recovery force, and ordered further study. Eventually, a watered-down proposal was adopted that assigned a Marine unit on Okinawa to be the dedicated reaction force.

Additionally, Moorer wanted to grant the commanders more flexibility in POW raids and he recommended that Laird permit U.S.-led rescue forces to enter Cambodia and Laos. By mid-August, Laird had reviewed and approved the request for U.S.-led forces to be used in POW recovery efforts in Laos and Cambodia. However, he wrote, crash-site "operations do not result in the recovery of personnel and should be conducted only when there is reasonable assurance of no contact with enemy forces and when there is minimal risk of incurring casualties."[22] Requests to send men into North Vietnam would be approved on a case-by-case basis.

While the problem of prisoner recovery was solved for the moment, Laird was still dissatisfied with POW intelligence from Laos. Moorer knew that despite the continual high-level interest, the recovery of any American POWs would be unsuccessful without more reliable intelligence. In September, Laird wrote a letter to Secretary of State William P. Rogers, stating, "There are some 250 U.S. personnel listed as missing in action in Laos, and from time to time there has been evidence that some U.S. personnel are held by the enemy in Laos. . . . In March, we asked the field to increase efforts aimed at the recovery of POWs and solicited comments on a number of specific proposals. Subsequent to that time I have reviewed the authorities for SAR and SAR-related operations and have approved measures to improve responsiveness and allow inspection of crash sites. Our efforts in this area continue, however, to be hindered by a lack of reliable intelligence information. I understand that Ambassador Godley believes that currently available CAS assets are adequate to collect all the available intelligence related to prisoners. I appreciate the effort which has been expended; however, in light of our lack of success to date I do not feel that we can be satisfied. Accordingly, I request that a renewed emphasis be directed toward an improvement of our intelligence regarding prisoners of war in Laos."[23]

Rogers assured Laird that the Vientiane embassy would take even greater measures to improve POW intelligence. Frank Sieverts at State forwarded to Godley a copy of the correspondence between the two Secretaries. Godley as usual wanted to minimize the U.S. military presence. On October 31, Godley wrote to Sieverts, "You may rest assured that we are doing everything conceivable in this domain. I would have no objection to increasing military personnel here to this end but for the life of me I cannot see what they would do other than harass already overworked persons.

"I am interested in your observation that Brigadier General Manor [Manor was overall commander of the Son Tay raid] cleared the telegram for the JCS. We are just as operationally oriented as is Washington and we recently sent in a special team into the Sam Neua area to look precisely into this problem. Unfortunately, its results as far as POW/MIA information is concerned was completely negative."[24]

What "special team" was sent into Sam Neua remains a puzzle. It appears that CAS was continuing to send Hmong teams to look for American POWs. Why the CIA will not disclose these efforts, the intelligence they were based on, and their results is just as much a mystery.

"I prayed for over an hour": The Escape of Jack Butcher

Air Force First Lieutenant Jack M. Butcher had arrived in South Vietnam in late February 1971. An OV-10 pilot, he was assigned as a "Covey" FAC, or Forward Air Controller, working the old *Prairie Fire* zone along the Trail in southern Laos. In February, when the JCS had denied the further use of American-led recon teams in Laos, the former SOG FACs had reverted to working normal air strikes against enemy supplies coming down the Trail. On March 24 Butcher and Captain Tom Yarborough took off in separate OV-10s to fly over the Trail area. Since Butcher was new in-country, it was necessary to have a more experienced FAC like Yarborough escort Butcher on familiarization flights before he would be allowed to handle strikes by himself. As his plane lifted off, Jack Butcher was about to start one of the most dramatic escapes and rescue attempts of the war.

Yarborough and Butcher had been given separate areas to reconnoiter. As Butcher was scanning a ford with binoculars looking for signs of enemy movement, an AAA shell slammed into the nose of his airplane, exploding below his left foot. Shrapnel tore into his body. Reacting instinctively, Butcher ejected. As he descended in his parachute, he blacked out.

Yarborough had finished conducting a sensor-laying mission when he radioed Butcher. Receiving no answer on any frequency, Yarborough became alarmed and flew toward Butcher's last known location. Unable to spot him, Yarborough dove into a fog bank covering the area. He "coasted into the clear about a thousand feet above ground. Within seconds, chills ran up and down my spine as the high-pitched shrill of an emergency beeper filled my helmet earphones."[25] Radioing back to headquarters, Yarborough alerted the SAR helicopters.

Butcher awoke on the ground, sitting next to a tree. He managed to get out his survival radio and turn it on. Unable to stand up and badly disoriented, he crawled into some bushes to hide and passed out. A few minutes later an NVA search party found him. They gave him first aid and moved him toward their base camp.

On the third day of his captivity, Jack Butcher woke up with an intravenous needle inserted into his arm. That evening he arrived at a huge camp and was taken to a hut. Butcher was being held at one of the major NVA military stations along the Trail, *Binh Tram* 34. An officer who spoke some English came by to see him, as did a doctor. As the NVA patched his wounds, Butcher sized up his situation.

"The fourth day was pretty bad for me," Butcher recalls. "The realization that I was a prisoner in Laos dawned on me. Although I had attended survival school at Clark Air Base in the Philippines, I had not done very well. I turned to my Christian faith and prayed for over an hour. I let God into my life and I mentally prepared myself for death. Afterwards I felt much better, and I believe God heard my prayers because the next day I managed to escape."[26]

Butcher noticed that after lunch each day, all the NVA took a siesta-type break. After lunch on the fifth day since his capture, he watched his guard get up and walk out of his hut. The guard sat down, leaned against a tree, and fell asleep. At first Butcher suspected a trap, as the guards had left Butcher's boots and a canteen full of water in the hut. Earlier, Butcher had inspected the doorway to a tunnel that was built into the hut. After a few minutes Butcher grabbed his boots and the canteen and crawled into the tunnel. He popped out a short distance away.

He was free. Alternately running and then stopping to listen, Butcher made his way west toward the sun. He climbed a ridge and noticed a wide, grassy open area below him. A trail meandered along the base of the ridge. As he was preparing to move further down the ridge, he heard loud voices coming down the trail. Suddenly, a large group of NVA soldiers appeared. They formed a line and began searching the ridge. Butcher carefully hid himself in a nearby bush. The NVA spent several hours combing the area but didn't find him. Finally they left.

Butcher waited an hour. He hadn't seen anyone in some time so he decided to risk moving. He left his hideout and worked his way carefully down the hill. As he entered the grassy area, almost a dozen NVA soldiers stood up around him, their AK-47s pointed directly at him. Each of their rifles had a long bayonet on it. Butcher raised his hands.

His few hours of freedom, though, had boosted his morale tremendously. "Now I knew my limits. I had carefully gone over in my head how I was going to face this ordeal. I realized that I hadn't even made it out of their base area. I was going to have to escape some other way."

Butcher was taken back to his hut. Over the next several days, the English-speaking officer began to interrogate him. The base commander wanted military information immediately. Butcher tried to play dumb and pretended he didn't understand the officer's English. Despite his stall tactics, the interrogator grimly pressed him for information. Butcher, however, refused to tell them anything. He was sticking to the Code of Conduct. Exasperated and in mounting fury, the communists threatened to shoot him. Butcher refused to cooperate.

"The next morning people gathered around the hut I was being interrogated in to look at me. When I still wouldn't answer their questions, the interrogator stood up and said, 'I'm sorry you've chosen not to answer; we've decided to execute you.' At that, all the guards except the one behind me left the room and the people outside started scattering. As the officer walked out the door, he said again that he was sorry I'd chosen not to talk. When he left, the guard behind me put his gun against my head. I heard him chamber the round into his pistol. My heart was pounding so hard in my chest, I could feel my life just stop. But I thought, 'To hell with them, I'm not breaking the Code.' I sat there waiting but he didn't shoot. After a few minutes the interrogator came back in and said that the North Vietnamese hadn't realized how much Nixon had brainwashed American soldiers. He would give me a day to think about it."

The interrogator left him alone after that. Butcher had now healed enough to begin the long walk to Hanoi. He departed on May 4 accompanied by two guards. He was given tennis shoes, socks, and a conical straw hat. At first, the guards bound him tightly, but as they moved north their vigilance quickly relaxed. As they moved slowly along the commo-liaison route, Butcher gathered information about his guards, their schedule, and how much ammunition each was carrying. He noticed that at each rest stop his guards would walk to a specific hut and present a set of orders for themselves and him. These were authorization passes needed by each traveler, passes that enabled them to receive rations and supplies at each stop.

Five days later, on May 9, Butcher noticed that his group was completely alone and that he had not seen anyone for several hours. Butcher told the guards he needed to go to the bathroom, hoping that they would ignore him. As he walked deeper into the forest, he watched them carefully. His guards moved to the other side of the trail to smoke. As Butcher ambled nonchalantly into the growth, one of the guards finally looked up and realized what he was doing. Figuring this was his best chance, Butcher took off running. The guards were unable to catch him. For the second time, Jack Butcher was free of his captors.

In Saigon, Kevin Kelly was sitting in the JPRC when the phone rang. Picking it up, he heard the excited voice of his friend, a Marine captain who worked in the Special Security Office (SSO), the staff section responsible for monitoring and handling intercepted enemy communications. Kelly was one of the few JPRC officers cleared for SIGINT, and the SOG SIGINT operation was one of the most tightly held areas in one of the most classified units in South Vietnam. "Get down here now," his friend said.

Kelly raced downstairs. Up till now, he had felt extremely frustrated in dealing with the out-of-date POW intelligence the JPRC had been receiving. Watching the news and listening to Nixon talk about the high priority the country was placing on POWs, Kelly felt that this was total hypocrisy; his disenchantment was growing daily. As he entered the room, the SSO turned to him and told him what he had wanted to hear for so long. "We just intercepted an enemy radio message: an OV-10 pilot has escaped along the Trail in southern Laos," the SSO said.

The great hunt was on.

"The entire 7th AF is at your disposal": Searching for the "Screeching Owl"

A second enemy message was shortly picked up describing Butcher's escape. Kelly went back upstairs to see Air Force Colonel Frank Zerbe. Normally, Zerbe was the second-in-command of SOG, but today he was the acting commander as Sadler was away on leave. Kelly entered Zerbe's office with one thought in mind: going after the OV-10 pilot. "This was timely intelligence, only hours old. I said to Zerbe, 'This is something we've been waiting for, we should respond.'"27

Zerbe agreed, and placed a call to Lieutenant General William Dolvin, the Chief of Staff for MACV. Zerbe, Kelly, and the SSO left to visit Dolvin, who saw them immediately. In the meantime, Kelly had searched the loss database and independently determined that the OV-10 pilot was Jack Butcher. Dolvin ordered Kelly to send up observation planes and to coordinate the search with 7th AF at Tan Son Nhut Air Base.

Upon arriving at the base, Kelly remembers meeting a one-star general and informing him of the need for search planes. "The Air Force general gave us only one plane because we had not yet been able to pinpoint Butcher's location. The general was afraid that this would detract from his primary mission of support. But one plane was ludicrous, we were trying to search a massive area."

Within twelve hours, the SSO shop had received a third radio intercept on Butcher. NSA had picked up that Butcher escaped near *Binh Tram* 33, and that the communists were intensifying their search in that sector. NSA had long ago plotted this area through previous SIGINT intercepts, and this greatly helped Kelly pin down Butcher's position. Armed with this information, the three went back again to see Dolvin, who this time called 7th AF personally and spoke to a two-star general. The 7th AF now would release a second plane for the search.

Back at the SSO shop, a fourth and fifth message were picked up. In the earlier intercepts, SOG overheard the communists warning their units to recapture Butcher, that he was "stubborn" and "a spy and very dangerous and if he was not captured, he may cause damage to the entire system."[28] On May 10, NSA overheard the NVA providing a description of Butcher. One NSA analyst states that "the Vietnamese . . . communications links sizzled with orders to recapture him at all costs. Butcher's name was mentioned many times in the clear by units who were assigned to search for him."[29]

Based on these intercepts, the JPRC was able to significantly narrow the search. Again the three asked to see General Dolvin. He agreed, ordering them to create a map board displaying plotted locations for Butcher. This time, the SSO briefed Dolvin. Kelly remembers his friend as "a very gung-ho guy. He was showing all the grid plots on the map board. When he finishes, Dolvin says to us, 'The old man needs to see this.' He picks up the phone and calls Abrams. Then we got up and Dolvin escorted us into Abrams' office. Abrams was sitting behind his desk chomping on a cigar. When we walked in, Abrams looks at Zerbe and he asks, 'Colonel, do you have anything to do with this briefing?' Zerbe says, 'No sir.' Abrams says, 'Then you wait outside.'

"I gave the briefing to Abrams, showing him the map plots, and I told him what had transpired at 7th AF. When I finished briefing him, he looked up at me and said, 'This guy's got balls, we got to save him.' He pushes the intercom, his aide comes in, we get ushered out and told to wait, that Abrams is going to Tan Son Nhut. A half hour later, he comes back. Dolvin goes in to see him and comes back out a few minutes later. Dolvin looks at me at says, 'You have the entire 7th AF at your disposal.'"

Kelly was ordered to set up a command post at Tan Son Nhut to coordinate the rescue attempt. He and the SSO started outlining the plan. The SSO wanted greater intercept concentration and he contacted NSA. This request, NSA later wrote, began "a series of events that was unprecedented in the history of SIGINT support to Search-and-Rescue efforts. . . . It was at this point NSA became actively involved for the first time in a real-time recovery of a downed pilot . . . for the next 20 days, [redacted] available on a 24-hour basis to assist in the recovery attempt."[30]

Butcher, meanwhile, headed west. He was feeling increasingly sick, and had unwittingly caught malaria. On May 11, he came across a grave. The body's personal possessions were lying on top. Butcher picked up a machete and a canteen. Although the lack of food and water and his growing illness were draining his energy, doggedly, Butcher kept going. Once he bumped into two Laotians and another time he was seen by two Vietnamese soldiers who were out for a stroll, but he managed to elude them. One night he stumbled onto some soft ground. Exhausted, he lay down and fell asleep immediately. An hour later he was awakened by the feeling of insects crawling all over his body. He had fallen asleep on an anthill.

Back at Tan Son Nhut, Kelly thought the situation room "was starting to look like the Pentagon." Abrams gave him his personal jet in case he needed to fly somewhere, or to go pick up Butcher if he was recovered. When Kelly discovered that Butcher had attended survival training at Clark, he had one of the Air Force training NCOs flown to Tan Son Nhut to serve in an advisory role. Kelly also had a million reward leaflets showered over the area, hoping maybe someone would come to Butcher's aid. The Coveys from Butcher's unit, the 20th TASS, were also conducting continual overflights of the area, hoping to spot him.

Massive amounts of aerial pictures were being taken and Kelly had marshaled every available photo interpreter in 7th AF. It soon paid off. One of the photo interpreters spotted a symbol laid out on the ground. Three E&E kits were immediately dropped. Kelly looked closely at the map to establish the precise position. SOG still had authority to put Vietnamese teams into the old *Prairie Fire* area, and Kelly was hoping he could use them. Then Kelly grimaced. The symbol was one kilometer outside that area. Now he had to get presidential authority to send in a *Bright Light* team.

CINCPAC reacted quickly to his request. By secure voice, McCain called Moorer personally and informed him of the events in Laos. In turn, Moorer wrote Laird that "COMUSMACV intends to launch a SAR-type recovery at approximately 1800 hours, 13 May 1971, Washington time. CINCPAC has requested one-time authority to commit Bright Light forces in the event SAR operations cannot generate sufficient force to extract pilot, or the pilot, when rescued, has additional perishable information on other US PWs in the immediate area."[31]

Laird gave permission for the team to enter Laos. But the kits remained unopened and the team did not go in. On the afternoon of May 16, another suspected code letter was spotted by Larry Thomas, one of the Covey FACs. The letter was "N," November, which was the code symbol for the month of March, the month Butcher went down. U.S. helicopters searched the area first. The decision was then made to insert SOG Recon Team *Georgia*.

The *Bright Light* team report states that they "moved to the vicinity of the survival letter and discovered that the letter was approximately 4–6 months old and the area about the letter showed no signs of recent activity. The letter was manmade. It had been formed by cutting the brush and bamboo level with the ground and obviously required a great deal of work to prepare. . . . The team noted movement to their north and . . . was extracted under fire. . . . Due to age of survival letter, RT leader felt the escaped PW is not connected with it. . . . The age of the survival letter indicates the letter may be a 'Z.'"[32]

The code symbol was not Butcher's. On May 18, however, Butcher was indeed making the symbol "N," he just was making it some distance away. The night before he had suffered through a hard, cold downpour. His malaria was getting worse, the headaches and fever severely weakening him. He came to an open grassy field and decided to make a letter here. He was cautious, though, as several days earlier he had come to a similar field and although he had carefully watched it, as he lay sleeping that night an AAA gun fired from close proximity. On either side of the field was a hidden AAA unit.

In Washington, NSA was still closely following the communist radio traffic. The NVA were baffled by their inability to catch a lone American pilot in what was essentially their own back yard. The communist search teams had crisscrossed different areas and still were unable to find him. Because he was so stealthy, the frustrated NVA gave Butcher a nickname, the "screeching owl."[33]

The NVA couldn't find Jack Butcher, but neither could Kelly, even with all the assets dedicated to the recovery. The RT's failure meant the time had come for more desperate measures. Aircraft equipped with loudspeakers were flown over the area the NSA knew the enemy was searching. The aircraft were broadcasting two messages. The first was a morale booster. The second was for Butcher to lay out a code letter, the first letter of his dog's name, D for Dominique. The NSA picked up the NVA radio traffic informing the search parties of the loudspeaker aircraft. They also picked up that the communists were afraid "that civilians were assisting the pilot. [Redacted] a proselytizing team was sent into the area to determine if civilians were hiding the POW."[34]

On May 19, with his hunger becoming overwhelming and after ten days of evading among one of the heaviest concentrations of NVA troops in Southeast Asia, Butcher's luck finally ran out. He sneaked into a nearby village during the NVA's siesta time and stole several pineapples. He was spotted by an elderly woman, so he quickly left the village and began walking down a nearby trail. As he was hurrying along, he noticed he had stumbled into another, more heavily camouflaged village. Just as he realized that the large bushes were really well-disguised huts, a Vietnamese soldier walked out of one of the huts to hang up some laundry. Butcher did the only thing he could think of. "I waved at him. He waved back to me and I kept going."

As his left the village after waving hello, he crossed a dry stream bed and was walking through the woods when he heard shouts behind him. Turning, he saw about ten NVA soldiers chasing him. He started running, but when they fired shots he simply stopped. He was exhausted, starving, and very sick. He knew it was hopeless. The NVA quickly surrounded him and ordered him to sit down. Within a half hour, an officer appeared who spoke very good English. He asked Butcher who he was. Butcher told him he was a missionary. He received a sharp blow to his back from a rifle butt for his insolence. He was taken to a nearby camp and thrown into a bunker. Logs were thrown over the top and dirt was piled on the logs to form a roof. Worn out physically, he fell into a deep sleep.

The next morning, Butcher awoke and banged on the roof, trying to get the guard's attention. The guard summoned the English-speaking officer, who ordered the roof raised enough so he could see in. Looking at Butcher, he said in a superior, condescending tone, "What do you want?" Butcher knew he was trapped, so "I told him I wasn't a missionary and he let me out of the bunker. Then he looked at me and said, 'I know who you are. If you are willing to cooperate, we will take care of you. But first I must tell you of an old Vietnamese proverb. It says that you will be forgiven for making the same mistake twice, but never the third time. You have escaped twice, and if you escape again we will shoot you on sight. Do you understand?' I said yes."

Unknown to Butcher, Kelly was still desperately searching for him. On May 26, another code letter was spotted, this time the letter "D," the same letter as his dog's name and what was being broadcast by the loudspeaker aircraft. A *Bright Light* team was inserted and searched the area. The code letter had been constructed with rocks. The team reported that the rock symbol was old and they did not think it was connected to Butcher. The team was extracted under heavy fire from an estimated platoon of enemy soldiers.[35]

The aerial search was resumed, but on May 27 the NSA picked up "information concerning the northward movement of an American POW who was very stubborn, had escaped once, and had to be tied up. . . . His name is Boots Sow, an apparent transliteration for Butcher."[36] At the JPRC, Kelly was informed of the new intelligence and "everyone was absolutely miserable."

Jack Butcher had successfully evaded NVA troops for ten days, all the time fighting a bout of malaria while trying to live off the land. He had made one fatal error. A later plot of his movements showed he was heading straight for Tchepone, the Lao town astride the Trail that had been occupied by NVA forces several years ago. Apparently he was recaptured on the outskirts. He now began anew the long walk to Hanoi. Fortunately for Jack Butcher, he survived and returned at *Homecoming*. Only one final question remains from one of the longest, most intense manhunts of the Vietnam war: who made the other symbols?

What the Agency Was Reporting

The military's criticisms of CAS over the lack of POW intelligence revolved around the often low-level and dated source reporting used by the CIA in its semiannual Lao POW camp studies. Part of the problem for the CIA was the high losses suffered among its guerrilla forces from the increased military pressure of the NVA. The communists were pushing the Hmong soldiers back in northern Laos, and although Vang Pao would launch counterattacks that would temporarily reclaim lost territory, the heavily outmanned Hmong would eventually have to retreat under the pounding of North Vietnamese artillery and massed infantry assaults. The Hmong villagers were also being driven out of their homes to prevent espionage and supply activity.

CAS did try to examine POW camps in those areas that were still relatively accessible to their forces. The CIA criteria for making an entry on the list was "two or more sources," either ground or photography. Just before the start of the October 1969 Lao camp conference, CAS reported that its "irregular forces participating in operations in Xieng Khouang and Savannakhet provinces investigated numerous locations that had been previously reported as POW camps. All investigated camps were found to be either abandoned or housing RLA prisoners."[37] Almost two hundred RLA prisoners were released from four camps, while another twenty camps were found abandoned.

The CIA semiannual Lao POW camp reports for 1968 and 1969 report that "500 enemy personnel were committed to guarding POWs." However, after the conference, that number jumped in 1970 and following years to 1,000. Standard language was used to describe the various sections, verbiage that often repeated itself from report to report. Beginning with the 1970 reports, any changes in intelligence were duly noted. For instance, the section on American POWs in the April 1970 report states, "Other than the Ban NaKay /VH 1956/ prison complex, American POWs are not believed to be permanently incarcerated in Laos. American personnel captured in Laos are escorted to the Ban NaKay prison complex or into North Vietnam through existing infiltration routes. American POWs are believed to receive better treatment than indigenous POWs, but occasionally are displayed for propaganda purposes. American POWs . . . are reported to receive milk and bread with their meals."[38]

Given Godley's continued insistence that the Vientiane Embassy's resources were sufficient to handle any intelligence tasking for POWs, and that they had placed the highest priority on gathering POW information, the CAS report was closely watched. Consequently, a memo was attached to several of the reports "clarifying" the sites that listed American POWs. For example, the memo for the April report states, "The confirmed detention sites for American PWs in Laos, including those through which Americans are known to have [word illegible], are grouped at the throats of the major access routes from Laos into NVN: Route 6 through Sam Neua in the north, the southern entrance to the Mu Gia pass in the south, and near Tchepone at the 17th parallel.

"Many Americans are believed to have passed through Laos or from Laos into North Vietnam. At the present time, however, there is only one confirmed case of an American PW being held in NVN who is known to have been captured in Laos: Mr. Ernie Brace. . . . there is only one site in Laos where American PWs are believed to be held "permanently" at the present time, site L-1 near Sam Neua."[39]

In December 1970, the CIA report now stated, "Until recently the Ban NaKay . . . prison complex was the only prison facility in Laos known to contain American POWs. Americans captured in northern Laos were escorted to this facility, where they were detained on a semipermanent basis. Recent reporting indicates, however, that all foreign POWs including the Americans held in this region may have been moved to an undisclosed location north of Ban NaKay. Americans captured in the Lao panhandle are not believed to be permanently detained in Laos, but rather are escorted . . . to North Vietnam."[40]

By March 1971, the CIA reported that the Americans in the Ban NaKay area whom it earlier recorded leaving for an undisclosed location "may have been moved to Muong Liet/VH1163/." Little else had changed from its December report, except three new prisons had been added and twelve dropped.[41]

In August, the Agency station in Laos sent a request to Langley asking for "All studies done by any intelligence organization dealing with POWs or POW camps in Laos, particularly in northeast Laos, models of POW camps drawn or made from these studies, and copies of photographs of suspected POW camps locations, particularly northeast Laos and adjacent areas of the DRV." CAS Vientiane needed this material because it was "currently refining its data bank of intelligence on POW camps in Laos and adjacent areas. This process has led us to believe if any American POWs are in Laos they are in the Sam Neua/Ban Tong complex in northeast Laos."[42]

Langley replied that "The conclusion mentioned . . . to the effect that 'if any American PWs are in Laos they are in the Sam Neua/Ban Tong complex in northeast Laos' was supported by a recent working-level interagency review of the problem. This review included all types of information available to the Washington community. A search was made for studies dealing with PWs and PW camps in Laos, particularly northeast Laos. We have found nothing to date other than photographs and collated bits of information on the previous sites mentioned in the Station's periodic report on PW detention sites. Only one model has been made of a site in Laos, the model of the Ban NaKay cave which was left at JPRC in 1968."[43]

By October 1971 the CIA study was over twice its normal page length. The CIA went into great detail about the camps and attempted to match ground reporting with aerial photography to provide precise grid locations for the prisons. The opening section on U.S. POWs states, "Americans captured in Laos fall into two categories—those who are captured in the Lao panhandle and those who are captured in northern Laos. . . . Those who are captured in northern Laos are escorted to prisons in Sam Neua province . . . or transferred to North Vietnam. The transfer of this latter category . . . has been the subject of conflicting reports. Several reports [redacted] have stated that all American prisoners have been sent to North Vietnam; however, other sources who have had access to [redacted] Pathet Lao officials have stated that all Americans who are captured in Laos remain in Laos."[44]

The write-up on Ban NaKay "indicates that the prison's location was shifted around from cave to cave . . . until the beginning of 1969 when it apparently settled down to a relatively stable location. This was probably due to the restrictions on bombing in the area which allowed the PL to stabilize. . . . It is unlikely that 20 American prisoners would be kept together in one location. If the reports of 20 American prisoners are anywhere near accurate, it is very probable that more than one cave is utilized at any given time for the detention of prisoners."

Several caves with building and vehicle activity were noted on aerial photography. Four other "probable prisons" were also located nearby. One cave was seen to have "A 35-by-70-foot rectangular area (fenced on at least three sides) with a possible net across the middle and judge's chair on one side (probable volleyball/tennis court) . . . located just outside the fence. An access road passed through zigzag trenches. There are rowcrop gardens across the road."

If this area was the same as the so-called "volleyball" photo taken in 1969, then two separate sources, human and photo, clearly noted the presence of twenty

Caucasians in this area. If they were U.S. POWs, they were in good enough shape to be playing volleyball.

A memo attached to the document dated October 7, 1971, noted that between "17–40 Americans (including an American female) reportedly being held in Laos." The next day, however, another memo from Langley sounded a more cautionary note. "The recent round-up report . . . indicates available information on this subject is sketchy and in some cases conflicting. . . . Much of the information is dated and from low-level sources. . . . Only four of the 27 prisons listed were reported to have contained Americans. . . ." Those prisons were Ban Tong, Ban NaKay, Hang Long, and Muong Nong in Savannakhet province. "In sum, we appear to have reporting in sufficient depth to confirm the existence of the four above-mentioned prison camps at their reported locations. Aerial photography tends to support our ground reports since it shows prison-like features, such as high fences. . . . The material contained in this report does not provide confirmed identities of known missing Americans, nor does it indicate that there are Americans currently being held at any of the cited locations. The most recent report of American detainees is dated April 1971 at Ban Tong in Sam Neua province. This report was of doubtful origin. . . ."[45]

The CIA report of an American female came from a Hmong guerrilla who claimed to have seen two older American males and a female near the village of Ban Tong, about twenty-five kilometers east of Sam Neua. The report, which wasn't even sent to other agencies, describes the source as having "a poor memory, is dull-witted and has poor judgment." That the Agency even included it in the round-up indicates the pressure it was under for any POW information at all.

Unfortunately, despite the CIA's assurances that it has declassified all of its POW holdings, no round-up reports for 1972 have ever been released. While the CIA continued to receive sporadic reports of American POWs, some of them quite interesting, the numbers of reports dropped off sharply, probably because the new Army interrogators were handling most of that burden. But the main question, other than were Americans alive in Laos, which most reports seem to accept, is who were they? The other big question is, did they stay in Laos or were they transferred to North Vietnam?

What the Pathet Lao Were Saying About POWs

While American intelligence knows a great deal about Vietnamese communist policy on the exploitation and political use of POWs, our understanding of Lao communist policy toward POWs is more limited. Few of their policy documents were captured during the war. But enough officials, Party members, and individuals who worked at the Lao Supreme Headquarters in Sam Neua defected, so that the United States possessed some indication of NLHS policies. How much the Pathet Lao units in the field adhered to these policies is another matter, but one can reasonably assume that PL military units close to the Supreme Headquarters followed policy fairly well.

A CAS report from May 1971 of a defecting Pathet Lao official describes PL policy towards POWs as one of "good treatment," after which "all foreign prisoners are to be moved to the Headquarters at Sam Neua." The official admitted that "it is possible that individual captors would not abide by such instructions. Furthermore, the food available in Sam Neua is not very good by Western standards, so it is probable that prisoners there are not well fed."[46]

The Pathet Lao and other news media also broadcast the occasional policy statement. At the World Peace conference in Budapest held in mid-May 1971, several relatives of POWs or MIAs were informed by PL General Singkapo that the Lao communists would release their captured Americans only when three conditions were met: a complete halt to the bombing, a cease-fire, and the formation of a coalition government. Mrs. James B. White, wife of an Air Force officer missing in Laos, informed the press that Singkapo had told her, "If the bombing halts, the Pathet Lao would release a list of all the prisoners and allow communications between the prisoners and their families. He also said if the U.S. accepts the three proposals the prisoners would be released immediately. The three conditions are the same as a peace formula stated earlier by Prince Souphanouvong."[47]

In March and again in October 1971, the Pathet Lao broadcast a "Statement on Policy towards Enemy Troops in Laos," which essentially said POWs were treated humanely and taken to a "safe" place. The Embassy "presumed up to now that this reference implicitly signified that Lao POWs were taken to NVN. . . ." To clarify, Ambassador Godley sent his deputy to visit Soth Petrasy, the head of the Vientiane branch of the Lao Patriotic Front.

As expected, Soth refused to focus on American attempts to emphasize the humanitarian aspects of the issue, and instead framed his answers within the usual politico-military context of a total bombing halt and an end to the war. Further, Soth "reiterated clearly LPF policy . . . that U.S. PWs were one of the few effective weapons his side possessed to barter withdrawal of American involvement from Laos. He stated that policy to refuse transmittal of PW information was specifically confirmed to him by Prince Souphanouvong during Soth's August visit to Sam Neua." Soth stated that "in view of LPF policy this subject . . . their policy included refusal to deliver mail to or forward mail from PWs. Soth reiterated that LPF refuses to divorce PW issue from question of bombing halt throughout territory of Laos. He said only total bombing halt will result in a list and information about PWs and end of war will result in their release."[48]

Finally, one high-ranking PL official, who defected in October 1973, stated that "the general rule was that any U.S. personnel captured prior to 1969 by the NVA were kept by the NVA and any captured by the PL were kept by the PL. Since the Indochinese conference held in Peking in April 1969, this policy had been changed throughout Indochina in general and Laos in particular."[49] At this conference, the Lao agreed to transfer their American POWs to the DRV, since the North Vietnamese had the financial resources and physical facilities to care for them.

The April 1969 time frame certainly fits the earlier CAS report on the movement of 27 Americans to North Vietnam. Many of the later wartime CAS and State documents accept this action, based partially on the transfer of Ernie Brace and partially on CAS reporting. Much of the current belief on the transfer of American POWs to North Vietnam is based on the October 1973 report. Were all the American POWs held in northern Laos gathered together, only to have the transfer halted at the last minute? How then to explain the few Americans, like Charles Riess and Norbert Gotner, who were captured in Laos and turned over to the North Vietnamese? What happened to the 27 Americans?

Rescue Offers in Laos

With the increased demand for POW intelligence in Laos, the JPRC finally convinced Godley to drop reward leaflets in his domain. In March 1971, the CIA station in Saigon cabled the Vientiane Station to inform them that the Saigon Embassy had approved five reward leaflets to use for American POWs in Laos. These leaflets had been developed jointly by the Embassy and the JPRC and their delivery could begin within 30 days after the Lao Embassy concurred.[50]

Although these reward leaflets didn't bring out the numerous shady characters that their counterparts had in Vietnam, one liberation scheme in 1971 is particularly noteworthy. The details are somewhat sketchy. In March 1971 a proposal to ransom American POWs in Laos was floated to the U.S. Embassy in Bangkok by a Thai national named Sompongs. Sompongs knew a prince of the Lao royal family who had contacts in Sam Neua, and for a price the prince and Sompongs were willing to help rescue 30 American POWs in that area. The Bangkok Embassy was informed that the "group were in good condition and even teaching

English to their PL captors. Sompongs said that his friend the Laotian prince proposed that he be paid $250,000 [US] per each prisoner recovered. . . . this is the amount that Commander Rainwater of the VFW [Rainwater had recently traveled to Vientiane and publicly offered a reward for American POWs] is willing to provide for recovery of American POWs. . . . Emboff [Embassy officer] told Sompongs of meeting with JPRC and that it was consensus that recovery of prisoners from Sam Neua was extremely unlikely. Sompongs said it was not necessary to go in and get them as PL was anxious to turn them over for a price. However, PL did not want North Vietnamese to know what they were doing. . . . Sompongs repeatedly said PL wanted to 'sell' prisoners but were 'embarrassed.'"[51]

On June 16, an officer at the U.S. embassy in Bangkok met again with Sompongs and "discussed further proposal to recover American prisoners being held in Sam Neua province of Laos. . . . We found it difficult to believe that prisoners could be brought out as Sompongs had earlier proposed because of PL and NVA policy on prisoners. Emboff suggested that Sompongs try again to persuade his friend to establish contact. . . . Sompongs said that he doubted that would do much good . . . since Prince was only passing on information which had been given him by high-ranking PL official (identified as General Singkapo) who would actually be responsible for seeing that the prisoners were removed from the camp. . . ."[52]

The U.S. efforts to make direct contact in Vientiane bore fruit in late July when the chief of the Embassy political section met Sompongs' source at a dinner party.[53] In conversation, the officer discussed his frustration in his recent dealings with Soth Petrasy, and that he had "reached conclusion afterwards that no progress could be made on this issue since all POWs had probably been removed from Laos and turned over to North Vietnamese, who now control them. Source immediately objected and said that thirty American POWs are still left in Laos, located in . . . Muong Soi (VH 5241)."[54]

The source indicated that Sinkapo was not involved nor was the source interested in money, since "he wanted to express his gratitude to USG for everything we had done to help Laos. . . ." The Embassy decided to cut off Sompongs "as intermediary" but stated that "nearest confirmed Alpha camp locations to site . . . are located some 30–35 kilometers west of Muong Soi near Sam Neua. We are somewhat skeptical but interested in his story . . ."

State cabled back several days later that it "appears to us that first point to establish is his accuracy of information that 30 US PWs are held in Laos. . . . One way to do this would be to obtain any word on identities of these prisoners. You could indicate that USG prepared to pay reward for such information. . . . As for

306 Code-Name Bright Light

rescue operation, this must be approached with extreme caution. . . . Any rescue attempt involving use of force in this area runs risk of gravest danger to prisoners. . . ." State also didn't want Sompongs cut off entirely, since he might pursue the matter on his own and cause problems. "We believe this should be done in way that keeps Sompongs somewhat on the string although cut off from actual discussions."[55]

Several weeks later, the Embassy contacted the source again to review the information about the POWs. "Discussion elicited report that 30 POWs were still detained in camp vicinity Muong Soi as of 31 March, that his information was received from reliable PL contacts who know the area and have precise information on layout of detention site and prisoner routines, that any liberation operation would have to be a hostile action, not a ransom scheme, as part of the guard detachment is composed of NVA troops. Source replied to Emboff's question that any attempt to obtain more precise information concerning the identities and condition of prisoners would compromise any possibility of their liberation."

The Embassy officer continued to emphasize that this conversation was strictly preliminary and that the most important consideration for the United States was learning the identities of the men in the camp. But the source "balked emphatically at the prospect of obtaining specific information . . . claiming it would compromise the entire venture. When he was reminded that the USG paid reward money for POW information, he remarked that he and others would participate only on humanitarian grounds. . . ." The officer went on to say, "In view of his dismissing Emboff's suggestion that more hard info on prisoners be obtained beforehand and seemingly illogical plan of operation for actual rescue, Embassy dubious at this stage that much can come of this affair. . . . we are not discounting possibility that we could end up with confirmation that some of our MIAs are being held in Sam Neua area."[56]

As far as is known, no rescue attempt was made nor did the Embassy try to ransom the prisoners. The CAS prison report does list Muong Soi as a viable prison, but it does not mention any American POWs. The number 30 is close to the probable number of POWs held based on the "volleyball" photo, but little else is known about this strange incident.

"Still moving quietly through the jungle": A Death in the JPRC

The NCO who served longest in the JPRC was First Sergeant Sebastian Deluca. Deluca had served three straight tours in SOG, having previously served at the SOG camp in Ban Me Thuot. Deluca led many patrols of Montagnards into

NVA-controlled territory and quickly won the respect of the mountain tribes for his skills in combat. He had an aggressive, outgoing personality, with a well-earned reputation as a man who could procure anything in Vietnam, especially those luxuries not normally found in the Army's spartan supply catalog.

He was widely liked and admired by those who worked with him. Major Dan Scott recalls traveling with "Top" Deluca to Ban Me Thuot to coordinate an operation. He was amazed at the great admiration still shown the JPRC sergeant by the indigenous troops. As they were about to leave, Scott was unable to contain his curiosity any longer and he asked one of the Montagnard team leaders why they loved Deluca so much. "Because he brings us back," the leader responded.

Like the rest of the JPRC, Deluca had grown extremely frustrated at the lack of success, the perceived lack of support, and the tremendous restrictions and bureaucracy involved in conducting POW raids. In particular, Deluca found Laos burdensome. On several occasions he mentioned conducting his own raid into Laos to free Americans. He would argue repeatedly with McImoyle about POWs held in Laos near Tchepone until McImoyle, wearied, told him to either produce some proof or shut up.

By March 1971 Deluca was also increasingly agitated at the slowness of the U.S. reactions to POW sighting reports. The failed raid on the MR-5 camp was still upsetting him. Fred Hopewell, then the JPRC's Air Force staff officer, remembers that Deluca began making statements to the effect that he would "go get some of his buddies in Bangkok and rescue the POWs himself. I kept telling him, 'Top, you're crazy,' but he wouldn't listen." An experienced combat soldier, Deluca believed he had information that 50 Americans were being held near Tchepone. His frustration level at maximum, Deluca decided to launch his own one-man rescue mission.

At the time Deluca was plotting his rescue mission, he also had a growing personal problem. Although he had a wife and family in Fayetteville, North Carolina, he was currently living with a Vietnamese woman in Saigon. They had a son together. For some reason, he had stopped sending money back to his family in North Carolina. The Red Cross was forwarding increasingly urgent letters to the Army informing them that Deluca's family in the States was suffering. Further, the Army had recently denied him a tour extension in Vietnam.

Deluca decided to take some leave and travel to Bangkok. He left on June 6 for a seven-day trip. When his was time up, he asked for a two-day leave extension, which was granted. When he did not return on June 15, inquiries began the next day. Unable to locate him, SOG declared him AWOL; they were frantic at the possibility of a man with Deluca's knowledge of SOG and JPRC operations falling into enemy hands. Messages began to flow to Bangkok and the SOG detachment at Nakhon Phanom, Thailand. "Find Deluca and find him now!"

But Deluca had already moved on. He linked up with a Thai bar girl working in Bangkok and they traveled together to Vientiane. The Embassy later discovered that Deluca had been seen at a bar "on June 20, in drunken state attempting to recruit Americans to assist him in a POW rescue mission."[57] No one took Deluca up on his offer, nor was anyone in Bangkok interested in his scheme. Unable to recruit any of his "buddies," Deluca and the girl, Nom Kusang, rented a motorized sampan (bamboo raft) and sailed down the Mekong toward southern Laos. They entered a tributary of the river and crossed back into Laos. Deluca was unarmed; he was carrying only some loose gems, some gold, and a map.

As they motored down the river, the pair were stopped by RLA troops at a bridge checkpoint. Because Deluca was without a passport, the RLA commander ordered him and the girl arrested. What happened next is still a bit of mystery. The two were held together in the guards' barracks. The SOG investigation states that at "About 0600 hours on 26 June Deluca told the girl he had to go relieve himself. Before leaving he gave her a note which she could not read. When the guards realized that Deluca had not returned the entire guard force was awakened and began a search."[58]

The guards returned around noon with Deluca's billfold. It had blood on it. The bar girl was sent on her way. Later, the RLA reported to the Embassy Army officer that Deluca had been accidentally killed by a patrol from a friendly unit the night of June 26. The autopsy report indicates he had been shot several times, twice in the back of the head as well "as an intact, small-caliber slug in the left leg . . . a piece of twine is tied about one wrist, and the opposite wrist features rope marks."

The RLA patrol claimed they had seen a man clothed in black pajamas walking down a trail in known enemy territory and opened fire, killing him. After learning of the incident, the G-2 for the RLA, Brigadier General Etam Singvongsa, sent an intelligence team into the area. The body was recovered on July 13 and taken to Nakhon Phanom Air Base. It was then flown to Saigon, where it was positively identified.

The conclusion reached in the SOG report was that Deluca "had gathered a significant piece of information that indicated prisoners were being detained near Tchepone, Laos. . . . The acts of Deluca to go AWOL, cross Laos, and attempt to traverse 80 km of contested terrain alone (after his escape from the RLA troops) was not in keeping with his normally rational and judicious behavior. . . . The obsession of a possible recovery of PWs obscured all logic and common sense. He apparently blindly kept going to Tchepone after being stopped by the soldiers. . . ." The recommendation was to change his status from AWOL to killed in the line of duty.[59]

When shown the information about Deluca having ventured into Laos un-armed, the men who served with him, both in the JPRC and in SOG, were stunned. Several feel he was murdered by the RLA troops, because the jewelry and gold he was carrying had disappeared. Whatever his motives, Deluca's death profoundly affected the JPRC, already disheartened after the Butcher incident.

The new Air Force officer, Gerry Bauknight, was extremely fond of Deluca. Learning of Deluca's death, Bauknight, like rest of the JPRC, was devastated by the loss. He kept a personal log of his JPRC days, and his diary expresses the sor-row and pain he felt. Bauknight wrote, "Here I sit waiting for a call from Vien-tiane to hear confirmation that a friend is dead. Morton Gould's orchestra plays a variation on 'Green Sleeves'. . . . Vientiane ARMA will send a canvas bag, so said the message. He was killed by friendly troops in Laos. Is that how it really hap-pened? Lightning and thunder of a tropical storm in Saigon. The rain pours down. I wonder what it was like out there in Thailand and Laos, that feeling knowing that you are on your last mission. A few weeks ago one of the maids, Ba Be, said 'Deluca *chet*' [dead]. I told her that she was crazy, but my face must have expressed the truth. She knew! I keep telling myself that he is safe and still mov-ing quietly through the jungle."[60]

14. "Wheel and Deal and Bring 'em Home"

—Unofficial motto of the JPRC, circa 1972

With America's decade-long involvement in fighting the war in Vietnam drawing to a close, the Joint Personnel Recovery Center geared itself to accomplish two last tasks: first, identify and inspect as many crash sites as possible; second, prepare for a post-hostilities environment. In the meantime, the final set of officers who served in the unit were still attempting to recover American POWs, only now they would have to use ARVN troops to accomplish those missions.

Lieutenant Colonel Gerald McImoyle left in March 1971, and was replaced by another U-2 pilot named James A. Black. Black departed in September, presenting Colonel John Sadler with the opportunity he had been waiting for. He nominated a Marine recon officer named Andy Anderson to head the unit. Anderson was a short, stocky, fiery leader who desperately wanted to rescue an American POW. To fill the unit, Anderson went looking for Special Forces officers with SOG or Vietnam experience. He found two Army officers, Major Ian Sutherland and Captain Don Lunday.[1] He got another outstanding Military Intelligence officer to replace Kelly, Robert Covalucci. Bauknight remained as the Air Force officer until April 1972.

A Final Flurry of E&E Symbols

In the seven months from the end of October 1971 until the end of May 1972, the JPRC encountered a rash of E&E symbols that left everyone involved in the POW rescue effort puzzled and confused.

The first symbol was spotted by an Air Force FAC in late October 1971. The symbol consisted of a long letter that looked like either a capital *I* or *L*, and a lower-case dotted *i* and *a*. The message relayed to the JPRC stated that all the symbols were in a plowed field. Their estimated width was three meters, their length eight to ten meters. All the edges were in sharp detail, and the symbol was so new that some of the grass was still green.[2]

When Bauknight briefed Zerbe and Sadler on the symbols, Zerbe ordered him to check the initials of MIAs, including Koreans, and also to scan the JPRC records for any possible aircraft losses in the area. No aircraft had gone down in the vicinity since May. Following the POW rescue concept agreed to by Abrams and McCain, the JPRC followed the new procedure and activated a Joint Recovery Task Force.

The plan called for an insertion of a SOG team to search the area. For two days the bad weather kept the team out. On October 28, a team of 11 Americans and 30 Montagnards landed near the symbol. They took pictures and "observed 8–10 footprints, one set a size nine with heel marks 2–3 days old. One set was clearly identified as lug soles. No barefoot tracks were observed. Appeared that someone disarranged symbol within past 24 hours."[3] The discovery of U.S. heel marks was not conclusive evidence that an American POW had made the symbol, since the enemy generally took the boots of captured prisoners, and many ARVN and RF/PF wore U.S.-type boots as well.

The flurry of E&E symbols continued. Another Air Force FAC reported on "30 Oct 71 the possible sighting of an E&E symbol X-Ray. . . . The symbol appeared to be man-made of plastic-type material found in survival gear, but no beeper or voice contact developed during friendly overflights."[4]

An E&E kit was dropped on the symbol and the FAC stayed in the general location for several hours. Nothing was picked up. However, the following day a "strong beeper was received for about 10 seconds from the area. Again, two more kits were delivered to the same target."[5]

While the planes were dropping the kits, a photo interpreter spotted a second *X*, or "X-Ray," at the same location.[6] Although FACs continued to monitor the frequencies, nothing was heard from any evader and the search was terminated on November 10. Again, no one could be certain it was an American because "X-Ray was the back-up code letter for this year, and because of possible compromise and numerous false sightings the back-up letter was changed. . . ." Additionally, an *X* symbol had been spotted in mid-September by a FAC about twenty kilometers away, but subsequent overflights had failed to respot it.

Several days later, a FAC from Udorn sighted the symbols *C* and *L* on a sandy riverbank. The code letters *C* and *L* were used in January 1970 and February 1971, respectively. A search of the records revealed no one down in the area, nor were there any confirmed POW camps located in the immediate vicinity. An OV-1 aircraft was launched with photo equipment and an E&E kit. This photo recon mission revealed that the letters covered a wide area and were definitely man-made. The following day it could not be determined if the kit had been used. No voice or beeper signals were transmitted from location and the vigil was terminated on November 18.[7]

Finally, on May 24, 1972, interpretation of photo imagery indicated the symbols *V* and *K* near Tchepone. Additional visual reconnaissance and further photos revealed that the letters were man-made and less than one week old. Although no correlation could be made with possible evaders in this area, and the letters were not formed using the standard modification, JPRC recommended that an E&E kit be dropped. The kit was never touched.[8]

This was the last code-letter symbol seen in the war. Despite all the efforts to create the program, monitor the SAFE areas, and drop E&E kits, just as Butcher's attempts to use ground symbols to signal would-be rescuers had been futile, no evadee was ever rescued as a result of the use of a symbol.

Last Chance in the Delta

Despite the withdrawal of the SEALs, the amount of intelligence flowing out of the Delta region, compared to the number of Americans held there, was impressive. Although reports continued to be received on American POWs in the Delta, their camps could not be precisely located. It was not until a year after their loss that good intelligence was first received confirming that the aviators White and Graf were alive.

On December 17, 1970, a unit of the Vinh Binh Popular Forces raided a POW camp and released 49 Vietnamese prisoners. One of the ex-POWs knew of another camp about seven kilometers away. Three days later he led the Popular Forces back into the area to raid the camp. When they hit the site, they discovered that the camp had been hastily evacuated only hours before. Documents were found, including the preliminary interrogation report of White and Graf, which noted that Graf was an intelligence officer who had served in Taiwan.[9]

Captain Bob Covalucci had recently joined the JPRC and this was his first assignment for the unit. He was a career military intelligence officer whose prior assignment was command of the Army intelligence unit in the Los Angeles area. He had served previously in South Vietnam, one of the many unlucky ones who arrived in January 1968, right before the Tet Offensive. An energetic, articulate officer, he worked diligently to create agent networks, hoping that he could bypass the lag normally found in following up reports from escapees. If he could get an agent into a camp and back out without raising suspicions, he felt their chances of success would be greatly improved.[10]

In mid-October 1971, two VC deserters reported the location of two Americans and 70 Vietnamese POWs in Vinh Binh province. Covalucci was dispatched to help coordinate the rescue effort. After further interrogation, it was learned that the complex was a series of four camps containing concrete bunkers used to house criminals and VC deserters. Although the two VC had not seen the Americans, the JPRC decided to launch a mission anyway.

On October 30, one of the deserters led a company of the Vinh Binh Regional Forces into the complex. Partially cooked meals and equipment were found, and a search of the area uncovered storage facilities and warm rice, indicating that the camp had been evacuated within the last three hours. The team reported back that there were no POWs sighted and no indications of American POWs having been in the area.[11]

One week later, at 1000 hours on the morning of November 6, two more Vietnamese walked into Tra Vinh, a town also located in Vinh Binh province. These men had just escaped that morning from the camp that had been hit on October 30. Following the escape of the previous two, only part of the camp had left the area. The pair said the first raid had come within 75 meters of their hidden location. Their group stayed within the area. Later, they escaped by killing one of the guards. When questioned separately, the two men agreed with the earlier deserters and confirmed the presence of two Americans and 70 Vietnamese POWs.

Wasting no time, the Province Senior Advisor ordered an immediate attack. Army Major Henry Dagenais, who was the province S-3, contacted the 7th ARVN Division and requested helicopters to assault the camp. Four hours after the escapees had entered Tra Vinh, the province intelligence platoon and Dagenais were airlifted into the area.

The platoon landed just short of the moving camp and instead hit a VC supply depot. "We got into a firefight and shot three VC," Dagenais recalls, "and we captured a prisoner who told us that the camp had come through earlier. We could see their tracks in the mud, it looked like a herd of cattle had been driven through. Everyone was walking in mid-calf-deep liquid mud, sloshing through swampy land that was covered in water from the rainy season."

At 1800 hours, Dagenais and his men ran into a tail sentry and killed him. The shots alerted the camp guards, and they and the POWs fled faster. Dagenais' men found a small piece of high ground sticking up about two feet out of the water. On the rise he found "a spoon belonging to a U.S. POW and a stick with a piece of cloth tied around it, like the old hoboes used to have. Cooking pots, sleeping mats, and other equipment lay scattered around. We were right on their tail, maybe thirty minutes behind them. We followed their footprints until darkness and a large canal stopped us. We could see the marks on the banks where they had met some boats and crossed the canal. Even though it was the middle of VC territory, we decided to stay overnight.

"The next morning, we searched the area until that afternoon, when some helicopters picked us up and landed us in what we thought was the enemy's direction of travel. Province intel gave us a location for their next probable camp, but it was too late, they had disappeared. We stayed a few more days but found nothing except some VC supply caches.

"Then we were told that no more helicopters were available, so I arranged by radio for ships from the 35th Coastal Group to pick us up. When we reached the South China Sea, I'm standing on the beach when I look over and I see this piece of metal sticking out of the sand dune. I started looking around and realized it was a crash site. I talked to a local fisherman who told me that several years back, an American plane had crashed there. Both pilots were killed and one had his head decapitated. The VC forced the villagers to drag the wreckage off the beach and into the swamp to hide it from aerial search. The bodies were buried on the beach. The fisherman used a piece of wing as the roof of his hut.

"Just as the ships showed up, so did the VC. We were wading out to the ships and the VC were firing at us from the beach. I can remember bullets hitting the water as my men and I reached the ships, but we all got on board safe. Later, I went back and pinpointed the crash site, which I was told was identified as an O-1. We believed that we had found Dale and Demmon's crash site from 1965."[12]

Thus, we come full circle back to Charles Dale and David Demmon, the two Army aviators lost on June 9, 1965, and never found. From their loss, to the Vietnamese camp guard who rallied in 1966, to the intriguing possibility unfulfilled during *Cobra Tail*, to the ARVN raid in January 1971, and finally to the U.S. government's excavations in 1992 on that same beach, the mystery of Dale and Demmon's fate is symbolic of the entire POW/MIA issue. If they died in a plane crash on that beach in a VC-controlled area, then every later sighting and report associated with them is flat-out wrong. If they survived, and Demmon was seen alive in Cambodia in December 1970, why have the Vietnamese been lying to the United States for so many years, claiming they have no knowledge of the pair? Why in 1995 did they supply a report of their unilateral investigation claiming that the two died in the crash of their plane several kilometers out to sea, when U.S. records clearly show the wreckage on a beach? It is questions like these that keep the POW/MIA issue burning.

The Final *Bright Light* Missions

A document captured in early January 1971 revealed that indeed two, rather than four, Americans were currently being held in the Delta. An ARVN unit seized a report from the Political Staff of the VC regional command addressed to the Political Staff Department at COSVN. The report stated that there were six POW camps in various Delta provinces and one higher-level camp at region headquarters. The main region camp was headed by a five-member management committee and a well-trained guard force, while the province-level camps were poorly run and did not send accurate reports even on the number of prisoners they held. The report further stated that the region camp held one American sergeant and five "Puppet" servicemen. Among the prisoners in the other provinces was one American first lieutenant in Vinh Binh province. At that time it was impossible to evacuate him to the regional camp.[13]

The camp guard force was not as well trained as the Political Staff believed. In October 1971, six ARVNs managed to break out of this camp, killing six guards in the process. One escapee was the translator for Bowers and Arroyo-Baez's team, Nguyen Van Nguyen. According to the translator, Richard Bowers was killed the night he and Arroyo-Baez were captured. A helicopter gunship made an air strike on their position, and in the confusion both Americans escaped. They were recaptured several hours later. Nguyen observed one of the VC guards, in a fit of anger, shoot and kill Bowers. He was stopped by his commander when he also attempted to shoot Arroyo-Baez. Bowers' body was weighted down with stones and dropped in a nearby canal.

The remaining prisoners were marched north to the U-Minh Forest. One of the escapees had last seen Arroyo-Baez thirty days ago. The escapee said that Arroyo-Baez had been quite ill and had developed a cough. They heard that Arroyo-Baez had escaped several weeks ago but had been caught.[14] During their escape, the prisoners ran into a VC who decided to join them. He was an Assistant District Chief for the area, a medium-level cadre who immediately led an operation back into the area. A VC hospital was found and some medical supplies were destroyed, but no POWs were recovered.

On the same day and on the other side of the Delta from Covalucci's efforts, the JPRC dispatched Army Major Ian Sutherland to the Delta to interview

Nguyen. Sutherland had served three tours in Vietnam, two with Special Forces. His current third tour was with SOG. He had also previously worked for the CIA on the South Vietnam–Cambodia border. Because of his long experience, Anderson had recruited Sutherland from SOG to work for the JPRC. He was the epitome of the legendary snake-eating Green Beret, and like Anderson he wanted to rescue an American.

Traveling to Bac Lieu, he met the American advisor to the Delta's interrogation center, Captain Woods E. Gray. A native of Louisiana, Gray had come down to assist in the interrogation of Nguyen and to provide technical assistance in making a map of the route Nguyen had taken to escape. Initially, Sutherland did not want to attack the camp immediately, since he felt that the VC had probably already moved on.

Sutherland waited two weeks, all the while preparing an unusual plan. Instead of the normal pattern of gathering recon photos and then inserting a team to locate the camp, following up with a classic helicopter assault, Sutherland wanted a new approach. He felt that "the VC learned early that planes flying a pattern meant pictures and pictures meant an operation. The U.S. military had developed this noncreative mind-set, a conventional, do-it-by-the-book bureaucratic process that eventually begins to erode all initiative. Under this mind-set, success or failure is not what matters, what counts is following procedures."[15]

Sutherland wanted to use a SOG Sea Commando Team (SCT) to attack from the ocean, penetrate to the camp, and then call in helicopters for extraction. Much as the SEALs had done in the summer, the SCT would launch in rubber boats from a World War II–vintage landing craft located offshore. Radar would be used to precisely guide the force to a preselected beachhead. A rainstorm helped hide their movements. Since the camp where Nguyen had been held was within three kilometers of the ocean, in an area called by the VC the "Dam Doi Secret Zone" the team would disguise themselves as VC, hoping to fool any enemy they encountered.

The SCT was composed of South Vietnamese SEALs lead by a Marine Force Recon officer named Captain Robert Lewis. By a strange set of coincidences, Lewis was a childhood friend of Gray, the interrogation advisor. Gray remembers attending a premission briefing. When it was his turn to speak, he stood up and suddenly heard this voice from the back of the room call out, "E [his childhood nickname], is that you?" Looking to the back, "I saw Robert. Suddenly for me the old pucker factor for this operation had dramatically increased. I was sending into a very dangerous situation someone I had gone to Cub Scouts with."[16]

Despite Gray's newfound apprehension, the SOG Sea Commando Team launched on November 8. The concept worked perfectly and the team moved swiftly toward the POW camp. Sutherland was in an airplane circling out at sea. As the team approached the immediate vicinity of the camp, a VC checking an animal trap discovered them. At first, the VC fell for the disguises and believed the team members were fellow VC. He told the SCT that the American had been moved the day after the escape and that the camp was now mined and booby-trapped. When the team pressed him for the location of the new camp, the VC discovered the ruse and refused to lead them to its new location.

As the team were moving back to the pick-up point, a VC column discovered them and attacked. Sutherland remembers Lewis calling him on the radio, saying, "We have a VC prisoner, they are all around us, get us out now!" Naval gunfire hammered three sides of the beachhead while a helicopter swooped in and picked them up.

The VC prisoner was taken back to Saigon and interrogated. He described a hard life, limited food, sickness, and continual threat of death from the air. Slowly he became receptive to the idea of starting a "new life," and after more sessions he decided he would attempt to reenter the secret zone and help secure the release of Arroyo-Baez. On November 13, the VC was sent back into the area carrying a radio, two small high-durability files to saw off the locks, and a note written in Spanish to Arroyo-Baez. He was never heard from again.

Later in November, another VC defector brought information of a POW camp in nearby Ba Xuyen province. With the defector acting as a guide, two American advisors and an ARVN unit air–assaulted into the camp. They were met by heavy ground fire and one helicopter was shot down. Eventually the camp was reached and evidence indicated that it had been evacuated a short time earlier. There was no evidence that Americans had been held there.

Based on the near misses of the prior operations and the excellent results from using the old World War II Landing Ship Tank (LST), the JPRC spent the next two months conducting a thorough study of all reported POW detention facilities along the coastal area of South Vietnam. The information developed indicated that An Xuyen province on the southern tip of Vietnam would be the most logical place to conduct raids. The JPRC wanted to use Sutherland's concept and place Sea Commando Teams on the LST for extended periods and conduct snatches of the enemy from the beaches and villages. The prisoners would be returned to the ship and interrogated for intelligence.

In early February, the first Sea Commando Team deployed. Although it was unable to develop any useful intelligence, the concept proved feasible and it was tried again in late February. This time an enemy prisoner revealed that he knew the location of a POW camp. The team did not attack the camp but instead passed the information to the 21st ARVN Division. On February 25, with the commander of the 21st and Dr. Roger Shields (the Pentagon official who had been directly responsible since 1971 for coordinating all DOD POW matters) monitoring the operation from a command helicopter, the ARVNs made an air mobile assault using two regimental recon companies.[17]

With important officials on the ship watching the operation, Sutherland was told by a senior SOG officer that if the communications lines between the 21st ARVN and SOG collapsed he, Sutherland, would be relieved. If the JCS and CINCPAC want an answer, he was told, then you better have an answer right then.

The search by the 21st ARVN found nothing except some civilians who had no knowledge of any detention facilities in the area. Everyone involved returned home disappointed. Sutherland, however, was happy that the commo link stayed up the entire time. After the SCT launched one last time on March 14, Sutherland joined up with a Navy SEAL named Tommy Norris to spend ten days wandering through the U-Minh Forest on a private foray looking for Arroyo-Baez. Despite their best efforts, they never found any trace of him. In February 1973 the communists reported that he had died in captivity in August 1972. His remains were returned in 1985.

The 21st ARVN operation was the last *Bright Light* mission of the war. *Bright Light* ended much as it began, with desperate American officers frantically searching for their comrades while stymied by poor intelligence and grudging cooperation. Although the end of the JPRC was near, Andy Anderson, the Center's commander, would give it one last chance to go home proud.

Once More into the Breach: *Bat 21*

One of the greatest efforts ever undertaken by the JPRC occurred in April 1972 with the rescue of Lieutenant Colonel Iceal Hambleton in the famous incident known as *Bat 21* near the town of Dong Ha in Quang Tri province. Hambleton was a veteran Air Force officer nearing the end of his career. He was fifty-three years old and had spent 30 years in the Air Force, much of it in the Strategic Air Command. The effort to recover Hambleton eventually grew into one of the most complicated and costly post-SAR efforts of the entire war. It became the stuff of legend; indeed, a movie was later made about it, starring Gene Hackman as Hambleton and Danny Glover as a FAC who shepherds him to safety. More important, the huge expenditure in ammunition, aircraft, and, ultimately, men's lives brought up the old, haunting question: how much is one life worth?

The massive NVA operation called the Easter Offensive had just rolled across the DMZ in a conventional, almost *Blitzkrieg*-style attack. Gone were the days of small infantry units engaging in short but sharp battles. This was a multidivision attack, backed up with recently acquired Soviet armor and fully supported by highly trained air defense troops. The NVA's target was the upper provinces of South Vietnam adjacent to the DMZ, which were flanked by the communist sanctuaries in Laos. The NVA assault overran several ARVN units, and while many ARVN soldiers fought well, others turned and fled in the face of the onslaught. One unit in particular, the ARVN Third Division, quickly found itself surrounded by strong NVA forces.

The North Vietnamese planned the offensive to take advantage of the poor seasonal weather. Low cloud cover prevented U.S. tactical air power from supporting the ARVN troops. In order to relieve some of the pressure on the embattled ARVN Third Division, on April 2 a B-52 strike was ordered against an advancing NVA column. The Air Force knew the enemy had SAM, or surface-to-air, missiles in the area, so they added additional support aircraft to suppress them. These included two EB-66s, sent to jam the enemy SAM radar and locate the sites. Their call signs were *Bat 21* and *Bat 22.*

Despite these precautions, the enemy SAM batteries quickly picked up the approaching aircraft and fired three different salvos at the U.S. planes. The first two volleys missed, but a missile from the third barrage directly struck *Bat 21.* Of the crew of six, only Hambleton is known to have ejected safely.[18] His chute was quickly spotted by a nearby FAC, who radioed for a rescue attempt on the downed airman.

Fortunately, some SAR forces were close by, having launched earlier to recover another aviator. As two of the heavily armed prop-driven A-1s used for SAR support entered the area, intense enemy antiaircraft fire immediately opened up. The A-1s subdued the fire enough so that several U.S. helicopters from F Troop, 8th Cav, could make the rescue attempt. As one of the Hueys came in, it was struck repeatedly by concentrated enemy ground fire and crashed. One man made it out and was captured alive by North Vietnamese troops, who carried him back across the DMZ. The other three crew members were killed. With night falling, however, further SAR efforts were called off. Air strikes hit enemy locations around Hambleton, who had landed four kilometers beyond the ARVN lines. Worse, his position was in the middle of one of the NVA's main avenues of attack against the beleaguered ARVN units.

On April 3 the valiant SAR forces returned for another try, but the communist antiaircraft fire was simply overwhelming. Two Jolly Green rescue helicopters were badly hit but limped back and essentially crash-landed at Phu Bai airbase. That afternoon, another U.S. plane was also shot down. An OV-10 observation plane carrying Captain William Henderson and First Lieutenant Mark Clark was hit by a shoulder-fired SA-7 missile. They managed to escape their burning plane before it exploded. Safely reaching the ground, Henderson was captured hiding in bushes ten meters from the river. But Clark evaded the enemy ground troops searching for him. Now two pilots needed rescuing. That night Hambleton reported that the NVA were searching for him using flashlights.[19]

On the April 4 and 5, the weather worsened and little could be done for the airmen. But on April 6 the storms had passed and the sun shone brightly in the morning sky. The A-1s returned with a vengeance, pounding the exposed NVA. Tremendous quantities of air bombardment poured down on the NVA antiaircraft positions, so much so that air strikes which normally would have gone to support the surrounded South Vietnamese were diverted to attack the enemy forces around Hambleton and Clark. The American advisors to the ARVN units bitterly complained to their superiors about the Air Force's lack of response to their pleas for help, but the Air Force ignored them and continued to support the SAR effort instead.

Despite the enormous tonnage of U.S. explosives dropped on the NVA, their AAA units fought back with grim determination. However, by midmorning, a FAC who was directing the aerial assault decided to make another pick-up attempt. He ordered a Jolly Green rescue helicopter to make a run for them. Spotting the SAR helicopter, the NVA attacked it. Taking enemy fire from all sides, the incredibly brave Jolly Green pilot attempted to reach Hambleton. As he came to hover over Hambleton, the heavy enemy fusillade intensified and the helicopter was struck numerous times. The pilot was forced to break off but the relentless hail of gunfire followed the helicopter along his path of retreat. Unable to shake the ferocious barrage, the Jolly Green took numerous hits and crashed about three kilometers away from Hambleton's position. The wreckage burned for several days, sending black clouds billowing into the air and marking the spot where six Americans gave their lives trying to rescue the downed airmen.

Back in Saigon, after reviewing the high losses in aircraft and the diversion of air power away from the ARVN, General Abrams reluctantly made the decision to call off further helicopter rescues. But Andy Anderson at the JPRC had been closely following the operation, and when Abrams stood his men down, Anderson decided it was his turn.

"I want to know some success before we stand down"

Andy Anderson knew the history of the JPRC, its failures and its many frustrating efforts over a six-year period to rescue American POWs. Like all the other officers who had served there, during his short time as head of the unit he burned to rescue a fellow American from the clutches of the communists. Like the rest, however, he quickly encountered enormous logistical problems and political roadblocks that stood in the way of success.

As he carefully watched the events unfold in the area around Dong Ha where Hambleton and Clark were hiding, an idea began to form in his mind that perhaps a ground team could do what the courageous SAR helicopters could not: sneak in undetected and steal the two airmen from underneath the NVA's nose. But meanwhile the situation had grown more tense. On April 7 a second OV-10 was shot down, adding another evading pilot to the picture. The pilot, First Lieutenant Bruce Walker, was communicating with the SAR forces, but his backseater, Marine First Lieutenant Larry Potts, was ominously silent.[20]

When General Abrams made his difficult decision to stand down the operation, Anderson went to see Major General Winton W. Marshall, second-in-command of the 7th AF. In doing so, Anderson deliberately stepped outside the chain of command, knowing full well that if he went first to Colonel Sadler at SOG or to Abrams, his idea would be rejected. By approaching the Air Force instead, he exposed himself to possible disciplinary action and jeopardized his career. Anderson took a calculated risk that they would listen and support him.

General Marshall agreed to see the stocky Marine. When Anderson arrived on April 8, he asked him what he could do for him. In a nonchalant manner, Anderson told the general he thought he could get a small team in to rescue the three pilots. He explained his plan to Marshall, who listened with growing interest. When Anderson finished, Marshall asked him why he was doing this. Anderson explained the bitter history of the JPRC and finished by telling Marshall that the JPRC was slated to leave SOG shortly and move to the J-2 intelligence shop. He wanted the unit to know some success before it stood down and he felt that this was its last, best chance. Marshall understood and resolved to assist this last-ditch effort.

With Air Force backing, Anderson immediately flew to the coastal city of Danang to visit the Navy's Advisory Group, which had been part of SOG since its inception. Anderson's plan called for getting a Navy SEAL with six Vietnamese commandos to swim up the Mieu Giang River, have the airmen meet them at the river, and then E&E to the ARVN lines by floating back down. Upon reaching Danang, Anderson was startled to find the unit ready to close down in three days; virtually everyone had already departed. He begged the Navy officer, Craig Dorman, to find him someone who could help. Dorman called the Navy office back in Saigon. As luck would have it, Tommy Norris, the SEAL who had helped Sutherland in the Delta, was sitting there. Norris agreed to the mission, and the Air Force quickly flew him north to rendezvous with Anderson.

Anderson and Norris went together to see the ARVN Third Division commander. He was extremely reluctant to assist these crazy Americans, but told them he would comply with their requests if ordered to. Anderson, already out on a limb, called back to Colonel Frank Zerbe at SOG. Zerbe convinced the ARVNs to go along with Anderson, but he forced Anderson to promise him that he would not swim in the river and that he would coordinate the operation from behind the front lines. Although Anderson agreed, he had no intention of keeping his promise.

On April 10, Norris, Anderson, and the Vietnamese commandos reached the ARVN outpost closest to the downed airmen, an old French bunker complex along the Route 9 motorcade route that led into Laos. It was manned by an understrength platoon of ARVN Rangers supported by two tanks.

Coordinating constantly with the FACs flying overhead, Anderson devised a plan to move all three airmen to the river for pick-up. The plan was passed to all three using an ingenious method of communication. Hambleton was an avid golfer. Using the layout of different courses, the strategy was passed to him describing how he was to proceed undetected to the river. Successive course changes would enable him to bypass the large concentration of enemy forces in the area. One of the FAC pilots who maintained contact with Hambleton relayed the messages to the exhausted officer. One message read, "Make like Esther Williams and head for Big Muddy." No NVA listening in would be able to crack that code. A similar but less elaborate plan was passed to Clark and Walker via their survival radios.

On the night of April 10, Norris entered the waters of the Mieu Giang. Anderson ordered Norris to go no further than one kilometer up the river from the outpost. Norris agreed, but like Anderson, he had no intention of obeying. He believed Anderson's plan was badly flawed; moreover, as a highly trained Navy SEAL, he was accustomed to being given wide latitude in carrying out orders.

As Norris entered the water, Anderson watched the area for enemy movement using a night vision device. He also acted as a radio relay to the orbiting aircraft, who in turn passed on the information to the survivors. Clark made the first move, since he was the closest to the river. However, he entered the water early and floated past the pick-up point. Norris chased him down the river, eventually located him and brought him back. To Anderson, Clark was only the first one. He had two more to go.

The morning of April 11, the NVA spotted the ARVN tanks, which, like magnets, immediately drew heavy enemy fire. The NVA pounded the outpost with artillery, resulting in five ARVN dead and fifteen wounded. During a lull in the barrage, Anderson jumped out to help pull some of the wounded into a nearby bunker. Suddenly, a mortar round slammed into the turret of a tank about ten meters away. A piece of shrapnel flew off and hit Anderson above the left eye, lodging in his nasal passage. The shrapnel hit him "like a baseball bat," knocking him unconscious for a few minutes. When he awoke, he was unable to see out of either eye, but thirty minutes later his sight returned.[21] Although he was only slightly wounded, he became the first and only JPRC military man ever to receive a wound during an official mission.

The incident created a great stir back in Saigon. Senior commanders began asking Bauknight pointed questions about Anderson's whereabouts and intentions. An officer with his security clearances and knowledge of U.S. operations would be a tremendous catch for the enemy. Anderson was ordered back to Saigon. Although he was forced to return to base, his concern for Hambleton was growing. He was by far the oldest of the airmen and he had been on the ground longer. Anderson feared that Hambleton's stamina was fading rapidly, and on the night of April 12, his fears came true. After a harrowing run to the river, Hambleton collapsed. He was completely exhausted and lay in the water all night propped against the riverbank. Time now was of the essence.

For once, luck was on the Americans' side. The batteries in the survival radio Hambleton carried should never have held out this long, but surprisingly they did. On April 13, with Anderson en route back from Saigon, Norris and one of the South Vietnamese commandos entered the river again. Using an abandoned sampan, they moved toward Hambleton's position. Reaching Hambleton, they placed him in the bottom of the shallow boat and covered him. Slowly they began to move back down the river. As they neared friendly lines an enemy machine gun spotted them and opened fire. Out in the open on the water, Norris ducked into some nearby reeds to hide. He quickly called in an air strike. An A-1 dropped a load of bombs directly on the nest and silenced the position. They continued unopposed and made it back safely.

Both Clark and Hambleton were suffering from cuts and bruises, but were otherwise okay. Anderson immediately informed the JPRC of the successful recovery. His message read, "With much delight and much pleasure, report Quang Tri Bright Light Operation a success. 2nd pilot on ground 12 days brought out by Sea Commando Team. Condition unknown, but alive and all right. LTC Anderson released this morning and at Naval Advisory Group."

The rescue operation, though, wasn't over yet. Bruce Walker, the pilot of the second OV-10, was still on enemy ground. The new plan called for Walker to move through a "no-fire" zone to the river while the ARVN made an obvious thrust west along their side of the river, hoping to draw the NVA away from the area Walker was to traverse. On April 15, the plan commenced but Walker was unable to move through the massed enemy troops. The plan was changed and he was instructed to move east. In the predawn hours of April 18, he was discovered by an enemy patrol. They began chasing him. Unfortunately, no FAC was overhead at this point to assist him. When a FAC did reach the scene at first light, he discovered Walker's difficult situation, and he called in air strikes to keep at bay the NVA who were following Walker.

However, after a short time the FAC was no longer able to reach Walker on the radio. In 1993, interviews with several of the enemy soldiers revealed that they had literally been in running pursuit of the fleeing Walker. They chased him into an open field, and with dawn breaking and the air strikes slamming into the earth around them, they realized that they could not capture him. An enemy soldier crept up close to Walker and shot him with five rounds of rifle fire. Of the three evading airmen, only Bruce Walker would never come home.

The mission now over, Anderson returned to the JPRC, but his tour was finished. He departed Vietnam within days and returned to the States. He retired within the year and took a job as a banker in Albany, New York. In a letter to Gerry Bauknight, he wrote, "I finally got my Bronze Star for 'meritorious service' for the Dong Ha swim. . . . The Commandant of the Marine Corps was livid with rage when he [only] saw 'meritorious service' after all the high-level messages from McCain to Moorer crossed his desk about the operation. His comment was 'I bet if you were Army Special Forces it would have been a Distinguished Service Cross.'"[22]

For his extraordinary effort, Tommy Norris received the Medal of Honor for his actions during the *Bat 21* mission. His South Vietnamese assistant, Nguyen Van Kiet, received the Navy Cross—the only Vietnamese ever to do so.

Darrell Whitcomb, a Vietnam combat veteran who served as a FAC in South Vietnam, Laos, and Cambodia, is an expert on the *Bat 21* operation and has studied the incident thoroughly. He states that the price for the operation was extremely high, including "two UH-1 Hueys, one Jolly Green SAR helicopter, two OV-10s, and one A-1 shot down and numerous airplanes so badly damaged they never flew again. Additionally, almost eight hundred and fifty plus air strikes and millions of dollars worth of ammunition were expended. The human toll, however, was the worst part. Eleven men killed and two captured. Why go to all this trouble and effort for one man?

"Anderson's motivations, of course, are for the JPRC to walk out with at least one success under their collective belt. But I believe the greater answer is that the war had dragged on for so long and we were so frustrated that our only goal left was to get our men and leave. We, the U.S. military, simply had to get this guy. In doing so, however, we stepped on the ARVNs and raised the ultimate, perhaps unanswerable question: how much is one man worth? The military is still wrestling with that question today."[23]

SIGINT in Southeast Asia: The NSA and the Execution Messages

In the early years of the war, POW/MIA intercepts were sent to the tactical commanders via "one-liners," single-sentence messages that provided information but left out the source and method of collection. More important, no analysis was conducted by NSA, which left the intelligence open to interpretation. After the field commanders complained about this reporting procedure, a modification of the tactical reporting system was instituted and a more formal system for POWs, using the code-name *Songbird*, was begun in early 1970.[24]

In March and April 1970 the new system was put to the test. On March 19, 1970, an F-4D fighter plane carrying two pilots, Captain William Rash and First Lieutenant Dennis Pugh, was shot down in Laos over the Ho Chi Minh Trail. Both ejected safely. Rash ducked into a cave and Pugh hid in some thickets. The NSA picked up the NVA radio messages that "two pilots parachuted down near the command post of the 57th Battalion," and that "the pilot . . . ran into a cave. All different types of planes arrived to rescue the pilot and *Binh Tram* (BT) 12 again shot down . . . 6 more planes."[25]

Contact with both pilots was established, but the SAR effort was hampered by the high concentration of enemy AAA fire. A later evaluation of the incident states that on the evening of March 20, Rash heard Pugh's voice on the radio that "the enemy was within ten meters of his position. Lt. Pugh then depressed the transmitter button on his radio and continued to hold it down. Excited 'bad guy' voices were heard. Capt. Rash heard Lt. Pugh say 'Wait' just before the mike went dead. This was followed by 15–20 gun shots. Contact with Lt. Pugh was never reestablished. Capt. Rash was extracted around noon on 21 March 1970."[26]

Retired Air Force Sergeant Jerry Mooney worked AAA and SAM intercepts for NSA during the war. Mooney has been one of the very few ex-NSA employees to ever speak publicly about the National Security Agency and its wartime efforts. Mooney recalls the Pugh incident vividly and notes that the NSA intercepted a "post-fire" report, i.e., a report given by the enemy AAA unit after the engagement, which indicated that Pugh was in fact captured. This became critical when several weeks later the NSA intercepted NVA communications indicating that the communists were attempting to secretly move one firing unit of the 238th SAM Regiment across the Ban Karai Pass, one of the major crossing points from North Vietnam into Laos. The aim was to shoot down the SIGINT U-2, code-named *Olympic Torch,* whose flight path followed directly along the Ho Chi Minh Trail.

At first, Mooney remembers, DIA didn't believe the NSA analysis. However, faced with the possibility that the U-2 could encounter a serious threat, DIA ordered a B-52 bomber strike on the location of the SAM site. Several days later, NSA picked up a signal emanating from the Ban Karai Pass communications center, from the commander of the AAA unit sent into Laos to guard the SAM unit. He was reporting that both units had been badly damaged in the bombing and had suffered severe losses in equipment and men. Shockingly, the NVA 367th Air Defense Division, the headquarters unit for the AAA commander, ordered that the next captured American pilot be executed in retaliation.

Several SIGINT reports partially confirm Mooney's account. The NSA Southeast Asia Daily Summary for April 8, 1970, noted that "8 April [redacted] an unidentified battalion in the BT 14 area near the Ban Karai pass [redacted] when American aircraft are shot down, the pilots are to be killed in order to avenge for those comrades who were struck on 5 April."[27]

Two months later the Chairman of IPWIC, DIA's POW-intelligence committee, asked the assembled group to consider possible U.S. government responses to a hypothetical question. He asked, what if "high-confidence reports are received indicating that certain lower-echelon enemy units have ordered that downed American pilots be killed rather than captured, and that these units should report to high authorities that the pilots died as a result of shoot-down? If such a situation developed, what should the USG do? What options are available?"[28]

The IPWIC members offered several options and afterwards the matter was quietly dropped. Given the time frame and the wording of the "question" by a senior DIA intelligence officer, the connection to the April incident is obvious.

The Vietnamese definitely know Pugh's ultimate fate but have offered no explanation. In October 1992 a DIA researcher found Pugh's identity and Geneva Convention cards in the Hanoi Central Military Museum.[29] His remains have never been returned.

Mooney states that after receipt of the message, they were ordered to review NVA traffic for any similar messages. Looking back to 1965, Mooney discovered that they could predict when an execution would occur. According to Mooney, "We noticed that whenever one of the AAA or SAM units' senior officers was killed by U.S. bombing, Air Defense headquarters would order a retaliatory execution. While this only happened a few times during the war, the correlation could be seen."[30]

The significance of these reported executions of American POWs came into sharp focus in the summer of 1972 when NSA intercepted another execution message. This time the stakes were far higher. During the Easter Offensive the NVA sent some of their premier antiaircraft units across the border for the first time to provide air defense for the communist divisions that swarmed across the DMZ into upper South Vietnam. As the offensive was sputtering to a close in July, the NSA picked up information that several U.S. F-4s had struck an AAA unit headquarters and killed a senior officer of the 284th AAA Regiment.

Several days later, the NSA intercepted the message that it had been dreading. Sending a "Flash" message, the highest priority for a communication, the NSA alerted MACV that the "NVN 377th Air Defense . . . plans to execute 10 *Americans* [redacted]. On 6 July . . . the 284th AAA Regiment . . . directed the execution of 10 Americans [redacted] on 8 July [redacted] the cadres shall be left behind to kill the 10 Americans. [Redacted] complete the task and return [redacted]. . . . The 284th AAA Regiment departed Quang Tri city on 5 July and is presently located in the areas of Cam Lo, Dong Lon and Tan Vinh."[31]

When NSA's Vietnamese Air Defense linguist, Berkeley Cook, translated the message and showed it to Mooney, the message included the location—Highpoint 310, near Khe Sanh on the Laos-South Vietnam border—and the time of the execution, noon. They had only a few hours to alert DIA and the White House so that the field could take action. However, an internal authorization problem forced them to wait several hours before they were allowed to transmit the message to MACV. By then it was too late.

The NSA listed the "10 Americans executed" message in their Daily Summary of events in Southeast Asia.[32] This report lists only the most important intercepts, which indicates that NSA believed the message was authentic, otherwise they would not have listed it for the senior echelons of the U.S. government. Dr.

Roger Shields, the DOD's POW/MIA coordinator, recalls reading the execution message, and he states that "the message simply did not strike him as real. No one knew for sure, of course, but it was not widely believed. This had occurred several other times and as a matter of policy we sent a message to them vehemently protesting and threatening dire consequences." Dr. Shields does not recall if a similar message was sent over this particular execution intercept.

In his 1995 book *Inside Hanoi's Secret Archives,* Malcolm McConnell reveals that the North Vietnamese deliberately hid the fact that "many" Americans died as a result of widespread torture, although the Vietnamese also seem to deny that they purposely killed Americans. One illuminating story in McConnell's book, however, discloses possibly corroborating details about the "10 Americans executed" message. An important Vietnamese officer working closely with Ted Schweitzer, a DIA researcher at the NVA Central Military Museum in Hanoi, told Schweitzer that a "colleague" of the Vietnamese officer admitted that late in the war ten American POWs held in a cave prison in southern Laos had escaped and were later recaptured by the Pathet Lao, who returned them to the control of the NVA at the cave prison. Afterward, the North Vietnamese guards threw grenades into the cave and killed the Americans.[33] While the story does not precisely match the NSA intercept, the broad elements of ten Americans executed late in the war certainly does. The location of the NSA intercept was extremely close to southern Laos.

Nothing further has been revealed about a deliberate NVA policy that dictated executions of downed American pilots in retaliation for the loss of senior officers. The returnees from North Vietnam disclosed that they were often subjected to mob violence and threats by militia, but generally when American POWs were killed it was done by villagers or undisciplined troops engaged in heat-of-the-battle-type slayings. Without the corroborating NSA intercepts, we would have only Mooney's statements.[34] The heavy redaction of the NSA messages makes it difficult to ascertain for certain whether Mooney's memory is completely accurate, but the text left untouched certainly provides strong support for Mooney's recollection of these wartime events. The U.S. government denies that either incident ever happened and the Vietnamese certainly aren't refuting that position. Who the ten Americans were remains a mystery no one seems very eager to uncover.

"A plan of escape": Operation *Thunderhead*

Air Force Major Tom Pugh and his copilot, Major Ronnie Rice, approached Hanoi from the south at 75,000 feet in an SR-71 reconnaissance plane. From the east, a second SR-71 was flying an intercept course above them. A third SR-71, in reserve in case either airplane had to abort its mission, advanced from the west.[35]

This was Tom Pugh's second flight over Hanoi in three days. Pugh's squadron of four SR-71s was based at Kadena airfield on Okinawa. The planes conducted high-altitude aerial photography of the North Vietnamese countryside, looking for a variety of supply movements and military installations. On May 1, Pugh had been ordered to fly his SR-71 so as to create a sonic boom over the North Vietnamese capital. Another SR-71 would make a second sonic boom within 15 seconds of Pugh's. When Pugh asked why an extremely valuable and scarce national resource was being used simply to make a loud noise over the city, he was told it was classified. Tom Pugh (unrelated to Dennis Pugh) shrugged his shoulders and got to work laying out the flight plan.[36]

The two aircrews followed a carefully laid-out series of timed flight checkpoints so as to arrive over the city precisely at noon. No special training was conducted, but the timing was critical. May 2 was their first try and the plan worked perfectly. Today was May 4, the second attempt. Promptly at noon, Pugh's SR-71 again broke the sound barrier over Hanoi. Ten seconds later, the SR-71 above them also smashed through. Below them, in a cellblock in the "Hanoi Hilton," two POWs looked at each other and nodded. Unknown to both flight crews, they had just signaled the start of Operation *Thunderhead,* the most highly classified POW effort of the war, a last-ditch, desperate attempt to escape from the heavily guarded prison the North Vietnamese called Hoa Lo.

The history of *Thunderhead* has its origins in the raid at Son Tay. The grouping of the prisoners enabled the POWs to set up an Escape Committee to formulate plans and gather supplies for an escape from the "Hilton." Two previous escapes had already been attempted and failed. The first occurred in 1967 by pure chance when two POWs, George Coker and George McKnight, watched their door swing open during a bombing raid. Although the pair got out of the "Hilton" and made it to the Red River, the two big Caucasians were quickly spotted in a city of much smaller Orientals and recaptured within several hours. The next escape happened in 1969 when John Dramesi and Edwin Atterberry executed a second breakout. Although they remained at large for a longer period of time, they were also caught.

Because of the deliberate planning involved, the second escape sent the Vietnamese wardens into a fit of rage. Dozens of Americans were cruelly tortured to extract information on their communication systems and internal chain of command. Atterberry was beaten so badly he died under the brutal treatment. After the purge, several of the higher-ranking POWs decreed that no other escape attempts would be allowed unless the escapees could prove they had "outside" assistance, which was a clever way of shutting off further efforts without having to directly countermand the Code of Conduct's injunction that prisoners should try to escape.

The Escape Committee included Dramesi, Jim Kasler, George McKnight, and others. They notified DIA of their intentions through various covert methods. Several plans were contemplated and rejected, including making a break toward the mountains to the north of Hanoi. A more promising scheme was what the POWs called the "Mole Plan," which was an attempt to tunnel from the "Hilton" to the Red River. The POWs would then float down the river to its mouth in the Gulf of Tonkin and there be picked up by a SAR helicopter at one of four designated points. This plan reached the Pentagon in late January 1972 and was called Operation *Diamond* by the military. When the plan was first presented to Secretary of Defense Laird, his initial reaction was completely negative. But after discussing it further, he did an about-face and gave his approval.[37]

The original strategy was changed, however, either by the POWs or by JCS. Eventually, the tunneling portion was dropped; the POWs would have to escape to the river by another route. They acknowledged they could accomplish this, and on April 28, Admiral Moorer sent a memo to Admiral McCain at CINCPAC approving the escape. The Strategic Air Command, which controlled the air movements of the SR-71s, was directed to execute the sonic booms. CINCPAC's recovery efforts, however, were placed on hold until mid-May.[38]

The POWs had notified the national command that between one and five men would be coming out. The sonic boom was necessary for two reasons. First of all, to overcome the stricture against escaping without "outside" help, the POWs who wanted to escape, primarily Dramesi and Kasler, needed proof that in fact "outside" help was available. Second, they wanted confirmation that the Navy was waiting for them at the mouth of the Red River. When the boom signal was given, they would leave between June 1 and 15. Either they would signal their location using a mirror they had purloined or they would steal a boat and fly a red or yellow flag from the mast. More significantly, the military command believed that the POWs had somehow secured Vietnamese assistance. According to General Manor, "After the Son Tay raid, the government was very reluctant to authorize any further attempts into North Vietnam because of the international repercussions and the fear of getting men killed. The belief the POWs had inside help was an important factor in approving the plan."

In fact, both Dramesi and Kasler are adamant that they did not have Vietnamese help and never implied that they did.[39] While Dramesi was not one of the covert communicators, he believes this misunderstanding probably arose because of the crude communication methods.[40] The Escape Committee, according to Dramesi, had set up a separate channel outside the one normally used by the POWs.

Some of the POWs had been preparing for the escape for years. Kasler notes that "we secured lots of supplies. We made Vietnamese costumes and even the style of hats they wore. We saved bread and rice for food and stole anything else we could use. The Vietnamese were careless about leaving stuff lying around." Dramesi agrees, and recalls that "we used lime mixed with the heavy toilet paper to form a cardboard-like material. We hid our supplies in the holes in the ceilings and covered them with this stuff. We then used charcoal to blend the cardboard into the color of the walls. We had a ladder, mirrors, and other supplies. I even had a key to the cell door hidden in the ceiling.

"Our plan was to wait until the flooding season when the river was moving at a speed of seven to twelve knots. We would put on our disguises, go through the roof and get over the wall at a spot where the guards no longer resided, using the ladder and some poles we had. Once in the river we would hitch a ride on flotsam. When we reached the rendezvous point at a given time at the Gulf, we had to rely on the Navy to find us. We didn't want to steal a boat until the very end or unless we had to. The Escape Committee had received a map of the area from the States which, during a rainstorm, they floated down to me wrapped in plastic and concealed inside a twig. It showed us the easiest way to get to the river and the island. We believed we had an excellent chance of success."

After the sonic boom signal was given, both groups began preparations. Kasler states, "Dramesi and I immediately wanted to go. There was just us and maybe a third man. We sent a message to the senior POW officers asking permission to escape."

Back in Hawaii, the military also was planning on how to accomplish the recovery. The mission was so tightly held that at first only McCain and two other senior CINCPAC officers knew about the escape attempt. That was expanded slightly to include Captain Andy Porth, an Air Force E&E specialist working at the Pacific Air Force (PACAF) in Hawaii. Jack Reisner had been his boss for several years. Porth was summoned to CINCPAC by a special back-channel message. McCain believed an E&E officer was needed and Porth was chosen. He was forbidden to speak to anyone about the operation, including the commander of PACAF.[41]

Lieutenant Commander Edwin L. Towers was the navy officer who did much of the planning and who participated in the operation. Towers coordinated the movement of various Navy assets to assist in the observation and possible rescue of the POWs—and later wrote a book about *Thunderhead*.[42] The Navy would use their SAR helicopters to conduct most of the inspections of the smaller rivers that comprised the delta of the Red River. The SEAL submarine, the USS *Grayback*, would be used to launch SEAL teams in small motorized vehicles called SDVs. These teams would be used to cover the back side of a small island, called Point Delta by the Americans, which was considered the main rendezvous.

Thunderhead, however, wasn't the only highly-classified POW operation at this time. On May 5, Marine Colonel William J. Davis was escorted to the Pentagon by Marine Lieutenant General Hugh Elwood to see General Manor. Davis was nominated as the Marine liaison to a new team planning a major operation: raiding the "Hanoi Hilton" to liberate the American POWs.[43] That the JCS was creating plans to raid the prison in central Hanoi at the same time as *Thunderhead* was just starting indicates both the desperation concerning POWs felt in Washington and their true estimate of the escape attempt's chances for success.

Davis immediately ran into the same fierce interservice rivalries that had dogged POW rescue operations since 1965. He wanted to use the two Marine Battalion Landing Teams already prepositioned on ships off the coast of Vietnam. With special training, the Marines could be ready in three days. But the Army and Air Force representatives wanted a repeat of the Son Tay raid, using Army Special Forces carried in Air Force helicopters.

By the time the various services had finished drafting the contingency plans, a quickly executed raid by fifteen hundred Marines had turned into a multidivisional occupation of Hanoi. The plan eventually died.

Meanwhile, the Navy's *Thunderhead* planning was completed by mid-May. Moorer wrote to McCain, "You are authorized to execute plan. . . . signals were executed without incident. . . . Therefore, we assume movement to Point Delta."[44] Operation *Thunderhead* was on.

"*Thunderhead* is now in progress"

On May 31 everything was set in motion. Required orders were issued and the surveillance phase had begun. A message was flashed to McCain from the commander of the Pacific Fleet that "Operation *Thunderhead* is now in progress." The USS *Long Beach* would act as commanding vessel for the operation. Heavily armored HH-3 Navy SAR helicopters would be used for the aerial-search portion while the SEAL submarine USS *Grayback* would conduct searches in the operational area around the island and twelve nautical miles out to sea.[45]

To insure operational security, the term "agents" was used in all of the electrical communications, even on secure radio channels. The use of "agents" was part of a cover story devised to hide the true nature of the mission. Most of the American personnel involved were told they were picking up agents or possibly high-level defectors.

Of greater concern than a security breach was the effect the war would have on the POWs' escape. In accordance with a presidential directive, the Navy had earlier sowed the mouth of the Red River and Haiphong harbor with lethal mines. The Navy noted to McCain that "if the agents attempt their entrance into the Gulf by boat from within any of the mined rivers, the probability is not favorable of surviving a transit of the river mouths through the mined segments in anything but a very small wooden boat entirely free of metal. . . . If a fishing boat sets off a mine, the chance of the passengers surviving would be small. . . . Since we are unable to communicate with the agents, we can hope for the best but must recognize the low probability of successful exit if transit to the coast is by boat." The message went on to say that if they had the help of local Vietnamese, perhaps they would warn the POWs of the mines.[46]

The Navy immediately ceased mining operations in the area and declared the rivers a "no-fire" zone for aircraft and naval gunfire. But it was too late; the deadly mines were blocking the POWs' escape route and there was no way to let them know.

Lieutenant Commander Towers and the SAR helicopters began making thrice-daily reconnaissance flights looking for a red or yellow flag hanging from a boat. Surprisingly, even when they penetrated North Vietnamese air space, they were not fired on by communist air defenses. Operations continued smoothly for the first five days, but no sign of the POWs was discovered. Then on the night of June 4 the first problem cropped up. The *Grayback* had attempted to place a SEAL team on the shore of the island closest to the North Vietnamese coast. They launched the team in an SDV, but the current sweeping out from the river mouth was so strong that the SEAL vehicle could make little headway. Halfway to the island the vehicle's batteries died and the SEALs were stranded in the open ocean.

An NVA garrison was known to be on the small river island, and fearing for the SEALs' safety the *Grayback* radioed Towers the next morning and asked the SAR helicopter to find and pick up the men. The men were quickly found, but it was decided to sink the SDV to prevent it from falling into enemy hands.

On the night of June 5 the helicopter attempted to rendezvous with the sub and drop the SEALs back into the water so they could rejoin the *Grayback*. After great difficulty in locating the sub's signal, the strobe was finally found. Unknown to everyone, the *Grayback* had launched its second SDV earlier that night. The second team also fell victim to the strong current and quickly foundered and capsized their SDV. Instead of the sub's signal, what the helicopter crew were seeing was the flares and lights of the second stranded SEAL team.

As the helicopter came to a hover, the first SEAL team jumped out of it into the darkness. Flying conditions were terrible that night and the helicopter pilot was unable to clearly discern the surface of the water. The SEALs wanted to be dropped from a height of no more than ten feet—but instead of ten feet up, the helicopter was hovering at thirty. The first SEAL out the door, Lieutenant Melvin S. Dry, slammed into the water. A heavy floating object crushed his throat and he died instantly. Another SEAL suffered a broken rib. The helicopter pilot, unaware of the catastrophe and low on fuel, returned to the *Long Beach.* Alone in the rough waters of the Gulf of Tonkin, the seven surviving SEALs miraculously linked up and stayed afloat the remainder of the night. At first light, Towers and the helicopter returned to the scene and rescued the SEALs. Luckily the men were carrying emergency beepers that helped pinpoint their location. In a long message, McCain explained the entire incident to Moorer. He finished by remarking, "Our hopes remain high."[47]

But not without another near disaster. On the morning of June 10, the *Grayback* was near the surface recharging her batteries when a sharp-eyed lookout on a nearby frigate, the USS *Harold E. Holt,* spotted the telltale wake of the sub's snorkel. No one was aware of the *Grayback's* presence in the area, so the *Holt* assumed it was an enemy submarine. Without hesitation, the *Holt* turned and began firing. Fortunately, its aim was not as good as the eyesight of its lookouts and the rounds from its five-inch guns missed. The submarine captain was none too happy at being used for target practice.

By June 15, despite repeated surveillance flights around the islands and rivers that form the mouth of the mighty Red River, no POWs were found. The mission that began with such high hopes among the military leadership of the country was reluctantly called off. Moorer sent a message to McCain stating, "It must now be concluded that for reasons unknown the escape attempt which generated *Thunderhead* either did not occur or was unsuccessful. . . . Unfortunately, the real purpose of *Thunderhead* cannot be divulged to most of the personnel who participated in the operation. However, please convey my personal thanks and appreciation for a job well done in this vital humanitarian task."[48]

What happened to Kasler and Dramesi? Shortly after the sonic booms hit, a request was sent to the senior POW, John Flynn, asking permission to make the attempt. After discussions between several of the leading POWs, including Stockdale and Robinson Risner, Flynn made a decision. The command was passed to Kasler ordering them not to escape. It was too risky and the possible NVA retaliation on the remaining POWs would disrupt their hard-won and newly formed communication systems. At least those were the reasons passed down to Kasler and Dramesi.

Both men were furious but followed orders.[49] Two years' worth of planning had just been washed away, a SEAL had died, and many Navy men had worked long hours waiting for POWs who had been ordered not to leave three days after Pugh's second sonic boom. But why risk an escape this late in the war? Kasler remarks that "I had been held longer than any American from a previous war and I had no hope of getting out in the near future." For Dramesi, the reason was simple: escape was dictated by the military Code of Conduct.

Word was eventually received in the camp that the Navy had been waiting for them. The small problem of the mines appears never to have been mentioned and Dramesi was unaware of them. Although the POWs did not plan to steal a boat unless forced to do so, if they had sailed or drifted into a minefield the chances are not good that they would have survived.

A question also arises about some strange NVA behavior during this time. In mid-May, the North Vietnamese inexplicably moved over two hundred POWs from Hanoi north to a mountain camp within five miles of the Chinese border. No adequate explanation has ever been offered as to why the communists suddenly moved this contingent of men out of Hanoi. The synchrony with *Thunderhead* is certainly interesting. When asked whether the North Vietnamese had picked up indications of the raid, both Dr. Shields and General Manor answered that they did not believe they had.

Towers finishes his book by providing this explanation of why the SAR helicopter was not fired on. He states that he was told by U.S. intelligence that the North Vietnamese had noted the movement of the USS *Duluth* closer to the mouth of the Red River. The *Duluth* was a troopship carrying Marines. The combination of renewed bombings in the area, helicopter overflights, and the suspicious movements of Navy vessels led the NVA to believe that the United States planned an amphibious assault in the area.

How did the North Vietnamese know which ships were in the area? Probably through Soviet intelligence, which may have known more about U.S. intentions than has previously been suspected. Further, the only way U.S. intelligence would have fathomed what the North Vietnamese were thinking was through signal intercepts. The NSA was involved in monitoring NVA radio frequencies as part of *Thunderhead,* probably hoping to pick up news of the POWs' escape. However, one cryptic NSA product report dated May 31 sheds light on possible NVA foreknowledge. "North Vietnam may be anticipating another 'Son Tay raid' by Allied forces [redacted] probable Allied forces were preparing 'helicopters to land troops and free prisoners. The action is also to involve 'the capture of NVN cadres.' Maintain a high state of combat readiness and work . . . to counter the [redacted] raid."[50]

The mention of a prisoner raid, the use of helicopters, and the date of this message correspond to the broad outlines of *Thunderhead.* Did the North Vietnamese have some inkling of the true intentions of *Thunderhead,* an operation held far closer than Son Tay ever was? Perhaps. Or was the movement of the POWs to the Chinese border and the NSA message all just part of the fog of war—another in a seemingly never-ending maze of odd coincidences and bad karma that haunted the Americans' efforts throughout the war?

Preparing for the End

As *Bat 21* was struggling to reach the river, both SOG and the JPRC were preparing for their final months of existence. SOG stood down and turned its operations over to a new unit called the Strategic Technical Directorate (STD). Colonel David Presson took command of the STD in mid-May, but his forces were extremely limited and he was unable to run any *Bright Light* missions.[51]

On March 16, 1972, JPRC became a staff element of MACV J-2 and terminated its relationship with SOG. As a member of the J-2, the JPRC in its final months was focused on preparing for its eventual stand-down. The reports for the last seven months of 1972 are filled with sightings of Americans in locations from which Americans never returned, but the JPRC could only stand by helplessly and watch. With no forces to launch rescue attempts and the ARVN tied up in fighting off the NVA offensive in the north, no prisoner raids were launched from April to December 1972. The *Bat 21* operation had probably been the final blow to running rescue missions. While successful, these operations also posed the risk of a major embarrassment to the United States at a time of delicate negotiations.

Air Force Lieutenant Colonel Bob Case, who replaced Anderson and was the last commander of the JPRC, recalls that "about 50 percent of my time was spent preparing for the follow-on organization, the Joint Casualty Resolution Center (JCRC). I flew to Hawaii on several occasions to discuss the planning for the new unit. At the same time, I was being told by the MACV J-2, General George Godding, to be very careful about any operations as we didn't want to screw up Kissinger. The mind-set had become to negotiate guys out; rescue operations were no longer desired, especially if they failed and proved to be an embarrassment. The other part of the time we would receive CAS or 525 MI sighting reports which we would try to correlate with our files. DIA had instructed us that our number one priority was determining who was alive versus KIA. Number two was inspecting crash sites. The JPRC had truly become a staff job."[52]

In addition to implementing the JCRC, the JPRC's other major task was creating a new Bright Light database program. Navy Lieutenant Commander Cliff Barney oversaw the implementation of the new database, but upgrades in computer technology mandated starting from scratch. The new program was begun in December 1971; it used the three files previously developed in early 1970 by Howard Daniel and Jack Thomas as a base. The program was still being feverishly worked on when the JPRC stood down on January 23, 1973, and became the JCRC. All the hard-copy files and the computer database were transferred to Thailand.[53]

Another major command concern was the number of American deserters. The notion of U.S. deserters being responsible for some of the postwar live-sighting reports has been conjectured for years. Military policy was to drop from the rolls any serviceman who was absent without leave for more than thirty days. Many men deserted before they ever departed the States for Vietnam. Their files were then turned over to the FBI. The report of the Senate Select Committee on POW/MIA Affairs noted that "DOD did not consider deserters to be military casualties," and that between the Committee and the FBI they believed there were only "1,198" total deserters during the war, of which DIA concluded that "fewer than 100 are known to have deserted while assigned to units in Vietnam."[54]

However, recently discovered records indicate a far larger pool of possible deserters than the Select Committee determined. In 1971, when MACV began addressing the number of deserters, they noted that "As of 31 December 1970, there were approximately 2,200 personnel of this command in deserter status. . . . According to debriefings of several longtime deserters returned to military control, the majority of absentees are attracted to an underground 'AWOL Community' in Saigon."[55]

MACV began to track the number of deserters per month and implemented a program to regain control of these men by using the South Vietnamese police to track them down. This program began to have success. For the first five months of 1971, the number of new deserters was only 134.[56] However, of the 2,200 deserters noted earlier by MACV, the Army was still reporting in February 1972 that it had "1,100 deserters in South Vietnam."[57]

In November 1972 CINCPAC queried MACV requesting a figure for how many men were AWOL in Vietnam. The 7th AF replied to the request by stating that "Army CID [Criminal Investigation Division] and Air Force AFOSI [Office of Special Investigations] estimate that there are 180–800 deserters in RVN at present time; one-third to one-fourth are thought to be Air Force personnel; if there is a rapid withdrawal it is estimated that a large number of these personnel will turn themselves in. . . ."[58]

The military was concerned that with the imminent return of the POWs, the remaining number of deserters in Vietnam needed to be added for planning. Some deserters "may try to surface as bona fide returnees from PW status; others will be AWOLs who were detained by enemy forces incident or subsequent to misbehavior; others may be deceased. . . . In the absence of positive guidance to the contrary, CINCPAC will process all returnees IAW [In Accordance With] normal Egress Recap procedures. Returnees who are accused of misbehavior will be removed from PACOM Egress Recap channels only on request of the service department concerned."[59]

Despite the large swings in numbers, few deserters appeared. "Initially more than 1,600 individuals were listed on various rosters as being AWOL or in desertion status on morning reports of units in RVN. A major coordination effort was initiated . . . to review the status of every individual on the rosters and purify this list, leaving only names of persons still missing. This effort reduced the list by approximately 50%. A detailed plan was developed to handle the large number of deserters expected to surface after the cease-fire. However, the plan never had to be implemented since only four deserters turned themselves in."[60]

Despite continual attempts to precisely determine the true number of American deserters in Vietnam, the conflict between the current DOD figures and the military reports at the end of the war is strange.

POW or Traitor?

Without greater research and a more forthcoming attitude from the Vietnamese, we may never learn the truth about how many Americans were working for the communists at the end of the war, or if the foreigners sighted with communist forces were Americans. What does seem clear is that some "non-Asians" were appearing in odd places.

Dozens of reports were received in 1972 concerning whites or blacks helping the communists fight their war. DIA logged in so many sightings it created a chronological listing, a document that comprises almost a dozen pages. Several of the more interesting ones discuss whites and blacks fighting for the enemy against ARVN troops. These are rare reports, since most sightings indicate that the collaborators were engaged in supporting roles.

During the April offensive, the *New York Times* reported that "American intelligence officers . . . here believe that the enemy forces that have occupied northern Binh Dinh province have two Caucasians, possibility Americans, operating with them in either an advisory role or a combatant role. . . . 'We've ruled out the possibility that they were prisoners,' one officer said. 'Refugees . . . said that the two were . . . talking in excellent Vietnamese with a North Vietnamese lieutenant. . . .'"[61]

Reports of Americans teaching English or operating radios that monitored U.S. radio nets are more common. Many of these reports remain uncorrelated to a specific individual and are far too numerous to all be Robert Garwood or McKinley Nolan, the other well-known collaborator. Some can probably be written off as the inventions of enterprising intelligence agents trying to stay on the American payroll. Others, however, are compelling, and require more of an in-depth look before they can be so easily dismissed.

One of the most fascinating incidents occurred in the Mekong Delta in January 1973. An enemy unit attacked the 494th Regional Force (RF) Battalion in Chuong Thien province on January 7. Survivors of the attack reported both blacks and whites fighting with the enemy unit. MACV reported to CINCPAC that several RF soldiers had described spotting eleven foreigners participating in the attack. They noted, "This headquarters has received a number of reports of US collaborators participating in enemy activities. These reports normally indicate three or less collaborators engaged . . . [in] monitoring US radio nets. This report is considered unique based on size of force and direct participation in the assault. . . . It is more likely they are defector/deserters or even civ rather than US PWs. . . . This conclusion based on [POW] debriefings . . . and reporting from human sources and are probably recent arrivals in the Delta. . . . JPRC records indicate only two Negroes MIA in Delta, neither fit descriptions of Negro participants in attack. . . ."[62]

The wounded RF soldiers were taken to the hospital in Vi Thanh and questioned. One survivor saw a "black American handling a . . . machine-gun. He was approx. fifty meters away when he spotted this individual, who he described as obese with short black hair. When questioned on the possibility of this man being a Cambodian, source became adamant . . . that the man he saw was a black American. Source described him as being very tall. . . ."

Another injured man reported he saw "a Caucasian dressed in camouflaged green fatigues handling an AK-47. . . . He was approx. forty meters away . . . and [had] a paler complexion than a Vietnamese and was tall. . . . His uniform was covered with twigs, leaves and small branches. . . . in no way did he appear to be a PW, his hands were not tied and he did not wear handcuffs. This man fired his weapon at source and source became a casualty. The next individual interviewed stated his present wounds were caused . . . by a black American."[63]

The report goes on to describe fighting by other foreigners in this attack. The report is detailed, with numerous witnesses describing blacks and Caucasians firing weapons. The 525th MI Group noted that "Although there have been periodic reports of collaborators operating with enemy units throughout RVN for several years, this report is unusual in the size of the foreign force involved. Previous sightings have usually indicated two or three collaborators, generally in support roles."[64]

Dr. Roger Shields, the head of DOD's POW/MIA affairs, remembers the incident. He recalls that "this was an extremely interesting report. We tried to follow up on this and later reinterviewed the witnesses. My memory is that based on the second debriefs, the Caucasians sort of disappeared, but they were quite convinced about the blacks. We could only assume that they were dark-skinned Asians, but we directed a psy-ops effort at this unit, trying to turn up information on them. We never did."[65]

At the same time as the incident with the "foreigners" occurred in the Delta, the JPRC received another, even more intriguing report. A recon team was inserted in Binh Dinh province on January 4, 1973, and observed an occupied camp the next day. They reported that "The camp consisted of six houses, two barracks and one guard tower. The total number of guards was not reported, however the guards are armed with M-16 rifles. An estimated 100 Vietnamese prisoners are in the camp."[66]

The recon team was extracted on January 8. In their debrief they noted "a camouflage network of sticks, branches, and shrubs was in the process of being prepared. . . . On 6 Jan, the team heard unidentified voices, one individual, speaking in a North Vietnamese accent said, 'Hurry up, move faster.' That command was followed by the command 'Move fast!' given by a person speaking in a South Vietnamese accent. Immediately after the second command a male, non-Vietnamese-speaking foreigner attempted to reply in Vietnamese. The team leader said the third voice was that of an American attempting to speak Vietnamese. The team did not observe any of the individuals who passed their position, nor did they observe any Caucasians. . . ."[67]

What makes the recon team report even more interesting is the rumor that floated out of Binh Dinh province in March 1973. A cable from the Saigon Embassy to the JCRC reported that the political officer in Qui Nhon (the capital city in Binh Dinh) was told by the province S-2 that according to low-level, unconfirmed reports from villagers, the VC intended to propose two points in Central

Binh Dinh province for exchange of prisoners including some Americans. One location given was the Phu Cat District, the scene of the 1971 sightings of collaborators.[68]

The JCRC replied that their records reflected POW sightings in the general area, particularly in the 1971–72 time frame. However, they replied, "these reports indicated the PWs were ARVN. Occasional sightings of one or two US PW are on file, but there is insufficient data to provide identification or adequate evaluation. Debriefings of *Homecoming* returnees have located all remaining US personnel on the PRG release list in Hanoi. All indications are that these personnel will be released from Hanoi rather than RVN. It is unlikely that any personnel named on the official PRG list would be released in Binh Dinh if the *Homecoming* information is correct."[69]

The JCRC was wrong in supposing that all remaining POWs on the NLF list would be released in Hanoi. Captain Robert White was freed on April 1 from his prison in the Delta. He was the last American returned by the Vietnamese. They were also wrong about there being only a few reports of American collaborators in this area. The communication mentions the Phu Cat area. Over a dozen reports of Americans working with the communists near Phu Cat Air Base were received in the winter of 1970–71. The report mentioned earlier about the American seen popping smoke originated from Binh Dinh province. Further, the release point listed in the cable is approximately twenty kilometers from the camp where the team heard what they reported as an American trying to speak Vietnamese. No American POW who returned home was in MR-2 during this time frame, with the possible exception of Robert Garwood. Garwood, however, is fluent in Vietnamese. The 27 Americans who were released at Loc Ninh in February were held in Cambodia. Since the team never saw the American, the report appears not to have been acted on in the turmoil of the final days. If accurate, this recon team report provides tantalizing evidence that at least one American was still in the jungle in Binh Dinh province after everyone came home.

Another Three from Hanoi

As the peace talks struggled to reach a conclusion, Hanoi sought to use the POW issue to once again pressure the United States into offering concessions in Paris. More importantly, they wanted to offer complete backing to Cora Weiss' Liaison Committee, especially since she had become the only conduit for the transmittal of letters. On September 2, the DRV's National Day, the announcement was made that three additional American POWs would be turned over to the visiting peace group. The group included Cora Weiss, David Dellinger, William Sloane Coffin, the Chaplain of Yale University, and Professor Richard Falk. The three POWs were two Navy officers, Norris Charles and Markham Gartley, plus recently shot down Air Force pilot Edward Elias.

In late June and early July both Charles and Elias were displayed at a press conference with Jane Fonda. She lectured the pilots about their acts of genocide against the people of North Vietnam and destroying civilian targets.[70] She made broadcasts asking American pilots to not fly missions against the North and was photographed sitting on a Vietnamese antiaircraft gun, a PAVN-style helmet perched on her head. Elias claimed he was forced to attend because the NVA were withholding medical treatment from a POW with a wounded leg.[71]

The prisoners were released on September 25. Before being permitted to return home they were forced to undergo a tour of bomb-damaged buildings in Hanoi, after which they were placed on a Soviet Aeroflot airliner, which took them first to Peking and then to Moscow. The activists stated they chose this route because they feared that if a stop were made in Laos, American authorities would attempt to "kidnap" the POWs. Fearing a possible defection, DOD ordered NSA to track the flight and report its destination and arrival times to the White House.[72]

In private, Hanoi had dictated to the peace group explicit terms on both the flight and the pilots' post-release behavior. The DRV wanted no repeat of the Frishman-Hegdahl incident in 1969, when it had to defend itself against charges of brutal treatment of POWs. Publicly, they claimed that the U.S. government had impeded earlier releases by asserting military control over the pilots and had misused them for propaganda attacks against the North Vietnamese.[73]

Arriving in Moscow, the Americans were met by a U.S. Embassy representative, who promptly got into an argument with the peace activists over whether the POWs would continue by commercial aircraft or military transport. Eventually, the POWs flew with the antiwar group to New York. Based on their debriefs, the military men confirmed who was alive in North Vietnam, especially the presence of Ernie Brace, the pilot shot down in Laos in 1965. The confirmed presence of Brace in a Hanoi prison led some in the government to believe that all the American POWs in Laos had been moved to North Vietnam. Others, however, were not so sure.

Looking in Laos

Because of Laird and Moorer's obvious interest in locating any American prisoners in Laos, the military continued to keep a close watch on that country. The military interrogation team sent by CINCPAC was reaping major dividends in intelligence, not only on POWs, but on the NVA/PL Order of Battle and on supply caches. By the spring of 1972, the main focus turned away from launching raids and toward examining crash sites. The CIA noted that "CAS was tasked with responsibility for investigating known crash sites in Laos, exclusive of the *Prairie Fire* Area of Operations. . . ."[74]

But the CAS teams were operating under a severe budget restriction imposed by Senator Stuart Symington, an outspoken opponent of the war and especially of the U.S. campaigns in Laos. The senator sponsored a bill placing a low ceiling on government expenditures in that country, and the CAS crash site inspections withered.

The same conflict of responsibilities concerning Laos that had existed since the beginning of the war continued to divide the U.S. effort. Since SOG was forbidden to cross the Lao and Cambodian borders, no recon teams were dispatched to check out sites in those areas. Instead, SOG concentrated its remaining assets on searching locations in South Vietnam. In coordination with the Graves Recovery personnel, they searched over forty crash sites between mid-March and mid-April, mainly in lower South Vietnam. The crash site teams recovered six remains.

On March 12, 1972, an Australian journalist named John Everingham arrived in Vientiane claiming to have spent 29 days in northern Laos as a captive of the Pathet Lao. Everingham stated that he was captured by some Pathet Lao villagers and was taken first by boat and then by truck deeper into Xieng Khouang province. He expressed regret to the Embassy officer that he was not taken to Sam Neua, as he had heard of an underground hotel there for Western journalists.[75] The Embassy immediately sought him out for an interview. Everingham was opposed to the U.S. intervention in Laos and was a supporter of the Pathet Lao. He related his story of imprisonment and subsequent travels and indicated he hoped to sell his story to *Life* magazine. He also claimed that his Pathet Lao guards told him that between one and two hundred American POWs were being held in caves in the Sam Neua area.

The Embassy dug deeper into Everingham's story and came to believe that he was only held in a local jail for a few days until a Pathet Lao officer determined that he was a journalist. Everingham was then allowed to travel around communist-controlled territory under escort until he was sent back to Vientiane. Furthermore, based on the fabrications of his captivity, his hearsay report of up to two hundred Americans in the caves of Sam Neua was immediately discounted.

In May, a far more important source provided information on American POWs in the northern part of Laos. The head of Lao military intelligence, Brigadier General Etam Singvongsa, reported that a high-level defector had just appeared in Paris after living in Sam Neua for the last two years. Although the message from him is heavily redacted, it does state that a man named Chou Norindr, who claimed to have lived for two years in the principal cave housing the Pathet Lao Supreme Headquarters, stated that "During that two years, he never saw or heard of any US prisoner in that area or any other place in Sam Neua province."[76]

Etam disclosed the information during a dinner for Rear Admiral Epes, the head of the DOD's newly formed POW/MIA Task Force. Epes was on a tour of Southeast Asia. Etam told the assembled diners that "debriefing of Chou was in direct response to longstanding requests by US mission to Etam to provide any available information concerning US PW and PW camps in Laos. Etam further stated that he is personally of the opinion that all US PW taken in Laos have been turned over to the North Vietnamese who are holding them in North Vietnam until the PL need them for use in negotiations. Etam has no concrete basis for this opinion; he bases it on the lack of reporting of any information concerning US PWs in Laos and the fact that life for the NLHS east of Sam Neua is difficult enough without having the political and logistical problem of guarding and taking care of US PWs."[77]

A contrary view was expressed at the dinner by some members of the U.S. mission and by the ICRC representative, Werner Blatter, that perhaps some American POWs had been moved to North Vietnam but that there were also some held in Laos, if for no other reason than cosmetics for the Pathet Lao. It was felt that statements by Soth Petrasy alleging that U.S. prisoners were held in the country supported this view.[78]

Whether any other information on Chou Norindr was provided by Etam is unknown. The attaché reported that because the date of his eventual return to Laos was uncertain, it was doubtful whether Chou could even be contacted because of the position of his family. Certainly a defector who had lived that long in the NLHS headquarters would have been thoroughly debriefed. Etam's belief that, since no reports on American POWs had been received in some time from that area, obviously the prisoners were no longer there. This is a typical intelligence officer's assessment: no smoke, no fire.

Most of the reports by ralliers or captured NVA prisoners dealt with American POWs being seen moving up the Ho Chi Minh Trail or at locations around the Trail. That was about to change. In December 1972 a Pathet Lao soldier rallied who had worked previously as a telephone repairman in the Ban NaKay area. He stated he had recently seen seven male Caucasians and three Thai females held in a cave called Ban Eune. Although the source was wounded and would occasionally lapse into unconsciousness, this was "the second report this office has now seen on this particular facility. This is the first PL source to report PWs in Sam Neua province in nearly two years. Previous reporting suggested that US PWs had been evacuated to NVN and there may have been no PWs near Ban NaKay after 1971."[79]

When U.S. intelligence compared the first source's description to the PL soldier's report, it became apparent that he was discussing an "identical cave facility." Because the telephone repairman was now the second source to report American POWs in this area, Godley believed he was important enough to authorize "US exploitation team personnel to conduct face-to-face interrogation of source including use of polygraph in order to fully develop this subject."[80]

The PL repairman was fully interrogated on January 20, 1973. He reported that "on 3 occasions during early 1972 he visited the PL PW cave near Ban NaKay Neua to repair the telephone line running to the cave." He described a "wooden bar" which ran across the road leading to the cave. According to the source, "there was a telephone at the cave which was connected directly to the intelligence office at the NLHS Hqs." He gave the telephone extension, but when the interrogator asked him why the telephone was in the cave if the door was locked and the guards were outside, he could not provide an answer.

The source noted that the pilots were relatively young and in good health. Then he added another surprising detail. He saw a film in 1970 or 1971 which depicted Prince Souphanouvong with two U.S. pilots. In October 1971, two Pathet Lao who worked in Soth Petrasy's office, one of whom was the film projectionist, defected and reported a similar film.[81] Neither of the pilots in the film were the same men as those in the caves.[82]

Within days, a third source reported a cave holding U.S. POWs in the same exact area. The source was a "staff photographer/journalist at the NLHS center. During his assignment . . . source learned of the existence of a PW detention facility to the north of Ban NaKay Neua. Although source never saw the cave, he deduced . . . that it was in the immediate vicinity of Ban Na Eune." The source went on to describe the visit by Ivan Shederov, a Soviet newsman who had interviewed Hrdlicka in 1966. The PL journalist claimed that only Prince Souphanouvong could grant access to the American POWs. The exploitation team noted that the source's latest information dated from July 1972. The team judged that "his information regarding this facility appears to be accurate," and that "it is probable that all three facilities reported by sources are the same facility. This office can neither confirm or deny the information contained in this report."[83]

Within two months, three separate sources had reported a cave containing

American POWs at virtually the same location. It was the first solid intelligence in two years, especially after Chou Norindr had badly dampened the belief that Americans were still held in Laos. Although the three were inconsistent as to certain details in their reports, that all three picked the same area is impressive. As *Homecoming* began, the Embassy's hopes for American POWs coming out of the caves in northern Laos was high.

"Show your displeasure at Pathet Lao footdragging": No POWs in Laos

As a result of the Paris Accords ending the war, on February 12, 1973, the first group of American prisoners departed Hanoi. On the same day, the 27 American prisoners still held in Cambodia were released at Loc Ninh airfield, but not without the usual political overtones. The communists at first refused to release the Americans until the senior GVN official arrived or until their POWs were returned by the South Vietnamese, even though this was not stipulated by the Paris Accords. Despite repeated requests for the American POWs, the communists continued to balk. When the GVN official and the enemy POWs finally arrived, the exchange took place. An interesting comment by a communist official was noted by one of the American officers present. According to him, "The second senior [communist] Rep said there were 125 US PW in SVN."[84]

Despite the difficulties encountered, the flow of prisoners continued from North Vietnam. But the release of the Americans thought to be held in Laos was a far different story. On February 20, a cease-fire in Laos was signed. The pact called for the release of all POWs held by Laotian forces within 60 days. The next day, two officials from the U.S. Embassy in Vientiane called on Soth Petrasy to discuss American prisoners held by the Pathet Lao. Soth was handed a list of all American MIAs in Laos through the end of December 1972 and a copy of an article in the *Bangkok Post* in which Soth had been quoted to the effect that there were Americans in Pathet Lao hands. Soth was asked to confirm the presence of American POWs, acknowledge how many they held, and provide their names.

The Vientiane Embassy reported to Washington that Soth "stated that the LPF [same as the NLHS] does hold foreign prisoners including Americans. He added that he does not know how many prisoners" or their identities. He "agreed to send a message directly to Prince Souphanouvong in Sam Neua asking for information on American PWs held by the Pathet Lao."[85] Ambassador Godley commented on this meeting by stating that "A direct dialogue between the LPF and the USG has been established on the prisoner/MIA question. . . . The ball is clearly in the LPF court."

National Security Advisor Dr. Henry Kissinger cabled Godley and suggested the Embassy "follow up . . . recent conversation with Soth by seeking detailed information concerning those held. . . . "[86] By the 24th no reply had been received, although the Embassy had again pressed both Soth, the head of the Vientiane office of the NLHS, and a more senior NLHS official over the importance of this issue. The Embassy officer noted to the senior NLHS official that even the Chinese were cooperating in identifying American POWs. Only the Pathet Lao were dragging their feet.[87] The Laotians promised an answer shortly.

Almost two weeks would pass before the Embassy could contact Soth Petrasy again. At another meeting, Soth said he had no news, although he reiterated that Americans were being held. It was becoming apparent to the Embassy officers, however, that "Soth really was not well informed on LPF intentions re US PWs captured in Laos."[88]

The CIA was asked to comment on the possible status and treatment of Americans being held in Laos based on the debriefs of the returnees. They noted that while they didn't have much definitive information on treatment, the debriefs of Klusmann and Dengler indicated that the "conditions of captivity, techniques of interrogation and pressures of indoctrination were quite similar to those practiced by the Vietnamese communists. Physical conditions in North Vietnam . . . [were] probably better than conditions in Laos. Near the Pathet Lao capital, however, there were prisons dug back into the cliffs and these may have been fairly tolerable."[89]

Given the fact that Americans apparently could survive captivity in Laos, especially near Sam Neua, Secretary of State Rogers was growing increasingly furious over the delays in prisoner exchanges there. He wrote to the Embassy, "Slow pace . . . raises our suspicions and is trying our patience. . . . You should show your displeasure at Pathet Lao foot-dragging in every quarter where it will register some effect."[90]

Several days later, on March 20, an Embassy officer met with Soth. Earlier, on March 17, Soth had told an American official that the United States already knew the names and numbers of American POWs to be released. When pressed on this comment, Soth replied that to "the best of his knowledge the Pathet Lao do not hold any PWs in addition to the names given the USG in Paris on 1 Feb. Officer replied that this was contrary to the impression Soth had given in Feb. Furthermore, we are inclined to believe that other American PWs captured in Laos, in addition to those given in Paris, are still alive."[91]

Besides Soth's, the Vientiane Embassy was getting other unconfirmed reports that Americans were being held in Laos. A Swedish television crew traveled to Sam Neua and held long discussions with Souphanouvong and General

Singkapo. They informed the Embassy "that subject of US PWs was too delicate a subject to bring up at that level. They were informed by one unidentified official that LPF did hold some US PWs. He stated there were not many captured because their artillery caught most US aircraft at low altitudes which did not allow time for pilots to eject."[92]

The military was also growing increasingly nervous about the lack of progress on American POWs in Laos. In a memorandum summarizing U.S. intelligence and the best estimate of the situation in Laos, DIA noted that "this Pathet Lao list was immediately suspect. It immediately generated speculation that there is, i.e., must be, a supplementary Pathet Lao list for the following reasons: All ten persons . . . are known to be held in North Vietnam. . . . There have been numerous intelligence reports over the past five years from Pathet Lao and NVA ralliers . . . of sightings of American POWs held in the Sam Neua area. Most of the reports have been obtained by the CIA. CIA has attempted to put ground recon teams into these areas with the mission of scouting suspect camps. Due to NVA security precautions . . . none of these have been successful.

"There is no communications intelligence referring directly to POW camps in Laos. Nonetheless, over the years, COMINT (chiefly intercepted NVA messages) has indicated that there are U.S. POWs in Laos. Overflights and photography have showed active caves . . . though none have ever been positively identified as holding prisoners. . . . DIA has reason to believe that the communists in Laos should have some information on at least 215 Americans downed in Laos. This is based on such known evidence as a good chute, beeper on the ground. . . . Many of these men could have been killed on the spot or have died later, but the communists should have information on what happened to them."[93]

Based on the DIA assessment and the history of U.S. intelligence in Laos, Admiral Moorer, the Chairman of the Joint Chiefs of Staff, thought "it was 'highly likely' that the Pathet Lao were holding live US POWs in addition to the nine on the DRV/Laos list. In discussions with other members of the National Security Council . . . the Admiral learned that there was general agreement on this point among high-level national security officials."[94]

Moorer immediately sent a cable to CINCPAC ordering a halt to U.S. troop withdrawals until a more complete list of American POWs was forthcoming. Years later, the Senate Select Committee attempted to determine if this order was based on hard intelligence. Moorer insisted that such an order could only have been given with White House approval, but in a letter to the Committee President Nixon denied telling Moorer to issue this order on the basis of any direct knowledge the United States possessed on additional POWs in Laos.

Faced with the Pathet Lao's apparent denial that they were holding any Americans, and the possibility that the nine Americans and one Canadian who had been captured in Laos and were now being held in Hanoi would be released in Vientiane, on March 22 Godley made a fateful recommendation.[95] He wrote to Rogers, "We believe the LPF holds, throughout Laos, more prisoners than found on the DRV list. But we believe that, for the time being, we should concentrate our efforts on getting these nine listed men repatriated as soon as possible . . . and deal with the question of accounting for our MIAs and determining whether there are additional PWs to be repatriated within the framework and time limits of the Laos cease-fire [accords]."[96]

The next day, Moorer's cable halting troop withdrawals was rescinded.

On March 26, Soth Petrasy urgently requested that the Embassy send a representative to his office. When the Americans arrived, he noted that he had just received a response from Souphanouvong in Sam Neua saying that the LPF had decided to release their nine American POWs in Hanoi. Despite their outrage at this transparent fiction, the officers "took note of LPF message and . . . [stated] that we hoped after release of these nine prisoners, LPF would work with U.S. . . . to clarify fate of other U.S. missing in Laos. Specifically . . . to [account for] at least one U.S. prisoner [David Hrdlicka] who had been alive in Laos . . . but whose name had not appeared on the Feb. 1 list. Soth replied to the best of his knowledge LPF did not hold any U.S. prisoners other than 9 being released."[97]

The final group of prisoners, including the nine Americans, were released on March 28. Certain military officers in DOD were furious. Richard Secord, who had been involved with Laos earlier and was intimately familiar with the 1966 rescue attempt, drafted a memorandum calling for sterner measures to force the Pathet Lao to acknowledge the status of any American POWs. This memorandum outlined a series of steps to be taken, including direct military intervention in the form of a resumed bombing campaign if the Pathet Lao continued to refuse U.S. requests for information. Eventually, only the diplomatic aspects of the memo were used.

By early April, with no further names forthcoming from the Pathet Lao, Ambassador Godley wrote to State saying, "in absence of any evidence to the contrary, Embassy is reluctantly approaching conclusion that LPF does not hold additional U.S. prisoners. . . . Although U.S. mission through the years has utilized every possible means to obtain valid information concerning MIAs in Laos, we have been unable to identify conclusively any U.S. personnel being held captive or identify conclusively a specific detention facility for U.S. prisoners . . ."[98]

While the JCRC hoped to enter Laos once the agreement was finalized, they were never allowed to search in Pathet Lao–controlled areas. The CIA believed that it should remain unattached to any JCRC operations. Instead, the Agency informed DIA it was engaged in what it termed a "highest priority effort" directed specifically at determining what happened to the American MIAs in Laos.[99]

At the same time the CIA was telling DIA about its "highest priority effort," the CIA's Chief of Station in Vientiane was reporting to Langley that "We are of the opinion that until . . . a final peace settlement [is reached] . . . operations directed at determining the presence of American POWs in Laos will be extremely difficult. Areas where Americans have been reported incarcerated, rather than simply in transit, are in NLHS controlled territory. . . . As far back as early 1965 and until August 1970, American POWs were reported being held at Ban NaKay Neua and Hang Long, both in Sam Neua province. No American POWs have been cited at Hang Long since August 1970. Based on available information it is our speculation that there are no American POWs remaining in South Laos and it is doubtful if any remain in North Laos. We realize the above leans toward the pessimistic side but wish to assure you Station is fully cognizant of the importance of determining the status of missing American personnel."[100]

The long postwar nightmare of determining what happened to the Americans missing in Laos had begun.

15. Afterword

And what would you do with that knowledge, Senator, bomb Hanoi?
—Sarcastic response by former Secretary of State Alexander Haig to a question by
  Senator John Kerry, Chairman of the Senate Select Committee on POW/MIA
  Affairs, regarding whether Haig knew if Americans were left behind in captivity

The JPRC was disbanded on January 23, 1973, by order of CINCPAC. On the same day, the JPRC's replacement, the Joint Casualty Resolution Center (JCRC), was born. For the first week the JCRC was manned by the former members of the JPRC, but unlike the JPRC, which labored with at best ten or eleven men, the JCRC was authorized over two hundred.

Edward Alan Brudno, the courageous Air Force officer who like many other POWs supplied critical intelligence to the United States through their letters, found it very difficult to adjust to life outside a Hanoi prison. Brudno suffered from extreme mood swings. Several times while in the prison he was stopped by his cellmates from committing suicide. He was a brilliant man, able to compose and memorize, entirely in his head, a ninety-minute poem to his wife, whom he worshipped. Despite his great joy at returning home and being reunited with his family, he was apparently unable to reconcile his long years in captivity with the antiwar activities of his wife and her parents. On June 3, 1973, he swallowed a handful of barbiturates and killed himself. His suicide note was written in

French. Claude Watkins recalls that it was "one of the real tragedies of the war. The Air Force simply didn't notice his problem in time."

The Brudno family, much like the nation, was particularly split by the long, bitter conflict. Alan's brother Bob, contemplating the passions and emotions caused by the war, notes that much of this harm "we did to ourselves. From my vantage point, the antiwar crowd often took the position that if you were against the war, you could not concurrently be for the POWs. The issue seemed to be of no great concern to the Left, who sometimes had the attitude that a prisoner 'got what he deserved.' Subsequently, Senator Kennedy and his ilk were compelled to downgrade the treatment of the POWs by the North Vietnamese. But think about this situation for a moment. What would have happened if the antiwar crowds, while protesting the continuation of the war, had also protested over the treatment of the POWs? Given the obvious North Vietnamese efforts to create and sustain the antiwar movement to force the U.S. to withdraw, I believe it would have enormously improved their treatment."[1]

Besides reflecting about the impact on the POWs of the actions of the antiwar movement, the battle of the U.S. military to identify, locate, and rescue its prisoners of war also offers a chance to learn valuable lessons for future conflicts. Looking back at their efforts, we find that between the ARVN and U.S. forces more than 125 rescue operations were launched over the course of the war. Almost a dozen JPRC-sponsored ransoms or swaps were attempted, not counting those involving the Saigon Embassy or the State Department. More than 20 post-SAR operations were conducted and over a dozen code-letter symbols were reviewed and acted on. While almost five hundred Vietnamese prisoners had been liberated and 110 American bodies recovered, no living Americans were freed. Given the sizable number of U.S. agents in Southeast Asia (the 525th MI Group alone had over thirteen hundred) and the number of attempts, one would think that allied forces would have succeeded occasionally. Even a 1-percent success rate would have been *something*. How then to explain the failure?

As a staff organization the JPRC had the responsibility for rescuing POWs but lacked any authority to fulfill that mission. At first, SOG thought its soldiers would handle most of the missions, but that concept quickly broke down. MACV also made a critical early mistake in allowing only the JPRC to authorize a raid. By the time the JPRC adjusted that policy and shifted more of the burden to the field commanders, it was too late in the war. After the Tet Offensive, political momentum began to swing away from the United States, and the desire to hold down casualties precluded making risky assaults into enemy territory with units whose morale was badly eroding.

Strong consideration should have been given later in the war to moving the JPRC under the overall SAR umbrella to create a unified rescue command. By 1969, Colonel Cavanaugh and other commanders were fighting a different war than that of 1965–66. Other recommendations, such as the SEAL-team rescue concept, should also have been given greater weight.

Some raids were certainly compromised. Enemy foreknowledge is indicated in those particular instances when allied forces entered hastily abandoned camps. The VC's effective early-warning system, nimble movement by guards along pre-planned escape routes, or the quick concealment of POWs in the dense foliage can account for only a portion of the near-misses. How these raids were compromised remains a great unknown.

Success was also badly hampered by slow response time. Though most of the JPRC commanders agree that they received any assistance they requested whenever they requested it, the process of doing so created delays which directly led to the repeated failures. It would frequently take an escapee several days to reach friendly forces. At that point the camp was already long gone. Many JPRC officers have remarked that they felt like a salesman going door to door asking for troops or support to launch an operation. Although they realized that their project was often based on flimsy intelligence and aimed into the heart of enemy territory, the mind-set they encountered from commanders who balked at sending their troops on these missions, fearing the possibility of ambush, does not speak well for the American military tradition of doing anything humanly possible to recover one's comrades.

The disaster of *Crimson Tide* undoubtedly colored the effort and attitudes of some senior officers. SOG was so highly classified that the details of the mission were probably not widely known, but military staff organizations possess a subconscious ability to perceive the feelings of the big bosses. Those impressions are rapidly transmitted to the main body and eventually the need for ever more "intelligence" before launching raids became entrenched.

The JPRC, however, shoulders only part of the blame and was only one of the many fronts that crashed against the calculated communist intransigence. The total POW/MIA effort included diplomatic initiatives carried out by State, attempts by the CIA in Laos and exchanges with the NLF, military attacks against POW camps in South Vietnam and to a smaller extent in Cambodia, and the combined exertions of the intelligence community to identify and locate the men in North Vietnam and Laos.

The effort in South Vietnam and Cambodia was defeated by a multitude of factors. The inhospitable terrain, the inability to generate definitive intelligence, cultural differences, numbing political restrictions, and tremendous amounts of disinformation and fraud contributed to the failure. The efforts of the outstanding communist intelligence services plus the ability of the Vietnamese to conceal their prisons and their policy of repeatedly moving their camps directly contributed to defeating the American efforts to find them. One can add to this mix an often overlooked but critical ingredient: bad luck, and lots of it.

The U.S. effort to identify the men in the prisons of North Vietnam fared remarkably well, despite the failure at Son Tay—and assuming no one was held in a second camp system or smuggled to China or Russia. However, the effort in Laos, even given the need for the "secret war" and outside of the SAR efforts, can only be construed as an utter failure magnified by U.S. policies.

The United States added to these burdens with shortsighted goals and restrictions mandated by the political makeup of the war. The fractured and polarizing interservice rivalries and the military/civilian conflicts that delayed the implementation of the rescue outfit, the micromanaging by upper echelons of the government, and the creation of a unit without dedicated reaction forces doomed the effort. It was a failure of results, not effort, but the effort often reeks of half-measures and an apparent willingness by the U.S. ambassadors in Laos and South Vietnam to sacrifice American prisoners because of the need to support national policies.

Ultimately, it was the communist war-fighting system against our war-fighting system, and their system won, or more accurately, survived, largely due to having the home-court advantage and a clearer overall strategic vision.

If there were suspicions about men being held back by the North Vietnamese or the Lao, one should reasonably ask why there wasn't a louder outcry from informed military and intelligence officers. If there is a single cause for that lack of clamor, it is this. Claude Watkins spent much of 1971 and all of 1972 giving daily briefings to virtually every senior military and civilian official in the government about the efforts to identify and locate the POWs. He reported that, despite the communist refusal to provide complete lists of prisoners, U.S. intelligence had identified all the POWs in the North Vietnamese camps save one man. Watkins relates that "we used over a dozen methods, including foreign media material, films, early returnees, letter writers, and foreign journalists to help identify the men in the north." Watkins' discussion of the success of that program, and the subsequent confirmation of the numbers and identities of the prisoners by the returnees, convinced most U.S. officials that all American POWs had returned. Many, though, still had deep reservations. George Carver, the former high-ranking CIA officer whose main responsibilities were in Vietnam for almost a decade, succinctly outlines the pressure to conform. "The Nixon White House had little time or patience for the unproved and unprovable doubts of second-echelon officials or intelligence officers."[2] All the POWs were home, period.

Lastly, in terms of whether men were still alive or held back after the war, I made an informal and by no means scientific survey of over fifty former JPRC officers, NCOs, and enlisted men. Overall, roughly 50 percent believe other men besides the deserters Robert Garwood and McKinley Nolan were left behind in Vietnam. Although they have no proof (and it would be surprising if they did), most base their opinions on their experiences during the war. About 25 percent are unsure, while the other 25 percent do not believe anyone was held back. This last group believes that most men died in their loss incident, were killed by communist troops before they could be moved to a camp, or succumbed to the harsh conditions in the prisons.

When questioned directly about Laos, however, the percentage jumps dramatically. Almost 75 percent believe men were still alive in Laos in 1973. Repeatedly they point to the intelligence reports indicating that Americans were being held in the caves of northern Laos. They admit it was difficult to acquire confirming evidence of Americans in the caves, but the low-level although consistent information they observed led them to accept this intelligence as factual.

The wartime effort was in many ways a mirror image of the postwar challenge. The struggles the men of the JPRC faced provide a vivid illumination of the bureaucratic mind-set and the barriers faced by rescue forces during the war. I trust that scholars will continue to investigate in greater detail the mountains of declassified material concerning the wartime and postwar response of the United States to the POW/MIA issue, for there was a vast array of efforts to recover American POWs. Just as important, the reader should not automatically assume that because the wartime military tried desperately to recover its missing soldiers, that effort is proof against criticism of its postwar conduct over the POW/MIA issue. Our national reaction and policies to the POW/MIA issue need deeper scrutiny instead of relegation to the fringes. A vital companion effort is understanding the motivations and policies of the Indochinese communists. Learning to understand how they saw our weaknesses and perceived our strengths can only serve to enhance future American military and diplomatic efforts.

For the men who served in the JPRC, one JPRC officer, Bob Covalucci, summed up their feelings best. "We as a group followed our convictions and employed whatever tactics we could devise to accomplish our mission. Sometimes I truly believe we were out there alone making things happen for folks who did not have a clue to the complexity of the task at hand. Our failures do not bring shame on the men who served in JPRC, for they gave more than a full measure of time, effort, and talent, but rather highlight the ill-conceived organizational concept for the execution of post-SAR operations in Southeast Asia. This is the lesson we at JPRC learned: You cannot conduct successful post-SAR operations without a dedicated reaction force under the direction of a qualified ground commander. Frankly, the national resolve was lacking in POW operations as it was with the total war effort, and soldiers died in captivity who could have been saved.

"In spite of it all, if you asked me to go back and do it again, I would gladly try! It was the most meaningful assignment of my 30 years in the Army, including command at every echelon and serving as the G-2 of the VII Corps in Germany. To those who were fortunate enough to be called, JPRC was a labor of *love*, and the personal risks taken by us in the jungles and swamps of Vietnam were worth the opportunity to save our fellow soldiers and return them to their families, as we returned to ours."

Despite all these difficulties, the military and most individuals in the government tried desperately to save their comrades, often with breathtaking courage. If history should judge the complete U.S. POW effort harshly, it should also remember Fred Caristo running across a minefield and smashing through the back of a hut trying to rescue two men whose names he doesn't even know, or the crew of the Jolly Green flying through a storm of enemy fire to recover Iceal Hambleton knowing full well they were on a suicide mission, or John Regan fearlessly advancing his men across an open field to free Nick Rowe, all the while expecting enemy soldiers to open fire from close range.

Whatever one thinks of the Vietnam war, the sacrifices, bravery, and stunning heroism of the men who valiantly tried to rescue their comrades hopefully have now been recognized and made more widely known. They deserve that much and more.

Notes

Acronyms of sources used herein are listed and expanded in the Glossary of Acronyms on pages 393–396.

Preface

1. Pham Teo is a pseudonym.

2. Telephone interview with Brigadier General Heinie Aderholt, USAF (Ret.), Fort Walton Beach, FL, September 29, 1995. Aderholt remains bitter over the delay in launching *Crimson Tide*. He compared this to when he worked with the CIA in Laos, noting that when they received important information they acted the next day. Aderholt recalls that McChristian wasn't very optimistic about their chances.

3. Telephone interview with Alden Egg, Portland, OR, September 15, 1996.

4. For insights into Johnson's behavior, see some of the interrogation reports in the case file of Staff Sergeant Leonard M. Tadios, REFNO 0048, which is currently on microfilm at the Library of Congress, Federal Research Division POW/MIA Microfilm Collection, Reel 202, Washington, DC. Tadios was held prisoner in the U-Minh with Johnson and Jackson, but he died of malaria in March 1966. This database hereafter referred to as "LOC FRD."

5. Despite the constant attempts to reeducate Johnson, he was faithful to his country. Before his release in late 1967, along with Sergeants James Jackson and Daniel Pitzer, he became very sick and was near death. When the three were finally sent to Cambodia to be released, Pitzer was ordered to keep Johnson alive "or else." For Pitzer's fascinating description of the release and Johnson's condition, see Al Santoli's book *To Bear Any Burden* (New York: E.P. Dutton, 1985), p.357.

6. Telephone interview with Lt. Col. Frank Jaks, USA (Ret.), Fayetteville, NC, December 15, 1995.

7. Aderholt interview.

Chapter 1

1. The Central Intelligence Agency had a wide-ranging role during the war and also had much input on POW intelligence because of its preeminent position in the Washington intelligence hierarchy. CIA attempts to recruit agents from the enemy ranks were largely unsuccessful, however, and the majority of POW intelligence the CIA did gather came from its interrogation of enemy prisoners, monitoring of foreign media, other overseas agent networks, or exploitation of "national tech-

nical means," which is a clever way to say satellites and photo interpretation. The CIA also provided a liaison officer to SOG known as the Special Assistant. The CIA and SOG held monthly coordination meetings at Udorn to discuss such items as POWs and placement of teams into Laos. If any records were kept of those meetings, they have never been declassified. Communication between SOG and the CIA at Udorn was by secure phone or by a dedicated secure teletype link. The unit designator for the CIA in Thailand was the 4802nd Joint Liaison Detachment (JLD). The Agency maintains a station in each of the overseas embassies, headed by an Agency employee known as the Chief of Station (COS). To preserve the secrecy of the CIA's clandestine operations, the cover name of Controlled American Source (CAS) was always used to denote the CIA. For example, the CIA staff at the Saigon embassy was referred to as "CAS Saigon." Cables would read that they were from "CAS Vientiane," as opposed to CIA Station Vientiane.

2. Gerry Carroll, *North SAR: a Novel of Navy Combat Pilots in North Vietnam* (Simon & Schuster, New York, 1991). Mr. Carroll was a Navy SAR pilot during the war and his story, although fiction, is nonetheless an accurate and at times hilarious description of the Navy and their Vietnam SAR efforts.

3. "Brig. Gen. Robert Kingston, CDR, Joint Casualty Resolution Center, End of Tour Report (January to December 1973)." BG Kingston was the first commander of the JPRC successor unit, called the Joint Casualty Resolution Center (JCRC). The JCRC initially had a strength level of almost 200 men, but after the death of an officer in a Viet Cong ambush in December 1973 during a JCRC remains recovery attempt, operations were suspended and the unit rapidly lost funding and manpower although it continued in existence. In 1992, a new unit, called the Joint Task Force-Full Accounting (JTF-FA), was formed to replace the JCRC.

4. Interview with Garnett "Bill" Bell, Fort Smith, AR, June 15, 1995. Mr. Bell worked for many years in the Joint Casualty Resolution Center. He is a fluent Vietnamese speaker and is considered an expert on both the POW/MIA issue and the Vietnamese communists.

5. Malcolm McConnell, with research by Theodore G. Schweitzer, *Inside Hanoi's Secret Archives: Solving the MIA Mystery* (Simon & Schuster, New York, 1995).

6. As an example of the difficulties of piecing together this story, at the request of the Senate Select Committee on POW/MIA Affairs, the sections dealing with POWs from both the yearly *Command Histories* of the Military Assistance Command, Vietnam and the JPRC section of the separate SOG annexes were almost completely declassified in 1992. The LOC microfilmed them and placed them on Roll 61 of the Photo Duplication Service (PDS) set under the innocuous title "Intel files." In April 1995 I visited the main FOIA office of the Pentagon to look at what was presented to me as the most current declassified JPRC sections of the SOG annexes. Three years after the JTF-FA had declassified them, the main FOIA office of DOD still had not received the latest released versions.

7. In the parlance of intelligence, any individual who provides information to the U.S. government is called a *source*. A *method* is any procedure used by U.S. intelligence agencies to acquire information. The government agency currently responsible for investigating the fates of the missing soldiers is called the Defense Prisoner of War/Missing Persons Office, known by its acronym of DPMO. DPMO maintains a database of roughly 3,750 Americans and selected foreign nationals who became prisoner and returned, who escaped or were released early, who or are still missing in action today, or whose remains have since been recovered. This list is headed "US Personnel Missing, Southeast Asia." No government document would be complete without an acronym, and the short name for this list is called PMSEA. DPMO also maintains a database of over 16,000 sources, almost 95 percent of whom are Southeast Asians and who have provided information on missing or returned Americans to U.S. investigators. This process of determining whether the information is

true or false is called *analysis*. Matching true information to a particular individual is known as *correlation*.

8. Normally, Senate committee files remain closed for twenty years. House committee files remain closed for fifty years.

Chapter 2

1. "Handling and Indoctrination of Foreign Prisoners of War." This captured enemy document was translated by the Combined Document Exploitation Center, hereafter referred to as CDEC. All CDEC documents possess a Bulletin and a Log Number to help identify them for retrieval. The CDEC records are currently housed at the National Archives (NARA), and several other locations around the country. The records are contained on 954 rolls of microfilm and are also in hard copy format. The CDEC records can be found in RG 472, Records of the U.S. Military Command, Vietnam, 1955–1975. This particular document is Bulletin #339, Log #04-1257-66. The Bulletins came out on a daily basis and listed summaries of individual documents. The first two numbers stand for the month, the middle series is the sequence number, and the last two are the year. Therefore, this document was the 1257th translation made in April 1966. What is intriguing about this document is that it was sent to the Vietnamese by the Liaison Department of the Chinese Politburo in May 1960. The document is a "Lessons Learned" from the Chinese Army in Korea on handling foreign POWs, the vast majority of which were Americans.

2. "Experience on American Soldiers' Psychology," RG 472, MACV J-2, Department Of Defense (DOD) 1965 Intelligence Information Reports (IIR), Box 4, NARA, College Park, MD. Hereafter referred to as "DOD IIR."

3. Every missing soldier listed on the DPMO list has a Reference number, called a REFNO. Duffy is 0002. Because Duffy disappeared under circumstances for which the Pathet Lao should easily be able to provide answers, Duffy is considered a "Priority Discrepancy Case." A Priority Discrepancy Case is one in which the U.S. believes the communists should have intimate knowledge of and should be able to quickly resolve. A photograph of a dead American pilot published in a North Vietnamese newspaper whose remains have never been returned is an example. Over three hundred cases out of 2,200 have been labeled Priority Discrepancy Cases, although more could reasonably be added.

4. Col. Lawrence Bailey and Ron Martz, "Lost in Laos," *Vietnam* (August 1994), p. 42.

5. Edgar Weitkamp's family is still deeply involved in attempting to discover the truth about their brother's loss. Although Bailey did not see any other parachutes, a French military advisor in Xieng Khouang informed the French Embassy that they had observed a second parachute. Others claim that the second chute unfortunately didn't open. In 1991, the JCRC excavated the graves of the seven American crewmen from the plane. When they exhumed the graves, only four bodies were discovered. None of them was Edgar Weitkamp, although his Identification Card was found in the 1990s in pristine condition in the Central Military Museum in Hanoi.

6. Lawrence R. Bailey and Ron Martz, *Solitary Survivor* (Brassey's, New York, 1996).

7. The CIA received a report dated February 20, 1962, about a prison camp in Laos holding an American, and another report, dated August 9, 1962, headed "Location of U.S. Prisoners in Laos."

8. The finished document, complete with a photo showing Moon with a head bandage, was entitled "Biography of a Prisoner." It was discovered by Bill Bell in a refugee camp. A copy can be seen in Moon's case file at the LOC.

9. Grant Wolfkill, *Reported to Be Alive* (Simon & Schuster, New York, 1965).

10. "Directive on the Execution of the Policy toward Prisoners and Surrenderers." Some impor-

tant documents were fully translated and given an Intelligence Information Report number. The document can be found in Bulletin #7096, Log #08-3652-67, IIR #6-027-0239-68.

11. "The Party's Policy towards POWs and Defectors," History of the Vietnam War on Microfilm, Section V: POW/MIA, Folder January 1968, Indochina Archive, University of California at Berkeley, Oakland, CA. The Archive is now located at Texas Tech University's Center for the Study of the Vietnam Conflict in Lubbock, Texas.

12. "VC/NVA Policy for the Handling of Free World/RVNAF Prisoners of War," CDEC Bulletin #47,271, Log #01-1336-72, IIR #6-028-0024-72.

13. Interview with Douglas Pike, Oakland, CA, December 12, 1994.

14. "Missing G.I. Held by Vietnam Reds," *New York Times,* June 12, 1962, p. 15.

15. "Initial I.P.W. Report of Sr. Captain Tran Xuan Vy, Assistant Chief of the Political Bureau of COSVN in charge of Troop and Enemy Proselytizing Section," RG 472, MACV J-2 DOD IIR's for 1964, Box 5, Log #1-25-64, p. 12, NARA, College Park, MD.

16. From COMUSMACV to CINCPAC, Date/Time Group (DTG) 020920Z Jul 62.

17. "Vietnam Reds Exploit Letter Attributed to G.I.," *New York Times,* June 14, 1962, p. 8, quoting an NLF broadcast.

18. Telephone interview with George Groom, Hogdenville, KY, October 30, 1996.

19. Telephone interview with Colonel Harry Munck, USA (Ret.), Honolulu, HI, November 6, 1996.

20. "Special Report Vietnam: Viet Cong Treatment of American POWs," dated February 1963. This report was ordered at the request of Maj. Gen. Albert Kuhfeld, then Judge Advocate General of the Air Force. It was based on the debriefs of the returnees. A copy of the report can be obtained from Maxwell Air Force Base in Montgomery, AL, where much of the Air Force Archives are kept. In reference to the VC's ability to obtain any military intelligence they needed, Groom noted that after their release, the District Security Chief was discovered to be a VC agent.

21. The Quang Da Special Zone was the VC military name for the area surrounding the city of Danang. The cadre in charge of the camp came from the Zone Military Proselytizing Section and the unit that captured Groom and Quinn were Zone sapper forces. Sappers were more highly trained units, similar to our Special Forces. Information on the capture of Groom and Quinn came from an Oral History interview of Nguyen Thanh Nam conducted by JTF-FA Special Assistant Garnett "Bill" Bell on January 16, 1993. Copies of JTF-FA Oral Histories can be acquired through a FOIA request to the JTF-FA, Camp Smith, HI. These documents are hereafter referred to as "Oral History."

22. On March 20, 1965, a document was captured in Phu Yen province headed "Impressions of two American POW's in Quang Nam before their release." It was the release document signed by Francis Quinn, who had signed his name "Francis Queen."

23. "G.I.'s in Vietnam Lied As Ordered," *New York Times,* May 5, 1962, p. 8.

24. Telegram from AmEmbassy Saigon to SecState, dated September 8, 1962, RG 46, Files of Frank Sieverts, Assistant to the Secretary of State for POW Affairs, Box 22, NARA, Washington, DC. Unfortunately, for any researcher attempting to locate documents from a particular box in the files of Mr. Sieverts, the boxes are completely unindexed and documents could easily have been moved into any of the other 43 boxes. This archive is hereafter referred to as "Files of Frank Sieverts."

25. Ibid., p. 1.

26. *New York Times,* July 12, 1962, p. 2, quoting the NLF radio station.

27. "Subj: SRV Oral History, Mr. Nguyen Khac Tinh," From CJTF-FA Det One To CDR, JTF-FA, dated 190922Z May 93 by JTF-FA Special Assistant Garnett "Bill" Bell. Bell believes that the VC deliberately kidnapped Dr. Vietti and Mitchell to help meet their own pressing need for

medical care and at the same time deny it to the ARVNs. One factor adding to the confusion is the loss of another male and a female, Betty Olsen and Henry Blood, in the same area in 1968.

28. "American Depicts Viet Cong Jailing," *New York Times,* January 9, 1963, p. 3.

29. "Policy towards U.S. POW's," CDEC Bulletin #7131, Log #09-1134-67.

30. "Experience on American Soldiers' Psychology," p. 2.

31. "Vietnam Reds Free German Sightseer," *New York Times,* June 10, 1962, p. 1, quoting Herr Mueller.

32. Telephone interview with Arthur A. Krause, Winnetka, CA, November 18, 1996.

33. "Subj: Interview of Requested Source Mr. Phan Tu," From CDR JTF-FA to DIA, JTF-FA Oral History Interview DTG 221802Z Jun 93, Senator Kerry List of Persons for Interview, Entry Number 18 of 83, p. 3. Mr. Phan Tu was a former member of the Enemy Proselytizing Department during the war against the French, and wrote a book entitled *ST-18* that describes the conditions of a fictional POW camp.

34. Of the aliases given to the JTF-FA interviewer, none was "Bon."

35. Oral History, Phan Tu, p. 4.

36. Telegram from SecState to AmEmbassy Saigon, no date, Declassified Documents Research System (DDRS), Document #90, 1993. Hereafter referred to as "DDRS." Nguyen Huu Tho died of a heart ailment on December 24, 1996.

37. Telegram from SecState to AmEmbassy Saigon, dated October 20, 1964, DDRS #101, 1991.

38. Translated captured document, Indochina Archive, Section V: POW/MIA section, Folder 12/63.

39. Jane Hamilton-Merritt, *Tragic Mountains: The Hmong, the Americans, and the Secret Wars for Laos, 1942–1992* (University of Indiana Press, Bloomington, 1995), p. 124.

40. "Accounts of the shooting down of a Supply Plane in Savannakhet," CIA Information Report TDCS-3/560,051 dated September 25, 1963. The CIA maintains a database of records that have been released under the provisions of the Freedom of Information Act (FOIA). The database is called MORI, Management of Released Information. Requesters looking for information on a particular subject can request a keyword search of this database. A printout listing all of the hits is mailed to the requester, who then can specify which records they want. This archive is hereafter called "MORI."

41. "Status of survivors of the C-46 crash and Pathet Lao plans for them," CIA Information Report TDCS-3/561,471, dated October 10, 1963, p. 6, MORI.

42. Telegram from AmEmbassy Vientiane to SecState, dated October 19, 1963, Files of Frank Sieverts, Box 23.

43. "Apparent good condition of the C-46 crash survivors and Pathet Lao plans to send them to Khang Khay," CIA Information Report TDCS-3/563,830, n.d., p. 2, MORI.

44. Telegram from AmEmbassy Vientiane to SecState, dated December 13, 1963, Files of Frank Sieverts, Box 24.

45. Both the communist Lao government and the JTF-FA have attempted to excavate some alleged grave sites for Debruin. All have proved empty. The Debruins have probably had the lengthiest involvement in the POW/MIA issue of any family. They have worked tirelessly for over thirty years to find Eugene, and they are a living testimony to fidelity, doggedness, and courage.

46. James N. Rowe, *Five Years to Freedom* (Ballantine Books, New York, 1984), p. 54.

47. The Communist Party Military Proselytizing cadres were directly responsible for penetrations by "fifth columnists." They would recruit a young Vietnamese, have him join the organization, and then wait until he learned when the camp was at its weakest, such as when everyone was

on leave for a major holiday. The VC would then attack the camp, often destroying it. The enemy agent would escape and would appear later with a miraculous story of how he had survived by fleeing into the jungle. He would be transferred to another post and the cycle would begin again.

48. *Philadelphia Inquirer,* dated December 26, 1996, p. 1, c. 5.

49. Dr. Earl H. Tilford, *Search and Rescue in Southeast Asia* (Center for Air Force History, 1992), p. 39. Dr. Tilford's book, written when he was a captain in the Air Force, remains the only authoritative text on the enormous SAR efforts conducted during the war.

50. Case file of Captain Carl Berg Mitchell, REFNO 0027-01, LOC FRD Reel 138.

51. Cable from CIA to SecState, DTG 121929Z February 1964, DDRS Document #3204, 1992.

52. Telegram from AmEmbassy Vientiane to SecState, dated June 6, 1964, DDRS Document #1957, 1992.

53. The alphanumeric designations for military aircraft reveal their purpose. "F" stands for fighter, while the "R" in front indicates it is a reconnaissance version of the original model. "B" means bomber; "C" means cargo.

54. Tilford, *Search and Rescue in Southeast Asia,* p. 48.

55. Klusmann debrief, DDRS, document #2344, 1989. Klusmann tentatively identified the civilian as Prince Souphanouvong.

56. Most Lao figures are commonly referred to by Westerners by their first names. For example, Souvanna Phouma is often simply called Souvanna.

57. Klusmann debrief, loc. cit. Navy Cdr. Everett Alvarez was the first U.S. POW in North Vietnam. He was shot down on August 4, 1964, while conducting bombing strikes in retaliation for the Gulf of Tonkin incident.

58. Telegram from AmEmbassy Vientiane to SecState, dated June 8, 1964, DDRS #1694, 1992.

59. Subject: [redacted], CIA Intelligence Information Cable, TDCS [redacted], date [redacted], MORI. The text mentions that it is probably Klusmann. CIA documents are hereafter referred to as "CIA Cable."

60. Mr. Klusmann states that the PL told him he could send mail. His wife did get one of his early letters a few weeks before his escape, which is the only known instance of an American POW in Laos after the 1962 Geneva Accords getting mail out, especially considering that Debruin was captured before him and was still alive at this time. The PL told Klusmann that they were holding one other American, who was undoubtedly Debruin.

61. Telegram from AmEmbassy Vientiane to SecState, dated August 18, 1964, DDRS Document #3332, 1991.

62. Telegram from AmEmbassy Vientiane to SecState, dated August 19, 1964, DDRS Document #3320, 1991.

63. "Subject: US Search and Rescue Operations — Southeast Asia," Memorandum for the Secretary of Defense, JCSM-839-64, dated October 2, 1964, RG 46, JCS files, Box 2, NARA, Washington, DC.

64. Telegram from AmEmbassy Vientiane to SecState, dated October 13, 1964, DDRS Document #1971, 1991.

65. Interview with Charles Klusmann, November 8, 1996, Columbia, MD. A massive search operation was conducted for Klusmann, but only after it was authorized by the Commander of the U.S. Air Force in the Pacific. Approval was also needed from the Thai government for the use of Thai airfields by Air America. None of this would have been necessary, however, if Air America had been given permission early on to cross the "no fly" zone.

Chapter 3

1. "Memorandum for the Deputy Secretary of Defense from the Secretary of the Air Force," dated July 16, 1967, p. 1, LOC FRD, Reel 376, Miscellaneous POW Folder, Washington DC.

2. Ibid., p. 1.

3. Telegram from AmEmbassy Saigon to SecState, dated April 12, 1965, LBJ Library, National Security file, Vietnam country file, POW/MIA file, document 111B, Austin, TX. These documents hereafter referred to as "LBJ, POW/MIA" and the document number.

4. Ibid., p. 5.

5. Telegram from SecState to AmEmbassy Saigon, dated March 24, 1965, LBJ, POW/MIA, #70.

6. "Vietcong Threaten to Kill U.S. Hostage if Terrorist is Shot," *New York Times,* April 8, 1965, p. 17, c. 6, quoting NLF radio.

7. "Memorandum of Conversation," DDRS #189, 1995.

8. Ibid., p. 2.

9. "Vietnam Reds Kill U.S. Aid Official Seized in August," *New York Times,* April 14, 1965, p. 1, c. 1.

10. A unilateral Vietnamese investigation reported in 1995 that Mr. Do Trang Chau, a former guerrilla who helped capture Grainger, was told in May 1966 to return and assist in recovering the remains. According to Chau, he dug for three hours, cleaned the remains and put them in a bag, which was subsequently given to Mrs. Grainger. Bell recalls that the Vietnamese pointed out this error in U.S. records to the American side in 1991.

11. "To: District Security Sections and Sub-Sections," CDEC Bulletin #16, Log #11-1056-65, RG 472, MACV J-2 files, Box number 2, NARA, College Park, MD.

12. Telegram from AmEmbassy Saigon to SecState, dated June 20, 1965, Case file of Gustav Hertz, REFNO 0052, LOC FRD Reel 214, p. 7.

13. Ibid.

14. Ibid. Underlined in original.

15. Significantly, Hertz was not among the American POWs held in this camp. Hertz was being held in the COSVN camp run by their security forces.

16. In an interview with a cadre named Nguyen Hung Tri by DPMO Senior Historian Robert DeStatte on December 26, 1992, Tri acknowledged working as an interpreter in the HQ's SVNLAF U.S. POW camp. Mr. Tri was told that Donald Dawson was at first taken to a temporary POW camp north of Saigon; there he was given what the VC said was a piece of his brother's flight gear. Although Dawson was promised that the NLF would return his brother's remains after the war, Mr. Tri remarked that he doubted the item belonged to Dawson or that anyone knew the location of his grave.

17. Rowe, *Five Years to Freedom,* pp. 143–146.

18. "Subject: Tear Gas," Memorandum to the President, dated March 12, 1965, LBJ Library, National Security Files, Vietnam Country File, Box 194, Folder 1/65–3/65, Document 11.

19. 1965 MACV *Command History,* J-3 Annex, p. 96.

20. MACV Military Report of Weekly Operations from 191601Z to 261600Z December 1964.

21. "Subject: Combat Operations After Action Report," RG 472, MACV J-3 After Action Reports File, Folder 1, NARA, College Park, MD, p. 2. Who these American POWs were remains a mystery.

22. Ibid., p. 4.

23. Bennett and an Army private named Charles Craft were advisors to the ARVN 33rd Ranger

Battalion when they were captured during a battle with a VC force in Ba Ria-Vung Tau Province. A few days later, a U.S. Marine officer named Donald Cook was also captured nearby. Together, they were marched to the NLF's main POW camp in Tay Ninh province. Although Craft reported after his release that the VC told him in late May that Bennett had been shot because he was unable to keep up, an ARVN sergeant released in September related that he had been held with Bennett, and that Bennett's firm resistance to the VC's attempts at political education had caused them to shoot him.

24. "Status of US Prisoners of the Viet Cong in South Vietnam," CIA Intelligence Memorandum, dated June 28, 1965, LBJ Library, National Security file, Vietnam country file, Southeast Asia Special Intelligence Material, Box 49, document 3b, Austin, TX.

25. "Vietcong Reds Announce Execution of U.S. Sergeant," *New York Times,* June 26, 1965, p. 2, c. 7.

26. Telegram from AmEmbassy Saigon to SecState, dated June 26, 1965, DDRS #348, 1993.

27. "Wounded U.S. Soldier Escapes Vietcong Captors," *New York Times,* December 14, 1965, p. 5, c. 3.

28. "U.S. Civilian Tells of His Rescue From Vietcong," *New York Times,* December 22, 1965, p. 5, c. 3, quoting Mr. Hudson.

29. Each ARVN unit had an American advisor assigned to it. At high staff levels, the U.S. officer who worked directly with the ARVN Military Region Commander was called the Senior Advisor. Each Vietnamese province and district also had an American advisor.

30. Telephone interview with Paul Rusidorf, Largo, FL, December 16, 1996.

31. Oral History interview with Mr. Pho Bien Cuong, September 22, 1993. Mr. Cuong was the former Director of the Phuoc Long Province Detention Camp.

32. Oral History interview with Mr. Tran Ngoc Khanh, current Province Party Secretary, September 27, 1993, and Mr. Do Van Nguyen, former wartime Province Party Secretary, July 2, 1993, Song Be Province, SRV.

33. "Prison camp 247 of K.4 District, Phuoc Long Province," CDEC Bulletin #465, Log #05-1582-66.

34. Telephone interview with Jasper Page, Calhan, CO, December 2, 1996.

35. Debriefing report of Jasper Page by the 704th Intelligence Detachment, dated November 23, 1965, Case File of Samuel Adams, REFNO 180-02, LOC FRD Reel 214, pp. 44–45.

36. "Sergeant Escapes Vietcong," *New York Times,* November 7, 1965, p. 4, c. 1.

37. The 1995 unilateral Vietnamese investigation into this case reported finding only hearsay witnesses to the deaths of the three Americans. They could not find the burial site and they recommended the case be closed.

38. The U.S. government has unsuccessfully sought to find the grave sites of Bennett, Roraback, and Versace. In several Oral History interviews with Vietnamese cadres, they claim that only Roraback was shot. The other two died of malaria and the communists simply used their deaths to pressure the GVN government. Bennett probably was shot, but the circumstances of Versace's fate are a little more uncertain. The commander of the U-Minh Forest camp, Senior Captain Nguyen Chi Cong, reported to Garnett "Bill" Bell that Versace was taken away by elements of the Military Proselytizing section when he became ill. Cong never saw Versace again and was later told that Versace died of an illness. Roraback, on the other hand, was definitely shot. Robert DeStatte, DPMO's Senior Historian in Hanoi for several years, told the author that he had interviewed the man who confessed to shooting Roraback.

39. Liberation Radio broadcast, September 26, 1965.

40. "Concerning the Handling of Prisoners of War," CDEC Bulletin #6450, Log #07-3510-67. The document was fully translated under DOD IIR #6-027-1309-67.

41. "Americans Treated Better," *New York Times*, July 28, 1965, p. 2, c. 2.

42. Telegram from SecState to AmEmbassy Saigon, dated December 15, 1965, LBJ, POW/MIA, #69.

43. "Memo for the Director, J-1, Subject: US Prisoners of War," dated October 5, 1965, LOC Photo Duplication Set (PDS) POW/MIA microfilm Reel 61, JCS Intel file, Washington, DC. Hereafter referred to as "LOC PDS."

44. Interview with H. Fremen Matthews, Chevy Chase, MD, August 9, 1995. Matthews worked at the Embassy until June 1966, when he returned to Washington to join the State Department's Vietnam Working Group as the Vietnam desk officer. He held that post until 1970.

45. Ibid.

46. 1965 MACV *Command History*, p. 431.

47. Telegram from AmEmbassy Saigon to AmEmbassy Vientiane, dated June 20, 1965, RG 39, Records of the Department of State, Laos, Box 2428, Folder POW, NARA, College Park, MD.

48. Telegram from AmEmbassy Vientiane to AmEmbassy Saigon, June 21, 1965, Files of Frank Sieverts, Box 2.

49. 1966 MACV *Command History*, p. 681.

50. Letter to AmEmbassy Saigon, from COMUSMACV, DTG 151136 Nov 65.

51. 1965 MACV *Command History*, p. 431. Major General Joseph A. McChristian, *The Role of Military Intelligence 1965–1967* (Department of the Army, Washington, DC, 1974), p. 145.

52. Telephone interview with Arthur J. Kyle, Falls Church, VA, August 22, 1996.

53. Message from CINCPACAF to 1127th FAG, dated September 23, 1965, "Uncorrelated Reports Pertaining to Americans Missing in Southeast Asia, December, 1978," Volume 11, p. 128. The 15-volume Uncorrelated set was produced by DOD under pressure from the National League of Families to release all the intelligence reports on American POWs that it held but could not match to an individual. The massive volumes that were reproduced provided an insight into the vast amounts of intelligence collected during the war by U.S. intelligence. That so many reports could not be matched to a particular missing man shocked many people. These reports are hereafter referred to as "Uncorrelated."

54. "Circular," CDEC Bulletin #173, Log #02-1231-66.

55. "Release of RVNAF and American Prisoners," CDEC Bulletin #2982, Log #03-2045-67, is one example, noting that when Smith and McClure were released by the NLF they had "promised to explain the real situation of the Vietnam War, and would, with the American people, struggle for the end of the war."

Chapter 4

1. In 1982, the League of Families visited the cave area of northern Laos where the two purportedly were held. The League's Executive Director, Ann Mills-Griffiths, was shown a large bomb crater near the entrance to one of the caves. The Laotian official claimed that a U.S. bomb had destroyed the location of Shelton and Hrdlicka's grave site. The League noted that the Lao official's report was an obvious orchestration.

2. William Sullivan, *Obbligato* (W. W. Norton & Company, New York, 1984), p. 213.

3. The CIA strongly believed that the war in Laos should be controlled by the Agency, and it never hesitated to make this view known to the American military.

4. Telegram from AmEmbassy Vientiane to SecState, dated March 22, 1965, DDRS #894, 1989.

5. Telegram from AmEmbassy Vientiane to SecState, dated April 9, 1965, DDRS #2629, 1988.

6. Telegram from AmEmbassy Vientiane to SecState, dated May 13, 1965, LBJ Library, National Security file, Laos Country file, Folder April 1965, Document #139, Austin, TX. Hereafter referred to as "LBJ, Laos," followed by the document number.

7. Telegram from AmEmbassy Vientiane to SecState, dated April 23, 1965, LBJ, Laos, #154.

8. Telegram from AmEmbassy Vientiane to SecState, dated August 13, 1965, DDRS #2794, 1991.

9. Telegram from AmEmbassy Vientiane to SecState, dated May 1, 1965, LBJ, Laos, #150.

10. Telegram from AmEmbassy Vientiane to SecState, dated May 15, 1965, LBJ, Laos, #134.

11. Ibid. Klusmann had a similar interview, which would indicate that the PL leadership had a much greater role in POW processing than is recognized. Certainly one of their top-ranking military leaders, General Singkapo, had contact with Klusmann and Debruin. In 1967, the CIA reported that Shelton and Hrdlicka had also been seen being taken to Singkapo's house.

12. Lima Sites were a variety of installations in Laos, including communication facilities, airstrips, and small outposts.

13. Telegram from AmEmbassy Vientiane to SecState, dated May 18, 1965, DDRS #2790, 1992.

14. Telephone interview with Carol Hrdlicka, Wichita, KS, December 3, 1996.

15. Ibid.

16. Telegram from AmEmbassy Vientiane to SecState, dated April 23, 1965, LBJ, Laos, #155.

17. "Fate of POWs Eludes Truth," *The Press-Enterprise* (Riverside, CA), dated April 29, 1995, p. 1.

18. Telegram from AmEmbassy Vientiane to SecState, dated June 20, 1965, LBJ, Laos, #105.

19. Telegram from SecState to AmEmbassy Vientiane, dated June 10, 1965, NARA, State Laos files, Box 2428, Folder POW.

20. Telegram from AmEmbassy Vientiane to SecState, dated July 1, 1965, LBJ, Laos #175.

21. Telegram from AmEmbassy Vientiane to SecState, dated July 1, 1965, LBJ, Laos, #175.

22. Telegram from AmEmbassy Vientiane to SecState, dated August 13, 1965, NARA, State Laos files, Box 2428, Folder POWs.

23. "Pathet Lao [redacted] account of his witnessing the capture of two American pilots," CIA cable TDCS DB-315/04026-65, dated December 10, 1965, p. 2, MORI.

24. "Pathet Lao [redacted] subsequent account of his witnessing the interrogation of two American pilots," CIA cable TDCS DB-315/04216-65, dated December 28, 1965, p. 2, MORI.

25. "Pathet Lao [redacted] account of seeing American pilots in captivity in Houa Phan Province," CIA cable TDCS-314/00624-66, dated January 11, 1966, p. 1, MORI. Tham Sadet means "Comet Cave" in Lao.

26. "Information on captured United States Air Force pilots in Houa Phan Province," CIA cable TDCS-314/04249-66, dated March 29, 1966, p. 2, MORI.

27. "Subject: JCRC Report T85-300, Firsthand sighting of an American POW in Houaphan Province, Laos in 1966," From JCRC Liaison Bangkok to CDR JCRC Barbers Pt, HI, DTG 060858Z Nov 85.

28. "Establishment of a major Pathet Lao Political and Military Headquarters 12 Kilometers east of Sam Neua," CIA cable TDCS-314/04279-66, dated March 30, 1966, p. 3, Uncorrelated Volume 1, p. 009.

29. "Report from Defector of American Prisoners near Ban Na Kay in January 1966," CIA cable TDCS-314/11752-66, dated September 17, 1966, p. 2, MORI. The DIA analysis of this report states that "the identity of the third alleged prisoner by source cannot be determined."

30. "Fragmentary report of imprisoned American pilots and Pathet Lao Headquarters in the Sam Neua area of Houa Phan Province," CIA cable TDCS-314/10305-66, dated August 14, 1966, p. 3, MORI.

31. "Subject: [redacted]," CIA cable, dated November 9, 1966, MORI.

32. "American and Thai prisoners near Ban Na Kay in Houa Phan Province," CIA cable TDCS-314/14211-66, dated November 3, 1966, p. 2, MORI.

33. "Death of an American pilot held in Ban Na Kay and movement of the two other American pilots to a new location near the Lao/Vietnam Border," CIA cable TDCS-314/16404-66, dated December 20, 1966, p. 2, MORI.

34. Telegram from SecState to AmEmbassy Paris, dated August 21, 1965, NARA, State Laos files, Box 2428, Folder POW.

35. Telegram from AmEmbassy Vientiane to SecState, dated May 26, 1966.

36. Ibid., p. 2.

37. Hrdlicka interview.

38. "Subject: Possible Release of Detainee," from OSAF to CINCPACAF, dated May 26, 1966, p. 2. This document was provided to the author by Carol Hrdlicka. The message basically deals with how to provide information to the press on Hrdlicka if he was released. The Embassy's viewpoint that he was on a reconnaissance mission dominated.

39. "Memorandum of Conversation," Airgram A-329 from AmEmbassy Vientiane to SecState, dated June 3, 1966, Files of Frank Sieverts, Box 15.

40. "Captured Pilot on Radio in Laos," *New York Times,* August 4, 1966, p. 12, c. 5.

41. Telegram from AmEmbassy Vientiane to SecState, dated October 11, 1966, Files of Frank Sieverts, Box 15.

42. CAS Vientiane cable to CIA Director, cite IN 74235, dated August 11, 1966.

43. "Subject: [redacted]," CIA cable, dated November 9, 1966, MORI.

44. Testimony of Maj. Gen. Richard Secord, USAF (Ret.), before the Senate Select Committee on POW/MIA Affairs, September 24, 1992, p. 638.

45. Telephone interview with Maj. Gen. Richard Secord, USAF (Ret.), Fort Walton Beach, FL, December 12, 1996.

46. Letter from Casualty Branch, Randolph AFB, Texas, to 7th Air Force, dated November 1, 1966. Document supplied by Carol Hrdlicka.

47. Letter from 7th AF to Casualty Branch, dated November 9, 1966. Document supplied by Carol Hrdlicka.

48. Another odd item in the saga of rescuing the men in the caves comes from a senior USAF officer who recently wrote to Carol Hrdlicka concerning her husband David. The commanding officer at McConnell Air Force Base in Kansas when David was shot down was Colonel Carlos Dannacher. In May 1966 Dannacher was assigned as the Director of Operations at 7th AF in Saigon. One night in mid-January 1967 Dannacher received a phone call from Colonel John Singlaub, the commander of SOG. Dannacher and Singlaub had gone to the War College together and he was glad to hear from his old friend. Singlaub asked Dannacher to report to SOG immediately for something very urgent. Upon arriving, Dannacher was told that David Hrdlicka was about to come across the southernmost part of the Laotian border into South Vietnam the next morning. Dannacher asked what his role was. He was needed to positively identify Hrdlicka if it was really him. Later that night, a distraught Singlaub called Dannacher and told him the mission was delayed and to forget about it. While it seems impossible that Hrdlicka would have been marched several hundred miles through enemy country to the South Vietnamese border, the general time frame does fit with the CIA's botched bribe attempt.

49. "Subject: Status on Shelton, Charles E.," dated March 7, 1973.

50. "U.S. Flier Who Fled Prison Camp Tells of Ordeal," *New York Times,* dated September 14, 1966, p. 5, c. 3.

51. Dieter Dengler, *Escape from Laos* (Presidio Press, San Rafael, 1979).

52. William Leary, "Mahaxay: Secret Rescue in Laos," *Vietnam* (June 1995), p. 24.

53. "Freeing of Prisoners held in a Pathet Lao Prison in Khammouane Province," CIA cable TDCS-314/00482-67, dated January 10, 1967, MORI.

54. "Debriefing of Thai National imprisoned by Pathet Lao," CIA cable TDCS-314/00482-67, dated January 11, 1967, MORI.

55. Secord interview.

56. Maj. Gen. John K. Singlaub and Malcolm McConnell, *Hazardous Duty: An American Soldier in the Twentieth Century* (Summit Books, New York, 1992), pp. 310–311.

57. Telegram from AmEmbassy Vientiane to SecState, dated October 11, 1966, LOC PDS Reel 78.

Chapter 5

1. Telegram from SecState to AmEmbassy Saigon, dated December 15, 1965, LBJ, POW/MIA, #69, p. 2.

2. Telegram from SecState to AmEmbassy Saigon, dated November 24, 1965, DDRS #23e, 1977.

3. H. Fremen Matthews interview.

4. Telegram from AmEmbassy Saigon to SecState, dated September 1, 1966, Files of Frank Sieverts, Box 16.

5. Telegram from AmEmbassy Saigon to SecState, dated January 10, 1966, LBJ, POW/MIA, #150.

6. "Subject: U.S. Prisoner Exchanges," Memorandum for McGeorge Bundy by Benjamin Read, Executive Secretary, January 17, 1966, LBJ, POW/MIA, #131.

7. Ibid., quoting Mr. Gottlieb.

8. "Memorandum of Telephone Conversation, Subject: ICRC rep de Heller meeting with NLF rep Tam," from Abba Schwartz, dated January 21, 1966, LBJ, POW/MIA, #127.

9. Ibid.

10. "Subject: Prisoner Exchange with the NLF," Memorandum of Telephone Conversation, from Abba Schwartz, dated January 26, 1966, LBJ, POW/MIA, #126a.

11. Telegram from SecState to White House, dated January 20, 1966, LBJ, POW/MIA, #15.

12. Telegram from SecState to AmEmbassy Saigon, dated January 20, 1966, LBJ, POW/MIA, #151.

13. Telegram from AmEmbassy Saigon to SecState, dated January 21, 1966, LBJ, POW/MIA, #142.

14. Telegram from SecState to White House, dated January 20, 1966, LBJ, POW/MIA, #14.

15. Craig R. Whitney, *Spy Trader: Germany's Devil's Advocate and the Darkest Secrets of the Cold War* (Times Books, New York, 1993), p. 341.

16. Telegram from AmEmbassy Saigon to SecState, dated March 4, 1966, LBJ, POW/MIA, #52.

17. "U.S. Aides Confirm Bids to Repatriate Captive of Vietcong," *New York Times*, March 28, 1966, p. 2, c. 5, and May 4, 1966, p. 3, c. 1.

18. Telegram from AmEmbassy Vientiane to SecState, dated May 20, 1966, POW/MIA, #53.

19. "Subject: Current efforts to assist U.S. Prisoners in Viet-Nam," Memorandum for Walt Rostow, dated June 23, 1966, LBJ, POW/MIA, #144a.

20. Telegram from AmEmbassy London to SecState, dated July 18, 1966, LBJ, POW/MIA, #4.

21. SpeCat [Special Category] Exclusive from CINCPAC to JCS, 150411Z July 66, LBJ, POW/MIA, #83.

22. Telegram from AmEmbassy Saigon to SecState, dated July 25, 1996, Files of Frank Sieverts, Box 16.

23. "Some Experiences on the Capture, Evacuation, Handling and Indoctrination of US Prisoners," CDEC Log #6-2654-67, DOD IIR 6-027-0219-67.

24. "Assertion that many captured American pilots are willing to stay in North Vietnam and may be used to train North Vietnamese pilots," CIA cable TDCS-314/06263-66, dated May 18, 1966, MORI.

25. "Hanoi Called Fair to Captive Fliers," *New York Times,* October 12, 1966, p. 3. c. 4.

26. Telegram from Amembassy Paris to SecState, dated November 22, 1966, LOC PDS Reel 78.

27. Jim and Sybil Stockdale, *In Love and War* (Harper & Row, New York, 1984), pp. 194–195.

28. Interview with Cdr. Robert Boroughs, USN (Ret.), Annandale, VA, January 11, 1997.

29. "3 Navy Officers, Believed Dead, Now Listed as Captives," *New York Times,* February 4, 1967, p. 10, c. 2.

30. Telephone interview with Colonel Robert Work, USAF (Ret.), Saratoga, CA, January 14, 1997.

31. Jim and Sybil Stockdale, *In Love and War,* p. 159.

32. Interview with Claude Watkins, Reston, VA, May 23, 1995.

33. Letter from Edward Alan Brudno to Mrs. Edward Alan Brudno, dated November 30, 1966. The author wishes to thank Mrs. Brudno for sharing her husband's wartime letters with him. This particular letter is filled with obscure references that Mrs. Brudno doesn't understand, nor did Watkins' group ever decipher all of them.

34. Letter from Edward Alan Brudno to Mrs. Edward Alan Brudno, dated July 15, 1966. Letter supplied to the author by Mrs. Edward Alan Brudno.,

35. "U.S. Units Sweep Jungle—Overran a Prison Camp," *New York Times,* February 23, 1966, p. 8, c. 5.

36. "Foe Kills 12 Prisoners," *New York Times,* October 12, p. 3, c. 5.

37. Charles McDonald, "The Phu Yen Prison Raid," *Behind the Lines* (March/April 1995), p. 20.

38. Daily 1/327th S-3 Staff Journal, 101st Airborne Division, RG 472, NARA, College Park, MD, p. 3.

39. Telephone interview with Charles McDonald, Pittsburgh, PA, December 12, 1966. Mr. McDonald brought the information, including the location of the camp with the graveyard, to the U.S. government in the mid-1980s. He was assigned source number 2920. There is no information in the source file as to whether the JCRC/JTF-FA has ever attempted a remains recovery at the location of the camp.

Chapter 6

1. "Memorandum for the Assistant Secretary of Defense, International Security Affairs," DJSM-500-66, dated April 19, 1966, LOC PDS Reel 61, Folder JCS Intel file, Washington, DC.

2. Ibid., p. 3.

3. Memorandum for: [redacted], Subject: U.S. POW Project, dated September 2, 1966. This document was found in the unindexed 200-plus volumes of POW/MIA material housed by the CIA FOIA office. This document is numbered 02886. The emphasis is in the original. This huge volume of material is hereafter referred to as "Unindexed."

4. Memorandum for the Assistant Vice Chief of Staff of the Air Force, dated May 27, 1966.

5. Telephone interview with Colonel Barney Cochran, USAF (Ret.), Fort Walton Beach, FL, December 11, 1996.

6. "Meeting of the Study Group on Prisoners and Detainees—24 Mar 66," Uncorrelated Volume 11, p. 125.

7. Interview with Brigadier General Heinie Aderholt, USAF (Ret.), Fort Walton Beach, FL, December 17, 1996.

8. Interview with Major General John Singlaub, USA (Ret.), Arlington, VA, March 15, 1995.

9. "Personnel Recovery Center," from CINCPAC to COMUSMACV, dated April 27, 1966. This document was obtained through FOIA from an index of JCS POW/MIA documents created during the Senate Select Committee hearings and provided to the author by the DOD FOIA office.

10. 1966 MACV *Command History,* Annex A, p. 682.

11. Ibid.

12. Telephone interview with Lieutenant Colonel Lester Hansen, USAF (Ret.), Bonita Springs, FL, February 20, 1995.

13. "Proposed Terms of Reference, Joint Personnel Recovery Center," from CINCPAC to COMUSMACV, dated August 16, 1966.

14. "Subj: JPRC Terms of Reference," from JCS to CINCPAC, dated September 1, 1966.

15. "Subj: Status of JPRC," from COMUSMACV to CINCPAC, dated September 21, 1966, JCS index.

16. Telephone interview with Lt. Col. Charles Boatwright, USA (Ret.), Reno, NV, December 6, 1996.

17. "Subject: Status of JPRC," from CDR, MACSOG to JCS, DTG 260201Z Aug 66.

18. CINCPAC messages 230045Z Oct 66 and 1223020Z Nov 66 provided guidance on the suspense and formatting requirements.

19. 1966 MACV *Command History,* SOG Special Annex, Appendix V, Joint Personnel Recovery Center (JPRC), p. 105, LOC PDS Reel 61, Folder JCS Intel, Washington, DC. Waggoner was a returnee at *Homecoming.*

20. Telephone interview with Robert Deane Woods, Grainger, IN, December 19, 1996.

21. Meadows was one of the most accomplished Special Forces operators of the war. He would eventually help lead the famous raid on Son Tay in November 1970.

22. The JPRC section to the SOG Annex of the MACV *Command History* provides a different version. The reason for the delay is given as "bad weather." Additionally, the dates for the JPRC operation are incorrect by two days. Woods' and Hansen's accounts agree in terms of timing and sequence. Years later, Woods met Dick Meadows, the leader of Team *Ohio.* Oddly, whoever did the declassification for the SOG annex apparently believed that acknowledging that Woods was in North Vietnam was still a serious violation of the national security of the United States, and so blacked out that portion. Also redacted was the mention of the U.S. Embassy in Laos in the subsection on *Commando 01.* We are fortunate to have such vigilant censors guarding our national secrets.

23. Singlaub, *Hazardous Duty,* p. 308.

24. 1966 MACV *Command History,* SOG Special Annex, Appendix V, Joint Personnel Recovery Center (JPRC), pp. 105–106, LOC PDS Reel 61, Folder JCS Intel, Washington, DC.

25. Hansen is positive that the team arrived at the carrier on the night when Woods went down. The *Command History* relates that it wasn't until October 14 that the JPRC was even notified, and not until October 16 that the team was sent in. It seems odd that a team would have been sent in if voice contact had been lost for two days. Woods believes that the team wasn't inserted until after he was captured, but is unable to pinpoint exactly when. If Hansen's version is correct, the team was

placed on the ground shortly after Woods was captured. If they had gone in on October 13, Robert Woods would not have spent the next five-plus years as a guest in Hanoi.

26. The PMSEA spells the crew chief's name as Piittmann, while documents from the time list it as Pittman.

27. "Subject: U.S. Personnel captured in Laos—Airman Pittman," no date. This document was a memorandum relaying the contents of the CIA Operational Report providing the details of the search for Pittman.

28. "Subj: Status of JPRC," from COMUSMACV to CINCPAC, DTG 130821Z September 1966.

29. From the Introduction to the PACOM Selected Area For Evasion Brief, dated January 1970.

30. "Subj: Bright Light report for period 2–8 Jan 67," from COMUSMACV to CINCPAC. Hereafter referred to as "Bright Light report for period."

31. Bright Light report for period 26 Dec 66–1 Jan 67, p. 2.

32. Bright Light report for period 23–29 Jan 67, p. 2.

33. Several senior cadres Bell interviewed, including Sr. Col. Pham Van Ban, Deputy of COSVN's Enemy Proselytizing Section, indicated that the United States and the COSVN Military Proselytizing Section secretly traded one American prisoner in 1970. When Bell tried to follow up on this report, JTF-FA told him they had no information in their files.

34. "Subj: Bright Light," from COMUSMACV to CINCPAC, DTG 150707Z Oct 66, p. 2. This was the first JPRC Bright Light update sent.

35. "Subj: Bright Light Report for the period of 30 Jan–5 Feb 67," pp. 1, 2. The author was unable to locate the complete set of JPRC reports, although he was able to put together 82 percent of them. The majority of those missing are from the early years, especially 1967. The weekly reporting format continued until the end of 1969, when the JPRC changed to a monthly format. Almost all the weeklies were less than five pages in length, while the length of the monthlies varied considerably.

36. 1967 MACV *Command History,* SOG Special Annex G, Appendix V, p. G-V-11, LOC PDS Reel 61, JCS Intel file, Washington, DC.

37. Boatwright interview.

38. This account was provided to the author by Lester Hansen, who at the request of General Aderholt several years earlier had written a detailed first-person report of his involvement in *Cobra Tail.* The author wishes to thank Mr. Hansen for generously sharing this document.

39. Singlaub, *Hazardous Duty,* p. 307.

40. Telephone interview with Lt. Col. Fred Caristo, USA (Ret.), Arlington, VA, December 12, 1996.

41. Citation for Distinguished Service Cross for Major Frederic J. C. Caristo, United States Army. Document provided by Fred Caristo.

42. Bright Light report for period 26 Dec–1 Jan 67, p. 2.

43. In a 1970 interrogation report, CMIC IIR 6 029 0004 70, a defecting NVA officer who was present at Ortiz-Rivera's capture, relates how the source, a Sr. Lt. in charge of the telephone communications section of the NVA 22nd Regiment, described the incident. The NVA officer said that the 9th Bn of the NVA 22nd Regiment had attacked and overrun a bunker containing one Caucasian and one "Negro." The "Negro" was sleeping when the NVA burst into the bunker. The NVA ordered them to follow the enemy back toward their base camp. The Caucasian refused and was shot and killed. Ortiz-Rivera dressed quickly and was moved back to the Regimental CP, where he was turned over to the Enemy Proselytizing officer. By the day of the raid, January 2, he was already

at the NVA 3rd Division Hqs. Eventually, he was sent to the MR-5 U.S. POW camp, where he was held with Garwood and others.

44. For Kline's account of his rescue, see PACAF Evasion and Recovery Report No. 76, LOC PDS Reel 84.

45. Aderholt relates that when Momyer found out he was going to take over the AF commando wing, he called Aderholt and asked him to stay, saying he was more valuable where he was because he was representing Air Force interests at SOG. According to Aderholt, Momyer hated the commandos and wanted an all-jet fighter force, but Aderholt had no desire to continue working with an Army task force like SOG; he felt his talents lay with the Air Commandos.

Chapter 7

1. The author finally located and briefly spoke with Rod Foster on July 11, 1996. A veteran of two tours on aircraft carriers who had logged over 18,000 hours in airplanes, Rod Foster was deeply involved in organizing the Escape and Evasion Kits that the JPRC produced to be deployed by aircraft to downed fliers. In addition, he professionally represented the Navy while assigned to the JPRC and was instrumental in arranging the desperate attempts to recover several downed Navy fliers in the spring of 1967. In a tragic twist of fate, Foster an airline pilot, was a passenger aboard the ill-fated TWA Flight 800, which went down off Long Island, New York, on July 17, 1996. There were no survivors.

2. "Reward Offered for U.S. Fliers," *New York Times,* January 16, 1967, p. 1, c. 3.

3. 1967 MACV *Command History,* SOG Annex G, JPRC Appendix V, p. G-V-13.

4. Tape of radio conversations supplied by Red McDaniel to George Patterson. The author would like to thank Mr. Patterson for providing a copy of this transcript.

5. Interview with George Patterson, Orange, CA, September 5, 1995.

6. Statement of Lt. JG Carpenter, September 5, 1967. Document supplied by George Patterson. Carpenter would also be shot down late in the war and is currently listed as MIA.

7. Ibid.

8. The Vietnamese returned Patterson's ID card in 1985 in pristine condition. According to them, he had been shot and killed by the militia during his capture. In a JTF-FA interview with the man who shot Patterson, he claimed that when he saw the American, the man reached around behind him as if searching for a gun. The Vietnamese then shot and killed Patterson. The Vietnamese have supplied different locations for his purported grave site, stating at first that wild pigs dug it up and later that the rains washed away the grave site. Even the U.S. government was skeptical. Summarizing Patterson's loss, DIA wrote that in "numerous recent reports the Vietnamese have stated graves containing remains of U.S. personnel have been destroyed by wild beasts, natural calamities, reforming of the terrain, and U.S. bombing. The mounting incidence of such alleged loss of graves borders on the incredible."

9. Bright Light report for period 17–23 July 1967, p. 2.

10. DPMO correlated this report to Hartmann, although Bell believes that it was probably one of the helicopter crewmen. Bell cites two reasons; when the JTF-FA excavated the helicopter crash, they could find remains of only three of the four crewmen. Second, the presence of bandages running from the unknown pilot's knees to his chest suggests burns, rather than a leg wound. Since Vietnam has returned Hartmann's remains, DPMO is not pursuing what really happened to him.

11. "G.I.'s Rescue 51 Vietnamese from Jungle Prison," *New York Times,* February 11, 1967, p. 3, c. 5.

12. 1967 *Command History,* p. G-V-2.

13. Letter from Les Hansen to the author, dated January 15, 1997.

14. Bright Light report for period 17–23 July 67, p. 1.

15. Bright Light report for period 29 Jan–5 Feb 67, p. 4.

16. Telegram from SecState to AmEmbassy Saigon, dated January 26, 1967, Files of Frank Sieverts, Box 13.

17. Telegram from AmEmbassy Saigon to SecState, dated January 30, 1967, Files of Frank Sieverts, Box 13.

18. "Subject: Efforts to Bring about Viet Nam POW *de facto* Exchange," Memo to Governor Harriman, dated March 2, 1967, Files of Frank Sieverts, Box 12. Emphasis in the original.

19. "Memorandum for Governor Harriman," dated April 4, 1967, Files of Frank Sieverts, Box 12.

20. Telegram from AmEmbassy Saigon to SecState, n.d., Files of Frank Sieverts, Box 15.

21. Ibid.

22. "Subject: Recap of JPRC records concerning Douglas K. Ramsey, FSO, USOM Hau Nghia Province, RVN," Case file of Douglas Ramsey, REFNO 0234, LOC FRD Reel 212, p. 41.

23. Telephone interview with Charles Crafts, Livermore, ME, February 18, 1997.

24. Bright Light report for period 6–12 March 67, p. 3.

25. "Memorandum for Governor Harriman," dated April 4, 1967, Files of Frank Sieverts, Box 22.

26. 1967 MACV *Command History,* SOG Annex G, JPRC Appendix V, p. G-V-1.

27. OPLAN Liberty Blackjack, HQ, 5th Special Forces Group. This document was supplied by Steve Sherman of Radix Press, Houston, TX.

28. Ibid.

29. Telegram from AmEmbassy Saigon to SecState, dated April 7, 1967, Files of Frank Sieverts, Box 11.

30. Telegram from SecState to AmEmbassy Saigon, dated April 27, 1967, DDRS #2673, 1993.

31. "Communist attempts at propaganda exploitation of prisoners of war (POW's) in Vietnam," CIA Working Paper dated June, 1967, CIA unindexed files, Vol. 211, p. 19376.

32. 1967 MACV *Command History,* Volume II, *Prisoners of War,* p. 971, quoting Harriman's letter.

33. Telegram from SecState to AmEmbassy Saigon, dated April 8, 1967, Files of Frank Sieverts, Box 22.

34. "Subject: Indications of Impending North Vietnamese Psychological Offensive," dated March 13, 1967, from Edwin Buchanan, Chairman, Interagency POW Intelligence Group. Buchanan was a CIA officer.

35. *New York Times,* April 17, 1967, p. 13, c. 1.

36. "February 1967 Monthly Report—[Redacted] POW Working Group," CIA unindexed files, Vol. 211, p. 12036.

37. Ibid.

38. "Supplement to Monthly Report, 26 March–25 April 1967," CIA unindexed files, Vol. 207, p. 3068.

39. [Redacted] Contribution to Monthly Report, 26 April–25 May 1967," CIA unindexed files, Vol. 207, p. 3171.

40. Ibid, p. 2.

41. [Redacted] Contribution to Monthly Report, 26 April–25 May 1967," CIA unindexed files, Vol. 207, p. 3171.

42. "Terms of Reference for IPWIC," dated October 23, 1967, LOC PDS Reel 520, Folder Misc. IPWIC material.

43. Telephone interview with Colonel Rudy Koller, USAF (Ret.), Walnut Creek, CA, August 25, 1995.

44. Interview with a confidential source, Arlington, VA, June 12, 1995.

45. "The 500th U.S. Aircraft Downed in Central and Lower Laos," *Vietnam Courier,* #109, May 8, 1967, Indochina Archive, Lao files for May 1967.

46. "Limitations on Military Actions in Laos," Memorandum to William Bundy from Ambassador William H. Sullivan, DDRS #2821, 1995, p. 3.

47. Airgram from SecState to US Mission Geneva, dated August 11, 1967, LBJ, POW/MIA, #82.

48. Uncorrelated Reports, Volume 1, p. 464.

49. "Visit of Souphanouvong to three Americans held in a cave on the Houei Vong in Houa Phan Province," CIA cable TDCS-314/05071-67, dated April 8, 1967, MORI.

50. "Presence of three rather than two American pilots prisoners near the Nam Sim east of Sam Neua," CIA cable CS-311/05019-67, dated April 27, 1967, MORI.

51. "Location in relation to Ban Kang Muong of cave on Houei Vong where American pilots are held; visits by the pilots to Ban Kang Moung," CIA cable [redacted], dated May 1, 1967, MORI.

52. "Death of an American flier in Houa Phan Province and use of American prisoners for propaganda purposes," CIA cable TDCS DB-315/01734-67, dated May 24, 1967, MORI.

53. "Two American pilots held captive in Khang Khay, Xieng Khouang Province, in May 1965," CIA cable TDCS-314/05325-67, dated April 13, 1967, MORI.

54. "Capture of four American pilots near Ban Hang Long in Houa Phan Province in January 1966," CIA cable TDCS-314/17426-67, dated November 28, 1967, MORI.

55. "Enemy prisons in Laos," CIA cable CS-311/10503-67, dated October 5, 1967, MORI.

56. "PW Intelligence Highlights for the month ended Friday, 25 August 1967," CIA unindexed files, Vol. 211, p. 03252.

57. Telegram from AmEmbassy Vientiane to SecState, dated November 6, 1967, LBJ, POW/MIA #28.

58. Excerpt from document summarizing message traffic, Liberation Radio broadcast of June 15th, Case file of Gustav Hertz, REFNO 0052, LOC FRD Reel 214, p. 13.

59. "Enemy in Vietnam Hints at Execution," *New York Times,* June 28, 1967, p. 2, c. 5.

60. Telegram from SecState to AmEmbassy Saigon, dated June 19, 1967, Files of Frank Sieverts, Box 23.

61. Excerpt from document summarizing message traffic, Liberation Radio broadcast of June 15th, Case file of Gustav Hertz, REFNO 0052, LOC FRD Reel 214, p. 13.

62. "White House Plea Sent to Vietcong," *New York Times,* July 18, 1967, p. 1, c. 1.

63. Telegram from SecState to AmEmbassy Saigon, dated July 3, 1967, Files of Frank Sieverts, Box 23.

64. Truong Nhu Tang, *A Vietcong Memoir* (Harcourt, Brace, Jovanovich, Orlando, FL, 1985), p. 103.

65. "Hertz Reported Dead," *New York Times,* November 8, 1967, p. 11, c. 1. The 1995 unilateral Vietnamese investigation into Hertz's death indicates he was actually held in the COSVN Security camp as opposed to a military-controlled camp. The document states, "The zone security prison camp primarily held puppet prisoners. But during the years 1964–1968 it held two American and one Englishman (Wallis), suspecting them of intelligence operations. One American by the name of 'Hot' was stricken with malaria and died. . . . Conclude investigations no remains can be found."

66. Frank Snepp, *Decent Interval* (Random House, New York, 1977), p. 32.

67. From Ambassador Bunker to the White House via the CIA, dated November 29, 1967, LBJ, POW/MIA #33c.

68. Telegram from AmEmbassy to SecState, dated December 6, 1967, Files of Frank Sieverts, Box 12.

69. "Background Data Possibly Relevant to the Current Vietnamese Communist Prisoner Exchange Overture," Memo from Richard Helms, Dir., CIA, to Dr. Henry A. Kissinger, dated October 29, 1971, JCS files, CIA folder, Box 3.

70. Telegram from SecState to AmEmbassy Saigon, dated February 7, 1968, Files of Frank Sieverts, Box 5.

71. Truong Nhu Tang, *A Vietcong Memoir,* pp. 1123–128.

Chapter 8

1. Telephone interview with Col. Horace "Jack" Reisner, USAF (Ret.), Roseville, CA, January 16, 1995. After Reisner left the JPRC in 1968, he spent three years at PACAF running the E&E shop and was instrumental in producing the PACAF book on missing Air Force personnel. In 1982, Reisner wrote a fictional account of his days in the JPRC entitled *The Last Hope,* published by Mead Press, Honolulu, HI. The novel uses many of the true-life incidents that occurred while he was Chief, JPRC. Despite its fictional disclaimer, it presents a fairly accurate and often funny portrayal of the personalities and events that happened on his watch.

2. "Memorandum for the Record," dated September 14, 1967, CIA unindexed files, Volume 187, n.p. Unfortunately, the CIA heavily redacted most of this three-page memo, thus denying the reader insight into a critical period in the JPRC's history.

3. *"Attachment A,* DIA Questions for JPRC," CIA unindexed files, Vol. 187, n.p. Emphasis in original.

4. Telephone interview with Colonel Charles Ogle, USA (Ret.), Tampa, FL, December 6, 1995.

5. Telephone interview with Colonel David McNabb, USAF (Ret.), Tampa, FL, March 18, 1995.

6. Letter from Edward Alan Brudno to Mrs. Edward Alan Brudno dated July 15, 1966.

7. Telegram from AmEmbassy Saigon to SecState, dated July 28, 1967, Files of Frank Sieverts, Box 22.

8. Telegram from AmEmbassy Saigon to SecState, dated August 10, 1967, Files of Frank Sieverts, Box 22.

9. Telegram from SecState to AmEmbassy Saigon, dated August 18, 1967, Files of Frank Sieverts, Box 22.

10. Bright Light report for period 1–7 January 1968, p. 1.

11. "Fate of U.S. POWs held at B-3 Front," n.d. Document provided to author by Bill Bell.

12. Bright Light report for period 24–30 July 1967, p. 1.

13. Telegram from AmEmbassy Saigon to SecState, dated July 13, 1967, Files of Frank Sieverts, Box 26.

14. 1967 MACV *Command History,* JPRC Appendix V, p. G-V-11.

15. Bright Light report for period 7–13 November 1967, p. 1.

16. "Viet Cong permission to release American Negro Prisoners in Phnom Penh for the sake of international publicity," CIA cable [redacted], dated November 9, 1967, MORI database.

17. "3 U.S. PW's Not Brainwashed, U.S. Says," *New York Times,* dated November 18, 1967, p. 3, c. 2.

18. Telegram from AmEmbassy Saigon to SecState, dated November 11, 1967, Files of Frank Sieverts, Box 9.

19. "Monthly Report, 26 Nov–25 Dec 67," CIA unindexed files, Vol. 211, p. 03336. The sys-

tem before MORI was called ORIS, Officially Released Information System. A note was stapled on the monthly reports which reads, "Please do not put into ORIS system." The CIA, although it had declassified this material, was obviously trying to limit its distribution.

20. Bright Light report for period 5–11 December 1967, p. 5.

21. MACV J-3 Daily Journals, dated January 9, 1968, Item #56, NARA, College Park, MD.

22. Upon his return, Anderson wrote an article for *Parade* magazine in which he claimed to have left his guard post because he was told by some Vietnamese kids that a young girl had been hurt in a fall from a coconut tree. *Parade,* March 10, 1968, pp. 9–10.

23. Interview with Lt. Col. Frederic Seamon, USA (Ret.), San Jose, CA, December 13, 1994. The pilot was Capt. Robin K. Miller of the 114th Assault Helicopter Company, based in Vinh Long.

24. NSA SIGINT Spot Report, LOC FRD Reel 268, Folder 1967. The NSA released approximately 4,000 intercepted enemy communications from the war. They were microfilmed together on reels 268–271.

25. Telephone interview with Lt. Col. John Alison, USAF (Ret.), Niceville, FL, February 21, 1997.

26. Bright Light report for period 27 Feb–5 Mar 68, p. 2.

27. From COMUSMACV to AmEmbassy Vientiane, dated March 19, 1968, case file of John Hartzheim, REFNO 1062, LOC FRD Reel 113, Washington, DC.

28. Fax dated September 20, 1995, from confidential DPMO source to author. Document in author's possession.

29. Bright Light report for period 6–12 Feb 67, p. 2.

30. Bright Light report for period 20–26 Feb 67, p. 2.

31. Interview with Mike Benge, Falls Church, VA, January 30, 1997.

32. Bright Light report for period 10–16 April 68, pp. 1, 2.

33. Bright Light report for period 29 May–4 June 68, pp. 1, 2.

34. For his heroic efforts at rescuing eleven Americans during the Ban Me Thuot battle plus another dozen Vietnamese and Montagnards, Benge was presented the State Department's highest award for valor. He continues to work today at USAID helping refugees in Southeast Asia.

Chapter 9

1. Bright Light report for period 23–30 January 1968, pp. 1, 2.

2. "Monthly Report, 26 January to 25 February 1968," CIA unindexed files, Vol. 211, p. 03661.

3. Minutes of IPWIC meeting, dated February 23, 1968, p. 1, LOC FRD Reel 520. All IPWIC minutes are located on Reel 520.

4. Minutes of IPWIC meeting, dated April 12, 1968, p. 3.

5. 1968 MACV *Command History,* Prisoners of War Section, p. 842, quoting Hanoi radio.

6. Telegram from AmEmbassy Vientiane to SecState, dated February 16, 1968, LBJ, POW/MIA #66.

7. Bright Light report for period 20–26 Feb 68, p. 3.

8. "Monthly Report, 26 January to 25 February 1968," CIA unindexed files, Vol. 211, p. 03661.

9. Telegram from AmEmbassy Vientiane to SecState, dated February 18, 1968, Files of Frank Sieverts, Box 22.

10. "VC Collection of personnel items of U.S. dead and wounded to forward to U.S. anti-war organizations," CDEC Bulletin #5210, Log #06-1632-67.

11. "Memorandum concerning fair treatment to be given to foreign captives," CDEC Bulletin #369, Log #04-1430-66.

12. Telephone interview with Col. Ted Guy, USAF (Ret.), Sunrise Beach, MO, August 24, 1996.

13. 1968 MACV *Command History,* Prisoners of War Section, p. 844.

14. "Peace Workers Tell of Delay in 3 Pilots' Return," *New York Times,* August 6, 1968, p. 2, c. 4, quoting Mrs. Scheer.

15. "Freed U.S. Pilots remain in Hanoi," *New York Times,* July 27, 1968, p. 8, c. 3.

16. "3 Captured U.S. Pilots Freed in Ceremony in Hanoi," *New York Times,* July 19, 1968, p. 3, c. 5, quoting Captain Carpenter.

17. "VC Committee for Solidarity with People of the United States," CDEC Bulletin #8646, Log #12-2664-67.

18. U.S. Department of State, Director of Intelligence and Research Intelligence Note, dated October 20, 1967, Files of Averell Harriman, Box 4, Folder Releases, NARA, College Park, MD.

19. "Subject: Pilot Interrogation," from AIRA Vientiane to CSA, DTG 030950Z Aug 68, LBJ, POW/MIA, #113.

20. Minutes of IPWIC meeting, dated August 16, 1968, p. 2.

21. "Toan Dan Thi Dua Lam Cong Tac Binh Van" (All People Emulate the Work of Proselytizing the Troops), undated, journal unknown, National Liberation Front document, Indochina Archive.

22. "Monthly Report, 26 January to 25 February 1968," CIA unindexed files, Vol. 211, p. 03661.

23. Statement of Donald E. Martin, Ireland Army Hospital, Fort Knox, KY, 30 April 1968, p. 21.

24. Bright Light report for period 10–16 April 68, p. 3. Although Dunn returned at *Homecoming,* Ray apparently died in captivity. At the end of March, the ARVN 23rd Ranger Battalion conducted a raid looking for the pair but found nothing.

25. "Subj: Debriefing of Sgt. Albert Potter and Cpl. Frank Iodice," From CG TF X-Ray to CO-MUSMACV, DTG 051827 Jul 68.

26. Bright Light report for period 29 May–4 June 68, p. 3.

27. Bright Light report for period 17–23 April 1968, pp. 2, 3.

28. "Summary and Location report," Chief of Station, Vietnam, April 6, 1968, CIA unindexed files, Vol. 156, p. 17519.

29. "NSA's Mission Statement," World Wide Web site of the National Security Agency, October 23, 1996.

30. The title of this report is redacted, but it is dated July 12, 1968, and it can be found on LOC FRD Reel 373. The entire reel, along with 374 and 375, contains a wealth of NSA wartime and post-wartime material.

31. Bright Light report for period 5–11 June 1968, p. 2.

32. "Subject: JPRC—U.S. POW's and MIA in Laos." The date of this internal memo is unclear. A typed date at the bottom says 3 September 1968, and a handwritten note at the top says 2 July 1968.

33. "Subject: [redacted]," CIA cable from COS Vientiane and COS Saigon to [redacted], dated August 1, 1968, CIA unindexed files, Vol. 176, p. 3943.

34. "Subj: Verification of POW sites," Memorandum for the Chairman, JCS, dated September 26, 1968, RG 46, Files of the Senate Select Committee on POW/MIA Affairs, JCS files, Box 2.

35. "American, Thai, and Philippine prisoners of War held in Laos—Locations of four

Enemy Prisons in South Laos," CIA cable TDCS-315/04550-68, dated December 6, 1968, MORI. A corrected copy of this cable indicated that fifteen Americans were being held by the Pathet Lao.

36. Captain Edward Valentiny, USAF, *The Fall of Site 85,* Project CHECO Report, August 9, 1968, p. viii.

37. Telegram from AmEmbassy Vientiane to SecState, dated December 28, 1967, LBJ, Laos, #69.

38. "Subject: Significance of Phu Pha Thi (Site 85) in Northeastern Laos," Memo to the Secretary of State, DDRS, #3482, 1995.

39. "Subj: Interview with LTC Truong Muc, Leader of Attack on Lima Site 85—Case 2052," DTG 250902Z Oct 94, from Cdr JTF-FA to SecDef Washington.

40. Telegram from AmEmbassy Vientiane to SecState, dated March 13, 1968, LBJ, Laos, #60.

41. Telegram from SecState to AmEmbassy Vientiane, dated March 19, 1968, LBJ, Laos, #93.

42. Telegram from AmEmbassy Vientiane to SecState, dated March 19, 1968, LBJ, Laos, #58.

43. This document is the result of the debriefing of the source by an Army interrogation team that had been assigned to Laos in 1971. The author wishes to thank Mrs. Ann Holland, who kindly supplied a copy.

44. "Monthly report, dated 26 December 1972–25 January 1973," CIA unindexed files, Vol. 228, p. 23098.

45. Dr. Timothy N. Castle, *At War in the Shadow of Vietnam: U.S. Military Aid to the Royal Lao Government 1955–1975* (Columbia University Press, New York, 1993), p. 97. Intrigued by Singkapo's revelation, Dr. Castle is engaged in a thorough study of the loss of the radar site. His book on the fall of Site 85 will be published by Columbia University Press.

46. Summary Report of 95-2L Joint Field Activity in Laos, 4 Dec–20 Dec 94.

47. "Lao Company 18 to disinter the remains of Americans killed at Phou Pha Thi," DTG 071949Z Jun 77, NSA SIGINT Spot Report, LOC PDS, Reel 271, Folder 1977. In the NSA, message summaries are known as "Spot Reports," or "Product Reports." When quotation marks appear around words it indicates a direct quote of the speaker. The word "probable" is deliberately used in NSA reports because they are forbidden by what are called Technical Instructions, created by the State Department, from making statements of fact. Therefore, while an outside reader unfamiliar with NSA instructions would normally assign caution to an evaluation of this message because of the use of the word probable, in fact it is done intentionally. The origin and purpose of Office 208 remains a mystery.

48. "Lao People's Liberation Army to Disinter remains of Americans killed in Laos," DTG 071939Z Jun 77, NSA SIGINT Product Report, LOC FRD Reel 375, Folder 1977.

49. Letter from Mrs. Ann Holland to the author, dated October 6, 1994.

50. Telegram from AmEmbassy Saigon to SecState, dated December 19, 1968, LBJ, POW/MIA, #69.

51. Minutes of IPWIC meeting, dated September 20, 1968, p. 1.

52. Col. Douglas Moore, "Face-off in the Jungle: And Three came Home," *ARMY* (March, 1982), p. 26, quoting Harriman. Colonel Moore piloted the Medevac helicopter that eventually flew the three POWs back to Saigon. His article is an excellent summation of the meeting and of Colonel Gibney's reactions and impressions of the affair.

53. Ibid., p. 28.

54. Telegram from AmEmbassy Saigon to SecState, dated December 26, 1968, LBJ, POW/MIA, #59.

55. Telegram from AmEmbassy Saigon to SecState, dated December 26, 1968, LBJ, POW/MIA, #56.

56. Telegram from AmEmbassy Saigon to SecState, dated December 28, 1968, LBJ, POW/MIA, #55.

57. "US PW Interrogation Reports by Element of Sub-Region (SR) 5 Party Committee, COSVN," CDEC Bulletin #19,018, Log #12-2191-68, fully translated under DOD IIR 6-029-3050-68.

58. "Opinion of PW Release," CMIC IIR 6-029-0100-69.

59. This information was taken from Oral History interviews with Nguyen Hung Tri and Pham Van Ban. Tuoi defected from Vietnam in 1979 and was interviewed in Malaysia. At the time of his interview in December 1992, Tri was a senior officer in Vietnam's National Petroleum Import-Export Corporation.

Chapter 10

1. "Vietnamese, Ex-Prisoners of Vietcong, Describe Starvation, Brutality and Terror of B-52's," *New York Times,* January 9, 1969, p. 10. The news article recounts the experiences of two Vietnamese prisoners who escaped during the continued ARVN raids into the U-Minh Forest in the days following Rowe's escape.

2. Telegram from AmEmbassy Paris to SecState, dated January 16, 1969, LBJ, White House POW/MIA files, #6.

3. Telegram from AmEmbassy Paris to SecState, dated January 19, 1969, DDRS #2713, 1996.

4. Reisner remained there until his retirement in 1970. He was instrumental in creating the PACAF Missing in Action book, a listing of all Air Force MIA's. This book can be seen on LOC PDS Reel 464.

5. Telephone interview with Colonel Robert Bradshaw, USAF (Ret.), Dunedin, FL, June 27, 1995.

6. Telephone interview with John Mitchell, Springfield, VA, April 19, 1995.

7. "Subject: US POWs in Laos," from COS Vientiane, dated June 9, 1969, CIA unindexed files, Vol. 167, p. 19422.

8. Interview with Robert Shackleton, Arlington, VA, May 23, 1995.

9. Lunday and Firth are deceased. Lunday died in a tragic airplane accident in 1977 that also claimed his father, whereas Firth passed away in 1985.

10. Telephone interview with Charles Roberts, Ojai, CA, April 22, 1995.

11. "Monthly Report 26 November–25 December 1968," CIA unindexed files, Vol. 236, p. 07749.

12. "Subject: Movement of American Prisoners into North Vietnam," October 30, 1968, CIA unindexed files, Vol. 187, p. 18593.

13. Bright Light report for period 21–27 Aug 67, p. 2.

14. "Subject: After Action Report: Operation Lucky Leaf," RG 472, USARV After Action Reports, Box 2, NARA.

15. Interview with Richard Childress, Washington, DC, January 10, 1997.

16. Bright Light report for 28 Aug–3 Sep 68, p. 1.

17. Ibid., p. 2.

18. CIA Station cable, dated September 1, 1968, CIA unindexed files, Vol. 189, p. 18144.

19. From DIA to USDAO Saigon, dated June 9, 1974, LOC PDS Reel 354.

20. Barry Enoch and Greg Walker, "The POW Raid," *Behind the Lines* (September/October, 1996), pp. 37–42.

21. Bright Light report for period 9–15 Oct 68, pp. 1, 2.

22. Bright Light report for period 16–22 Oct 68, pp. 1, 2.

23. Bright Light report for period 27 Nov–3 Dec 68, p. 2.

24. Bright Light report for period 4–10 Dec 68, p. 1.

25. Bright Light report for period 11–17 Dec 68, p. 2.

26. Rowe, *Five Years to Freedom,* pp. 406–408.

27. Telephone interview with John Regan, Providence, RI, October 29, 1996.

28. "Subj: Brightlight," From COMUSMACV to CINCPAC, DTG 310718Z Dec 68.

29. From Walt Rostow to the President, dated January 1, 1969, LBJ, POW/MIA, #56.

30. "Subj: Brightlight," From COMUSMACV to CINCPAC, DTG 010819Z Jan 69.

31. Bright Light report for period 4–10 Sept 68, pp. 2, 3.

32. In 1992, an F-111 life pod capsule, the portion that was designed to eject with the pilots, was found in a Soviet museum. It was later determined that it came from a 1972 loss. Several of the pilots lost on F-111s in the war, however, were believed to have survived ejection and were captured by the Vietnamese. Only two men of the twelve F-111 crew members came home.

33. Telegram from AmEmbassy Vientiane to SecState, dated April 1, 1968, LBJ, Laos, #54.

34. Telegram from AmEmbassy Vientiane to SecState, dated April 2, 1968, LBJ, Laos, #55.

35. Bright Light report for period 20–26 Nov 68, p. 3.

36. Minutes of IPWIC meeting, dated April 12, 1968, LOC FRD Reel 520, p. 1.

37. Telegram from AmEmbassy Vientiane, dated October 5, 1968, Files of Frank Sieverts, Box 11.

38. Telephone interview with Arthur Hesford, Jensen Beach, FL, February 21, 1997.

39. Telegram from AmEmbassy Vientiane to SecState, dated November 23, 1968, LBJ, Laos, #24.

40. Ibid.

41. "POW Issue in Laos Linked to Bombing," *Washington Post,* dated April 23, 1969, p. 4.

42. Telegram from AmEmbassy Vientiane to SecState, dated September 8, 1969, Case file of Peter Hesford, REFNO 1100, FRD LOC Reel 186.

43. Telegram from AmEmbassy Vientiane to SecState, dated September 3, 1969, Files of Frank Sieverts, Box 12.

44. "Pathet Lao claim 158 U.S. fliers held," *Washington Post,* dated November 12, 1969, p. 24. The government's press backgrounder informed the journalists that Soth was mistaken, that the figure of 158 was derived from a list of the total number of American missing in Laos.

45. Bright Light report for 27 Nov–3 Dec 68, pp. 2, 3.

46. "Copter Crews Busy Rescuing Pilots Downed in Laotian Hills," *New York Times,* dated December 10, 1969, p. 4.

47. Telegram from SecState to AmEmbassy Vientiane, dated December 15, 1968, Files of Frank Sieverts, Box 19.

48. "Subject: SAR Efforts—Laos," from AIRA Vientiane to CINCPAC, DTG 170915Z Jan 69.

49. "Glorious Feats of the Lao Army and People," Editorial, *Quan Doi Nhan Dan,* Hanoi, Feb. 13, 1969, pp. 1, 4.

50. From CINCPAC to DIA, DTG 092240Z Nov 68, LOC PDS Reel 61.

51. Bright Light report for period 9–15 Apr 69, p. 2.

52. Bright Light report for period 18–24 Dec 68, p. 2.

53. *Report of the Select Committee on POW/MIA Affairs,* United States Senate, January 13, 1993, pp. 365, 366.

54. Bright Light report for period 5–11 Mar 69, p. 2.

55. Telephone interview with Thomas H. Van Putten, Lowell, MI, February 24, 1997.

56. Bright Light report for period 18–24 Sep 68, p. 3. The ARVN was a 525th MI Group source who had escaped on April 25, 1968.

57. The Dale and Demmon case is typical of the challenges faced by families. According to the JTF-FA's best guess, the plane crashed in the Delta in Vinh Binh province, part of NVA MR-9, which is the same area as VC MR-3. The former commander of the B-2 Front's U.S. POW camp, Le Quang Huy, stated that communist POW policy was such that Americans captured in MR-9 would only be moved to the MR-9 camp, which is where Rowe et al. were held, and not to the B-2 Front camp, as the distance was too great. Is there any evidence that Dale and Demmon were held in the MR-9 complex? Not from any of the Americans who were released or escaped from there, but the notes of the Detainee Committee for February 1966 state that a defecting VC guard from the MR-9 camp indicated that two other Caucasians besides the Rowe group were held in the area. The Detainee committee believed that these could only be Dale and Demmon. Although Huy denied that any Americans were ever transferred from MR-9 to B-2, he did say that it would take an exception to policy to move the men. Bell was told in March 1993 that in fact MR-9 did have an evacuation route by boat up to the B-2 Front area. The intelligence study done on Ba Thu mentions that the area was a major supply depot for the upper Delta. The communists could easily have moved Dale and Demmon out of the MR-9 area into Cambodia if they desired. Why they would do this is the unanswered question.

Chapter 11

1. "Subj: Bright Light," From COMUSMACV to CINCPAC, DTG 111005Z Apr 69.

2. Telephone interview with Col. George R. Reinker, USAF (Ret.), Valparaiso, FL, March 9, 1995.

3. "Subject: CIA Information Reports on PW camps in Laos," undated, CIA unindexed files, Vol. 223, p. 00062.

4. Minutes of IPWIC meeting, dated March 11, 1968, p. 1.

5. CIA Monthly Report, 25 March–25 April 1969, LOC FRD Reel 403, Folder 225.

6. Ibid.

7. "Subject: Inclusion of Civilians in DIA 'book' of missing and captured personnel," dated April 15, 1969.

8. Telephone interview with Frank Sieverts, Washington, DC, January 24, 1997.

9. "Monthly report, 26 May–25 June 1969," CIA unindexed files, Vol. 223, p. 19335.

10. Letter to Sieverts from unknown author at AmEmbassy Saigon, June 26, 1969, Files of Frank Sieverts, Box 18.

11. "Subject: Opening Report Monroe Bay," Case file of Arthur Ecklund, REFNO 1422, LOC FRD Reel 195.

12. Bright Light report for period 16–22 Apr 69, p. 3.

13. 1969 MACV *Command History,* SOG Annex, JPRC Annex, p. X-50.

14. In 1991 Bill Bell interviewed a nurse who was working at the hospital on the day of the raid. She told Bell that she had developed a relationship with an American POW who remained hidden in the jungle until the raiding party left. This individual is currently a Priority Discrepancy Case.

15. Telephone interview with Col. Robert Gleason, USAF (Ret.), Clemmons, NC, July 16, 1995.

16. Telephone interview with Col. Steven Cavanaugh, USA (Ret.), San Diego, CA, March 29, 1995.

17. "Subject: PW Recovery Operations," From COMUSMACV to MACV, DTG 211137Z Mar 70.

18. Bright Light report for period 11–17 June 1969, p. 2.

19. "G.I. Who Fled Vietcong Says He Missed Coffee," *New York Times,* June 1, 1969, p. 23, c. 3.

20. "Subject: Bright Light," from COMUSMACV to JCS, DTG 220650Z Oct 69.

21. "2 Copter Crewmen Set Free by Enemy Near Duclap Camp," *New York Times,* December 13, 1969, p. 44, c. 3.

22. "Subject: Returned American POWs," memo from Headquarters, Advisory Team 16, Quang Tin Province, dated 15 November 1969, Advisory Team 16 Daily Journals, Box 7, NARA, College Park, MD.

23. Telephone interview with Col. James Rabdau, USA (Ret.), Boise, ID, February 22, 1997.

24. Bright Light report for period 24 Jan–24 Feb 1970, p. 2.

25. Bright Light report for period for 25 Feb–24 Mar 1970, p. 2.

26. Bright Light report for period 25 Mar–24 April 1970, p. 2.

27. Bright Light report for period 21 May–13 Jun 1970, p. 2.

28. Bright Light report for period 21 April–22 May 1970, p. 3.

29. The League still works diligently to account for those Americans who remain Missing in Action, ably led by its long time Executive Director Ann Mills-Griffiths. Her brother, Lt. Cdr. James Mills, USN, is still unaccounted for in Vietnam. The League's headquarters is in Washington, DC, and the organization is still called the "National League of Families of American Prisoners and Missing in Southeast Asia."

30. Lt. Col. Charles F. Kraak, *Family Efforts on Behalf of United States Prisoners of War and Missing in Action in Southeast Asia* (Army War College, Carlisle Barracks, PA, May 23, 1975), p. 8. This was an individual research project by a Military Police officer who spent four years involved with the issue.

31. "Subject: Government Handling of Prisoner of War Matters," dated August 29, 1969, RG 46, JCS Files, Box 3.

32. "Subject: Briefing on PWs," Files of Frank Sieverts, Box 26.

33. Telegram from AmEmbassy Paris to SecState, dated July 10, 1969, Files of Frank Sieverts, Box 22.

34. 1970 MACV *Command History, Prisoners of War,* p. X-22, quoting Mr. Davis.

35. "3 Freed U.S. Servicemen, Pale and Thin, Reach Laos from Hanoi," *New York Times,* August 6, 1969, p. 4.

36. "Subject: Apparent condition of returned POWs," from OUSAIRA Vientiane to DIA, DTG 060256Z Aug 69.

37. Minutes of the DOD POW Policy meeting, dated January 20, 1970.

38. "Six American pilots held in a two-story building in Sam Neua," CIA cable TDCS-314/11944-67, dated August 9, 1967, MORI.

39. "Transfer of two American pilots held captive in Laos to North Vietnam," CIA cable [redacted], dated January 5, 1969, MORI.

40. "Pathet Lao transfer of all American Prisoners from Laos to North Vietnam," CIA cable TDCS-314/09796-69, dated July 1, 1969, MORI.

41. "Subject: PW camps in Laos," from 7th AF to AmEmbassy Vientiane, DTG 170220Z Oct 69.

42. "Seventh Air Force POW Camps Listing Laos," dated October 1, 1969. This document was generously supplied to the author by POW/MIA researcher Roger Hall.

43. "Subject: PW camps in Laos," from 7th AF to AmEmbassy Vientiane, DTG 170220Z Oct 69.

44. Ibid.

45. "Subject: PW camps in the Hang Long area," from 7th AF to JPRC, DTG 040800Z Nov 69.

46. "Subject: PW camps in the Hang Long area," from 7th AF to 432 TRW Udorn, DTG 100205Z Nov 69.

47. "Subject: PW camps in Laos," from 7th AF to JPRC, DTG 061000Z Dec 69.

48. "Subj: POW Relief Operations in Laos and South Vietnam," Memorandum to the President, dated February 12, 1970, Nixon Presidential Archive, College Park, MD.

49. Roger Hall, "Abandoned in Laos," *Conservative Review* (January/February 1997), p. 12. Reinker believes that the photos were probably taken by reconnaissance aircraft and not Buffalo Hunter drones.

50. "General Location of Prison Camp containing about 20 United States Air Force pilots in the Ban NaKay region," CIA cable TDCS-314/00217-70, dated January 6, 1970, MORI.

51. "Current Status of American PWs in SVN," December 23, 1969, CIA unindexed files, Vol. 223, p. 00060.

52. Interview with SMSGT Thomas "Jack" Henry, USAF (Ret.), San Antonio, TX, April 1, 1995.

53. Interview with MSGT Howard A. Daniel III, USA (Ret.), Dunn Loring, VA, March 12, 1995.

54. Shortly after completion of the program, the JPRC held a party for everyone involved. In a terrible accident, one of the 519th database coders, a young Specialist/4 named Helring, drowned in a pool after becoming intoxicated.

55. Bright Light report for period 19 Dec 69–23 Jan 70, p. 3.

56. Minutes of the DOD POW Policy Committee meeting, dated February 18, 1970, JCS files, Box 3.

57. "Conversation with Frank Sieverts," dated January 6, 1970, CIA unindexed files, Vol. 145, p. 08099.

58. DIA letter, S-3811/AP-7, dated November 6, 1968.

59. "American Prisoners of War," Memorandum of Conversation, August 17, 1970, Files of Frank Sieverts, Box 2.

60. 1969 MACV *Command History,* SOG Annex, JPRC Annex F, p. 6.

Chapter 12

1. Interview with Colonel Fred Hopewell, USAF (Ret.), Malvern, PA, July 15, 1995. See also 1970 MACV *Command History,* SOG Annex B, JPRC Appendix XII, p. B-XII-9.

2. The Navy in particular badly wanted to recover Graf. Several JPRC officers remarked separately that the Navy told the JPRC to back off, that they would rescue Graf. What steps the Navy took to realize that ambition is unknown.

3. Bright Light report for period 13 June–30 July 1970, p. 2.

4. Darryl Young, *The Element of Surprise: Navy SEALs in Vietnam* (Ivy Books, New York, 1990), p. 45.

5. Bright Light report for period 31 July–4 September 1970, p. 2.

6. Telephone interview with Captain Louis Boink, USN, Arlington, VA, March 1, 1995.

7. Bright Light report for period 31 July–4 September 1970, pp. 3, 4.

8. T. L. Bosiljevac, *SEALs. UDT/SEAL Operations in Vietnam* (Paladin Press, Boulder, CO, 1990), p. 185.

9. Ibid., p. 184. Many of the books written by former SEALs incorrectly state that the raids they participated on were the first *Bright Light* operation of the war. Mr. Bosiljevac's work utilizes the SEAL *Command Histories* and is the most accurate source for the dates and outcomes of the missions.

10. "American prisoners in VC POW camps," CIA unindexed files, Vol. 187, no page number.

11. Telephone interview with Barry Enoch, Sisters, OR, February 10, 1997.

12. "VC/NVA PW camp of the Ca Mau Province Party Committee," CMIC IIR 6-029-0048-71.

13. Bright Light report for period 1 Jul–1 Aug 71, pp. 2, 3.

14. Benjamin Schemmer, *The Raid* (Harper & Row, New York, 1976), p. 34.

15. "Subj: Confirmed PW camp," from DIA to CINCPAC, DTG 012244Z Apr 70.

16. "Ba Vi (a.k.a. C30P) PW Prison," IIR 1-516-0596-70, June 1, 1970, Uncorrelated Volume 11, p. 468.

17. "Sontay is Described as Empty Sometime," *New York Times,* December 3, 1970, p. 11, c. 4.

18. Telephone interview with Lieutenant General Leroy Manor, USAF (Ret.), Shalimar, FL, March 22, 1997.

19. "Discord Building over Sontay Raid," *New York Times,* December 13, 1970, p. 5, c. 1.

20. "Reactions of Official North Vietnamese to the November, 1970 raid on the Son Tay camp and eye witness details on the episode," CIA cable TDCS-317/09026-72, dated March 3, 1972, MORI.

21. "Raid on Son Tay prison camp," DOD IIR 1-515-0015-73.

22. Monthly report for 26 December 1970–25 January 1971, p. 5.

23. Senate *Congressional Record,* January 26, 1994, p. S-163. Senator Bob Smith of New Hampshire is quoting from a just-declassified CIA photographic study of selected prison facilities in North Vietnam. The study was done in 1976.

24. Manor interview.

25. Bright Light report for period 1 December 70–1 January 71, p. 2.

26. Letter from JPRC to Chief, Casualty Branch, dated April 6, 1971, Case file of David Demmon, REFNO 0094, LOC FRD Reel 202.

27. "Futile Cambodia POW Raid Reported," *New York Times,* January 20, 1971, p. 6.

28. Letter from JPRC to Chief, Casualty Branch, dated April 6, 1971, Case file of David Demmon, REFNO 0094, LOC FRD Reel 202.

29. Bright Light report for period 1 Jan 71–1 Feb 71, p. 2.

30. Bright Light report for period 1 February–1 March 1971, p. 2.

31. Bright Light report for period 1 February–1 March 1971, p. 4.

32. "Subject: Combat Operations After Actions report," dated March 18, 1971.

33. Interview with WO4 Frank Anton, USA (Ret.), Washington, DC, June 19, 1997. Mr. Anton has recently published a memoir of his days in captivity, entitled *Why Didn't You Get Me Out?* (Summit Books, Arlington, TX, 1997). During Mr. Anton's movement north along the Ho Chi Minh Trail, he encountered a recently captured American aviator, a helicopter warrant officer, who appeared to be in good health. Although unable to positively identify this individual, based upon the time and location, Mr. Anton is fairly certain he saw WO1 William Milliner. WO1 Milliner never returned home and never appeared in the Hanoi prison system. The Vietnamese deny any knowledge of Milliner's fate.

34. "Enemy Proselytizing Interrogator's Notebook," CDEC Bulletin #48,709, Log #04-1527-72, fully translated in DOD IIR 6-028-0166-72.

35. Letter from John Schermerhorn to the author, dated December 12, 1996.

36. "Statistical Reports on RVNAF PWs Detained in PW Camps in Binh Dinh Province," CDEC Bulletin #50,799, Log #12-1007-72.

37. "Subj: Security Directives, Current Affairs Committee, VC Quang Da Province Party Committee, VC MR-5," CDEC Bulletin #40,926, Log #12-1517-70.

38. Bright Light report for period 1 February to 1 March 1971, p. 3.

39. "Subj: Bright Light," from OSI Det 5009 Phu Cat AB to OSI Dist 50, DTG 250859Z Feb 71.

40. Bright Light report for period 1 March to 1 April 1971, p. 2.

41. Bright Light report for period 31 July to 4 September 1970, p. 2.

42. Telephone interview with Carl Kraft, Rigby, ND, January 25, 1996.

43. Bright Light report for period 1 Oct–1 Nov 70, p. 3.

44. Telephone interview with John McFadyen, Bay City, MI, June 25, 1995.

45. Snepp, *Decent Interval*, p. 32.

46. Ibid.

47. Telegram from AmEmbassy Saigon to SecState, dated October 9, 1971, Files of Frank Sieverts, Box 23.

48. "Subject: Bright Light," from COMUSMACV to CINCPAC, DTG 120930Z Oct 71.

49. "New Vietnamese Communist Overture on Prisoner Exchange," Memo from Richard Helms to Dr. Henry C. Kissinger, dated October 27, 1971, JCS files, CIA folder, Box 3.

50. Ibid.

51. Snepp, *Decent Interval*, p. 33.

52. "Further Developments Related to NLF Prisoner Exchange Offer," Memo from Adm. Elmo R. Zumwalt, Jr., to SecDef, dated October 29, 1971, LOC PDS Reel 86.

53. The author was unable to locate any additional documentation on the Ramsey exchange beyond October, but the documentation he did find supported Snepp's account. Therefore, the author believes that Snepp's account is accurate except concerning the death of Tai. Bill Bell was told by some of the ARVN officers running the National Interrogation Center that Tai was still in his cell the day the communists overran Saigon. Several of Bell's Vietnamese POW/MIA counterparts also told him that Tai was currently Vietnam's Deputy Director of Customs.

Chapter 13

1. *Report of the Senate Select Committee on POW/MIA Affairs*, p. 136.

2. "PW Recovery efforts in SVN, Laos, and Cambodia," from CINCPAC to JCS, DTG 160435Z May 71, JCS files, Box 3.

3. Kuno Knoebl, translated by Bernard Fall, *Victor Charlie: The Face of War in Vietnam* (Frederick A. Praeger, New York, 1967), p. 296.

4. "Five-Year Trial on the Trail," *Bangkok Post*, March 21, 1971, magazine section, p. 46.

5. DOD IIR 1-775-0073-71, Uncorrelated vol. 12, pp. 243–247.

6. The pages from this book describing this incident can be found in the POW/MIA file of the Indochina Archive, Texas Tech University, Center for the Study of the Vietnam Conflict, folder for June 1972.

7. "Subj: CIA Station Efforts Aimed at the Rescue of American Prisoners of War in Laos," CIA Memorandum, dated February 6, 1970, included as an Appendix to the earlier listed Memorandum to the President, dated February 12, 1970.

8. "Contributions by Vientiane and Vietnam Stations," April 14, 1970, CIA unindexed files, Vol. 211, n.p.

9. Minutes of IPWIC meeting, dated June 12, 1970, p. 1.

10. Bright Light report for period 13 Jun–30 July 1970, p. 4.

11. "U.S. Prisoners of War in Laos," from CINCPAC to JCS, DTG 2603577 Aug 1970, RG 46, JCS files, Box 3.

12. "Subj: U.S. Prisoners of War in Laos," from JCS to CINCPAC, DTG 102009Z Sep 70, RG 46, JCS files, Box 3.

13. "Discussion with Col. Dan Hatch, SACSA," dated January 21, 1971, CIA unindexed files, Vol. 211, n.p.

14. Telegram from SecState to AmEmbassy Vientiane, dated March 6, 1971, Files of Frank Sieverts, Box 3.

15. Telegram from AmEmbassy Vientiane to SecState, dated March 10, 1971, Files of Frank Sieverts, Box 22. This is an extremely interesting comment. If Godley is talking about the "volley-ball" photo, then he is confirming that a team was sent to determine the presence of Americans.

16. "U.S. Prisoners in Laos," from CINCPAC to JCS, DTG 140410Z Mar 71, JCS Files, Box 3.

17. Telegram from SecState to AmEmbassy Vientiane, no date, Files of Frank Sieverts, Box 12.

18. "US Mission, Laos Intra-Agreement regarding processing of PW, ralliers, and captured documents," from OUSARMA Vientiane Laos to DIA, DTG 150245Z May 71.

19. "PW rescue forces and crash teams," from CINCPAC to JCS, DTG 182259Z Apr 71, JCS files, Box 3.

20. "PW recovery efforts in SVN, Laos, and Cambodia," from COMUSMACV to CINCPAC, DTG 150630Z May 71, JCS files, Box 3.

21. "PW Recovery efforts in SVN, Laos, and Cambodia," from CINCPAC to JCS, DTG 160435Z May 71, JCS files, Box 3.

22. "Subject: PW recovery efforts in Southeast Asia," Memo for the CJCS, dated August 13, 1971, JCS files, Box 2.

23. Letter from Secretary of Defense Melvin Laird to Secretary of State William Rogers, dated September 9, 1971, JCS files, Box 2.

24. Letter from Ambassador G. McMurtrie Godley to Special Assistant to the Under Secretary of State Frank Sieverts, dated October 31, 1971, Files of Frank Sieverts, Box 36.

25. Tom Yarborough, *Danang Diary* (St. Martin's Press, New York, 1990), p. 262.

26. Telephone interview with Jack Butcher, Tacoma, WA, March 8, 1997.

27. Telephone interview with Kevin Kelly, Las Vegas, NV, March 7, 1997.

28. "The Jack Butcher Case," LOC FRD Reel 373. This document is an after-action report which details NSA's role in helping to recover Butcher. It appears to be written shortly before *Homecoming*. The day after President Nixon had the returned POWs to the White House for dinner, Butcher was summoned to the JCS for a meeting with over a dozen people. The group included Marlene Barger, one of NSA's top analysts on the NVA's Group 559, the military organization that ran the Trail, Berkeley Cook, a Vietnamese linguist considered as good as a native speaker, and Kevin Kelly. Normally the most reticent of intelligence agencies, this is the only instance the author has ever found of the NSA actually discussing its involvement in an operation.

29. Interview with Marlene Barger of NSA, dated February 12, 1992, by Tom Lang of the Senate Select Committee, RG 46, Files of William Codinha, NSA Folder, NARA.

30. "The Jack Butcher Case," FRD LOC Reel 373.

31. "Subject: US Escapee Rescue in Laos," Memorandum for the Secretary of Defense, CM-896-71, dated May 13, 1971, JCS files, DIA folder, Box 2.

32. "US PW escapee in Laos," from COMUSMACV to CINCPAC, DTG 190710Z May 71, JCS files, Box 2.

33. "The Jack Butcher Case," FRD LOC Reel 373, p. 4.

34. Ibid., p. 5.

35. Bright Light report for period 1 May–1 June 1971, p. 3.

36. NSA Southeast Asia Daily Summary for May 27, 1971, LOC FRD Reel 373.

37. "Investigation of reported POW camps by Lao Irregular troops in Xieng Khouang and Savannakhet provinces," CIA cable TDCS-314/14495-69, dated October 9, 1969, MORI.

38. "Enemy prisons in Laos," CIA cable [redacted], dated April 1, 1970, MORI.

39. "Memorandum: Laos locations," dated April 3, 1970, attachment to April CIA prison study.

40. "Enemy prisons in Laos," CIA cable TDCS-314/12572-70, dated December 1, 1970, MORI.

41. "Enemy prisons in Laos," CIA cable TDCS-314/02438-71, dated March 5, 1971, MORI.

42. Memo from COS Vientiane to CIA Director, dated August 25, 1971, CIA unindexed files, Vol. 167, p. 13613.

43. "Subject: Background on Suspected Detention Sites in Laos," from Director, CIA, to COS Vientiane, undated, but sometime after September 1, 1971, CIA unindexed files, Vol. 156, p. 00386.

44. "Enemy prisons in Laos," CIA cable [redacted], dated October, 8, 1971, MORI.

45. "Subject: Comments of Round-up Report on Prisoner of War Camps in Laos," dated October, 8, 1971, CIA unindexed files, Vol. 157, n.p.

46. "Pathet Lao policy toward handling of foreign prisoners of war," CIA cable TDCS-314/05243-71, dated May 19, 1971, MORI.

47. "Peking, Lao Reds Air POW Terms," *Stars and Stripes,* May 21, 1971, p. 3.

48. Telegram from AmEmbassy Vientiane to SecState, dated November 5, 1971, Files of Frank Sieverts, Box 13.

49. From USDAO Vientiane to DIA, DTG 190950Z Oct 73, IIR 2-237-0435-73.

50. CIA cable from Saigon to Vientiane, dated March 13, 1971, CIA unindexed files, Vol. 167, p. 09473.

51. Telegram from AmEmbassy Bangkok to SecState, dated May 22, 1971, Uncorrelated files, Volume 13, p. 260.

52. Telegram from AmEmbassy Bangkok to SecState, dated June 16, 1971, Files of Frank Sieverts, Box 13.

53. It is unknown if this is the Prince. His name is redacted out, but he is referred to as a "72-year-old man."

54. Telegram from AmEmbassy Vientiane to SecState, dated July 23, 1971, Uncorrelated files, Volume 13, p. 276.

55. Telegram from SecState to AmEmbassy Vientiane, dated July 28, 1971, Uncorrelated files, Volume 5, p. 663.

56. Telegram from AmEmbassy Vientiane to SecState, dated August 12, 1971, Files of Frank Sieverts, Box 13.

57. Telegram from AmEmbassy Vientiane to SecState, dated July 5, 1971, Files of Frank Sieverts, Box 13.

58. "Report of Investigation of First Sergeant Sebastian E. Deluca," USARV POW/MIA materials, Box 18, Folder Deluca, NARA, College Park, MD.

59. The event was obviously embarrassing to SOG and it was hushed up. A recently discovered

internal SOG investigation, noted above, conducted at the time by JPRC Army Major Robert Mann, plus State Department cables have been used to clarify Deluca's death.

60. Personal log of Gerry C. Bauknight, entry for 3 July 71. At the time, Bauknight was an Air Force major. The author wishes to express his thanks to Mr. Bauknight for sharing his personal diaries.

Chapter 14

1. Don Lunday was the brother of JPRC officer Robert Lunday.

2. Personal log of Major Gerry C. Bauknight, entry for 25 Oct 71.

3. Personal log of Major Gerry C. Bauknight, entry for 28 Oct 71.

4. Bright Light report for period 1 November–1 December 1971, p. 11.

5. Ibid.

6. Personal log of Major Gerry C. Bauknight, entry for 3 Nov 71. His diary also notes that on 7 Nov a C-130 got a strong beeper for five seconds. It is unclear if this pertains to the X-Ray symbol, but since no other SAR effort is mentioned in his log, the author believes it probably is.

7. Bright Light report for period 1 Nov–1 Dec 1971, p. 12.

8. Bright Light report for period 1 May–31 May 1972, p. 3.

9. Bright Light report for period 1 Dec–31 Dec 70, p. 2. Stan Sirmans, a retired Navy captain who served in the area during the war, has interviewed White extensively. According to Sirmans, White denies that Graf was heavily interrogated and was surprised at the amount of information in the document. Apparently, this information was collected during the first several months of their captivity. In February, after the VC learned this information, Graf was visited by a six-foot-tall Oriental believed by White to be Chinese. Several days later, Graf escaped. Different witnesses later reported that Graf either had been shot near a river or had drowned while attempting to cross it. According to the Vietnamese, he was buried in the river bank and his remains were washed away.

10. Telephone interview with Col. Robert Covalucci, USA (Ret.), Sierra Vista, AZ, February 13, 1995.

11. Bright Light report for period 1 October to 1 November 1971, p. 4.

12. Telephone interview with Colonel Henry Dagenais, USA (Ret.), Columbia, MD, March 5, 1997.

13. "US PWs in MR-3," CDEC Bulletin #42, 122, Log #02-1060-71.

14. Bright Light report for period 1 October to 1 November 1971, p. 10.

15. Telephone interview with Col. Ian Sutherland, USA (Ret.), Cape Girardeau, MO, February 20, 1995.

16. Telephone interview with Woods E. Gray, Baton Rouge, LA, March 31, 1997.

17. Bright Light report for period 1 February to 1 March, 1972, pp. 4–6.

18. The possibility exists that one other EB-66 crew member got out. Hambleton remarked to an interviewer that he is uncertain, but he may have heard another seat also eject. No other chutes, however, were spotted. Hambleton was the navigator and his actual call-sign was Bat 21 Bravo. Bat 21 was the plane's call-sign.

19. Personal diary of Major Gerry C. Bauknight, entry for April 4, 1972. Bauknight kept both a personal log, which contained his notes of daily events, and a personal diary, which recorded his feelings about Vietnam and his job.

20. Potts survived but was quickly captured. Most reports indicate he died in captivity while moving toward Hanoi.

21. Personal diary of Major Gerry C. Bauknight, entry for April 17, 1972.

22. Letter from Andy Anderson to Gerry Bauknight, dated December 31, 1973.

23. Telephone interview with Darrell Whitcomb, Fairfax, VA, April 2, 1997. The author wishes to thank Mr. Whitcomb for generously sharing his extraordinary knowledge of the *Bat 21* operation. His book, *The Rescue of Bat 21,* will be published by the Naval Institute Press in the winter of 1997–98.

24. Interview of Charles Semich at NSA on February 12, 1992, by Tom Lang, Investigator for the Senate Select Committee, RG 46, Files of William Codinha, NSA folder.

25. NSA SIGINT Product Report, LOC FRD Reel 269, Folder 1970. Most of the NSA reports are so heavily redacted that it is impossible to find dates or titles.

26. LOC FRD Reel 376, no folder. The documents on the reel were microfilmed in no apparent order or logical sequence.

27. NSA Southeast Asia Daily Summary, no date, LOC FRD Reel 375.

28. Minutes of the IPWIC meeting, dated June 12, 1970, p. 3.

29. Case file of Dennis Pugh, REFNO 1573-01, LOC FRD Reel 145.

30. Telephone interview with SMSGT Jerry Mooney, USAF (Ret.), Billings, MT, June 15, 1995.

31. "NVN 377th Air Defense Division Plans to Execute 10 *Americans,*" NSA SIGINT Spot Report, DTG 071545Z Jul 72, LOC PDS Reel 270, Folder 1972.

32. "NSA Southeast Asia Daily Summary," DTG 072000Z Jul 72, LOC FRD Reel 375.

33. McConnell, *Inside Hanoi's Secret Archives,* p. 351.

34. Mooney has come under fire in the past from the government and their supporters in the press for not buttressing his claims with documentary evidence. However, both seem to conveniently forget that former NSA employees do not walk out the front door with an armload of highly classified material from the most security-conscious intelligence agency in the country.

35. Paul Crickmore, *Lockheed SR-71: The Secret Missions Exposed* (Osprey, London, 1989), p. 139.

36. Telephone interview with Col. Tom Pugh, USAF (Ret.), Lancaster, CA, April 5, 1997.

37. "POW Task Force meeting for April 25, 1972," CIA Memorandum, CIA unindexed files, Vol. 145, p. 12186.

38. "Subject: [redacted]," dated April 28, 1972, Memo from Chairman, JCS, to Admiral McCain, LOC PDS Reel 61.

39. Telephone interview with Col. James Kasler, USAF (Ret.), Momence, IL, November 13, 1995.

40. Telephone interview with Col. John Dramesi, USAF (Ret.), Pittsburgh, PA, March 31, 1997.

41. Telephone interview with Col. Andy Porth, USAF, Warsaw, Poland, January 22, 1996. See also an interview with Porth in RG 46, Senate Select Committee, Case files of Senate Investigator Robert Taylor, Covert Ops folder.

42. Edwin L. Towers, *Hope for Freedom: Operation Thunderhead* (Lane and Associates, La Jolla, CA, 1981), p. 6. Tower's book is an excellent account of the Navy's three-week surveillance effort waiting for the POWs to arrive.

43. Michael R. Conroy, "POW Rescue Game Plan," *Vietnam* (December 1992), pp. 47–53.

44. SpeCat Exclusive to Admiral McCain from Admiral Moorer, DTG 152358Z May 72, LOC PDS Reel 61.

45. From CINCPACFLT to CINCPAC, DTG 312255Z May 72, LOC PDS Reel 61.

46. From CINCPACFLT to CINCPAC, DTG 221220Z May 72, LOC PDS Reel 61.

47. Orr Kelly, *Never Fight Fair: Navy SEALs' Stories of Combat and Adventure* (Presidio Press, Novato, CA, 1995), pp. 205–219. From CINCPACFLT to CJCS, DTG 070555Z Jun 72, LOC PDS Reel 61.

48. "Subj: Termination of Thunderhead," from CJCS, no date, LOC PDS Reel 78.

49. The perceived lack of resistance so angered Dramesi that in 1975 he published a book, *Code of Honor.* His book was a hard-hitting portrayal of what he viewed as the faulty leadership of some of the officers in the camps and their willingness to acquiesce to Vietnamese pressure. His work incensed the former POWs and he has essentially been ostracized by some of them ever since.

50. "Unidentified NVA element possible attempt to free prisoners," NSA SIGINT Product Report, DTG 302052Z May 72, LOC FRD Reel 271.

51. Telephone interview with Col. David Presson, USA (Ret.), San Antonio, TX, June 16, 1995.

52. Telephone interview with Lt. Col. Robert Case, USAF (Ret.), Fort Myers, FL, January 16, 1995.

53. Letter from Col. Fredwin Odom, USA (Ret.), to the author, n.d.

54. *Senate Select Committee Report,* pp. 133–134.

55. "Subject: Deserters and AWOL's," letter dated March 6, 1971, from Maj. Gen. William G. Dolvin, MACV Chief of Staff, to the Commanders of the 7th AF, US Army, US Naval Forces, and III Marine Amphibious Force.

56. "Sub: Military Discipline," SpeCat Exclusive from General Abrams for Admiral McCain, DTG 150800Z Jun 71.

57. Minutes of the PW Intelligence Task Force meeting, February 8, 1972, CIA unindexed files, Vol. 156, p. 12950.

58. "Subj: AF Personnel in Deserter Status," from 7th AF to CINCPACAF, DTG 020705Z Nov 72.

59. "Deserters in SEASIA," from CINCPAC to JCS, DTG 180113Z Nov 72.

60. "After Action Report—Operation *Countdown,*" Volume 1, p. 38. This is the USARV/MACV report of the U.S. military departing Vietnam.

61. "U.S. Aides Believe Two Whites are Active in Enemy's Invasion," *New York Times,* May 1, 1972, p. 6.

62. From COMUSMACV to CINCPAC, DTG 090900Z Jan 73, Uncorrelated vol. 7, pp. 098, 099.

63. From CDR 525th MI Group to DIA, DTG 100530Z Jan 73, Uncorrelated vol. 7, pp. 101–106.

64. Ibid.

65. Telephone interview with Dr. Roger Shields, Short Hills, NJ, April 2, 1997.

66. "Subj: Bright Light," from CG SRAC to COMUSMACV, DTG 071220Z Jan 73.

67. "Subj: Bright Light," from CG SRAC to COMUSMACV, DTG 101315Z Jan 73.

68. Telegram from AmEmbassy Saigon to CDR, JCRC, dated March 16, 1973, Files of Frank Sieverts, Box 33.

69. Telegram from CDR, JCRC, to AmEmbassy Saigon, dated March 19, 1973, Files of Frank Sieverts, Box 33.

70. Carole Hack, "In a bizarre incident, Air Force POW Ed Elias was freed through the propaganda efforts of American collaborators," *Vietnam* (June 1996), p. 55.

71. Minutes of IPWIC meeting, dated October 7, 1972, CIA unindexed files, Vol. 213, #11610.

72. "Scheduled Flight probably carries *American* POW's from North Vietnam," NSA SIGINT Spot Report, DTG 251925Z Sept 72, LOC FRD Reel 375.

73. 1972 MACV *Command History,* p. 52, LOC FRD Reel 451.

74. "Subject: Crash site investigations," dated April 21, 1972, CIA unindexed files, Vol. 211, no page number.

75. Telegram from AmEmbassy Vientiane to SecState, dated March 14, 1972, Uncorrelated Vol. 6, p. 411.

76. "Subject: Initial debriefing of Lao returnee from Sam Neua province," from JANAF Attaches to DIA, DTG 090555Z May 72, Uncorrelated Vol. 11, pp. 24, 25.

77. Ibid.

78. "Subject: RADM Epes trip report," dated May 31, 1972, p. 5.

79. From JANAF Vientiane Laos to DIA, DTG 190922Z Jan 73, Uncorrelated Vol. 11, p. 288.

80. Telegram from AmEmbassy Vientiane to SecState, dated January 20, 1973, Uncorrelated Vol. 13, p. 270. The November source report can be found in Vol. 11, pp. 289–291.

81. Despite the efforts of the JTF-FA Lao Archival research team in Vientiane, no such film has ever been located.

82. Later in March the repairman was reinterrogated. He changed his story to indicate that he saw only three Caucasians instead of eight. He attributed this to the head wound he was suffering from at the time. See CIA cable dated 5 March 1973, DDRS #1493, 1991.

83. From JANAF Vientiane to DIA, DTG 060400Z Feb 73, Uncorrelated Vol. 9, pp. 203–205.

84. "Subject: PW Negotiations Bien Hoa," Memorandum for the Record from Major Leon C. Matassarin, USA, dated February 12, 1973.

85. Telegram from AmEmbassy Vientiane to SecState, dated February 21, 1973, Files of Frank Sieverts, Box 27.

86. *Report of the Senate Select Committee on POW/MIA Affairs,* p. 87.

87. Telegram from AmEmbassy Vientiane to SecState, dated February 24, 1973, Files of Frank Sieverts, Box 27.

88. Telegram from AmEmbassy Vientiane to SecState, dated March 10, 1973, Files of Frank Sieverts, Box 27.

89. "Status and Treatment of Prisoners of War in Laos," dated March 14, 1973, CIA unindexed files, Vol. 211, p. 14786.

90. Telegram from SecState to AmEmbassy Vientiane, dated March 15, 1973, Files of Frank Sieverts, Box 29.

91. Telegram from AmEmbassy Vientiane to SecState, dated March 20, 1973, Files of Frank Sieverts, Box 27.

92. Telegram from AmEmbassy Vientiane to SecState, dated March 23, 1973, Files of Frank Sieverts, Box 27.

93. "Subject: The status of U.S. Prisoners in Laos," Memorandum dated March 24, 1973, LOC FRD Reel 63.

94. *Senate Select Committee Report,* p. 89.

95. Godley appears to be reacting to Moorer's earlier cable about halting troop withdrawals, although in Senate testimony he claimed not to remember.

96. Telegram from AmEmbassy Vientiane to SecState, dated March 22, 1973, Files of Frank Sieverts, Box 31.

97. Telegram from AmEmbassy Vientiane to SecState, dated March 26, 1973, Files of Frank Sieverts, Box 27.

98. Telegram from AmEmbassy Vientiane to SecState, dated April 5, 1973, Files of Frank Sieverts, Box 13.

99. "Subject: US Prisoners of War in Laos," dated June 4, 1973, JCS files, Box 3.

100. Cable from COS Vientiane to Director, CIA, dated June 9, 1973, CIA unindexed files, Vol. 234, p. 21187.

Chapter 15

1. Interview with Robert Brudno, Washington, DC, February 7, 1997.

2. George A. Carver, Jr., "Submission on Vietnam POW/MIA Matters," House Subcommittee on Asia and Pacific Affairs, June 30, 1993, p. 4.

Glossary of Acronyms, Abbreviations, and Foreign Terms

AAA	Antiaircraft Artillery
ADP	Automated Database Program
AF	Air Force (US)
AFOSI	Air Force Office of Special Investigations
AmEmb	American Embassy
AO	Area of Operations
ARVN	Army of the Republic of (South) Vietnam
CAS	Controlled American Source (cover term for CIA)
CCC	Command and Control, Central
CCN	Command and Control, North
CCS	Command and Control, South
CDEC	Combined Document Exploitation Center
CIA	Central Intelligence Agency (US)
CICV	Combined Intelligence Center, Vietnam
CI	Counter Intelligence (US)
CIDG	Civilian Irregular Defense Group (indigenous)
CINCPAC	Commander in Chief, Pacific (the organization as well as the man)
CJCS	Chairman, Joint Chiefs of Staff
CMIC	Combined Military Interrogation Center
COD	Carrier on Demand

COMUSMACV	Commander, Military Assistance Command, Vietnam
COS	Chief of Station (CIA)
COSVN	Central Office for South Vietnam (of the DRV)
CSD	Combined Studies Division
CSSP	Combined Services Support Program
DCI	Director of Central Intelligence (CIA)
DIA	Defense Intelligence Agency (US)
DOD	Department of Defense (US)
DMZ	Demilitarized Zone
DPMO	Defense Prisoner/Missing Persons Office
DRV	Democratic Republic of (North) Vietnam
E&E	Escape and Evasion
EO	Executive Order
FAC	Forward Air Controller
FAG	Field Activity Group; Forward Air Guide
FBIS	Foreign Broadcast Information Service
FOB	Forward Operational Base
FOIA	Freedom of Information Act
FRD	Federal Research Division
GPD	General Political Directorate
GVN	Government of (South) Vietnam
ICC	International Control Commission
ICRC	International Committee of the Red Cross
ID	Infantry Division; Identification
IDHS	Intelligence Data Handling System
IIR	Intelligence Information Report
IPWIC	Interagency Prisoner of War Intelligence Ad-Hoc Committee
JANAF	Joint Army Navy Air Force
JCRC	Joint Casualty Resolution Center
JCS	Joint Chiefs of Staff (US)
JLD	Joint Liaison Detachment (CIA)
JPRC	Joint Personnel Recovery Center
JSARC	Joint Search and Rescue Center
JTF-FA	Joint Task Force—Full Accounting
JUSPAO	Joint United States Public Affairs Office
KIA	Killed in Action
KIA/BNR	Killed in Action/Body Not Recovered

LOC FRD	Library of Congress Federal Research Division, POW/MIA Microfilm Collection
LPLA	Lao People's Liberation Army
LS	Lima Site
LST	Landing Ship Tank
LZ	Landing Zone
MACV	Military Assistance Command, Vietnam
MIA	Missing in Action
MOA	Memorandum of Agreement
MOI	Ministry of the Interior (DRV)
MORI	Management of Released Information
MPS	Ministry of Public Security (DRV)
MR	Military Region (VC/NVA)
NARA	National Archives Record Administration
NBLs	No-Bomb Lines
NCO	Non-Commissioned Officer
NKP	Nakhon Phanom (air base)
NLHS	Neo Lao Hak Set (Lao Patriotic Front [communist])
NLF	National Liberation Front (Viet Cong)
NSA	National Security Agency (US)
NVA	North Vietnamese Army
NVA/PL	North Vietnamese Army/Pathet Lao
NVN	North Vietnam
OB	Order of Battle
OHP	Oral History Program
ONI	Office of Naval Intelligence
OPLAN	Operations Plan
OSD	Office of the Secretary of Defense
PACAF	Pacific Air Force (US)
PACOM	Pacific Command (US)
PAVN	People's Army of Vietnam
PDS	Photo Duplication Service
PF	Popular Forces
PL	Pathet Lao (Lao communist army)
PO	Political Officer
POW or PW	Prisoner of War
PRU	Provisional Reconnaissance Units (noncommunist)
RF	Regional Forces

RLA	Royal Lao Army
RLAF	Royal Lao Air Force
RLG	Royal Lao Government
ROK	Republic of (South) Korea
RTS	Recon Technical Squadron
SAAT	Safe Area Activation Team(s)
SACSA	Special Assistant for Counterinsurgency and Special Activities (the section as well as the man)
SAFE	Selected Area for Evasion
SAM	Surface-to-Air (Missile)
SAR	Search and Rescue
SCT	Sea Commando Team
SEAL	Sea-Air-Land (US Navy Special Forces)
SecDef	Secretary of Defense (US)
SecState	Secretary of State (US)
SERE	Survival, Evasion, Resistance and Escape
SF	Special Forces (Green Berets)
SIGINT	Signals Intelligence
SOG	Studies and Observation Group
SSO	Special Security Office
STD	Strategic Technical Directorate
SVN	South Vietnam
TACAN	Tactical Air Navigation
TSN	Tan Son Nhut (air base)
USAF	United States Air Force
USAID	United States Agency for International Development
USG	United States Government
UW	Unconventional Warfare
VC	Viet Cong (= Vietnamese Communists; armed insurgents in South Vietnam)
VCI	Viet Cong Infrastructure
VFW	Veterans of Foreign Wars
VNAF	(South) Vietnamese Air Force
VR	Visual Reconnaissance
XO	Executive Officer

Index

Hai, Nguyen Van, 40–42, 46, 51, 83, 149
Haig, Alexander, 351
Hambleton, Iceal, 318–324, 356
Hamilton, Walter D., 46
Hamm, Gerald A., 240
Hang Long, 302. *See also* Ban Hang Long area
Hansen, Lester, 106–114, 117–120, 122, 127, 129–131, 133, 154, 155
Haoi, Le Van, 278, 279
Harriman, W. Averell, 75, 77, 87–91, 100, 135–137, 141, 142, 159, 181, 183, 196, 198, 199, 202–203, 220, 222, 243–245
Harris, Carlyle Smith, 96
Harris, Hunter, 104, 105, 124
Harris, Jesse B., 238–240
Harris, John S., 145
Hartmann, Richard, 131–132
Hatch, Don C., 232, 285
Hatzheim, John, 167
Hau Nghia province, 46, 138
Hayden, Tom, 162, 182
Hayhurst, Robert, 170
Hegdahl, Douglas B., 245, 246, 256, 342
Helicopter Support Squadron 17 (HC-17), 5
Helms, Richard, 252, 279
Henderson, William, 320
Henry, Thomas "Jack," 253–255
Hertz, Gustav, 39–42, 45, 46, 51, 53, 75, 83, 84, 138, 149–150, 152, 161
Hertz, Mrs. Gustav, 36, 40, 152
Hesford, Arthur, 221–223
Hesford, Peter, 221–223
Hiep Hoa village, 29, 46, 55
Hilbert, Phillip, 103
Hmong (Meo), 7, 13, 15, 27, 31, 59, 60, 63, 65, 70, 72, 122, 148, 190, 191, 248, 252, 299
Hoa Hao, 160, 161
Hoai, Le Van, 279
Hoa Lo (Hanoi Hilton), 95, 329, 330
Ho Chi Minh, 91, 244
Ho Chi Minh Trail, xi, 3, 27, 32, 58, 62, 69, 77, 146, 205, 281–283, 285, 288, 291
Holland, Ann, 195
Holland, Melvin, 195

Homecoming, 30, 58, 130, 159, 167, 229, 264, 299, 341, 346
Hopewell, Fred N., 260, 307
Hot Snap, 118, 127
Houei Het camp, 73, 74
Houei Vong, 146
Hrdlicka, Carol, 64, 68, 71, 72
Hrdlicka, David, 57–59, 63–66, 68–69, 71, 72, 75–77, 103, 146, 148, 194, 345, 349
Hudson, Henry, 47
Hue, 169–171, 234
Hung Vuong I, 44

Iles, George, 266
Indochina Archive, 10–11
Indochina War, 12, 27
Indoctrination efforts, 12–13, 20, 21, 176, 199
In Love and War (Stockdale), 96
Interagency POW Intelligence Working Group, 95, 143–145
Interagency Prisoner of War Intelligence Ad-hoc Committee (IPWIC), 145, 233, 268, 326
Interdepartmental Committee on Prisoners of War, 143
International Committee of the Red Cross (ICRC), 37, 65, 68, 80–84, 87, 89, 90, 92, 93, 95, 97, 98, 100, 116, 142, 146, 175, 184, 203, 221
International Control Commission (ICC), 37, 89, 178
Iodice, Frank C., 186, 187

Jackson, James E., xiii, 161–163, 201, 208
Jaks, Frank, xiv–xviii, 121–123
Jefferson, Perry H., 235
Johns, Ernest, 104
Johnson, Edward R., xiii, xiv, 161–163, 201, 208
Johnson, Lyndon B., 3, 36, 40, 44, 77, 84, 87, 175, 202, 216, 219, 223
Johnson, Sandra, 177
Johnson administration, 37, 83, 150, 202, 204
Johnson Library, Austin, Texas, 10
Joint Casualty Resolution Center (JCRC),